Exam 70-448: TS: Microsoft SQL Server 2008, Business Intelligence Development and Maintenance

OBJECTIVE

IMPLEMENTING AN SSIS SOLUTION		
Implement control flow.	Chapter 1	Lesson 2
	Chapter 2	Lesson 1
Implement data flow.	Chapter 1	Lesson 3
	Chapter 2	Lesson 1
	Chapter 2	Lesson 2
	Chapter 2	Lesson 3
Implement dynamic package behavior by using property expressions.	Chapter 3	Lesson 1
Implement package logic by using variables.	Chapter 1	Lesson 2
Implement package configurations.	Chapter 3	Lesson 1
Implement auditing, logging, and event handling.	Chapter 2	Lesson 2
	Chapter 2	Lesson 3
Extend SSIS packages by using .NET code.	Chapter 1	Lesson 2

CONFIGURING, DEPLOYING, AND MAINTAINING SSIS		
Install and maintain SSIS components.	Chapter 1	Lesson 1
	Chapter 2	Lesson 1
	Chapter 4	Lesson 1
Deploy an SSIS solution.	Chapter 3	Lesson 2
Manage SSIS package execution.	Chapter 4	Lesson 2
Configure SSIS security settings.	Chapter 4	Lesson 1
Identify and resolve issues related to SSIS solution deployment.	Chapter 1	Lesson 1
	Chapter 2	Lesson 2
	Chapter 2	Lesson 3
	Chapter 3	Lesson 2

IMPLEMENTING AN SSAS SOLUTION		
Implement dimensions in a cube.	Chapter 5	Lesson 2
	Chapter 5	Lesson 3
	Chapter 6	Lesson 1
Implement measures in a cube.	Chapter 5	Lesson 2
	Chapter 5	Lesson 4
Implement a data source view.	Chapter 5	Lesson 1
Configure dimension usage in a cube.	Chapter 6	Lesson 1
Implement custom logic in a cube by using MDX.	Chapter 6	Lesson 2
	Chapter 6	Lesson 3
Implement data mining.	Chapter 9	Lesson 1
	Chapter 9	Lesson 2
	Chapter 9	Lesson 3
	Chapter 9	Lesson 4
Implement storage design in a cube.	Chapter 7	Lesson 1

CONFIGURING, DEPLOYING, AND MAINTAINING SSAS		
Configure permissions and roles in SSAS.	Chapter 8	Lesson 1
Deploy SSAS databases and objects.	Chapter 7	Lesson 2
Install and maintain an SSAS instance.	Chapter 8 Chapter 8	Lesson 2 Lesson 3
Diagnose and resolve performance issues.	Chapter 8	Lesson 3
Implement processing options.	Chapter 7	Lesson 3
IMPLEMENTING AN SSRS SOLUTION		
Implement report data sources and datasets.	Chapter 10 Chapter 12	Lesson 1 Lesson 3
Implement a report layout.	Chapter 10 Chapter 10 Chapter 11	Lesson 1 Lesson 3 Lesson 2
Extend an SSRS solution by using code.	Chapter 11	Lesson 4
Create an SSRS report by using an SSAS data source.	Chapter 10	Lesson 2
Implement report parameters.	Chapter 11 Chapter 11	Lesson 1 Lesson 2
Implement interactivity in a report.	Chapter 10 Chapter 11	Lesson 3 Lesson 2
Implement report items.	Chapter 10 Chapter 10 Chapter 11	Lesson 1 Lesson 4 Lesson 2
Embed SSRS reports in custom applications.	Chapter 11	Lesson 3
CONFIGURING, DEPLOYING, AND MAINTAINING SSRS		
Configure report execution and delivery.	Chapter 12 Chapter 12	Lesson 2 Lesson 3
Install and configure SSRS instances.	Chapter 13 Chapter 13	Lesson 1 Lesson 2
Configure authentication and authorization for a reporting solution.	Chapter 12	Lesson 2
Deploy an SSRS solution.	Chapter 11	Lesson 3
Configure SSRS availability.	Chapter 13 Chapter 13	Lesson 1 Lesson 2

Exam Objectives   The exam objectives listed here are current as of this book's publication date. Exam objectives are subject to change at any time without prior notice and at Microsoft's sole discretion. Please visit the Microsoft Learning Web site for the most current listing of exam objectives: http://www.microsoft.com/learning/en/us/exams/70-448.mspx.

Microsoft® SQL Server® 2008— Business Intelligence Development and Maintenance

MCTS Self-Paced Training Kit (Exam 70-448)

Erik Veerman,
Teo Lachev, and
Dejan Sarka of
Solid Quality
Mentors

PUBLISHED BY
Microsoft Press
A Division of Microsoft Corporation
One Microsoft Way
Redmond, Washington 98052-6399

Library of Congress Control Number: 2009920806

Printed and bound in the United States of America.

4 5 6 7 8 9 10 11 12 13 QGT 6 5 4 3 2 1

Distributed in Canada by H.B. Fenn and Company Ltd.

A CIP catalogue record for this book is available from the British Library.

Microsoft Press books are available through booksellers and distributors worldwide. For further information about international editions, contact your local Microsoft Corporation office or contact Microsoft Press International directly at fax (425) 936-7329. Visit our Web site at www.microsoft.com/mspress. Send comments to tkinput@microsoft.com.

Microsoft, Microsoft Press, Active Directory, Excel, Internet Explorer, MSDN, PivotTable, SharePoint, SQL Server, Visio, Visual Basic, Visual C#, Visual Studio, Windows, Windows Server, and Windows Vista are either registered trademarks or trademarks of the Microsoft group of companies. Other product and company names mentioned herein may be the trademarks of their respective owners.

The example companies, organizations, products, domain names, e-mail addresses, logos, people, places, and events depicted herein are fictitious. No association with any real company, organization, product, domain name, e-mail address, logo, person, place, or event is intended or should be inferred.

This book expresses the author's views and opinions. The information contained in this book is provided without any express, statutory, or implied warranties. Neither the authors, Microsoft Corporation, nor its resellers, or distributors will be held liable for any damages caused or alleged to be caused either directly or indirectly by this book.

Acquisitions Editor: Ken Jones
Developmental Editor: Laura Sackerman
Project Editor: Maureen Zimmerman
Editorial Production: Online Training Solutions, Inc.
Technical Reviewer: Rozanne Murphy Whalen; Technical Review services provided by Content Master, a member of CM Group, Ltd.
Cover: Tom Draper Design

Body Part No. X15-52846

To my children . . . Meg, Nate, Kate, and Caleb.
—ERIK VEERMAN

To my family, for tolerating my absence during the writing of this book.
—TEO LACHEV

To my son.
—DEJAN SARKA

Acknowledgments

First, thank you to Teo and Dejan for their excellent work and dedication to the effort to make this book project a success. Also thanks to my many clients who have provided real-life BI experiences—both the good and the ugly, but I won't tell you which ones! Next, there's no better place to work than with Solid Quality Mentors—a special thanks to Douglas McDowell and Brian Moran, who make our firm one of the best in the world. My book dedication is to my children, but it is my wonderful wife, Amy, who makes this all possible. Thank you for your patience. *Sola gratia, sola fide, solo Christos.*

—Erik Veerman

I would like to thank Erik Veerman and Solid Quality Mentors for entrusting me to write the Analysis Services part of *MCTS Self-Paced Training Kit (Exam 70-445): Microsoft SQL Server 2005 Business Intelligence—Implementation and Maintenance* and this book. Over the past several years, I've been privileged to personally know and work with bright and talented developers who have contributed tremendously to the success of the Microsoft Business Intelligence Platform. Erik and Dejan are two of the best. Their professionalism, experience, and dedication have shown through this book again. Thank you for making this project a smooth ride!

—Teo Lachev

It was a great pleasure to work with Erik and Teo again. In addition, thanks to all friends from Solid Quality Mentors.

—Dejan Sarka

Contents at a Glance

Contents

What do you think of this book? We want to hear from you!

Microsoft is interested in hearing your feedback so we can continually improve our
books and learning resources for you. To participate in a brief online survey, please visit:

www.microsoft.com/learning/booksurvey/

Chapter 8   Securing and Administering SSAS   315

Chapter 10   Developing SSRS Reports   445

What do you think of this book? We want to hear from you!

Microsoft is interested in hearing your feedback so we can continually improve our
books and learning resources for you. To participate in a brief online survey, please visit:

www.microsoft.com/learning/booksurvey/

Introduction

This Training Kit is designed for business intelligence (BI) developers and administrators who plan to take the Microsoft Certified Technology Specialist (MCTS) Exam 70-448, *Microsoft SQL Server 2008, Business Intelligence Development and Maintenance*. The primary objective of this exam is to certify that BI developers and administrators know how to develop and maintain solutions built on the Microsoft SQL Server 2008 BI platform, which includes SQL Server Integration Services (SSIS), SQL Server Analysis Services (SSAS), and SQL Server Reporting Services (SSRS). We assume that before you begin using this Training Kit, you have experience developing or implementing BI solutions. We also assume that you have experience managing or supporting BI project security, deployment, and maintenance. The Preparation Guide for Exam 70-448 is available from *http://www.microsoft.com/learning/exams/70-448.mspx*. The practice exercises in this Training Kit require you to use Microsoft SQL Server 2008 Enterprise or Microsoft SQL Server 2008 Developer. A 180-day evaluation edition of SQL Server 2008 Enterprise is included on this book's SQL Server 2008 evaluation DVD. If you do not have access to this software, you can download a 180-day trial of SQL Server 2008 from *http://www.microsoft.com/sqlserver/2008/en/us/trial-software.aspx*. You can also consider purchasing SQL Server 2008 Development, which contains all of the required features.

By using this Training Kit, you will learn how to:

- Install and configure the SQL Server 2008 BI components.
- Work with the design and management tools in SQL Server 2008 for BI.
- Develop and deploy SSIS projects.
- Secure, manage, and troubleshoot SSIS packages.
- Develop and deploy SSAS solutions.
- Secure SSAS cubes and dimensions.
- Implement, configure, and deploy SSRS reports.
- Manage and secure SSRS report servers.

Hardware Requirements

We recommend that you use a test workstation, test server, or staging server to complete the exercises in each practice. However, it would be beneficial for you to have access to production-ready data in your organization. If you need to set up a workstation to complete the practice exercises, the minimum 32-bit system (X86) requirements for installing SQL Server 2008 are:

- A computer with a 1-GHz Pentium III compatible or faster processor (2 GHz or faster recommended).
- 512 MB of RAM or more (2 GB or higher recommended).
- 2.1-GB free hard disk space for the SQL Server installation files and samples (which include all of the BI services, client components, developer and management tools, sample databases and projects, and online help files).
- A DVD-ROM drive for installing SQL Server 2008 from the evaluation software DVD.
- A Super VGA (1024 × 768) or higher resolution video adapter and monitor.
- A keyboard and Microsoft mouse, or compatible pointing device.

For detailed SQL Server 2008 hardware requirements, see *http://technet.microsoft.com/en-us/library/ms143506.aspx*. You can also install SQL Server 2008 on a virtual machine instead of on standard computer hardware by using the virtual machine software Virtual PC 2007, Virtual Server 2005 R2, Hyper-V, or third-party virtual machine software. To download an evaluation of Virtual Server 2005 R2, go to *http://www.microsoft.com/virtualserver*. For more information about Hyper-V, go to *http://www.microsoft.com/hyperv*. To download Virtual PC for free, go to *http://www.microsoft.com/windows/products/winfamily/virtualpc/default.mspx*.

Software Requirements

Note that you will need SQL Server 2008 installed with the BI components, tools, and samples in order to complete the practices included with each chapter. Although these products can be installed on a production server, it is not recommended that you use a production installation for this Training Kit. Instead, install these products and execute the practices on a single development computer. The following software is required to complete the practice exercises:

- **A compatible operating system**   SQL Server 2008 can be installed on many versions of Windows server and desktop operating systems, including Windows XP (with Service Pack 2 [SP2] or later), Windows Server 2003 (with SP2), Windows Vista, and Windows Server 2008. See *http://technet.microsoft.com/en-us/library/ms143506.aspx* to help you choose a compatible SQL Server 2008 version.

  In general, SQL Server 2008 Enterprise can be installed on many of the server operating system products (such as Windows Server 2003 SP2 or Windows Server 2008), but it cannot be installed on the desktop operating systems.

SQL Server 2008 Developer can be installed on the same Windows Server editions that the Enterprise edition can be installed on, and it can also be installed on the desktop operating systems, such as Windows XP SP2 and Windows Vista.

- **SQL Server 2008** A 180-day evaluation of SQL Server Enterprise is included on the evaluation software DVD. A 180-day evaluation of SQL Server 2008 is also available as a free download from the Microsoft Developer Network (MSDN) Web site at *http://www.microsoft.com/sqlserver/2008/en/us/trial-software.aspx*. Instructions for installing the BI components of SQL Server 2008 are included in the next section.

- **Microsoft .NET Framework 3.5** This is required to be installed before the SQL Server 2008 installation setup process can be initiated. This prerequisite is available with the installation files on the SQL Server 2008 evaluation DVD.

- **Microsoft Visual Studio 2008 (optional)** You use Visual Studio 2008 Standard or Visual Studio 2008 Professional installed with the Microsoft Visual Basic .NET library to complete the practice exercises for Chapter 11. You must also install Visual Studio 2008 SP1 (or later).

  A 90-day trial version of Visual Studio 2008 Professional is available at *http://www.microsoft.com/downloads/details.aspx?FamilyID=83c3a1ec-ed72-4a79-8961-25635db0192b&displaylang=en*. You can download Visual Studio 2008 SP1 by going to *http://www.microsoft.com/downloads/details.aspx?FamilyId=FBEE1648-7106-44A7-9649-6D9F6D58056E&displaylang=en*.

  You should install Visual Studio 2008 only when you are ready to start Chapter 11, because doing so changes the menu options you see in Business Intelligence Development Studio (BIDS). For example, to create a new project in BIDS when you have Visual Studio installed, you choose File and then New Project. In contrast, to create a new project in BIDS when you do not have Visual Studio installed, you choose File, New, and then Project.

> **NOTE** USING BIDS AND VISUAL STUDIO TOGETHER
>
> With the exception of Chapter 11, this book was written under the assumption that you do not have Visual Studio installed. If you already have Visual Studio installed, you will find that your menu options in BIDS will differ slightly from what is written in the book for the procedures and practice exercises.

- **The sample relational databases named AdventureWorks2008 and AdventureWorks-DW2008** These are available through the Microsoft open source community Web site *http://www.codeplex.com*. Search for "SQL Server 2008 databases," or navigate to *http://www.codeplex.com/MSFTDBProdSamples/Release/ProjectReleases.aspx?ReleaseId=18407*.

- **The sample SSAS database named Adventure Works DW 2008** The sample SSAS database is available with the SQL Server 2008 product samples on the Microsoft open source community Web site *http://www.codeplex.com*. Search for "SQL Server 2008 product samples," or navigate to *http://www.codeplex.com/MSFTDBProdSamples/Release/ProjectReleases.aspx?ReleaseId=18407*.

- **The AdventureWorks report samples** The AdventureWorks report samples consist of report definition files for SQL Server Reporting Services that reference the AdventureWorks 2008 databases. To download the samples, go to the Microsoft open code source community Web site at *http://www.codeplex.com* and search for "SQL Server 2008 Reporting Services samples," or navigate to *http://www.codeplex.com/MSFTRSProdSamples/Wiki/View.aspx?title=SS2008%21AdventureWorks%20Sample%20Reports&referringTitle=Home*. After you download and install the sample reports, you must deploy the reports within BIDS. The instructions for doing so are on the Codeplex Web page from which you download the sample reports.

For detailed hardware requirements, see *http://technet.microsoft.com/en-us/library/ms143506.aspx*. It should also be noted that Internet Information Services (IIS) is not required for Reporting Services 2008 installation.

Installing SQL Server 2008

Either SQL Server 2008 Enterprise or SQL Server 2008 Developer is required to run the code samples and practices provided in this book. A 180-day evaluation edition is available on this book's SQL Server 2008 evaluation DVD. Alternatively, a free 180-day evaluation edition of SQL Server 2008 Enterprise is available for download from *http://www.microsoft.com/sqlserver/2008/en/us/trial-software.aspx*. This version can be installed on both the server operating system and desktop operating system with which SQL Server 2008 is compatible.

The SQL Server 2008 platform includes the core Database Engine, BI components, and tools to support development and administration. SQL Server 2008 is available in different editions and languages. The editions include feature subsets intended for a variety of purposes and applications. The primary editions of SQL Server 2008 are:

- **SQL Server 2008 Enterprise** Includes the full features of SQL Server 2008 and provides enterprise performance and capabilities.

- **SQL Server 2008 Developer** Includes the full features of SQL Server 2008 and can be used for development.

- **SQL Server Standard** Includes the core functionality of SQL Server 2008 but does not contain the scalability options and advanced capabilities that SQL Server 2008 Enterprise and SQL Server 2008 Developer contain.

- **SQL Server 2008 Workgroup**   Contains the core database components but is limited in functionality, with only a small subset of BI features.

- **SQL Server 2008 Web**   Contains the core database components with limited functionality and also includes Reporting Services with limited functionality. This version is intended for Web applications and workloads.

- **SQL Server 2008 Express**   Freely distributable lightweight edition of SQL Server 2008. This version has limitations but can be used for development and to embed in applications.

- **SQL Server 2008 Compact**   The lightweight mobile version of SQL Server 2008 Database Engine.

For a comprehensive description of each edition's capabilities, see *http://www.microsoft.com/ Sqlserver/2008/en/us/editions.aspx*. The focus of this Training Kit is the implementation and management of the BI components found in the Enterprise, Developer, and Standard editions of SQL Server 2008.

EXPLORING THE SQL SERVER INSTALLATION CENTER

All the features of SQL Server 2008 are available on the SQL Server 2008 evaluation DVD and can be installed on the same server. You can also install the features on separate servers if that works best within your BI architecture.

The installation of SQL Server 2008 components are launched through the SQL Server Installation Center, which runs automatically when the evaluation DVD is inserted and provides installation and setup resources for stand-alone installations, upgrades, failover cluster installs, tool installs, and so on. Figure I-1 shows the Installation page of the SQL Server Installation Center.

For a new installation or to modify an existing installation, click the New SQL Server Stand-alone Installation Or Add Features To An Existing Installation link on the Installation page.

IMPORTANT   **LICENSING SQL SERVER 2008**

A SQL Server 2008 license is required for each server on which you install any of the server components; however, running multiple components of SQL Server 2008 on the same server requires only a single license. You can find complete licensing details at *http://www.microsoft.com/sqlserver/2008/en/us/licensing.aspx*.

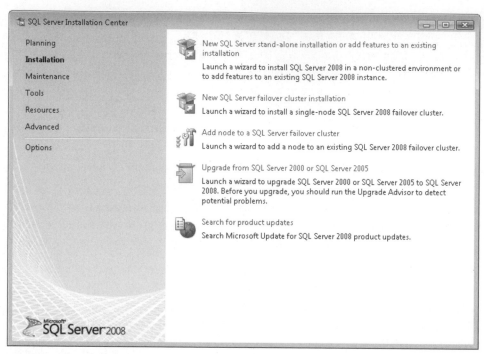

FIGURE I-1 The Installation page of the SQL Server Installation Center provides links that launch the SQL Server 2008 installation.

Selecting Installation Components

The first step of the installation will check the minimum hardware requirements and will install Microsoft .NET Framework 3.5 and SQL Server Native Client. These prerequisites are included on the SQL Server 2008 evaluation DVD. Furthermore, during the initial setup, the installer will identify other required supporting applications and Windows components you might need.

The SQL Server installation process will then scan your computer for the required configuration. The System Configuration Check results will indicate whether configuration changes need to be made before the installation proceeds. If any configurations are not correct, Setup will block the installation of SQL Server 2008. After the prerequisites and configuration check, you will be able to select the features for installation on the Feature Selection page of the SQL Server 2008 Setup Wizard. For a complete installation, select all the components, as shown in Figure I-2.

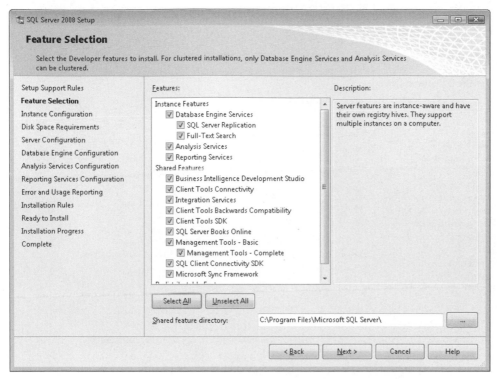

FIGURE I-2 On the Feature Selection page, select all the components for a complete SQL Server installation.

Choosing Installation Details

After the component selections are complete, the next installation steps are determining the installation details, such as selecting the instance name, setting the program and data file locations, and identifying the appropriate security accounts.

SPECIFYING AN INSTANCE NAME

The first selection you will be prompted to make will determine the instance name. Several components of SQL Server 2008 can be installed on the same computer multiple times. Each time the same component is installed, it needs a new instance name for that installation. Instances apply to the Database Engine, Analysis Services, and Reporting Services.

- Choosing the Default Instance means that the installation components that you selected will be installed with no name.

- Alternatively, you can name the new installation instance by using the Named Instance option.

Figure I-3 shows the Instance Configuration page of the SQL Server 2008 Setup Wizard with the Default Instance option selected.

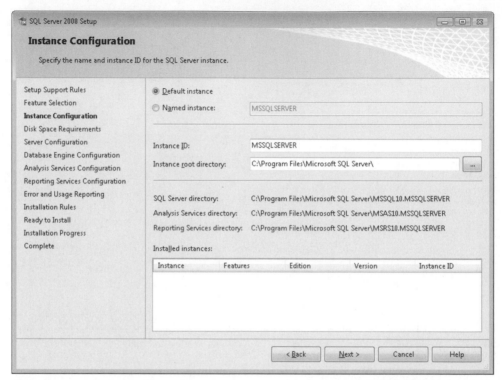

FIGURE I-3 The Instance Configuration page allows you to either choose the Default Instance or create a Named Instance for all the installation components.

When you choose the default instance, the connection strings to access the servers need to contain only the server name and not the named instance extension. Having multiple named instances also allows you to install different versions and editions of SQL Server on the same physical computer. For example, you can have multiple installations of SSAS on the same physical computer, each at different service pack levels.

CUSTOMIZING SERVICE ACCOUNTS

The Server Configuration page allows you to customize the security accounts that each service will use to run. On the Service Accounts tab of the Server Configuration page, shown in Figure I-4, you can indicate the service account to be used. For each service, the Account Name can use a local account or domain account where you specify the account password. Alternatively, you can also choose the LOCAL SYSTEM or Network Service account and a password is not required. However, access to local and external domain resources might be limited.

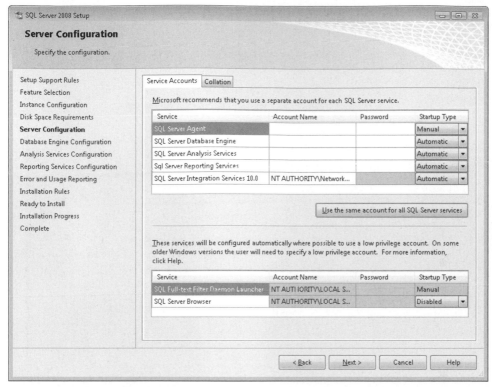

FIGURE I-4 On the Service Accounts tab of the Server Configuration page, you can define the security accounts that are used when each service starts.

To build a test system, such as for the purposes of this Training Kit, you can set all the services to use the LOCAL SYSTEM account. Click the Use The Same Account For All SQL Server Services button, and then choose the LOCAL SYSTEM account.

The Collation tab defines how the Database Engine handles data sorting based on locale settings, case sensitivity, and binary order.

The Database Engine collation settings can be defined independently from Analysis Services collation settings. To define separate collations, select the Customize For Each Service Account check box, and then change the value of the Service drop-down list for each service on the Server Configuration page.

SETTING THE AUTHENTICATION MODE

The Authentication Mode setting is specific to the SQL Server Database Engine and defines the way in which users are able to log on to SQL Server. Figure I-5 shows the Database Engine Configuration settings.

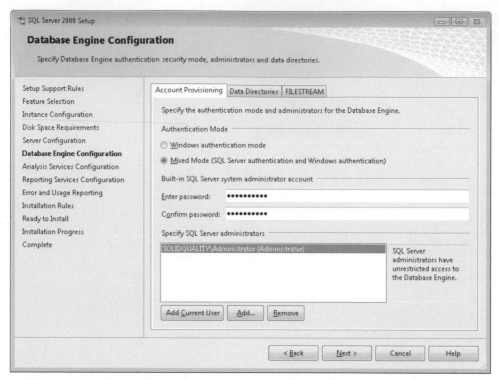

FIGURE I-5 The Database Engine Configuration page is used to set the SQL Server security authentication mode.

- The Windows Authentication Mode option specifies that a user can connect only with a local computer account or domain account.
- The Mixed Mode option allows users to connect with Windows Authentication or with authentication defined in SQL Server.

Note that you can change the Authentication Mode setting after installation by using the Server Properties dialog box in SQL Server Management Studio.

Click the Add Current User button or the Add button to add your personal account as a SQL Server administrator or another account as an administrator. Furthermore, the folders for storing files such as log files, data files, backup files, and temp folders can be set on the Data Directories tab. Filestream can be enabled on the FILESTREAM tab for accessing unstructured file data through SQL Server.

CONFIGURING ANALYSIS SERVICES

The installation settings for Analysis Services include defining the administrator accounts and setting folders for the data, backup, and log files, as shown in Figure I-6.

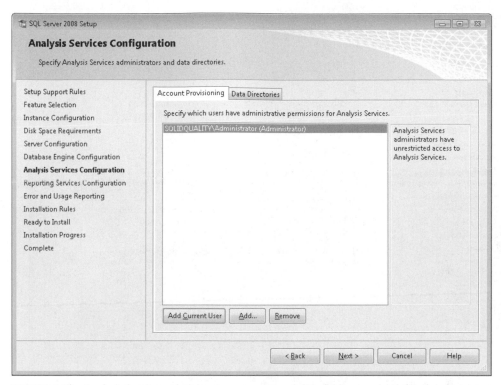

FIGURE I-6 The Analysis Services administrator accounts and data folders can be defined during setup.

CONFIGURING REPORTING SERVICES

For SQL Server 2008 implementations that include Reporting Services, during the installation, you can either choose the default SSRS configuration or choose to configure the SSRS service later, but you cannot customize the SSRS installation settings. In other words, you can choose to have Reporting Services configured with the default configurations, or you can have Setup install Reporting Services but leave it unconfigured and then configure it after installation. Chapter 13, "Configuring and Administering the SSRS Server," reviews the custom configuration for Reporting Services. Figure I-7 shows the Reporting Services Configuration page of the SQL Server 2008 Setup Wizard.

If SharePoint Services is installed, Reporting Services can also be installed in SharePoint integrated mode so that you can administer the report server and users can access reports through SharePoint.

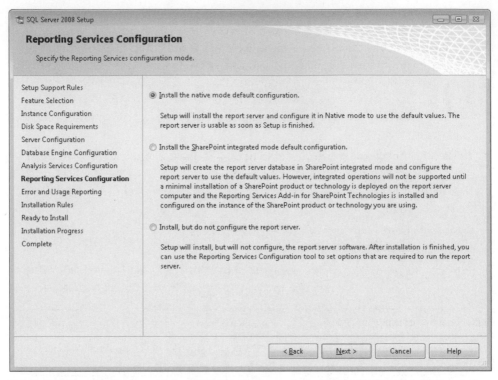

FIGURE I-7 Reporting Services can be installed in native mode, installed with SharePoint integrated mode, or installed but not configured.

COMPLETING THE INSTALLATION

On the remaining wizard pages, you can specify whether to send errors to Microsoft, perform final installation checks, and to confirm the installation detail summary. Clicking Install on the Ready To Install page will run the file copy and installation process until the setup process is complete.

Using the SQL Server Evaluation DVD and the Companion CD

A companion CD and a SQL Server 2008 evaluation DVD are included with this Training Kit. The companion CD contains the following:

- **Practice tests** You can practice for the 70-448 certification exam by using tests created from a pool of 200 realistic exam questions. These questions give you many different practice exams to ensure that you are prepared to take the real test.

- **Chapter practice exercises** Many chapters in this book include sample files associated with the practice exercises at the end of every lesson. Most exercises have a project or solution that you can use to complete the exercise and a version of the completed exercise for your review. To install the sample files on your hard disk, run Setup.exe from the Practice folder on the companion CD. The default installation folder is C:\Users*username*\Documents\Microsoft Press\MCTS Training Kit 70-448\Source\. Within the Source folder, you will find a separate folder corresponding to each chapter in the book.

- **An eBook** An electronic version of this book (an eBook) is included for times when you do not want to carry the printed book with you. The eBook is in Portable Document Format (PDF), and you can view it by using Adobe Acrobat or Adobe Acrobat Reader, available from *http://www.adobe.com*.

- **Sample chapters** Sample chapters from related Microsoft Press titles are offered on the CD. These chapters are in PDF format.

- **Glossary** A glossary of terms used in this book is included on the companion CD. The glossary is in PDF format, viewable by using Adobe Acrobat or Adobe Acrobat Reader.

> **Digital Content for Digital Book Readers:** If you bought a digital-only edition of this book, you can enjoy select content from the print edition's companion CD.
> Visit **http://go.microsoft.com/fwlink/?LinkId=144373** to get your downloadable content. This content is always up-to-date and available to all readers.

Installing the Practice Tests

To install the practice test software from the companion CD on your hard disk, perform the following steps:

1. Insert the companion CD into your CD drive, and then accept the license agreement. A CD menu appears.

> *NOTE* **IF THE CD MENU DOES NOT APPEAR**
>
> If the CD menu or the license agreement does not appear, AutoRun might be disabled on your computer. Refer to the Readme.txt file on the CD for alternative installation instructions.

2. Select the Practice Tests item, and then follow the instructions on the screen and then follow the instructions in the Microsoft Press Training Kit Exam Prep Suite 70-448 Wizard.

Using the Practice Tests

To start the practice test software, follow these steps:

1. Click Start, select All Programs, select Microsoft Press Training Kit Exam Prep, and then select Microsoft Press Training Kit Exam Prep again. A window appears that shows all the Microsoft Press training kit exam prep suites that are installed on your computer.

2. Double-click the practice test that you want to use.

CHOOSING PRACTICE TEST OPTIONS

When you start a practice test, you choose whether to take the test in Certification Mode, Study Mode, or Custom Mode.

- **Certification Mode** Closely resembles the experience of taking a certification exam. The test has a set number of questions, it is timed, and you cannot pause and restart the timer.

- **Study Mode** Creates an untimed test in which you can review the correct answers and the explanations after you answer each question.

- **Custom Mode** Gives you full control over the test options so that you can customize them to suit your needs. You can click OK to accept the defaults, or you can set the number of questions you want to answer, define the way the practice test software works, choose the exam objectives to which you want the questions to relate, and indicate whether you want your lesson review to be timed. If you are retaking a test, you can indicate whether you want to see all the questions again or only those questions you previously missed or did not answer.

In all modes, the user interface you see when taking the test is essentially the same, but depending on the mode, different options will be enabled or disabled.

After you click OK, your practice test starts.

- To take the test, answer the questions, and then use the Next, Previous, and Go To buttons to move from question to question.

- After you answer an individual question, to see which answers are correct and to see an explanation of each correct answer, click Explanation.

- If you would rather wait until the end of the test to see how you did, answer all the questions, and then click Score Test. You will see a summary of the exam objectives you chose, the percentage of questions you answered correctly overall, and the percentage of questions you answered correctly for each objective. You can print a copy of your test, review your answers, or retake the test.

When you review your answer to an individual practice test question, a "References" section lists the places in the Training Kit in which you can find the information that relates to that question and provides links to other sources of information. After you click Test Results to score your entire practice test, you can click the Learning Plan tab to see a list of references for every objective.

Uninstalling the Practice Tests

To uninstall the practice test software for a Training Kit, use the Add Or Remove Programs option in Windows Control Panel.

System Requirements for the Companion CD

To use the companion CD, you need a computer running Windows Server 2008, Windows Vista, Windows Server 2003, or Windows XP Professional. The computer must meet the following minimum requirements:

- 1 GHz 32-bit (x86) or 64-bit (x64) processor (depending on the minimum requirements of the operating system)
- 1 GB of system memory (depending on the minimum requirements of the operating system)
- A hard disk partition with at least 1 GB of available space
- A monitor capable of at least 800 x 600 display resolution
- A keyboard
- A mouse or other pointing device
- An optical drive capable of reading CDs

The computer must also have the following software:

- A Web browser such as Windows Internet Explorer 7 or later
- An application that can display PDF files, such as Adobe Acrobat Reader, which can be downloaded at *http://www.adobe.com/reader*

These requirements support the use of the companion CD. To perform the practice exercises in this training kit, you need additional hardware and software. See the preceding sections for detailed requirements.

Microsoft Certified Professional Program

The Microsoft certifications provide the best method to prove your command of current Microsoft products and technologies. The exams and corresponding certifications are developed to validate your mastery of critical competencies as you design and develop or implement and support solutions with Microsoft products and technologies. Computer professionals who become Microsoft-certified are recognized as experts and are sought after industry-wide. Certification brings a variety of benefits to the individual and to employers and organizations.

> **NOTE** **THE MICROSOFT CERTIFICATIONS**
>
> For a full list of Microsoft certifications, go to *http://www.microsoft.com/learning/mcp/default.asp*.

Technical Support

Every effort has been made to ensure the accuracy of this book and the contents of the companion CD. If you have comments, questions, or ideas regarding this book or the companion CD, please send them to Microsoft Press by using either of the following methods:

E-mail:

- tkinput@microsoft.com

Postal Mail:

- *Microsoft Press*
Attn: MCTS Self-Paced Training Kit (Exam 70-448): Microsoft SQL Server 2008—Business Intelligence Development and Maintenance *Editor*
One Microsoft Way
Redmond, WA 98052-6399

For additional support information regarding this book and the companion CD (including answers to commonly asked questions about installation and use), visit the Microsoft Press Technical Support Web site at *http:/www.microsoft.com/learning/support/books*. To connect directly to the Microsoft Knowledge Base and enter a query, visit *http://support.microsoft.com/search*. For support information regarding Microsoft software, please visit *http://support.microsoft.com*.

Evaluation Edition Software Support

The 180-day evaluation edition software provided with this Training Kit is not the full retail product and is provided only for the purposes of training and evaluation. Microsoft and Microsoft Technical Support do not support this evaluation edition.

Information about any issues relating to the use of this evaluation edition with this Training Kit is posted to the Support section of the Microsoft Press Web site at *http://www.microsoft.com/learning/support/books*. For information about ordering the full version of any Microsoft software, please call Microsoft Sales at (800) 426-9400 or visit the Microsoft Web site at *http://www.microsoft.com*.

CHAPTER 1

Developing SSIS Packages

A *package* is the core object within SQL Server Integration Services (SSIS) that contains the business logic to handle workflow and data processing. You use SSIS packages to move data from sources to destinations and to handle the timing precedence of when data is processed. You can create packages by using the SQL Server Import And Export Wizard in SQL Server Management Studio (SSMS) or by using the SSIS Designer in the Business Intelligence Development Studio (BIDS). This chapter looks at creating and defining packages in SSIS and using the main components of the control flow and data flow objects with sources and destinations.

SSIS is designed for many data integration and processing applications. One of those applications is the processing of data into a data mart or data warehouse, where data is used exclusively for business intelligence (BI) analytics and reporting. Although many businesses use SSIS for BI, there are many other applications of SSIS. For example, many organizations use SSIS to move data from legacy systems into new systems during application migrations, to integrate data from multiple systems by passing data back and forth, to extract data for sending to vendors or partners, to cleanse data, to import data from vendors or partners—the list goes on. Because this Training Kit focuses on BI, part of the SSIS content and lessons cover using SSIS for data warehouse extraction, transformation, and loading (ETL), but the SSIS chapters and lessons also explain how to take advantage of SSIS for other purposes.

This initial chapter explains how to create SSIS packages and defines the basic objects contained in the control flow and data flow. Later chapters describe the advanced features, deployment, and implementation details of SSIS.

Exam objectives in this chapter:

- Implement control flow.
- Implement data flow.
- Implement package logic by using variables.
- Extend SSIS packages by using .NET code.
- Identify and resolve issues related to SSIS solution deployment.
- Install and maintain SSIS components.

Before You Begin

To complete this chapter, you must have:

- Knowledge of Microsoft SQL Server 2008, including SSIS features and components.
- Experience working with SQL Server Business Intelligence Development Studio (BIDS) projects and solutions.
- Experience working in SQL Server Management Studio (SSMS).
- The AdventureWorks2008 and AdventureWorksDW2008 sample databases installed. You can download these databases from the CodePlex community Web site at *http://www.codeplex.com/MSFTDBProdSamples*.

Lesson 1: Creating SSIS Packages and Data Sources

Estimated lesson time: 50 minutes

The core object within SSIS is a *package*. A package contains the business logic to handle the data extraction, manipulation, and transformation tasks needed to move data to destinations. Packages also contain workflow elements to help process data. These workflow elements might involve running a stored procedure, moving a file from an FTP server to a destination folder on your server, or sending an e-mail message when an error occurs. When you execute a package, the logic within performs the designed steps.

Packages also contain connections to data sources and data destinations. You set up these connections to connect to different external systems such as databases, files, File Transfer Protocol (FTP) servers, Simple Mail Transfer Protocol (SMTP) servers, and so on. Connections are used for the SSIS data processing engine (called the *data flow*) as well as the workflow engine (called the *control flow*).

Creating SSIS Packages

The first step in getting started with SSIS is to create a package. You can accomplish this in one of two ways:

- By using the built-in Import And Export Wizard in SQL Server 2008, which asks you about moving data from a source to a destination and then automatically generates an SSIS package. After you create a package in the wizard, you can execute it immediately, schedule it, or associate it with an SSIS project.
- By explicitly creating a package inside an SSIS project in BIDS. BIDS in SQL Server 2008 uses the Microsoft Visual Studio 2008 interface with specific templates installed to create BI objects such as SSIS packages. Within the BIDS development environment, you first create an SSIS project and then create and develop new packages.

The remainder of this lesson explains using both methods to develop SSIS packages.

Using the Import And Export Wizard

With SQL Server 2008, you use the Import And Export Wizard to copy data without going through the process of creating an SSIS project. When you use the wizard, it generates an SSIS package that you can execute immediately or save and then manually modify or schedule.

You typically start the Import And Export Wizard through SSMS when you are connected to the SQL Server relational engine. SSMS is the SQL Server management tool designed primarily for managing databases, and you will be using SSMS many times in the lessons throughout this Training Kit. To launch SSMS, from the Start menu, select Microsoft SQL Server 2008 and then SQL Server Management Studio. Figure 1-1 shows the Connect To Server dialog box, where you first connect to the Database Engine.

FIGURE 1-1 Start SSMS by selecting Microsoft SQL Server 2008 from the Start menu and then selecting SQL Server Management Studio. Connect to the Database Engine to manage SQL Server relational databases.

Starting the Import And Export Wizard

As its name states, the Import And Export Wizard can both import and export data. Use the following considerations to determine which part of the wizard to use:

- Importing data with the wizard lets you bring into a SQL Server table any data contained in accessible sources. Sources include other SQL Server databases, flat files, data in Microsoft Office Excel spreadsheets or Microsoft Office Access databases, and data in Oracle databases.

- Exporting data with the wizard lets you send data from SQL Server tables, views, or custom queries to flat files or database connections.

To start the Import And Export Wizard, follow these steps:

1. Through SSMS, connect to the instance of the SQL Server 2008 Database Engine that contains your source or your destination.

2. Open Object Explorer. You will find a list of various object containers under the SQL Server connection. The Databases folder shows all the databases attached to that instance of SQL Server. The System Databases subfolder contains the system databases.

3. To start the Import And Export Wizard, right-click the database that you want to use as your source or destination.

4. Click Tasks. If the database is the source of data that you want to send to a different system, select Export Data. If the database is the destination for files that currently exist outside the system, select Import Data, as Figure 1-2 shows.

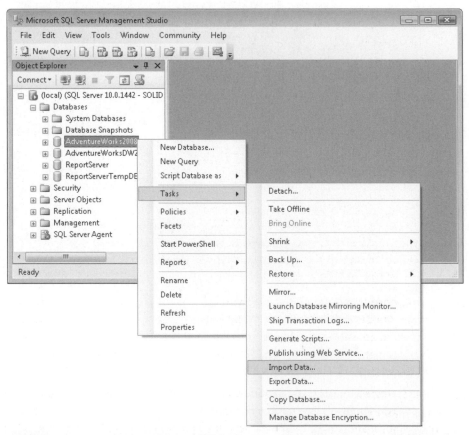

FIGURE 1-2 Start the Import And Export Wizard by right-clicking the database in SSMS and then clicking Tasks.

The wizard then walks you through several pages of questions, the answers to which are used to build the resulting package. The wizard pages include the following:

1. The Choose A Data Source page lets you specify where your data is coming from, such as a SQL Server database, an Excel file, a flat file, or other source. If your source is a relational database, you can also configure the security for the connection. Figure 1-3 shows the first page of the Import And Export Wizard.

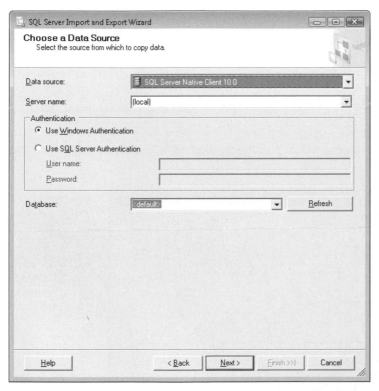

FIGURE 1-3 The Import And Export Wizard first lets you choose the data source where the data will be coming from, such as a SQL Server database, an Excel spreadsheet, or a flat file.

2. The Choose A Destination page lets you specify where your data will be sent. You specify the destination type and, if applicable, the server name and security settings needed to access the data. If you chose Import Data in SSMS to start the wizard, the data destination settings will match those of the database you selected prior to starting the wizard.

3. If you selected a relational database source that allows custom queries, on the Specify Table Copy Or Query page, you can choose to copy the data directly from the source to the destination or to specify a query. If you choose to specify a query, an additional page, named Provide A Source Query, enables you to manually enter the query.

4. If your source is a relational database and you do not specify a query, you can choose tables and views from your source on the Select Source Tables And Views page. If your source is a flat file or you specified a query, only the file or query is available as a choice. Also on this page, you can rename the destination table and edit the column mappings by clicking the Edit Mappings button to define column NULL settings, identity insert, and whether the table should be dropped and recreated every time.

5. Use the Save And Run Package page to execute the package immediately or save the package for later execution. If you save the package, you can later go back and edit the package by using the SSIS Designer, which is demonstrated in the rest of this chapter.

Saving and Editing Packages Created in the Wizard

The wizard's last page lets you execute the package immediately or save it. If you choose to save the autogenerated package within an Integration Services project in BIDS, as Figure 1-4 shows, you can modify its contents later. At times, you might want to use the wizard to generate a basic package to which you can add more advanced logic that the wizard cannot generate.

FIGURE 1-4 The final page of the Import And Export Wizard lets you execute and/or save packages.

In general, the Import And Export Wizard provides a quick way to move data from one source to a destination, especially for a one-time use, but there are some limitations:

- You can specify only one source and one destination in the wizard.
- Advanced workflow precedence is not available through the wizard.
- The wizard does not share data sources with other packages.

You need to evaluate whether your data processing requirements enable you to use the wizard or whether you need to develop a new package from scratch in BIDS.

Creating an SSIS Project in BIDS

Although the Import And Export Wizard is useful for generating a quick package that moves data from one source to one destination, these packages are frequently only a starting point. More often than not, you will need to either develop a package that has more complicated requirements or create a set of coordinated packages. For these cases, you first need to create a new SSIS project in BIDS.

> **NOTE OBJECTS IN BIDS**
>
> Remember that any one project in BIDS can contain only objects from the same project type, such as SSIS, SQL Server Analysis Services (SSAS), or SQL Server Reporting Services (SSRS). However, a single project can be associated with projects of different types in the same solution.

All of the SQL Server BI components are generated in a similar fashion through the BIDS development tool. To launch BIDS, from the Start menu, select Microsoft SQL Server 2008 and then SQL Server Business Intelligence Development Studio. Follow these steps to create a new SSIS project:

1. In BIDS, choose New, Project from the File menu. (If you have Visual Studio 2008 installed separately from BIDS, you can simply select New Project from the File menu.) Figure 1-5 shows the resulting New Project dialog box.

2. Fill out the New Project dialog box as follows:

    a. Under Project Types, select Business Intelligence Projects.

    b. Under Templates, select Integration Services Project.

    c. Assign a name to your project in the Name box.

    d. In the Location box, either leave the default folder location for storing new projects (in the ..\Documents\Visual Studio 2008\Projects\ folder) or change to a location of your choice.

3. When you have finished, click OK to build the project. The project contains several SSIS logical object folders, which Solution Explorer displays. You use these objects in your SSIS projects to point to connections and process data. Figure 1-6 shows a new project, with the default Package.dtsx package (created with the project) in the SSIS Designer and Solution Explorer on the right.

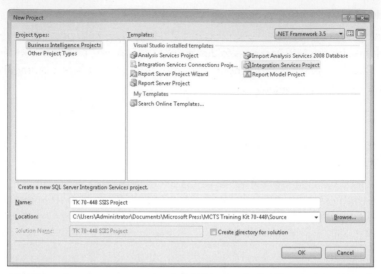

FIGURE 1-5 Creating a new project in BIDS begins in the New Project dialog box.

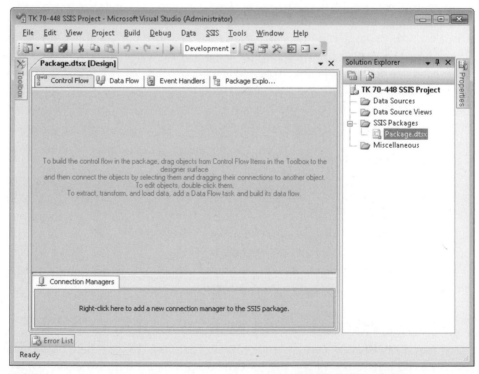

FIGURE 1-6 Creating a new project automatically creates a new SSIS package named Package.dtsx and several logical folders in Solution Explorer in BIDS.

You are now ready to configure and develop your package.

To add an existing package—such as one created by the Import And Export Wizard—to your project, right-click the SSIS Packages folder in Solution Explorer, and then click Add Existing Package. This dialog box lets you import packages from other projects or import packages that have already been deployed.

EXAM TIP

When you create packages in BIDS, the package is stored in the file system with the .dtsx file extension. This .dtsx file is an XML file that contains the logic and the layout for the design you have developed in BIDS, and you can move the file to a different project, manually deploy it to different servers, or make it part of a deployment package. In Chapter 3, "Deploying and Configuring SSIS Packages," and Chapter 4, "Administering, Securing, and Executing SSIS Packages," you will work with .dtsx files during deployment and execution.

Developing Project Data Sources and Package Connections

Because the main purpose of SSIS is to move data from sources to destinations, the next most important step is to add the pointers to these sources and destinations. These pointers are called *data sources* and *connections*. Data sources are stored at the project level and are found in Solution Explorer under the logical folder named Data Sources. Connections, on the other hand, are defined within packages and are found in the Connection Managers pane at the bottom of the Control Flow or Data Flow tab. Connections can be based on project data sources or can stand alone within packages. The next sections walk you through the uses and implementation of project data sources and package connections.

Creating a Data Source

A *data source* is an SSIS project object. Data sources contain connection strings that point to files or databases, and you can reference them within one or more packages. Data sources are optional within SSIS, but they are beneficial during development if you have a large number of packages that need to use the same database or file connection. Using a data source also helps if you need to change a connection used in many packages. You simply change the data source once and then open each package in your project, which will automatically synchronize the connection string stored in the package with the data source.

> **IMPORTANT** **PROJECT DATA SOURCES ARE FOR DEVELOPMENT PURPOSES ONLY**
>
> Be aware that after a package is deployed to a new environment and executed outside the project, the connection string is no longer updated by the project data source. Instead, you must use package configurations to share connection strings. See Chapter 3 to find out about sharing connection strings by using package configurations.

Using data sources in your project and packages is a two-step process:

1. **Creating the data source**   Within Solution Explorer, right-click the Data Sources folder, and then click New Data Source. On the Welcome page of the wizard, click Next. Figure 1-7 shows the Data Source Wizard.

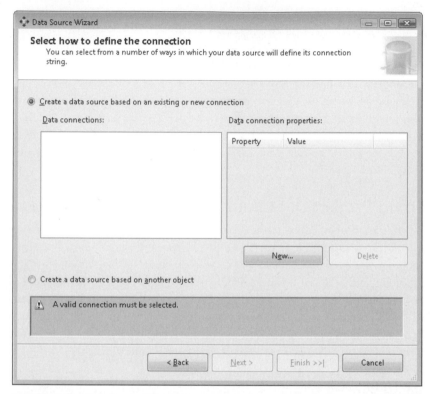

FIGURE 1-7 The Data Source Wizard lets you create a new connection in your project that can be shared between packages. The New button starts the Connection Wizard to create a new connection.

If you have made connections in the past on your server, a cached list of those connections appears in the Data Connections area, and you can choose an existing connection or click the New button to create a new connection. Figure 1-7 shows the connection page of the wizard without any cached connections.

2. **Adding the data source to a package**   After you create your data source in the project, you need to add the data source to your packages.

Creating Package Connection Managers

A *package connection manager*, sometimes simply called a *package connection*, is independent of project data sources. However, package connections can reference a project data source. A package connection lets the different components in SSIS communicate with an object (such as a database, file, or server) outside the package. You can use package connections as source adapters, FTP or e-mail servers, or flat files.

If you link the package connection to the project data source, when the project data source is edited, the package connection is also updated when the package is being developed. In the BIDS design environment in Figure 1-8, Solution Explorer shows a project data source, and two package connections appear in the Connection Managers pane at the bottom of the SSIS Designer.

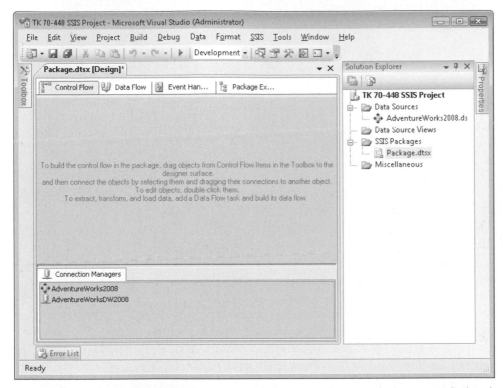

FIGURE 1-8 SSIS projects contain data sources, and packages contain connection managers. Project data sources can be linked to package connection managers, or connection managers can stand alone within a package.

Packages can be based on data sources defined in the SSIS project, or they can be stand-alone connections within a project. In Figure 1-8, the project has a data source named AdventureWorks2008, which is also referenced in the package's Connection Managers pane. In this example, the package contains another connection named Adventure-WorksDW2008, which does not reference a project data source. The icon used to identify a project data source matches the icon for the package connection if a package connection references a project data source.

Adding Connections in the Connection Managers Pane

To create a new connection, right-click in the Connection Managers pane at the bottom of the Control Flow tab, as Figure 1-9 shows.

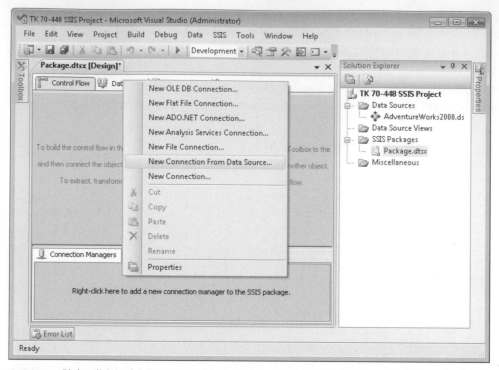

FIGURE 1-9 Right-click in the Connection Managers pane to create a new connection for your package.

You can create a connection from a project data source by selecting New Connection From Data Source, as Figure 1-9 shows, or you can create a stand-alone connection within a package by selecting New Connection and then choosing another connection provider from the Connection Manager Type list. A stand-alone connection is a connection that is not shared during development with other packages using a project data source. Stand-alone connections in a package that have the same name as a connection or connections in another package can, however, be updated together at run time through package configurations.

> **IMPORTANT MODIFYING A PROJECT DATA SOURCE**
>
> When you create a package connection from a data source, that connection is updated only during development whenever the package is opened and the data source has been changed. Package connections are not updated when they are run separately from the associated SSIS project—for example, when they are run from the command line.

The first step in creating a package connection is choosing the connection type, as Figure 1-9 shows. If you select a connection based on a data source, the connection has been created. However, if you choose another type of connection, you must perform at least one more step before the connection is complete. For example, if you are connecting to a relational database, you must select either New OLE DB Connection or New ADO.NET Connection (depending on which connection provider you want to use to access an underlying database). After you select the connection type, you need to configure that connection.

When you select the connection type, SSIS prompts you to either select a connection string that has been cached on the machine you are working on or create a new cached connection. If the connection string is already cached on your machine, simply select that connection from the list to add it to the list of connections in the Connection Managers pane in your package.

If a connection string does not exist in the cache, you need to create a new connection string. For example, to define a new connection string for an OLE DB connection, in the Connection Managers pane, right-click and then click New OLE DB Connection. Next, in the Configure OLE DB Connection Manager dialog box, click New. In the Provider list, choose from the list of OLE DB providers that are installed on your machine, and then specify the database name and the connection security credentials, as Figure 1-10 shows, and then click OK. After you specify the connection options, you can choose the newly cached connection from the list, which then adds the new connection to the Connection Managers pane in the package.

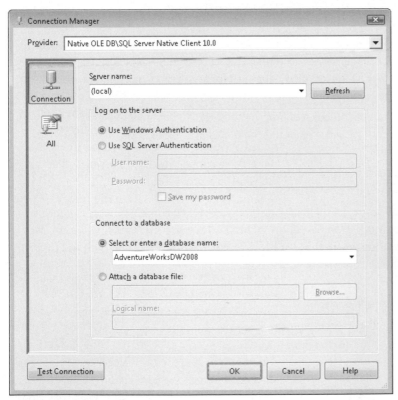

FIGURE 1-10 The Connection Manager dialog box lets you specify the provider, server, database, and security for the new connection.

Now that you have finished creating your package and package connections, you are ready to start developing package components. Connections are used in several package components, including control flow tasks, data flow adapters and transformations, event handlers, package logging, and package configurations—all of which are described in other chapters of this Training Kit.

PRACTICE   Creating New Packages, Data Sources, and Connections

The following exercises familiarize you with the common tasks of creating a new project in BIDS and working with data sources and connections. All the practice files can be installed from the Practice folder on the companion CD.

EXERCISE 1   Create the Project and Packages

In this exercise, you will create a new SSIS project and then work with a couple of SSIS packages by adding data sources and connections.

1. Start SQL Server Business Intelligence Development Studio (BIDS), by clicking the Start button and then selecting All Programs, Microsoft SQL Server 2008, SQL Server Business Intelligence Development Studio.

2. Choose New, Project from the File menu. (If you have Visual Studio 2008 installed separately from BIDS, simply choose New Project from the File menu.) The New Project dialog box displays all the installed templates for Microsoft Visual Studio, including the Business Intelligence Projects templates.

3. In the New Project dialog box, confirm that Business Intelligence Projects is selected in the Project Types area, and then in the Templates area, select the Integration Services Project template.

4. Near the bottom of the New Project dialog box, in the Name box, type **TK 70-448 SSIS Project** as the name of your SSIS project.

5. In the Location box, type the path, starting with the Documents folder in your user profile: **..\Documents\Microsoft Press\MCTS Training Kit 70-448\Source**. This is the same location where the practice exercise files for the Training Kit will be installed by default.

6. Next, clear the Create Directory For Solution check box, which stores the SSIS project in the folder you specified in step 5.

7. Click OK to have BIDS create the new SSIS project.

8. When the project is created, SSIS automatically creates a new SSIS package named Package.dtsx and opens it in the SSIS Designer. In Solution Explorer, right-click Package.dtsx, and then click Rename.

9. Rename the package by typing **MyPackage.dtsx**. BIDS might prompt you to rename the package object. If a message box appears that prompts you to rename the package object as well, click Yes. Always click Yes if you are prompted to change the package object when renaming a package because this updates the internal name of the package.

10. Click the Save button on the toolbar, and then close the package by clicking the Close button in the upper-right corner of the SSIS Designer.

11. To create a new package, right-click the SSIS Packages folder in Solution Explorer, and then click New SSIS Package. This creates a new package object named Package1.dtsx (the number depends on how many packages you have created) in the SSIS Packages folder in Solution Explorer.

12. To rename the new package, right-click the package, and then click Rename. Rename the package to **DimCustomer.dtsx** because this package will contain logic to process the customer dimension table. When prompted, click Yes to rename the package object.

13. Following the same steps, create one more package in your SSIS Project named **DimPromotion.dtsx**.

EXERCISE 2 Create Project Data Sources

In this exercise, you will create two project data sources, which will be used in your packages as the source and the destination.

1. If necessary, start SQL Server Business Intelligence Development Studio (BIDS), open the project you created in Exercise 1, *TK 70-448 SSIS Project*, and then open Solution Explorer (if it is not already displayed). You can open Solution Explorer by clicking the Solution Explorer button on the Standard toolbar.

2. In Solution Explorer, right-click the Data Sources folder, and then click New Data Source. When the Welcome page of the Data Source Wizard appears, click Next.

3. On the Select How To Define The Connection page, select Create A Data Source Based On An Existing Or New Connection.

4. Click New to open the Connection Manager dialog box.

5. In the Provider drop-down list, select the Native OLE DB\SQL Server Native Client 10 provider and click OK. Type **(local)** in the Server Name field.

6. In the Select Or Enter A Database Name drop-down list, select AdventureWorks2008.

7. Click the Test Connection button, and then click OK. Click OK again to close the Connection Manager dialog box.

8. Select the (local).AdventureWorks2008 data connection in the Data Connections list, and then click Finish in the Data Source Wizard.

9. The Completing The Wizard page prompts you to enter a name for the new project data source. Type **AdventureWorks2008** in the Data Source Name box, and then click Finish. Be sure to remove the space between Adventure and Works2008.

10. Next, repeat steps 2 to 9 to create a new project data source for the (local).AdventureWorksDW2008 database, and name this data source **AdventureWorksDW2008.**

11. When you are finished creating the data sources, click the Save All button on the BIDS toolbar.

EXERCISE 3   Create New Package Connections from the Project Data Sources

In this exercise, you will add the project data sources you just created to the two packages that you have developed.

1. If necessary, start SQL Server Business Intelligence Development Studio (BIDS), open the project you created in Exercise 1, *TK 70-448 SSIS Project*, and then open Solution Explorer. Edit your MyPackage.dtsx package by double-clicking the package in Solution Explorer.

2. Locate the Connection Managers pane (at the bottom of the SSIS Designer window), right-click in the pane, and then click New Connection From Data Source.

3. In the Select Data Source dialog box, select both the AdventureWorks2008 and AdventureWorksDW2008 data sources from the list, and then click OK to accept. This puts the two project data sources into the package's Connection Managers pane.

4. Perform the same steps in the *DimCustomer.dtsx* package to add the AdventureWorks2008 and AdventureWorksDW2008 project data sources as connection managers for the package.

5. When you are finished creating the connection managers, click the Save All button on the BIDS toolbar.

✔ Quick Check

1. You are asked to combine data from an Excel workbook and a database table and then push the results to a fixed-width flat file. Can you accomplish this task by using the Import And Export Wizard?

2. You need to create both SSIS packages to process your data and SSAS cubes to perform analysis. Can you create both objects in a single project?

3. What is the difference between a project data source and a package connection?

4. If a connection references a data source and the data source is changed, when will the connection be updated?

Quick Check Answers

1. No. The Import And Export Wizard lets you work with only a single source and a single destination. To combine data merging or data cleansing tasks, you need to either create a new package specifically for that purpose or modify a package previously created by the wizard.

2. No. You cannot create both SSIS and SSAS objects in one project because BIDS does not let you combine objects used for different platforms. You need to build two separate projects in BIDS: one for the SSIS packages and another for the SSAS cubes and dimensions.

3. Both project data sources and package connections are connection strings. However, a data source resides outside the package and can be used as the connection reference for more than one package. A package connection does not have to be associated with a data source.

4. Connections are updated by their associated data sources only when the package is opened for editing in BIDS.

Lesson 2: Creating and Editing Control Flow Objects

Estimated lesson time: 45 minutes

Now that you have created an SSIS project, packages, and package connections, it is time to start using SSIS features for data integration and for processing logic. This lesson and Lesson 3, "Using Data Flow Adapters and Transformations," focus on the two main components within SSIS: the control flow and the data flow. The *control flow* is the workflow engine and contains control flow tasks, containers, and precedence constraints, which manage when tasks and containers execute. The *data flow*, in contrast, is directly related to processing and transforming data from sources to destinations.

This lesson looks at defining control flow objects with the Control Flow design surface. When you have an SSIS project open within BIDS and are designing a package, the tabs across the top of the SSIS Designer let you choose an SSIS component to work with. The Control Flow design surface is the first tab and displays a workspace where you configure control flow objects. There are three primary types of control flow objects:

- **Control flow tasks**   Workflow objects that perform operational-level jobs
- **Control flow containers**   Provide a grouping mechanism for tasks and other containers
- **Constraints**   Let you connect tasks and containers and define execution ordering and precedence

Creating Control Flow Tasks

A *control flow task* is an SSIS component that performs an operation such as sending an e-mail message, executing an SQL statement, or copying a file from an FTP server. When a control flow task is complete, it either succeeded or failed. You use the control flow to coordinate the execution of tasks in parallel or to set precedence constraints based on the tasks' completion status. See Chapter 2, "Debugging and Error Handling in SSIS," to learn more about precedence constraints.

To create a new control flow task in your package, drag the task from the toolbox to the Control Flow tab in the SSIS Designer. Figure 1-11 shows the Toolbox window when the Control Flow tab is clicked in the SSIS Designer.

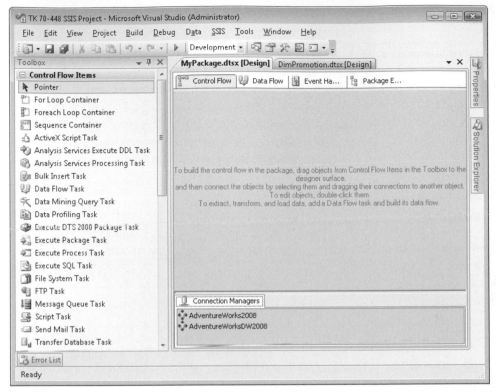

FIGURE 1-11 Control flow objects are found in the BIDS toolbox when you click the Control Flow tab in the SSIS Designer.

After you add a task to the control flow workspace, you need to configure the task to perform the specific operation you selected. To allow configuration, every task has an editor that you can open by double-clicking the task or by right-clicking the task and then clicking Edit. Table 1-1 lists the tasks in SSIS under the Control Flow Items list in the toolbox.

You might have noticed that there is also a list of Maintenance Plan Tasks for the control flow. These are primarily for database administrators (DBAs) who are managing SQL Server 2008 databases through the SSMS maintenance plan interface or DBAs who are creating packages in BIDS for database maintenance.

As you can see, SSIS features the ability to perform a host of different processing and integration operations. It is beyond the scope of this Training Kit and Exam 70-448 to discuss the design patterns for the components, but you will use several of these tasks in some lesson examples, and a couple of tasks are highlighted here.

TABLE 1-1 Common Tasks in SSIS

TASK	DESCRIPTION
ActiveX Script Task	Runs Microsoft Visual Basic Scripting Edition (VBScript) and JScript code and is included mainly for legacy support when a Data Transformation Services (DTS) package is migrated to SSIS.
Analysis Services Execute DDL Task	Runs XML for Analysis (XMLA) code against an SSAS database. XMLA is the data definition language (DDL) for SSAS; therefore, this task lets you perform common structure changes such as adding partitions to cubes.
Analysis Services Processing Task	Allows the processing of SSAS objects through an SSIS package.
Bulk Insert Task	Allows the execution of bulk copy operations for SQL Server. This task works only against a SQL Server Database Engine.
Data Flow Task	Allows data processing from sources to destinations. Lesson 3 in this chapter covers the data flow task in more detail.
Data Mining Query Task	Performs data mining queries and lets you capture the results for analysis.
Data Profiling Task	Allows the analysis of source data for patterns, missing data, candidate keys, and statistics. These results typically inform developers about what logic to include in their SSIS packages based on their data needs.
Execute DTS 2000 Package Task	Runs a DTS package within SSIS.
Execute Package Task	Runs other SSIS packages either deployed to SQL Server or in the file system.
Execute Process Task	Runs a command-line operation such as program or batch file execution.
Execute SQL Task	Runs SQL code against any underlying database connection in the SQL language of the connected database engine.
File System Task	Lets you copy, move, and delete files as well as perform other file and folder operations.
FTP Task	Sends and receives files between the file system and an FTP server and performs simple file and folder operations on the FTP server.

TASK	DESCRIPTION
Message Queue Task	Integrates with Message Queuing (MSMQ) on a server running Windows to read and send messages.
Script Task	Runs Microsoft Visual Basic 2008 or Microsoft Visual C# 2008 within an SSIS package.
Send Mail Task	Sends an e-mail message through an SMTP server.
Transfer [Object] Task	Tasks that copy SQL Server objects from one system to another, including databases, SQL Server Agent jobs, error messages, logins, master stored procedures, and database-level objects.
Web Service Task	Lets you connect to a Web service to send or receive information.
WMI Data Reader Task	Lets you run a Windows Management Instrumentation (WMI) query against the operating system to capture server information.
WMI Event Watcher Task	Waits for a particular event before executing.
XML Task	Combines, queries, and differentiates multiple XML files on the server.

Using Control Flow Containers

Your package must contain at least one task that performs a specific operation; however, most of the time, packages will have several tasks that coordinate with each other, and you need a way to organize those tasks. This is where a control flow container can help. A *control flow container* lets you group tasks together to control how tasks are run in parallel as well as ordering, logging, and transactions. Containers can also execute the tasks within them several times based on iterative requirements.

As with tasks, you find containers in the toolbox when you are working in the control flow. To use a container, you simply drag the container from the toolbox onto your control flow workspace. The screen in Figure 1-12 shows a package control flow containing a single container that holds several tasks.

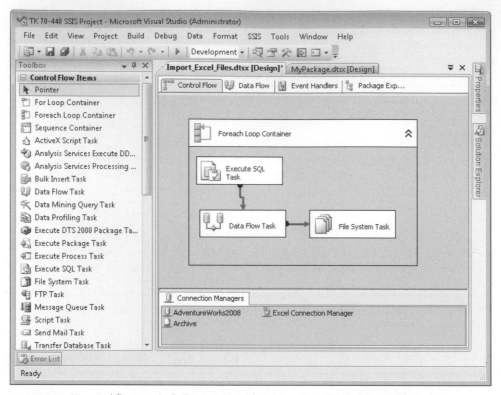

FIGURE 1-12 A control flow can include containers that group together tasks and subcontainers.

Additionally, you can drag task objects and other containers into your container.

There are three primary containers in SSIS: a Sequence Container, a For Loop Container, and a Foreach Loop Container.

- **Sequence Container** Lets you organize subordinate tasks by grouping them together, and lets you apply transactions or assign logging to the container.

- **For Loop Container** Provides the same functionality as the Sequence Container except that it also lets you run the tasks within it multiple times based on an evaluation condition, such as looping from 1 to 10.

- **Foreach Loop Container** Also allows looping, but instead of providing a condition expression, you loop over a set of objects, such as files in a folder.

Figure 1-13 shows the Foreach Loop Editor, which you open by double-clicking the container or by right-clicking the container and then clicking Edit.

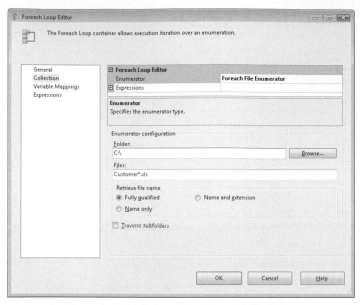

FIGURE 1-13 The Foreach Loop Editor lets you iterate over files in a folder and return the file names (one at a time) into a variable.

As described, the Foreach Loop Container can iterate over different types of objects, and the configuration choices let you specify the objects over which to loop and the detailed settings. Furthermore, the values of the enumerated objects can be put into user variables. For example, the Foreach Loop Container can iterate over files in a folder and return the file names into a variable.

Working with Package Variables

Variables within SSIS are a way to integrate objects by passing values between tasks and containers, accepting values from external sources, or building code dynamically that is then executed. You can also use variables for auditing and logging.

To work with variables within a package, choose Variables from the SSIS menu (when designing a package). Figure 1-14 shows the Variables window within BIDS.

At the top of the Variables window are buttons that let you create and delete variables as well as view other variables within a package. As Figure 1-14 shows, all SSIS variables are given a name, scope, data type, and value. The *scope* defines at what level within a package the variable is created. For example, if you select a Foreach Loop Container and then click the Add Variable button on the toolbar for the Variables window, the variable is scoped at that level. When no tasks or containers are selected, the variable is scoped at the entire package level.

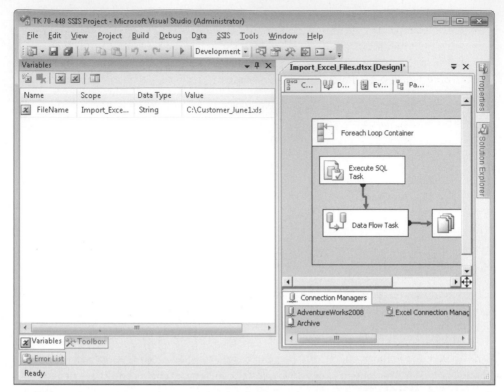

FIGURE 1-14 The Variables window lets you add, delete, or modify variables in a package.

EXAM TIP

Variables are viewable to a task or container only if the variables' scope is at the scope of the task or container in question, at the scope of a parent container level, or at the package scope itself. For example, if an Execute SQL Task has a variable directly assigned to it through the variable's scope, only the Execute SQL Task can see and use the variable. Other tasks or containers will not be able to reference the variable. On the other hand, if a Foreach Loop Container has a variable scoped to it, all the tasks within the Foreach Loop Container (including the container itself) can reference and use the variable. Variables are referenced as *User::[VariableName]* or *System::[VariableName]*.

Within SSIS, there are two types of variables: system variables and user variables.

- **System variables**   System variables are not editable but can be referenced within tasks and containers. System variables are set by the package for tracking metadata such as the package name and the user that executes the package. To view all system variables, click Show System Variables (the button labeled with an X) on the Variables window toolbar.

- **User variables**   You can create and define user variables for any purpose in the package. For example, the Foreach Loop Container updates user variables with values for every loop it iterates through. In Figure 1-13, shown earlier, file names for all files on the C drive that begin with the word *customer* will be mapped to a variable named *FileName*. Figure 1-15 shows the Variable Mapping tab in the Foreach Loop Editor.

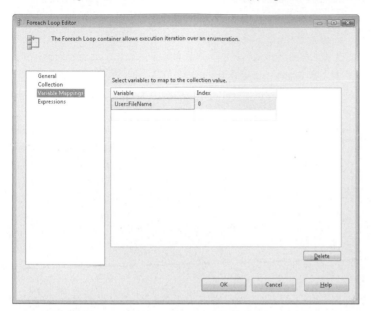

FIGURE 1-15 The Variable Mapping tab in the Foreach Loop Editor allows the values that are looped through to update an assigned variable for each iteration in the loop.

Using the Script Task and Data Profiling Task

Although this Training Kit focuses on development and maintenance rather than design, it is worth highlighting a few key control flow tasks. The exam objective domain covers using code within a package as well as performing data profiling, so let's look at the Script Task and the Data Profiling Task.

Script Task

You use the Script Task within SSIS to execute VB.NET or C#.NET code. The Script Task has the following features:

- Uses the Visual Studio Tools for Applications 2.0 (VSTA) interface, which lets you run VB.NET and C#.NET code with the full host of methods and functions.
- Variables can be referenced and updated within a script.
- Connections can be referenced and updated within a script.
- SSIS breakpoints can be applied within the script's code (for the Script Task). Chapter 2 will discuss breakpoints.
- Runs in both a 32-bit environment (X86) and a 64-bit environment (X64).

If you want to reference SSIS variables within a Script Task, you need to include the variables in the ReadOnlyVariables or ReadWriteVariables list, depending on whether you will be just accessing the variable for read purposes or updating the variable.

In the control flow example shown earlier in Figures 1-13, 1-14, and 1-15, the package is looping through Excel files and storing the Excel file path in a package variable. The package contains a connection to Excel that needs to be updated with the value of the variable, because each time the package loops, the variable needs to be updated.

Using a Script Task, you can update the Excel connection with the value of the variable. The first step is to drag a Script Task into the Foreach Loop Container from the toolbox. The script needs to be the first task that runs in the Foreach Loop Container, so place it before the Execute SQL Task and connect it to the Execute SQL Task with a precedence constraint. (Precedence constraints are covered in Chapter 2.) Figure 1-16 shows the Script Task Editor.

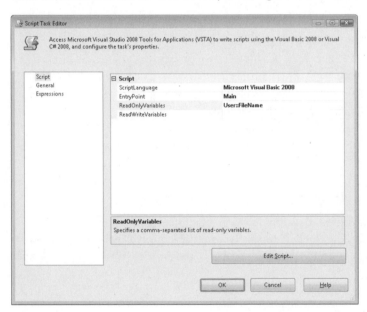

FIGURE 1-16 The Script Task Editor lets you select the programming language (VB.NET or C#.NET) as well as define any uses of variables within the script itself.

This example uses Microsoft Visual Basic 2008 as the *ScriptLanguage* and specifies the *User::FileName* variable in the *ReadOnlyVariables* property. To design the script, in the Script Task Editor, click Edit Script.

For this example, the script needs to update the Excel connection manager to point to the value of the variable, as the following code shows:

```
Dts.Connections("Excel Connection Manager").ConnectionString() = _
    "Provider=Microsoft.Jet.OLEDB.4.0;Data Source=" + _
    Dts.Variables("FileName").Value.ToString() + _
    ";Extended Properties=""EXCEL 8.0;HDR=YES"";"
```

The reference to the connection begins with *Dts.Connections* and the reference to the variables begins with *Dts.Variables*.

This code executes for every loop in the Foreach Loop Container and updates the Excel connection manager.

Data Profiling Task

You use the Data Profiling Task to review source data entities, to check the cleanliness and completeness of the data, and to understand how the data is organized structurally, such as possible key columns and relationships between columns.

The Data Profiling Task has two parts: the Data Profiling Task in the control flow that performs the analysis and the Data Profile Viewer to review the results.

To use the Data Profiling Task, first create an ADO.NET connection where the source tables or views reside. The Data Profiling Task requires an ADO.NET connection for sources. Next, drag the task from the toolbox onto the control flow, and then open the task to edit its properties. The easiest way to perform a data profile is to click the Quick Profile button in the Data Profiling Task Editor. Figure 1-17 shows the Single Table Quick Profile Form dialog box configured to run against the [Sales].[vPersonDemographics] view.

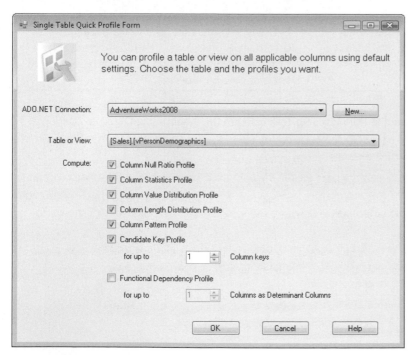

FIGURE 1-17 The Data Profiling Task can gather accuracy, completeness, and statistics information about the data within source tables or views.

As you can see, the Data Profiling Task can analyze data in various ways, which Table 1-2 describes.

TABLE 1-2 Data Profiling Task Features

PROFILE	DESCRIPTION
Column Null Ratio Profile	Evaluates the column and returns the percent of NULLs in the column relative to the total number of rows in the table.
Column Statistics Profile	For numeric and datetime columns, returns the spread and averages of the values.
Column Value Distribution Profile	Identifies the uniqueness of the values in a column across all the rows for that column.
Column Length Distribution Profile	Shows the various value lengths for a text column and the percentage of all the rows that each length takes up.
Column Pattern Profile	Displays any patterns found in the column data and returns the regular expression pattern that matches the pattern.
Candidate Key Profile	Identifies one or more columns that are unique across all the rows; the percentage of uniqueness is shown.
Functional Dependency Profile	Lists any columns that have value dependencies on other columns within the table, where a value from one column is found only when the value of another column is distinct.

After you configure the Data Profiling Task through the Single Table Quick Profile Form dialog box, you need to specify the output XML file in the *Destination* property. This is where the task stores the profiling results.

To view the results, open the Data Profile Viewer. (Click Start and then select All Programs, Microsoft SQL Server 2008, Integration Services, Data Profile Viewer.) Click Open on the toolbar, and browse to the output XML file where the results are stored. Figure 1-18 shows the Data Profile Viewer.

The Data Profile Viewer displays each profile type. The left pane lets you navigate between the profile types and source tables that were profiled. The right pane displays the results.

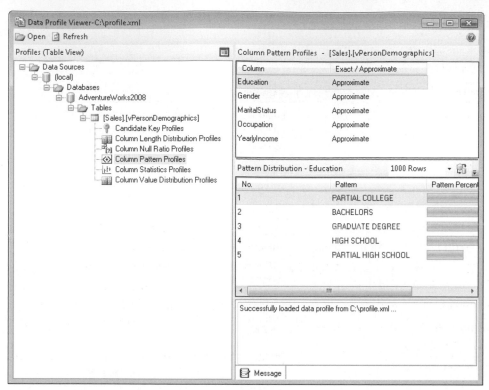

FIGURE 1-18 The Data Profile Viewer displays the results of the Data Profiling Task in a graphical form that demonstrates each profile type.

Testing Package Execution in BIDS

During the development of a package, you need to test its execution to validate that your package and tasks are configured correctly.

You can execute a package from within BIDS in three primary ways:

- Choose Start Debugging from the Debug menu on the menu bar.
- Click Start Debugging (the button containing an arrow that resembles the Play button on a DVD player) on the Standard toolbar.
- Press F5 on your keyboard.

After a package is run in BIDS, a new tab named the Progress tab appears in the SSIS Designer. This tab shows the execution results and lets you troubleshoot any package errors you might find. The Progress tab is renamed as Execution Results when you are back in design view.

Creating and Editing a Control Flow Task

The following exercises will familiarize you with creating and editing a control flow task and executing the package within the design environment.

EXERCISE 1 Create a Control Flow Task and Test Package Execution

In this exercise, you will work with control flow tasks and execute packages in the SSIS Designer.

1. If necessary, start SQL Server Business Intelligence Development Studio (BIDS), open the project *TK 70-448 SSIS Project* you created in Lesson 1, "Creating SSIS Packages and Data Sources," or open the completed exercise file from the companion CD, and then edit the package named MyPackage.dtsx (right-click the package in Solution Explorer, and then click Open).

2. Open the Toolbox window by selecting Toolbox from the View menu, locate the Execute SQL Task item, and drag it to the control flow workspace of your package.

3. Edit the Execute SQL Task object by double-clicking the task icon or by right-clicking the task icon and then clicking Edit.

4. Change the Connection property to use the AdventureWorks2008 connection.

5. In the SQL Statement property of the Execute SQL Task Editor dialog box, type the following code:

```
UPDATE Production.Product
SET ProductLine = 's'
WHERE ProductLine IS NULL
```

6. Click OK in the Execute SQL Task dialog box to return to the SSIS Designer. Right-click the Execute SQL Task, click Rename, and type **Update ProductLine**.

7. Next, drag a Sequence Container object from the toolbox onto the control flow workspace.

8. Drag the Update ProductLine Execute SQL Task you just created into the Sequence Container so that the task is nested in the Sequence Container box.

9. To test the execution of the package, click Start Debugging on the Standard toolbar or choose Start Debugging from the Debug menu.

10. When the package execution is complete, your Sequence Container and Execute SQL Task should be green.

11. Click the Execution Results tab (named Progress while the package is executing) in the SSIS Designer to view the execution details.

12. Select the Stop button from the tool menu to stop the debugger (or choose Debug, Stop Debugging from the Debug menu).

13. Click the Save All button on the BIDS toolbar.

EXERCISE 2   Modify the DimCustomer ETL Package Control Flow

In this exercise, you will start the process of building the DimCustomer SSIS package that will handle the ETL process from the AdventureWorks2008 database to the AdventureWorks-DW2008 database.

1. If necessary, start SQL Server Business Intelligence Development Studio (BIDS), open the project *TK 70-448 SSIS Project* you created in Lesson 1, "Creating SSIS Packages and Data Sources," or open the completed exercise file from the companion CD, and then open the empty DimCustomer package.

2. From the toolbox, drag two Execute SQL Tasks onto the control flow workspace and then drag one Data Flow Task onto the workspace.

3. Next, connect the first Execute SQL Task to the Data Flow Task by dragging the green precedence constraint from the Execute SQL Task onto the Data Flow Task. Then connect the green precedence constraint from the Data Flow Task to the second Execute SQL Task.

4. Rename the first Execute SQL Task to **Truncate Update Table**, and rename the second Execute SQL Task to **Batch Updates**. Figure 1-19 shows what your resulting control flow should look like.

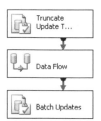

FIGURE 1-19 Your control flow for the DimCustomer package should contain an Execute SQL Task, followed by a Data Flow Task, followed by another Execute SQL Task.

5. Before editing the tasks in SSIS, open SSMS, connect to the Database Engine, and create a new query against the AdventureWorksDW2008 database. Execute the following code, which you can find in the CreateCustomerUpdateTable.sql file in the ..\Source\Ch 01\ folder of the practice exercise files.

```
USE AdventureWorksDW2008
GO

CREATE TABLE [dbo].[stgDimCustomerUpdates](
    [CustomerAlternateKey] [nvarchar](15) NULL,
    [AddressLine1] [nvarchar](60) NULL,
    [AddressLine2] [nvarchar](60) NULL,
    [BirthDate] [datetime] NULL,
    [CommuteDistance] [nvarchar](15) NULL,
    [DateFirstPurchase] [datetime] NULL,
    [EmailAddress] [nvarchar](50) NULL,
    [EnglishEducation] [nvarchar](40) NULL,
    [EnglishOccupation] [nvarchar](100) NULL,
    [FirstName] [nvarchar](50) NULL,
    [Gender] [nvarchar](1) NULL,
    [GeographyKey] [int] NULL,
    [HouseOwnerFlag] [nvarchar](1) NULL,
    [LastName] [nvarchar](50) NULL,
    [MaritalStatus] [nvarchar](1) NULL,
    [MiddleName] [nvarchar](50) NULL,
    [NumberCarsOwned] [tinyint] NULL,
    [NumberChildrenAtHome] [tinyint] NULL,
    [Phone] [nvarchar](25) NULL,
    [Suffix] [nvarchar](10) NULL,
    [Title] [nvarchar](8) NULL,
    [TotalChildren] [tinyint] NULL,
    [YearlyIncome] [nvarchar](100) NULL) ON [PRIMARY]
```

6. After you have successfully created the table, switch back to the DimCustomer SSIS package and edit the Execute SQL Task named Truncate Update Table.

7. In the Execute SQL Task Editor dialog box, set the Connection property to Adventure-WorksDW2008, and then enter the following SQL code in the SQLStatement property before clicking OK to save it:

```
TRUNCATE TABLE dbo.stgDimCustomerUpdates
```

8. Edit the last Execute SQL Task, named Batch Updates, and set the Connection property to AdventureWorksDW2008.

9. In the SQLStatement property, enter the following UPDATE statement. (You can find this statement in the UpdateCustomerTable.sql file in the ..\Source\Ch 01\ practice exercise folder.)

```
UPDATE dbo.DimCustomer
   SET AddressLine1 = stgDimCustomerUpdates.AddressLine1
     , AddressLine2 = stgDimCustomerUpdates.AddressLine2
     , BirthDate = stgDimCustomerUpdates.BirthDate
     , CommuteDistance = stgDimCustomerUpdates.CommuteDistance
     , DateFirstPurchase = stgDimCustomerUpdates.DateFirstPurchase
     , EmailAddress = stgDimCustomerUpdates.EmailAddress
     , EnglishEducation = stgDimCustomerUpdates.EnglishEducation
     , EnglishOccupation = stgDimCustomerUpdates.EnglishOccupation
     , FirstName = stgDimCustomerUpdates.FirstName
     , Gender = stgDimCustomerUpdates.Gender
     , GeographyKey = stgDimCustomerUpdates.GeographyKey
     , HouseOwnerFlag = stgDimCustomerUpdates.HouseOwnerFlag
     , LastName = stgDimCustomerUpdates.LastName
     , MaritalStatus = stgDimCustomerUpdates.MaritalStatus
     , MiddleName = stgDimCustomerUpdates.MiddleName
     , NumberCarsOwned = stgDimCustomerUpdates.NumberCarsOwned
     , NumberChildrenAtHome = stgDimCustomerUpdates.NumberChildrenAtHome
     , Phone = stgDimCustomerUpdates.Phone
     , Suffix = stgDimCustomerUpdates.Suffix
     , Title = stgDimCustomerUpdates.Title
     , TotalChildren = stgDimCustomerUpdates.TotalChildren
  FROM dbo.DimCustomer DimCustomer
 INNER JOIN dbo.stgDimCustomerUpdates
    ON DimCustomer.CustomerAlternateKey
       = stgDimCustomerUpdates.CustomerAlternateKey
```

10. Click OK in the Execute SQL Task Editor dialog box, and then save the package. In the next lesson, you will complete the data flow portion of this package and then test the execution.

Lesson 3: Using Data Flow Adapters and Transformations

Estimated lesson time: 45 minutes

Lesson 2, "Creating and Editing Control Flow Objects," showed how to use control flow tasks and containers. One of the most valuable control flow tasks is the Data Flow Task. A package can have zero, one, or more data flows. To work with the Data Flow Task, you can either drag a Data Flow Task from the Control Flow toolbox onto the workspace and then double-click it, or you can click the Data Flow tab within the SSIS Designer. After clicking the Data Flow tab, you see the Data Flow Designer, where you can use the data flow to handle and transform datasets. The Data Flow Task has three types of objects in the toolbox:

- Data flow source adapters
- Data flow transformations
- Data flow destination adapters

Figure 1-20 shows the Data Flow tab with the toolbox open, highlighting the data flow sources and some of the data flow transformations. Notice the difference between the Control Flow toolbox items and the Data Flow toolbox items.

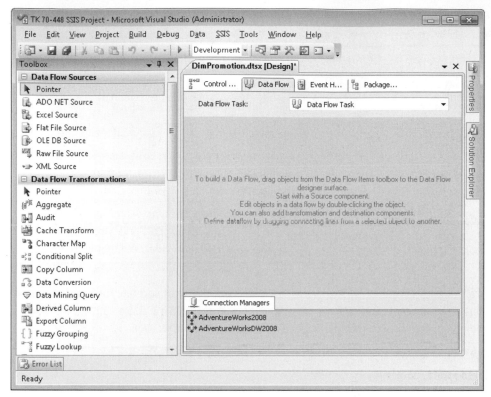

FIGURE 1-20 When you are working in the data flow, the toolbox shows items related to data flow development, including data flow sources, data flow transformations, and data flow destinations.

In this lesson, you will look at the details of the source and destination adapters as well as the transformations.

Defining Data Flow Source Adapters

Data flow source adapters use package connections, which point to the server instance or file location of the data source. (The only exception is the raw file adapter, which does not use a package connection.) A source adapter extracts data from sources and moves it into the data flow, where it will be modified and sent to a destination. You create data flow source adapters by dragging a source adapter from the Data Flow toolbox onto the Data Flow tab in the SSIS Designer. Table 1-3 describes the different data flow sources and their uses.

TABLE 1-3 Data Flow Sources and Their Uses

DATA FLOW SOURCE	PURPOSE
ADO.NET Source	Provides connections to tables or queries through an ADO.NET provider.
Excel Source	Allows extractions from an Excel worksheet defined in an Excel file.
Flat File Source	Connects to a delimited or fixed-width file created with different code pages.
OLE DB Source	Connects to installed OLE DB providers, such as SQL Server, Access, SSAS, and Oracle.
Raw File Source	Stores native SSIS data in a binary file type useful for data staging.
XML Source	Allows raw data to be extracted from an XML file; requires an XML schema to define data associations.

As an example, Figure 1-21 shows the OLE DB Source Editor dialog box for a package that is pulling special offer sales data from the AdventureWorks2008 database with the intention of loading it into the DimPromotions table in AdventureWorksDW2008.

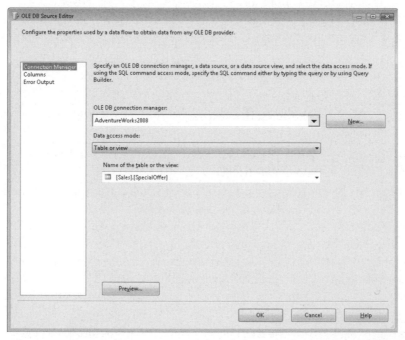

FIGURE 1-21 The OLE DB Source Editor displays that the DimPromotions package is configured to select data from the [Sales].[SpecialOffer] table.

The OLE DB source adapter is similar to the ADO.NET adapter in that a connection manager is required and either a table needs to be selected or a query needs to be written. In this example, the Data Access Mode drop-down list is set to Table Or View, and the [Sales]. [SpecialOffer] table is selected. If the Data Access Mode was set to SQL Command, you could enter a query for the source.

Creating Data Flow Destinations

Data flow destinations are similar to sources in that they use package connections. However, destinations are the endpoints in a package, defining the location to which the data should be pushed. For example, if you are sending data to an Excel file from a database table, your destination will be an Excel Destination adapter.

EXAM TIP

Many SSIS objects have a *ValidateExternalMetadata* property that you can set to *False* if the object being referenced (such as a table) does not exist when the package is being designed. This property is most commonly used for source or destination adapters, such as when a destination table is created during package execution.

All the source adapters (except the Data Reader source) have matching destination adapters in the SSIS data flow. And there are other destination adapters that let you send data to even more destinations. Table 1-4 lists the destination adapters in the SSIS data flow.

TABLE 1-4 Data Flow Destinations and Their Uses

DATA FLOW DESTINATION	PURPOSE
ADO.NET Destination	Allows insertion of data by using an ADO.NET managed provider.
Data Mining Model Training	Lets you pass data from the data flow into a data mining model in SSAS.
DataReader Destination	Lets you put data in an ADO.NET recordset that can be programmatically referenced.
Dimension Processing	Lets SSAS dimensions be processed directly from data flowing through the data flow.
Excel Destination	Used for inserting data into Excel, including Excel 2007.
Flat File Destination	Allows insertion of data to a flat file such as a comma-delimited or tab-delimited file.
OLE DB Destination	Uses the OLE DB provider to insert rows into a destination system that allows an OLE DB connection.

DATA FLOW DESTINATION	PURPOSE
Partition Processing	Allows SSAS partitions to be processed directly from data flowing through the data flow.
Raw File Destination	Stores native SSIS data in a binary file type useful for data staging.
Recordset Destination	Takes the data flow data and creates a recordset in a package variable of type *object*.
SQL Server Compact Destination	Lets you send data to a mobile device running SQL Mobile.
SQL Server Destination	Provides a high-speed destination specific to SQL Server 2008 if the package is running on SQL Server.

EXAM TIP

You can configure the OLE DB Destination adapter to insert data from the data flow through bulk batches of data, instead of one row at a time. To use this destination-optimization technique, edit the OLE DB Destination and set the Data Access Mode to Table Or View— Fast Load. When the OLE DB Destination is not configured with fast load, only one row at a time will be inserted into the destination table.

Figure 1-22 shows a simple data flow with one source and one destination. The data flow extracts records from the AdventureWorks2008 SpecialOffers table and inserts them into the AdventureWorksDW2008 DimPromotions table.

FIGURE 1-22 This simple data flow shows data being extracted from a source and inserted into a destination.

Like the source, the destination adapter requires configuration, both in the connection and table that the rows should be inserted into as well as in mapping the data flow columns to the destination table columns. Figure 1-23 shows the OLE DB Destination Editor for the preceding example.

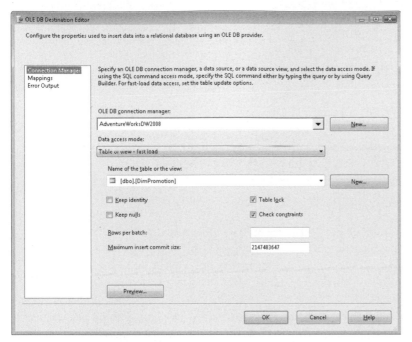

FIGURE 1-23 The destination adapter for the DimPromotions table is configured to connect to the AdventureWorksDW2008 database and insert rows into the DimPromotions table by using the fast-load feature.

Notice that this OLE DB Destination uses the AdventureWorksDW2008 connection and is configured by default to use the Table Or View—Fast Load option of the Data Access Mode drop-down list. This means that records will be processed with bulk insert statements rather than one row at a time.

Figure 1-24 shows the Mappings tab of the same OLE DB Destination Editor. This is where you map columns available from the data flow to the destination columns in the destination adapter. All the destination adapters have a Mappings tab.

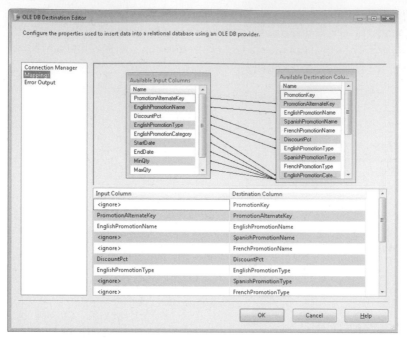

FIGURE 1-24 Each destination adapter requires you to map data from the data flow input columns to the destination columns.

Notice that not all columns are mapped. However, if one of the unmapped destination columns is marked as NOT NULL, the destination fails the package when it is run. In the section titled "Using Transformations" later in this lesson, you see how to use the Slowly Changing Dimension Transformation to handle new records and updates.

Working with Data Flow Transformations

Transformations give you the ability to modify and manipulate data in the data flow. A transformation performs an operation either on one row of data at a time or on several rows of data at once.

As with the source and destination adapters, you drag transformations from the Data Flow toolbox onto the Data Flow tab of the SSIS Designer, and edit them by right-clicking the transformation you want to change and then clicking Edit. You connect sources, transformations, and destinations through data paths, which you create by dragging the output arrow onto another component in the data flow. The green data path arrows are for rows that are successfully transformed, and the red output path arrows are for rows that failed the transformation because of an error, such as a truncation or conversion error. Figure 1-25 shows a data flow that connects a source to several transformations through data paths and onto a destination.

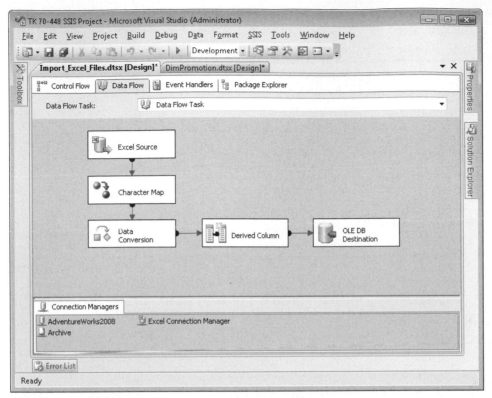

FIGURE 1-25 You use data paths to connect data flow transformations with sources, destinations, and other transformations.

Selecting Transformations

Transformations perform a wide variety of operations on the underlying data, and the transformation you choose depends on your data processing requirements. Some transformations operate similarly to other transformations; therefore, we can categorize them into natural groupings of like components.

LOGICAL ROW-LEVEL TRANSFORMATIONS

The most common and easily configured transformations perform operations on rows without needing other rows from the source. These transformations, which logically work at the row level, often perform very well. Table 1-5 lists the logical row-level transformations.

Some common uses of these transformations include performing mathematical calculations, converting a text value to a numeric or decimal data type, and replacing NULLs with other values. Because the Import Column and Export Column Transformations work with large binary data types, these two transformations carry an increased workload.

TABLE 1-5 Logical Row-Level Transformations

DATA FLOW TRANSFORMATION	PURPOSE
Audit	Adds additional columns to each row based on system package variables such as *ExecutionStartTime* and *PackageName*.
Cache Transform	Allows data that will be used in a Lookup Transformation to be cached and available for multiple Lookup components.
Character Map	Performs common text operations, such as Uppercase, and allows advanced linguistic bit conversion operations.
Copy Column	Duplicates column values in each row to new named columns.
Data Conversion	Creates new columns in each row based on new data types converted from other columns—for example, converting text to numeric.
Derived Column	Uses the SSIS Expression language to perform in-place calculations on existing values; alternatively, allows the addition of new columns based on expressions and calculations from other columns and variables.
Export Column	Exports binary large object (BLOB) columns, one row at a time, to a file.
Import Column	Loads binary files such as images into the pipeline; intended for a BLOB data type destination.
Row Count	Tracks the number of rows that flow through the transformation and stores the number in a package variable after the final row.

MULTI-INPUT OR MULTI-OUTPUT TRANSFORMATIONS

Multi-input and multi-output transformations can work with more than one data input or can generate more than one output, respectively. These transformations provide the capability to combine or branch data and give the data flow the overall ability to process data from one or more sources to one or more destinations. Table 1-6 lists the multi-input and multi-output transformations.

TABLE 1-6 Multi-Input and Multi-Output Transformations

DATA FLOW TRANSFORMATION	PURPOSE
Conditional Split	Routes or filters data based on Boolean expressions to one or more outputs, from which each row can be sent out only one output path.
Lookup	Allows matching between pipeline column values to external database tables; additional columns can be added to the data flow from the external table.
Merge	Combines the rows of two similar sorted inputs, one on top of the other, based on a defined sort key.
Merge Join	Joins the rows of two sorted inputs based on a defined join column(s), adding columns from each source.
Multicast	Generates one or more identical outputs, from which every row is sent out every output.
Union All	Combines one or more similar inputs, stacking rows one on top of another, based on matching columns.

As Table 1-6 describes, the Merge and Merge Join Transformations require sorted inputs. When these components are used in a data flow, the transformation waits for rows from either input, based on the defined sort order, to preserve the sorted output or match across the sorted rows; this means that rows might not immediately be sent out the output path.

EXAM TIP

When trying to determine which transformation to use that brings more than one data source together, remember that the Merge Join Transformation brings two sorted sources together and matching rows together with either an Inner Join, a Full Outer Join, or a Left Outer Join. Merge Join can match more than one row across the join columns. This behavior is different from that of the Lookup Transformation, which brings back only a single match across the join columns of the Lookup table.

The Union All Transformation does not join rows together but rather brings each row separately from the sources, stacking the rows together. The number of rows in the output of Union All is the combined row counts of all the inputs. The Merge Transformation is similar to Union All, except that the sources have to be sorted and the sort position is preserved.

MULTI-ROW TRANSFORMATIONS

Some transformations perform work based on criteria from multiple input rows or generate multiple output rows from a single input row. These transformations can be more intensive in operation and memory overhead, but they provide valuable functions to meet business requirements. Table 1-7 lists the multi-row transformations.

TABLE 1-7 Multi-Row Transformations

DATA FLOW TRANSFORMATION	PURPOSE
Aggregate	Associates records based on defined groupings and generates aggregations such as *SUM*, *MAX*, *MIN*, and *COUNT*.
Percent Sampling	Filters the input rows by allowing only a defined percent to be passed to the output path.
Pivot	Takes multiple input rows and pivots the rows to generate an output with more columns based on the original row values.
Row Sampling	Outputs a fixed number of rows, sampling the data from the entire input, no matter how much larger than the defined output the input is.
Sort	Orders the input based on defined sort columns and sort direction and allows the removal of duplicates across the sort columns.
Unpivot	Takes a single row and outputs multiple rows, moving column values to the new row based on defined columns.

In the cases of the Sort, Aggregate, and Row Sampling Transformations, all the input rows are blocked, allowing the transformations to perform the work before sending rows down the output path. These transformations often require more server resources, memory, and processor capacity than do other transformations.

ADVANCED DATA-PREPARATION TRANSFORMATIONS

The final grouping of transformations lets you perform advanced operations on rows in the data flow pipeline. Table 1-8 lists these advanced data-preparation transformations.

TABLE 1-8 Advanced Data-Preparation Transformations

DATA FLOW TRANSFORMATION	PURPOSE
OLE DB Command	Performs database operations such as updates and deletes, one row at a time, based on mapped parameters from input rows.
Slowly Changing Dimension	Processes dimension changes, including tracking dimension history and updating dimension values. The Slowly Changing Dimension Transformation handles these common dimension change types: Historical Attributes, Fixed Attributes, and Changing Attributes.
Data Mining Query	Applies input rows against a data mining model for prediction.
Fuzzy Grouping	Associates column values with a set of rows based on similarity, for data cleansing.
Fuzzy Lookup	Joins a data flow input to a reference table based on column similarity. The Similarity Threshold setting specifies the closeness of allowed matches—a high setting means that matching values are closer in similarity.
Script Component	Provides VB.NET scripting capabilities against rows, columns, inputs, and outputs in the data flow pipeline.
Term Extraction	Analyzes text input columns for English nouns and noun phrases.
Term Lookup	Analyzes text input columns against a user-defined set of words for association.

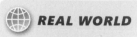 **REAL WORLD**

Erik Veerman

Most customers I've worked with have numerous systems that host all kinds of data—from sales transaction systems, to human resources, to custom business apps. Many of these systems even run on different database platforms such as SQL Server, Oracle, DB2, or legacy systems that aren't even sold any more. The complexity of data within organizations extends beyond just the enterprise relational database, often including Excel files and departmental Access applications. Navigating through these systems can be difficult, to say the least.

SSIS delivers real benefits in these situations because it helps you efficiently consolidate data.

In one customer engagement I was involved with, our task was to simplify a complicated process that pulled in five different data sources. Two of them were in SQL Server, one was in Oracle, another was in Excel, and the last was a large binary flat file created from an IBM AS/400 system.

Before we redesigned the processing of this data, the operation required a nightly job that ran for 7.5 hours. The job included a batch process to convert the AS/400 binary file to ASCII, and the job pulled the Oracle and Excel data into a staging environment inside SQL Server and then through a rather large stored procedure. Custom logic joined data (numbering in the millions of rows) across servers through linked servers and staged the data into about 15 staging tables before the finished product was produced. Sound familiar?

The redesign in SSIS reduced a lot of the complexities because we could extract data from these sources directly into the data flow in SSIS and join different sources together. We also were able to convert the complicated T-SQL logic involving the staging tables to a series of transformations and tremendously reduce the overall disk I/O by going from 15 to 3 staging tables.

The net result was three SSIS packages that ran together in 25 minutes. What a time gain. In addition, using SSIS reduced hardware overhead and management of the old process, allowing the customer's IT professionals to do much more with time they didn't think they could ever recoup.

Using Transformations

Each transformation has an editor window to define the way the operation is applied to the data. For example, the Derived Column Transformation specifies an expression that generates a new column in the data flow or replaces an existing column. To open the Transformation Editor, either double-click the transformation or right-click the transformation and then click Edit. Figure 1-26 shows the Derived Column Transformation Editor.

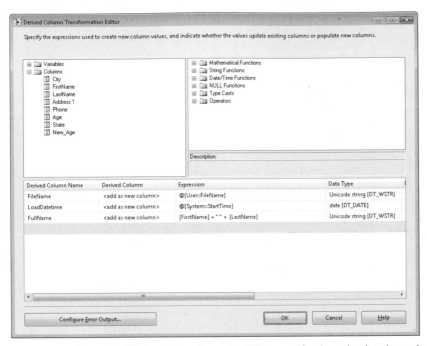

FIGURE 1-26 The Derived Column Transformation Editor specifies how the data is manipulated as it flows through a transformation.

In the Derived Column example in Figure 1-26, one of the new columns added to the data flow is named FullName, which is based on the concatenation of the FirstName column and the LastName column using the following SSIS expression:

```
[FirstName] + " " + [LastName]
```

Other transformations contain similar functionality. Each transformation has an editor specific to the chosen operation.

The next example uses the Slowly Changing Dimension Transformation in the DimPromotion package to identify new records versus updated records. Figure 1-27 shows the data flow that results.

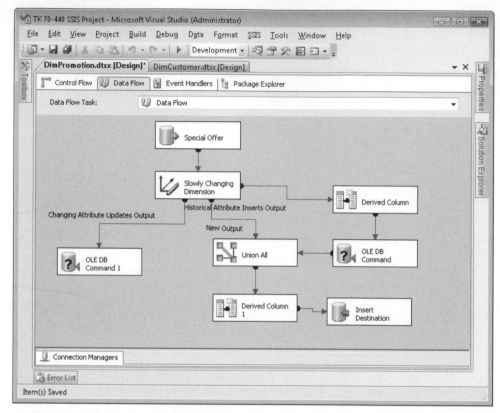

FIGURE 1-27 The Slowly Changing Dimension Transformation sends rows out multiple outputs depending on whether there is a new record or a change and on what kind of change.

Figure 1-27 shows the output of the Slowly Changing Dimension Transformation. All the output transformations and destinations were created by the Slowly Changing Dimension Wizard, which built the rest of the data flow.

Figure 1-28 shows the Slowly Changing Dimension Columns page of the wizard, which defines which dimension columns should cause what kind of change to the output. The options are Fixed Attribute, which means the change should not happen; Changing Attribute, which means that an update happens; or Historical Attribute, which means that the change creates a new record.

A detailed review of all the SSIS transformations is outside the scope of this Training Kit, but you can find information about them in the References section at the end of this book.

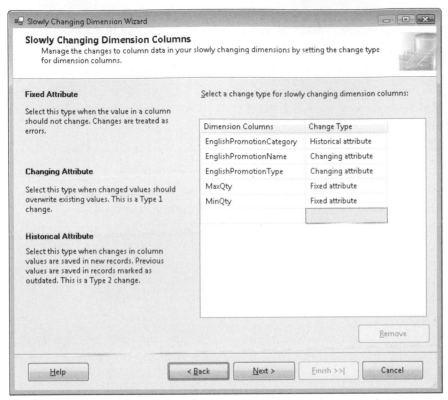

FIGURE 1-28 The Slowly Changing Dimension Wizard lets you define what kind of output should be created depending on the kind of change that occurs.

PRACTICE **Creating Simple and Complex Data Flows**

These exercises walk you through creating data flows that include sources, destinations, and one or more transformations. You will begin with a rather simple data flow but will then build a more complex data flow.

EXERCISE 1   Create a Simple Data Flow

In this exercise, you will develop a simple data flow that contains a source adapter, an Aggregate Transformation, and a destination adapter.

1. If necessary, start SQL Server Business Intelligence Development Studio (BIDS), open the project *TK 70-448 SSIS Project* you created in Lesson 2, "Creating and Editing Control Flow Objects," or open the completed exercise file from the companion CD, and then open the *MyPackage.dtsx* package for editing.

2. On the Control Flow tab of the SSIS Designer, drag Data Flow Task from the toolbox into the Sequence Container object. The Sequence Container object should now include an Execute SQL Task named Update ProductLine and a Data Flow Task object.

3. Drag the output arrow from the Update ProductLine Task onto the Data Flow Task object. The output arrow is green, which means it represents a precedence constraint; see Chapter 3 for more information about precedence constraints.

4. Click the Data Flow tab at the top of the SSIS Designer.

5. In the toolbox, drag OLE DB Source, located under the Data Flow Sources group, onto the data flow workspace. Right-click the OLE DB Source item and then click Edit to open the OLE DB Source Editor dialog box.

6. Select AdventureWorks2008 in the OLE DB Connection Manager list and then click OK.

7. From the Data Access Mode drop-down list, select SQL Command.

8. In the SQL Command text box, type the following query (available in the SQLCommandQuery.sql file in the ..\Source\Ch 01\ folder for the practice exercises):

```
SELECT SH.OrderDate, SD.LineTotal, P.ProductLine
FROM Sales.SalesOrderHeader SH
INNER JOIN Sales.SalesOrderDetail SD
ON SH.SalesOrderID = SD.SalesOrderID
INNER JOIN Production.Product P
ON SD.ProductID = P.ProductID
```

9. Click the Columns tab on the left, and then verify that the OrderDate, LineTotal, and ProductLine columns are shown as available columns in the source adapter.

10. Click OK in the OLE DB Source Editor dialog box.

11. From the Data Flow toolbox, drag an Aggregate Transformation onto the Data Flow design surface, just below the OLE DB Source adapter.

12. Link the OLE DB Source output to the Aggregate Transformation by dragging the green output arrow onto the Aggregate Transformation.

13. Edit the Aggregate Transformation by double-clicking it or by right-clicking it and then clicking Edit.

   a. In the Aggregate Transformation Editor dialog box, select OrderDate from the Input Column drop-down list, and then verify that the default operation Group By is selected for the new row.

   b. Add a second Input Column row by selecting the LineTotal column from the drop-down list. For the Operation column of the newly added LineTotal, select Sum from the list. And last, type **SubTotal** in the Output Alias column for the LineTotal row.

   c. Add a third Input Column row by selecting the ProductLine column from the list.

   d. Verify that the default operation Group By is selected for the new row.

   e. Click OK in the Aggregate Transformation Editor dialog box.

14. In the Data Flow toolbox, navigate to the Data Flow Destinations grouping of objects, and then drag the OLE DB Destination object onto the Data Flow design surface.

15. Connect the output of the Aggregate Transformation to the new OLE DB Destination object by dragging the output arrow from the Aggregate Transformation onto the OLE DB Destination adapter.

16. Right-click the OLE DB Destination adapter, and then click Edit to display the OLE DB Destination Adapter Editor dialog box.

    a. In the OLE DB Destination Adapter Editor dialog box, verify that the OLE DB Connection Manager drop-down list is set to AdventureWorks2008.

    b. Click the New button next to the Name Of The Table Or The View drop-down list.

    c. In the Create Table dialog box, change the name of the new table to **Sales_Summary**. The CREATE TABLE code listed in the window should look like the following:

    ```
    CREATE TABLE [Sales_Summary] (
        [OrderDate] DATETIME,
        [SubTotal] NUMERIC (38,6),
        [ProductLine] NVARCHAR(2)
    ) ON [PRIMARY]
    ```

    d. Click OK in the Create Table dialog box.

    e. On the Mappings tab of the OLE Destination Editor dialog box, ensure that the columns are all mapped from source to destination.

    f. Click OK to save your settings.

    Figure 1-29 shows the completed data flow, with the source, aggregate, and destination components.

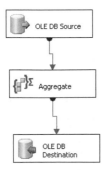

FIGURE 1-29 The data flow for this exercise contains an OLE DB Source adapter, an Aggregate Transformation, and an OLE DB Destination adapter.

17. Right-click the Data Flow design surface, and then click Execute Task. Observe the execution of the data flow to confirm successful completion of this exercise.

18. Click the Stop button on the toolbar to stop the debugger (or choose Debug, Stop Debugging from the Debug menu).

19. Click the Save All button on the BIDS toolbar.

EXERCISE 2   Create a Data Flow Destination

In this exercise, you will create a data flow that loads new records into the DimCustomer table of the AdventureWorksDW2008 database and that performs updates for existing records.

1. If necessary, start SQL Server Business Intelligence Development Studio (BIDS), open the project TK 70-448 SSIS Project, and then open the DimCustomer.dtsx package for editing. Your DimCustomer.dtsx package should contain an Execute SQL Task named Truncate Update Table, a Data Flow Task object, and a second Execute SQL Task named Batch Updates that was created in Lesson 2.

2. Click the Data Flow tab at the top of the SSIS Designer to navigate to the Data Flow design surface.

3. Drag an OLE DB Source adapter from the toolbox onto the design surface. Rename the OLE DB Source adapter **Customer Source**. Edit the source adapter and set the following properties as shown:

OLE DB Connection Manager	AdventureWorks2008
Data Access Mode	SQL Command
SQL Command Text (Code available in the CustomerSourceQuery.sql practice exercise file in the ..\Source\Ch 01\ folder.)	select convert(nvarchar(15),SC. AccountNumber) as CustomerAlternateKey, C.Title, C.FirstName, C.MiddleName, C.LastName, C.Suffix, C.EmailAddress, C.AddressLine1, C.AddressLine2, D.BirthDate, D.MaritalStatus, D.YearlyIncome, D.DateFirstPurchase, D.Gender, D.TotalChildren, D.NumberChildrenAtHome, D.Education, D.Occupation, D.HomeOwnerFlag, D.NumberCarsOwned from Sales.vIndividualCustomer C inner join Sales.Customer SC on C.BusinessEntityID = SC.PersonID inner join Sales.vPersonDemographics D on C.BusinessEntityID = D.BusinessEntityID

4. Drag a second OLE DB Source adapter from the toolbox onto the Data Flow design surface, rename it to **Customer Dim**, and then edit it. Edit the source adapter and set the following properties as shown:

OLE DB Connection Manager	AdventureWorksDW2008
Data Access Mode	Table or view
Name Of The Table Or View	[dbo].[DimCustomer]

5. For this next set, you will be sorting the data from the sources on the business key. First, drag two Sort Transformations from the Data Flow toolbox onto the Data Flow design surface, and then connect the output arrow for the Customer Source adapter to the first Sort Transformation and the Customer Dim to the second Sort Transformation, as Figure 1-30 shows.

FIGURE 1-30 The initial data flow for this exercise contains two OLE DB Source adapters and two Sort Transformations.

6. Edit the first Sort Transformation and select the check box on the left side of the CustomerAlternateKey column in the Available Input Columns. Click OK to save the transformation.

7. Edit the second Sort Transformation and select the check box on the left side of the CustomerAlternateKey column in the Available Input Columns. Click OK to save the transformation.

8. From the Data Flow toolbox, drag a Merge Join Transformation to the design surface, and then connect the output arrow from the first Sort Transformation (originating from Customer Source) to the Merge Join Transformation. When prompted with the Input Output Selection dialog box, choose Merge Join Left Input from the Input drop-down list, and then click OK.

9. Also connect the output arrow of the second Sort Transformation (originating from Customer Dim) to the Merge Join Transformation.

10. Edit the Merge Join Transformation to display the Merge Join Transformation Editor dialog box.

   a. Change the Join Type drop-down list setting to Left Outer Join, which will retrieve all the rows from the originating Customer Source query (the left source of the Merge Join Transformation) and any matching rows from the right side (which is from the *dbo.DimCustomer* source).

   b. To return all the columns from the Customer Source query, select the check box immediately to the left of the Name column header in the left Sort list. Doing this will select all the check boxes for every column that is the desired result.

   c. In the right list of columns from Customer Dim, select only the check box next to the CustomerAlternateKey column.

   d. Scroll down the Output Columns list at the bottom of the Merge Join Transformation Editor dialog box to the very bottom, and for the CustomerAlternateKey column, change the Output Alias value to **Dim_CustomerAlternateKey**.

   e. Click OK to save the changes to the Merge Join Transformation.

11. From the Data Flow toolbox, drag a Conditional Split Transformation onto the Data Flow design surface, and then connect the output arrow from the Merge Join Transformation to the Conditional Split Transformation.

12. Edit the Conditional Split Transformation to display the Conditional Split Transformation Editor dialog box.

   a. Create a new output by typing **New Records** in the Output Name box for the first row of the output list.

   b. In the same row of the output list, type the following code in the Condition field:

   ```
   ISNULL([Dim_CustomerAlternateKey]) == TRUE
   ```

   c. In the Default Output Name box, change the value from Conditional Split Default Output to **Updated Records**.

   d. Click OK to save your changes in the Conditional Split Transformation Editor dialog box.

13. From the Data Flow toolbox, drag an OLE DB Destination adapter to the Data Flow design surface (be sure not to drag the similar source adapter but rather the destination adapter), and then change its name to **DimCustomer Table**.

14. Drag the output arrow of the Conditional Split Transformation onto this new OLE DB Destination adapter. When prompted in the Input Output Selection dialog box, select New Records from the Output drop-down list, and then click OK.

15. Right-click the DimCustomer Table Destination adapter that you just created and click Edit to display the OLE DB Destination Editor dialog box. Set the following properties in the OLE DB Destination Editor dialog box:

OLE DB Connection Manager	AdventureWorksDW2008
Data Access Mode	Table Or View—Fast Load
Name Of The Table Or View	[dbo].[DimCustomer]

    a. While you are still in the OLE DB Destination Editor dialog box, click the Mappings tab in the left area of the dialog box. This automatically maps the columns from the data flow to the DimCustomer table based on column name and data type.

    b. Not all columns will be mapped. From the Available Input Columns list, locate the Education column and drag it on top of the EnglishEducation column of the Available Destination Columns list. Do the same for Occupation to EnglishOccupation and HomeOwnerFlag to HouseOwnerFlag.

    c. Click OK to save your changes in the OLE DB Destination Editor dialog box.

16. Add a second OLE DB Destination adapter to the Data Flow design surface, and then connect another output arrow from the Conditional Split Transformation to the new OLE DB Destination adapter. Rename the destination adapter **DimCustomer Update Table**.

17. Edit the DimCustomer Update Table destination adapter you just created to display the OLE DB Destination Editor dialog box. Set the following properties in the OLE DB Destination Editor dialog box:

OLE DB Connection Manager	AdventureWorksDW2008
Data Access Mode	Table Or View—Fast Load
Name Of The Table Or View	[dbo].[stgDimCustomerUpdates] (This table was created in Lesson 2.)

a. While you are still in the OLE DB Destination Editor dialog box, click the Mappings tab. This automatically maps the columns from the data flow to the DimCustomer table based on column name and data type.

b. Not all columns will be mapped. From the Available Input Columns list, locate the Education column and drag it on top of the EnglishEducation column of the Available Destination Columns list. Do the same for Occupation to EnglishOccupation and HomeOwnerFlag to HouseOwnerFlag.

c. Click OK to save your changes in the OLE DB Destination Editor dialog box.

Your data flow should now resemble the one shown in Figure 1-31. You can find the completed exercises in the ..\Source\Ch 01\ folder of the Training Kit materials.

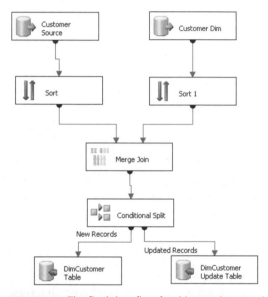

FIGURE 1-31 The final data flow for this exercise contains several sources and destinations, with transformation logic to handle inserts and to stage updates for the DimCustomer table.

18. Confirm the correct development of your package by executing the package in BIDS.

19. Choose Debug, Stop Debugging from the Debug menu to stop the debugger, and then click the Save All button on the BIDS toolbar.

✔ Quick Check

1. How would you use SSIS to import a file from an FTP server to a SQL Server table?

2. You need to migrate a user-created Access database to SQL Server, but the Data Flow toolbox does not contain an Access source adapter. How do you import this data into SQL Server?

3. The Multicast Transformation and the Conditional Split Transformation both can have multiple outputs. Which transformation would you use if you needed to send rows matching certain conditions out one output and rows matching different conditions out another?

4. Describe the transformations you could use to combine data from two different database tables that exist on two different servers.

Quick Check Answers

1. First, you would use an FTP Task to copy the file to the machine on which SSIS is installed. You can then import the file into a SQL Server table by using a Data Flow Task configured with a Flat File Source adapter and either a SQL Server Destination adapter or an OLE DB Destination adapter.

2. Although not listed in the toolbox, Access is one of the many database sources and destinations that SSIS works with. To extract data from Access, you first need to make a package connection to the Microsoft Jet OLE DB Provider. You can then use the OLE DB Source adapter to select the table or perform a custom query.

3. The Conditional Split Transformation lets you define expressions against which the rows from the source are evaluated. For every row, the expressions are evaluated in order, and a row is sent out the first output when the matching expression evaluates to True. Therefore, any single row can go out only one output. With a Multicast Transformation, on the other hand, all rows go out every output.

4. To combine data from two different database tables that exist on two different servers, you could use the Merge Join Transformation, which combines datasets by joining the rows across a set of common keys. This transformation allows an inner join, a left outer join, or a full outer join. You could also use a Lookup Transformation to associate data from two sources. The Lookup can cache a table in memory and, through matching columns, can return new columns to the data flow.

Case Scenario: Creating an ETL Solution

The business development department of Adventure Works has requested that you implement a data mart that it can use to analyze reseller sales against salesperson sales targets. Your first task is to create a series of SSIS packages that move data from the source Enterprise Resource Planning (ERP) system to a data mart database that contains fact tables and dimension tables.

1. How would you work within BIDS to create SSIS project structures, packages, project data sources, and package connections?

2. What transformations would you use, and how would you implement the data flow that loads dimension tables?

3. What transformations would you use, and how would you implement the data flow that loads fact tables?

Chapter Summary

- Creating SSIS packages involves working with BIDS and creating a new SSIS project.

- The main object in an SSIS project is a package, which contains the business logic to manage workflows and process data.

- Within a package, the control flow lets you create tasks and containers, which provide the ability to run process-oriented operations.

- The Data Flow Task is the second core object (behind the control flow) in an SSIS package, enabling data-processing operations.

- The data flow uses source adapters, destination adapters, and transformations.

CHAPTER 2

Debugging and Error Handling in SSIS

Package development and implementation goes beyond using transformations to connect sources to destinations. You must also implement error handling and test and troubleshoot your packages as you develop them. SQL Server 2008 Integration Services (SSIS) provides several ways to handle errors at different levels of the SSIS architecture. For example, at the control flow level, you can add a failure constraint that, if an error occurs, redirects the workflow to a specified alternative task. Similarly, in the data flow, if a row causes an error in a transformation, you can send the row out an error path. SSIS even includes event-handling capabilities that let you trap *OnWarning* and *OnError* events, and you can have all these events logged to a table or a file for review and troubleshooting.

In this chapter, you look at the various capabilities in SSIS for debugging packages during development and for dealing with errors during production execution, including execution logging. You begin by looking at how to configure package transactions and checkpoints and then see how to identify package status, handle task errors, and log your package execution. Last, you learn about data flow error handling and debugging.

Exam objectives in this chapter:
- Implement control flow.
- Implement data flow.
- Implement auditing, logging, and event handling.
- Install and maintain SSIS components.
- Identify and resolve issues related to SSIS solution deployment.

Before You Begin

To complete this chapter, you must have:
- Knowledge of SSIS features and components.
- Experience working with SQL Server Business Intelligence Development Studio (BIDS) projects and solutions.
- Practice working in the control flow and data flow.
- The AdventureWorks2008 databases installed.

Lesson 1: Configuring Package Transactions and Checkpoints

Estimated lesson time: 30 minutes

Most relational databases such as Microsoft SQL Server perform operations in atomic units. This means that a single statement or series of statements is either successful and affects data or is not successful and the system returns the data to the state it was in before the attempted statement execution. The unit of work that needs to be completed successfully in order for the data to be applied is called a *transaction*.

In SSIS, transactions can be set at various levels of the package, and you can coordinate transactions through package restartability features. In other words, you can configure a package to start from the point of failure or from an earlier step when the package is rerun. In SSIS, this configuration process is called *adding checkpoints*. Checkpoints work together with transactions to enable package restartability.

Defining Package and Task Transaction Settings

You can set package transactions at the entire package level or at any control flow container level or task level. Transactions in SSIS use the Microsoft Distributed Transaction Coordinator (MSDTC); the MSDTC service needs to be started on the computer for transactions to work. Any service or program that is enabled to work with the MSDTC can be part of a transaction in SSIS.

To enable a transaction within a package, you need to set the TransactionOption property of the task or container to Required. Figure 2-1 highlights the properties of a package at the control flow level, which means that the properties apply to the package as a whole. The TransactionOption property is the same on any control flow object.

When deciding whether and how to implement a transaction, follow these guidelines:

- For transactions to be enabled in SSIS, you need to start the MSDTC service, and the tasks that you want to be part of the transaction must work with the MSDTC service natively.

- If a series of tasks must be completed as a single unit in which either all the tasks are successful and committed or an error occurs and none of the tasks are committed, place the tasks within a Sequence Container and then set the TransactionOption property of the container to Required.

- A task can inherit the transaction setting of its parent when the TransactionOption property is set to Supported, which is the default setting when creating a task or container.

- You can prevent a task from participating in a transaction by setting its TransactionOption property to NotSupported.

- If you set the TransactionOption property of a Foreach Loop Container or For Loop Container to Required, a new transaction will be created for each loop of the container.

- Transactions work at the control flow level and not within a data flow. Therefore, you can turn on a transaction for a Data Flow Task, but you cannot turn it on separately for selected components within the data flow; either the entire data process will be successful or it will be rolled back.

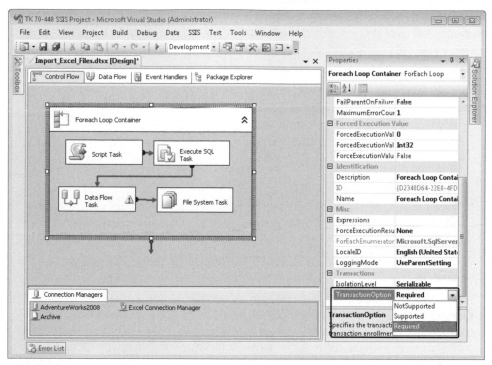

FIGURE 2-1 A task's or container's TransactionOption property must be set to Required to enable a transaction within a package.

EXAM TIP

At times, you might want to enable a transaction for a container but exclude some of the tasks within the container. For example, if you have a couple of Execute SQL Tasks in the container that are used for auditing purposes but the TransactionOption property for the container is set to Required, if an error occurs, the logging tasks will also be rolled back. To prevent the auditing tasks from rolling back, set the TransactionOption property for those tasks to Not Supported. This will still let the other tasks in the container be in the transaction, but it will not include the auditing tasks as part of the transaction.

Implementing Restartability Checkpoints

Sometimes you want the ability to restart a package if it fails and have it start at the point of failure, especially if you are working with complicated or long-running packages. In other words, you might not want successfully completed tasks to run again if you restart the package. You can accomplish this restartability by enabling checkpoints in the package.

Enabling restartability within a package requires first enabling a package to use checkpoints and second setting the specific tasks and containers to write checkpoints. To turn on checkpoints within a package, follow these steps:

1. Within the package, open the Properties window if necessary, and then click the Control Flow tab of the SSIS Designer, which will reveal the package properties.

2. Set the SaveCheckpoints property at the package level to True. This allows SSIS to save checkpoints during package execution.

3. For the CheckpointFileName property, provide a valid path and file name to a checkpoint file. Packages use files to maintain their state information, so if a package fails and is then restarted, the package can read the checkpoint file to determine where it left off and to track the state information at the last successful task.

4. Set the CheckpointUsage property to IfExists, which causes the package to run from the beginning if the checkpoint file is not present or to run from the identified point if the file exists.

EXAM TIP

If you set the CheckpointUsage property to Always, the checkpoint file must be present or the package will not start. In addition, using checkpoints is not allowed if you have set the TransactionOption of the package to Required.

Figure 2-2 shows the package properties, highlighting the checkpoint properties set in steps 1 through 4.

5. After you enable checkpoints in a package, the final step is to set checkpoints at the various tasks within your package. To do this, set the FailPackageOnFailure property at each task or container to True.

In the previous example, the Truncate Update Table, Data Flow, and Batch Updates Tasks have the FailPackageOnFailure property set to True.

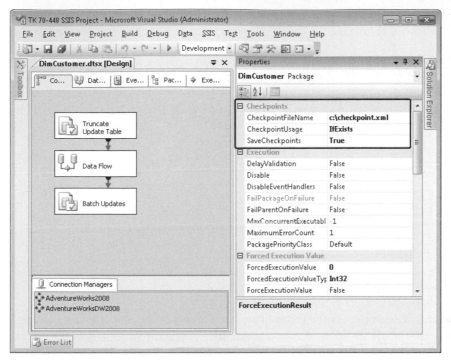

FIGURE 2-2 Setting checkpoint properties for a package requires modifying the package-level properties CheckpointFileName, CheckpointUsage, and SaveCheckpoints.

After you have performed steps 1 through 5 to set up checkpoints for your package, including the control flow objects, your packages are set up to restart in case of failure. Here is what happens when you run a package that has checkpoints enabled:

1. The package checks to see whether the checkpoint file exists.

   - If the checkpoint file does *not* exist, the package begins at the first task (or parallel tasks) in the control flow.

   - If the checkpoint file does exist, the package reads the file to find out where to start (including updating the value of variables and connections at the time of the last failure).

2. At each successful checkpoint in the package (when the Data Flow Task has FailPackage-OnFailure set to True and the task is successful), the checkpoint file is updated.

3. If the package fails, the checkpoint file stays in the file system and keeps the last update it had from the last successful checkpoint.

4. If the package is successful, the checkpoint file is deleted. Therefore, the next time the package runs, the checkpoint file will not exist, and the package will start from the first task(s).

Figure 2-3 shows the first execution of the package. At this point, no checkpoint file exists, so the package begins at the Execute SQL Task.

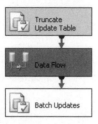

FIGURE 2-3 During the first execution of this package, the Truncate Update Table Task succeeds and is green, and the Data Flow Task fails, and is red.

During the execution of the control flow shown in Figure 2-3, the Truncate Update Table Task succeeds, and SSIS writes a checkpoint to the checkpoint file. However, the Data Flow Task fails, which does not update the checkpoint file, and the package stops.

At this point, the failure is corrected in the Data Flow Task, and the package is rerun. Figure 2-4 shows the control flow of the rerun package. As you can see, this package failed at step 2 of the first run. After the problem was corrected, the second execution of the package started at step 2 and continued to completion.

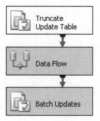

FIGURE 2-4 During the second execution of this package, the Data Flow Task is the first task to run, and the package finishes to completion.

After completion of the last step, called Batch Updates in Figure 2-4, the checkpoint file was deleted.

PRACTICE Implementing Package and Task Transactions

In this practice, you will turn on transactions at the container level and observe the results when a task fails within the container. You will also enable checkpoints for a package and observe the results.

EXERCISE 1 Enable Transactions and Observe a Transaction Rollback

In this exercise, you will enable a transaction for a Sequence Container and observe the data results after an error occurs in another task within the same container.

1. In Control Panel, select Administrative Tools and then Services to open the Services console. If necessary, start the Distributed Transaction Coordinator (MSDTC) service.

2. Open the SSIS project named *TK 70-448 SSIS Project* in SQL Server Business Intelligence Development Studio (BIDS) that you created in Chapter 1, "Developing SSIS Packages," and then open the package named MyPackage.dtsx. Alternatively, you can use the 448-ch02 Start Here project in your Documents\Microsoft Press\MCTS Training Kit 70-448\Source\Ch 02\ folder.

3. Choose Properties Window from the View menu to open the Properties window. Click the Auto Hide button, which resembles a pushpin, in the Properties window to lock the window in the open position.

4. In the Control Flow design surface, select the Sequence Container object by clicking it, and then note the Sequence Container properties listed in the Properties window.

5. Set the TransactionOption property to Required using the drop-down list.

6. Save the package by clicking the Save button on the toolbar.

7. Next, drag a new Execute SQL Task from the toolbox to the bottom of the Sequence Container workspace just below the Data Flow Task.

8. Connect the Data Flow Task to the new Execute SQL Task by dragging the output arrow from the bottom of the Data Flow Task onto the Execute SQL Task.

9. Edit the Execute SQL Task by double-clicking the task.

    a. In the Execute SQL Task Editor dialog box, change the Connection property to the AdventureWorks2008 connection.

    b. Modify the SQLStatement property and type the following statement:

```
SELECT CONVERT(int,ProductLine) FROM Sales_Summary
```

    This SQL code intentionally forces an error in the Execute SQL Task when trying to convert a text value to an integer. Click OK to close the Enter SQL Query dialog box.

    c. Change the Name property within the Execute SQL Task Editor dialog box to **Force Failure**.

    d. Click OK in the Execute SQL Task Editor dialog box to return to the Control Flow design surface. Figure 2-5 shows what your control flow should look like with the new Execute SQL Task.

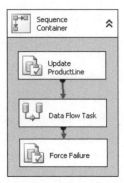

FIGURE 2-5 The new Force Failure Execute SQL Task in the MyPackage.dtsx package is added below the Data Flow Task.

10. Open SQL Server Management Studio (SSMS) and connect to the Database Engine. Open a new database query against the AdventureWorks2008 database.

11. Run the following SQL statement, and then observe the results:

```
SELECT COUNT(*) FROM Sales_Summary
```

12. Return to BIDS, and then execute the SSIS package you just modified, which intentionally fails at the last step. Before stopping the package in Debug mode, open the Data Flow Task and note that the SSIS Designer shows a couple thousand rows inserted into the Sales_Summary table.

13. Stop the package execution, and then rerun the query from step 11. You should see the same number of rows.

14. Observe that even though the Data Flow Task was successful, the data was rolled back. This is because the Sequence Container was configured with the TransactionOption setting as Required and the last task within the Sequence Container failed, therefore rolling back the Data Flow Task data.

EXERCISE 2 Set and Observe Checkpoints in a Package

In this exercise, you will turn on checkpoints in the DimCustomer.dtsx package and observe how checkpoints work when an error occurs.

1. If necessary, start SQL Server Business Intelligence Development Studio (BIDS), open the project *TK 70-448 SSIS Project*, and then edit the DimCustomer.dtsx package by double-clicking it in Solution Explorer.

2. Open the Properties window on the Control Flow tab, and then change the following package-level properties:

   a. Set CheckpointFileName to **c:\DimCustomer_Checkpoint.xml**.

   b. Set CheckPointUsage to IfExists.

   c. Set SaveCheckpoints to True.

3. Select all three tasks in the control flow (hold down the Ctrl key and click each of the tasks). By doing this, you can change the FailPackageOnFailure property for all the tasks at the same time.

4. In the Properties window, while the tasks are selected, change the FailPackageOnFailure property to True.

5. Now, select just the Data Flow Task object and then change the ForceExecutionResult property to Failure. The ForceExecutionResult property is located in the Misc properties grouping and is used for testing when you want to simulate a failure to check error handling or checkpoint logic.

6. Run the DimCustomer.dtsx package in BIDS, and observe that the package intentionally fails at the Data Flow Task.

7. Stop the package in the debugger, and then check the C drive in Windows Explorer for the existence of the DimCustomer_Checkpoint.xml file. This file contains the state information when the package failed.

8. Before restarting the package, select the Data Flow Task object, and then change the ForceExecutionResult property to None, which will let the Data Flow Task run successfully.

9. Restart the DimCustomer.dtsx package in the Control Flow design surface, and notice that the package starts at the Data Flow Task and then completes with the final Execute SQL Task.

10. Last, return to the C drive in Windows Explorer, and confirm that the DimCustomer_Checkpoint.xml file no longer exists because it was automatically deleted after the successful package execution.

11. Return to BIDS and click the Stop button on the toolbar to return to the SSIS Designer.

Lesson 2: Identifying Package Status, Enabling Logging, and Handling Task Errors

Estimated lesson time: 35 minutes

A package run in the BIDS SSIS Designer shows the progress of execution, including the status of tasks and containers. In the data flow, when a package is executing in the BIDS debug environment, you can monitor package progress through row counts as data flows through the data flow components, and you can see color changes that indicate the status. Overall, this progress functionality lets you easily test packages and identify errors as you are developing.

In addition, the control flow allows precedence constraints that let you control the workflow steps in a package, specifying the tasks that should be run based on simple completion status (success, failure, or complete) and those that should use advanced evaluation criteria. This lesson looks at ways to monitor package execution status during development and how to configure control flow constraints to handle errors and enable advanced precedence handling.

Viewing Package Status

While a package is running in the debug environment (that is, when you execute a package in BIDS), you can see the status of both control flow and data flow components. BIDS highlights tasks in different colors, as follows, to help you see what is happening in the package:

- Objects that are not highlighted when a package is running have not yet started.
- Objects highlighted in yellow are in progress. In the data flow, you will also see the number of rows that have gone through the source, transformation, and destination components.
- A task or data flow component highlighted in red has failed. Even after an error has occurred, other components in the package might still be executing.

> **IMPORTANT** **ALLOWING MULTIPLE ERRORS IN A PACKAGE DURING EXECUTION**
>
> The MaximumErrorCount control flow property lets a package continue to run to completion even after errors have occurred. The maximum number specifies the number of errors that can occur before the package will stop executing and report failure.

- When components are highlighted in green, either the control flow task or container is complete or all the available rows have gone through the components successfully.

If you are using either a For Loop Container or a Foreach Loop Container, the embedded tasks might turn the various status colors at different times as the loops are performed. Even when all the tasks in a package have been completed, the package will remain in the debug/execution state until the package has been stopped. This behavior lets you easily see the final status of tasks and the row counts in the data flow.

In addition to the visual aids that help you see what a package is doing, while you are running a package in the debug environment, you can also read the execution details on a new tab in the SSIS Designer named Progress. Figure 2-6 shows the Progress tab results of a package during execution.

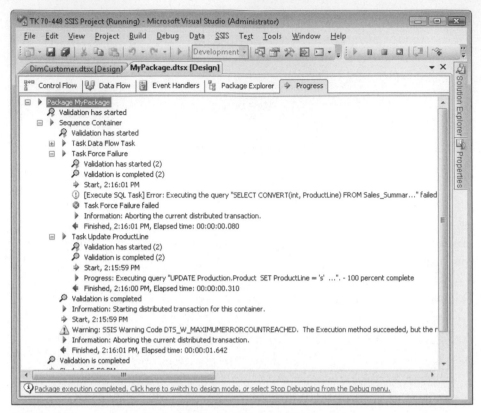

FIGURE 2-6 You can view package execution details on the Progress tab.

When a package is executed outside the debug environment, this tab's name changes to Execution Results. The listed results include error and warning descriptions, execution times, final destination row counts, and other execution information (such as validation steps and configuration usage).

Configuring Execution Logging

The same information captured on the Progress tab when a package is executed in BIDS can also be captured to a logging table or logging file by using the SSIS built-in logging features.

You enable logging on a package-by-package basis, and you turn on logging for a package by first opening a package in BIDS and then selecting Logging from the SSIS menu. You can also open the Configure SSIS Logs dialog box by right-clicking in the Control Flow tab and then clicking Logging. Figure 2-7 shows the Configure SSIS Logs dialog box.

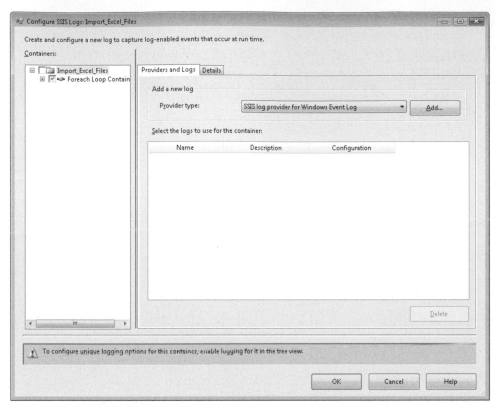

FIGURE 2-7 You use the Configure SSIS Logs dialog box to set up package logging.

Enabling logging in a package involves the following three steps:

- **Choosing the container to log** The left navigation section of the Configure SSIS Logs dialog box lets you define what part of the package you want to enable logging for. Typically, you want to log an entire package, in which case, you should select the check box for the entire package at the upper left of the navigation tree. But you can also log part of a package by selecting the check box for just the appropriate container or task.

- **Setting the log provider type** The log provider is the log events destination location, such as a table or file. You select the provider from the Provider Type drop-down list in the Providers And Logs tab of the dialog box and then click Add. The most common log types are Text Files or SQL Server, but you can also log to the Windows Event Log, SQL Server Profiler, or an XML file. If required by the provider type you selected, specify a connection in the Configuration drop-down list and then select the check box to enable logging on this provider. The practice exercises at the end of the lesson walk through the logging configuration process.

- **Selecting the log events** The log events are the details that SSIS captures on the provider when a package runs. These events are found on the Details tab in the Configure SSIS Logs dialog box. Figure 2-8 shows several events selected on the Details tab.

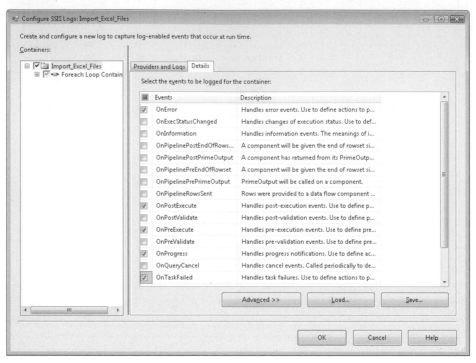

FIGURE 2-8 The Details tab of the Configure SSIS Logs dialog box lets you select different log events.

The most common log events selected are OnError, OnPostExecute, OnPreExecute, On-Progress, and OnTaskFailed. The OnPreExecute and OnPostExecute events are captured at the start and end of each container and task when the package runs and allows a method to determine the execution times of each task.

If you select SQL Server as the log provider, the log details are stored in a system table named dbo.sysssislog. Figure 2-9 shows the table contents after a package is executed.

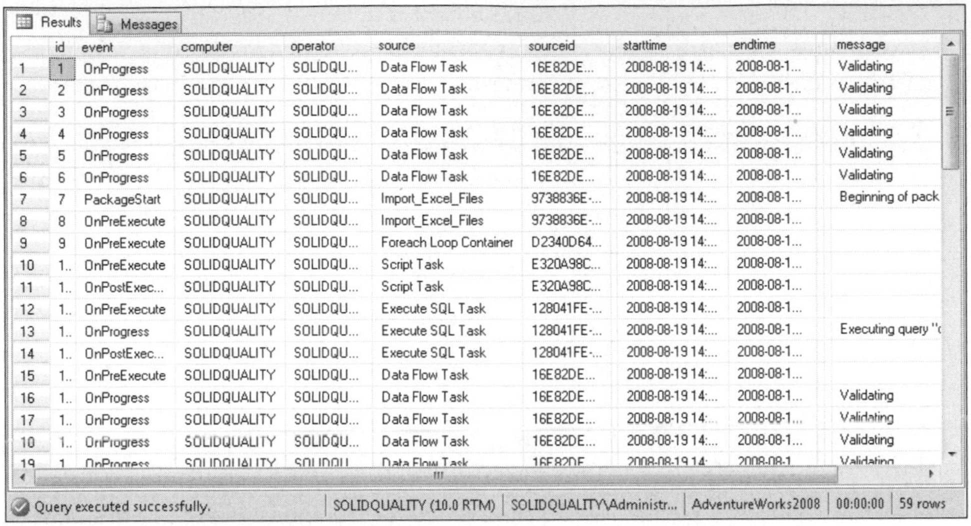

	id	event	computer	operator	source	sourceid	starttime	endtime	message
1	1	OnProgress	SOLIDQUALITY	SOLIDQU...	Data Flow Task	16E82DE...	2008-08-19 14:...	2008-08-1...	Validating
2	2	OnProgress	SOLIDQUALITY	SOLIDQU...	Data Flow Task	16E82DE...	2008-08-19 14:...	2008-08-1...	Validating
3	3	OnProgress	SOLIDQUALITY	SOLIDQU...	Data Flow Task	16E82DE...	2008-08-19 14:...	2008-08-1...	Validating
4	4	OnProgress	SOLIDQUALITY	SOLIDQU...	Data Flow Task	16E82DE...	2008-08-19 14:...	2008-08-1...	Validating
5	5	OnProgress	SOLIDQUALITY	SOLIDQU...	Data Flow Task	16E82DE...	2008-08-19 14:...	2008-08-1...	Validating
6	6	OnProgress	SOLIDQUALITY	SOLIDQU...	Data Flow Task	16E82DE...	2008-08-19 14:...	2008-08-1...	Validating
7	7	PackageStart	SOLIDQUALITY	SOLIDQU...	Import_Excel_Files	9738836E-...	2008-08-19 14:...	2008-08-1...	Beginning of pack
8	8	OnPreExecute	SOLIDQUALITY	SOLIDQU...	Import_Excel_Files	9738836E-...	2008-08-19 14:...	2008-08-1...	
9	9	OnPreExecute	SOLIDQUALITY	SOLIDQU...	Foreach Loop Container	D2340D64...	2008-08-19 14:...	2008-08-1...	
10	1..	OnPreExecute	SOLIDQUALITY	SOLIDQU...	Script Task	E320A98C...	2008-08-19 14:...	2008-08-1...	
11	1..	OnPostExec...	SOLIDQUALITY	SOLIDQU...	Script Task	E320A98C...	2008-08-19 14:...	2008-08-1...	
12	1..	OnPreExecute	SOLIDQUALITY	SOLIDQU...	Execute SQL Task	128041FE-...	2008-08-19 14:...	2008-08-1...	
13	1..	OnProgress	SOLIDQUALITY	SOLIDQU...	Execute SQL Task	128041FE-...	2008-08-19 14:...	2008-08-1...	Executing query "(
14	1..	OnPostExec...	SOLIDQUALITY	SOLIDQU...	Execute SQL Task	128041FE-...	2008-08-19 14:...	2008-08-1...	
15	1..	OnPreExecute	SOLIDQUALITY	SOLIDQU...	Data Flow Task	16E82DE...	2008-08-19 14:...	2008-08-1...	
16	1..	OnProgress	SOLIDQUALITY	SOLIDQU...	Data Flow Task	16E82DE...	2008-08-19 14:...	2008-08-1...	Validating
17	1..	OnProgress	SOLIDQUALITY	SOLIDQU...	Data Flow Task	16E82DE...	2008-08-19 14:...	2008-08-1...	Validating
18	1..	OnProgress	SOLIDQUALITY	SOLIDQU...	Data Flow Task	16E82DE...	2008-08-19 14:...	2008-08-1...	Validating
19	1..	OnProgress	SOLIDQUALITY	SOLIDQU...	Data Flow Task	16E82DE...	2008-08-19 14:...	2008-08-1...	Validating

Query executed successfully. | SOLIDQUALITY (10.0 RTM) | SOLIDQUALITY\Administr... | AdventureWorks2008 | 00:00:00 | 59 rows

FIGURE 2-9 The dbo.sysssislog table includes the events and event details of a package during execution.

Connecting Control Flow Objects with Precedence

Precedence constraints are the control flow connectors between tasks and containers. In fact, in the practices you completed in Chapter 1 and in Lesson 1 in this chapter, you created simple precedence constraints by dragging output arrows from one task to another. Usually, these connectors are green, red, or blue, indicating the execution success, failure, or completion, respectively. For example, if a task fails, the constraints that are blue or red are evaluated as True. Even though a task failed, it is considered complete, and therefore, blue constraints (completion) are followed to the next task or container.

> ***IMPORTANT*** **COMPARING CONTROL FLOW PRECEDENCE CONSTRAINTS AND DATA FLOW PATHS**
>
> **Precedence constraints are used only in the control flow of a package and not in the data flow. When looking at objects configured in the control flow and comparing these to components configured in the data flow, the objects look very similar, but they are very different. The connectors between objects in the control flow are precedence constraints, whereas the connectors in the data flow are data paths. You will look at paths in Lesson 3, "Handling Data Flow Errors and Debugging."**

SSIS also provides advanced constraint capabilities, which allow conditional and/or expression evaluation criteria. Figure 2-10 shows a complicated control flow that has been configured with several precedence constraints.

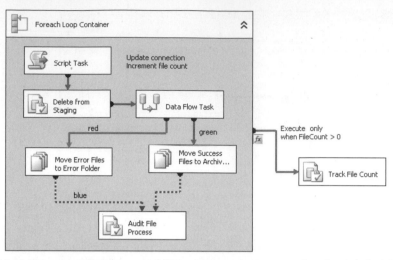

FIGURE 2-10 You can configure a control flow with precedence constraints that handle failures, either/or logic, and evaluation expressions.

Notice that some constraint lines are solid, some are dashed, and some have function symbols (*Fx*) associated with them. Each of these indicates the implementation of a different precedence constraint feature, as follows:

- Solid lines represent logical AND precedence, meaning that a task will run only when all the constraint conditions are met.

- Dashed lines are logical OR statements between tasks. For example, if a task has dashed constraints pointing to it, the task will run when either of the precedence conditions is met.

- Function symbols show that an SSIS expression has been embedded in the constraint for evaluation. When you use embedded expressions, constraints can determine task execution unrelated to preceding task results.

Within the control flow, you can edit a precedence constraint by double-clicking the constraint or by right-clicking the constraint and then clicking Edit. Figure 2-11 shows the Precedence Constraint Editor.

As you look at the Precedence Constraint Editor dialog box in Figure 2-11, notice the two general groupings of properties: the Evaluation Operation properties and the Multiple Constraints properties.

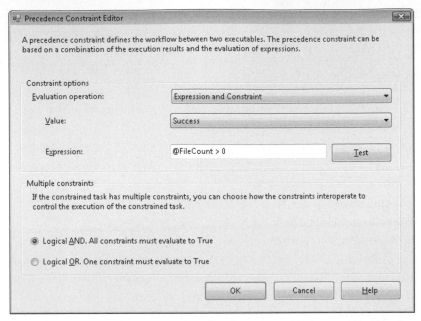

FIGURE 2-11 The Precedence Constraint Editor lets you modify the constraint for advanced features.

Evaluation Operation Properties

The Evaluation Operation properties let you define the conditions that determine the successful evaluation of the constraint. There are two primary evaluation indicators:

- Constraints are simply the execution status of the upstream (preceding) task (completion, failure, or success), which you can select from the Value drop-down list. For example, if an upstream task fails and the constraint is set to Failure, the constraint requirement is met.

- Expressions in the precedence constraints are advanced Boolean evaluators (meaning that they must evaluate to True or False) that you can write in the SSIS Expression language. Expressions can include mathematical and string functions and can reference package variables. When the evaluation operation allows an expression, you can type it in the Expression box.

You can specify different combinations of these two evaluation indicators that work together to determine whether the precedence constraint allows a downstream (subsequent) task to execute. The Evaluation Operation drop-down list includes four options:

- **Constraint** By selecting Constraint, you specify that only the execution completion status will be used to evaluate the precedence constraint.

- **Expression** By selecting Expression, you specify that only an expression will be used to evaluate the precedence constraint.

- **Expression And Constraint** If you select Expression And Constraint, the precedence constraint will evaluate to True only if both expressions evaluate to True and the execution status matches the constraint setting.

- **Expression Or Constraint** If you select Expression Or Constraint, the precedence constraint will evaluate to True if either of the expressions evaluate to True or if the execution status matches the constraint setting.

All the properties mentioned here relate directly to the specific precedence constraint that you are editing. These options give you granular control over how SSIS should evaluate a precedence constraint. Whenever you use an expression as the evaluation operation or as part of the evaluation operation, SSIS will display a small function symbol next to the precedence constraint line.

Multiple Constraint Properties

When you have multiple precedence constraints connected to the same task or container, you also have the option to apply comparisons across the constraints. Your two Multiple Constraints options are as follows:

- **Logical AND** Is the default and means that all the precedence constraints connected to the task or container need to meet their conditions in order for the downstream task or container to execute.

- **Logical OR** Lets you specify that only one of the precedence constraints needs to meet its requirements in order for the task or container to execute.

When you change the logical condition to either Logical AND or Logical OR, the change propagates to all the precedence constraints connected to the same downstream task or container. When you set the logical condition to Logical OR, the precedence constraint lines become dashed for all the related precedence constraints.

Returning to the example in Figure 2-10, the constraints shown control the workflow of the control flow in the following way:

1. Each loop in the Foreach Loop Container will check for files and first perform a Script Task and an Execute SQL Task. The precedence constraints after each of these tasks are marked as Success; therefore, both tasks need to be completed successfully for the Data Flow Task to run.

2. The Data Flow Task has two precedence constraints, one Success and one Failure. If the Data Flow Task is successful, a File System Task runs that archives the successfully processed file to a folder named Archive. If the Data Flow Task fails, a different File System Task moves the file to a folder named Error_Files.

3. The final task in the Foreach Loop Container is an Execute SQL Task that audits the processing of the file. It has two precedence constraints connected to it, and they are marked as Logical OR with a Completion constraint. This means that when either the File System Task that moves the successful file completes or the File System Task that moves the error file completes, this Execute SQL Task runs.

4. When the Foreach Loop Container completes, it has a precedence constraint tied to another Execute SQL Task. Figure 2-11 showed the editor for this constraint, which requires that the Foreach Loop Container is successful and that the FileCount variable has a value greater than 0. This variable is updated in the Script Task within the Foreach Loop Container. If there are no files to process, the FileCount value is 0, and the final Execute SQL Task in the control flow does not run.

PRACTICE Creating and Configuring Precedence Constraints

In the following exercises, you will create precedence constraints to specify when your control flow tasks should run, and then you will observe the implications of defining precedence constraints during execution. You will also turn on package logging for the DimCustomer.dtsx package.

EXERCISE 1   Set Up Constraints

In this exercise, you will configure a precedence constraint to handle failures and also create a Script Task that displays a message box demonstrating that the task ran.

1. If necessary, start SQL Server Business Intelligence Development Studio (BIDS), open the project *TK 70-448 SSIS Project*, and then open the MyPackage.dtsx package.

> **NOTE PRACTICE FILES**
>
> The installed practice files contain the completed SSIS projects for Lessons 1 through 3 in the ..\Source\Ch 02\ folder.

2. Drag a Script Task onto the Control Flow design surface, but not inside the Sequence Container.

3. Drag the output arrow from the Sequence Container onto the Script Task.

4. Right-click the precedence constraint you just created, and then click Edit in the drop-down list.

5. In the Precedence Constraint Editor dialog box, change the Value drop-down list to Failure, and then click OK to save the changes.

6. Edit the Script Task by double-clicking it.

7. Click Edit Script, which opens the Microsoft Visual Studio code editor.

8. Look for the comment in the editor *// TODO: Add your code here*, which is in the *public void Main()* section of the code, and add the following code:

```
MessageBox.Show("Script Task ran!");
```

Be sure to delete the whole *// TODO: Add your code here* line.

9. On the File menu, choose Exit, and then click OK in the Script Task Editor dialog box.

10. Execute the MyPackage.dtsx package you just modified in BIDS.

11. Click OK when the Script Task message box is displayed, and then stop the package.

12. Delete the Force Failure Execute SQL Task embedded in the Sequence Container by right-clicking the Force Failure Execute SQL Task and then clicking Delete.

13. Rerun the package in BIDS; you see that the Script Task does not run because the Sequence Container was successful.

14. To allow the Script Task to run regardless of whether the Sequence Container is successful or fails, right-click the precedence constraint that connects the Sequence Container and the Script Task, and then click Completion.

15. Rerun the package, and when the Script Task message box appears, click OK. You see that the Script Task ran because you configured the precedence constraint to execute whether the Sequence Container succeeded or failed.

16. Stop the package, and then close it.

EXERCISE 2 Turn On SSIS Logging for the DimCustomer.dtsx Package

In this exercise, you will enable logging in a package to capture the package execution details into a SQL table. Then you will run the package and query the table after the package has completed.

1. If necessary, start SQL Server Business Intelligence Development Studio (BIDS), open the project *TK 70-448 SSIS Project*, and then open the DimCustomer.dtsx package that you modified in Exercise 1 by double-clicking it in Solution Explorer.

2. Choose Logging from the SSIS menu, which opens the Configure SSIS Logs dialog box.

   a. To enable logging for the entire package, select the check box next to the top-level DimCustomer folder in the left navigation tree.

b. In the Provider Type drop-down list, choose SSIS Log Provider For SQL Server, and then click Add. This adds an entry to the list for configuring a log.

c. In the new log entry added to the list, select the check box to enable it.

d. On the same log entry line, click in the Configuration column to display a drop-down list of package connections. Select AdventureWorksDW2008 from the list.

e. Click the Details tab, and in the list of events, select the check boxes next to the following events: *OnError*, *OnPostExecute*, *OnPreExecute*, and *OnTaskFailed*.

f. Click OK to save the changes to the logging configuration.

3. To generate log entries, run the DimCustomer.dtsx package in BIDS.

4. After the package completes, switch to SSMS, open a new query, and then execute the following SQL statement to view the new entries in the log table:

```
SELECT * FROM dbo.sysssislog
```

✔ Quick Check

1. When a package fails while you are developing it, where should you look to identify what happened?

2. You have a package that includes a step that occasionally fails because of network connectivity problems. When a network connectivity error occurs, you need to perform an alternative step to run the same operation in a slower but more reliable way. At the completion of the alternative step, you would like to run the next step in the original workflow. How can you accomplish this?

Quick Check Answers

1. The Progress or Execution Results tabs in the SSIS Designer show package execution details, including any warnings that were displayed or errors that occurred during execution. Often, you will need to scroll through the results and look for the errors and their descriptions. A single error might produce multiple error messages.

2. From the first task, create a red failure precedence constraint to the alternative task. You then need to create Success constraints from both the alternative task and the original task to the third task. You need to set the Success constraints to Logical OR so that when either the first task or the second task is successful, the final task will run.

Lesson 3: Handling Data Flow Errors and Debugging

Estimated lesson time: 45 minutes

In the real world, no data source is perfect. Therefore, you will need to handle anomalies and bad data as you process data in your SSIS data flow. By default, when an error occurs in a data flow row, the Data Flow Task fails. However, SSIS includes the capability to route the bad rows away from the data flow and handle the data problem without affecting the good rows. Furthermore, within the data flow, you can pause execution and monitor the actual data as it is flowing through the SSIS engine.

In this lesson, you look at using error paths to route failed rows to a different subset of components, and you review how to use data viewers to debug data flows. Last, you explore how to use event handlers to take care of package errors and how to use breakpoints to debug the control flow.

Using Error Paths to Handle Data Flow Errors

Paths in the data flow are similar to precedence constraints in the control flow, except that data flow paths handle rows of data rather than the execution status of tasks. There are two primary paths in the data flow:

- **Data paths** The green connectors that go from one component to another. For these paths, the rows that have successfully gone through a component are output, as are error rows when the error output is set to ignore failures.

- **Error paths** The red connectors between data flow components. They contain data rows that fail in a component when the error rows are set to be redirected.

Not all components in the data flow use error paths. For example, the Multicast component only copies data; it does not perform any operation on the data itself, so there is no possible point of failure, and there are no error paths. Components that use error paths include all source adapters, destination adapters, Lookup Transformations, Conditional Split Transformations, Derived Column Transformations, and so on.

Figure 2-12 shows a completed data flow containing a Data Conversion Transformation with two outputs. The error path, which displays in red in the SSIS Designer (and is labeled *red* in the figure), handles rows that fail in the Data Conversion Transformation operation.

In this example, the error row output is passed to a Derived Column Transformation named Fix Age, and this Derived Column Transformation is sent to a Union All Transformation, which brings the error row output data back together with the successfully converted data from the Data Conversion Transformation.

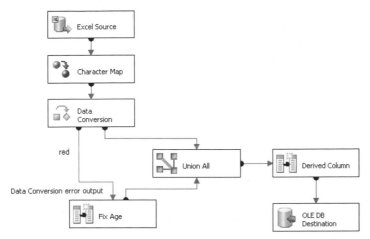

FIGURE 2-12 A red arrow indicates the error path for rows that fail in the Data Conversion Transformation.

To use error paths, you need to configure the error output. You have three options for handling errors in the data flow components:

- Setting the error output to Fail Transformation causes the data flow to fail if an error is encountered.

- Using the Ignore Failure option will let the row continue out the normal green data path, but the value that resulted in the error is changed to NULL in the output.

- Setting the error output to Redirect Row sends the error row out the red error path; this is the only way to handle errors with separate components.

These error-handling options are available for the entire row as well as for the operation for each column within the row. This does not mean that a single column gets redirected, but rather that some columns can be set to ignore failures, while errors in other columns cause redirects. Figure 2-13 shows the Configure Error Output dialog box, which you use to set these properties. To navigate to this dialog box, you can either double-click to edit the component and then select Configure Error Output, or you can simply drag the red error path output arrow onto the next component, which opens the same dialog box.

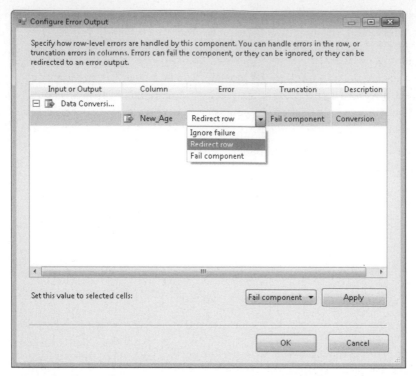

FIGURE 2-13 The Configure Error Output dialog box lets you set what happens when an error occurs in an upstream transformation.

In the example shown earlier in Figure 2-12, the Data Conversion Transformation is converting a column named Age from a *DT_WSTR* data type (Unicode string) to a *DT_NUMERIC* data type (numeric string). However, some of the values coming from the Age column are 43, 31, None, 26, and NA. As you can see, SSIS cannot successfully convert the text values to a numeric type, and the Data Conversion Transformation fails if the error rows are not redirected.

Instead, the error rows are configured to be redirected as Figure 2-13 shows, and the red error output is sent to a Derived Column Transformation. All this transformation does is create a new column that has a 0 as the age because the age is indeterminate. The Union All Transformation brings the converted Age column together with the 0 value from the Derived Column Transformation, and the rows can now be passed down eventually to the destination without error.

Common uses of the error path output are when text file source data does not match the data type specified in the data flow or when a Lookup Transformation does not find a match. Sometimes a destination runs into an error row if a constraint is violated when the inserts are performed. In addition, the error rows can be handled differently depending on whether you need to send them to a temporary table for review or whether you need to clean up the data and bring the rows back into the data flow through a Union All.

Using Data Viewers to Identify Data Flow Issues

Troubleshooting data issues can be frustrating, especially when you are not able to easily identify the problem row or issue. Therefore, SSIS also includes the capability to watch rows in the data flow as they are passing through the pipeline. SSIS implements this capability through data viewers, a feature you can use when you are running packages in BIDS during development. For any path in the data flow, you can add a data viewer that pauses the execution of the data flow and displays the data in the data viewer in one of four formats.

You add a data viewer by right-clicking the path and then clicking Data Viewers. Figure 2-14 shows the Data Flow Path Editor dialog box with the Data Viewers tab selected.

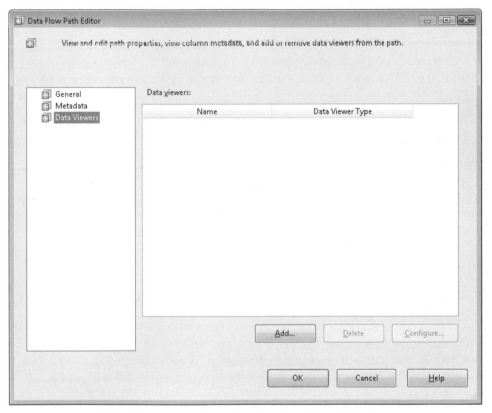

FIGURE 2-14 You add data viewers through the Data Flow Path Editor dialog box.

After clicking Add on the Data Viewers tab in the Data Flow Path Editor dialog box, you can configure your data viewer. You first need to choose the type of data viewer you want to use. Four types are available:

- **Grid**   Shows the raw data in columns and rows; the grid is the viewer most commonly used to identify row-level data.
- **Histogram**   Used for numeric columns; shows the distribution of data across a range.

- **Scatter Plot** Reveals data relationships between two numeric columns, highlighting outliers.
- **Column Chart** Displays the summary values of a column selected in the data flow.

After you select the type of data viewer, click OK to accept the defaults.

> **NOTE DATA VIEWERS DO NOT WORK WHEN A PACKAGE IS RUN FROM THE COMMAND LINE**
>
> You can use a data viewer only when running a package in the debug environment. If you have an error path configured in a package, it will be ignored when you run the package programmatically or from the command line.

The most commonly used data viewer is Grid, because it shows the actual rows of data. When you choose the Grid type and then execute the package in BIDS, the data viewer displays a set of rows at a time. Figure 2-15 shows the Data Viewer dialog box as a package is executing.

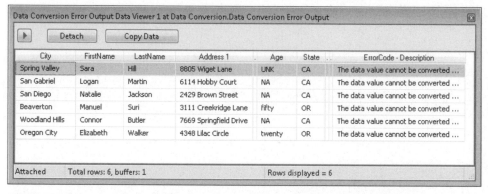

FIGURE 2-15 Error rows display in the data viewer window as a package is executing.

After reviewing the rows, you can choose to allow the data to move on until completion by clicking Detach in the Data Viewer window, or you can return the next batch of rows to look at by clicking the Play button. If you use a data viewer on an error path, you can add the Error and Error Code columns to the output to identify the column in the row that caused the row to fail a component.

Handling Package Errors with Event Handlers

In the data flow, using data viewers gives you the ability to easily debug problems while processing data. The control flow is different, however, because the focus is on workflow and execution rather than on data and transformations. Taking advantage of the capabilities in Visual Studio, the control flow supports visual debugging and breakpoint features. You will first look at the event handlers that SSIS provides, and you will then explore the debugging capabilities in the control flow.

SSIS provides the capability to listen for certain execution events and perform other operations when an event happens (depending on the execution event). For example, if an error occurs, the error event handler can send an alert or potentially fix a data problem. Event handlers use the control flow paradigm for workflow processing, which includes all the same control flow tasks and containers that are in the Control Flow toolbox.

You can define zero, one, or more than one event handler for a package. To add an event handler to a package, you need to click the Event Handlers tab in the SSIS Designer. To create a new package event handler, you select a task from the Executable drop-down list and the an event from the Event Handler drop-down list, as Figure 2-16 shows.

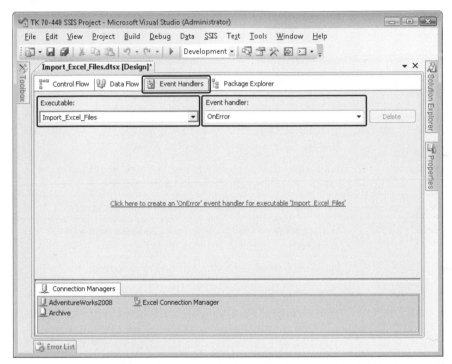

FIGURE 2-16 You define event handlers on the Event Handlers tab of the SSIS Designer, choosing the executable task and specific event for the event handler.

The executable component is the task or container scope that triggers the event. You can also choose the package itself (the highest-level container) as the executable component for an event. The event handler is the actual event that causes the event workflow to execute. Table 2-1 describes the package event handler types.

In addition, event handlers assigned to an executable scope propagate down to child events when the event fires. If an event is assigned to a container, the child executable files include the tasks and containers that are embedded within the parent container. This means that if you assign an OnError event to the package and an OnError event occurs at a task, the event handler fires for both the task and the package (and for any containers between). You can use an event handler for tracking error details, for sending failure messages in e-mail messages, and for implementing manual rollback logic.

Using event handlers is a great way to track package execution; you can use them to audit the execution, capturing the errors that occur in a task. In addition, you can use the event handler Send Mail Task for notification purposes—for example, it can notify an administrator of a certain predefined condition that requires a special response.

> **BEST PRACTICES** **CAPTURE ERROR INFORMATION WITH THE ONERROR EVENT**
>
> Each package contains a set of system variables that are updated for the various levels in the package during package execution. With event handlers, you can capture these variables and values, which provide contextual information such as the ErrorCode, ErrorDescription, and SourceName (the task), when the event fires.

TABLE 2-1 Package Event Handler Types

EVENT HANDLER	DESCRIPTION
OnError	Runs when a task or container reports an error.
OnExecStatusChanged	Runs for all tasks and containers when the execution status changes to In Process, Success, or Failed.
OnInformation	Runs when SSIS outputs information messages during the validation and execution of a task or container.
OnPostExecute	Runs after a container or task successfully completes.
OnPostValidate	Executes after a container or task has successfully been validated.
OnPreExecute	Runs just before a container or task is executed.
OnPreValidate	Runs before the component is validated by the engine.
OnProgress	Executed when a progress message is sent by the SSIS engine, indicating tangible advancement of the task or container.
OnQueryCancel	Invoked when an Execute SQL Task is cancelled through manual intervention, such as stopping the package.
OnTaskFailed	Similar to OnError, but runs when a task fails rather than each time an error occurs.
OnVariableValueChanged	Runs when the value changes in a variable for which the RaiseChangeEvent property is set to True.
OnWarning	Runs when a task returns a warning event such as a column not being used in a data flow.

REAL WORLD

Erik Veerman

A common practice with SSIS is creating a template SSIS package—sometimes called a *package framework*—that contains a set of preconfigured tasks and event handlers for auditing purposes. Then when you start to create a new package, you begin with the package template so that all your packages have the same logging, auditing, configurations (SSIS configurations are reviewed in Chapter 3, "Deploying and Configuring SSIS Packages"), and event handling set up.

One of the first things I do when working with a client to implement an SSIS solution is drop in the SSIS framework that I have created over the years. It includes logging and auditing tables, a way to perform incremental extraction, and even a set of SQL Server Reporting Services (SSRS) reports that run off the tables to show status for execution times and for troubleshooting. The framework package I developed includes an *OnError* event handler that captures the error task and description to a table with the time of the error. In addition, it uses the *OnVariableValueChange* event handler and captures the changes in variable values as the package is executing. All this functionality together provides a nice way to ensure consistency and gain better insight into your SSIS execution environment.

The drawback to not beginning with a package template is the challenge of trying to add auditing after the fact, which can be difficult because you are trying to copy and paste tasks and create user variables for auditing. It is my experience that you would be well served to create a package template up front, or you can even start with some of the frameworks available for copying!

After you have created a package that you want to use as a template, you can copy it to the following folder, which will make it available from Visual Studio:

C:\Program Files\Microsoft Visual Studio 9.0\Common7\IDE\PrivateAssemblies\ ProjectItems\DataTransformationProject\DataTransformationItems

After your package is in this templates folder, any time you need to create a new SSIS package, select the Project menu on the Visual Studio menu bar, and then select Add New Item. Your package will appear in the list.

Debugging the Control Flow with Breakpoints

Package debugging lets you know via the SSIS Designer what is going on during the execution of a package so that you can troubleshoot or validate processing logic. Control flow debugging involves setting breakpoints in the package, which will pause the control flow execution so that you can observe the execution state. SSIS takes advantage of the breakpoint functionality that comes with Visual Studio, which means that you have the capabilities to view execution information about the package when you execute a package in the SSIS Designer.

> **IMPORTANT BREAKPOINTS WORK IN CONTROL FLOW ONLY**
>
> Breakpoints function in the control flow but not in the data flow. For scripting, this means that you can set breakpoints only in a control flow Script Task but not in a data flow Script Component Transformation.

To set a breakpoint, select the task or container, and either press F9 or navigate to the Debug/Toggle Breakpoint menu. You can set multiple breakpoints in a package, and you can embed a breakpoint within a Script Task at a line of code. Figure 2-17 shows a package that is running but is paused at execution.

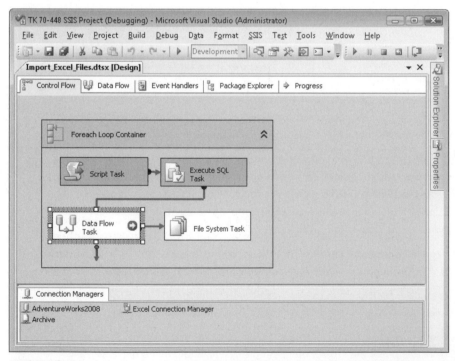

FIGURE 2-17 A package can have a breakpoint enabled at any task or container, such as on the Data Flow Task in this example, and when the package is run, it will pause its execution at the breakpoint.

In this screen, the arrow next to the breakpoint icon, which appears as a small red circle containing a yellow arrow, indicates which task the package is currently waiting to run. When you are paused in the debug environment, you can do the following things to help troubleshoot your package:

- Open the Locals window to see all the variable values and the package status. To open this window, choose Windows and then Locals from the Debug menu. If you have several variables in a package that you actively use to control logic and precedence, you can use a breakpoint to pause the execution, which lets you troubleshoot variable values handling before the package execution completes. Figure 2-18 shows the Locals window with the package variables displayed.

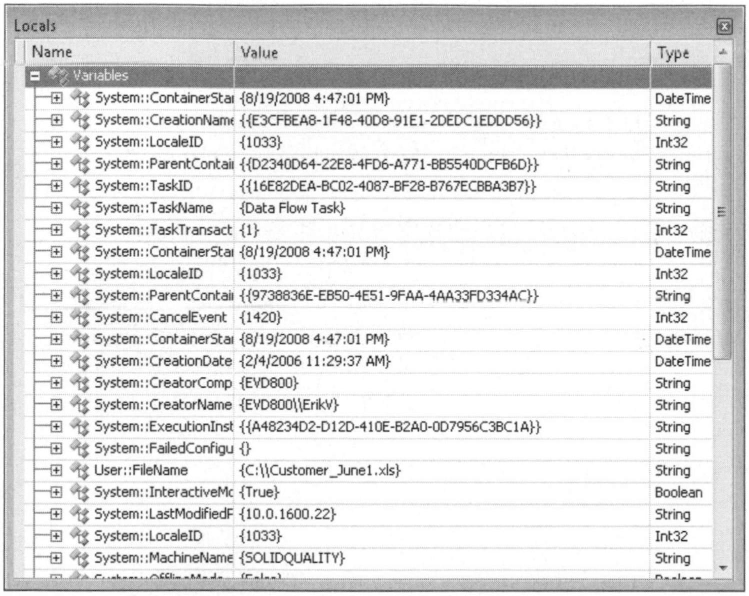

FIGURE 2-18 You open the Locals window by choosing the Debug menu and then choosing Windows. The Locals window shows the value of variables when a package is paused with a breakpoint during execution.

- When you have completed working during a pause and are in a Script Task, you can continue the execution of the script and package to the next breakpoint either by clicking the Continue button on the Debug toolbar or by pressing F5. Alternatively, you can stop the package from continuing by clicking the Stop button on the toolbar. Breakpoints in a Script Task are very useful because they help you validate the code logic and branching that you are performing with the script.

- When the package is paused on a task (as opposed to within the code of a Script Task, as described in the preceding list item) in the control flow, you can also continue running the package to completion (or to the next breakpoint) by clicking the Continue button on the Debug toolbar or by pressing F5.

- You can stop the package during execution, whether the package is paused at a breakpoint or executing, by clicking the Stop button on the toolbar or by pressing Shift+F5.

In all, breakpoints are powerful tools for resolving errors and validating functionality. Combined with data views in the data flow, they provide comprehensive debugging support during your package development.

PRACTICE Identifying Data Flow Errors

In this practice, you will add an error flow path and then identify the error by observing the rows in the output through a data viewer.

EXERCISE Add Error Flow Paths

In this exercise, you will use the error path to handle insert errors when a constraint is violated and then use a Data Viewer to identify the error.

1. In SSMS, create a new database query connected to the AdventureWorks2008 sample database, and run the following code. (The code is available in the practice exercise files at ..\Source\Ch 02\AlterSalesSummaryConstraint.sql.)

```
USE [AdventureWorks2008]
GO
TRUNCATE TABLE dbo.Sales_Summary
GO
ALTER TABLE dbo.Sales_Summary  WITH CHECK
ADD CONSTRAINT [CK_Summary_ProductLine]
CHECK  ((upper([ProductLine])='R' OR upper([ProductLine])='M'
OR upper([ProductLine])='T'))
GO
```

The preceding code uses the Sales_Summary table that you created in Chapter 1 and used in Lessons 1 and 2 of this chapter.

2. If necessary, start SQL Server Business Intelligence Development Studio (BIDS), open the project *TK 70-448 SSIS Project*, and then edit the MyPackage.dtsx package that you modified in Lesson 2 by double-clicking it in Solution Explorer.

3. Click the Data Flow tab in the SSIS Designer, right-click the OLE DB Destination adapter, and then click Edit.

4. In the Data Access Mode drop-down list, select Table Or View, and then verify that the Sales_Summary table is still selected in the Name Of The Table Or The View drop-down list.

5. Click OK in the OLE DB Destination Editor dialog box to return to the SSIS Designer.

6. Right-click in the Data Flow workspace, and then click Execute Task to run the Data Flow Task. Before stopping the package, click the Progress tab and observe that the OLE DB Destination adapter failed because of a constraint violation.

7. Stop the package to return to the SSIS Designer. Click the Control Flow tab, and then click somewhere in the control flow other than a task or container to deselect any objects.

8. Choose Variables from the SSIS menu; this opens the Variables window.

9. Click Add Variable (the leftmost button on the Variable window toolbar) to create a new variable for the package, and then name the variable **ErrorCount**. Again, be sure that you are on the Control Flow tab and that no task or container is selected. This ensures that the variable is created at the package level.

10. Return to the data flow, and display the toolbox. Drag a Row Count Transformation onto the data flow workspace.

11. Select the OLE DB Destination adapter, and then drag the red error output path onto the Row Count Transformation.

12. When the Configure Error Output dialog box appears, change the value in the Error column drop-down list to Redirect Row, and then click OK to return to the Data Flow design surface.

13. Open the Row Count Transformation by double-clicking it, and then change the VariableName property to User::ErrorCount.

14. Click OK in the Row Count Editor dialog box to return to the Data Flow tab of the SSIS Designer.

15. Right-click the red error path, and then click Data Viewers.

16. Click Add in the Data Flow Path Editor, select Grid in the Type list, click OK in the Configure Data Viewer dialog box, and then click OK in the Data Flow Path Editor dialog box.

17. Right-click in the Data Flow design surface, and then click Execute Task.

18. A new data viewer appears, which reveals the OLE DB Destination Error Output rows. Observe that the ProductLine column for all the error rows is "S," which violates the defined constraint that you created in step 1.

19. Click the Detach button in the Data Viewer window, and then stop the package execution.

20. In SSMS, run the following database query, which adds "S" as a valid value of the ProductLine column in the Sales_Summary table. (The code is available in the practice exercise files at ..\Source\Ch 02\AlterSalesSummaryConstraint2.sql.)

```
USE [AdventureWorks]
GO
ALTER TABLE dbo.Sales_Summary
DROP CONSTRAINT [CK_Summary_ProductLine]
GO
ALTER TABLE dbo.Sales_Summary  WITH CHECK
ADD CONSTRAINT [CK_Summary_ProductLine]
CHECK  ((upper([ProductLine])='R' OR upper([ProductLine])='M'
OR upper([ProductLine])='T' OR upper([ProductLine])='S'))
GO
```

21. Return to BIDS and rerun the data flow, observing that the OLE DB Destination is now successful, with no rows being routed to the error path output or data viewer.

✔ **Quick Check**

1. A Data Conversion Transformation is failing in the middle of the data flow execution, and you need to determine what is causing the error. How should you proceed?

2. Your package contains a string variable that you are updating, using a Script Task, to be a file path and file name. Your package is failing at a File System Task that is configured to use the variable to move the file to a different folder on the server. How do you troubleshoot the package?

3. You would like to log all the package errors to a custom database table that you have created for auditing purposes. How can you accomplish this task?

Quick Check Answers

1. To determine what is causing the error, configure the Data Conversion Transformation error path to Flat File so that any rows that are failing conversion are sent to a file. Then create a data viewer on the error path, and run the package in BIDS. This technique will capture the errors in a file and display the rows in the SSIS Designer for troubleshooting.

2. Because the Script Task can contain embedded breakpoints in the code, set a breakpoint in the script so that you will be able to execute the package and step through the lines of code, observing the value of the variable to check the code and accuracy.

3. By using the *OnError* event handler assigned to the package level, you can also use an Execute SQL Task that calls a stored procedure, passing in the *SourceName* and *ErrorDescription* variable values. The procedure can then track these details into a metadata storage table for auditing.

Case Scenario: Troubleshooting and Handling Errors in SSIS Packages

You are creating a set of SSIS packages that move data from a source transactional system to data mart tables. As you develop the packages, you need a way to troubleshoot both your control flow development and your data flow development. You also need to ensure that the data in your destination database is in a consistent state and not in an intermediate state when an error occurs. In addition, you need to provide an audit trail of information and build alerts into your package design. How would you handle the following requirements during your package development and implementation?

1. In SSIS, you need to use debugging techniques in the control flow and data flow to speed up package development and troubleshooting so that you can complete your packages quickly with minimal frustration.

2. Each destination table in your data mart must have the inserts, updates, and deletes fully complete and committed, or you need to roll back the changes so that the table is in a consistent state. You also need a way to restart your packages from the point of failure.

3. You need to capture both the count of rows that are inserted into the destination within your data mart and the time when the last row was sent to each destination in the data flows.

4. When a package fails, you must immediately send e-mail messages that identify the task that failed and describe the error in detail.

Chapter Summary

- When you run packages in the BIDS SSIS Designer, the debug environment shows the execution status of tasks, the row counts of transformations, and the execution results.

- SSIS includes package logging that can capture events during the execution of a package such as errors, warnings, and start times and end times for troubleshooting packages when a failure occurs outside of BIDS.

- The control flow includes flexible precedence constraints to handle success, failure, and completion workflows and more complicated expression and logical AND/OR precedence. In addition, event handlers give you the ability to run processes when conditions that you have defined are met.

- The data flow allows routing of failed rows out an error path and includes data viewers that give you the capability to observe the data during execution as you are developing a package.

- By using breakpoints during package debugging, you can pause a package during execution to observe package state information so that you can troubleshoot potential problems.

CHAPTER 3

Deploying and Configuring SSIS Packages

After you have finished developing your SQL Server Integration Services (SSIS) packages—as discussed in Chapter 1, "Developing SSIS Packages," and Chapter 2, "Debugging and Error Handling in SSIS"—your next task is to make your packages ready for execution. To do this, you must set up your environments and packages so that they are ready to be deployed to a new environment. You can also configure your packages to be dynamic so that they easily handle changes in connections and properties.

For deployment, you prepare your packages by updating various environmental settings, such as connection strings and file paths, without manually editing each package. You then need to move them to a new server. SSIS includes methods for configuring your packages and for handling the deployment process. This chapter discusses how to configure your package to eliminate the need to make changes as you move from one environment to the next and then covers how to use the Business Intelligence Development Studio (BIDS) to deploy a package.

Exam objectives in this chapter:

- Implement dynamic package behavior by using property expressions.
- Implement package configurations.
- Deploy an SSIS solution.
- Identify and resolve issues related to SSIS solution deployment.

Before You Begin

To complete this chapter, you must have:

- Knowledge of how to work in Business Intelligence Development Studio (BIDS) to create new packages and develop basic objects.
- Experience working in SQL Server Management Studio (SSMS) to connect to databases.
- An understanding of the basics of file copying and security.
- Knowledge of system environment variables.

Lesson 1: Using Package Configurations and Expressions

Estimated lesson time: 45 minutes

SSIS provides package configurations that let you update properties, variable values, and connections at run time. You can have the package look to an external source for configuration information that changes the settings within the package when it executes. Package configurations are optional, but they provide several benefits in your execution environment such as letting you update package settings without having to open each package in BIDS. They also give you a central location for settings that can be shared between packages. For example, using package configurations lets you maintain the connection strings and the variable settings for all your packages in a single location. This can save you time and effort when you need to change multiple packages to deploy them to a new server environment.

Understanding Package Configurations

When you work in BIDS, all values that you set up during development are stored as XML in the package's .dtsx file; the package is also stored in that .dtsx file. The file is located in the folder in which you created the SSIS project. When you execute your package, either in the development environment or in another way (see Chapter 4, "Administering, Securing, and Executing SSIS Packages," for details about executing packages), the first action a package takes is to look at its configurations and overwrite the package's current settings with the new settings from the configuration. Some common elements that are configured by using package configurations are:

- **Connection properties**   These include the connection string itself, server name, and connection user name and password.
- **Package variable properties**   These include variable values, variable descriptions, and the Raise Change Event property.
- **Package properties**   These include any property that you defined at the package level, such as package-level transaction options, checkpoint settings, and security settings.
- **Task and container properties**   These include transaction settings at the container or task level and specific properties directly related to the task or container type.

> **IMPORTANT   DATA FLOW COMPONENT PROPERTIES CANNOT BE UPDATED BY CONFIGURATIONS**
>
> Most data flow properties cannot be configured by using package configurations. You can configure only the Data Flow Container itself. However, outside configurations, there are ways to make some of the data flow components dynamic at run time, such as by using variables and SSIS expressions to modify properties.

Enabling SSIS Package Configurations

By default, each package has its package configurations turned off. To work with configurations, you use the Package Configurations Organizer, which lets you perform the following tasks:

- Enable or disable a package's package configurations.
- Add and remove configurations assigned to the package.
- Define the order in which the configurations are applied.

To open the Package Configurations Organizer, open the package for which you want to turn on configurations, and then choose SSIS Configurations from the SSIS menu. Figure 3-1 shows the Package Configurations Organizer dialog box.

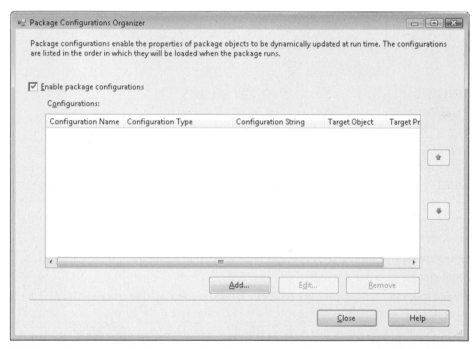

FIGURE 3-1 The Package Configurations Organizer lets you add, remove, and manage configurations assigned to your package.

To enable configurations for a package, select the Enable Package Configurations check box at the top of the dialog box, as Figure 3-1 shows.

Creating a Configuration

After you turn on package configurations, the next step is to create or edit the configurations. To create a new configuration, click Add in the Package Configurations Organizer dialog box to open the Package Configuration Wizard. Figure 3-2 shows the wizard's first page (after the Welcome page) with the Configuration Type drop-down list expanded.

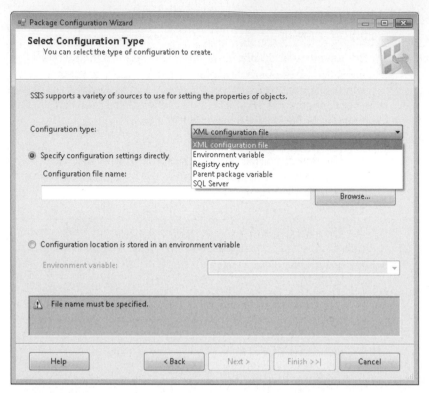

FIGURE 3-2 The Package Configuration Wizard lets you specify the type of configuration for your package.

On the Select Configuration Type page, choose a configuration type. Table 3-1 describes the configuration types you can choose from.

Choose the most appropriate configuration for your environment and your project requirements. Ensure that you consider how the packages will be supported in a production environment and how other technologies are supported and configured. If the configurations include connection string information, be sure to evaluate any security and industry-compliance requirements that you might need to fulfill.

The most commonly used configuration types are XML Configuration File and SQL Server configurations. Let's look more closely at each of these types.

TABLE 3-1 Package Configuration Types

TYPE	DESCRIPTION
XML Configuration File	Stores configuration settings in an XML file in the file system. Select XML Configuration File if you are comfortable working with configuration files and your project requirements let you store configuration information in a file system file. You can store multiple configurations in a single XML file.
Environment Variable	Saves the configuration information inside the system's global variables collection, which is called an *environment variable*. When you add an Environment Variable configuration, you can choose only one property for each Environment Variable configuration.
Registry Entry	Lets you save package properties and settings inside your computer's registry. You can select multiple configuration settings at a time and store them in the registry.
Parent Package Variable	Provides a way to inherit the value of a variable from a parent package. When a package is executed from another SSIS package by using the Execute Package Task, the values of its variables are available to the child package through the Parent Package Variable configuration. With this configuration type, you can choose only one package property setting at a time.
SQL Server	Uses a SQL Server table to store the package setting information. This configuration setting lets you store multiple configurations in a single table.

Creating an XML File Configuration

If you choose the XML Configuration File type, you can specify the location for your configuration file. Figure 3-3 shows the option you can configure for the XML Configuration File type.

There are two ways to specify the location of the XML file:

- You can type the file name in the Configuration File Name box. This is, in a sense, hard-coding the configuration location. But if your configuration file will always have the same location and name, this is a good choice because it simplifies the configuration environment.

- Alternatively, you can use an environment variable that contains the location of the configuration file. To use this approach, you need to create a system environment variable in your computer's system properties. The value of the environment variable needs to contain the full path, name, and extension of the file.

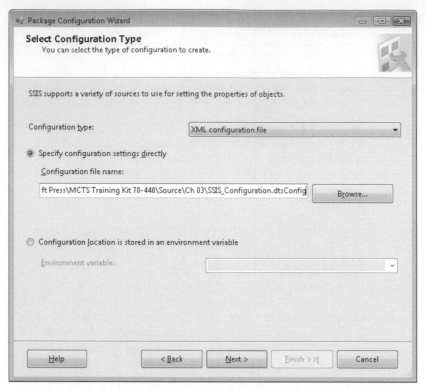

FIGURE 3-3 The XML Configuration File type lets you enter the location of the file or use an environment variable that contains the location.

EXAM TIP

When you use an environment variable as the pointer to the XML file, it is called an *indirect configuration*. Indirect configurations are useful when the location of the file changes from the development server to the deployment server. To use the indirect configuration, you first need to create the file by using the wizard and then go back to edit the configuration and assign the environment variable.

Using an environment variable for the file location pointer is called the *indirect file location approach* and is very valuable if your XML file location or file name might change in the future or already changes between environments. If you choose to use an environment variable, be sure to add it to the servers that the package will run on.

You use System Properties to create an environment variable. To open System Properties in Windows Vista, in Control Panel, open System, and then click Advanced System Settings. In Windows Server 2008, click the Advanced tab. Click Environment Variables to display the Environment Variables dialog box, as shown in Figure 3-4.

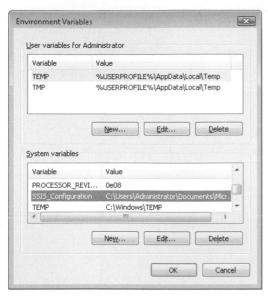

FIGURE 3-4 The server's Environment Variables dialog box lets you create system environment variables that are available to SSIS configurations.

Be sure to click the New button in the System Variables section to make the environment variable available to all applications. The environment variable value needs to be the full path, including the name and extension of the SSIS configuration file. Last, be sure to close and then relaunch BIDS so that it can see the newly created configuration.

As with all the configuration types, more than one package can use the same XML Configuration File. So if you have several packages that have common properties, such as configuration strings, you might want to have all of them use one XML file for configurations.

Next, you need to define the server settings and properties that the XML Configuration File should contain. Because these are common among all configuration types, we will review the SQL Configuration setup before describing the server settings and property definition.

Creating a SQL Server Configuration

If you decide to store your package configurations in a SQL Server table, select SQL Server from the Configuration Type drop-down list in the Package Configuration Wizard. Using Microsoft SQL Server as the storage mechanism for your configurations requires a different group of settings from what the other configuration types, such as the XML Configuration File, use. Figure 3-5 shows the SQL Server configuration options available for setting up configurations.

FIGURE 3-5 Using the SQL Server configuration type requires that you specify a package connection, table, and grouping (called a filter) that the configurations will use for their storage.

Just like the XML Configuration File type, you can specify an environment variable as the location of your configuration (which is the data source name), or you can specify the configuration settings directly. The SQL Server configuration type has several settings. Using SQL Server as your storage area requires defining the table location details. Table 3-2 describes the configuration settings for the SQL Server configuration type.

EXAM TIP

Packages can share SQL Server configurations even if they are running on different servers because the SQL Server configuration does not have to be stored on the local server, unlike the other configuration types.

TABLE 3-2 SQL Server Configuration Properties

PROPERTY	DESCRIPTION
Connection	This must be a SQL Server–based connection that sets the server and database in which your configurations will be stored and from which they will be read. If a connection does not exist, you can click New next to Connection to open the Configure OLE DB Connection Manager dialog box.
Configuration Table	The configuration table is the table in which the configurations will reside. This table has strict column name and data type requirements. To create the table, you can click New next to Configuration Table to open the Create Table dialog box in which you can change the name of the table and execute the table-creation statement on the connection that you specified.
Configuration Filter	Multiple SQL Server configurations can share the same table, which you can specify by using the Configuration Filter drop-down list. You can either enter a new filter or choose one that already exists in the table. The name you select or enter for this property is used as a value in the Configuration Filter column in the underlying table.

Adding Properties to Your Configuration

No matter which SSIS configuration type you select, on the next page in the wizard, selecting Properties To Export allows you to select the SSIS package and object properties that need to be used in the configuration. After you define the configuration type properties in the Package Configuration Wizard, click Next.

At this point, SSIS prompts you to verify whether configuration entries already exist for the configuration type you selected. If they do, SSIS prompts you to either reuse the configuration entries or overwrite them. Figure 3-6 shows the dialog box that lets you specify what to do with the existing entries.

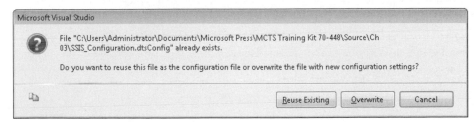

FIGURE 3-6 If entries already exist in the configuration you selected, you can either reuse them or overwrite them with new entries.

If you see this dialog box, you will likely want to share the existing configurations between packages. If you do, click the Reuse Existing button. If you want to clear the existing entries and create new ones, click Overwrite.

If configuration entries do not already exist in this configuration or if you clicked Overwrite, you see the Select Properties To Export page, shown in Figure 3-7.

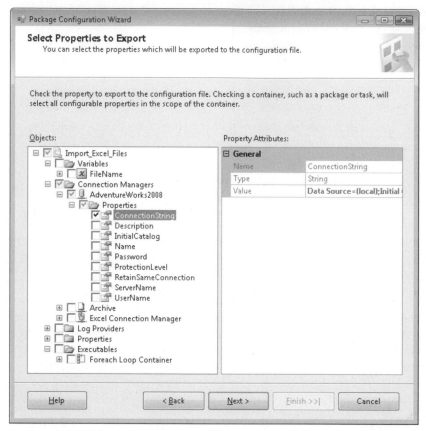

FIGURE 3-7 You can choose the properties that you want to include in your configuration by selecting from the options in the property tree view of your package.

The Select Properties To Export page uses a tree view structure of your package properties and lets you select the properties for the SSIS configuration you selected. Properties are grouped by the following folders:

- **Variables** Contains a list of all the package variables and their corresponding properties to select from for configuration entries.
- **Connection Managers** Shows a list of all the package connections and lets you choose the specific properties of your connections.
- **Log Providers** Lets you dynamically set the log configuration, which is the connection that the log provider will use.
- **Properties** Displays all the package-level (rather than task-level or container-level) properties that you can use to configure your package.
- **Executables** Contains the tree structure of your tasks and containers. By navigating through this tree, you can configure the specific properties of your tasks and containers.

If you are using the XML Configuration File, Registry Entry, or SQL Server configuration type, you can set multiple configuration properties at one time by selecting multiple property check boxes. For the other configuration types, you simply select the one property that you will use for the configuration.

The wizard's final page lets you name the configuration so that you can identify it in the configurations list.

Sharing, Ordering, and Editing Your Configurations

If you have several configurations in your list, you can define the order in which configurations are applied in a package. The configurations are called in the order in which they are listed in the Package Configurations Organizer. This is an important consideration if you have multiple configurations updating the same property or if you have configurations that have a dependency on a prior configuration. For example, you might have a configuration that updates a connection string, which is then used as the location of the configuration entries in a second configuration. The last-applied property update will be the value that is used in the package.

A common approach is to share configurations between packages. If you do this, you might have configuration entries that apply to one package and not another. This does not affect the package execution, but you will receive a warning to indicate that a configuration property does not exist in the package.

As a final note, you can modify all SSIS configuration entries you have made by simply editing the file, SQL Server, registry, or environment variable value. Look for the Configured Value property, and change it as necessary.

You can use the Package Configurations Organizer to order the configurations you create in your package; just use the up and down arrows on the right side of the window, as Figure 3-8 shows. Configurations are applied one at a time in the order that they are listed. This means that if you have two configurations updating the same property, the last one applied (lower in the configuration list) is in effect in the package.

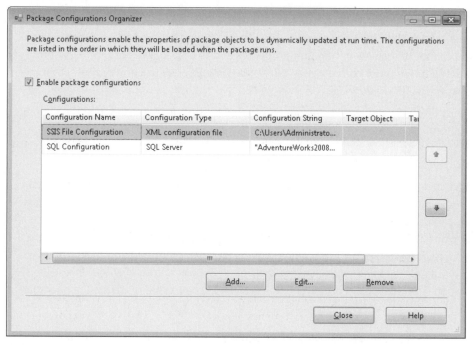

FIGURE 3-8 The Package Configurations Organizer lets you order the configurations by using the up and down arrows on the right side of the dialog box.

REAL WORLD

Erik Veerman

I often come across customer requirements that specify that connection user names and passwords cannot be stored as a clear text string in an XML file. This is a reasonable policy for security. If the password is stored as clear text, anyone who has access to the file can access the user name and password. Storing these values in a SQL Server table can be more secure because users can more easily be denied permissions on the table. However, if you plan to deploy packages between servers, the connection to the configuration table also needs to be in a configuration. So if you store everything in a SQL Server configuration table, you might create a circular reference: you don't want to put the connection string configuration in the database of that same connection!

A common solution to the circular-reference problem is to create two configurations. The first configuration (listed at the top of the configuration list) contains a single entry that points to the SQL Server configuration connection. The connection string uses Windows Authentication to avoid user names and passwords, and the connection type could be an XML Configuration File, a Registry Entry, or an Environment Variable configuration type. To ensure that the connection string is updated immediately when the package loads, this configuration, which points to a SQL Server database storing your SQL Server configuration table, needs to be the first in the list of configurations. The rest of your configurations can then use the SQL Server configuration type, and the connection would be up to date for your environment.

In summary, here's how to set up the two-configurations workaround:

1. Create a single XML configuration that has only one entry—the connection string to the database that contains the file.

2. Create a second configuration (below the XML configuration) that is a SQL Server configuration, and then use that configuration for all your other configurations.

Configurations are very beneficial when you are moving packages from one environment to another and when you need to update connections or settings for multiple packages at one time.

Determining Which Configuration Type to Use

As you can see, you have a lot of choices for package configurations. The natural question is which configuration should you use, depending on your requirements? Here is some guidance as you work through your choices:

- If you have multiple packages that need to share a configuration but the packages are executing on different computers, you should use the SQL Server configuration type. All the packages can point to the SQL Server database, which can reside on a different server. You need to create all the other configuration types locally on the server, so you cannot share those configurations across servers.

- If you are executing packages together, with one package executing a second package by using the Execute Package Task, and you need to pass the value of a variable from the parent package to the child package, you should use the Parent Package Variable configuration. Conversely, if your requirements specify that you cannot have any package-to-package dependencies, you should not use the Parent Package Variable configuration.

- If you are planning to move packages from a development server to a test server and then to a production server and each environment needs to use a different location for the configuration (such as the path to an XML Configuration File), you should use the indirect configuration setup for the configuration. This uses an environment variable on the system, which points to the correct XML file.

- If you have more than one configuration entry that you want to put in a single SSIS configuration, you need to use either the XML Configuration File or the SQL Server configuration because these configuration types allow the inclusion of more than one property (such as a connection string and a variable value) per configuration. The other configuration types (Environment Variable, Registry Entry, Parent Package Variable) allow only one property per configuration.

Using SSIS Expressions and Property Expressions

SSIS includes an expression language to help generate dynamic properties or to test Boolean logic. Several components reviewed in Chapter 1—including containers, tasks, and transformations—use the SSIS expression language. In addition to the built-in components that use expressions, SSIS also allows properties of control flow objects to be dynamically updated through SSIS property expressions. The rest of this lesson reviews expressions and their use.

The most common use of an expression is in a data flow conditional split or derived column. Figure 3-9 shows the Derived Column Transformation Editor.

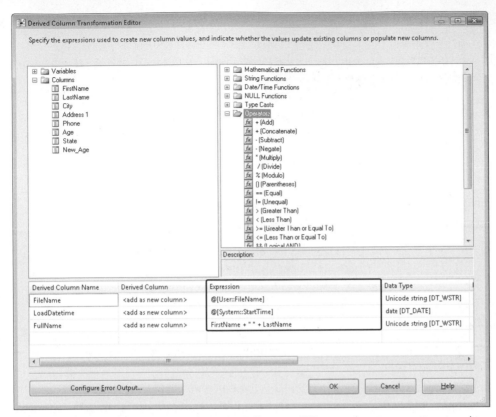

FIGURE 3-9 The Derived Column Transformation Editor uses SSIS expressions to generate new columns or update the value of existing columns.

SSIS expressions, such as the one highlighted in Figure 3-9, are used to generate the value of a new column or update the value of an existing column. In the upper-left section in Figure 3-9 is a list of package variables and a list of columns in the data flow. Both are available to reference in the expression. In the upper-right section is a comprehensive list of SSIS expression functions that you can use for this transformation.

Table 3-3 lists all the places you can use expressions in an SSIS package.

TABLE 3-3 Using SSIS Expressions

COMPONENT	DESCRIPTION
Derived Column Transformation	The Derived Column Transformation uses the SSIS expression language to generate the value of a new column or change the value of an existing column.
Conditional Split Transformation	The Conditional Split Transformation uses the SSIS expression language to evaluate the Boolean result of conditions that determine to which output a row should be sent.

COMPONENT	DESCRIPTION
For Loop Container	The For Loop Container uses an expression to set the initial condition of the loop and the change for each loop and then to determine whether the loop is complete. This uses a combination of Boolean checks and set operations.
Variable Expression	Variables can be dynamically set through an SSIS expression. This is done when a variable is selected in the Variables window and the Properties window is open. To use this capability, you need to set the EvaluateAsExpression property to True and then enter an expression in the Expression property.
Property Expressions	Property expressions are a way that SSIS can dynamically update the value of properties while a package is running. Instead of using a hard-coded value for a property, you can use an expression to generate the value. These properties include package properties at the control flow level and container and task properties and are accessed through the editors and the Properties window. We will discuss property expressions at the end of this section.

Expression Syntax

As shown in the upper-right pane in Figure 3-9, the expression language includes mathematical functions, string functions, date/time functions, NULL functions, type casts, and standard operator functions. To better understand how the expressions work, here are some common functions and operators:

- **Mathematical Functions**   Used to perform complex mathematical operations, including *ABS*, *Log*, and *Power*.

- **String Functions**   Take the value of a string and then apply logic to modify the value or find a specific location in the value—for example, *Len*, *LTrim*, and *Replace*.

- **Date/Time Functions**   Apply either date-manipulation functions, such as *DateAdd*, where a date value is changed by adding or subtracting an attribute of the date (for example, days, weeks, or months), or date-evaluation functions that perform date checks, such as *DateDiff*, which compares two dates and returns the difference, or *DatePart*, which pulls out a specific part of a date (for example, day, week, or month).

- **NULL Functions**   Either evaluates whether a variable or column is null (*IsNull*) and returns True or False or uses a Null value of a specific data type, such as *DT_I4* (4-byte integer).

- **Type Casts**   Converts a value from one data type to a different data type. For example, *(DT_I4)"10.0"* converts 10.0 to 10 as an integer.

- **Operators** Operators can be anything from standard mathematical operators such as
  +, -, and % to operators that can perform Boolean evaluations. Here are some of the
  Boolean-like operators:
  - Equal: ==
  - Not equal: *!=*
  - Logical AND: *&&*
  - Logical OR: ||
  - Conditional: <boolean> ? <true part> : <false part>

The conditional operator is a particularly useful aspect of the SSIS expression language. It
performs like a conditional *if* statement or *cast* statement. It first checks a Boolean expression,
and if the Boolean returns *True*, the first clause is returned; if the Boolean returns *False*, the
second part is returned. In the following example, if the *Color* column is *null*, the expression
returns a value of *"Unknown"* (as an ANSI string of length 20); otherwise, the trimmed value of
Color is returned:

```
ISNULL( [Color] ) ? (DT_STR, 20, 1252)"Unknown" : TRIM( [Color] )
```

Property Expressions

One practical use of SSIS expressions is *property expressions*, which let you update properties of
the control flow during package execution. You can apply a property expression in two ways.
First, you can set the property as an expression through the Properties window. Figure 3-10
shows the Expressions property in the Properties window for a package. You open the Property
Expressions Editor by clicking the ellipsis button of the Expressions property, and in this dialog
box, you can select a property from the drop-down list and then type an expression.

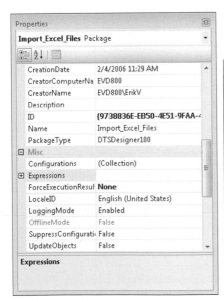
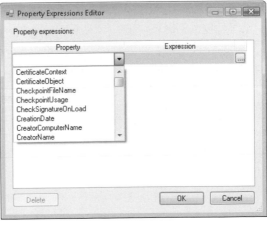

FIGURE 3-10 You can set property expressions through the Properties window by expanding the Expressions property.

Notice the ellipsis button in the Expression field of the Property Expressions Editor. Clicking this button opens an expression editor, which looks similar to the Derived Column Transformation Editor you saw earlier in Figure 3-9.

The second way to set property expressions is to use the task or container editors, which have one or more ways to set properties through an expression. Figure 3-11 shows the Foreach Loop Editor. The Collection tab has a method to set properties with an expression. The Property Expressions Editor dialog box, also shown in Figure 3-11, was opened by clicking the ellipsis button in the Expressions property you see directly above the dialog box. Also notice the Expressions property tab on the left—this tab lets you set properties for the Foreach Loop Container in general (not specific to the collection).

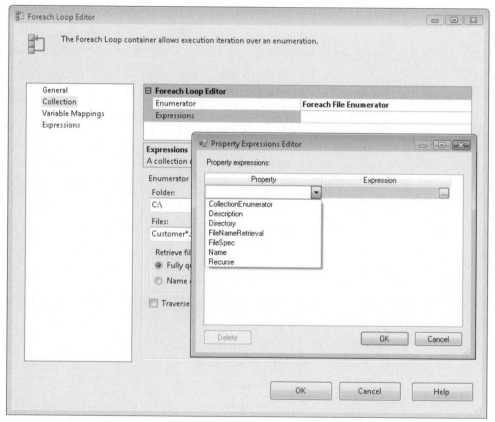

FIGURE 3-11 You can also set property expressions through the task and container editor windows. This figure shows the Foreach Loop Editor with the Property Expressions Editor window open on the Collection tab.

EXAM TIP

Not only can you set package, task, and container properties through expressions, but you can also update the value of connection properties while a package is running. This capability is especially useful when you have a *ForEach* loop that is iterating over files. You can use the variable that the full path is being captured to and update the connection for the file with a property expression. In Exercise 3 in this lesson's practice section, you will update the value of the Microsoft Office Excel connection while the package is running.

PRACTICE Using Configurations and Expressions to Make Package Properties Dynamic

In this practice, you will create an XML Configuration File, share it between two packages, and then create a SQL Server configuration type. You will then use property expressions to update the value of a connection string in a package connection. You can access the practice files in the Documents\Microsoft Press\MCTS Training Kit 70-448\Source\Ch 03\ folder.

EXERCISE 1   Create an XML Configuration

In this exercise, you will use SSIS Configurations to create an SSIS XML Configuration File that will contain the connection string property of the AdventureWorks2008 connection manager.

1. In BIDS, open the SSIS project named *TK 70-448 SSIS Project* you modified in the Chapter 2 practice exercises, or open the 448-ch03 Start Here project in the ..\Source\ Ch 03\ folder of the installed companion disk files.

2. Open the DimCustomer.dtsx package in BIDS by double-clicking the package in Solution Explorer.

3. Choose Package Configurations from the SSIS menu.

    a. Select the Enable Package Configurations check box in the Package Configurations Organizer dialog box.

    b. Click Add to create a new configuration.

    c. Click Next on the Welcome To The Package Configuration Wizard page.

    d. In the Configuration Type drop-down list, select XML Configuration File.

    e. Click the Browse button next to the Configuration File Name box, browse to the installed files folder ..\Source\Ch 03\, and then type **SSIS_Connections.dtsConfig**. Click Save to save the file name and path.

    f. Click Next in the Package Configuration Wizard to go to the Select Properties To Export page.

g. Below Objects, expand the Connection Managers folder, expand Adventure-Works2008, and then expand the Properties folder for the AdventureWorks2008 connection.

h. Select the check box next to the ConnectionString property, and then click Next.

i. Name the configuration **Primary XML Configuration**, and then click Finish, which completes the process of generating the XML Configuration File and updating the package configurations to reference it.

4. In the Package Configurations Organizer dialog box, click Close.

5. Save and close the DimCustomer.dtsx package.

6. Open the DimPromotion.dtsx package by double-clicking the package in Solution Explorer.

7. Repeat steps 3a through 3e on the DimPromotion.dtsx package. After step 3e, click Next in the Configuration Type page, and you will be prompted to overwrite the existing file or reuse the configurations that it contains. Click the Reuse Existing button.

8. Name the XML Configuration **Primary XML Configuration**, and then click Finish.

9. Save and close the DimPromotion.dtsx package.

EXERCISE 2 Create a SQL Server Configuration

In this exercise, you will create a second SSIS Configuration entry by using the SQL Configuration type, and then you will add several package, connection, and task properties to the configuration.

1. If necessary, start BIDS, open the project *TK 70-448 SSIS Project*, and then edit the DimCustomer.dtsx package by double-clicking the package in Solution Explorer. If you are promoted to synchronize the connection strings, click OK.

2. Choose Package Configurations from the SSIS menu to open the Package Configurations Organizer dialog box.

3. Click Add in the Package Configurations Organizer. In the next few steps, you will add a SQL Configuration entry that will contain several package properties that might need to be changed without editing the package.

   a. Click Next on the Welcome page, and then on the Select Configuration Type page, change the Configuration Type in the drop-down list to SQL Server.

   b. Change the Connection drop-down list setting to AdventureWorks2008 (or confirm that AdventureWorks2008 is selected).

   c. Click the New button next to the Configuration table drop-down list, which generates a SQL script to create a table named [dbo].[SSIS Configurations]. Click OK in the Create Table dialog box to execute the CREATE TABLE statement and return to the Package Configuration Wizard.

d. Type **PackageProperties** in the Configuration Filter box. The Select Configuration Type page should resemble the one shown in Figure 3-12.

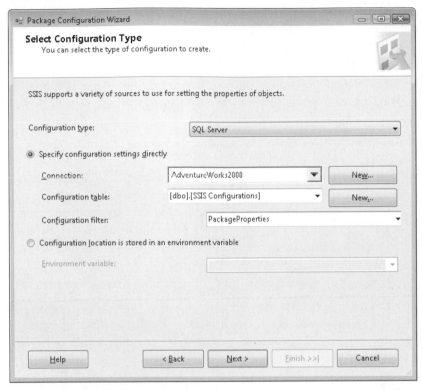

FIGURE 3-12 After following steps 1 through 3d in Exercise 2, your SQL Server configuration should look like this.

e. Click Next, and then below Objects, scroll through the list to configure the following three properties by selecting their corresponding check boxes:

Connection Managers\AdventureWorksDW2008\Properties\ConnectionString

Properties\TransactionOption

Executables\Data Flow\Properties\Disable

f. Click Next, name the configuration **Package Property Configurations**, and then click Finish to complete the configuration.

g. Click Close in the Package Configurations Organizer dialog box.

4. Switch to SSMS, and then connect to the Database Engine. In the Object Explorer window, browse to the AdventureWorks2008 database and then expand the Tables Container.

5. Right-click the [dbo].[SSIS Configuration] table, and then click Edit Top 200 Rows.

6. Locate the record where the PackagePath value is \Package\Data Flow.Properties[Disable], and then change the ConfiguredValue column from False to **True** by typing over the value in the column. This will force the Data Flow Task to not run.

7. Close the table, and then return to BIDS.

8. Execute the DimCustomer.dtsx package, and observe that the Data Flow Task did not run even though the task was not disabled in the SSIS Designer. This is because the configuration value was updated when the package started.

9. Return to SSMS, and repeat step 6, changing the ConfiguredValue column of the Disable property from True to **False**.

EXERCISE 3 Use a Property Expression to Update a Connection

In this exercise, you will work with the Import_Excel_Files.dtsx package, replacing the Script Task that updates the Microsoft Office Excel connection with a property expression. This package is available by opening the 448-ch03 Start Here project located in the ..\Source\Ch 03\ folder or by importing the package into your existing project (see the following note).

> **NOTE** ADDING THE IMPORT_EXCEL_FILES.DTSX PACKAGE TO AN EXISTING PROJECT
> You can add the Import_Excel_Files.dtsx package to your existing SSIS project by right-clicking SSIS Packages in Solution Explorer and then clicking Add Existing Package. Select File System from the Package location drop-down list, and then browse to the file in the Package Path field.

1. Open the Import_Excel_Files.dtsx package by double-clicking the package in Solution Explorer.

2. Delete the Script Task inside the Foreach Loop Container by right-clicking the task and then clicking Delete. Confirm the deletion when prompted.

3. In the Connection Managers window at the bottom of the SSIS Designer, select Excel Connection Manager.

4. Open the Properties window, and then click the pushpin to lock the window in the open position.

5. While the Excel Connection Manager is still selected, click the Expressions property in the Properties window.

6. Click the ellipsis button to the right of the Expressions box to open the Property Expressions Editor.

   a. In the drop-down list that appears when you click the Property value, select ExcelFilePath.

b. On the same line, click the ellipsis button to the right of the Expression column to open the Expression Builder window.

   c. In the upper-left section, expand the Variables folder, find the User::FileName variable, and drag it into the Expression text box, which should then read @[User::FileName].

   d. Click OK to save your changes, and then click OK again in the Property Expressions Editor to return to the package.

7. Navigate to the Data Flow tab, and then select the Excel Source adapter.

8. In the Properties window, change the value of the ValidateExternalMetadata property to **False**. This will ensure that the package will not break during validation if the variable does not initially have a valid value before the Foreach Loop Container runs.

9. Navigate to the ControlFlow tab and select the Foreach Loop Container. In the Properties Window, set DelayValidation to true.

10. Execute the package in BIDS to test execution. The connections assume that the logged-on user is the administrator and that the path to the files is:

   C:\Users\Administrator\Documents\Microsoft Press\MCTS Training Kit 70-448\ Source\Ch 03\Chapter Examples

   You might need to change the Archive connection and Foreach Loop folder to enable the package to execute successfully.

✔ Quick Check

1. What are some reasons to use package configurations in your SSIS architecture?
2. When does a package read and use the configuration entries?
3. When are property expressions evaluated as a package is running?

Quick Check Answers

1. SSIS package configurations are valuable when you have an SSIS environment in which you need to deploy packages from one server to another and the properties of those packages, such as their connections, need to be updated.

2. Configuration entries are read at the start of the package execution. In BIDS, configurations are applied only when you execute a package in the debug mode; they are not applied when you are designing your package.

3. Unlike configuration entries that are read at the start of the package execution, property expressions are updated when the property is accessed by the package during package execution. A property expression can change the value of a property in the middle of the package execution, and the new value is read when the property is needed by the package.

Lesson 2: Deploying SSIS Packages

Estimated lesson time: 30 minutes

After you have set up configurations and expressions in a package, you are ready to move the package to its new environment. SSIS provides the tools to handle package deployment, and when you make use of these built-in deployment tools, the deployment process requires only two steps:

1. Creating a package installer set by using the Package Deployment Utility.
2. Deploying the installer set to your new deployment destination.

However, you do not have to use the deployment tools to move your package from one environment to another. Packages are merely XML files, and you can copy them from the project folder to the destination folder or import them into SQL Server. This lesson begins by describing the package deployment methods in SSIS and then describes package deployment with the built-in deployment tools.

Understanding Package Deployment

To best understand deployment, you first need to understand package storage. When you create SSIS projects, packages reside in the system folder in which the SSIS project was defined; they have a .dtsx extension. When you move your packages from the development environment to your test or production machines, you have two options for package storage:

- **SSIS Deployment To The File System**   Independently of the projects in which they were created, packages can be placed on file shares or in file folders from which they can then be executed.

- **SSIS Deployment To SQL Server**   Packages can be imported into SQL Server, from which they can be executed. When packages are stored in SQL Server, SSMS connects to SSIS to manage them. Chapter 4 covers the details of package execution and SQL Server storage.

EXAM TIP

When you deploy a package to SQL Server, the package is stored in the msdb database in a table named dbo.sysssispackages. Therefore, if you want to back up packages that have been deployed to SQL Server, you can back up the msdb database.

For SSIS packages, deployment—the process of moving a file from one environment to another—involves either placing the SSIS package files into folders or importing the SSIS package files into SQL Server. Deployment can be manual or can be driven through the deployment utility.

- **Manual package deployment** You can move your SSIS packages to a destination folder by copying them manually, by using a source-control tool that handles file deployment, or by creating a script or an application that handles the deployment. If you store your package in SQL Server, you can either use the DTUtil command-line utility that comes with SSIS to deploy your packages to SQL Server or manually import them through SSMS. Using DTUtil is discussed in the section titled "Using the SSIS DTUtil Command-Line Management Utility" later in this chapter. If you choose to import your packages manually, connect to the SSIS service through SSIS, open the Stored Packages folder, right-click the MSDB folder, and then click Import Package to open the Import Package dialog box, shown in Figure 3-13. Chapter 4 covers the SSIS service in more detail.

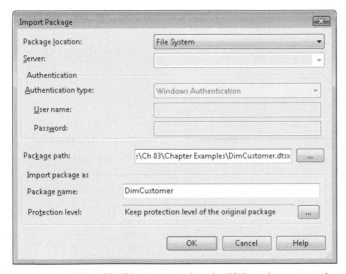

FIGURE 3-13 When SSMS is connected to the SSIS service, you can import package files manually.

- **Deployment utility** The SSIS built-in automated tool, the Package Deployment Utility, can also deploy packages either to a file system or to SQL Server. The benefit of using the SSIS deployment utility is that you can deploy an entire project at the same time to either the file system or SQL Server. The Package Deployment Utility first generates a set of files that are packaged and ready to be deployed, and you then run the package installer to perform the deployment. The rest of this lesson covers the Package Deployment Utility and the Package Installation Wizard.

Creating an Installer Kit by Using the Package Deployment Utility

The Package Deployment Utility helps you create what is called a *deployment set* that contains all the files you need to deploy the packages in a project.

You work directly in the BIDS project settings to generate the deployment set. Each SSIS project has a property for enabling the deployment utility. When this property is enabled, every time the project is built (or the debugger begins to run), the following items in the project are copied to a single folder location:

- Packages
- Miscellaneous files
- Project Deployment Manifest (the installer kit configuration file, discussed later in this section)

To turn on the deployment utility for an SSIS project, follow these steps:

1. Right-click the SSIS project listed in the BIDS Solution Explorer, and then click Properties. Figure 3-14 shows the Deployment Utility property page in the SSIS Project Property Pages dialog box.

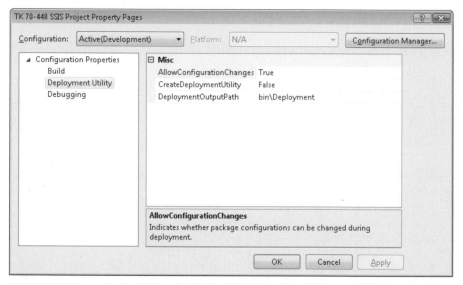

FIGURE 3-14 Properties for SSIS projects contain settings that define whether and in what way the deployment utility will create a deployment set.

2. Change the CreateDeploymentUtility property from False to **True**.

3. Set the location in which the deployment files should be stored when the project is built by modifying the DeploymentOutputPath property. This property can be a relative path, starting with the SSIS project folder, or you can enter a share or drive letter and path. The default location is the ..\bin\Deployment\ folder in your project folder.

4. At the time of deployment, you have the option to allow the package configurations to be modified. By default, the AllowConfigurationChanges property is set to True, but this can be changed to False if you need to limit configuration changes to the deployment kit when it is being deployed.

5. Click OK.

The next step is to run a build process on the SSIS project to generate the deployment set. To do this, right-click the SSIS project in Solution Explorer and then click Build.

> **IMPORTANT TURN OFF DEPLOYMENT WHEN FINISHED**
>
> If the CreateDeploymentUtility property is set to True, any time any package in the project is debugged (for example, if it is executed in BIDS), a new deployment set will be created. This will overwrite existing deployment sets, so be sure to set the CreateDeploymentUtility to False after you have created the deployment set.

At this point, it is a good idea to open the Deployment folder path to verify that the files have been generated successfully. In this folder, you should see your package .dtsx files, any miscellaneous files that were defined in your project, and a package deployment configuration file with the file extension .SSISDeploymentManifest. This file contains the package lists and is used when you deploy the installer set. Figure 3-15 shows the files that are part of the deployment set for the chapter examples.

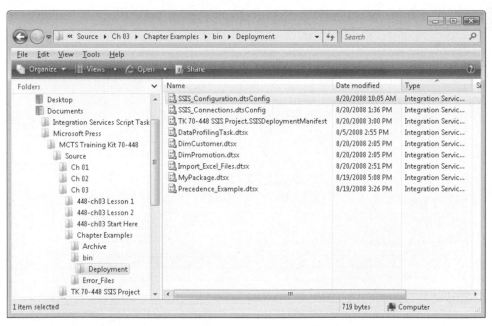

FIGURE 3-15 The Package Deployment Utility generates the set of packages in the project, adds any configuration files, and generates the .SSISDeploymentManifest file.

Deploying Packages

As noted earlier, because SSIS packages are stored in the project folder, you can manually move the actual .dtsx files to a new server environment on a share or manually import them into SQL Server through SSMS or the DTUtil command-line utility (discussed in the following section, "Using the SSIS DTUtil Command-Line Utility"). However, you can also use the automated deployment process, which can perform a batch deployment of all SSIS packages in your project either to a destination folder or into SQL Server. Using the deployment features can make configuration management and multipackage deployment easier.

After the Package Deployment Utility creates the installer kit, as shown earlier in Figure 3-15, your next objective is to take the set of files and deploy them to a destination by using the Package Installation Wizard. To begin the deployment of the installer kit, take the following actions:

1. The optional first step is to move the installer kit to the destination computer. If your destination is a network share or a SQL Server to which you have security access from the development server, the deployment files can remain in place.

2. To launch the installer kit, locate the folder containing the deployment files, and find the file named [Project Name].SSISDeploymentManifest. To open the Package Installation Wizard, double-click the deployment manifest file. When you run the wizard, you will have the option to deploy the package to either a SQL Server database or a file system. If you select a database deployment, you need to provide the server name to which the package will be deployed and credentials; you also still need to provide a location in which to place your files.

3. On the Deploy SSIS Packages page, you select the deployment destination, as Figure 3-16 shows. Choose either File System Deployment or SQL Server Deployment, and then specify whether the packages should be validated after deployment. Click Next.

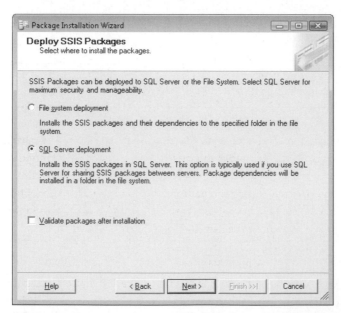

FIGURE 3-16 The Deploy SSIS Packages page prompts you to choose the location in which your project packages will be stored.

4. Based on what you selected on the first page, you will now be able to define the specific storage location, using either the SQL Server connection details or a file and folder path. Figure 3-17 shows the Specify Target SQL Server page. You need to set a Package Path, which is the virtual SSIS subfolder within the msdb database storage. Click Next.

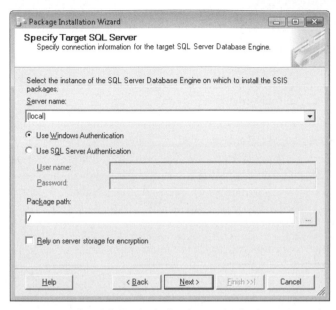

FIGURE 3-17 When SQL Server is the chosen destination, you need to specify the deployment server and package path.

5. The Select Installation Folder page lets you designate a location for all dependent files. Click Next.

EXAM TIP

Whether you are deploying to SQL Server or to the file system, the Package Installation Wizard copies dependent files to the folder you specify. This includes XML configuration files that are used by any package in the project (but only where the XML configuration path is hard-coded in the package and does not use an environment variable). The Package Installation Wizard will also update the XML configuration entries in the package and change them to point to the new XML Configuration File path.

6. Clicking Next on the Confirm Installation page will initiate the deployment.

7. If your package includes configuration files, at this point, the Configure Packages page lets you change any of the properties that exist, as Figure 3-18 shows. Only XML configuration files are updatable during deployment; you cannot update other configuration types. Click Next.

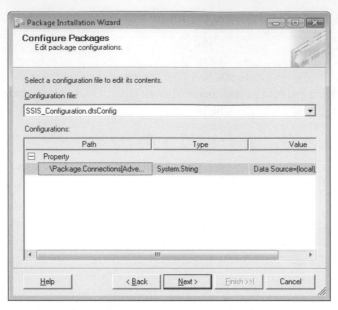

FIGURE 3-18 During the Package Installation Wizard deployment, you can set configuration values for SSIS configurations.

8. The wizard's final page displays the deployment results. Click Finish to complete the deployment.

The result of the deployment is the copying of packages to the specified destination as well as the update of the configuration file locations to where the new configuration files are placed. Figure 3-19 shows the Object Explorer in SSMS after the packages have been deployed to SQL Server.

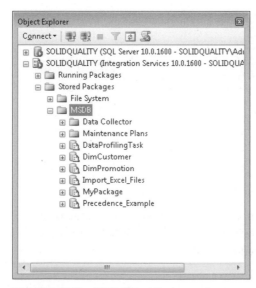

FIGURE 3-19 The SSMS Object Explorer, when connected to the SSIS service, shows the packages deployed to the server.

Using the SSIS DTUtil Command-Line Utility

SSIS comes with the command-line utility DTUtil, which lets you perform package-management tasks, such as deployment, through command-line or batch file processes. DTUtil can work with packages that are stored in the file system, in SQL Server, or in a designated folder on the SSIS computer named the SSIS Package Store. This section covers using DTUtil for package management. Chapter 4 covers how to use DTUtil to manage package security.

DTUtil Operations and Parameters

DTUtil uses standard command-line parameters to perform its operations. For example, the package storage location references use the */SQL*, */FILE*, and */DTS* parameters for sources and destinations.

Operationally, DTUtil can perform various management-focused package operations. Table 3-4 lists some of the command-line switches that perform operations on packages; you can use these switches with other command parameters to locate source and destination packages.

TABLE 3-4 DTUtil Command-Line Parameters

COMMAND-LINE PARAMETER	DESCRIPTION
/COPY	Copies packages from a source to a destination
/MOVE	Moves packages from a source to a destination
/DELETE	Deletes packages from a destination
/EXISTS	Checks for the existence of a package
/ENCRYPT	Encrypts an existing package
/DECRYPT	Decrypts a package by using a package password
/SIGN	Digitally signs a package
/FCREATE	Creates and manages folders for the SSIS Package Store and in the SQL Server msdb database

To illustrate the usefulness of DTUtil for SSIS management and operations, we will look at a few common examples. In the first example, shown here, the DTUtil operation copies a file named MyPackage.dtsx from a local folder to the same local folder with the new file name MyCopiedPackage.dtsx. (Note that parentheses are needed if any spaces exist in the path.)

```
dtutil.exe /FILE c:\MyPackage.dtsx /COPY FILE;c:\MyCopiedPackage.dtsx
```

The next example deletes MyPackage.dtsx from the local SQL Server msdb database with a specified SQL login and password. If */SOURCEUSER* and */SOURCEPASSWORD* are not provided, the statement will use Windows Authentication, as the second line shows:

```
dtutil.exe /SQL MyPackage /SOURCEUSER SSIS_User /SOURCEPASSWORD [password] /DELETE
dtutil.exe /SQL MyPackage /DELETE
```

The following example checks for the existence of MyPackage on the local SQL Server. (Note that the .dtsx file extension is not needed for any package referenced in SQL Server.) If the package does not exist, the command-line result will read *The specified package does not exist*.

```
dtutil.exe /SQL MyPackage /EXISTS
```

The next example deploys (copies) a package from the file system to SQL Server:

```
dtutil.exe /FILE c:\MyCopiedPackage.dtsx /COPY SQL;\MyCopiedPackage
```

> **NOTE** **DTUTIL EXECUTION DETAILS**
>
> For a detailed review of the DTUtil command-line parameters, see SQL Server 2008 Books Online or run the command-line command *DTUtil /Help* on a server that has SSIS installed.

DTUtil Execution Methods

You can execute DTUtil through any command-line scheduling and utility, including SQL Server Agent or Windows Scheduler. In addition, you can create batch files that you can use to automate common or recurring processes.

When you execute DTUtil through an automated command-line utility, you can use Table 3-5 to interpret the return codes.

TABLE 3-5 DTUtil Command Return Codes

RETURN CODE	DESCRIPTION
0	Success
1	Failure
4	Package not found
5	Package cannot load
6	Bad syntax

PRACTICE **Deploying SSIS Packages**

In this practice, you will generate an SSIS installer kit for deployment. You will then deploy the installer kit set to a SQL Server instance.

EXERCISE 1 Create an Installer Kit

In this exercise, you will set the properties of the SSIS project to create the installer kit. Then you will build the project, which actually generates the files that are needed for deployment.

1. If necessary, start BIDS and open the project *TK 70-448 SSIS Project*. The installed practice files contain the completed projects for both Lesson 1 and Lesson 2 in the ..\Source\Ch 03\ folder.

2. In Solution Explorer, right-click the project, and then click Properties.

   a. In the Configuration Properties list in the left section, click the Deployment Utility Properties tab.

   b. Change the value of CreateDeploymentUtility to **True**.

   > **NOTE DEPLOYMENTOUTPUTPATH**
   >
   > Notice the DeploymentOutputPath property, which defines where the project will deploy the packages and the installer kit.

   c. Click OK to save your changes.

3. Choose Build [Project Name], where [Project Name] is the name of your project, from the Build menu. Alternatively, you can initiate the build process by right-clicking the project in Solution Explorer and then clicking Build.

   This will copy all the packages, XML configuration files, and miscellaneous files stored in the project to the project's DeploymentOutputPath property. An installer kit configuration file will also be created in this location. By default, this will be located in the ..\bin\Deployment\ folder under your project location.

EXERCISE 2 Deploy Your Packages by Using an Installer Kit

In this exercise, you will launch the SSIS Deployment Wizard by using the SSIS Deployment Manifest file, and then you will configure the deployment to move the packages to the msdb database in SQL Server.

1. Browse to the DeploymentOutputPath as defined on the project properties tab in Exercise 1. The default path will be [project path]\bin\Deployment\. If your project is stored with the installed chapter files for Chapter 3, you will find it in the ..\Source\Ch 03\ folder.

   > **NOTE LOCATING YOUR PROJECT PATH**
   >
   > If you are unsure where your project path is, select the project in Solution Explorer in BIDS, and then open the Properties window. The FullPath property will direct you to the correct location.

2. In the Deployment folder, you will find an installer kit named {project name}.SSIS-DeploymentManifest. Double-click this file to open the Package Installation Wizard.

   a. Click Next on the Welcome page.

   b. On the Deploy SSIS Packages page, select SQL Server Deployment, and then click Next.

   c. On the Specify Target SQL Server page, type **(local)** as the Server Name, and then select Use Windows Authentication.

   d. Click the ellipsis button next to the Package Path box. In the SSIS Package window, confirm that the top-level SSIS Packages folder is selected, and then click OK.

  e. Click Next to display the Select Installation Folder page. This is where any related files will be placed in the file system, such as configuration files.

  f. Click Next to confirm the installation.

  g. Because a configuration file was created in the Lesson 1 exercises, you will see the Configure Packages screen. Click Next to accept the values already defined in the configuration files.

  h. Click Finish to conclude the deployment.

 3. Verify that the packages were deployed successfully by taking the following steps:

  a. Open SSMS.

  b. In the Connect To Server dialog box, choose Integration Services from the Server Type drop-down list and Localhost from the Server Name drop-down list.

  c. In Object Explorer, expand Stored Packages—MSDB. Verify that all the packages from the project exist.

✔ Quick Check

1. What items are created when the CreateDeploymentUtility property for the SSIS project is set to True and the project is built? Where can you find these items?

2. What are the two types of destinations to which an installer kit can deploy SSIS packages?

3. Can you use DTUtil to delete a package that is deployed to SQL Server?

Quick Check Answers

1. A copy of all the packages, XML configuration files, the project's miscellaneous files, and the installer kit configuration file are all created with the deployment utility. These files are copied to the location specified in the project's Deployment-OutputPath property. The default value is [project path]\bin\Deployment, where [project path] is the location of the project you are working on.

2. SSIS packages can be deployed to either a file system or a SQL Server database, and the installer kit will prompt you to choose one of these.

3. Yes, you can use DTUtil to delete packages in the file system and in SQL Server by using the */DELETE* command-line switch.

Case Scenario: Deploying SSIS Packages

You are asked to manage a set of 25 SSIS packages generated by a development team. These packages perform data consolidation from three source systems: IBM DB2, Oracle, and flat files exported from a legacy system. The destination is a SQL Server database that is used for Customer Relationship Management (CRM) and call-center reporting. The sources do not support Windows Authentication, but a user name and password are provided immediately after the monthly password change as part of the company's security-compliance policy. You need to define deployment procedures and make the packages independent of source user-connection information. How would you satisfy the following requirements?

1. The packages must point to the correct servers and be updated with the user names and passwords—all without editing the packages in production. However, the packages the development team gave you contain hard-coded connections. How can you implement a flexible architecture to handle the changes?

2. Your organization has invested in a test environment that mirrors the production environment, so the deployment objective is to deploy all the packages for a development cycle to the test server, on which the packages can go through an extensive quality-assurance process before they are deployed to production. Your deployment strategy needs to include a complete set of files with an automated deployment process, and your packages need to be deployed to SQL Server for both environments so that the packages can be backed up through your database backup procedures. How do you proceed?

3. Occasionally, as bugs are identified, you are given a single SSIS package to deploy. To minimize human error in the deployment, you need an automated procedure to deploy the file to the test and development servers. How can you achieve this?

Chapter Summary

- Through SSIS package configurations, you can store package properties outside the package. The available properties can come from various source objects: package-level objects, control flow objects, variables, connections, and so on.

- Configurations can be stored in the registry, in an XML file, in an environment variable, in a parent package variable, or in a SQL Server table.

- Packages can use more than one configuration. Multiple configurations are applied in order, and packages can share configuration entries.

- SSIS includes an expression language for dynamically configuring some control flow and data flow objects. One valuable application of the expression language is property expressions, which allow properties in a package to be updated at run time.

- You can deploy packages to SQL Server or the file system either manually or by using the Package Deployment Utility in BIDS.

- The SSIS built-in deployment is a two-step process that consists of creating a deployment installation kit through the Package Deployment Utility and then deploying the installation kit by using the Package Installation Wizard.

- SSIS comes with the DTUtil command-line utility, which can copy, move, delete, encrypt, and digitally sign packages.

CHAPTER 4

Administering, Securing, and Executing SSIS Packages

The final aspects of SQL Server Integration Services (SSIS) covered in this Training Kit are administering the SSIS service and securing and executing SSIS packages. The installation of SSIS includes a Windows service that assists with the availability, management, and security of packages deployed to Microsoft SQL Server. SSIS packages also have security settings in the form of encryption. In many environments, package security is a matter of protecting data, processes, and structure definitions from access by individuals outside of an organization or by someone inside an organization who does not need to or should not see them. SSIS security in packages, in the service, and even in the file system can help you meet many of the security requirements in your organization.

In terms of package execution, in Chapter 1, "Developing SSIS Packages," and Chapter 2, "Debugging and Error Handling in SSIS," we worked in Business Intelligence Development Studio (BIDS) to test execution through the debug environment during development. In addition, Chapter 3, "Deploying and Configuring SSIS Packages," covered deploying packages from a development environment to the test environment and, ultimately, to the production environment. The last step in the life cycle of your package is to implement an execution strategy. This chapter covers package security and execution as well as several management aspects that we have not discussed yet.

Exam objectives in this chapter:

- Install and maintain SSIS components.
- Manage SSIS package execution.
- Configure SSIS security settings.

Before You Begin

To complete this chapter, you must have:

- Knowledge of how to work in BIDS to create new packages and develop basic objects.
- Experience working in SQL Server 2008 and using SQL Server Management Studio (SSMS) to connect to databases.
- Knowledge of package deployment and package storage.
- An understanding of the Database role and experience with file system security.

Lesson 1: Managing the SSIS Service and Configuring Package Security

Estimated lesson time: 30 minutes

The SSIS service is installed when you install the Integration Services components of SQL Server 2008 on a server. The Introduction to this Training Kit provides those installation steps.

The SSIS service assists in the management of packages deployed to SQL Server by enabling SSMS to connect to the service and then manage, secure, monitor, and execute packages. The SSIS service is not required to run packages, but it can be beneficial to package execution because the service caches the SSIS components into memory, allowing a faster startup time during execution. The biggest benefit to using the SSIS service is the management and securing of packages deployed to SQL Server.

This lesson begins by looking in more detail at the SSIS service in conjunction with SSMS and then explores the considerations you need to think through if you are planning to use SSIS in a cluster environment. Last, this chapter will address the important security aspects of packages deployed to SQL Server as well as security encryption within a package.

Managing the SSIS Service

The SSIS service is a Windows service named SQL Server Integration Services 10.0, and it runs the executable file MsDtsSrve.exe. You can manage this service as you do other Windows services. However, be sure to use the SQL Server Configuration Manager to configure the startup requirements and the service account.

After the service is started, you can connect to it through SSMS. In the Connect To Server window, change the server type to Integration Services. After you connect to the SSIS service, the Object Explorer window in SSMS lets you manage, secure, and execute packages deployed to the server. Figure 4-1 shows SSMS connected to the SSIS service.

In Object Explorer, you'll find two top-level folders: Running Packages and Stored Packages.

> **IMPORTANT INSTALLING CUSTOM COMPONENTS**
>
> If you need to install a custom component (such as a custom task, log provider, source, transformation, or destination), the component needs to be installed on all servers that require the component's use. Copy the component's assembly in the %Program Files%\ Microsoft SQL Server\100\DTS\ folder, and then register the assembly with the gacutil.exe with the /i switch for installation. After the component is registered, you can add it to the BIDS toolbox by right-clicking in the toolbox and then selecting Choose Items. See the References section at the end of this book for a related MSDN article on using custom objects.

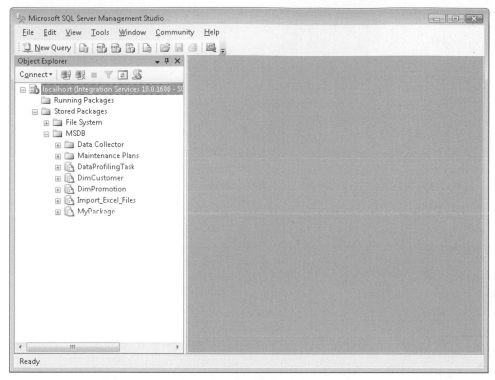

FIGURE 4-1 When SSMS is connected to Integration Services, Object Explorer shows deployed packages and lets you manage the virtual folders in SSMS.

The Running Packages Folder

The SSIS service monitors packages that are executed on the server, whether they are stored in the server or are just executed from a project or the file system. Therefore, you can connect to the SSIS service in SSMS and refresh the Running Packages folder to see which packages are currently running. In addition, you can right-click a running package and then select Stop to terminate package execution after the next task completes (not necessarily immediately).

The Stored Packages Folder

The Stored Packages folder has two subfolders—File System and MSDB—as you can see in Figure 4-1. The File System folder does not show all the files on the server, but instead shows only files that are stored in the package store location. The package store is located by default in the %Program Files%\Microsoft SQL Server\100\DTS\Packages\ folder. However, you can change this to a different location. The service uses an XML configuration file that contains the path to the package store, as follows:

C:\Program Files\Microsoft SQL Server\100\DTS\Binn\MsDtsSrvr.ini.xml

You can edit this XML file and change the *<StorePath>* element value to a different full path. The value also accepts relative paths. The service sees any subfolders under this package store location, and SSMS displays them as subfolders in the SSMS console.

The MSDB folder displays packages that have been deployed to SQL Server. These packages are stored in the SQL Server msdb database in a table named [dbo].[sysssispackages]. You can create virtual folders under the MSDB folder and import packages directly to those subfolders. Figure 4-1 shows two subfolders under the MSDB folder: Data Collector and Maintenance Plans. These are for system packages either generated by the maintenance plan or used by the SQL Server 2008 Data Collector subsystem.

Managing Packages in SSMS

After you have deployed or imported a package into SQL Server or the package store, you can perform some package management tasks. Figure 4-2 shows the shortcut menu for a package in SSMS.

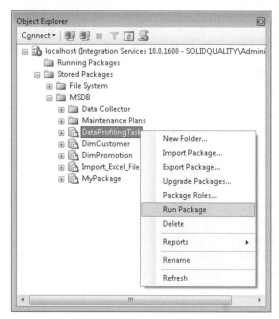

FIGURE 4-2 When connected to the SSIS service in SSMS, you can use the shortcut menu to manage packages.

The shortcut menu shows several options. The New Folder and Import Package options are for the MDSB folder itself, to create a virtual folder or add a new package from the file system.

The Export Package option lets you take a deployed package and move it either to the file system or to another SQL Server. Upgrade Packages is for SQL Server 2005 SSIS packages that need to be upgraded to SQL Server 2008 SSIS packages. A wizard will take you through the upgrade process.

Package Roles is for the security management of packages deployed to the msdb database, which is discussed later in this lesson. You can also execute a package by using the Run Package option or delete the deployed package by using the Delete option.

Configuring the SSIS Service in a Windows Cluster Environment

SSIS is one of the SQL Server 2008 components that does not support instances. This means that there can be only one service for SSIS installed per server. In addition, the SSIS service is not cluster aware during the installation, so you need to configure it separately if you are working with a Windows cluster.

You can find details about configuring SSIS in a cluster environment in the "Configuring Integration Services in a Cluster Environment" white paper (*http://msdn.microsoft.com/en-us/library/ms345193.aspx*), which is also referenced in the References section at the end of this book. Simply put, there are two ways to configure the SSIS service in a clustered environment:

- **Installing the SSIS service independent from the cluster resources**   You can install the SSIS components on all nodes of the cluster, and by default, they will not be part of any cluster resource group. The service will be started on all nodes, and you can run packages from any node in the cluster. If all your packages are stored on a network share that is not part of the package store, no further configuration is needed.

  If you want to centralize all your packages in SQL Server, you need to change the MsDtsSrvr.ini.xml file. Change the *<ServerName>* element to reference a specific server and instance; if the SQL Server is in the cluster, use the virtual server name and instance. Last, change this file on all the nodes so that you can connect to the SSIS service on any machine and see the same packages.

- **Integrating the SSIS service in a cluster group**   You can add the SSIS service as a cluster resource, a process detailed in the "Configuring Integration Services in a Cluster Environment" white paper mentioned earlier. If you want to store packages in the package store, you would choose this approach because the shared service would be running on only one node at a time and you could reference the virtual name of the server. The service would need to point to a shared MsDtsSrvr.ini.xml file on a shared drive in the same cluster resource group as the service. This requires a registry change, which is also documented. The package store location also must be on the shared drive in the same cluster resource group.

EXAM TIP

When you are running a package on a server node of a Windows cluster environment and the node fails, the restartability rules apply. You can turn on checkpoints in your packages and have the checkpoint file created on a share so that if the package needs to be restarted, it can locate and use the checkpoint file.

Adding SSIS Package Security

The SSIS built-in security feature lets you add security encryption to each of your packages or set security roles for packages deployed to msdb. SSIS packages themselves do not contain any source or destination data, but they could provide information about the underlying data they are processing. Securing SSIS is important for two main reasons:

- **Connection information** Although package definitions do not contain any data from your sources or destinations, you have connection information in those packages, so you need to limit access to them.

- **Schema information** Your packages pull data from sources and push it to destinations, so although someone might not be able to access the source or destination directly, if that person acquires an unencrypted package, he or she would have access to what those sources and destinations look like.

Therefore, you need to consider how to prevent access to either the connections or the entire package. There are three ways to limit access to packages:

- You can apply SQL Server security roles to any package that has been deployed to the SQL Server msdb database. You can define which SQL logins or Windows groups or users have read and write access to a package, which controls whether someone can execute or export a package.

- You can employ security encryption by using the package protection level, in which either part or all of a package is encrypted. You can set security encryption properties when developing a package in BIDS, when deploying a package, or when importing or exporting a package. You can apply these properties either to the entire package or to the sensitive data only. It is important that you thoroughly understand what securing a package means regarding connection information and schema information.

- You can use file-level security, in which you can apply access rights to the file or folder if your packages reside on a computer's file system.

This section begins by looking at the package roles in msdb and how to encrypt part of a package or the whole package through package protection levels and package passwords. You can also use the DTUtil.exe command-line tool to help you manage security.

Assigning Roles and Securing Packages Stored in msdb

If you have deployed a package to SQL Server in the msdb database, you can implement additional security regarding who can view, execute, or modify a package by taking advantage of database roles. The roles are fixed database-level roles, and you assign them through the msdb database. Roles are assigned read and/or write actions as follows:

- Read actions focus on viewing and executing packages.

- Write actions apply to moving packages in and out of msdb without executing the packages.

You can secure packages through roles in msdb by connecting to the SSIS service in SSMS.

After connecting to the SSIS service, you need to open the Package Roles dialog box. Follow these steps to secure your package by using roles:

1. In the console tree, expand the Stored Packages folder and then the MSDB folder.

2. Right-click the name of the package to which you want to apply the security roles, and then select Package Roles to display the Package Roles dialog box, shown in Figure 4-3.

FIGURE 4-3 The Package Roles dialog box lets you assign read and write access to a package.

When you open the Package Roles dialog box for a package the first time, the dialog box displays defaults for both the Reader role and the Writer role. The default roles are created with the msdb database during SQL Server 2008 installation and can be used by the SSIS service and your packages. You can either use the built-in roles and assign users to the roles or create new database roles in msdb and then have your packages use those custom roles; you cannot do both. You also cannot select multiple roles in the Reader Role or Writer Role drop-down lists. But this limitation is balanced by the flexibility of the built-in roles and the ability to assign users or database logins to these roles in msdb. Table 4-1 defines the security for the built-in SSIS roles in msdb.

Consider the following guidelines when deciding which roles to use:

- For SSIS execution managers who should have execute privileges but should not be adding packages to SQL Server, you should assign the db_ssisoperator role, which can view, execute, and export packages.

- For users who should be able to work only with packages that they created, you should assign the db_ssisltduser role, which has limited access rights and enables those users to execute and export only packages that those particular users imported to the SQL Server. Users assigned to the db_ssisltduser role cannot work with other users' folders.

TABLE 4-1 Security Attributes of the Built-in SSIS Roles in msdb

ROLE	READ ACTIONS	WRITE ACTIONS
db_ssisadmin	View all packages. Execute all packages. Export all packages. Execute all packages in SQL Server Agent.	Delete all packages. Change all package roles. Import packages.
db_ssisltduser	View user's packages. Execute user's packages. Export user's packages.	Delete user's packages. Change user's package roles. Import packages.
db_ssisoperator	View all packages. Execute all packages. Export all packages. Execute all packages in SQL Server Agent.	None.
Windows Admin	View execution details of currently running packages.	Stop currently running packages.

Understanding and Setting the Package Protection Level

A package's ProtectionLevel property encrypts package definition information that resides in the underlying XML file. You set the ProtectionLevel property at the package level when you are editing the package in BIDS. This means that you define what should be encrypted and how it should be encrypted for the entire package. You can also set a PackagePassword property, which you use when the ProtectionLevel requires encrypting metadata in the package with a password. Figure 4-4 highlights the relevant security properties of the package.

By default, the package is set to use the ProtectionLevel EncryptSensitiveWithUserKey. This means that if you create a package with the default ProtectionLevel and your package contains sensitive information (such as a connection with a password), the connections that contain the password will be encrypted and viewable only by you, the package author, if the package is opened in BIDS on the computer on which it was developed. In this case, you can open the package and will not have to retype the connection passwords; other users can open the package, but they will have to know the connection passwords to test the package in BIDS. Out of the box, the only package properties marked as sensitive are connections with user names and passwords; however, if you write a custom task, component, or connection manager, you can specify which properties are sensitive.

Table 4-2 summarizes the available package ProtectionLevel options.

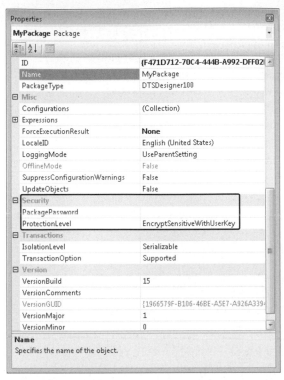

FIGURE 4-4 The ProtectionLevel and PackagePassword security settings are defined at the package level.

TABLE 4-2 ProtectionLevel Options

OPTION	DESCRIPTION
DontSaveSensitive	Sensitive information is not saved in the package at all. Each time the package is reopened in BIDS, the connection passwords must be reentered. For package execution, the password needs to be stored in a package configuration or passed to the package through the command-line setting. This is the recommended setting if you are exclusively using Windows Authentication for your connections.
EncryptAllWithPassword	The entire package is encrypted with a password that is set in the PackagePassword property. To open the package in BIDS, you need to enter the correct package password, and the package cannot be executed without passing the password to the package at execution.

OPTION	DESCRIPTION
EncryptAllWithUserKey	The entire package is encrypted based on the current user and computer. Only the user who last designed or exported the package can design or execute the package.
	A package cannot be opened in BIDS unless it is opened by the user who developed it, on the computer on which it was developed. The package can be executed only through the same user account on the same computer.
EncryptSensitiveWithPassword	The sensitive information in the package is encrypted based on a package password, which is set in the PackagePassword property. Each time the package is reopened, a password must be provided. If the password is not provided, the package will open, but all sensitive data will be replaced with blanks. If a user attempts to execute the package without a password, the execution will fail.
EncryptSensitiveWithUserKey	The sensitive information (connection passwords) in the package is encrypted based on the current user and computer. If the same user reopens the package, nothing is changed. If a different user opens the package, all the sensitive information is cleared out. Other users can still design or execute the package, but they need to enter the password or pass the password into the package through the command line or SSIS configurations.
ServerStorage	This setting can be used only when a package is stored in a SQL Server database. Server storage means that nothing in the package definition is encrypted. Instead, the entire package is protected by using a SQL Server database role. This option is not supported when a package is saved to the file system.

If encryption is enabled in the package by using any of the ProtectionLevel options except ServerStorage and DontSaveSensitive, the encrypted data is saved along with the rest of the package's information in the .dtsx file. If the entire package is encrypted, all the .dtsx file's XML code is encrypted, and the XML cannot be read by a text editor. SSIS encrypts the data by using the Microsoft Data Protection Application Programming Interface (DPAPI).

When choosing a package ProtectionLevel setting, consider these key points:

- If all your connections use Windows Authentication and, therefore, do not require passwords because users are authenticated through Windows, you do not have sensitive information in your package (with the exception of a custom component that has sensitivity defined). In this situation, you should choose DontSaveSensitive because there is nothing to be encrypted. Your package can be executed on any computer by any user as long as the Windows account running the package has the appropriate security privileges for the connections.

- Sensitive information cannot be stored in clear text in a package file stored in the file system. So if you have sensitive information in a package, such as a connection password, you have to use an SSIS configuration to update the connection password at run time or be able to decrypt the password either by using the package password or by running the package on the same computer by the same user account. Similar to storing connection passwords in an SSIS configuration, you can also pass the connection password to the package through the DTExec command-line utility.

Assigning a Package Password

If you choose the protection level EncryptSensitiveWithPassword or EncryptAllWithPassword, you need to set a package password. You can assign a package password in the Properties window when you access the Control Flow tab of the SSIS Designer. Use the PackagePassword property, above the ProtectionLevel setting, as shown earlier in Figure 4-4. To assign a password, click the ellipsis button next to the PackagePassword box to display the Property Editor dialog box where you can type the password twice.

For either of these protection levels, if you try to execute the package without entering the valid password, the execution fails.

> **NOTE   THE IMPLICATIONS OF ENCRYPT ALL**
>
> If the entire package is encrypted and you try to view the package in BIDS without providing a valid password, the package will not open. If only the sensitive data is encrypted, the package will open, but all the sensitive data will be replaced with blanks.

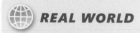
Designing an SSIS Extraction, Transformation, and Loading (ETL) solution that you need to deploy to a different server can sometimes be a frustrating experience when working with the encryption settings—especially because passwords cannot be included in the package file in clear text.

Particularly when you are working in a team environment, the encryption settings can be challenging because the default protection level is EncryptSensitiveWith-UserKey. So if you want to pass the development of a package to someone else, that person will see an error the first time he or she tries to open it.

My favorite approach is to create a consistent SSIS configuration environment on every computer that will be running the packages, whether that is on a development workstation, a development server, a quality assurance (QA) server, a test server, or a production computer. The configuration can be an XML file or a registry entry, as long as it has the passwords included for any connection that does not allow Windows Authentication. With this configuration in place, you can change the ProtectionLevel setting to DontSaveSensitive for all your packages, and when the package executes, it gets the password from the configuration entry.

Some people do not like this approach because the password is still available somewhere. But the bottom line is that the password has to be stored somewhere, and the configuration location you choose needs that extra level of security, whether that means putting file restrictions on it or locking down the SQL Server table where it exists.

Managing Package Security with DTUtil

Chapter 3 reviewed the capabilities of the DTUtil command-line utility to perform deployment operations such as moving, copying, and verifying packages. The DTUtil command-line utility can also perform security operations such as encrypting a package and digitally signing a package.

To apply encryption to a package, you can use the */ENCRYPT* command-line parameter with DTUtil. This parameter requires the package location and encryption level in the parameter string and a package password if the encryption requires it. The encryption level is a numeric indicator related to the EncryptionLevel property of a package, with the following equivalence:

- 0 = DontSaveSensitive
- 1 = EncryptSensitiveWithUserKey
- 2 = EncryptSensitiveWithPassword

- 3 = EncryptAllWithPassword
- 4 = EncryptAllWithUserKey
- 5 = SQLServerStorage

The following example encrypts MyPackage.dtsx with the password EncPswd:

```
dtutil.exe /file MyPackage.dtsx /encrypt file;MyPackage.dtsx;3;EncPswd
```

To digitally sign a package, you can use the *SIGN* command parameter in conjunction with the location and the hexadecimal certificate identifier. The following example signs a package named MyPackage, located on the local SQL Server instance:

```
dtutil.exe /SIGN SQL;MyPackage
```

PRACTICE Encrypting a Package and Assigning Package Roles

In the first exercise in this practice, you will turn on package encryption by using a password and then see how security affects execution. In the second exercise, you will change the security roles for packages stored in SQL Server.

EXERCISE 1 Turn On Package Encryption by Using a Package Password

In this exercise, you will set the protection level of a package to EncryptAllWithPassword and then set the PackagePassword property.

1. Open the SSIS project you created in the exercises in Chapter 3, or open the 448-ch04 Start Here project in the Documents\Microsoft Press\MCTS Training Kit 70-448\Source\Ch 04\ folder. Edit the MyPackage.dtsx package by double-clicking the package in Solution Explorer.

2. In the SSIS Designer, click the Control Flow tab, and then open the Properties window for the control flow. (One way to open the Properties window is to press the F4 function key.) In the Properties window, browse to the ProtectionLevel property, and select EncryptAllWithPassword in the drop-down list.

3. Click the PackagePassword property, and then click the ellipsis button to the right of the property. When prompted, type **EncPswd** for the package password, type it again in the Confirm New Password text box, and then click OK to save it.

4. Save the package, and then close it.

5. Double-click the package again from Solution Explorer. When prompted to enter the package password, click Cancel. You will receive an error message stating that the package cannot open. Click OK. You will then see a message that says *Document contains one or more extremely long lines of text....* This is because the encrypted package content is seen as one long line of text. Click No.

6. This time, try to open the package and type **EncPswd** when prompted to enter the package password. Click Yes in the dialog box that says *Document contains one or more extremely long lines of text....* Now the package opens in the SSIS Designer.

EXERCISE 2   Change Security Roles for Packages Stored in SQL Server

In this practice exercise, you will work with the msdb roles for SSIS by first importing a package into the SSIS service and then defining the security roles for the package. In addition, the package is encrypted with a password, and you will enter the package password when the package is imported.

1. Open SSMS, and when prompted to connect to a service, change the service type to Integration Services, and specify **localhost** as the server. If you have problems connecting, be sure your SSIS and SQL Server services are started.

2. Browse to the Stored Packages, MSDB folder, and then right-click the MSDB folder and select Import Package.

   a. In the Package Location drop-down list, select File System.

   b. In the Package Path box, either type the path to MyPackage.dtsx in the file system or click the ellipsis button to browse to the package location. Be sure to select the exact package from the project exercises; if you are unsure which project you are working on, use the MyPackage.dtsx file from the completed lesson files in the ..\Source\Ch 04\448-ch04 Lesson 1\ folder.

   c. After identifying the package path, confirm that the Package Name text box is set to MyPackage, and notice that the protection level is set to Keep Protection Level Of The Original Package.

   d. Click OK to import the package into the msdb database. When you are prompted to enter the password, type **EncPswd**, and then click OK again.

   e. If you performed the deployment steps from Chapter 3, you are also prompted to overwrite the existing MyPackage. Click Yes.

3. Right-click the MyPackage package you just imported into the MSDB folder, and then select Package Roles.

4. Change the Reader Role drop-down list value to db_ssisadmin, which allows only users who are members of the db_ssisadmin MSDB role to execute the package.

5. Click OK in the Package Roles dialog box to apply the setting.

Lesson 2: Executing and Scheduling Packages

Estimated lesson time: 30 minutes

Outside the development environment, you can execute a package in one of two primary ways: by programmatically using the SSIS object model or by using command-line tools (including SQL Server Agent).

Using the SSIS object model, you can load and execute packages programmatically inside an application. You can find the methods to execute a package programmatically in the two different classes within the *Microsoft.SqlServer.Dts.Runtime* namespace:

- **The *Application* class**   Includes two methods—the *LoadFromSQLServer* method and the *LoadPackage* method—to load a package from either SQL Server or the file system, respectively.

- **The *Package* class**   Includes an *Execute* method, which runs the package and returns the *DTSExecResult* enumeration with the success or failure of the execution.

You can find more details about programmatic execution and the object model under the Integration Services Class Library reference on the MSDN Web site or in SQL Server 2008 Books Online.

The more common execution method is through the command line. SSIS ships with a command-line utility named DTExec, which can be embedded in any other command-line execution or scheduling tool, and a command-line UI utility named DTExecUI, which helps you build the command line. In addition, with SQL Server 2008, SQL Server Agent has direct support for SSIS command-line execution.

In this lesson, you will learn how to execute packages through SSMS, SQL Server Agent Jobs, the Package Execution Utility (DTExecUI) and the command-line execution tool, DTExec.

Using DTExecUI to Configure Package Execution

The command-line executable file DTExec is a fully featured utility with broad parameterization capabilities. You can generate the command line manually by applying the command parameters to meet the execution circumstance, but to save time and avoid errors, you can use the command-line builder utility named DTExecUI.

DTExecUI is a visual tool that naturally groups the command parameter options. The server on which you run DTExecUI must have SSIS installed. To open DTExecUI, type **DTExecUI** either from a command prompt or by choosing Start and then Run to open the Run dialog box. You can open the tool from the Run dialog box or from the command prompt without specifying the path. Figure 4-5 shows the DTExecUI tool, which groups the command parameters in the left pane.

To use DTExecUI, follow these steps:

1. Open the Execute Package Utility by executing DTExecUI either by choosing Start and then Run, and entering **DTExecUI** in the Run dialog box, or through a command prompt.

2. On the General property page, select the package for execution so that you can modify a property on the other pages. In the Package Source drop-down list, select File System, SSIS Package Store, or SQL Server, depending on where your package is located.

3. After identifying the package location, select the specific package for execution. If your package is stored in SQL Server or the SSIS Package Store, you need to specify the connection details to the SQL Server 2008 server by providing the server name. SQL Server also requires you to either provide a user name and password or specify Windows Authentication. All location choices require that you specify the package in the Package box by clicking the ellipsis button to the right of the Package box.

4. Next you need to specify how the package should be executed by configuring other package execution properties. Selecting the various property pages on the left from Configurations down through Verification will let you override settings such as connections, logging, and outputs. Table 4-3 describes the execution configuration options.

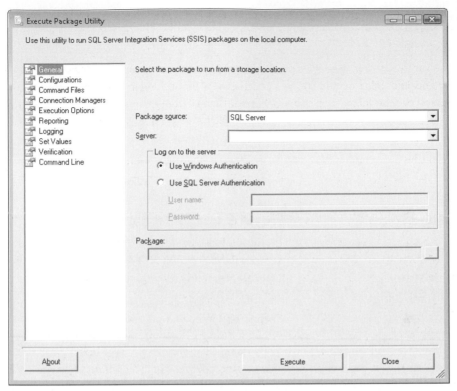

FIGURE 4-5 The DTExecUI tool uses property pages to group the command parameters.

TABLE 4-3 DTExecUI Execution Configuration Options

PAGE	DESCRIPTION
General	As described earlier in steps 2 and 3, you can specify the package location and name on this property page.
Configurations	In addition to the configurations already defined in the package, you can add XML configurations to a package at execution time through this property page. These XML configurations are added to the configurations that currently exist in the package.
Command Files	The DTExec.exe parameters can be stored in a separate file, and the Command Files properties let you specify the text file that will contain the parameters.
Connection Managers	For the selected package, the connections can be over-written at run time with new connection information. Select the connections to overwrite, and then manually alter the connection string.

PAGE	DESCRIPTION
Execution Options	The Execution Options property page allows advanced execution details for the package execution, including the following: ■ Validate Package Without Executing ■ Maximum Concurrent Executables ■ Enable Package Checkpoints ■ Browse To Checkpoint File ■ Override Restart Options ■ Restart Options
Reporting	The Reporting properties define the information returned to the command-line output. The selected events determine the level of information returned.
Logging	Log providers can be added at run time.
Set Values	The Set Values properties let you override package properties, including package variables.
Verification	On this property page, you set verification options that allow a package to run, using the following: ■ Execute Only Signed Packages ■ Verify Package Build ■ Build ■ Verify Package ID ■ Package ID ■ Verify Version ID ■ Version ID
Command Line	The Command Line property page shows the command line that will be passed to DTExec. All the options you configured on the other property pages will be accounted for in the command-line text, which you can edit manually.

5. The final configuration step is to either run the package immediately or use the command-line output. Clicking Execute immediately runs the package, showing execution details in a separate window similar to the Execution Results window in BIDS.

   Alternatively, selecting the contents of the Command Line text box on the Command Line property page lets you copy the resulting command-line parameter output. You can then paste it into a batch file, a command-line tool, or a Command Prompt window. Be sure to use the prefix *DTExec* on the execution line. Figure 4-6 shows the Command Line property page in the DTExecUI interface.

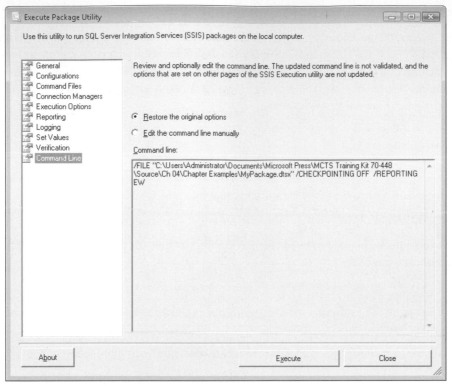

FIGURE 4-6 The DTExecUI Command Line property page lets you copy the command-line parameters and use them in conjunction with DTExec from a command line or in a command-line tool.

The Set Values property page in DTExecUI lets you override package properties at run time. The page has two input fields: Property Path and Value. To populate the property path for a variable, you need to use the following syntax:

\Package.Variables[user::MyVariable].Value

For example, if you had a string variable named *strUserName* and you wanted to set the value from DTExecUI, you would use the following value to specify the Property Path in the Set Values property page:

\Package.Variables[user::strUserName].Value

In the Value text box, you then type the name of the user you want to assign to the *strUserName* variable when you execute the package.

The result of setting the execution details through DTExecUI is a command-line output that you can find on the Command Line property page of the DTExecUI utility and use for command-line parameters with DTExec.

Using DTExec for Package Execution

You can run SSIS packages through any command-line utility by referencing the DTExec executable file in the command-line utility or a batch file. As described in the preceding section, "Using DTExecUI to Configure Package Execution," the DTExec utility comes with many command-line parameters. The details of these parameters are outside the scope of this coverage, but here are a few examples:

To execute an SSIS package saved to SQL Server with Windows Authentication, use the following code:

```
dtexec.exe /sql MyPackage /server SQLProd
```

To execute a package in the file system, use the following code:

```
dtexec.exe /file "c:\MyPackage.dtsx"
```

To run a package that has been saved in the file system with additional logging options, use the following code:

```
dtexec.exe /f "c:\MyPackage.dtsx" /l "DTS.LogProviderTextFile;c:\SSISlog.txt"
```

To run a package stored in the file system, passing in an XML configuration file, run the following code:

```
dtexec.exe /f "c:\pkgOne.dtsx" /conf "c:\pkgOneConfig.cfg"
```

EXAM TIP

If you are running an SSIS package and you want to create a logging dump file if an error occurs, you can use the */DumpOnErr[or]* switch. This is different from the */Dump* switch, which creates the dump when a specified event occurs.

When a package is executed from the command line, the package will always execute at the location from which DTExec is run—not the location at which it is stored. SSIS packages can be located on remote file shares or remote SQL Servers, but the package will execute where the DTExec statement is located.

Executing Packages in SSMS with the SSIS Service

As you learned in Lesson 1, you can use SSMS to connect to the SSIS service. The SSIS service gives you the ability to manage and secure packages stored in SQL Server. In addition to providing security, the SSIS service also lets you run packages manually when you are connected to the SSIS and SSMS services.

To execute a package manually in SSMS, follow these steps:

1. Connect to the SSIS service from SSMS, and browse to the package you want to execute, either in the File System folder (the package store) or in the MSDB folder.

2. Right-click the package, and then select Run Package, as shown earlier in Figure 4-2.

At this point, SSMS will open the DTExecUI utility. DTExecUI will be preconfigured with the package location information on the General property page of the tool, and you can configure the other property pages as previously described. You run the package by clicking the Execute button at the bottom of the DTExecUI interface. The Running Packages folder in SSMS will show all the currently running packages under the SSIS service.

Creating SQL Server Agent Jobs to Execute SSIS Packages

SQL Server Agent is a Windows service that can schedule and execute jobs in much the same way other scheduling tools do. You can schedule these jobs to run on a specific schedule or in response to a specific event, or you can run the jobs manually. Each SQL Server Agent job can have one or more steps.

After the SQL Server Agent service is started, follow these steps to create a new job that schedules and executes packages:

1. Open SSMS, and then connect to the SQL Server database instance where SQL Server Agent is started. The management of SQL Server Agent is embedded in the Database Engine Object Explorer connection in SSMS.

2. Within the Object Explorer window, expand the SQL Server database instance and then expand SQL Server Agent, as Figure 4-7 shows.

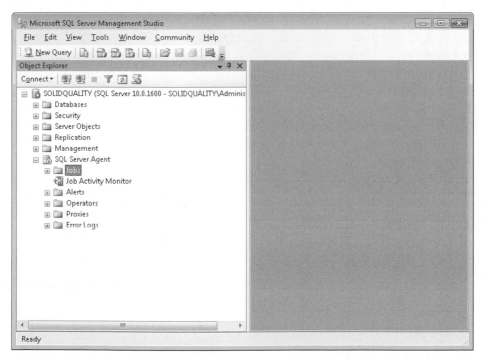

FIGURE 4-7 SQL Server Agent management is found by connecting to the Database Engine instance within SSMS and then expanding SQL Server Agent.

To schedule an SSIS package, you need to create a new step within a SQL Server Agent job.

1. To create a new job, right-click the Jobs folder in Object Explorer, and then select New Job. Provide a descriptive name for the job in the Name box so that the job can be identified among the other jobs.

2. On the Steps property page in the New Job window, click New to open the New Job Step window. This step is the one that you configure to execute a package, so you need to enter a name that describes the job step.

3. In the Type drop-down list, select SQL Server Integration Services Package to update the interface for the rest of the window, customizing it for the execution of an SSIS package. Figure 4-8 shows the New Job Step window set to execute an SSIS package.

4. Notice that at this point, the New Job Step window uses the DTExecUI interface, so you can set the same options as you can set in DTExecUI. Before configuring the other properties, select the package to be executed by selecting the Package Source (SQL Server, File System, or SSIS Package Store) and then selecting the package.

5. After you have configured the options, click OK in the New Job Step window to return to the New Job window. From here, you can define a schedule on the Schedules property page as well as set alerts and notifications for your package execution.

You can schedule SQL Server Agent jobs to run in the typical way, through a recurring schedule, or trigger them to run at other server events, such as when the service is idle or when the service starts. The following list defines your scheduling options for a SQL Server Agent job:

- **Recurring** Configures the job to run at daily, weekly, or monthly intervals as defined in the scheduling interface.

- **One Time** Schedules the job to run only once, at a predefined date and time.

- **Start Automatically When SQL Server Agent Starts** Configures the job to run when the SQL Server and SQL Server Agent services start.

- **Start Whenever The CPUs Become Idle** Based on a predefined idle utilization, schedules a job to run a package during idle times.

You can set up notifications, such as sending e-mail messages or writing log events, to run when a package fails, completes, or succeeds.

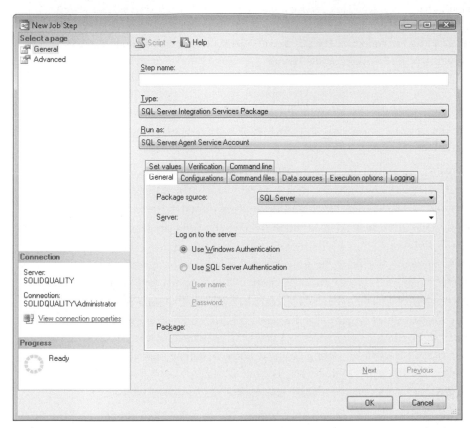

FIGURE 4-8 Create a new job and then a new job step with the Type set to SQL Server Integration Services Package.

IMPORTANT   **SQL SERVER AGENT OR PROXY ACCOUNT**

Any job scheduled under SQL Server Agent will run under the account through which SQL Server Agent is logged in. By default, this is the Local System. (This account is set under SQL Server Configuration Manager.) If your packages are set up to use Windows Authentication and no configurations have been set up, the user will need permissions to perform each of the database tasks in the package.

Executing Packages by Using DTExecUI, DTExec, and SQL Server Agent

In these practice exercises, you will use DTExecUI to create a command-line statement that runs the SSIS package loaded into SQL Server in Lesson 1. You will then execute the package from the command line. You will also schedule a package to be executed with SQL Server Agent.

EXERCISE 1 Create and Execute a Command-Line Statement

In this practice exercise, you will use the Execute Package Utility, DTExecUI, to build the command-line parameter switches that will then be used with DTExec to run a package from the command line.

1. From the Start menu, select Run, and in the Open box, type **DTExecUI** and then click OK.

2. With the Package Source set to SQL Server, type **(local)** in the Server box, and then confirm that the Use Windows Authentication option is selected as the Log On To The Server choice.

3. Click the ellipsis button to the right of the Package box, and then select MyPackage from the SSIS Packages folder. Click OK to close the Select An SSIS Package dialog box and automatically enter \MyPackage in the Package box.

4. Click the Reporting property page in the left pane, and if you completed Lesson 1 of this chapter, you will be prompted to enter the package password. Type **EncPswd**, and then click OK. On the Reporting property page, select the Verbose check box in the Console Events area.

5. Select the Command Line property page in the left pane.

6. On the Command Line property page, select the command-line parameters, right-click the selected text, and then select Copy.

7. Open a Command Prompt window by choosing Start and then Run, typing **cmd** in the Open box, and then clicking OK.

8. At the command prompt, type **DTExec** (adding a space at the end), right-click where the cursor is flashing, and then select Paste. Your command line should match the following:

    ```
    dtexec.exe /SQL "\MyPackage" /SERVER "(local)" /DECRYPT /CHECKPOINTING OFF
    /REPORTING V
    ```

9. Before executing the statement, add the package password after the */DECRYPT* line. Enclose the password in quotation marks, and your statement should look like the following:

    ```
    dtexec.exe /SQL "\MyPackage" /SERVER "(local)" /DECRYPT "EncPswd" /CHECKPOINTING
    OFF /REPORTING V
    ```

10. Press Enter to watch the package execute from the command line. If prompted with the Script Task Ran message box, click OK.

EXERCISE 2   Execute a Package through SQL Server Agent

In this second exercise, you will create a SQL Agent job that runs an SSIS package. The package used, DimCustomer.dtsx, has a package password set on it from the Lesson 1 exercises, which will require entering it during the job configuration steps.

1. In SSMS, connect to the local Database Engine instance.

2. In Object Explorer, expand SQL Server Agent Container, right-click the Jobs folder, and then select New Job.

3. In the Name box, type **Daily DimCustomer Execution**, and then select Steps in the property page list in the left pane.

4. Click New at the bottom of the Steps property page.

    a. In the Step Name box, type **DimCustomer**.

    b. In the Type drop-down list, select SQL Server Integration Services Package.

    c. On the General tab at the bottom of the New Job Step window, confirm that SQL Server is defined as the Package Source, and type **(local)** in the Server box.

    d. Click the ellipsis button to the right of the Package box, select DimCustomer from the list, and then click OK. (The DimCustomer package was deployed to SQL Server in the exercises in Chapter 3; if DimCustomer does not exist, you might need to import this package into SSMS by following the procedure in Lesson 1, Exercise 2, step 2 of this chapter).

    e. Click OK in the New Job Step window.

5. Select the Schedules property page, and then click New to create a new schedule.

    a. In the New Job Schedule window, type **Daily** for the schedule name.

    b. Leave Recurring entered in the Schedule Type drop-down list, and change the Occurs drop-down list selection to Daily.

    c. Change the Occurs Once At box to **8:00:00 AM**, and then click OK in the New Job Schedule window.

6. In the New Job window, click OK to complete the new job creation and run the package at 8:00 each morning.

7. Notice that in Object Explorer, under SQL Agent Jobs, the Daily DimCustomer Execution job is listed. You can manually start the job by right-clicking it and then selecting Start Job At Step.

Quick Check

1. What are the benefits and drawbacks of storing packages in SQL Server?

2. Can you schedule packages to execute through SQL Server Agent if you have the EncryptSensitiveWithUserKey or EncryptAllWithUserKey value set for the ProtectionLevel property?

3. If you have a package for which a variable must be updated at the start of execution, what methods are available to you?

Quick Check Answers

1. When packages are stored or deployed to SQL Server, you can back them up by backing up the msdb system database. In addition, when packages reside in SQL Server, you can assign package roles to manage security. However, packages stored in the msdb database require more management than packages that are not stored there. For example, to modify packages stored in the database, you have to export them and then reimport them to SQL Server.

2. A package can be executed through SQL Server Agent with the user key encryption only if the package is executed on the server on which it was created and by the user who created it. If the ProtectionLevel is set to EncryptSensitiveWith-UserKey and Windows Authentication is used for the connection, a package can be executed on a different server or by a different user, but a warning will be returned.

3. Variables can be updated at execution by using a configuration or by using the Set Value command-line parameter, where the property path is typed as **\Package.Variables[user:: strUserName].Value** and the value is passed in.

Case Scenario: Securing and Scheduling SSIS Packages

Your SSIS ETL packages have been deployed to SQL Server, and it is now your responsibility as the database administrator (DBA) to secure and schedule the packages for execution on your production server. One of the shared connections references a legacy database system that requires a user name and password. Therefore, a SQL Server configuration has been set up to manage the user name and password and to share them between packages. Your task is to secure the packages and schedule them for execution, taking into account the following requirements:

1. The packages contain schema information about a financial database, so you need to be sure that the packages are encrypted. You also need to ensure that the shared connection password in the SQL Server configuration table is secure.

2. The packages need to be scheduled to run at 8:00 every morning by using SQL Server Agent.

Chapter Summary

- The SSIS service assists in the management and securing of SSIS packages deployed to SQL Server. You can include this service in a Windows cluster installation as needed.

- When you import or deploy packages to SQL Server, you can secure them by using msdb roles.

- By using the package ProtectionLevel setting, you can encrypt packages with a password or by the user account and server. You can encrypt either the entire package or just the sensitive information in the package.

- Besides providing package deployment capabilities, DTUtil can also set the encryption settings and digitally sign packages through command-line scripts.

- The DTExecUI command-line utility provides a user interface that builds SSIS command-line execution commands.

- The DTExec command-line utility can reference and execute a package, giving you several parameters for controlling the execution, such as changing connections, setting logging options, and applying configuration files.

- Packages can be loaded in SQL Server and executed in SSMS by connecting to the SSIS service.

- SQL Server Agent provides the ability to schedule packages for execution.

CHAPTER 5

Developing SSAS Cubes

Microsoft SQL Server Analysis Services (SSAS) is a multidimensional server that provides online analytical processing (OLAP) and data mining services. OLAP lets end users analyze data by using a host of tools such as Microsoft Office Excel, SQL Server 2008 Reporting Services (SSRS), ProClarity, custom-developed applications, and third-party tools. Data mining helps users discover data patterns that are not easily discernable, such as understanding what products customers tend to buy together. This chapter focuses on the OLAP functionality of SSAS, exploring the process of developing basic SSAS cubes and dimensions.

Exam objectives in this chapter:

- Implement dimensions in a cube.
- Implement measures in a cube.
- Implement a data source view.

Before You Begin

To complete this chapter, you must have:

- Knowledge of dimensional modeling.
- A basic understanding of SSAS concepts and features.
- Experience working with SQL Server 2008 Business Intelligence Development Studio (BIDS) projects and solutions.
- The SQL Server 2008 AdventureWorksDW2008 database installed.

Lesson 1: Creating Data Sources and Data Source Views

Estimated lesson time: 30 minutes

Although you can build an SSAS solution on top of an arbitrary database schema, SSAS works best with database schemas that are designed to support data analytics and reporting needs. You achieve such schemas by reducing the number of tables available for reporting, denormalizing data, and simplifying the database schema. The methodology you use to architect such schemas is called *dimensional modeling*.

The AdventureWorksDW2008 sample database has been designed in accordance with the dimensional modeling methodology. Compared with the AdventureWorks2008 highly normalized database schema, which has more than 70 tables, AdventureWorksDW2008 is less complex and contains fewer than 30 tables. Figure 5-1 shows only the tables that contain data about sales from individual customers.

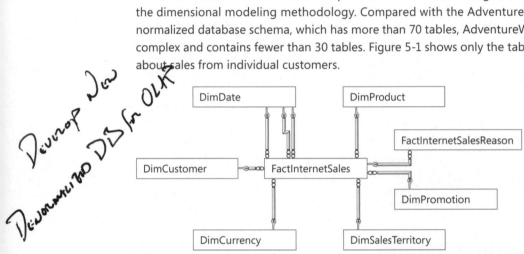

FIGURE 5-1 The AdventureWorksDW2008 schema is optimized for data analytics and reporting.

The FactInternetSales table stores the numeric data called *facts* used to measure sales to individual consumers. Dimension tables—such as DimDate, DimCustomer, and so on—let the user slice the consumer sales data in the fact table by subject areas called *dimensions*.

As you might have noticed, the fact table (FactInternetSales) and its related dimension tables form the star pattern that is typical of OLAP. With a star schema, the dimension data is contained in a single table. This requires denormalizing the dimension data, which is another common OLAP data modeling technique. For example, a Product dimension table might contain all product-related data, such as products, product category, model, and color. Discussing dimensional modeling in detail is outside the scope of this book, but Ralph Kimball's book *The Data Warehouse Toolkit: The Complete Guide to Dimensional Modeling* (Wiley, 2002) provides good coverage of this subject.

After the dimensional schema is in place, you can build the Unified Dimensional Model (UDM), also known as an *SSAS cube*, on top of it. The cube is a logical storage object that combines dimensions and measures to provide a multidimensional view of data. The term *Unified Dimensional Model* promotes the idea that an SSAS cube is more than a traditional OLAP cube because it combines characteristics of relational models (attributes and flexible relationships) and dimensional models (dimensions, measures, and hierarchies). Thus, we will use the terms *UDM* and *cube* interchangeably throughout this book.

REAL WORLD

Teo Lachev

Ad hoc reporting—letting business users create their own reports—is a popular data analytics requirement. A good ad hoc reporting solution should be designed with the end user in mind and shouldn't require the user to know the database schema and query language. SSAS is designed from the ground up to efficiently support ad hoc reporting needs.

One reporting project I was involved in required implementing an ad hoc solution on top of an existing operational database. Because the database schema was highly normalized and the database contained gigabytes of data, we quickly overruled ad hoc reporting tools that are layered on top of the database and autogenerate SQL queries. Instead, we designed a "classic" OLAP solution in which data is extracted from the operational database and loaded into a data mart. We followed the data dimensional methodology to architect the data mart schema. From some 200 tables in the operational database, the data mart schema contained about 10 dimension tables and 2 fact tables.

On top of the data mart, we built an SSAS Unified Dimensional Model (UDM) layer, which provided several important benefits. To start, SSAS is designed to deliver exceptional performance for large data volumes. Unlike relational databases, which have no notion of the hierarchical relationships in data, SSAS understands the semantics of data. This helped us extend our cube with important business calculations in the form of Multidimensional Expressions (MDX). For example, we defined Key Performance Indicators (KPIs) that measure company performance. We also benefited from the flexible, role-based security model that SSAS provides. This security model is enforced when the user connects to the cube. Last, many Microsoft-provided and third-party tools support SSAS and its MDX query language. In our case, we designed a Microsoft Office SharePoint dashboard to help executive managers understand the company's performance. End users could use Microsoft Office Excel or the SQL Server Report Builder from SQL Server Reporting Services to author ad hoc reports.

So if your task is to design an ad hoc reporting solution, your first stop should be SSAS.

The UDM consists of several components, as follows:

- **Data source**   Represents a connection to the database where the data is stored. SSAS uses the data source to retrieve data and load the UDM objects when you process them.

- **Data source view (DSV)**   Abstracts the underlying database schema. Although a DSV might seem redundant, it can be very useful by letting you augment the schema. For example, you can add calculated columns to a DSV when security policies prevent you from changing the database schema.

- **Dimensional model**   After you've created a DSV, the next step is to build the cube dimensional model. The result of this process is the cube definition, consisting of measures and dimensions with attribute and/or multilevel hierarchies.

- **Calculations (optional)**   Only in rare cases will the dimensional model alone fully meet your needs. As a UDM designer, you can augment your cube with custom business logic in the form of MDX expressions, such as Quarter-To-Date (QTD) and Year-To-Date (YTD).

- **End-user model (optional)**   The main design goal of the dimensional model is to provide an intuitive end-user reporting and data navigation experience. The end-user model defines the additional features you can build on top of the dimensional layer to provide even richer data semantics. These features include key performance indicators (KPIs), actions, perspectives, and translations. For example, if international users will be browsing the cube, you can localize the dimension levels by using translations.

- **Management settings**   As a last step, a savvy administrator would configure the cube to meet various operational requirements, including availability, latency, and security. At this stage, for example, the cube administrator will configure which users can access the cube, when and how the cube data can be updated, the cube storage model, and so on.

This lesson explains how to implement the first two layers of the UDM: the data source and the DSV.

Defining a New Data Source

You define a new data source by first creating a new SSAS project using BIDS, as follows:

1. Start SQL Server Business Intelligence Development Studio from the Microsoft SQL Server 2008 program group.

2. Choose New and then Project from the File menu to open the New Project dialog box, shown in Figure 5-2.

3. BIDS includes several project templates for creating business intelligence (BI) projects. Select the Analysis Services Project template.

4. Specify the project name and location, and then click OK.

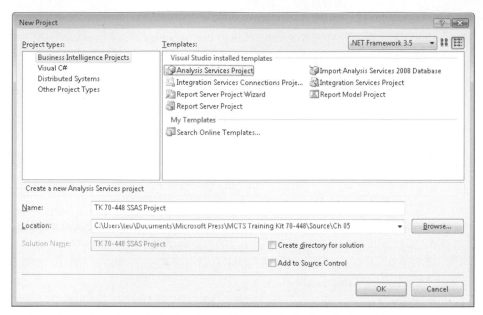

FIGURE 5-2 Select the Analysis Services Project template in the New Project dialog box.

After the new project is created, follow these steps to create a data source:

1. Right-click the Data Sources folder in Solution Explorer.

2. Select New Data Source from the shortcut menu to launch the Data Source Wizard. On the Welcome To The Data Source Wizard page, click Next.

3. On the Select How To Define The Connection page, click New to set up a new connection by using the Connection Manager dialog box.

4. From the Provider drop-down list, choose an appropriate provider for your data source.

5. Next, you need to specify how SSAS will connect to the data source. This includes entering a connecting string and choosing an authentication option.

> **BEST PRACTICES** **CHOOSE NATIVE DATA SOURCE PROVIDERS**
>
> When setting up a data source, you can select either a native OLE DB data provider or a Microsoft .NET managed data provider. Because SSAS is implemented in native code, you should always choose a native provider if available. If you choose a .NET provider, you will experience performance overhead associated with marshaling .NET types to native code for all data source operations. When processing fact tables with millions of rows, this overhead could add up and increase processing times. Other types of data providers, such as Open Database Connectivity (ODBC) and Java Database Connectivity (JDBC), are not supported.

When setting the connection information, you also need to decide what authentication option the server will use to connect to the data source to read data. The options are Windows integrated security and standard authentication (user name and password). What is not so obvious is that both BIDS and the SSAS server use these settings to connect to the data source. BIDS will use the connection for all interactive data source operations (for example, browsing a relational table). The SSAS server will use the same data source definition to connect to the data source when processing dimensions and cubes to load them with data.

- **Standard authentication**   Standard authentication (select the SQL Server Authentication option in the Connection Manager dialog box) requires you to enter a user name and password to connect to the database. Standard authentication is straightforward because the same credentials will be used for both BIDS and SSAS connections. Standard security is also supported by all commercial databases. However, standard authentication is less secure than Windows authentication (requiring you to know and manage passwords), and you should avoid it in favor of Windows Integrated authentication.

  The Connection Manager gives you an option to save the password by selecting the Save My Password check box. The password is saved in an encrypted format. For an added level of security, BIDS will ask you to reenter the password under certain circumstances. For instance, copying the data source definition between projects invalidates the password and requires you to reenter it.

- **Windows authentication**   This option connects to the data source under the identity of a Windows account. If you decide to use Windows authentication (select the Windows Authentication option in the Connection Manager dialog box), you need to be aware of the process identity under which the data operations are carried out. Data source operations initiated in BIDS are performed under the identity of the interactive user (you). Thus, assuming you have local administrator rights, all interactive operations—such as browsing data and retrieving data schemas in DSV—will succeed.

6. Expand the Select Or Enter A Database Name drop-down list, and select the database that you want to connect to. Optionally, click the Test Connection button to verify that that you can connect to the database. Click OK to return to the Data Source Wizard.

7. In the Impersonation Information page, shown in Figure 5-3, you specify the identity under which a server-side data operation will be carried out. SSAS supports several impersonation options that are applicable only with Windows authentication.

FIGURE 5-3 The Data Source Wizard Impersonation Information page

8. Follow these guidelines to choose the appropriate impersonation settings:

- The Use A Specific Windows User Name And Password setting lets SSAS connect to your data source through a predefined Windows account.

- The Use The Service Account option performs the data source operations under the identity of the SQL Server Analysis Services Windows services. This option is appropriate if your SSAS service account is a domain or local account and has read access to the underlying data source data.

- The Use The Credentials Of The Current User option impersonates the identity of the interactive user (you) for all operations. This option is rarely used because it applies only to certain data retrieval scenarios involving querying data mining models.

- Last, the Inherit option lets the server decide which impersonation mode is appropriate. The server will use the service account for cube processing and the credentials of the current user for querying data mining models. For more information about this option, see the topic "New Database Dialog Box" in SQL Server 2008 Books Online (see References).

9. Select the Use The Service Account option, and then click Next. On the Completing The Wizard page, click Finish. You have now finished creating and defining the data source.

EXAM TIP

SSAS supports specifying the identity of the user by using the *EffectiveUserName* connection setting, such as *"Provider=SQLNCLI10.1;Data Source=(local);Integrated Security=SSPI;Initial Catalog=AdventureWorksDW2008;EffectiveUserName=bob"*. When *EffectiveUserName* is passed in the connection string, the server will impersonate the specified user account. This option requires the interactive user to be an SSAS administrator (a member of the SSAS Server role). For this reason, *EffectiveUserName* might present a security vulnerability and should be used with caution.

Selecting Objects for a DSV

After you create a data source in your project, the next step is creating a DSV that describes the underlying relational database structure. To begin, follow these steps:

1. In BIDS, in Solution Explorer, right-click the Data Source Views folder, and then select New Data Source View. This launches the Data Source View Wizard.

2. On the Select A Data Source page, select a data source from the list of data sources you have created. (If necessary, you can click New Data Source to define a data source for the DSV.)

3. The Data Source View Wizard displays a list of available objects (tables and views) from the underlying database that you can add to the DSV. Select the objects you want to work with, and then move them to the Included Objects list by clicking the single right arrow (>) button, as Figure 5-4 shows. After you have added all the necessary objects to the Included Objects list, click Next.

4. On the Completing The Wizard page, accept the default name that has been copied from the data source name or type in a new name for the DSV, and then save your new DSV by clicking Finish.

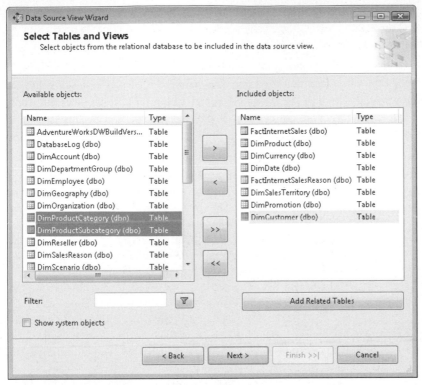

FIGURE 5-4 Add only the tables and views needed to support the creation of other objects within the SSAS solution.

Creating DSV Keys and Table Relationships

One purpose of a DSV is to identify both the primary keys for dimension tables and the table relationships between dimension and fact tables. Many of the designers and wizards you use to develop other SSAS objects rely on this information to do their jobs. If the primary keys and table relationships are physically defined within the underlying relational database, the Data Source View Wizard will detect and automatically add them to the DSV. If they are not defined, you must manually add logical (rather than physical) primary key and table relationship definitions to your DSV. For example, if you create a DSV by using SQL views instead of regular tables, the DSV will not include any relationships or primary keys because none exist in the underlying database schema. In this case, you must extend the DSV by defining appropriate relationships and logical primary keys.

Defining the logical primary keys for the dimension tables within the DSV is relatively simple. Just follow these steps:

1. Within the Data Source View Designer, select one or more columns that make up the key for the table by holding down the Control key and then clicking the relevant columns.

2. Right-click the selected columns, and then select Set Logical Primary Key on the shortcut menu. A key icon will appear beside the column or columns you have identified as the primary key or keys for the table.

To define a logical table relationship, drag the foreign key from a given fact table to its related primary key within a dimension table. The resulting relationship will appear as an arrow leading from the foreign key table to the primary key table. If you accidently drag the columns in the wrong direction, simply right-click the relationship arrow and then click Edit Relationship; you can then use the Reverse button to reverse the direction of the relationship.

After you have created the primary keys and table relationships, the DSV is ready to support the creation of other objects, particularly dimensions and cubes, within your SSAS solution. Figure 5-5 shows a DSV created by using the FactInternetSales fact table and its related dimension tables from the AdventureWorksDW2008 database.

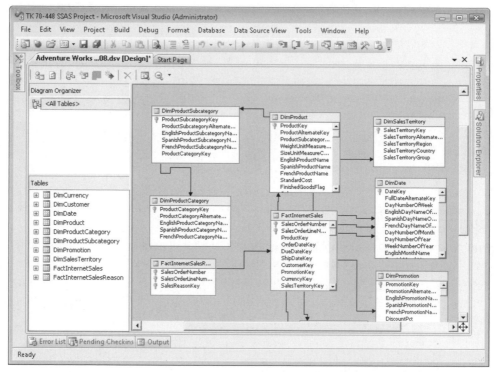

FIGURE 5-5 The DSV for the FactInternetSales fact table and its related dimension tables shows the primary keys for each table, along with the relationships between the tables.

Defining DSV Named Calculations and Named Queries

When defining a DSV, you might sometimes find that the underlying relational database design does not meet the requirements defined for the SSAS solution. For example, a specific table might have columns, such as first name and last name columns, that need to be combined, or the information for a needed dimension might be in more than one table. In these cases, you can augment the DSV by using named calculations and named queries.

As its name suggests, a *named calculation* is a column based on an expression. The expression syntax is data source–specific and must conform to the dialect of the underlying relational database. If you have experience with SQL Server, think of a named calculation as a computed column in a table. Unlike a computed column, however, a named calculation is part of the DSV, not the relational table definition. To add a named calculation to a DSV, follow these steps:

1. Right-click an existing table within the DSV, and then select New Named Calculation.

2. In the Create Named Calculation dialog box, give the calculation a name and a description, and then in the Expression field, enter the SQL expression that will generate the needed result.

3. Click OK to save the new named calculation.

EXAM TIP

A named calculation can reference another table. Suppose that you have a data source view (DSV) that has Product and ProductCategory tables. Both tables have a ProductCategoryID column, and there is a relationship on ProductCategoryID. The ProductCategory table has a CategoryName column. You need to add a named calculation column to the Product table that shows the product category by referencing the CategoryName column from the ProductCategory table. You can use the following SQL *SELECT* statement for the named calculation source:

```
(SELECT CategoryName FROM  ProductCategory
WHERE ProductCategoryID = Product.ProductCategoryID)
```

Similar to a SQL view, a named query creates a new logical table that is added to the DSV and then treated like a physical table from the underlying relational database. Again, similar to a SQL view, you create a named query by using a full *SELECT* statement that returns one or more columns. The *SELECT* statement can contain any SQL code that is compatible with the underlying database, including a *WHERE* clause, query hints, *JOIN* clauses, *GROUP BY* statements, and so on. To add a named query to your DSV, follow these steps:

1. Right-click the background of the design surface for the DSV, and then select New Named Query.

2. Give the query a name and a description by using the Name and Description fields of the Create Named Query dialog box.

3. In the Query Definition field, enter the full *SELECT* statement that will return the desired results. Notice that the Query Definition field lets you create the *SELECT* statement graphically, set returned column properties, and test the query.

4. Click OK in the Create Named Query window.

Note that in addition to specifying the *SELECT* statement for a named query, you also need to set a logical key and define relationships to related tables or other named queries.

EXAM TIP

As your requirements evolve, you might need to replace a table in the DSV with another table that exists in the data source or with a named query. To do so, simply right-click the DSV table, and then select Replace Table. A submenu with two options will appear. Select With New Named Query to replace the table with a new named query. This opens the Create Named Query dialog box. The With Other Table option opens a dialog box that shows all tables and views in the data source to let you select a different table.

PRACTICE **Creating an SSAS Project, a Data Source, and a DSV**

The following exercises will familiarize you with the tasks necessary to create an SSAS project, add a data source, and create a DSV.

EXERCISE 1 Create an SSAS Project

Start by creating a new SSAS project, as follows:

1. From the Start menu, select Microsoft SQL Server 2008 and then SQL Server Business Intelligence Development Studio (BIDS).

2. On the File menu, select New, and then select Project.

3. Select the Analysis Services Project type from the list of available templates.

4. In the Name box, change the project name to **TK 70-448 SSAS Project**.

5. If necessary, clear the Create Directory For Solution check box, and then click OK to create the project.

EXERCISE 2   Create a Data Source

Follow these steps to set up a data source that points to the AdventureWorks2008 database:

1. In BIDS, select Solution Explorer on the View menu (or press Ctrl+Alt+L) if the Solution Explorer window is not shown.

2. Right-click the Data Sources folder within Solution Explorer, and then select New Data Source.

3. On the Welcome page of the Data Source Wizard, click Next. On the Select How To Define The Connection page, click New to define a new connection.

4. Because you will use a SQL Server database, in the Provider drop-down list at the top of the Connection Manager dialog box, make sure that the Native OLE DB\SQL Native Client 10.0 provider is selected. Type **(local)** in the Server Name box.

5. Leave the Use Windows Authentication option selected, and then select the AdventureWorksDW2008 database in the Select Or Enter A Database Name drop-down list.

6. Click Test Connection to test connectivity to the AdventureWorksDW2008 database, and then click OK to save the connection information.

7. Click Next in the Data Source Wizard. On the Impersonation Information page, select Use The Service Account, and then click Next.

8. Accept the default name assigned in the Data Source Name box, Adventure Works DW2008, and then click Finish to save the new data source. Notice that the Data Source Wizard creates the Data Source Name based on the name of the database you selected, but inserts spaces within the name between words.

EXERCISE 3   Create a DSV

When the data source is in place, you need to create a data source view that represents and augments the underlying database schema. Follow these steps to create a data source view:

1. In BIDS, select Solution Explorer on the View menu (or press Ctrl+Alt+L) if the Solution Explorer window is not shown.

2. Right-click the Data Source Views folder, and then select New Data Source View.

3. In the Data Source View Wizard, select Adventure Works DW 2008 from the Relational Data Sources list, and then click Next.

    Suppose that the Adventure Works data warehouse currently handles only direct sales to Internet customers and stores them in the FactInternetSales table.

4. Below Available Objects, select the FactInternetSales (dbo) table , and then move it to the Included Objects list by clicking the single right arrow (>) button.

5. Select the FactInternetSales table by clicking it in the Included Objects list. Next, click Add Related Tables to automatically add all the dimension tables that are related to the FactInternetSales table to the Included Objects list.

6. Hold down the Control key and select the DimProductCategory (dbo), dbo.DimProduct-Subcategory (dbo), and DimSalesReason (dbo) tables in the list of Available Objects, and then move them to the Included Objects list.

    At this point, the Included Objects list (see Figure 5-4, shown previously) should include the FactInternetSales, DimProduct, DimSalesTerritory, DimCurrency, FactInternetSales-Reason, DimDate, DimPromotion, DimCustomer, DimProductCategory, DimProduct-Subcategory, and DimSalesReason tables.

7. Click Next, accept the default DSV name of Adventure Works DW2008, and then click Finish to create the new DSV.

8. Explore the resulting DSV within the Data Source View Designer; notice the primary key definitions and the table relationships the wizard created.

9. In Solution Explorer, double-click the Adventure Works DW2008 view to open it in the Data Source View Designer.

    Typically, end users prefer to see the customer's full name instead of first and last name as separate attributes. Recall that named calculations can help you enrich the database schema by implementing such derived columns.

10. Add a new named calculation to the DimCustomer table and name it FullName. Configure the named calculation to use the following expression to return the customer's full name:

```
FirstName + ' ' + LastName
```

    Add named calculations to the DimDate table as shown in Table 5-1.

TABLE 5-1 Named Calculations for the DimDate Table

NAME	EXPRESSION
SimpleDate	DATENAME(mm, FullDateAlternateKey) + ' ' + DATENAME(dd, FullDateAlternateKey) + ', ' + DATENAME(yy, FullDateAlternateKey)
MonthName	EnglishMonthName+' '+ CONVERT(CHAR (4), CalendarYear)
CalendarQuarterOfYear	'CY Q' + CONVERT(CHAR (1), CalendarQuarter)
FiscalQuarterOfYear	'FY Q' + CONVERT(CHAR (1), FiscalQuarter)

11. Save the new DSV by selecting either the Save Selected Items or the Save All option from the File menu in BIDS; alternatively, you can click the Save button on the main toolbar in BIDS.

12. Close the Data Source View Designer by selecting Close on the BIDS File menu.

Lesson 2: Creating and Modifying SSAS Cubes

Estimated lesson time: 45 minutes

After you have created a data source and a DSV that model your underlying data structures, your next task is to create the dimensional layer of the UDM. This includes designing dimensions, cubes, measure groups, and measures. Although you can create these objects manually from scratch, BIDS includes a handy SSAS Cube Wizard to get you started with the dimensional layer. When the wizard is completed, you can refine the generated objects in the BIDS designers. For example, you can edit the cube definition in the BIDS Cube Designer. This lesson covers how to use the Cube Wizard to create cubes and then how to modify an existing cube by using the Cube Designer.

Using the Cube Wizard

After you have created your DSV, including appropriate primary key and table relationship definitions, you can use the BIDS Cube Wizard to quickly autogenerate the raw dimensional model. When the wizard is finished, you can review the resulting cube and dimension objects, augment them, and deploy them for testing and use.

To start the Cube Wizard, right-click the Cubes folder in Solution Explorer, and then select
New Cube. The wizard will walk you through a series of questions it uses to generate the cube.

1. On the Select Creation Method page, shown in Figure 5-6, you specify the way the
    wizard will create the cube and dimensions.

    The Cube Wizard provides three options for generating the cube definition:

    - **Use Existing Tables**   This option lets you generate the cube from the bottom up
      based on an existing data source. The wizard will examine the DSV you specify and
      identify suitable dimension and measure group candidates.

    - **Create An Empty Cube**   This option creates an empty cube and does not autogen-
      erate any dimensions. Consequently, you need to design the dimensional model
      from scratch.

    - **Generate Tables In The Data Source**   Select this option when you prefer to design
      the UDM from top to bottom in the absence of a data source. With this approach,
      you first architect the UDM. After the UDM is in place, you can autogenerate the
      supporting database schema. The Template drop-down list, which is available only
      when this option is selected, lets you select a predefined cube template that you
      have previously saved in the X:\Program Files\Microsoft SQL Server\100\Tools\
      Templates\olap\1033\Cube Templates\ folder, where X: is the letter assigned to
      the volume on which you installed SQL Server. Figure 5-6 shows the Adventure
      Works Enterprise Edition and Adventure Works Standard Edition templates, which
      are installed when you download and install the AdventureWorksAS2008 database
      included in the SQL Server 2008 version of the AdventureWorks All Databases sample
      files from CodePlex (see References). You can add your own cube templates to this
      folder to facilitate designing cubes from the top down.

The most common cube creation method is the first option, which lets you build the cube from an existing data source.

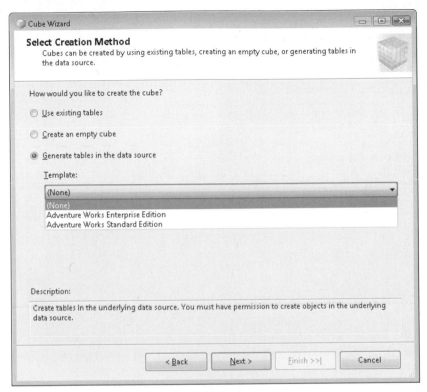

FIGURE 5-6 The Cube Wizard Select Creation Method page

2. On the Select Measure Group Tables page, shown in Figure 5-7, you select the DSV on which the dimensional model will be based and identify the source tables for the measure groups in the cube. A measure group is the UDM equivalent of a fact table in dimensional modeling. It contains numeric measures (facts) that change over time and that can be sliced by the cube dimensions. You can click the Suggest button to let the wizard identify tables for measure group candidates based on the table relationships in the DSV.

FIGURE 5-7 Use the Select Measure Group Tables page to specify which tables will be used as fact tables.

3. On the Select Measures page, shown in Figure 5-8, the wizard suggests numeric columns as measure candidates for the measure groups identified in the preceding step. If a suggested measure is not useful, clear its check box to instruct the wizard not to create this measure. You can rename measure groups and measures in place by selecting a measure and clicking its name to enter edit mode. Assigning meaningful names to the cube metadata is important because end users will see these names.

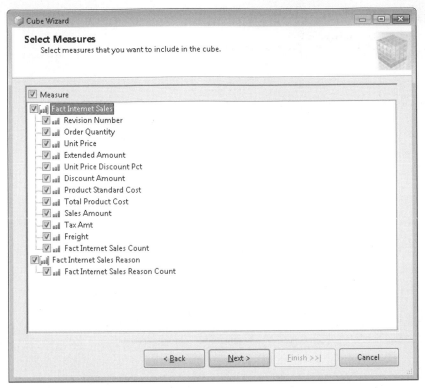

FIGURE 5-8 The Select Measures page lets you specify which columns will be used as measures in the cube.

4. On the Select New Dimensions page, shown in Figure 5-9, the Cube Wizard suggests dimension candidates. As on the Select Measures page, you can rename dimensions in place or remove dimensions that you do not want by clearing their check boxes.

5. To complete the wizard, provide the new cube with a name on the Completing The Wizard page. The wizard will then create all the dimensions and the cube that contains the measure groups and measures. In many cases, you will want to refine these objects after the Cube Wizard is completed, but the wizard can save you time and effort when you are building your first few SSAS solutions.

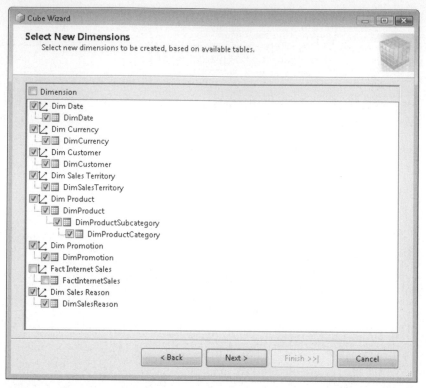

FIGURE 5-9 The Select New Dimensions page lets you identify the dimensions that the wizard will autogenerate.

Modifying a Cube with the Cube Designer

Although the Cube Wizard does a good job of building the raw dimensional model based on the metadata available within a given DSV, you will often need to modify the model to meet your users' specific needs. You can modify the model by using the BIDS Cube Designer and Dimension Designer. Next you will look at how the Cube Designer can help you fine-tune the new cube.

After the Cube Wizard is completed, BIDS opens the resulting cube within the Cube Designer, but you can open a cube at any time by double-clicking the cube within Solution Explorer or by right-clicking a cube name and then selecting Open. The Cube Designer interface has 10 design tabs across the top. You can use these tabs to view and modify various aspects of the cube. This chapter describes the basic development tasks related to each tab; more advanced tasks are discussed in Chapter 6, "Extending SSAS Cubes;" Chapter 7, "Managing SSAS Storage, Processing, and Deployment;" and Chapter 8, "Securing and Administering SSAS." Table 5-2 enumerates each tab and its purpose.

TABLE 5-2 Cube Designer Tabs

TAB NAME	PURPOSE
Cube Structure	Used to edit the basic structure of a cube.
Dimension Usage	Defines the relationship between the dimensions and measure groups within a cube.
Calculations	Contains MDX formulas and scripts to define calculated members and named sets.
KPIs	Defines key performance indicators within the cube, including formulas for KPI status and trends.
Actions	Used to create actions, such as running reports or launching URLs, that will be available to end users as they browse the cube.
Partitions	Defines the storage structures used for each measure group within a cube.
Aggregations	Used to create custom aggregation designs.
Perspectives	Used to create subsets of the cube content for easier end-user browsing.
Translations	Defines language translations for a cube's metadata, such as measure names and dimension names.
Browser	Used to browse the cube data.

Measure Properties

You can use the Cube Structure tab to modify the basic structure of a cube. The Measures pane lists the measure groups and measures defined in the cube. The Properties window in BIDS provides a list of the properties related to a selected object, so you can use it to change the properties for the overall cube, for a given measure group, or for a specific measure. For example, some of the most common measure properties you will use in the exercises included in the lesson are:

- The Name property, which specifies how the measure is referenced and called in the end-user tool.

- The FormatString property, which lets you tell the Database Engine how the measure should be formatted; it could be formatted as a currency or a percentage, for example.

You can find a complete list of properties related to measure groups in the topic "Configuring Measure Group Properties" in SQL Server 2008 Books Online (see References). And you can find a complete list of measure-related properties in the topic "Configuring Measure Properties" in SQL Server 2008 Books Online (see References).

Dimension Properties

The lower-left corner of the Cube Structure tab displays a list of dimensions (along with their hierarchies and attributes) in the cube. You can use the Properties window to change the properties of a selected object. Figure 5-10 shows the full Cube Structure tab within the Cube Designer.

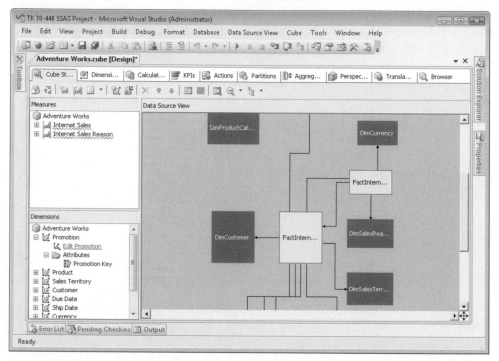

FIGURE 5-10 You can use the Cube Structure tab in the Cube Designer to modify a cube's structure.

It is important to note that any properties you change in a cube for a given dimension, hierarchy, or attribute do not affect the design of the dimension outside of the context of the cube. A dimension included within a cube represents an instance of a dimension (called a *cube dimension*) that is defined within the Dimensions folder of the project (called a *database dimension*).

> **BEST PRACTICES** **PAY ATTENTION TO WARNING RULES**
>
> A new feature in SSAS 2008 is *warning rules* that inform you about best practices you
> should follow. If a designer detects a conflicting rule, it underlines the object with a blue
> wavy line. When you point to the wavy line, a rule description appears as a tooltip. You can
> see all warning rules in the Error List window when you build the project (right-click the
> project node in Solution Explorer and then select Build). You can dismiss a rule by right-
> clicking the rule in the Error List window and then selecting Dismiss. You can disable the
> rule globally on the Warnings tab in the Properties window for the project database (in
> Solution Explorer, right-click the project node and then select Edit Database). As a best
> practice, you should examine the warning messages and incorporate best practices early in
> the design process. You can look up the message text in SQL Server 2008 Books Online to
> learn about a specific rule.

PRACTICE **Creating and Modifying a Cube**

The following exercises will help familiarize you with both the task of creating a cube and its
related dimensions by using the Cube Wizard and the task of editing the structure of a cube
by using the Cube Designer.

EXERCISE 1 Create a Cube

In this exercise, you will create the raw dimensional model on top of the Adventure Works
DW2008 data source view you implemented in the Lesson 1 practice. You will use the Cube
Wizard, which is capable of autogenerating the dimensional model.

1. Using the SSAS project that you created in the Lesson 1 exercises, right-click the Cubes
    folder in Solution Explorer, and then select New Cube to start the Cube Wizard. Click
    Next on the Welcome page.

    The installed practice files contain the completed SSAS projects and are located in the
    Documents\Microsoft Press\MCTS Training Kit 70-448\Source\Ch 05\ folder.

2. On the Select Creation Method page, ensure that Use Existing Tables is selected, and
    then click Next.

3. On the Select Measure Group Tables page, make sure that the Adventure Works
    DW2008 data source view is selected in the Data Source View drop-down list. Click the
    Suggest button to let the wizard identify the FactInternetSales and FactInternetSales-
    Reason measure group tables, and then click Next.

4. On the Select Measures page, clear the Revision Number and Unit Price Discount Pct check boxes to exclude them from the measure list because they cannot be meaningfully aggregated. Rename the Fact Internet Sales measure group to **Internet Sales** and the Fact Internet Sales Reason measure group to **Internet Sales Reason**. Rename the Fact Internet Sales Count measure, which the wizard automatically generates to count the records in the underlying fact table, to **Internet Sales Count**. Rename the Fact Internet Sales Reason Count measure in the Internet Sales Reason measure group to **Internet Sales Reason Count**. Click Next.

5. On the Select New Dimensions page, clear the Dim Product check box because you will add this dimension manually later. Rename all dimensions in place by removing the *Dim* prefix. For example, select Dim Promotion, and then click it to enter edit mode. Rename it in place to **Promotion**. Click Next to continue.

6. On the Completing The Wizard page, type **Adventure Works** as the cube name, and then click Finish.

   The Cube Wizard autogenerates the cube and dimension definitions and shows them in Solution Explorer. BIDS opens the Adventure Works cube definition in the Cube Designer. To make the cube available to end users, you must process and deploy the cube to an SSAS server.

7. In Solution Explorer, right-click the project node, and then select Properties. In the TK 70-448 Project Property Pages dialog box, below Configuration Properties on the left, select Deployment. Notice that by default, BIDS will deploy the SSAS database to localhost (the local computer) and will make the name of the SSAS database the same as the project name (TK 70-448 SSAS Project). If SSAS is not running locally or is running on a named instance, change the Server property to match your setup, and then click OK.

8. In Solution Explorer, right-click the project node, and then click Deploy. If a message stating that the server content is out of date appears, click Yes to build and deploy the database. BIDS deploys and processes the cube to load the cube and dimensions with data from the data source.

9. In the Cube Designer, click the Browser tab, and then explore the new cube by placing various measures in the Report pane of the PivotTable Viewer. For example, drag the Sales Amount from the Internet Sales measure group to the Drop Totals Or Details Fields Here area of the Pivot Viewer. To slice the measure by sales territory, drag the Sales Territory dimension to the Drop Row Fields Here area (if you prefer the sales territories to show on rows), or the Drop Column Fields Here area (if you prefer the sales territories to appear on columns).

   Although the dimension definitions are far from complete, slice the measures by dragging dimensions on rows or columns.

EXERCISE 2   Use the Cube Designer to Edit a Cube's Structure

In this exercise, you will use the Cube Designer to make changes to the Adventure Works cube. Specifically, you will use the Cube Structure tab of the Cube Designer to modify the cube measures.

1. If the cube definition is not open in the Cube Designer, double-click the Adventure Works cube in Solution Explorer.

2. Navigate to the Cube Structure tab, and in the Measures pane, expand the Internet Sales measure group. Select the Unit Price measure. If the Properties window is not open, select Properties Window from the View menu; you might want to "pin" the Properties window so that it is always open in BIDS by clicking the pushpin button in the Properties window title bar.

   By default, the Cube Designer shows the measures in a tree view, in which measures are listed under their containing measure groups. However, when making the same setting to multiple measures, you might find it more convenient to switch to the grid display mode so that you can change properties in all of them at once.

3. Click the Show Measures Grid button on the toolbar. If you want to switch back to tree view mode, click the same button. Hold down the Ctrl key and select the following measures: Unit Price, Extended Amount, Discount Amount, Product Standard Cost, Total Product Cost, Sales Amount, Tax Amt, and Freight. In the Properties window, choose Currency from the FormatString drop-down list.

4. Change the FormatString property to **#,#** for the following measures: Order Quantity, Internet Sales Count, and Internet Sales Reason Count.

5. For the sake of simplicity, reduce the number of measures. Select the Product Standard Cost, Total Product Cost, Tax Amt, and Freight measures, and then press Delete. In the Delete Objects dialog box, click OK to confirm that you want to delete these measures.

6. Save the changes to your cube by selecting either the Save Selected Items or the Save All option from the BIDS File menu; you can also use the Save Selected Items or Save All buttons on the main toolbar (under the menu options) in BIDS.

7. To propagate the changes to the deployed cube, right-click the project node in Solution Explorer, and then select Deploy. If a message stating that the server content is out of date appears, click Yes.

8. After the deployment completes, in the Cube Designer, click the Browser tab. A warning is displayed at the bottom stating that the cube has been reprocessed on the server. Click the Reconnect link to refresh the browser window. Alternatively, you can click the Reconnect button on the toolbar. Explore the cube changes that you performed in this practice.

Lesson 3: Creating and Modifying Dimensions

Estimated lesson time: 35 minutes

When the Cube Wizard generates a set of dimensions, it adds only primary key columns as dimension attributes. This is not very useful for analyzing data because end users will rarely use system-generated keys. Therefore, you need to revisit each dimension and modify its design as needed. As your requirements evolve, you might need to add new dimensions to the UDM dimensional model. This lesson describes both how to create new dimensions by using the BIDS Dimension Wizard and how to modify dimensions by using the BIDS Dimension Designer.

Creating a Dimension

BIDS includes a Dimension Wizard that helps you create a new dimension. To start the wizard, right-click the Dimensions folder in Solution Explorer, and then select New Dimension. The main pages of the Dimension Wizard are as follows:

1. The Select Creation Method page, shown in Figure 5-11, and just as you saw in the Cube Wizard, lets you specify how the dimension will be created.

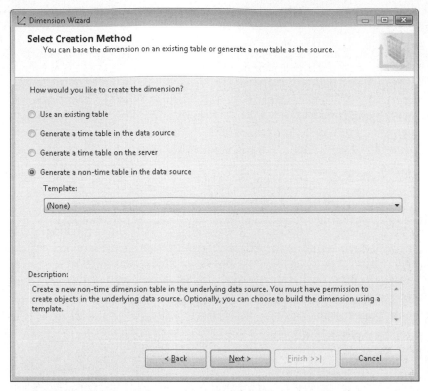

FIGURE 5-11 The Select Creation Method page of the Dimension Wizard

- Select the Use An Existing Table option to create a dimension from an existing table.

- Because analyzing data by time is a common requirement, the wizard provides two options to help you construct a time dimension. The Generate A Time Table In The Data Source option lets you generate a designated time dimension table in the data source and then populate the table with a range of dates. SSAS also supports autogenerating a server-based time dimension (the Generate A Time Table On The Server option). This option can be useful when the fact tables include columns of the DateTime date type and resolving these columns to a designated time table is not an option.

- Select the Generate A Non-Time Table In The Data Source option to create the dimension from the top down by designing the dimension definition first and then autogenerating a dimension table schema in the data source. Optionally, you can autogenerate the dimension from a dimension template.

2. On the Specify Source Information page, shown in Figure 5-12, you select the DSV and the source dimension table. This step also lets you specify which column(s) will be used for the dimension key attribute. A dimension must have a dimension key attribute that uniquely identifies the dimension records, called *dimension members*. You can think of the dimension key attribute as a primary key of a relational table. Similar to a primary key, the dimension key attribute can consist of one or more columns. Because system keys are rarely useful to end users, you can optionally specify a single name column that will be shown to the end user.

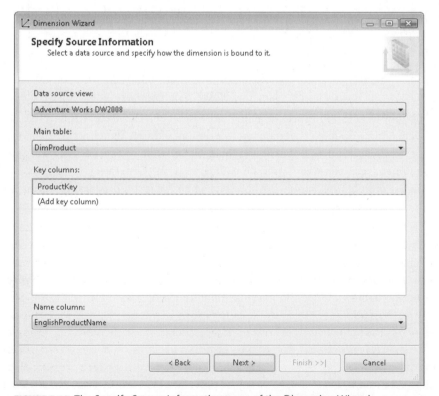

FIGURE 5-12 The Specify Source Information page of the Dimension Wizard

3. On the Select Related Tables page, shown in Figure 5-13, the Dimension Wizard displays a list of tables it detected that are related to the base dimension table through a one-to-many relationship. Including the related tables can be useful if you want to add columns from these tables, such as Product Subcategory, as dimension attributes.

FIGURE 5-13 The Select Related Tables page of the Dimension Wizard

4. The Select Dimension Attributes page, shown in Figure 5-14, lets you specify additional columns to add to the dimension as dimension attributes. By default, each attribute forms a hierarchy called an *attribute hierarchy* that lets the user analyze data by the members of this hierarchy. For example, the Color attribute hierarchy will contain the distinct values of the underlying Color column. This is incredibly useful because it lets the user see the aggregated measure values of each member of the attribute hierarchy. For example, the user can browse the Sales Amount measure by the product color. Some columns might not be meaningful to the end user. You can clear the Enable Browsing check box to hide the attribute when a user browses the cube. SSAS also supports assigning a predefined attribute type to an attribute. This is important when designing the time dimension because it tells the server which attributes represent time periods (year, quarter, month, and so on) when you write time-related calculations, such as Year-To-Date and Quarter-To-Date. The attribute type is optional for other dimensions, but it can be useful for providing hints about what this attribute represents to the client application, such as an OLAP browser.

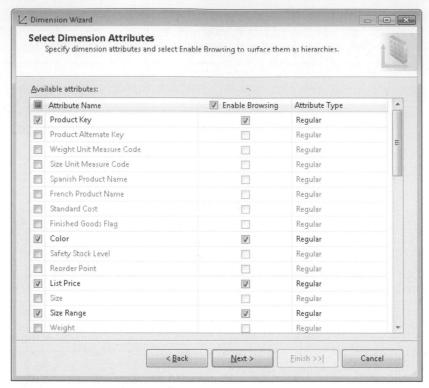

FIGURE 5-14 The Select Dimension Attributes page of the Dimension Wizard

5. On the Completing The Wizard page, give the new dimension a name, and then click Finish to create the new dimension. The new dimension will automatically be opened in the Dimension Designer, as Figure 5-15 shows.

After you create a dimension, you can use the Dimension Designer to modify the design of the dimension—adding, changing, and removing attributes and hierarchies. A new dimension is not automatically added to the cube in the projects. You need to manually add the dimension to the cube and associate the dimension with the related measure groups.

- To add a new attribute, right-click a source column within the Data Source View pane of the Dimension Designer, and then select New Attribute From Column. Alternatively, you can drag the column onto the Attributes pane.

- To remove an attribute, select the attribute within the Attributes pane and click Delete on the Dimension Designer toolbar, or simply press the Delete key.

- Modifying attributes (by changing attribute properties) is covered later in this lesson, and working with hierarchies is discussed in Chapter 6.

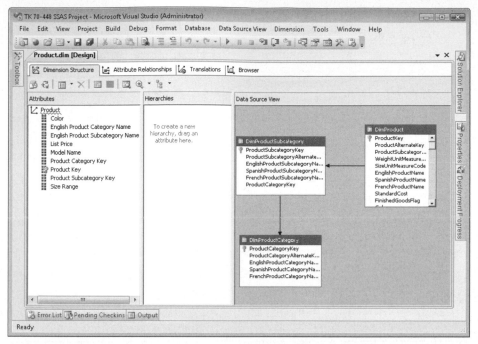

FIGURE 5-15 Use the Dimension Designer to modify the attributes and hierarchies in a dimension's design.

BEST PRACTICES   **DEFINE DIMENSION STORAGE MODE**

As you do in the Cube Designer, you use the Properties window within BIDS to modify many aspects of a dimension, its attributes, and its hierarchies. For the dimension itself, the following two properties define the storage mode for the dimension: StorageMode and ProactiveCaching. The StorageMode property determines whether the dimension is stored by using multidimensional OLAP (MOLAP) or relational OLAP (ROLAP) mechanisms. The ProactiveCaching property determines whether the SSAS service will process and update the dimension automatically. Most typical SSAS solutions use MOLAP storage and do not employ proactive caching. See Chapter 7 for a full discussion of the storage modes in SSAS.

Modifying Dimension Attribute Properties

As with the overall dimension, each attribute within a dimension has properties that control the use and behavior of the attribute. Table 5-3 describes some of the most commonly used properties for an attribute.

TABLE 5-3 Commonly Modified Dimension Attribute Properties

PROPERTY NAME	PURPOSE
Name	Provides the name for the attribute.
Usage	Determines whether the attribute represents the key for the dimension, defines a parent-child hierarchy, or is a regular attribute.
KeyColumns	Specifies the column(s) to use as the unique key for the members of the attribute.
NameColumn	Specifies the column that provides name values for the members of the attribute; NameColumn is optional.
AttributeHierarchy-Enabled	Determines whether the attribute is enabled as a hierarchy; this must be True if the attribute will be used in a multilevel hierarchy.
AttributeHierarchy-Visible	Determines whether the attribute can be seen and selected by end users as a single-level hierarchy.
IsAggregatable	Specifies whether measures aggregate across the members of the attribute into an "all" level.
OrderBy	Determines whether the members of the attribute are ordered by its own key or name column or by the key or name column of a related attribute.
OrderByAttribute	Provides the name of the attribute that determines ordering, if ordering is provided by a related attribute.
Type	Specifies the type of information contained by the attribute.

To modify the properties for a given attribute, select the attribute from the list of attributes, and then use the Properties window to modify its properties. You can toggle the list of attributes from a tree view to a grid view by using the View Attributes As List/View Attributes As Grid button on the toolbar in the Dimension Designer. By using a table or grid view, you can select more than one attribute at a time and then modify a given property value for all the selected attributes.

Assigning Dimensions to Cubes

New dimensions are not automatically added to existing cubes. If you design one or more new dimensions by using the Dimension Wizard rather than letting the Cube Wizard create them automatically, you need to add your new dimensions to a cube to let end users browse the cube data by those dimensions. To add a dimension to a cube:

1. Open the cube within the Cube Designer.
2. Ensure that the Cube Structure tab is active, and then click the Add Cube Dimension button on the toolbar.
3. In the Add Cube Dimension dialog box, add one or more database dimensions to the cube.

Be aware that you can add the same dimension to a cube more than once if the dimension will play different roles within the cube. For example, you might add a time dimension to a cube more than once to support analysis by different dates, such as order date, ship date, and due date. A dimension that is added multiple times to the same cube is called a *role-playing dimension*.

EXAM TIP

You can add the same dimensions multiple times to the cube to create role-playing dimensions, such as Due Date, Ship Date, and Order Date. You can use the Dimension Usage tab to assign meaningful names to the role-playing dimensions and associate them with the appropriate measure group.

PRACTICE **Working with SSAS Dimensions**

Work through the following exercises to familiarize yourself with the tasks involved in working with database and cube dimensions.

EXERCISE 1 **Use the Dimension Wizard to Create a Dimension**

As user requirements evolve, you might need to enhance an existing cube by adding new dimensions. Recall that in the previous practice you excluded the DimProduct table when you used the Cube Wizard to generate the raw Adventure Works cube. In this practice, you will use the Dimension Wizard to create the Product dimension from scratch.

1. Using the SSAS solution defined during the practices in this chapter's preceding lessons, right-click the Dimensions folder in Solution Explorer, and then select New Dimension to launch the Dimension Wizard. On the Welcome page, click Next.

2. On the Select Creation Method page, leave the Use An Existing Table option selected, and then click Next.

3. On the Specify Source Information page, leave Adventure Works DW2008 selected. In the Main Table drop-down list, select the DimProduct table. Notice that the Key Columns grid shows the Product Key column. This column will be used as a source of the dimension key attribute. In the Name Column drop-down list, select English-ProductName. This will be the column the user will see when browsing the cube data by dimension key attribute.

4. On the Select Related Tables page, leave the DimProductSubcategory and Dim-ProductCategory tables selected, and then click Next.

5. On the Specify Dimension Attributes page, select the following attributes in addition to the attributes that are already selected: Color, ListPrice, SizeRange, ModelName, EnglishDescription, EnglishProductCategoryName, and EnglishProductSubcategory-Name.

6. On the Completing The Wizard page, name the new dimension **Product**, and then click Finish. The Dimension Wizard will create the definition of the Product dimension, add it to the Solution Explorer, and open the dimension in the Dimension Designer.

7. Within the Dimension Designer, deploy and process the new dimension by clicking the Process button on the toolbar. If a message stating that the server content is out of date appears, click Yes to build and deploy the database. When the Process Dimension dialog box appears, click Run to fully process the new dimension.

8. When the processing actions are complete, click Close in the Process Progress dialog box, and then click Close again in the Process Dimension dialog box.

9. In the Dimension Designer, click the Browser tab, and then explore the attributes and the single hierarchy available within the new dimension to get a sense of how the dimension will behave when used.

EXERCISE 2 Modify Dimension and Attribute Properties

The BIDS designers are very useful to get you started with the raw dimension model, but that is as far as they can go. As a UDM designer, you need to take additional time to refine the dimensional model and make it easier for the end users to understand and navigate. In this exercise, you revisit all cube dimensions and make appropriate changes.

1. In Solution Explorer, double-click the Currency dimension to open it in the Dimension Designer.

2. In the Attributes pane, rename in place the Currency Key attribute, which is the dimension key attribute, to **Currency**.

3. With the Currency attribute selected and the Properties window open, click the ellipsis (...) button in the NameColumn property. In the Name Column dialog box, select the CurrencyName column, and then click OK. As a result, the values in the CurrencyName column will be shown when the user browses data by the Currency attribute of the Currency dimension. Save your changes, and then close the Dimension Designer.

4. Open the Customer dimension in the Dimension Designer. Rename the Customer Key attribute in place to **Customer**. Set the NameColumn property of the Customer attribute to the FullName column in the DimCustomer table. (Note: The column probably appears at the bottom of the list of columns because you just added it.) Click OK to close the Name Column dialog box.

5. You can sort the attribute members by key, name, or another attribute. By default, UDM will sort the attribute members by the attribute key. Change the OrderBy property of the Customer attribute to Name to sort the customers in alphabetical order by their names.

Recall that the Cube Wizard adds only the keys of the dimension tables as dimension attributes. Most real-life dimensions will require additional attributes. In this exercise, you revisit the dimensions generated by the Cube Wizard and refine their design.

6. In the Data Source View pane of the Dimension Designer, hold down the Ctrl key and select the following columns: AddressLine1, AddressLine2, BirthDate, Commute-Distance, DateFirstPurchase, EmailAddress, EnglishEducation, EnglishOccupation, Gender, HouseOwnerFlag, MaritalStatus, NumberCarsOwned, NumberChildrenAtHome, Phone, Title, TotalChildren, and YearlyIncome.

   Drag the selected columns to the Attributes pane to add them as dimension attributes. Notice that the Dimension Designer automatically inserts an empty space to delimit the words in each attribute name, such as Number Cars Owned.

7. Rename the English Education attribute in place to **Education** and the English Occupa-tion attribute to **Occupation**.

8. It is not uncommon for a dimension to include many attributes. You can reduce clutter by organizing related attributes in display folders, which are supported by most OLAP browsers that target SSAS 2005 and later. In the Attributes pane, hold down the Ctrl key and select the Address Line 1, Address Line 2, Email Address, and Phone attributes. Type **Contact** for the AttributeHierarchyDisplayFolder property. Select the Commute Distance, Education, Gender, House Owner Flag, Marital Status, Number Cars Owned, Number Children At Home, Occupation, Total Children, and Yearly Income attributes. Type **Demographic** for their AttributeHierarchyDisplayFolder property. Save your changes, and then close the Dimension Designer.

9. Open the Date dimension in the Dimension Designer. In the Attributes pane, select the root node (Date). In the Type drop-down list in the Properties window, select Time. This tells the UDM that this dimension is the time dimension.

   Setting the dimension type is useful for two main reasons. First, the Business Intel-ligence Wizard uses this information to generate time-dependent MDX expressions, such as year-to-date and quarter-to-date calculations. Second, OLAP browsers can interpret the dimension type and change the user interface accordingly. For example, when you select a time dimension in Excel, the Excel PivotTable report puts the dimen-sion automatically in columns because most users would prefer this report format.

10. Rename the Date Key dimension key attribute to **Date**. Set the NameColumn property to the SimpleDate column.

11. In the Type property drop-down list, expand Date, expand Calendar, and then select Date.

12. In the Data Source View pane, hold down the Ctrl key and select the following attributes: MonthNumberOfYear, CalendarQuarter, CalendarYear, FiscalQuarter, and FiscalYear. Drag these columns to the Attributes pane to create corresponding dimension attributes.

13. Select the CalendarQuarter attribute, and then set its NameColumn property to the CalendarQuarterOfYear column and its Type property to Date, Calendar, Quarters. The CalendarQuarterOfYear column provides a more descriptive name for the attribute members, such as *CY Q1*.

14. Select the FiscalQuarter attribute, and then set its NameColumn property to the FiscalQuarterOfYear column and its Type property to Date, Fiscal, FiscalQuarters.

15. Rename the Month Number Of Year attribute to **Month Name**. Set the NameColumn property to the MonthName column and its Type property to Date, Calendar, Months.

16. Select the Calendar Year attribute, and then change its Type property to Date, Calendar, Years. Select the Fiscal Year attribute, and then change its Type property to Date, Fiscal, FiscalYears.

17. Attempt to process the Date dimension. Notice that the process operation results in the following error:

```
Errors in the OLAP storage engine: A duplicate attribute key has been found when
processing: Table: 'dbo_DimDate', Column: 'MonthNumberOfYear', Value: '11'. The
attribute is 'Month Name'.
```

This error is shown because the MonthNumberOfYear attribute, which serves as a key column of the Month Name attribute, does not contain unique values for each value of the MonthName column, which defines the attribute name (NameColumn property). To resolve this error, you need to set up a composite key that includes the MonthNumberOfYear and CalendarYear columns.

18. In the Dimension Designer, select the MonthName attribute, and then click the ellipsis button (...) in the KeyColumns property. Add the CalendarYear column to the collection because the year-month combination defines each month uniquely. Click OK.

19. Select the Calendar Quarter attribute, and then add the CalendarYear column to the KeyColumns collection of the Calendar Quarter attribute.

20. Select the Fiscal Quarter attribute, and then add the FiscalYear column to the KeyColumns collection of the Fiscal Quarter attribute. Save your changes, and then close the Dimension Designer.

21. In Solution Explorer, double-click the Promotion dimension to open it in the Dimension Designer.

22. Rename the Promotion Key attribute in place to **Promotion**, and then set its NameColumn property to the EnglishPromotionName column. Set the OrderBy property of the Promotion attribute to Name to sort the Promotion attribute by name.

23. In the Data Source View pane, select the DiscountPct, StartDate, EndDate, EnglishPromotionType, EnglishPromotionCategory, MinQty, and MaxQty columns. Drag these columns to the Attributes pane. Rename the EnglishPromotionType attribute to **Promotion Type**. Save your changes, and then close the Dimension Designer.

24. In Solution Explorer, double-click the Sales Reason dimension to open it in the Dimension Designer. Rename the Sales Reason Key attribute to **Sales Reason**, and then bind its NameColumn property to the SalesReasonName column. Set the OrderBy property of the Sales Reason attribute to Name. Save your changes, and then close the Dimension Designer.

25. In Solution Explorer, double-click the Sales Territory dimension to open it in the Dimension Designer. Rename the Sales Territory Key attribute to **Sales Territory Region** because it represents the lowest level of the Sales Territory Group, Sales Territory Country, and Sales Territory Region hierarchy. Bind its NameColumn property to the SalesTerritoryRegion column. Set the OrderBy property to Name.

26. In the Data Source View pane, select the SalesTerritoryCountry and SalesTerritoryGroup columns, and then drag them to the Attributes pane to add them as new attributes. Save your changes, and then close the Dimension Designer.

27. In Solution Explorer, double-click the Product dimension to open it in the Dimension Designer. Rename the Product Key attribute to **Product** and the English Description attribute to **Description**.

28. Rename the Product Category Key attribute to **Category**, and then bind its NameColumn to the EnglishProductCategoryName column. Change the OrderBy property of the Category attribute to Name.

29. Rename the Product Subcategory Key attribute to **Subcategory**, and then bind its NameColumn to the EnglishProductSubcategoryName column. Change the OrderBy property of the Subcategory attribute to Name.

> **BEST PRACTICES   USE INTEGER ATTRIBUTE KEYS**
>
> In general, you should use integer columns in the attribute KeyColumns collection. For example, when the dimension spans multiple tables, use the primary keys of the related tables for the attribute keys. You should use the DimProductCategory.ProductCategoryKey column, for instance, instead of the EnglishProductCategoryName column. Using integer keys improves the cube performance.

30. In the Attributes pane, select the English Product Subcategory Name and English Product Category Name attributes, and then delete them.

31. Save the changes to your dimension design by selecting either the Save Selected Items or the Save All option from the File menu in BIDS; alternatively, you can use the Save buttons on the main toolbar (under the menu options) in BIDS.

32. Right-click the project node in Solution Explorer, and then click Deploy to deploy the changes to the server and process the Adventure Works cube.

33. To test the changes, in Solution Explorer, right-click the Adventure Works cube, and then click Browse. If the Cube Designer is already open, click the Reconnect toolbar button to reconnect the browser window to the dimension. Create a report that

shows the Sales Amount measure broken by Sales Territory Region on rows and Order Date.Calendar Year on columns.

EXERCISE 3 Add a Dimension to an Existing Cube

When browsing the cube, notice that the Product dimension is not included in the cube. That is because this dimension was added outside the Cube Wizard. BIDS does not automatically include new dimensions in the cubes that exist in the project. Next you will add the Product dimension to the cube.

1. In Solution Explorer, double-click the Adventure Works cube to open it in the Cube Designer. Make sure that the Cube Structure tab is active.

2. Select Add Cube Dimension from the Cube menu to display the Add Cube Dimension dialog box.

3. In the Add Cube Dimension dialog box, select the Product dimension, and then click OK. This will add the Product database dimension to the cube as a cube dimension. Notice that the Product dimension now appears within the Dimensions pane in the lower-left corner of the Cube Designer. Also notice that the DimProduct, DimProduct-Subcategory, and DimProductCategory tables have been added to the Data Source View pane within the Cube Designer.

4. In the Cube Designer, click the Dimension Usage tab. Notice that the Cube Designer has automatically joined the Product dimension to the Internet Sales measure group because it inferred that the underlying tables are related. The Product dimension does not join the Internet Sales Reason measure group because the FactInternetSalesReason table does not reference the DimProduct table in the DSV.

   Also notice that although there is only one Date database dimension, there are three role-playing, date-related dimensions, named Date (Due Date), Date (Ship Date), and Date (Order Date). The Cube Wizard has detected that the FactInternetSales table references the DimDate table three times and has added the Date dimension three times as well.

5. Save the changes to your cube design by selecting either the Save Selected Items or the Save All option from the BIDS File menu; or you can use the Save buttons on the main toolbar (under the menu options) in BIDS.

6. Right-click the project node in Solution Explorer, and then click Deploy to deploy the changes and process the Adventure Works cube.

7. In the Cube Designer, click the Browser tab. If a warning related to reprocessing the cube appears at the bottom of the tab, click Reconnect to reconnect the browser window to the cube. Explore the measures by the various product attributes that are available now that the Product dimension is included in the cube.

✔ Quick Check

1. While using the Dimension Wizard, you inadvertently select the wrong primary key column and fail to select all the attributes you need for the dimension. Do you have to delete the dimension and start over?

2. When creating a new dimension by using the Dimension Wizard, can you specify the cubes to which the new dimension will be added after it is created?

3. Your FactInternetSales fact table references the DimDate table three times with OrderDateKey, DueDateKey, and ShipDateKey foreign keys. You want the end users to browse the cube data by these dates. Do you need to create separate Time database dimensions?

Quick Check Answers

1. Although you can certainly delete the dimension and start over, it is likely that you can make all necessary corrections by using the Dimension Designer. Simply update the key attribute to reflect the correct KeyColumns property and add the additional attributes as needed.

2. No, you cannot specify the cubes to which a new dimension will be added. The Dimension Wizard simply creates any new dimension as a database-level dimension. If you want to use the new dimension within one or more existing cubes, you must open each cube within the Cube Designer and add the dimension.

3. No, you add the same time dimension multiple times to the cube as a role-playing dimension.

Lesson 4: Creating Measure Groups and Measures

Estimated lesson time: 30 minutes

The Cube Wizard goes a long way toward helping you automatically generate the raw dimensional model from the existing physical model. Remember that based on your input, the Cube Wizard created the Internet Sales measure group over the FactInternetSales fact table. However, as business requirements evolve, you might need to add new measure groups and measures to the dimensional model.

Creating a Measure Group

There are two main scenarios in which you might need to add a new measure group:

- When a new fact table has been added to the database and you need to bring its data into the cube. Because a measure group typically is bound to a single fact table, you would need as many measure groups as there are fact tables in the data warehouse.

- When you need a Distinct Count measure that calculates the number of fact rows with unique values, such as the number of unique customers who have placed orders. Because of the required server overhead for storing Distinct Count measures, a measure group can have only one measure with a Distinct Count aggregation function.

Follow these steps to add a new measure group:

1. Make sure that the underlying fact table is included in the cube's DSV; if it is not, add the table to the DSV.

2. In the BIDS Cube Designer, click the Cube Structure tab. Right-click the Cube node in the Measures pane, and then select New Measure Group. Figure 5-16 shows the New Measure Group dialog box, which lets you select a fact table. The fact tables that are already in use are excluded from the list selector and are listed in the warning message at the bottom of the dialog box.

3. Select the fact table that will become the source of the new measure group, and then click OK to confirm the dialog box selection.

   A new measure group is created. Its name matches the space-delimited name of the underlying fact table.

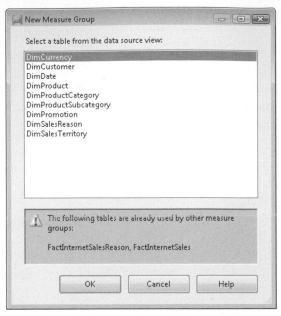

FIGURE 5-16 Select a fact table for the source of the measure group.

A measure group must contain at least one measure. By default, the Cube Designer adds all numeric columns from the source fact table as measures. In addition, the Cube Designer adds a system-generated measure that contains a Count aggregate function. This measure can be useful if you need the server to automatically calculate the number of fact table rows. For example, if the Internet Sales measure group represents a customer order and the user slices the cube by year, the Internet Sales Count measure will return the number of orders placed in each year. You can remove the Count measure after the Cube Designer has generated the measure group.

Understanding Measure Group Properties

After the new measure group is added to the cube, you can select it in the Measures pane to see its properties in the BIDS Properties window. Table 5-4 describes the most significant measure group properties.

TABLE 5-4 Measure Group Properties

PROPERTY	DESCRIPTION
ErrorConfiguration	Specifies whether the default or the custom error configuration will be used to handle error conditions. The default configuration uses the settings in the msmdsrv.ini server configuration file. With a custom configuration, you can control how error conditions—including duplicate, unknown, and null keys—will be handled when the measure group is processed.
EstimatedRows	Helps the server choose the optimum data structures and processing algorithms for a measure group when the number of rows in a fact table is already known. A measure group can load an unlimited number of rows.
IgnoreUnrelated-Dimensions	Defines the server behavior when the user browses the measures by dimensions that are not related to the measure group. By default, unrelated dimensions are ignored; if IgnoreUnrelatedDimensions is set to True, unrelated dimensions are used, but the data is considered missing.
ProactiveCaching	Specifies the proactive caching settings. See Chapter 8 to find out about proactive caching.
ProcessingMode	Defines the place in the cube processing at which data becomes available to users. By default, ProcessingMode is set to Regular, and users cannot access the measure group until processing is complete. If ProcessingMode is set to LazyAggregations, data is accessible as soon as it is processed, but processing takes longer.
StorageMode	Defines the default storage mode for the measure group partitions; options are Multidimensional Online Analytical Processing (MOLAP), Relational Online Analytical Processing (ROLAP), and Hybrid Online Analytical Processing (HOLAP).
Type	Provides client applications with information about the contents of the measure group (for example, Sales). This property is not used by the server. The client can inspect and interpret this property as needed (for example, change the display icon of the measure group).

Creating a Measure Group for Distinct Count

The New Measure Group dialog box does not let you select a fact table that is already being used by another measure group. Yet, as noted, a Distinct Count measure must be placed in a separate measure group. As a workaround, the Cube Designer will automatically create a new measure group when you attempt to add a measure that contains a DistinctCount aggregate function to an existing measure group. Here's how to create a Distinct Count measure:

1. In the Measures pane, right-click an existing measure group, and then select New Measure.

2. In the New Measure dialog box that appears, select Distinct Count in the Usage drop-down list.

3. If necessary, select the Show All Columns check box to display all columns in the fact table, as Figure 5-17 shows. This is necessary if the Distinct Count measure uses a foreign key column or a text-based column for the counting.

4. Select the column to be counted, and then click OK.

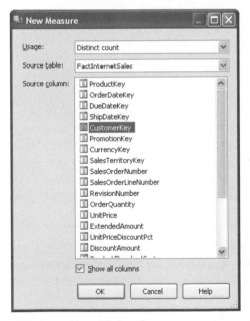

FIGURE 5-17 Use a Distinct Count measure to count the unique customers who have placed orders.

The Cube Designer creates a new measure group whose name matches the name of the original measure group and appends a consecutive number to it. So, for example, if the original measure group is named Internet Sales, the new measure group will be named Internet Sales 1. To rename the measure group, change its Name property or edit it in place by double-clicking the measure group's name in the Measures pane and then typing the new name.

Adding and Configuring Measures

Just as a relational table is a container for columns, a cube measure group contains related measures. As new columns are added to the fact table, you might need to add corresponding measures to the measure group and configure their behavior.

Adding a New Measure

To add a new measure, use the New Measure dialog box, shown earlier in Figure 5-17. After you select the source column of the measure, use the Usage drop-down list to select its aggregation behavior. Based on how they aggregate, measures can be classified as additive, semiadditive, or nonadditive.

Fully additive measures, such as Sales Amount, can be summed across all dimensions. Other measures, such as account and inventory balances, can be aggregated across all dimensions except Time. If you attempt to aggregate these measures across Time, you will get incorrect results. Suppose that a bank account has a balance of $100 in January, February, and March. If the server sums the account balance across Time, at the end of March, the balance will be $300, which is incorrect. Instead, you need to configure the account balance as a semiadditive measure so that the server does not sum the measure across Time but instead returns the account closing balance for the last time period selected.

EXAM TIP

Development and Enterprise editions of SSAS provide several functions—such as *LastChild*, *LastNonEmpty*, and *AverageOfChildren*—that help you handle semiadditive measures. For example, *LastNonEmpty* will let you get the closing inventory balance for a given time period that is not empty. Although you can use custom MDX expressions to aggregate semiadditive measures, you will get better performance if you use these standard functions. For the complete list of standard aggregation functions, see the topic "Configuring Measure Properties" in SQL Server 2008 Books Online (see References).

Last, nonadditive measures, such as rates and percentages, cannot be meaningfully aggregated across any dimension. Instead, you can use MDX expressions to specify how they aggregate—for example, by defining a weighted average calculation.

Configuring Measures

Measures have properties that control their storage, aggregation, and display behavior. To configure a measure, select it in the Measures pane. The BIDS Properties window shows the measure properties, which Table 5-5 lists.

TABLE 5-5 Measure Properties

PROPERTY	DESCRIPTION
AggregateFunction	Specifies the measure aggregate function.
DataType	Needs to be explicitly set for Count and Distinct Count measures only. The default option, Inherited, gets the data type from the underlying DSV.
DisplayFolder	Groups measures into logical folders.
FormatString	Defines the measure display format. Custom format strings such as #,##0;(#,##0) are supported.
MeasureExpression	Defines a measure expression (multiplication or division only) of two operands; the second operand must be in a different measure group. For example, assuming that the cube has a Currency Rate measure group with an Average Rate measure, you can convert the Sales Amount measure to USD by using the following expression: [Sales Amount] * [Average Rate]
Source	Defines the measure binding. Measures are typically bound to a single numeric column (fact) from the fact table that serves as the source of the measure group (column binding). However, a Count measure could be bound to a row (row binding) if it needs to count rows.
Visible	When set to False, hides the measure from the end user. The measure can still be used in MDX expressions.

PRACTICE   Adding Measure Groups and Measures

In this practice, you will learn how to create a new Reseller Sales measure group, add measures to it, and configure the new objects to support Adventure Works' decision to bring resale facts into the data source and store them in the FactResellerSales fact table.

EXERCISE 1   Add Measure Groups

Suppose that Adventure Works has enhanced its data warehouse database to store reseller sales and currency conversion. The reseller sales are stored in the FactResellerSales fact table, while the currency exchange rates are captured in the FactCurrencyRates fact table. You need to enhance the cube to make this functionality available to the end users. You will use the Cube Designer to add two measure groups that map to the FactResellerSales and FactCurrencyRates fact tables.

1. In Solution Explorer, double-click the AdventureWorks DW2008 DSV to open it in the Data Source View Designer. Notice that the FactResellerSales and FactCurrencyRates fact tables are not listed in the Tables pane.

2. Choose Add/Remove Tables from the Data Source View menu.

3. In the Add/Remove Tables dialog box, select both the FactResellerSales and Fact-CurrencyRates tables by holding down the Ctrl key in the Available Objects list and clicking the single right arrow (>) button to move them to the Included Objects list. Click OK to return to the Data Source View Designer.

4. Right-click an unoccupied space in the DSV pane, and then click Arrange Tables to arrange the objects on the diagram so that they do not overlap. Save your changes, and then close the Data Source View Designer.

5. In Solution Explorer, double-click the Adventure Works cube to open it in the Cube Designer. The Cube Structure tab should be active by default.

6. In the Measures pane, right-click the Adventure Works cube, which is the root node, and then click New Measure Group.

7. In the New Measure Group dialog box, select the FactResellerSales table, and then click OK.

   The Cube Designer creates a new measure group named Fact Reseller Sales and adds all numeric columns, including nonreferenced keys, as measures to this measure group. In addition, the Cube Designer discovers that some measures, such as Sales Amount, have names that are identical to those in the Internet Sales measure group. Because the measure name must be unique across all measure groups, the Cube Designer appends the name of the measure group to the name of the measure. So in this case, Sales Amount is renamed as Fact Reseller Sales. You will correct the names of the measure group and measures in Exercise 2 of this lesson.

   > **BEST PRACTICES** **VERIFY MEASURE GROUP–DIMENSION RELATIONSHIPS**
   >
   > After you add a new measure group, do not forget to navigate to the Dimension Usage tab and verify the relationships between the measure groups and the dimensions. The Cube Designer auto-configures these relationships based on the relationships that exist in the DSV.

8. Reseller Key, Employee Key, and Revision Number are not very useful as measures. Select them, one at a time. Then in each case, press Delete, and in the Delete Objects dialog box, confirm that you want to remove the measure by clicking OK. Alternatively, you can switch to the grid view by clicking the Show Measures Grid toolbar to select

and delete measures in one step. To reduce the number of measures, also delete the Product Standard Cost, Total Product Cost, Tax Amt, Freight, and Unit Price Discount Pct measures.

9. Repeat steps 6 and 7 to create a new Fact Currency Rate measure group that uses the FactCurrencyRate fact table.

EXERCISE 2   Configure Measure Groups and Measures

In this exercise, you will work with the properties of measure groups and measures to rename them and change their formatting.

1. Double-click the Adventure Works cube in Solution Explorer to open it in the Cube Designer. In the Measures pane of the Cube Structure tab, rename the Fact Reseller Sales measure group in place to **Reseller Sales**. Rename the Fact Currency Rate measure group to **Currency Rate**.

2. One by one, rename in place each measure in the Internet Sales measure group so that they all start with the word *Internet*. For example, rename Order Quantity to **Internet Order Quantity**.

3. One by one, rename in place each measure in the Reseller Sales measure group so that they all start with the word *Reseller*. For example, rename Order Quantity to **Reseller Order Quantity**. The Cube Designer adds the measure group name as a suffix to the end of all measures whose names match names of existing measures, to avoid duplicated names. This is because a cube cannot have measures with identical names. Because the measures in the Reseller Sales measure group have unique names already, remove the *Fact Reseller Sales* suffix from all measures whose names include it. Rename Reseller Fact Reseller Sales Count to **Reseller Sales Count**.

4. Click the Show Measure Grid button on the toolbar to switch to a grid view. The grid view is convenient if you want to set the properties of multiple measures to the same setting.

5. Hold down the Ctrl key and select the Reseller Unit Price, Reseller Extended Amount, Reseller Discount Amount, and Reseller Sales Amount measures, and then format them as currency by selecting Currency in the FormatString drop-down list of the BIDS Property window. To format Reseller Order Quantity and Reseller Sales Count measures as general numbers with a thousands separator, select these measures, and then type **#,#** in the FormatString property.

6. Optionally, convert some sales measures to United States dollars (USD) by specifying a measure expression. For example, to convert Reseller Sales Amount to USD, enter the following expression in its MeasureExpression property:

```
[Reseller Sales Amount] / [Average Rate]
```

EXERCISE 3   Create a Distinct Count Measure

In this exercise, you will create a Distinct Count measure that will count the unique customers who have placed sales orders.

1.   In the Measures pane of the Cube Designer's Cube Structure tab, right-click the Internet Sales measure group, and then click New Measure.

2.   In the New Measure dialog box, select the Show All Columns check box.

3.   Select the CustomerKey column, select DistinctCount in the Usage drop-down list, and then click OK. Note that the Cube Designer creates a new measure group named Internet Sales 1, which contains a single Customer Key Distinct Count measure.

4.   Rename the Internet Sales 1 measure group to **Internet Customers** and the Customer Key Distinct Count measure to **Customer Count**.

5.   In Solution Explorer, right-click the project node, and then click Deploy to deploy the changes to the server and process the AdventureWorks cube.

6.   Optionally, use the Cube Browser to create a report that uses the measures in the Reseller Sales and Internet Customers measure groups.

> ✔ **Quick Check**
>
> 1.   What is the difference between measures and a measure group?
>
> 2.   What types of measures can you identify based on the way they aggregate?
>
> 3.   How do you set the aggregation function of a measure?
>
> **Quick Check Answers**
>
> 1.   A measure group is a container of measures. Typically, a measure group repre-sents a fact table, and its measures represent the facts.
>
> 2.   Based on how it aggregates data, a measure can be additive, semiadditive, or nonadditive.
>
> 3.   You can set a measure's aggregation function by setting its *AggregationFunction* property to one of the SSAS standard aggregation functions.

Case Scenario: Building an SSAS Solution as a Prototype

The business development department at Adventure Works has asked you to develop a solution to analyze Internet and reseller sales by using Excel 2007. Given the strong support for working with cubes in Excel, you decide to create an SSAS solution that provides the requested sales data, with various dimensions, hierarchies, and attributes available to support a broad range of analysis needs.

1. How can you quickly create a prototype of your solution to gain a better understanding of the data and the end-user requirements?

2. What SSAS features are you likely to take advantage of to improve the usability of the cube from an end-user perspective?

Chapter Summary

- Every SSAS solution must include a data source view (DSV) that contains schema metadata to support the other objects within that solution. The solution might also include named calculations and named queries.

- The BIDS Cube Wizard and Dimension Wizard provide easy mechanisms for adding new cubes and dimensions to an SSAS solution.

- The BIDS Cube Designer provides tabs for reviewing and modifying various aspects of a cube. The two tabs you use to control the basic structure of a cube are the Cube Structure tab and the Dimension Usage tab.

- You use the BIDS Dimension Designer to modify a dimension and to add, modify, or delete specific attributes and multilevel hierarchies within the dimension.

- You can set various attribute properties to control the behavior of the attributes from an end user's perspective. Likewise, you can control the behavior of dimension attributes through various properties available within the Dimension Designer.

- A measure group is a container of measures. The most important property of a measure is *AggregationFunction*, which tells the server how to aggregate the measure. Additive measures aggregate across all dimensions joined to the measure group. Semiadditive measures aggregate across all dimensions except time. Non-additive measures require custom calculations that define their aggregation behavior.

CHAPTER 6

Extending SSAS Cubes

Y ou can extend SQL Server 2008 Analysis Services (SSAS) cubes in versatile ways to meet advanced business requirements. You can define attribute relationships and hierarchies to optimize the cube design and facilitate data analytics. In addition, you can further enrich the reporting experience by building an end-user layer consisting of key performance indicators (KPIs), actions, translations, and perspectives. You can also use Multidimensional Expressions (MDX) language expressions to define important business metrics not available in the fact tables or that require custom expressions.

This chapter builds on the Adventure Works cube implemented in Chapter 5, "Developing SSAS Cubes." The source code for the Chapter 6 practices can be installed from the companion CD. This chapter starts by discussing attribute and dimension relationships. You will learn how to extend the Unified Dimensional Model (UDM) with KPIs, actions, translations, and perspectives. And after describing the MDX query fundamentals, the chapter will explore MDX calculated members and named sets.

Exam objectives in this chapter:

- Implement dimensions in a cube.
- Configure dimension usage in a cube.
- Implement custom logic in a cube by using MDX.

Before You Begin

To complete this chapter, you must have:

- Knowledge of dimensional modeling and SSAS cubes.
- An understanding of SSAS dimensions and measures.
- Practical experience with Analysis Services projects in Business Intelligence Development Studio (BIDS).

Lesson 1: Defining User Hierarchies and Dimension Relationships

Estimated lesson time: 60 minutes

From an analytical standpoint, a *dimension* gives users the ability to analyze data by subject areas. Dimensions let users isolate, drill down, roll up, categorize, filter, summarize, and perform other actions on data. In the UDM, a dimension is a logical container of attributes. Understanding how dimension attributes relate to each other will help you optimize the UDM performance.

Defining Attribute Relationships

An SSAS dimension gets its data from one or more dimension tables that reside in the data source. If the dimension is based on a star schema, its source is a single dimension table. Dimensions based on a snowflake database schema typically span multiple dimension tables. In the Adventure Works cube, for example, the Product dimension is built on a snowflake schema that includes the DimProduct, DimProductSubcategory, and DimCategory tables. The rest of the dimensions are of a star type and use single dimension tables.

Unlike a relational database, which stores data in two-dimensional structures of rows and columns, the UDM is a multidimensional system that supports data hierarchies—such as the hierarchy formed by Year, Quarter, and Month levels—and the relationships that exist among the attributes forming these hierarchies. Table 6-1 summarizes such relationships for a subset of the attributes in the Product dimension you designed in Chapter 5.

TABLE 6-1 Understanding Attribute Relations

TABLE COLUMN	ATTRIBUTE TYPE	RELATIONSHIP TO PRIMARY KEY	OTHER RELATIONSHIPS
ProductKey	Primary key	Dimension key	
Description	Attribute	1:1	
Color	Attribute	Many:1	
Subcategory	Attribute	Many:1	Many:1 with Category
Category	Attribute	Many:1	

All dimension attributes are directly or indirectly related to the dimension key attribute with one-to-one (1:1) or many-to-one (Many:1) logical relationships. For example, the Description attribute has a 1:1 relationship with the dimension key attribute (ProductKey), assuming that each product has a unique description. In contrast, the Color attribute has a Many:1 relationship to the dimension key because multiple products can have the same color. Similarly, the Subcategory attribute has a Many:1 relationship with the dimension key because one subcategory can include multiple products. The Subcategory attribute has a logical Many:1 attribute with the Category attribute because one product category can include multiple subcategories.

BEST PRACTICES **DEFINE ATTRIBUTE RELATIONSHIPS**

By default, the UDM is not aware of the logical relationships among attributes. It defines Many:1 relationships between all attributes and the dimension key, except with snowflake dimensions, where it automatically creates separate Many:1 relationships among attributes from different tables. As a modeler, you must spend additional time to understand and define appropriate attribute relationships.

Setting up relevant attribute relationships provides the following benefits:

- SSAS can effectively store data. The server can optimize the storage of the attribute hierarchies.

- SSAS can effectively retrieve and aggregate data. In the absence of attribute relationships, the server must query the fact data and then group data by the attribute. For example, if there are no attribute relationships between the Subcategory and Category attributes, a query that groups data by product category will scan the fact data on the fly to summarize the individual products. However, if the attributes are related, the server could optimize the query and use the subcategory subtotals.

To learn more about the importance of defining attribute relationships, read the white paper "Microsoft SQL Server 2008 Analysis Services Performance Guide" (see References).

Compared with SSAS 2005, SSAS 2008 has simplified the process of analyzing and defining attribute relationships by introducing a new Attribute Relationships tab in the Dimension Designer, as Figure 6-1 shows.

This tab has a Diagram pane, an Attributes pane, and an Attribute Relationships pane. If the Attributes and Attribute Relationships panes are not visible, click the Show List Views button on the Dimension Designer toolbar on the Attribute Relationships tab.

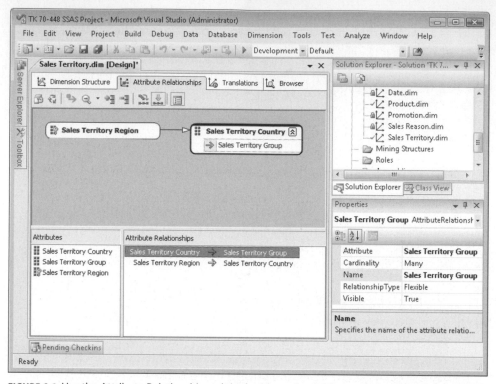

FIGURE 6-1 Use the Attribute Relationships tab in the Dimension Designer to view and change attribute relationships.

The Diagram pane shows an attribute relationship graph so that you can quickly visualize existing relationships. The Attributes pane shows the dimension attributes. And the Attribute Relationships pane lists existing attribute relationships. To select an attribute relationship, click the relationship in the Attribute Relationships pane or select the arrow that connects the attributes in the Diagram pane, and then use the Properties pane to modify the relationship properties. Table 6-2 describes the relationship properties.

TABLE 6-2 Attribute Relationship Properties

PROPERTY	PURPOSE
Attribute	Specifies the name of the related attribute.
Cardinality	Specifies the cardinality of the relationship between the two attributes (could be One or Many).
Name	Specifies the relationship name. This translates to the name of the member property that the end user will see when browsing the attribute in a browser that supports member properties, such as Microsoft Office Excel 2007.

PROPERTY	PURPOSE
RelationshipType	Specifies whether the relationship can change over time. Set this property to Flexible when you expect changes, such as for a product that can change a subcategory. Set it to Rigid if the relationship does not change, such as for a relationship between the Quarter and Year attribute in a Time dimension.
Visible	Defines the visibility of the member property. When set to False, the corresponding member property will not be shown to the end user.

To create a new attribute relationship, follow these steps:

1. In the Attributes pane, right-click the source attribute that is on the "one" side of the relationship, and then select New Attribute Relationship.

2. Configure the relationship by using the Create Attribute Relationship dialog box, shown in Figure 6-2.

FIGURE 6-2 Use the Create Attribute Relationship dialog box to set up a new attribute relationship.

Make sure that the Name drop-down list below Source Attribute shows the attribute that is on the "many" side of the relationship and that the Name drop-down list below Related Attribute shows the attribute on the "one" side of the relationship. Use the Relationship Type drop-down list to specify a Flexible or Rigid relationship type. You can also create a new relationship in the Dimension Designer by dragging the source attribute onto the related attribute in the Diagram pane. To delete an attribute relationship, select the relationship in the Attribute Relationships pane (or click the arrow connector in the Diagram pane) and then press Delete.

Creating and Modifying User Dimension Hierarchies

The UDM is an attribute-based model in which the cube space is defined by attribute hierarchies. In Chapter 5, you saw that each dimension attribute forms an attribute hierarchy whose members are formed by the distinct values of the attribute source column. For example, the members of the Sales Territory Country attribute hierarchy contain the distinct countries stored in the SalesTerritoryCountry column. Attribute hierarchies are incredibly useful because they let end users analyze data aggregated by the members of the hierarchy. As a modeler, you should consider setting up additional user hierarchies that combine attributes and define useful navigational paths.

For example, many users who interact with cubes through Excel or another user application need to be able to drill down into a hierarchy that provides expanding levels of detail. Such hierarchies might include the year, quarter, month, and day within a Date dimension; the category, subcategory, and product name within a Product dimension; or the country, state, and city within a Geography or Customer dimension. SSAS supports dimensions that have multiple user hierarchies, giving end users multiple options for exploring cube data.

You define hierarchies within the context of a given dimension by using the Dimension Structure tab of the Dimension Designer. The Hierarchies pane in Figure 6-3 shows a Sales Territory user hierarchy that has Group, Country, and Region levels.

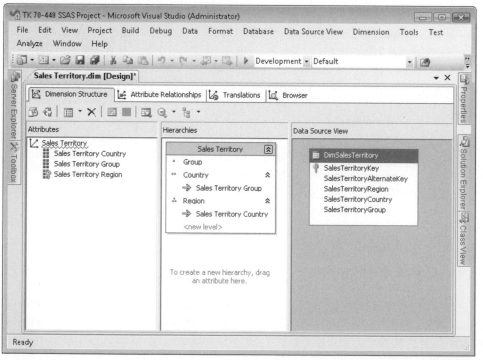

FIGURE 6-3 The Sales Territory user hierarchy lets end users drill down into the data by Group, Country, and Region.

You define hierarchies by following these steps:

1. To add a new hierarchy within a dimension, right-click the attribute that will be the top level, and then select Start New Hierarchy. For example, in the Sales Territory dimension, which you implemented in Chapter 5, you can create a new hierarchy by selecting the Sales Territory Group attribute as the top level. Alternatively, you can drag an attribute to the Hierarchies pane to serve as the top level of a new hierarchy.

2. To add additional levels, right-click each attribute that will serve as a level in the hierarchy, and then select Create Level. Alternatively, to create a new level, you can drag the attribute to the <new level> placeholder within the hierarchy's structure in the Hierarchies pane. You can add more hierarchies to the dimension's design by repeating this procedure.

After you have created a new hierarchy, you can use the Properties window to modify the properties for the hierarchy and each of its levels. For example, you can use the DisplayFolder property of the hierarchy to place it within the display folder used for attribute hierarchies or a different folder. Or you can use the Name property to change the name of a level from the name of the attribute used as the source for the level to a name that makes more sense from an end user's perspective. Alternatively, you can rename a level in place in the Hierarchies pane.

EXAM TIP

A user hierarchy typically assumes Many:1 relationships among its levels. For example, a territory group can have many countries, and a country can have many regions. Although you can set up user hierarchies without defining attribute relationships, you should avoid this structure because it results in a poor dimension design. When the Dimension Designer detects missing attribute relationships, it displays a warning icon next to the name of the hierarchy in the Hierarchies pane. You can expand the hierarchy levels in the Hierarchies pane to see the existing attribute relationships. To optimize your dimension design, switch to the Attribute Relationships pane and set up Many:1 attribute relationships. Also consider hiding attributes that are used in user hierarchies by setting their AttributeHierarchyVisible property to False to prevent redundancy in the user experience.

Associating Dimensions to Measure Groups

When you add a dimension to a cube, the Cube Designer determines which measure groups the dimension is related to by using the table relationships metadata within the data source view (DSV) on which the cube is based. In most cases, the associations the Cube Designer creates are correct. However, you can use the Dimension Usage tab to review the relationships between dimensions and measure groups and to correct any problems.

> **BEST PRACTICES**   **DEFINE DIMENSION USAGE WITHIN A CUBE**
>
> Within SSAS, a cube can contain multiple measure groups and multiple dimensions. Although many of the measure groups are likely related to the same dimensions, not every dimension will be related to every measure group. In addition, SSAS supports different types of measure group-to-dimension relationships to support different database modeling requirements. You can use the Dimension Usage tab within the Cube Designer to define the various relationships that should exist between each measure group and dimension within the cube.

Figure 6-4 shows the Dimension Usage tab within the Cube Designer, which displays along the top of the table the list of measure groups in the cube and along the left side of the table the list of dimensions in the cube.

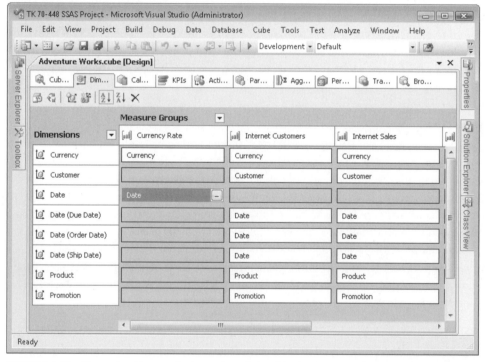

FIGURE 6-4 The Dimension Usage tab shows the relationships between a cube's measure groups and its dimensions.

You can sort the dimensions and measure groups alphabetically in ascending or descending order by clicking the appropriate toolbar button. The intersection of a given measure group and dimension defines the relationship between the two. If a dimension is not related to a measure group, the intersection will show an empty gray cell.

In Figure 6-4, the Date dimension joins only the Currency Rate measure group. This is a redundant Date dimension relationship that the Cube Designer defined when you added the Currency Rate measure group. To optimize the cube design and reduce the number of dimensions, consider deleting the Date dimension and reusing an existing role-playing Date dimension, such as Date (Order Date), to browse the Currency Rate data.

Selecting Relationship Types

If you select a cell within the table on the Dimension Usage tab, an ellipsis (…) button provides access to the Define Relationship dialog box, shown in Figure 6-5. You can use this dialog box to create or modify a relationship between a dimension and a measure group. The dialog box lets you select the relationship type and set various properties related to the relationship.

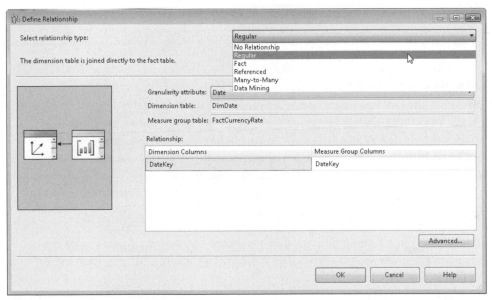

FIGURE 6-5 In the Define Relationship dialog box, you can add new relationships and modify existing ones.

When relating a given dimension to a measure group, you can select one of several types of relationships, depending on your specific need. Your choice will be driven primarily by the database design and model you are using to define the cube. Table 6-3 describes all the relationship types you can define in a cube.

TABLE 6-3 Dimension Usage Relationship Types

RELATIONSHIP TYPE	PURPOSE
Regular	Defines the relationship when a dimension is joined directly to a measure group through a specific attribute called the "granularity" attribute.
Fact	Used when the dimension is based on the fact table used to define the measure group.
Referenced	Used when a given dimension is related to a measure group through an intermediate dimension.
Many-To-Many	Specifies that a dimension is related to a given measure group through an intermediate measure group.
Data Mining	Defines the relationship between a dimension based on a data mining model and a given measure group.

EXAM TIP

Sometimes after analyzing the database schema and designing fact and dimension tables, you will be left with columns in the fact table that do not justify moving them to designated dimension tables, such as Sales Order Number. Yet reporting requirements might require you to let end users browse data by these columns—for example, to see all sales order line items for a given sales order. You can meet such requirements by building dimensions directly from the fact table and then joining them to the related measure groups through a fact relationship.

To select a given relationship type, open the Define Relationship dialog box, and then select the relationship type from the Select Relationship Type drop-down list at the top of the dialog box. Based on the relationship type you select, the other options available within the dialog box will change to reflect the required settings for that relationship type. Ensure that the appropriate values are entered for the options shown, and then click OK to close the dialog box.

A dimension does not need to join a measure group at the dimension key level. For example, the AdventureWorksDW2008 database has a FactSalesQuota fact table that stores the quarterly sales quota of salespersons. At the same time, the lowest level of the DimDate dimension table is days. However, SSAS supports joining DimDate to FactSalesQuota at the quarter level. When defining a relationship at a higher level, it is extremely important to define appropriate Many:1 relationships. Failure to do so might yield incorrect subtotals.

The following exercises will familiarize you with the tasks related to defining attribute relationships, working with dimension hierarchies, and creating relationships between dimensions and measure groups. When beginning the exercises, use the Start Here project from the Documents\Microsoft Press\MCTS Training Kit 70-448\Source\Ch 06\TK448-ch06 Start Here\ folder in the installed practice files.

EXERCISE 1   Define Attribute Relationships

In this exercise, you will define attribute relationships in the Date, Product, and Sales Territory dimensions.

1. In Solution Explorer, double-click the Date dimension to open it in the Dimension Designer.

2. Click the Attribute Relationships tab. Notice that the Diagram pane shows the Date dimension key attribute. All other attributes are related to the dimension key through Many:1 relationships; there are no relationships among the nonkey attributes.

   However, some attributes have logical Many:1 relationships with other attributes. For example, the Month Name attribute has a Many:1 relationship with the Calendar Quarter attribute, and the Calendar Quarter attribute has a Many:1 relationship with Calendar Year. Next, you will change the dimension design to reflect these relationships.

3. Right-click the Month Name attribute, and then select New Attribute Relationship. In the Create Attribute Relationship dialog box that appears, make sure that the related attribute is Calendar Quarter. Change the Relationship Type to Rigid (Will Not Change Over Time) because months cannot change quarters. Click OK.

4. The Month Name attribute also has a Many:1 relationship with fiscal quarters. Create a second Rigid relationship between the Month Name attribute and the Fiscal Quarter attribute.

5. Create a Rigid relationship between the Calendar Quarter and Calendar Year attributes and another Rigid relationship between the Fiscal Quarter and Fiscal Year attributes. Save your changes, and then close the Dimension Designer.

6. In Solution Explorer, double-click the Product dimension to open it in the Dimension Designer.

7. Click the Attribute Relationships tab, and notice that there are already attribute relationships between the Product and Subcategory attributes and the Subcategory and Category attributes. The Dimension Designer discovered that the Product dimension has a snowflake schema and automatically generated these attribute relationships.

Notice in the Attributes pane of the Attribute Relationships tab that warning icons appear in some attribute relationships to warn you that the relationship and related attribute names differ. Consequently, when end users browse the cube, they will see a member property that has the relationship name instead of the name of the related attribute.

8. In the Attribute Relationships pane, select the Product–Description relationship, and, in the Properties window, clear its Name property. If you do not specify the Name property, it defaults to the Attribute property.

9. Repeat step 8 for the Product–Subcategory and Subcategory–Category relationships. Save your changes, and then close the Dimension Designer.

10. In Solution Explorer, double-click the Sales Territory dimension to open it in the Dimension Designer.

11. Click the Attribute Relationships tab, and set up a Many:1 Flexible relationship between the Sales Territory Country and Sales Territory Group attributes. Save your changes, and then close the Dimension Designer.

EXERCISE 2 Define User Hierarchies

In this exercise, you will define user hierarchies in the Date, Product, and Sales Territory dimensions. These user hierarchies will provide logical navigational paths to explore the cube data.

1. In Solution Explorer, double-click the Date dimension to open it in the Dimension Designer. Currently, the Date dimension does not have any user hierarchies defined, but end users often browse data by year, quarter, month, and day. In this exercise, you will implement a Calendar user-defined hierarchy that includes these levels.

2. Click the Dimension Structure tab. Drag the Calendar Year attribute from the Attributes pane to the Hierarchies pane to start a new user hierarchy where the top level is the Calendar Year attribute.

3. Click the new hierarchy to select it. Rename the hierarchy by changing its Name property to **Calendar**.

4. Drag the Calendar Quarter attribute from the Attributes pane onto the <new level> placeholder in the Calendar hierarchy. This creates the second hierarchy level, which will let the user drill from years to quarters.

5. Repeat step 4 twice more to add the Month Name and Date levels to the Calendar hierarchy.

   Note that if you skipped Exercise 1, the Dimension Designer will show a warning indicator in the hierarchy caption. When you point to this indicator, the Dimension Designer will display the following tooltip:

   Attribute relationships do not exist between one or more levels of this hierarchy. This may result in decreased query performance.

   If this happens, follow the steps in Exercise 1 to set up attribute relationships.

6. Create a new Fiscal user hierarchy that contains the Fiscal Year, Fiscal Quarter, Month Name, and Date levels. Save your changes, and then close the Dimension Designer.

7. In Solution Explorer, double-click the Product dimension to open it in the Dimension Designer.

8. Define a Product Categories user hierarchy that contains Category, Subcategory, and Product levels. Save your changes, and then close the Dimension Designer.

9. In Solution Explorer, double-click the Sales Territory dimension to open it in the Dimension Designer.

10. Define a new user hierarchy that contains Sales Territory Group, Sales Territory Country, and Sales Territory Region levels.

11. Rename the hierarchy to **Sales Territories**. In addition, rename the Sales Territory Group level to **Group,** the Sales Territory Country level to **Country**, and the Sales Territory Region level to **Region**. Save your changes, and then close the Dimension Designer.

EXERCISE 3   Review and Modify Dimension Usage Relationship Types

In this exercise, you will create an Internet Sales Order Details fact dimension and set up a Fact relationship between this dimension and the Internet Sales measure group. You will also define a many:many dimension relationship. Last, you will optimize the Adventure Works cube by removing redundant dimension relationships.

Sometimes you might need to create a dimension directly from columns that exists in the fact table. For example, the FactInternetSales fact table includes SalesOrderNumber and SalesOrderLineNumber columns. Suppose that you need to support detail reports that will show sales orders and their associated sales items. Because there is not a designated Sales Order dimension table, you can create a Fact dimension (also called degenerate) directly from the fact table.

1. Open the Adventure Works DW2008 DSV, and then add a named calculation called LineItemDescription to the FactInternetSales table that uses the following expression:

```
CONVERT ( CHAR ( 10 ), SalesOrderNumber )  + 'Line '  +
CONVERT ( CHAR ( 4 ), SalesOrderLineNumber )
```

2. In Solution Explorer, right-click the Dimensions folder, and then select New Dimension. On the Select Creation Method page of the Dimension Wizard, accept the Use An Existing Table option.

3. On the Specify Source Information page, expand the Main Table drop-down list, and then select FactInternet Sales. Expand the Name Column drop-down list, and then select the LineItemDescription column.

4. On the Select Related Tables page, clear the check boxes for all suggested related tables.

5. On the Select Dimension Attributes page, clear the check boxes for all attributes except Sales Order Number.

6. On the Completing The Wizard page, name the new dimension **Internet Sales Order Details**, and then click Finish.

7. In Solution Explorer, double-click the Adventure Works cube to open it in the Cube Designer. On the Cube main menu, select Add Cube Dimension. In the Add Cube Dimension dialog box, select the Internet Sales Order Details dimension, and then click OK.

8. Click the Dimension Usage tab, and then review the existing dimension relationships. Notice that the Internet Sales Order Details dimension is related to the Internet Sales measure group through a Fact relationship. That is because the dimension is based on the same fact table that the measure group is based on.

   Notice too that the Sales Reason dimension does not join the Internet Sales measure group because the intersecting cell is empty. In the AdventureWorksDW2008 database, a sales order can be associated with one or more sales reasons, such as Promotion or Marketing, and a sales reason can be associated with one or more sales orders. The FactInternetSalesReason table represents the Many:Many relationship between sales reasons and orders. SSAS supports many-to-many dimension relationships.

9. Click the ellipsis (...) button in the intersecting cell between the Sales Reason dimension and the Internet Sales measure group.

10. In the Define Relationships dialog box that appears, expand the Select Relationship Type drop-down list, and then select Many-To-Many. Expand the Intermediate Measure Group drop-down list, and then select the Internet Sales Reason measure group whose source fact table is FactInternetSalesReason. Click OK to create the many-to-many dimension relationship.

    Notice that the Date dimension joins only the Currency Rate measure group. As it stands, this relationship is not useful because you cannot browse the data in the other measure groups by this dimension. You can optimize the cube design by deleting the Date dimension and reusing one of the existing Time role-playing dimensions, such as Date (Order Date).

11. Right-click the Date dimension in the Dimensions column, and then select Delete to remove the Date dimension. Click OK in the Delete Objects dialog box that appears, to confirm the deletion.

12. You will use the Date (Order Date) dimension to browse the data in the Currency Rate measure group. Click the ellipsis (...) button in the intersecting cell between the Date (Order Date) dimension and the Currency Rate measure group.

13. In the Define Relationship dialog box, expand the Select Relationship Type drop-down list, and then select Regular.

14. Expand the Granularity Attribute drop-down list, and then select the Date attribute, because the Date (Order Date) dimension will join the Currency Rate measure group at the date level.

15. Expand the drop-down list in the Measure Group Columns column in the Relationship grid, and then select the DateKey column. Click OK.

16. You can rename any cube dimension. Because the Date (Order Date) dimension now fulfills a more generic role, you will change its name to Date. Click the Date (Order Date) dimension in the Dimension column, and then rename it in place to **Date**. Save your changes.

17. In Solution Explorer, right-click the project node, and then select Deploy to deploy the changes and process the Adventure Works cube. If a message stating that the server content is out of date appears, click Yes to build and deploy the database.

18. Optionally, use the Cube Browser tab to test the changes. For example, explore the measures in the Internet Sales measure group by the Sales Reason dimension. Notice that the aggregate for the Other sales reason type correctly handles the fact that many sales reasons can be selected for a single Internet order (that is why you need to create a many-to-many relationship between the dimension and the measure group).

Quick Check

1. Why should you spend time defining appropriate attribute relationships?

2. When creating a dimension, can you create different hierarchies to represent every possible combination of attributes and to maximize the options available to end users for using the hierarchies to explore cube data?

3. Can you create hierarchies directly from columns within a dimension's table?

4. Can a dimension be related to a measure group if the underlying dimension table is not related to the appropriate fact table in a primary key–to–foreign key relationship?

5. Must every dimension you add to a cube be related to every measure group within that cube?

Quick Check Answers

1. Proper attribute relationships optimize storage and improve query performance because the server might be able to produce the totals from the related attribute totals instead of scanning the fact table.

2. Although technically you can create different hierarchies to represent every combination of attributes, a large number of hierarchies within a dimension design will likely offer too many options and confuse end users. Generally, users can create their own hierarchies by simply nesting (cross-joining) different attributes onto the rows or columns of a given query, although this capability is somewhat dependent on the applications they are using. So having attributes available only for the most commonly requested or needed hierarchies is probably your best design strategy.

3. No, you cannot create hierarchies directly from columns within a dimension's table. Hierarchies can be created only based on attributes that have been added to the dimension's design.

4. Although the dimension cannot be related to the measure group in a Regular relationship, you might be able to create a Referenced or Many-To-Many relationship if an intermediate dimension table or intermediate fact table related to the dimension and measure group in question is available. This capability within SSAS provides an elegant solution to various database modeling requirements.

5. No, you do not have to relate every dimension you add to a cube to every measure group in the cube. In fact, you can create a cube that includes multiple measure groups whose source fact tables are related to different sets of dimensions. This lets end users browse the data in a way that makes sense from a business perspective rather than forcing them to analyze data in a way that is constrained by the underlying database design.

Lesson 2: Creating KPIs, Actions, Translations, and Perspectives

Estimated lesson time: 75 minutes

Many organizations use key performance indicators (KPIs) to gauge their business performance. KPIs are quantifiable measures that represent critical success factors, and analysts use them to measure company performance, over time, against a predefined goal. For example, Sales Profit, Revenue Growth, and Growth In Customer Base are good KPI candidates. KPIs are typically used as part of a strategic performance measurement framework, commonly known as a *business scorecard*.

 REAL WORLD

Teo Lachev

KPIs are typically shown on a *dashboard* page. A digital dashboard, also known as an enterprise dashboard or an executive dashboard, is a business intelligence (BI) tool that helps track the status (or health) of a company via KPIs.

One of my recent projects involved building a Microsoft Office SharePoint–based dashboard page for displaying various KPIs—such as Return Of Assets, Growth In Customer Base, and Percentage Of Customers Profitable—that were defined in an SSAS cube. What makes SSAS suitable for KPIs is that the server automatically calculates the KPI properties as the user slices the cube data. For example, the user could drill down into the Time dimension, and the cube would calculate the KPIs across the hierarchy at year, quarter, and month levels.

In addition, we benefited from the supreme performance that SSAS offers. Besides showing KPIs for the current and previous periods, our dashboard page included several charts and report views that showed historical trends. The page would submit many queries to the SSAS server, and some of the queries would request a large number of calculated measures across many time periods. But by carefully fine-tuning the cube performance, we were able to render the page within seconds.

In addition to KPIs, you can take advantage of other user-oriented features to help you extend the functionality of a cube. For example, you can implement actions to request URL resources, to drill down into data, and to launch a SQL Server Reporting Services (SSRS) report. You can localize the cube metadata and data to target international users. And you can use perspectives to provide subviews of large and complex cubes.

Understanding KPI *Value*, *Goal*, *Status*, and *Trend* Properties

In SSAS, a KPI is an extended measure that has four main expression-based properties: *Value*, *Goal*, *Status*, and *Trend*. The *Value* property is required; the rest are optional.

Value

The KPI *Value* property represents the current value of the KPI. This property is typically mapped to a regular or calculated measure, such as Reseller Sales Amount.

Goal

The KPI *Goal* property defines what the KPI value should be in the perfect world. It could be set to a fixed number, such as 0.40 for 40 percent; a regular measure, such as Sales Target; or a calculated measure. The following expression sets the KPI goal to 40 percent more than the Reseller Sales Amount for the previous date period:

```
1.40 * ([Date].[Calendar].PrevMember, [Measures].[Reseller Sales Amount])
```

The *PrevMember* MDX function returns the previous member in a hierarchy. So if the current level is Year, the function returns the previous year; if the current level is Month, you get the previous month; and so on.

Status

The *Status* property indicates how the KPI value compares to the goal. Its expression should return an integer value of –1 for underperformance, 0 for acceptable performance, or 1 for good performance. SSAS provides several standard KPI-related MDX functions: *KPIValue* to retrieve the KPI value, *KPIGoal* to retrieve the KPI goal, *KPIStatus* to retrieve the KPI status, and *KPITrend* to retrieve the KPI trend properties. The following *Status* expression evaluates the range of the KPI value-to-goal ratio and then returns –1, 0, or 1 accordingly:

```
Case
When KpiValue( "Reseller Sales" ) /KpiGoal ( "Reseller Sales" ) >= 1 Then 1
When KpiValue( "Reseller Sales" ) / KpiGoal ( "Reseller Sales" ) < 1
    And KpiValue( "Reseller Sales" ) / KpiGoal ( "Reseller Sales" ) >= .85 Then 0
Else -1
End
```

Trend

The *Trend* property indicates how the KPI value is doing over time. As with the *Status* property, *Trend* should return a value between −1 and 1. For example, the following expression returns the growth ratio in Reseller Sales Amount compared to the previous period:

```
(
    [Measures].[Reseller Sales Amount] –
    ([Date].[Calendar].PrevMember,
    [Measures].[Reseller Sales Amount])
) /
[Measures].[Reseller Sales Amount]
```

Additional KPI Properties

KPIs have some additional metadata properties that could be helpful for a client application, including the following:

- **Associated Measure Group**   Used to identify the measure group with which this KPI should be associated.
- **Display Folder**   Used to organize related KPIs into logical folders.
- **Parent KPI**   Used to indicate the parent KPI of the current KPI. This is useful if a set of KPIs are shown together, as they might be in a scorecard.
- **Current Time Member**   Used to indicate the member of the Time dimension that should be used as the current member.
- **Weight**   Used to evaluate the importance of a KPI compared to its siblings.
- **Status Indicator and Trend Indicator**   Used to identify the images the client should use to display the values graphically.

Creating KPIs

You can use the KPIs tab in the Cube Designer to create and test KPIs. Follow these steps to create a new KPI:

1. Open the cube in the Cube Designer, and then click the KPIs tab, as shown in Figure 6-6.
2. Set the KPI properties.
3. Save your changes, and then deploy your project.

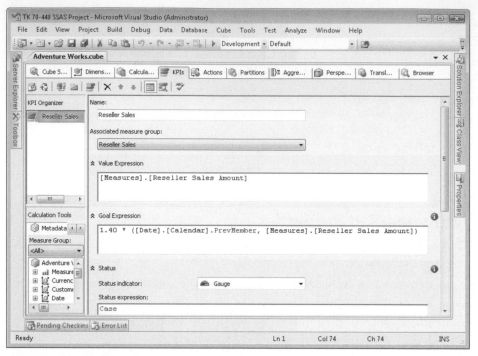

FIGURE 6-6 Use the KPIs tab to create and edit a KPI.

Viewing KPIs

There are a number of ways to test and display KPIs. For quick testing, use the built-in KPI Browser in BIDS, as follows:

1. Deploy the KPI changes to the server.

2. On the KPIs tab in the Cube Designer, select the KPI you want to test in the KPI Organizer pane.

3. Click the Browser View toolbar button to browse the KPIs, as shown in Figure 6-7.

4. Optionally, use the Filter pane of the KPI Browser to filter the KPI properties. For example, to see the Reseller Sales KPI for calendar year 2003, add the Date dimension to the Filter pane, and then set its Calendar hierarchy to 2003.

Although the KPI Browser lets you set up a dimension filter—for example, it will let you filter Calendar Year 2004 only—it does not let you browse the KPIs by multiple dimension members.

You can use KPI-aware client applications, such as Excel 2007 and SSRS, to display KPIs on a report. You can also write an MDX statement in SQL Server Management Studio (SSMS) to directly query the KPI properties by using the *KPIValue()*, *KPIGoal()*, *KPIStatus()*, and *KPITrend()* MDX functions.

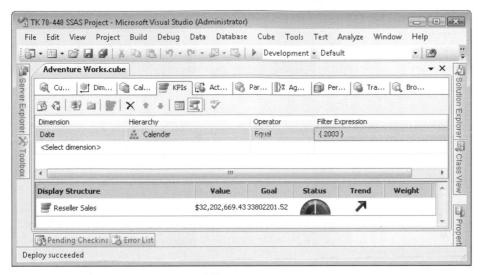

FIGURE 6-7 Use the KPI Browser to test a KPI.

EXAM TIP

You can write an MDX statement that uses the *KPIValue()*, *KPIGoal()*, *KPIStatus()*, and *KPITrend()* MDX functions to query KPIs. For example, the following MDX statement retrieves the properties of the Reseller Sales KPI that you implement in this chapter, sliced by Product Category for the year 2003:

```
SELECT {KPIValue("Reseller Sales"),
KPIGoal("Reseller Sales"),
KPIStatus("Reseller Sales"),
KPITrend("Reseller Sales")} ON COLUMNS,
[Dim Product].[Product Category].Members  ON ROWS
FROM [Adventure Works]
WHERE [Date].[Calendar].[Calendar Year].&[2003]
```

Implementing Actions

Actions can extend your cubes in versatile ways. For example, suppose that a user has drilled down to the lowest level of the Product dimension and wants to see the individual sales orders placed for that product. If the order information is not stored in the cube, you can implement a reporting action that lets the user request an SSRS report that displays the order data from another system.

> **BEST PRACTICES** **UNDERSTAND CLIENT-SPECIFIC FEATURES**
>
> SSAS actions are defined in the cube but are interpreted and initiated by the client application. Not all clients support actions. For example, Excel 2007 supports actions, but SSRS does not. Therefore, before implementing actions, you need to consider the reporting tools your users will use to browse the cube.

Understanding Action Types

You can define several action types to integrate your cube with client applications. The action type informs the client application about how it should interpret the action. There are three main action types that are consistent with the Cube Designer user interface:

- **Regular actions**   Multipurpose actions that can retrieve information from different places. Regular actions can be further subdivided based on the action content, as Table 6-4 shows.

TABLE 6-4 Regular Action Types

CONTENT TYPE	PURPOSE
Dataset	The action content is an MDX statement.
Proprietary	The action content is client-specific. The client is responsible for interpreting the semantic meaning of the action.
Rowset	The action content is a command statement to retrieve data. Unlike the Dataset action, however, a Rowset action targets any OLE DB–compliant data source, including a relational database.
Statement	The action content represents an OLE DB command. Unlike the Dataset and Rowset actions, the statement should not yield any results other than success or failure.
URL (default)	The action content is a URL and should indicate one of the standard protocols, such as HTTP, HTTPS, FTP, FILE, or MAIL. For security reasons, a client application might ignore protocols other than HTTP and HTTPS.

- **Drillthrough actions**   Let the client request the details behind aggregated cell values in the cube. This is the only action type that the client application can send to SSAS for execution.

- **Reporting actions**   Can be used to request SSRS reports. The action command is the URL report path along with optional report parameters.

Creating an Action

Follow these steps to implement a new action:

1. Open the cube in the Cube Designer, and then click the Actions tab, as shown in Figure 6-8.

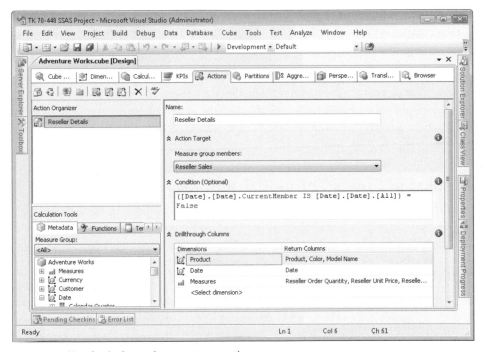

FIGURE 6-8 Use the Actions tab to create an action.

2. Click the New Action, New Drillthrough Action, or New Reporting Action toolbar button to create a regular, drillthrough, or reporting action, respectively.

3. Configure the action properties.

Common action properties that apply to all action types include action name, target, and condition. Each action type also supports specific properties. For example, when configuring a drillthrough action, you need to specify a list of drillthrough columns that the end user will see when the action is executed.

Understanding Action Discovery

In the process of configuring the action, you specify the action target, which consists of the target type and object. If you want to target an attribute hierarchy, for example, you would choose Attribute members as the target type and the attribute hierarchy as the target object.

Suppose that you have a Web page that takes a product identifier as a query parameter—for example, *http://www.adventureworks.com/olap/ShowTransactions.aspx?ProductName='Road Bike'*—and then displays the order transactions for a given product as the result of that query. Suppose also that the Product dimension has a *ProductName* attribute. For the query to work, you need this action to be available only when the user browses the cube by the *ProductName* attribute hierarchy, so you can get the product name from the *ProductName.CurrentMember. Name* expression. To scope the action this way, set its *Target Type* property to Attribute Members and its *Target Object* property to *Dim Product.ProductName*. Optionally, you can specify an action condition in the form of an MDX expression that further restricts the action scope.

As part of the action discovery stage, the client sends the server the user context, in the form of coordinates, to retrieve the actions defined for that scope. The server matches the action scope against the coordinates to identify the actions that are applicable for that scope. If such actions are discovered, the cube resolves the action command and returns it to the client. The client has final say over whether the action will be presented to and executed by the user.

Localizing Cubes Through Translations

SSAS makes it easy for you to support international users by defining translations in the cube. As its name suggests, a *translation* is a translated version of cube metadata (such as captions of measures, dimensions, perspectives, and KPIs) and data (members of attribute hierarchies).

Translating Cubes

To translate the cube metadata—including captions of cubes, cube dimensions, measure groups, measures, KPIs, actions, and named sets—open the Cube Designer, and then click the Translations tab. Click the New Translation button on the toolbar, and then select the language for which you want to define a translation. For each element in the cube, enter a caption that has been *localized* (translated to a given foreign language).

Translating Dimensions

Follow these steps to implement a dimension translation:

1. Open the dimension in the Dimension Designer, and then click the Translations tab.

2. Click the New Translation button on the toolbar, and from the drop-down list, select the language for which you want to define a translation. Enter a localized caption for each element in the cube.

3. To localize dimension members, select the intersecting cell between the attribute hierarchy and the language column, and then click the ellipsis (...) button.

4. In the Attribute Data Translation dialog box that appears, select the column of the dimension table that stores the translated caption, as shown in Figure 6-9.

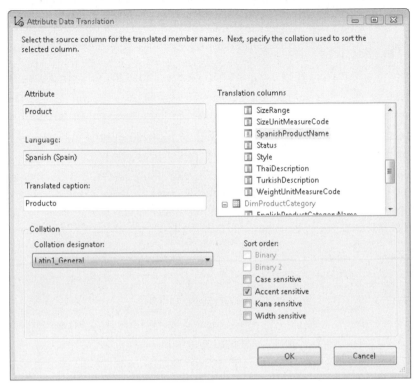

FIGURE 6-9 Use the Attribute Data Translation dialog box to localize the attribute caption and data.

By default, SSAS selects a translation based on the local culture of the current thread. At design time, the easiest way to test translations is to use the Cube Browser and select the desired language from the Languages drop-down list.

Implementing Cube Perspectives

SSAS cubes can become quite large and span several measure groups, but a large dimensional model might be overwhelming to end users. This is where perspectives can help.

A *cube perspective* represents a subset of the cube. Its main purpose is to reduce the perceived complexity of a large cube by exposing only a subset of the cube objects. For example, if the Adventure Works reseller sales department is mostly interested in browsing reseller sales, you can create a perspective that includes only the Reseller Sales measure group and its associated dimensions. By default, the cube has a single perspective that exposes the entire cube content.

> **IMPORTANT** **PERSPECTIVES ARE NOT A SECURITY MECHANISM**
>
> Perspectives are not a security mechanism, and you cannot use them to enforce restricted access to portions of the cube. Object security policies pass through the containing perspectives. For example, if the user does not have access to a given dimension, that dimension will not show in the perspectives that contain it.

Defining Perspectives

You can create new perspectives by using the Perspectives tab of the Cube Designer. To do so, follow these steps:

1. Open the cube in the Cube Designer, and then click the Perspectives tab.

2. Click the New Perspective button on the toolbar, and then specify the name of the perspective.

3. Select the objects to be included in the perspective. These objects can include measure groups, measures, dimensions, hierarchies, attributes, KPIs, actions, and calculations. For example, Figure 6-10 shows a cube that has Internet Sales and Reseller Sales perspectives to provide logical views pertinent to the Internet and reseller sales subject areas.

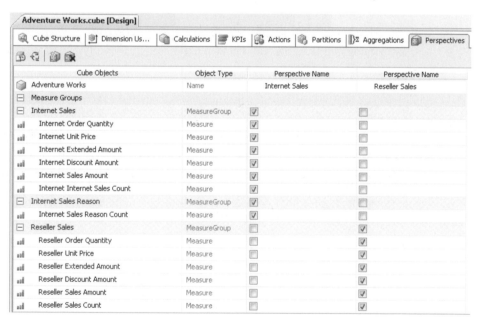

FIGURE 6-10 Implement perspectives to define logical views of the cube metadata.

In this practice, you will see how to create KPIs, actions, translations, and perspectives to help Adventures Works employees track reseller performance, drill through data, view cube information in Spanish, and see only the data they need to see.

EXERCISE 1 Implement the Reseller Sales KPI

In this exercise, you will learn how to implement a Reseller Sales KPI for Adventure Works to track the reseller sales against a predefined goal.

1. Open the TK 70-448 SSAS Project in BIDS (the ..\Source\Ch 06\TK448-ch06 Lesson 1\ folder in the installed practice files within the Documents folder for your user account).

2. Open the Adventure Works cube in the Cube Designer, and then click the KPIs tab.

3. Click the New KPI button on the toolbar.

4. Type **Reseller Sales** in the Name box.

5. Select the Reseller Sales measure group in the Associated Measure Group drop-down list.

6. For the sake of simplicity, the value of the Reseller Sales KPI will be supplied from the existing Reseller Sales Amount measure. Type **[Measures].[Reseller Sales Amount]** in the Value Expression box.

7. For the current period, Adventure Works wants to see reseller sales increase 40 percent over the previous period. Enter the following expression in the Goal Expression box:

```
1.40 * ([Date].[Calendar].PrevMember, [Measures].[Reseller Sales Amount])
```

Alternatively, you can select the Metadata and Functions tabs to drag metadata objects and MDX functions from the Calculations Tools pane to construct the expression. Note that the KPI Designer uses color coding in the expression to emphasize reserved words and functions.

8. Leave Gauge as the status indicator. Enter the following expression in the Status box:

```
Case
When KpiValue("Reseller Sales")/KpiGoal("Reseller Sales") >= 1
Then 1
When KpiValue("Reseller Sales")/KpiGoal("Reseller Sales")< 1
And KpiValue("Reseller Sales")/KpiGoal("Reseller Sales")>= .85
Then 0
Else -1
End
```

9. Leave the Trend Indicator drop-down list set to Standard Arrow. Enter the following expression in the Trend Expression box:

```
([Measures].[Reseller Sales Amount] -
([Order Date].[Calendar].PrevMember,
[Measures].[Reseller Sales Amount]))/
[Measures].[Reseller Sales Amount]
```

10. Deploy the solution to send the changes to the server and process the Adventure Works cube.

11. Now that the Reseller Sales KPI is ready, you will test it in the Browser view of the KPI Designer. With the KPIs tab still open, click the Browser View button on the toolbar, and then click the Reconnect button to create a new session.

12. In the Filter pane, expand the Dimension drop-down list, and then select the Date dimension. Expand the Hierarchy drop-down list, and then select the Calendar user hierarchy. Expand the Filter Expression drop-down list, and then select the year 2003 check box and click OK. The values of the Reseller Sales KPI change to reflect the filter selection.

EXERCISE 2   Implement a Drillthrough Action, a Translation, and Perspectives

In this exercise, you will learn how to implement a drillthrough action, a dimension translation, and two perspectives. Suppose that the end users want to see the individual resale order transactions behind a given aggregate cell in the cube. Follow these steps to implement the Reseller Details drillthrough action:

1. Open the Adventure Works cube in the Cube Designer.

2. Click the Actions tab.

3. Click the New Drillthrough Action button on the toolbar. The Cube Designer creates an empty action named Drillthrough Action.

4. Type **Reseller Details** in the Name box.

5. A drillthrough action can be associated with measure groups only. Expand the Measure Group Members drop-down list, and then select Reseller Sales.

6. A drillthrough action can potentially return many rows. You can use an MDX condition to limit the scope of the action. Suppose that you want the Reseller Sales drillthrough action to be activated only when the user drills down to the Date level of the Date dimension. To achieve this, enter the following expression in the Condition box:

```
([Date].[Date].CurrentMember IS [Date].[Date].[All]) = False
```

7. Use the Drillthrough Columns pane to specify the columns to show to the end user when the user initiates the drillthrough action. To do so, from the Dimensions drop-down list, select a dimension such as Product. Then, in the Return Columns drop-down list, select the check box for the columns you want to display. You can choose any measures from the targeted measure group and/or attributes from the dimension joined to it. Select the Product, Color, and Model Name attribute check boxes of the Product dimension, the Date attribute of the Date dimension, and all the measures that are part of the Reseller Sales measure group.

8. Expand the Additional Properties pane. To be sure that the action does not return too many rows and cause performance issues, type **100** in the Maximum Rows box.

9. Deploy the project. To test the drillthrough action, navigate to the Browser tab, and then create a pivot report with the Calendar hierarchy of the Date dimension on columns and the Reseller Sales Amount measure on data.

10. Assuming that the Calendar hierarchy is not expanded to its lowest level, right-click a Reseller Amount cell and notice that the Reseller Details action is not shown.

11. Expand the Calendar hierarchy to the Date level. Again, right-click a Reseller Amount cell, and notice that the Reseller Details action is now available, as Figure 6-11 shows.

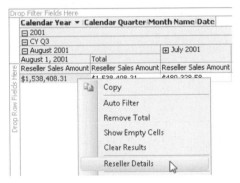

FIGURE 6-11 The client application is responsible for showing available actions for user selection.

12. Click Reseller Details to initiate the action, and notice that a new dialog box named Data Sample Viewer opens. The Data Sample Viewer dialog box shows the actual transactions that were loaded from the fact table when the cube was processed.

EXERCISE 3   Implement a Dimension Translation

Suppose that the Adventure Works cube will be browsed by Spanish-speaking users. Follow these steps to localize the Product dimension for Spanish speakers by implementing a dimension translation:

1. In Solution Explorer, double-click the Product dimension to open it in the Dimension Designer, and then click the Translations tab.

2. Click the New Translation button on the toolbar, select the Spanish (Spain) language in the Select Language dialog box that appears, and then click OK. A new column titled Spanish (Spain) is added to the grid.

3. Localize the dimension name to Spanish by typing **Producto** in the Dim Product row. Localize the name of the Product attribute hierarchy, the dimension key, by typing **Producto** in the Product row.

4. To localize the captions of the members in the Product hierarchy, select the intersecting cell between the Spanish (Spain) column and the Product attribute hierarchy. Click the ellipsis (...) button inside the cell to open the Attribute Data Translation dialog box.

5. In the Translation Columns list, select the SpanishProductName column, and then click OK. Notice that the Producto cell now has an icon that indicates that the attribute data for this attribute hierarchy has been localized.

6. To test the Spanish translation, deploy the solution, and then open the Adventure Works cube in the Cube Designer. Click the Browser tab. Create a report that uses the Product attribute hierarchy on rows and Internet Sales Amount on data.

7. Expand the Language drop-down list, and then select Spanish (Spain). Notice that the captions of the Product attribute hierarchy and its members are now in Spanish, as Figure 6-12 shows.

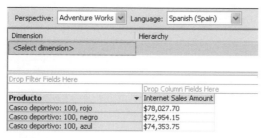

FIGURE 6-12 To test translations in the Cube Browser, set the Language drop-down list to the required language.

EXERCISE 4   Implement a Perspective

As the Adventure Works cube grows in complexity, users might find it difficult to navigate through its metadata. In this exercise, you will create Internet Sales and Reseller Sales perspectives to show only selected objects of the cube.

1. Open the Adventure Works cube in the Cube Designer, and then navigate to the Perspectives tab.

2. Click the New Perspective button on the toolbar. A new column is added to the grid.

3. Change the name of the new perspective from Perspective to **Internet Sales**.

4. Clear the check boxes for the Reseller Sales measure group, the Reseller Sales KPI, and the Reseller Details action.

5. Repeat steps 2 and 3 to create a new **Reseller Sales** perspective.

6. Clear the check boxes for the Internet Sales, Internet Sales Reason, and Internet Customers measure groups and the Customer, Sales Reason, and Internet Sales Order Details dimensions.

7. Deploy the solution, and then navigate to the Browser tab in the Cube Designer.

8. Expand the Perspective drop-down list, and then select the Reseller Sales perspective. Notice that the cube metadata pane changes to show only the objects that are included in the Reseller Sales perspective, as Figure 6-13 shows.

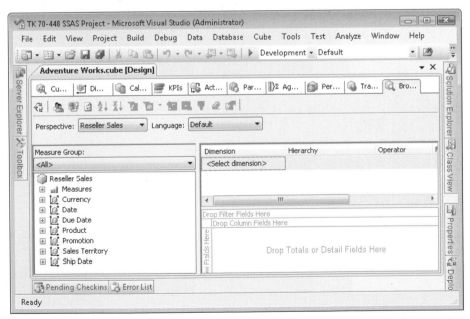

FIGURE 6-13 The Reseller Sales perspective filters the cube metadata to show only the cube objects that are included in the perspective.

Lesson 3: Creating Calculations and Queries by Using MDX

Estimated lesson time: 45 minutes

SSAS lets you quickly build dimensional models that provide essential OLAP and data mining features. However, chances are that in real life, business needs will require you to go beyond what the dimensional model can provide and enhance the cube with business logic. MDX gives you the programming power to implement custom calculations and unlock the full potential of SSAS. This lesson provides essential coverage of MDX programming by explaining how you can work with MDX queries, calculated members, and named sets.

Understanding MDX Syntax

Although originally developed for SSAS, over the years MDX has become the common language of OLAP. Most OLAP vendors have embraced or are currently adopting the XML for Analysis (XMLA) specification (see References), which describes the MDX language. As a result, there are many OLAP servers and browsers on the market that use MDX as a programming language in one form or another.

In SSAS, MDX is used in two main ways: to query and to extend multidimensional cubes. Client applications can send MDX queries to the cube to retrieve results. You can also use MDX expressions to extend your cubes. For example, you can use MDX to implement business metrics such as KPIs.

MDX Fundamentals

The results of an MDX query or expression depend on the current context in the cube. To use MDX effectively, you need to understand how to navigate the cube space by referencing tuples and sets.

TUPLES

A *tuple* is a multidimensional coordinate that identifies a single cell in the cube space. A tuple is produced by one member that is taken from one or more attribute hierarchies. For example, the tuple [Product].[Product].[Road Bike], [Date].[Year].[2004], [Measures].[Internet Sales] references a cell found at the intersection of product Road Bike, year 2004, and measure Internet Sales; the cube measures are treated as members of a special Measures dimension.

> **BEST PRACTICES** **REFERENCE DIMENSION MEMBERS**
>
> When you reference a dimension member in a tuple, you can use the member name (for example, [Product].[Product].[Mountain-100]). However, this syntax works only if there is a single product with that name. Rather than using the member name, you can resolve the member uniquely by using its key. To reference a member by key, you prefix the key with an ampersand (&). Assuming that you have a product with a key of 10, [Product].[Product].&[10] will resolve that member uniquely, even if there are other products with the same name.

Because the cube space typically consists of many attribute hierarchies, enumerating each of them is tedious. When you omit an attribute hierarchy, its default member (usually the hierarchy *All* member) is used.

SETS

An *MDX set* is a collection of tuples with the same dimensionality, or attribute hierarchies. For example, the following set is a valid set consisting of two tuples that have the same dimensionality:

```
{([Sales Territory].[Country].[All Countries],[Date].[Year].[2004], [Product].[Product].
[Mountain-100]),
([Sales Territory].[Country].[All Countries],[Date].[Year].[2004], [Product].[Product].
[Road-200])}
```

The following set is invalid because its tuples have different dimensionality: The first tuple uses the Customer dimension, and the second uses the Territory dimension:

```
{([Customer].[John Doe], [Date].[Year].[2003], [Product].[Product].[Mountain-100]),
([Sales Territory].[Country].[Canada],
[Date].[Year].[2003], [Product].[Product].[Road-200])}
```

Basic MDX Queries

The basic MDX query consists of a *SELECT* statement that has the following syntax:

```
SELECT [ * | ( <SELECT query axis clause>
    [ , <SELECT query axis clause> ... ] ) ]
FROM <SELECT subcube clause>
[ <SELECT slicer axis clause> ]
```

For example, the following MDX query returns the Internet Sales Amount measure on columns, broken down by product categories or rows, and filtered for calendar year 2004 only:

```
Select [Measures].[Internet Sales Amount] on Columns,
    [Product].[Category].Members on Rows
From [Adventure Works]
Where [Date].[Calendar Year].&[2003]
```

QUERY AXES

A query can have up to 128 axes (numbered from 0 to 127). The preceding query uses only two. The first five axes are named COLUMNS, ROWS, PAGES, SECTIONS, and CHAPTERS. Note that although you can project the results on many axes, you cannot skip axes. For example, you cannot request the ROWS axis without the COLUMNS axis. Rather than using the axis alias, you can use the ordinal position for the axis—for example, you can use 0 in place of COLUMNS.

Typically, the *FROM* clause specifies the name of the cube to query. Alternatively, the *FROM* clause can use another *SELECT* statement that defines a portion, or subcube, of the cube. The slicer axis filters the query results.

CALCULATED MEMBERS

Optionally, the query can request calculated columns in the form of calculated members by using a *WITH* clause before the *SELECT* statement. For example, the following query defines a *Gross Profit* calculated member as a sum between the Internet Sales Amount and Reseller Sales Amount measures:

```
With  Member [Gross Profit] AS
    '[Measures].[Internet Sales Amount] +
    [Measures].[Reseller Sales Amount]'
Select {[Measures].[Internet Sales Amount],[Gross Profit]}
on Columns,
    [Product].[Category].Members on Rows
```

```
From [Adventure Works]
Where [Date].[Calendar Year].&[2003]
```

Frequently used calculated members can be defined inside the cube so that they are readily available to all clients.

Applying MDX Functions

MDX provides a host of useful functions to navigate the cube space. Here are a few of the most commonly used functions.

The *CurrentMember* Function

The *CurrentMember* function takes a hierarchy and returns the current member in respect to a given cell coordinate. For example, the tuple [Order Date].[Calendar].CurrentMember, [Measures].[Reseller Sales Amount] returns the Reseller Sales Amount for the member of the Calendar hierarchy that references the current cell. The *CurrentMember* is the default property of a dimension member and often is omitted.

Functions for Navigating Hierarchies

MDX provides functions such as *PrevMember*, *Children*, and *Parent* for navigating hierarchies. *PrevMember* takes a member and returns a previous member in the hierarchy. For example, [Order Date].[Calendar].PrevMember returns the previous member with respect to the current member of the Calendar hierarchy. So if the Calendar hierarchy is expanded to the Year level and the current cell is referenced by year 2004, *PrevMember* will return year 2003.

EXAM TIP

The *PrevMember* function is frequently used to define the KPI Trend or Goal properties. For example, the Reseller Sales KPI uses the following expression to set the Goal property to 40 percent more than the Reseller Sales Amount for the previous date period:

```
1.40 * ([Date].[Calendar].PrevMember, [Measures].[Reseller Sales Amount])
```

Consequently, if the user browses the cube data by years, the *PrevMember* function will return the previous year for each year. If the user browses data by quarters, the *PrevMember* will return the previous quarter for each quarter, and so on.

The *Members* function returns all members of a hierarchy. For example, [Product].[Product].[Product].Members returns all products excluding the *All* member. The *Children* function returns the members below a given member. For example, [Date].[Calendar].[Calendar Year]. [2003].Children returns all quarters of year 2003, assuming that the level below the Year level in the Calendar hierarchy is Quarter. In contrast, the *Parent* function returns the member's parent in a given hierarchy. So [Product].[Categories].[Product]. [Road Bike].Parent returns the *Bikes* member of the Product Category hierarchy.

Functions for Navigating Time

MDX provides a few functions, such as *Lag* and *ParallelPeriod*, to help you navigate the Time dimension. The *Lag* function returns a member at a given offset from a given member—for example, [Order Date].[Calendar].Lag(1) returns the previous sibling of the current member. So if the current member is at the Quarter level, *Lag(1)* will return the previous quarter. If it is at the Year level, *Lag(1)* will return the previous year, and so on.

ParallelPeriod returns the member from a prior period in the same relative position as a specified member with an optional offset; if no member is specified, 0 is assumed. For example, ParallelPeriod ([Date].[Calendar].[Calendar Quarter], [Date].[Calendar].[Month Name].[October 2003]) returns October 2002.

EXAM TIP

Another time-related function commonly used in MDX expressions is the *PeriodsToDate* function. This function returns a set of sibling members from the same level as a given member, starting with the first sibling and ending with the given member. For example, the following query uses the *PeriodsToDate* function to return the Internet sales for the first 10 months of 2003:

```
select [Measures].[Internet Sales Amount] on 0,
PeriodsToDate([Date].[Calendar].[Calendar Year],
[Date].[Calendar].[Month Name].&[10]&[2003]) on 1
from [Adventure Works]
```

For a list of all MDX functions and how to use them, see the topic "Multidimensional Expressions (MDX) Reference" in SQL Server 2008 Books Online, included in the References section at the end of this book.

Creating Calculated Members

A calculated member is a dimension member whose value is calculated dynamically at run time. Remember that the cube measures are considered members of a special Measures dimension. The definitions of the cube calculated members and named sets become part of the cube MDX script, which can be accessed from the Calculations tab of the Cube Designer. Unlike a regular measure, a calculated member does not increase the cube size because the server stores only its definition, not its data.

Calculated Member Syntax

The following statement creates a *Sales Amount* calculated member as the sum between the Internet Sales Amount and Reseller Sales Amount measures:

```
CREATE MEMBER CURRENTCUBE.[MEASURES].[Sales Amount]
 AS [Measures].[Internet Sales Amount] +
   [Measures].[Reseller Sales Amount],
FORMAT_STRING = "Currency",
VISIBLE = 1;
```

You define a calculated member by using the *CREATE MEMBER* MDX statement, which uses an MDX expression. A calculated member has a few properties such as *FORMAT_STRING* and *Visible* that control its display behavior.

When to Use Calculated Members

As you investigate whether to implement a calculated member, you have the following options:

- If you need a measure that does not belong to a particular measure group, consider defining it as a calculated member. For example, the Sales Amount measure spans both Internet Sales and Reseller Sales measure groups. Thus, it is a good candidate to become a calculated member.

- Consider creating a calculated member when you need a nonadditive measure that operates uniformly across dimension levels. For example, a calculated member that calculates the average reseller profit amount (Reseller Sales Amount / Reseller Sales Count) returns the expected results no matter how the end user slices the cube. It simply takes the measure values at the current cube coordinate and divides them. In comparison, an additive measure with a *SUM* aggregate function will produce incorrect results because it will sum up the values.

> **NOTE SCOPE ASSIGNMENTS**
>
> Scope assignments let developers write to the cube space and overwrite the measure aggregation behavior. In general, however, calculated members do not have a default aggregation function. If you need to scope the expression at a certain level of a dimension—at the leaf member level, for example—and let the server aggregate the measure from that level up, it is probably better to use standard measure and scope assignments. Scope assignments are not covered in this book.

Defining Named Sets

As its name suggests, a named set is an MDX construct that has an alias and that returns a set of dimension members. You can explicitly specify the set tuples, or you can use standard set-producing MDX functions, such as *Children* or *Members*. For example, the following named set returns the top 50 customers:

```
CREATE SET CURRENTCUBE.[Top 50 Most Profitable Customers]
  AS
    TopCount (
      (Existing [Customer].[Customer].[Customer].Members),
               50,
               [Measures].[Internet Sales Amount]
        );
```

The *Members* function returns all members of the Customer attribute hierarchy in the Dim Customer dimension. Use the triple notation syntax, *Dimension.Attribute.Attribute*, to exclude the *All* member of the hierarchy. The *TopCount* function ranks the set by evaluating the customer *[Internet Sales Amount]* total and returns the top 50 customers only. Last, the *Existing* keyword forces the set to be reevaluated within the current context, such as when the user selects a different time period.

SSAS supports two types of named sets based on how the server evaluates them. A *static named set* is evaluated once by the server. In contrast, a *dynamic named set*, which was introduced in SSAS 2008, is evaluated for each query. By default, BIDS creates dynamic named sets. For more information about static and dynamic named sets, see the blog entry "MDX in Katmai: Dynamic Named Sets" by Mosha Pasumansky (see References).

PRACTICE Extending Cubes by Using MDX Expressions

In this practice, you will create MDX queries, calculated members, and named sets.

EXERCISE 1   Create and Execute MDX Queries

In this exercise, you will learn how to use SSMS to create and test an MDX query.

1. Open SSMS.

2. Press Ctrl+Alt+T to open Template Explorer.

3. In Template Explorer, click the Analysis Server button on the toolbar to see the Analysis Services templates only.

4. Expand the MDX node, expand the Queries node, and then double-click the Basic Query template. SSMS should generate the following query:

```
Select <row_axis, mdx_set,> on Columns,
     <column_axis, mdx_set,> on Rows
From <from_clause, mdx_name,>
Where <where_clause, mdx_set,>
```

5. When prompted, connect to the SSAS server.

6. Select the TK 70-448 SSAS Project database in the Available Databases drop-down list. SSMS shows the metadata of the Adventure Works cube in the Cube pane.

7. In the Cube pane, expand the Measures folder and the Internet Sales measure group, and then drag the Internet Sales Amount measure before the ON Columns clause of the query. Delete the <row_axis, mdx_set,> clause.

8. In the Cube pane, expand the Product dimension. Drag the Category attribute hierarchy onto the query ROWS axis. Type **.Members** after [Product].[Category] so that it becomes [Product].[Category].Members. Delete the <column_axis, mdx_set,> clause.

9. In the Cube pane, drag the root node, Adventure Works, so that it follows the FROM keyword. Delete the <from_clause, mdx_name,> clause.

10. Expand the Date dimension, expand Date.Calendar Year and Calendar Year, and then drag 2003 so that it follows the WHERE clause of the query. Delete <where_clause, mdx_set,>.

11. Click the Execute button on the toolbar to execute the query and see the results. Your screen should match the screen shown in Figure 6-14.

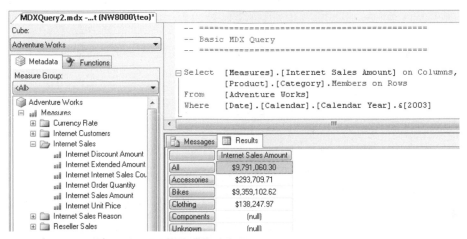

FIGURE 6-14 Use SSMS to write and test MDX queries.

EXERCISE 2 Implement a Calculated Member

In this exercise, you will use BIDS to implement a *Sales Amount* calculated member whose definition is saved in the cube script. You will define the *Sales Amount* calculated member as a sum of the Internet Sales Amount and Resellers Sales Amount measures.

1. Open the TK 70-448 SSAS Project in BIDS (the ..\Source\Ch 06\TK448-ch06 Lesson 2 folder of the installed practice files).

2. Open the Adventure Works cube in the Cube Designer, and then navigate to the Calculations tab. By default, the Form View button on the toolbar is selected, which lets you work with one script object at a time.

3. Click the New Calculated Member button on the toolbar.

4. Type **[Sales Amount]** as the calculated member name.

5. Enter the following expression in the Expression box:

```
[Measures].[Internet Sales Amount] +
[Measures].[Reseller Sales Amount]
```

6. Select Currency from the Format String drop-down list, as Figure 6-15 shows.

7. Click the Calculation Properties button on the toolbar.

8. In the Calculation Properties dialog box, expand the Calculation Name drop-down list, and then select the [Measures].[Sales Amount] calculated member.

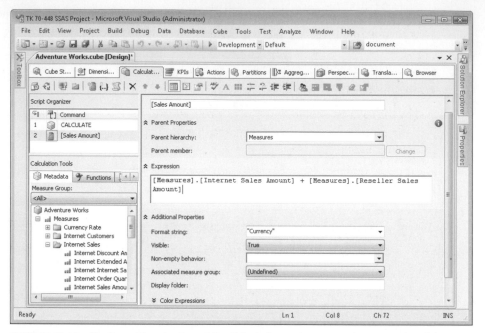

FIGURE 6-15 Use the Form View toolbar of the Calculations tab to enter the properties of the calculation member in predefined fields.

9. In the Display Folder column, type **Sales Summary**. Leave the Associated Measure Group column empty—because the Sales Amount calculated member spans two measure groups, it cannot be logically associated with either of them. Click OK to close the Calculation Properties dialog box.

10. Deploy the solution, and then click the Browser tab.

11. In the Measure Group pane, expand the Measures node, and notice that there is a new Sales Summary folder.

12. Expand the Sales Summary folder. Notice that the Sales Amount calculated member has a special icon to differentiate it from the regular measures.

13. To test the Sales Amount calculated member, drag it to the data section of the report.

EXERCISE 3 Implement a Named Set

In this exercise, you will implement a named set in BIDS that will return the top 50 customers by evaluating the Internet Sales Amount measure.

1. With the Adventure Works cube open in the Cube Designer, navigate to the Calculations tab.

2. Click the New Named Set button on the toolbar.

3. In the Name box, type **[Top 50 Most Profitable Customers]**.

4. Enter the following expression in the Expression box:

```
TopCount (
(EXISTING [Customer].[Customer].[Customer].Members),
50, [Measures].[Internet Sales Amount])
```

5. Deploy the solution, and then switch to the Browser tab. If the report pane has existing results displayed, select the results and then click the Clear Results button on the toolbar to clear them.

   The Browser does not support named sets on reports. However, you can test a named set as a filter to the report.

BEST PRACTICES   **USE A PIVOTTABLE REPORT TO TEST NAMED SETS**

You can create a PivotTable report in Excel 2007 to test named sets on report columns or rows.

---

6. Expand the Customer dimension. SSAS has discovered that the [Top 50 Most Profitable Customers] named set uses members of the Customer dimension, so it has automatically associated the named set with the Customer dimension. Although you cannot assign the named set to another dimension or measure group, you can use the Calculation Properties window to assign the named set to a display folder inside the Customer dimension.

7. Drag the [Top 50 Most Profitable Customers] named set onto the dimension filter.

8. Drag the Customer attribute hierarchy onto rows and Internet Sales Amount onto data, as Figure 6-16 shows. Notice that only the top 50 customers are returned.

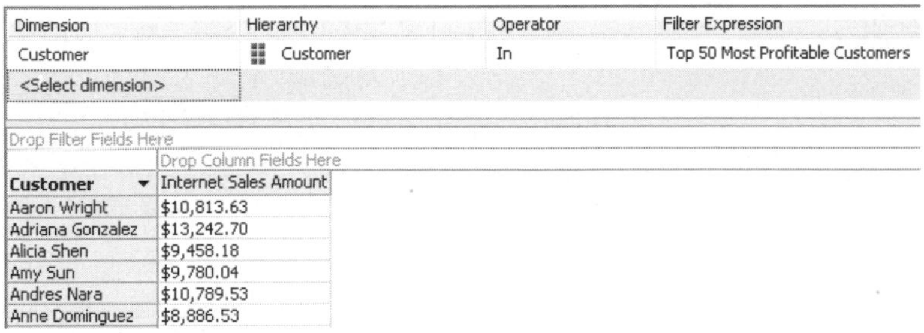

Dimension	Hierarchy	Operator	Filter Expression
Customer	Customer	In	Top 50 Most Profitable Customers
<Select dimension>			

Drop Filter Fields Here

	Drop Column Fields Here
Customer ▾	Internet Sales Amount
Aaron Wright	$10,813.63
Adriana Gonzalez	$13,242.70
Alicia Shen	$9,458.18
Amy Sun	$9,780.04
Andres Nara	$10,789.53
Anne Dominguez	$8,886.53

FIGURE 6-16 Test the named set in the Browser tab of Cube Designer by dragging it onto the dimension filter.

Case Scenario: Extending SSAS Cubes

As it stands, the Adventure Works cube has data only for Internet sales. However, the business requirements state that the reporting solution must support consolidated reports that show both Internet and reseller sales. Adventure Works is also in the process of developing a Web-based dashboard solution, which needs to display vital business metrics in the form of KPIs.

1. What do you need to change in the dimensional model to accommodate the reseller sales?

2. How could you implement the Adventure Works KPIs?

Chapter Summary

- The cube space is defined by attributes. Sometimes there are logical relationships among attributes within the same dimension. You should understand and explicitly define such relationships to optimize the UDM.

- In addition to attribute hierarchies, you can define user hierarchies that provide useful navigation paths in the UDM. A dimension can have several user hierarchies.

- You can browse data in a measure group by a dimension only if the dimension is joined to the measure group. You must review the Dimension Usage tab and correct the dimension relationships if needed. In addition to regular relationships, SSAS supports other relationship types to support more complex schemas.

- Key performance indicators (KPIs) are quantifiable measures that organizations can use to track business performance. A KPI has four main properties: *Value*, *Goal*, *Status*, and *Target*.

- You can use cube actions to extend your cube functionality. With the exception of the drillthrough action, which is handled by SSAS, all other actions must be handled by external applications.

- Translations let modelers localize cube metadata, dimension metadata, and dimension member captions to foreign languages to support international users.

- Perspectives expose subviews of the cube metadata to reduce the perceived complexity of the cube.

- You can implement business calculations in the form of MDX calculated members and named sets.

CHAPTER 7

Managing SSAS Storage, Processing, and Deployment

The dilemma that many people face with SQL Server Analysis Services (SSAS) and online analytical processing (OLAP) technologies is how to maximize query performance with large data volumes while using the smallest amount of storage space possible. An optimal storage strategy produces fast queries while maintaining reasonable cube-processing times. SSAS goes a long way toward meeting demanding performance and scalability requirements. And you can improve this performance and scalability even more by choosing an optimum storage mode and creating useful cube aggregations.

In the preceding SSAS chapters, you have been designing the Adventure Works data warehouse without knowing how SSAS stores multidimensional data. If your cubes are relatively small, they will probably perform well by using the default storage options. However, chances are that in real life, your cubes will be many times larger, and you might need to optimize their storage design and performance. In addition, you might need to implement low-latency OLAP solutions to minimize the time it takes new data to become available for querying. This chapter provides comprehensive coverage of SSAS storage options and optimization techniques. It also explores ways to partition measure groups to improve processing and query performance and describes ways to design and optimize cube aggregations.

In a typical SSAS enterprise environment, three groups of people are involved in the different phases of the SSAS cube's life cycle. Database developers focus on designing and programming the cube. Administrators are concerned with managing the cube. And end users query the cube and run reports.

As an SSAS administrator, you will perform various management tasks in different phases of the cube life cycle. Two ongoing activities that you need to master are deploying and processing SSAS objects. As this chapter demonstrates, SSAS provides a comprehensive management framework to help you perform these and other management activities.

The source code for this chapter is available in the ..\Source\Ch 07\ folder on the companion CD.

Exam objectives in this chapter:

- Implement storage design in a cube.
- Deploy SSAS databases and objects.
- Implement processing options.

Before You Begin

To complete this chapter, you must have:

- Knowledge of cube measure groups.
- Knowledge of dimensions.
- Two installed instances of SSAS to complete the practice exercises in Lesson 2.

Lesson 1: Defining Measure Group Partitions and Aggregations

Estimated lesson time: 40 minutes

The SSAS storage architecture is based on sound and flexible design goals. It lets administrators select a storage mode that provides an optimum balance between cube performance and storage space. The design is transparent to the client applications. As an administrator, you can change the design at any time after the cube is deployed.

Understanding Partitions

SSAS stores the measure group data in physical units called *partitions*. A partition defines the slice of the fact table data that is loaded into a measure group.

Reasons for Partitioning

By default, a new measure group has only one partition that stores all the data from the source fact table. However, creating additional partitions is beneficial for two main reasons:

- **Improved performance**   If a measure group has only one partition, the server must scan the entire partition to find the data it needs to satisfy a query, assuming that the data is not cached or stored as an aggregation. For example, suppose that the user queries the cube to find the Reseller Sales Amount total for year 2004. If the Reseller Sales measure group has only the default partition, the server must scan all the data in the measure group to calculate the total. In contrast, if the measure group is partitioned by year, the server needs to scan only the 2004 partition. Even if the query spans multiple years, partitioning can still yield better results because the server can query partitions in parallel.

- **Improved manageability**   Partitions can have different storage modes and aggregation designs, and you can manage them independently. For example, you can delete a partition without having to reprocess the cube. You can also process partitions independently of other partitions. For instance, you can process a partition that stores the most recent data more frequently than a partition that stores historical data. Last, partitioning reduces cube processing time because the server can process partitions in parallel.

To ensure that your application takes advantage of the power offered by partitioning, you should incorporate a good partitioning strategy early in the cube design cycle.

Considerations for Partitioning

A measure group is typically time dependent—that is, it has a foreign key to the Time dimension table. Therefore, a natural strategy is to partition by time (for example, by year, quarter, and month). Determining the best partition slice definition—that is, the number of records stored in the partition—is not an exact science. In general, you should avoid creating partitions that have fewer than 4,000 rows or more than 20 million rows, as well as partitions that are larger than 250 MB. You can find more guidelines about partition performance in the white paper "Microsoft SQL Server 2008 Analysis Services Performance Guide," by the Microsoft Analysis Services team (see References).

> **BEST PRACTICES USE A FORMAT CONVENTION FOR THE TIME PRIMARY KEY**
>
> Consider using a date format as the primary key of the Time dimension. For example, rather than using an identity column, consider an integer key with the format *YYYYMMDD* (for example, 20070412). Not only does this format make it easier to query the fact table because it will not have to be joined to the Time dimension table, but it also simplifies the partition slice definitions, especially if they need to be generated by the system—for example, if they need to be generated by using a SQL Server Integration Services (SSIS) package.

A measure group's partitions do not need to have uniform slice definitions. For example, a very volatile "hot" partition that stores the most recent data and is frequently queried could have a slice definition set to the current month. In contrast, a partition with historical data that spans different time periods, such as quarters, can have a coarser slice definition.

In addition, a measure group's partitions do not need to use the same fact table as a source. The database administrator (DBA) might have decided to split a large fact table into several smaller tables. As long as these tables have the same schema, you can bind partitions to separate fact tables.

Creating Measure Group Partitions

After you decide on the partition slice definition, you are ready to partition the cube measure group. You can create partitions during the design cycle by using Business Intelligence Development Studio (BIDS) or after the cube is deployed by using SQL Server Management Studio (SSMS). Both options use the same Partition Wizard and produce the same results. In general, you would use BIDS if you wanted your partition design to be part of the SSAS project, but to change the partition design after the cube is deployed, the administrator might prefer to use SSMS.

Changing the Default Partition Slice

Recall that, by default, a new measure group has a single partition that is bound to the entire fact table; this is called *table binding*. If both partitions will use the same fact table as a source, before adding a new measure group partition, you must change the default partition to use query binding. This narrows the partition slice of the default partition to leave space for the new partition.

Follow these steps to change the binding of the default partition:

1. In the Cube Designer in BIDS, click the Partitions tab, shown in Figure 7-1.

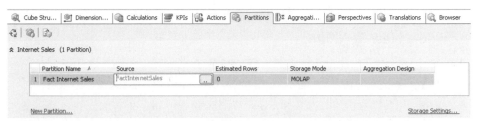

FIGURE 7-1 Use the Partitions tab to view the existing measure group partitions and create new ones.

2. Expand the measure group whose partition design you want to change.

3. Click the ellipsis (...) button in the Source column to open the Partition Source dialog box.

4. In the Binding Type drop-down list, select Query Binding, as Figure 7-2 shows.

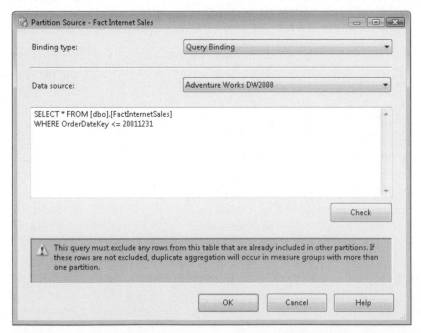

FIGURE 7-2 Before adding a new partition, change the binding type of the default partition to Query Binding.

5. Enter a *SELECT* query statement that defines the definition slice. Usually, you would select all rows whose date is less than or equal to the lower boundary of the new partition. Click OK.

BEST PRACTICES   **SPECIFY A CORRECT PARTITION SLICE**

The partition slice query specifies the fact table rows that will be loaded into the partition. As the warning message in the Partition Source dialog box indicates, when defining multiple partitions within a measure group, it is important to specify a correct *WHERE* clause so that no rows are lost or duplicated.

Adding a New Partition

After you rescope the default partition, you are ready to create a new partition by following these steps:

1. Note the upper boundary of the default partition, and then find the lower and upper boundaries of the new partition by querying the Time dimension table. Set the lower boundary of the next time period to be after the upper boundary of the default partition.

2. Back on the Partitions tab, select the default partition, and then click New Partition on the toolbar to launch the Partition Wizard.

3. Click Next on the wizard's Welcome page. On the Specify Source Information page, select the check box for the source fact table in the Available Tables list, and then click Next.

4. On the Restrict Rows page, select the Specify A Query To Restrict Rows check box, enter a *SELECT* query that defines the slice of the new partition For example, you might use the following query:

```
SELECT * FROM [dbo].[FactInternetSales]
WHERE OrderDateKey >= 20020101 AND OrderDateKey <= 20021231
```

5. Use the Processing And Storage Locations page, shown in Figure 7-3, to set up the partition location. By default, when the partition is processed, it stores data on the local server. An interesting feature that the SSAS storage architecture supports is *remote partitions*. A remote partition is processed by another SSAS server. In this deployment scenario, the local server receives queries and dispatches them to the remote server. Remote partitions give you additional options to scale a very large cube.

6. On the Completing The Wizard page, enter a name for the partition. This page also gives you the option to design aggregations, postpone the aggregation design, or copy the aggregation design from another partition. Click Finish.

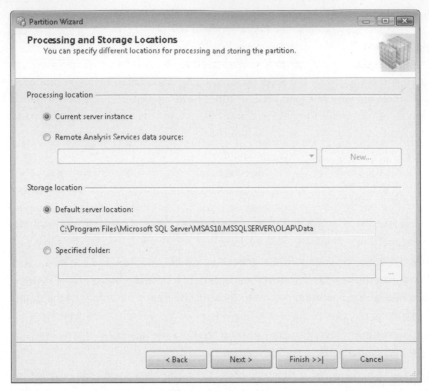

FIGURE 7-3 You can configure a new partition to be located and queried by a remote SSAS server.

Selecting Partition Storage Modes

The logical storage model of a cube consists of two layers: metadata and data. It might also include a third layer of aggregations. The metadata is what makes the cube appear as a logical entity to end users. The cube metadata is always stored on the SSAS server, but as an administrator, you can control the storage locations of the cube data and any aggregations.

Understanding Storage Modes

SSAS supports three storage modes: multidimensional OLAP (MOLAP), relational OLAP (ROLAP), and hybrid OLAP (HOLAP). Table 7-1 describes the effect the choice of storage mode has on query time, data latency, processing time, and storage size.

TABLE 7-1 Comparing Storage Modes

MODE	QUERY TIME	LATENCY	PROCESSING TIME	STORAGE SIZE
MOLAP	Fast	High	Fast	Medium
ROLAP	Slow	Low	Slow	Large
HOLAP	Medium	Medium	Fast	Small

The following discussion provides an overview of each storage mode.

MULTIDIMENSIONAL OLAP

With MOLAP, both data and aggregations are stored in file-based multidimensional structures created and managed by the SSAS server. MOLAP is the default storage mode because the MOLAP stores are very efficient; MOLAP cubes have the fastest query performance. With MOLAP, the server can index the data and aggregations for the best query performance, and MOLAP eliminates the network overhead that results if data is moved across the wire from the data source to the SSAS server.

With MOLAP, the server brings the cube data from the data source into the cube when the cube is processed. The data is duplicated because it exists in both the data source and the cube. MOLAP data latency is high because new data is available only when the partition is processed. However, the administrator can enable proactive caching on a MOLAP partition to implement real-time data refreshing. You will learn more about proactive caching in the section "Understanding Proactive Caching" later in this lesson.

MOLAP processing time is fast because the data is stored efficiently in a compressed format on the server rather than in a relational database. In general, the storage size of a MOLAP store is about 20 percent to 25 percent of the nonindexed relational data. Last, MOLAP scores in the middle in terms of storage space because the data exists both in the relational database and on the SSAS server.

RELATIONAL OLAP

With ROLAP, both the cube data and the cube aggregations remain in the relational database, so the SSAS server must create additional relational tables to hold the cube aggregations. If no aggregations are defined, ROLAP is the most efficient storage mode, but queries are slow because they must be satisfied from the relational database. If you need a low-latency partition and you cannot use proactive caching, ROLAP can be a practical solution.

HYBRID OLAP

As its name suggests, HOLAP is a hybrid between MOLAP and ROLAP. In HOLAP, the cube data remains in the relational store, but the aggregations are stored on the SSAS server. HOLAP is the most efficient mode in terms of disk space because detail-level data is not duplicated, as it is with MOLAP, and HOLAP requires less space to store aggregations than ROLAP does.

EXAM TIP

Choose the HOLAP storage mode if you want to store cube aggregations on the SSAS server but keep the fact data in the source database.

In terms of query performance, HOLAP scores in the middle. If the query can be satisfied entirely by existing aggregations, HOLAP performs as well as MOLAP. But if it cannot be satisfied, the query is sent to the relational database, and performance suffers. In terms of processing times, HOLAP cubes might be processed faster than either MOLAP or ROLAP cubes because data is read only once to create aggregations. However, because SSAS has an efficient storage architecture, in real life MOLAP and HOLAP should give you comparable processing times, so it is best to consider HOLAP only for large historical partitions that are queried infrequently.

Configuring Storage

You can configure the default storage mode for all partitions in a measure group by setting the StorageMode property for that measure group. However, you can overwrite the storage mode at the partition level. In BIDS, the easiest way to change the partition storage mode is to select the partition on the Partitions tab and then change its StorageMode property in the Properties window to one of the three standard storage modes, as Figure 7-4 shows.

FIGURE 7-4 You can set the StorageMode partition property to MOLAP, ROLAP, or HOLAP.

You can also select the partition, click the Storage Settings link (see Figure 7-1) displayed below it and to the right, and then click the Options button in the Partition Storage Settings dialog box. Next, in the Storage Options dialog box, expand the Storage Mode drop-down list and select the new storage mode.

To set the storage mode in SSMS, right-click the partition, and then select Properties. You can also open the Partition Storage Settings dialog box by clicking the Proactive Caching link in the Partition Properties dialog box.

Understanding Proactive Caching

As noted, with MOLAP and HOLAP storage modes, SSAS caches data (MOLAP storage mode only) and aggregations (both MOLAP and HOLAP) on the server. However, when you take a data "snapshot" by processing a cube, the data becomes outdated until you process the cube again. The amount of OLAP data latency that is acceptable will depend on your business requirements. In some cases, your end users might require up-to-date or even real-time information. A new feature of SSAS 2005, *proactive caching*, can help you solve data latency problems.

EXAM TIP

Proactive caching is especially useful when the relational database is transaction oriented and data changes at random. When data changes are predictable—such as when you use an extract, transform, and load (ETL) process to load data—consider processing the cube explicitly. When the data source is transaction oriented and you want minimum latency, consider configuring the cube to process automatically by using proactive caching.

How Proactive Caching Works

When you enable proactive caching, the server can listen for data change notifications and can update dimensions and measures dynamically in an "autopilot" mode. Figure 7-5 shows how proactive caching works.

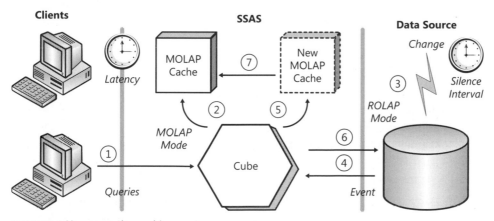

FIGURE 7-5 How proactive caching works

Look at this diagram closely to see how proactive caching works as data changes. For the sake of simplicity, assume that the cube being queried is a MOLAP cube.

STEADY STATE

In steady mode, no changes are happening to the relational data. Client applications submit Multidimension Expressions (MDX) queries to the cube, as shown in Figure 7-5, step 1. At step 2, the cube satisfies the queries from a MOLAP cache. The server listens for a data change notification event, which could be one of the following three types:

- **SQL Server**   This option uses the Microsoft SQL Server trace events that the relational engine raises when data is changed (SQL Server 2000 and later).

- **Client Initiated**   In this case, a client application notifies SSAS when it changes data by sending a NotifyTableChange XML for Analysis (XMLA) command.

- **Scheduled Polling**   With this option, the server periodically polls the required tables for changes.

UNSTEADY STATE

At some point, a data change occurs in the data source, as Figure 7-5, step 3 shows. This change triggers a notification event to the SSAS server (step 4). The server starts two stop-watches. The Silence Interval stopwatch measures the time elapsed between two consecutive data change events. This will reduce the number of false starts for building the new cache until the database is quiet again. For example, if data changes are occurring in batches, you do not want to start rebuilding the cache with each data change event. Instead, you can optimize proactive caching by defining a silence interval that allows a predefined amount of time for the batch changes to complete.

After data in the relational database is changed, the server knows that the MOLAP cache is out of date and starts building a new version of the cache (step 5). The Latency stopwatch specifies the maximum latency period of the MOLAP cache; the administrator can also predefine the maximum latency period. During the latency period, queries are still answered by the old MOLAP cache. When the latency period is exceeded, the server discards the old cache. While the new version of the MOLAP cache is being built, the server satisfies client queries from the ROLAP database (step 6). Last, when the new MOLAP cache is ready, the server activates it (step 7) and redirects client queries to it. Proactive caching enters a steady state again until the next data change event takes place.

Enabling Proactive Caching

For your convenience, SSAS supports several predefined partition storage settings, including settings for proactive caching. To view these settings in BIDS, open the Partition Storage Settings dialog box, shown in Figure 7-6, by clicking the Storage Settings link below the selected partition.

Table 7-2 describes the standard partition storage settings.

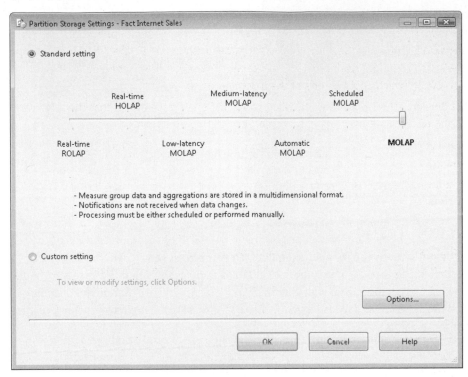

FIGURE 7-6 SSAS supports several predefined proactive caching modes.

TABLE 7-2 Standard Partition Storage Settings

MODE	QUERY TIME
Real-time ROLAP	As with standard ROLAP, partition data and aggregations are stored in the relational database. The server maintains an internal cache to improve query performance. When the change notification is received, the server drops the ROLAP cache to ensure that data is not out of sync with the data in the relational database.
Real-time HOLAP	As with standard HOLAP, partition data is stored in the re-lational database, and aggregations are stored in the cube. Aggregations are rebuilt as soon as a data change notifica-tion is received.
Low-latency MOLAP	The MOLAP cache expires in 30 minutes.
Medium-latency MOLAP	Similar to Automatic MOLAP except that the MOLAP cache expires in 4 hours.

MODE	QUERY TIME
Automatic MOLAP	The default silence interval is set to 10 seconds. As a result, the server will not react if the data change batches are fewer than 10 seconds apart. If there is not a period of silence, the server will start processing the cache in 10 minutes.
Scheduled MOLAP	Same as MOLAP except that the server will process the partition on a daily schedule.
MOLAP	The partition storage mode is standard MOLAP. Proactive caching is disabled. You need to process the partition to refresh data.

If the standard storage modes do not meet your data latency requirements, you can specify custom settings by clicking the Options button in the Partitions Storage Settings dialog box. The custom settings specify how often the MOLAP cache is rebuilt, whether the MOLAP cache is rebuilt on a schedule or as a result of a data change event, whether the server should revert to ROLAP when the cache is being rebuilt, and the type of data change notifications that will be used. Lesson 3, "Processing SSAS Objects," discusses the proactive caching custom settings in more detail.

Understanding Aggregations

No matter how you slice data, the cube always appears to contain every possible aggregated value. In reality, the aggregated values might not be stored in the cube. The server can derive the aggregated values in one of three ways:

- Assuming that the data has been requested before, the server can retrieve it from an internal cache.
- If the data is not found in the cache, the server searches for precalculated data aggregations stored in the cube.
- If no suitable aggregations are available, the server has no choice but to get the data from the partition and aggregate it on the fly.

As you can imagine, designing and building useful aggregations can speed query response times tremendously. Aggregations are precalculated summaries of data. Specifically, an aggregation contains the summarized values of all measures in a measure group by a combination of different attributes.

How Aggregations Are Used

To understand aggregations, consider the cube shown in Figure 7-7. This is a small cube consisting of two dimensions, Date and Product, and one measure, Sales Amount.

The cube has three aggregations based on different combinations of attribute hierarchies. The all-level aggregation stores the grand total Sales Amount. The intermediate aggregation stores the total Sales Amount for the year 2004 and Road Bikes product subcategories. Last, assuming that the fact table references Month and Product dimensions, there is also a fact-level aggregation for July 2004 and product Road-42.

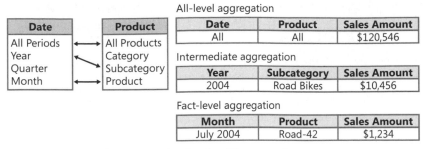

All-level aggregation

Date	Product	Sales Amount
All	All	$120,546

Intermediate aggregation

Year	Subcategory	Sales Amount
2004	Road Bikes	$10,456

Fact-level aggregation

Month	Product	Sales Amount
July 2004	Road-42	$1,234

FIGURE 7-7 Aggregations summarize data by different attributes.

Suppose that a query asks for the overall Sales Amount value. The server discovers that this query can be satisfied by the all-level aggregation alone. Rather than having to scan the partition data, the server promptly returns the result from the precalculated Sales Amount value taken from this aggregation. Even if there is not a direct aggregation hit, the server might be able to use intermediate aggregations to derive the result. For example, if the query asks for Sales Amount by product category, the server could use the intermediate aggregation, year 2004 and subcategory Road Bikes, to derive the total.

Why Not Create All Possible Aggregations?

If aggregations are so useful, why not create all possible aggregations in the cube to achieve the best performance? The short answer is that this would be counterproductive—all those aggregations would require enormous storage space and long processing times. The total number of aggregations would equal 2 raised to the power of the total number of attributes in the cube. For example, if you created all possible aggregations in the Adventure Works demo cube, you would end up with about 2 ^ 50 = 1.1258E+15 aggregations. You would need a lot of storage space!

Not only do excessive aggregations take more storage space, but they also increase cube processing time because aggregations are created when the cube is processed. Your goal should always be to find the optimal subset of aggregations that gives you the necessary increase in query performance without overwhelming the server.

You do not have to create aggregations manually. At design time, you can use the Aggregation Design Wizard to select useful aggregations for you. After the cube is deployed, you can use the query usage statistics to refine the aggregation design through the Usage-Based Optimization Wizard. Both tools are available in BIDS and SSMS. You can use the Aggregations tab in the Cube Designer to run the Aggregation Design Wizard or the Usage-Based Optimization Wizard. You can also use this tab to review and fine-tune the aggregation design.

This chapter covers the Aggregation Design Wizard. Chapter 8, "Securing and Administering SSAS," discusses the Usage-Based Optimization Wizard.

Defining Aggregations with the Aggregation Design Wizard

The Aggregation Design Wizard does not take into account the queries that will be submitted to the server or the dimensions that will be used most. This information is not available at design time. Instead, the Aggregation Design Wizard identifies suitable aggregations based on your dimensional design and data statistics. To do so, the Aggregation Design Wizard executes a sophisticated algorithm that consists of two main steps: identifying suitable aggregation candidates and performing a cost/benefit analysis for each aggregation.

The Aggregation Design Wizard does not consider all attributes for aggregations. Instead, it examines the attribute's AggregationUsage property. As Figure 7-8 shows, you will find the AggregationUsage property in the properties of the selected attribute in the Dimensions pane of the Cube Structure tab in the Cube Designer rather than in the Dimension Designer. This is because aggregations consist of the cube measures and the attributes of the dimensions referenced by the cube.

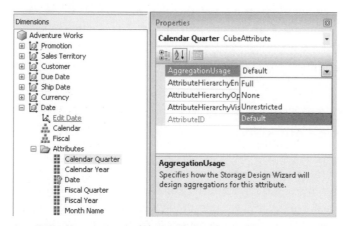

FIGURE 7-8 You can control the attributes that will be considered for aggregation design by changing the attributes' AggregationUsage property.

Table 7-3 explains each AggregationUsage setting.

TABLE 7-3 AggregationUsage Settings

SETTING	DESCRIPTION
Full	Every aggregation in this cube must include this attribute or a related attribute at a lower level of the attribute chain. For example, if you have Month->Quarter->Year attribute relationships and you set the AggregationUsage property of Year to Full, the server might favor Quarter instead of Year because the Year totals can be derived from Quarter totals.
None	No aggregations will include this attribute. Consider using this option for infrequently used attributes.

SETTING	DESCRIPTION
Unrestricted	Leaves it to the Aggregation Design Wizard to consider the attribute when designing aggregations.
Default	Escalates the All attribute, the dimension key attribute, and the attributes participating in the user hierarchies to Unrestricted. The aggregation usage of attributes participating in Many-To-Many, Referenced, and Data Mining dimensions will be set to None.

EXAM TIP

Suppose that you have a Customer dimension that includes a Phone Number attribute that stores customers' phone numbers. It is unlikely that end users will group data by the Phone Number attribute. So you can set this attribute's AggregationUsage property to None to instruct the Aggregation Design Wizard not to consider the Phone Number attribute when designing aggregations.

Estimating the Aggregation Cost/Benefit

When the Aggregation Design Wizard has identified attribute candidates, it performs a cost/benefit analysis to reduce the number of the aggregations. In general, the Aggregation Design Wizard favors smaller aggregations. When estimating the aggregation cost, the Aggregation Design Wizard examines the attribute member counts (EstimatedCount attribute property) and fact table counts (EstimatedRows measure group property). You can either manually overwrite these counts on the Specify Object Counts page of the wizard or let the wizard do the counting.

BEST PRACTICES   UPDATE DATA STATISTICS

To help the Aggregation Design Wizard make a correct cost/benefit analysis, be sure to keep the EstimatedCount and EstimatedRows counts up to date. This is especially important when moving the cube from development to production. When the cube is deployed, you can run the Aggregation Design Wizard again and enter the new counts on the Specify Object Counts page.

Last, the Aggregation Design Wizard estimates the benefit of each aggregation by analyzing its coverage. When doing this, the Aggregation Design Wizard analyzes the attribute relationships in the aggregation candidates and eliminates duplicate aggregations. For more information about the inner workings of the Aggregation Design Wizard, see the white paper "SQL Server 2008 Analysis Services 2005 Performance Guide" (see References).

Setting the Aggregation Options

The Set Aggregation Options page of the Aggregation Design Wizard, shown in Figure 7-9, gives you several options for designing the number of aggregations.

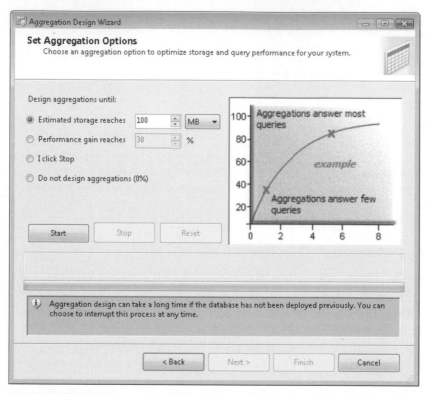

FIGURE 7-9 The Set Aggregation Options page offers several options for designing the number of aggregations.

The Estimated Storage Reaches option lets you limit the number of aggregations by the storage space they use. With this option, the Aggregation Design Wizard will create aggregations until they consume the specified amount of disk space or until the 100 percent aggregation threshold is reached.

Use the Performance Gain Reaches option to specify a hypothetical percentage improvement in query performance that you expect the aggregation design to yield. Contrary to what you might expect, a performance gain of 100 percent does not create all possible aggregations for the selected partition. Instead, it simply means that the wizard will keep adding aggregations until a hypothetical 100 percent improvement in query performance is reached. In general, a performance gain of 20 percent to 30 percent should be adequate for most cubes.

The I Click Stop option lets you start the aggregation and stop it when you are satisfied with the results. Last, the Do Not Design Aggregations (0%) option removes the current aggregation design.

PRACTICE   Defining Measure Group Partitions and Storage

In this practice, you will partition the Internet Sales measure group of the Adventure Works cube by year and configure the partition storage mode.

EXERCISE 1   Create Measure Group Partitions

The AdventureWorksDW2008 database stores data for four years (2001 to 2004). You can use the default partition for the first year. So to partition the Internet Sales measure group by year, you need to create three new partitions. In this exercise, you will change the default partition of the Internet Sales measure group to load data for year 2001 only.

1. In BIDS, open the Chapter 7 SSAS Start Project from the ..\Source\Ch 07\TK448-ch07 Start Here \TK 70-448 SSAS Project\ folder.

2. In Solution Explorer, double-click the Adventure Works cube to open it in the Cube Designer, and then click the Partitions tab.

3. If necessary, expand the Internet Sales measure group, and notice that it has only one partition, which binds to the entire fact table. This is a table binding. As noted earlier in this chapter, before you can create a new partition, you need to change the default partition so that it uses query binding.

4. Rename the default partition by typing **Internet Sales 2001** in the Partition Name column.

5. In SSMS, connect to the Database Engine, right-click the dbo.DimDate table and choose Select Top 1000 Rows to browse its data. Notice that the DateKey column of the last dimension member for year 2001 is 20011231. Browse the structure of the FactInternetSales table, and notice that the OrderDateKey column references the DateKey column of the DimDate table.

6. In BIDS, on the Partitions tab in the Cube Designer, click the ellipsis button in the Source column to open the Partition Source dialog box.

7. Expand the Binding Type drop-down list, and then change the binding type to Query Binding.

8. Change the default *SELECT* statement as follows:

```
SELECT * FROM [dbo].[FactInternetSales]
WHERE OrderDateKey <= 20011231
```

9. Click the Check button to verify the query syntax. Click OK to finalize the changes to the Internet Sales 2001 partition.

   Next, you will add three more partitions to the Internet Sales measure group for years 2002, 2003, and 2004.

10. On the Partitions tab of the Cube Designer, click the New Partition button on the toolbar in the Internet Sales section to start the Partition Wizard. On the Welcome page of the wizard, click Next.

11. On the Specify Source Information page, select the dbo.FactInternetSales table check box in the Available Tables list box, and then click Next.

12. On the Restrict Rows page, select the Specify A Query To Restrict Rows check box. Delete the default *SELECT* statement, and enter the following *SELECT* statement in the Query box:

```
SELECT * FROM [dbo].[FactInternetSales]
WHERE OrderDateKey >= 20020101 and OrderDateKey <= 20021231
```

13. On the Processing And Storage Locations page, accept the defaults, and then click Next.

14. On the Completing The Wizard page, name the partition by typing **Internet Sales 2002**. Select Design Aggregations Later, and then click Finish to create the partition.

15. Create a new Internet Sales 2003 partition with the following slice definition:

```
SELECT * FROM [dbo].[FactInternetSales]
WHERE OrderDateKey >= 20030101 and OrderDateKey <= 20031231
```

16. Create the last partition, Internet Sales 2004, with the following slice definition:

```
SELECT * FROM [dbo].[FactInternetSales]
WHERE OrderDateKey >= 20040101 and OrderDateKey <= 20041231
```

Figure 7-10 shows the completed partition design of the Internet Sales measure group.

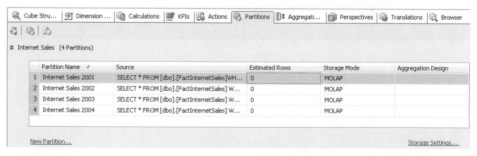

FIGURE 7-10 The Internet Sales measure group is partitioned by year.

17. Deploy the solution to send the changes to the server and process the cube. Option-ally, create a pivot report in the Browser tab for the Cube Designer that uses the Inter-net Sales measure group. The report should return the same results as it did before because changing the physical storage of a measure group does not change the data; it simply reorganizes the way the data is stored.

EXERCISE 2 Select Partition Storage Modes

In this exercise, you will use SQL Server Profiler to see the way different storage modes affect query execution.

1. Open SQL Server Profiler by clicking Start, clicking All Programs, clicking Microsoft SQL Server 2008, clicking the Performance Tools program group, and then selecting SQL Server Profiler.

2. Select New Trace from the File menu. In the Server Type drop-down list, select Data-base Engine, and then click the Connect button. Click Run in the Trace Properties dialog box to start a trace that monitors the activities in the relational databases.

3. Open the Adventure Works cube in the Cube Designer, and then navigate to the Browser tab.

4. Create a report that uses one or more measures (for example, the Internet Sales Amount measure) from the Internet Sales measure group. In SQL Server Profiler, you should not see any *SELECT* statements sent to the AdventureWorksDW2008 database because MOLAP queries are always satisfied from the multidimensional server store.

5. Suppose that the Adventure Works users only infrequently query data older than three years and that the historical data would take a lot of storage space if it were config-ured for MOLAP. To minimize the storage space on the server, you decide to leave the historical data in the database by changing the storage mode of the historical partition for year 2001 to HOLAP.

   To do so, in the BIDS Properties window, change the storage mode of the Internet Sales 2001 partition to HOLAP, and then deploy the solution.

6. On the Browser tab, drag the Date.Calendar user hierarchy onto columns to see the Internet Sales amount broken down by years.

7. In SQL Server Profiler, you should see an SQL *SELECT* statement that the server sends to retrieve the aggregated values for the report, as Figure 7-11 shows.

   If there are no aggregations and the storage is set to HOLAP, all queries that target a HOLAP partition are sent to the relational database, as if the storage is set to ROLAP. This might have a negative impact on performance with large data volumes.

8. Close SQL Server Profiler. Change the storage mode of the Internet Sales 2001 parti-tion back to MOLAP, and redeploy the solution.

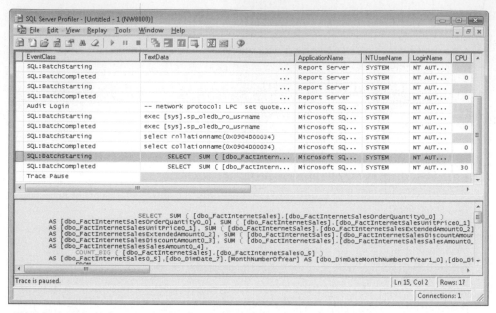

FIGURE 7-11 With the storage mode set to HOLAP, if there are no aggregations, queries are sent to the relational data source.

EXERCISE 3   Configure Proactive Caching

In this exercise, you will use the SSAS proactive caching feature to implement a low-latency partition. Suppose that you want the Adventure Works cube to synchronize data changes for the year 2004 as soon as they happen in the underlying data source.

Because you will use SQL Server notifications, the account that SSAS runs under must have System Administrator privileges to the SQL Server Database Engine. This is the case if the SSAS account is set to LocalSystem. You can use SQL Server Configuration Manager (found in the Microsoft SQL Server 2008 Configuration Tools program group) to verify and change the SSAS account. Alternatively, if changing the SSAS account is not an option, you can grant the SSAS account ALTER TRACE rights to the SQL Server Database Engine. To do so, right-click the SQL Server login, click Properties, and then select the Securables page. Click the Search button, select the Server option, and then click OK. In the Permissions grid, select the Grant check box on the Alter Trace row, and then click OK.

1. Now, in the Browser tab within the Cube Designer, open the Adventure Works cube, and then click the Partitions tab.

2. Expand the Internet Sales measure group, and then select the Internet Sales 2004 partition.

3. Click the Storage Setting link to open the Partition Storage Settings dialog box. Move the Standard Setting slider to Automatic MOLAP.

4. Click Options, and then click the Notifications tab, as Figure 7-12 shows. Notice that, by default, the system will use SQL Server trace notifications. One limitation of this notification option is that if the partition uses query binding, you must specify the tracking tables explicitly.

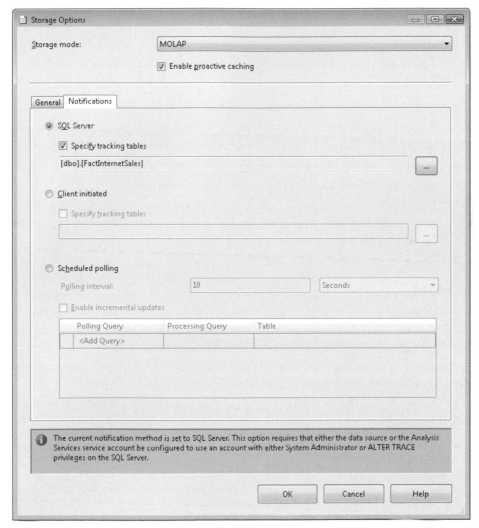

FIGURE 7-12 If the partition uses query binding, you must specify the tracking table explicitly with SQL Server notifications.

5. Select the Specify Tracking Tables check box. Click the ellipsis (...) button, select the FactInternetSales (dbo) table, and click OK to close the Relational Objects dialog box. Click OK to close the Storage Options dialog box, and then click OK again to close the Partition Storage Settings dialog box.

6. Deploy the solution.

7. Switch to the Browser tab, and then create the report shown in Figure 7-13 by dragging the Date.Calendar Year hierarchy onto columns and the Internet Sales Amount measure onto data.

Calendar Year ▼				
⊞ 2001	⊞ 2002	⊞ 2003	⊞ 2004	Grand Total
Internet Sales Amount	Internet Sales Amount	Internet Sales Amount	Internet Sales Amount	Internet Sales Amount
$3,266,373.66	$6,530,343.53	$9,791,060.30	$9,770,899.74	$29,358,677.22

FIGURE 7-13 Use this report to test the proactive caching settings of the Internet Sales 2004 partition.

8. Use SQL Server Profiler to connect to SSAS.

9. In SSMS, connect to the Database Engine. Right-click the dbo.FactInternetSales table in the AdventureWorksDW2008 database, and then click Open Table to browse its data.

10. Go to the last record in dbo.FactInternetSales, and then change the value in the Sales Amount column—for example, you might increase it by 1,000.

11. Navigate back to SQL Server Profiler. You should see a trace notification event, and in 10 seconds, additional events should follow, signaling that the server has started processing the MOLAP cache.

12. In the Browser tab in the Cube Designer, refresh the report, and notice that the Internet Sales Amount total for year 2004 has changed. This is because when proactive caching is enabled, the server automatically rebuilds the affected multidimensional structures.

EXERCISE 4   Design Aggregations with the Aggregation Design Wizard

This practice walks you through the process of implementing aggregation designs by using the Aggregation Design Wizard.

1. Open the Adventure Works cube in the Cube Designer, and then navigate to the Aggregations tab.

2. Notice that the Internet Sales node shows zero aggregation designs. Consequently, if the query results are not cached on the server, the server must query the fact data to answer any query that requests Internet sales.

3. Select the Internet Sales (0 Aggregation Designs) row, and then click the Design Aggregations button on the toolbar to start the Aggregation Design Wizard. On the Welcome page of the wizard, click Next.

4. On the Select Partitions To Modify page, select all four partitions to apply the same aggregation design.

5. The Review Aggregation Usage page shows the current values of the AggregationUsage setting for all attributes. You can overwrite the default values and set AggregationUsage for a given attribute to Full, None, or Unrestricted. Leave the Default column preselected and click Next.

6. On the Specify Objects Count page, you enter the estimated object counts manually. If you click the Count button, the wizard will count the objects, as Figure 7-14 shows.

FIGURE 7-14 Be sure to specify correct object counts so that the aggregations the Design Wizard suggests are useful.

BEST PRACTICES **SPECIFY OBJECT COUNTS**

If you let the Design Wizard count the objects, the wizard will not replace existing count values. When you move a cube from development to production, be sure to delete the counts that need to be replaced before clicking the Count button.

7. Expand the dimension objects, and notice that most of the attributes are shown in bold. These attributes represent those the wizard will consider for the aggregation design. Recall that the attribute AggregationUsage property controls the attributes that are considered for aggregation design.

8. On the Set Aggregation Options page, select the Performance Gain Reaches option, and then click Start. The Aggregation Design Wizard runs the cost/benefit algorithm to select aggregations that will give a hypothetical 30 percent increase in query performance, as Figure 7-15 shows.

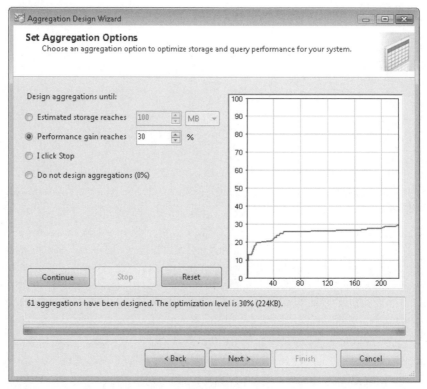

FIGURE 7-15 With the Performance Gain Reaches option, the server designs enough aggregations to yield the requested performance increase.

9. On the Completing The Wizard page, accept the default settings to save the aggregation design, but do not process the aggregations, and then click Finish.

10. On the Aggregations tab, notice that the Cube Designer has added the new aggregation design to the Internet Sales measure group. In our case, the aggregation design includes 61 aggregations.

11. Click the Advanced View button on the toolbar. Expand the Aggregation Design drop-down list, and then select the AggregationDesign item. The Aggregations tab displays the first 30 (0–29) aggregation designs, as Figure 7-16 shows. You can change the Range drop-down list to review the rest of the aggregation designs.

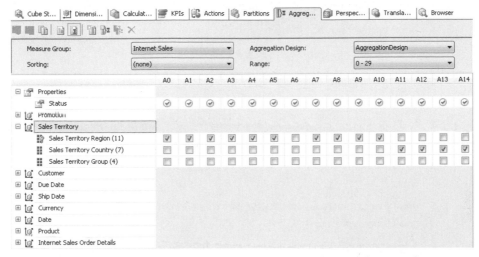

FIGURE 7-16 In advanced mode, the Aggregations tab lets you review and change each aggregation design.

You can expand a dimension, such as Sales Territory, to view which attributes are included in the aggregations. In our case, for example, the Aggregation Design Wizard has included the Sales Territory Region attribute in aggregations A0 to A5 and A7 to A10. Therefore, a query that groups data by Sales Territory Region will likely be answered by existing cube aggregations. You can use the Aggregations tab in advanced mode to change the aggregation designs or create new aggregation designs.

12. Deploy the solution to process the cube and create the aggregations.

BEST PRACTICES   **COPY THE AGGREGATION DESIGN**

You can use SSMS to copy the aggregation design from one partition to another. Simply right-click the partition, and then click Copy Aggregation Design. Alternatively, before the Partition Wizard completes, it lets you copy an aggregation design to use in creating a new partition.

Lesson 2: Deploying SSAS Objects

Estimated lesson time: 40 minutes

After your Unified Dimensional Model (UDM) is complete, you need to deploy it to a testing server for quality assurance (QA) testing or to a production server so that it is available to end users. More than likely, you will need to deploy periodically, such as after you have made enhancements and bug fixes to the UDM, so that you can synchronize the latest UDM definition with the deployed copy. SSAS supports several options to meet different deployment needs. Table 7-4 outlines these deployment options and describes when using the option is recommended.

So that you can choose the most appropriate technique for the deployment task at hand, you need to understand how each of these deployment options works, so we will look at each in turn.

TABLE 7-4 Deployment Options

OPTION	RECOMMENDED USE
BIDS	Deploying the latest changes to your local server for testing.
Deployment Wizard	Deploying to a test or production environment when you need more granular control.
XMLA script	Scheduling a deployment task.
Synchronize Database Wizard	Synchronizing two cubes, such as a staging cube and a production cube.
Backup and restore	Moving a cube from one server to another (covered in Chapter 8).
Analysis Management Objects (AMO)	Handling deployment programmatically (not covered in this book).

Deploying SSAS Projects with BIDS

As a developer, you would use BIDS to design cubes in an iterative edit, build, and deploy cycle to your local SSAS instance or a development server. You would typically use a small database to process and test your changes quickly on a local instance of SSAS. When the cube design is ready, you would publish the changes to a test server for testing. Use BIDS deployment when:

- You have created a BIDS Analysis Services project, and you work in project mode.
- You want to test your changes during the design cycle.
- You want to deploy your SSAS cube to a testing or production server, and you do not need to retain the existing management settings, such as roles and partitions.

Before discussing BIDS deployment, we will look at the design options available with BIDS.

BIDS Design Modes

Just as a relational database is a container of relational objects, an Analysis Services database contains SSAS objects, such as cubes, dimensions, and data source views. The BIDS equivalent of an SSAS database is an Analysis Services project. BIDS supports two design options for working with SSAS databases. The following list describes how these two options differ and how they affect deployment:

- **Connected mode** As its name suggests, in connected mode, you are directly connected to the SSAS database, so changes are applied immediately when the object is saved. To work in connected mode, from the BIDS File menu, select Open, Analysis Services Database. In the Connect To Database dialog box, type the SSAS server name and the name of the database you want to connect to. BIDS creates a project file, but in connected mode, this file contains only the server and database names. After the project is created, you can start making changes to the object definitions. Because changes are committed immediately to the SSAS database, you do not need to do anything extra to deploy them.

- **Project mode** This mode should be familiar to you because you have used it in the preceding chapters to design the Adventure Works cube. Project mode is the SSAS default and the recommended design option; BIDS defaults to project mode when you create a new Analysis Services project by selecting File, New, Project. In project mode, your changes are saved locally as XML files. The advantage of project mode is that it facilitates team development. When you put the project under source control, multiple developers can make changes to objects by checking out the corresponding files without worrying that they will overwrite each other's changes.

    In project mode, you make changes while you are disconnected from the server. To test your changes, you need to deploy the changes to an SSAS server—for example, you might deploy them to your local SSAS server.

Deployment Settings

The project properties, which you can access by right-clicking the project node in Solution Explorer and then clicking Properties, include deployment settings that specify where and how the project will be deployed, as Figure 7-17 shows.

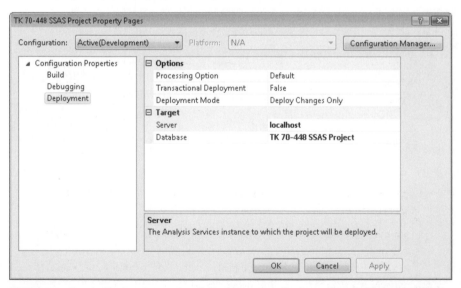

FIGURE 7-17 Use the Project Properties dialog box to specify the project deployment settings.

Table 7-5 describes these settings.

TABLE 7-5 Deployment Options

OPTION	SETTINGS	DESCRIPTION
Processing Option	Default	Applies the minimum processing tasks to bring the cube to a ready state.
	Full	Fully processes the database.
	Do Not Process	Deploys the changes only.
Transactional Deployment	False	Executes each command in the deployment script independently.
	True	Rolls back changes if a deployment command fails.
Deployment Mode	Deploy All	Overwrites the target database.
	Deploy Changes Only	Compares the project with the target database and deploys changes only.
Server		Specifies the name of the target server, such as localhost.
Database		Specifies the name of the target database; created by BIDS if it does not already exist.

Deploying a Project

After you configure the deployment settings, you can deploy the project by right-clicking the project node in Solution Explorer and then clicking Deploy. BIDS first builds the project to verify that all objects are defined correctly. If there are any inconsistencies, BIDS aborts the deployment and shows the errors in the Errors window.

Next, BIDS builds a deployment script named <project name>.asdatabase and saves it to the project bin folder. Last, it sends the deployment script to the server to synchronize the server database with the local project.

> **BEST PRACTICES** **USE THE DEPLOYMENT WIZARD TO AVOID OVERWRITING THE MANAGEMENT SETTINGS**
>
> Even if you set Deployment Mode to Deploy Changes Only, BIDS deployment overwrites the target database management settings, such as partition design and security roles. Thus, you need to be careful when deploying the project to a production server. If you need more control over deployment, consider using the Deployment Wizard.

Using the Deployment Wizard

As convenient as BIDS deployment is, it limits the amount of control you can exercise over the deployment process. The Deployment Wizard is specifically designed to support incremental deployment, so it gives you more control.

Understanding the Deployment Wizard

As you just learned, when you build an Analysis Services project, BIDS generates a deployment script and additional XML files in the project bin folder. The Deployment Wizard uses these XML files as a basis to deploy changes to the target database. Table 7-6 describes the build files.

TABLE 7-6 BIDS Build Files

FILE	DESCRIPTION
Projectname.asdatabase	The deployment script file; contains the definition of all objects in the project.
Projectname.configsettings	Includes environment settings, such as data source connection definitions.
Projectname.deploymentoptions	Contains the deployment options from the project properties and additional user-configurable deployment settings, such as partition overwrite and role membership settings.
Projectname.deploymenttargets	Contains the names of the target deployment server and database.

Deployment Modes

The Deployment Wizard supports two deployment modes: interactive and command-line. In interactive mode, the wizard reads the build files and shows you their settings. You can overwrite these settings if you need to. The end result is an XMLA script that you can run immediately or save for later execution.

The wizard also supports command-line mode, which you can use to automate the wizard so that, for example, you can run it as a scheduled job. In command-line mode, you can control the wizard execution by using various switches. For example, you can use the /a switch to make changes to configuration files that the wizard uses as a starting point the next time it runs. Or, you can use the /s switch to run the Deployment Wizard in silent mode. You can also automate the script generation by running the Deployment Wizard in command-line mode with the /o switch.

To see a list of all the switches, open the Command Prompt window, navigate to C:\Program Files\Microsoft SQL Server \100\Tools\Binn\VSShell\Common7\IDE\, and then type:

```
microsoft.analysisservices.deployment.exe /?
```

 REAL WORLD

Teo Lachev

One of my projects required an automated deployment of several SSAS databases to several test servers with the Microsoft MsBuild system. We prepared a batch file that performed the deployment in several steps. First, the batch file would use the following command to build the SSAS project and obtain the *.asdatabase file:

```
devenv.exe /Build projectfile
```

Next, the batch file started the Deployment Wizard in command-line mode to produce a deployment script file, as follows:

```
"C:\Program Files\Microsoft SQL Server\100\Tools\Binn\VSShell\Common7\
IDE\Microsoft.AnalysisServices.Deployment.exe" <filename>.asdatabase /s
/o:"<scriptfilename>.xmla"
```

Last, the batch file deployed the deployment script by using the SSAS asccmd sample utility, as follows:

```
ascmd.exe -S <servername> -i <scriptfilename>.xmla
```

You can download the asccmd command-line utility sample from the Analysis Services 2008 samples page (see References). If the deployment server has BIDS, you can alternatively use its deployment capabilities in one step, as follows:

```
devenv "<path to SSAS solution.sln" /deploy <project configurationname>
```

Working with the Deployment Wizard

You can run the Deployment Wizard by clicking the Deployment Wizard link in the Microsoft SQL Server 2008 Analysis Services program group. In interactive mode, the Deployment Wizard walks you through the following pages:

1. On the Specify Source Analysis Services Database page, you specify the location of the projectname.asdatabase deployment script file.

2. On the Installation Target page, you enter the names of the target server and SSAS database. If the database does not exist, the wizard will create it.

3. On the Specify Options For Partitions And Roles page, shown in Figure 7-18, you specify whether you want to overwrite or retain the existing partition and security role settings on the target server.

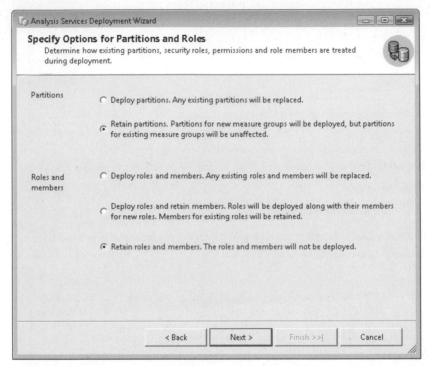

FIGURE 7-18 The Deployment Wizard lets you retain or change the partitions and security management settings for the target server.

 EXAM TIP

Suppose that you want to deploy the latest bug fixes that you have made to your SSAS project to a production server. You have already defined security roles and partitions on the server, and you want to preserve the server setup. You can use the Deployment Wizard to deploy the new changes and retain the existing role and partition settings. On the Specify Options For Partitions And Roles page, select the Retain Partitions and Retain Roles And Members options.

4. On the Specify Configuration Properties page, shown in Figure 7-19, you can specify configuration, optimization, and impersonation settings, such as the connection string to the data source, impersonation information, and location of error log files. You can also specify the storage locations at the cube, measure group, or partition level.

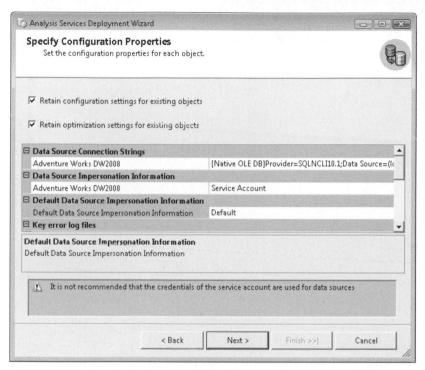

FIGURE 7-19 The Specify Configuration Properties page of the Deployment Wizard lets you retain or change the configuration and optimization settings for existing objects.

5. The Select Processing Options page lets you specify the processing mode. Select Default Processing if you want the server to choose the appropriate processing mode for each object on its own. Select Full Processing to fully process all objects or None to tell the server not to process the database.

6. On the Confirm Deployment page, shown in Figure 7-20, you can leave the Create Deployment Script check box cleared to start the deployment process immediately after you click Next. Or you can select the Create Deployment Script check box to save the deployment settings as a script file for later execution.

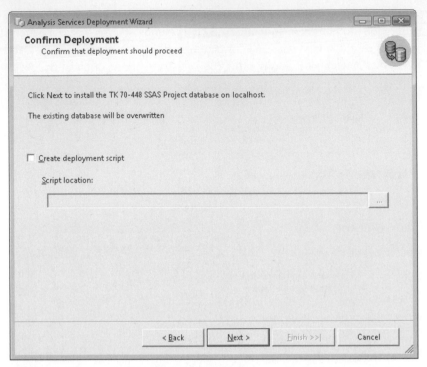

FIGURE 7-20 You can save the deployment settings to a script file for later execution.

Running XMLA Scripts for Deployment

If you tell the Deployment Wizard to create a deployment script, the wizard generates an XMLA file named projectname script.xmla and saves it in the specified location.

Understanding the Deployment Script

The deployment script consists of two sections. The first section starts with the *Alter* XMLA command followed by the definitions of all objects in the database.

The second section starts with a *Process* XMLA command. It instructs the server to process the database by using the processing mode you specified on the Select Processing Options page.

The following code shows a sample deployment script:

```
<Batch Transaction="false" xmlns="…">
  <Alter AllowCreate="true" ObjectExpansion="ExpandFull">
    <Object>
      <DatabaseID>TK 70-448 SSAS Project</DatabaseID>
```

```
      </Object>
      <ObjectDefinition>
        <Database xmlns:xsd="…">
          <ID>TK 70-448 SSAS Project</ID>
          <Name>TK 70-448 SSAS Project</Name>
          <DataSourceImpersonationInfo>
            <ImpersonationMode>Default</ImpersonationMode>
          </DataSourceImpersonationInfo>
…
    <Process>
      <Type>ProcessDefault</Type>
      <Object>
        <DatabaseID>TK 70-448 SSAS Project</DatabaseID>
      </Object>
    </Process>
```

Because the script is described in XMLA, you can modify it manually, or you can run the Deployment Wizard again and overwrite the existing script file.

IMPORTANT **GENERATING THE DEPLOYMENT SCRIPT IN COMMAND-LINE MODE**

You can automate the XMLA deployment script generation by running the Deployment Wizard in command-line mode with the /o switch.

Running the Deployment Script

When the deployment script is ready, you have several options for executing it. You can execute it manually in SSMS, you can schedule the script execution with the SQL Server Agent service, or you can use the Analysis Services Execute DDL Task.

To execute the deployment script manually, simply open the script file in SSMS, connect to the target server when prompted, and then click the Execute button on the toolbar (or press Ctrl+E) to run the script.

You can also schedule the script execution with the SQL Server Agent service, which is a component of SQL Server. SQL Server Agent supports a SQL Server Analysis Services Command step type, which you can use to execute any XMLA script.

Last, an SSIS package can use the Analysis Services Execute DDL Task to run any XMLA data definition language (DDL) command, including the *Alter* command.

Using the Synchronize Database Wizard

Synchronizing two SSAS databases is a common management task. For example, you might need to process a cube once on a dedicated staging server and then deploy it to load-balanced production servers. The traditional way to synchronize databases is to back up and restore the SSAS database, but this requires several steps and might take longer than you want. Instead, consider simplifying this task by using the Synchronize Database Wizard.

Understanding Database Synchronization

The output of the Synchronize Database Wizard is a single XMLA command named *Synchronize*. You need to send this command to the target server whose objects need to be updated. When the target server receives the *Synchronize* command, it forwards the command to the specified source server so that the target server can acquire a read lock on the source database. Next, the target server obtains a list of source database metadata and data files.

Having received the files, the target server releases the read lock on the source database because the target server can complete the remaining tasks on its own. The target server compares the source files against the state of the target database and identifies the differences. Last, the target server applies the metadata and data differences to the target database to make it identical to its source counterpart.

> **IMPORTANT**   **SETTING UP SECURITY**
>
> Because copying the database metadata and data is a sensitive task, the Windows account under which the target SSAS server runs must have administrative rights to the source database. When you connect to the source server in SSMS, you connect under your identity. However, the target server executes the *Synchronize* command under its service account. If this is the Local System Windows account, the command will fail. To avoid this, configure the target SSAS server to run under a domain account and grant that account administrative rights to the source database.

Using the Synchronize Database Wizard

You can start the Synchronize Database Wizard from SSMS, as follows:

1. In SSMS, connect to the Analysis Services on the target SSAS server.

2. Right-click the Databases folder, and then click Synchronize to start the Synchronize Database Wizard.

3. On the Select Database To Synchronize page, enter the name of the source server in the Source Server drop-down list box. Expand the Source Database drop-down list, and then select the source database.

4. On the Specify Locations For Local Partitions page, you can optionally overwrite the default location of the cube partitions. For example, if the data folder of the staging server is on the C drive, but the production server stores data on the D drive, you can change the partition locations to reflect that.

5. The wizard supports limited customization. For example, you can use the Synchronization Options page to preserve the security settings on the target server by selecting the Skip Membership option, as Figure 7-21 shows. Real-life cubes can be very large, so the Synchronize Database Wizard supports efficient compression to send the data changes to the target server. Leave the Use Compression When Synchronizing Databases check box selected to compress data.

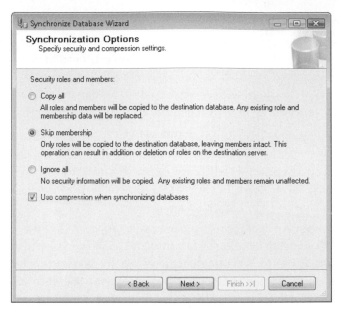

FIGURE 7-21 The Synchronize Database Wizard lets you retain the security settings on the target server and compress the synchronization files.

6. Use the Select Synchronization Method page to specify the deployment method. As with deployment, you can start the synchronization process immediately or generate a script and run it later.

EXAM TIP

Suppose that you have a farm of production servers and you need to deploy the latest changes to each server. You want to avoid processing the SSAS database on each production server because each cube would take very long to process. Instead, you decide to process the cube on a staging server and then synchronize each production server with the staging server. The Synchronize Database Wizard is designed specifically to handle this deployment model.

Understanding the Database Synchronization Script

The script file that the Synchronize Database Wizard generates is simple. It contains a single Synchronize command, as follows:

```
<Synchronize>
  <Source>
    <ConnectionString></ConnectionString>
```

```
    <Object>
      <DatabaseID>TK 70-448 SSAS Project</DatabaseID>
    </Object>
  </Source>
  <SynchronizeSecurity>SkipMembership</SynchronizeSecurity>
  <ApplyCompression>true</ApplyCompression>
</Synchronize>
```

The *Synchronize* command specifies the connection string to the source server and the name of the source database, as well as the synchronization options you selected when you ran the wizard. As with running a deployment script, you can run the synchronization script manually, automate it with SQL Server Agent, or use the SSIS Analysis Services Execute DDL Task.

SSAS also provides a management application programming interface (API) in the form of the AMO object library. AMO is intended for use by Microsoft .NET managed clients, such as VB.NET or C# applications. As you perform management tasks in SSMS and BIDS, behind the scenes, these tools use AMO to send commands to the server. Consider AMO when you need programmatic control over SSAS management, such as when you need to evaluate some conditions before processing an SSAS database.

Discussing AMO in detail is beyond the scope of this book and the exam, but you can learn about AMO by reading the topic "Analysis Management Objects" in SQL Server 2008 Books Online (see References).

PRACTICE   Deploying SSAS Objects

In this practice, you will deploy and synchronize SSAS databases by using the Deployment Wizard and the Synchronize Database Wizard.

EXERCISE 1   Deploy Databases with the Deployment Wizard

Suppose that you need to publish the latest changes in your local Adventure Works DW cube to a staging server and you want to retain the existing management settings on that server. In this exercise, you will use the Deployment Wizard to prepare a deployment script that you can execute on the staging server at a later time.

1. Open the TK 70-448 SSAS Project in BIDS (.\Source\Ch 07\TK448-ch07 Lesson 1\ folder).

2. To ensure that you have the latest deployment files, right-click the project node in the Solution Explorer pane, and then select Build.

3. Start the Deployment Wizard from the Microsoft SQL Server 2008 Analysis Services program group. On the Welcome page of the wizard, click Next.

4. On the Specify Source Analysis Services Database page, enter or use the ellipsis button to browse to the path of the TK 70-448 SSAS Project.asdatabase file, which you can find in the bin subfolder of the source project folder (..\Source\Ch 07\TK448-ch07 Lesson 1\bin\). Click Next.

5. On the Installation Target page, in the Server box, type the name of the target server to which the database will be deployed (or use **localhost** for testing). Expand the Database drop-down list and select the TK 70-448 SSAS Project database.

6. On the Specify Options For Partitions And Roles page, accept the default settings, and then click Next.

7. On the Specify Configuration Properties page, select the Retain Configuration Settings For Existing Objects and Retain Optimization Settings For Existing Object check boxes.

8. On the Select Processing Option page, accept the default settings by clicking Next.

9. On the Confirm Deployment page, select the Create Deployment Script option, and then specify the path to the deployment script file. Click Next to generate the file. The Deploying Database page shows the deployment progress. When the deployment completes, click Next and then click Finish.

10. Optionally, open and execute the deployment script in SSMS.

EXERCISE 2 Synchronize Databases Using the Synchronize Database Wizard

In this exercise, you will use the Synchronize Database Wizard to synchronize a production database with a staging database. As a prerequisite, you will need two SSAS server instances, one of which can be a named instance on your local machine.

1. Open SSMS, and then connect to Analysis Services on the target server for which you want to synchronize the database.

2. Right-click the Databases folder, and then select Synchronize to start the Synchronize Database Wizard.

3. On the Select Database To Synchronize page, shown in Figure 7-22, enter the names of the source server—in this case, **(local)**—and source database—in this case, **TK 70-448 SSAS Project**.

4. Skip the Specify Locations For Local Partitions page.

5. On the Specify Query Criteria page, accept the default settings.

6. On the Select Synchronization Method page, select the Save The Script To A File option, and enter the file path of the script file. Name the file **synchronize.xmla**.

7. On the Completing The Wizard page, review the summary, and then click Finish to generate the script file.

8. Optionally, open the synchronization file in SSMS and execute it.

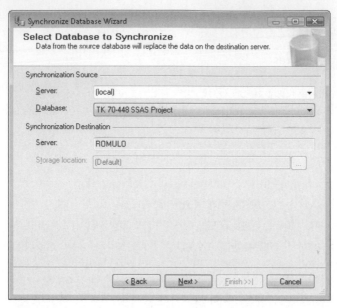

FIGURE 7-22 On the Select Database To Synchronize page, enter the names of the source server and database.

 Quick Check

1. Does BIDS deployment retain the partition design and security settings on the target server?

2. Which deployment option would you use to deploy your local changes to a production database without overwriting the partition and security settings?

3. Which deployment options can you use to synchronize a production database with a staging database?

Quick Check Answers

1. No, BIDS deployment overwrites the target database.

2. To deploy your changes to production, you would use the Deployment Wizard, which gives you more control over the deployment process than BIDS does.

3. The easiest option for synchronizing a production and a staging database is to use the Synchronize Database Wizard. But you could also execute a Synchronization XMLA command or back up and restore the database.

Lesson 3: Processing SSAS Objects

Estimated lesson time: 40 minutes

As you saw in Lesson 1, "Defining Measure Group Partitions and Aggregations," the MOLAP storage mode is essentially a disk-based cache of the source data in the relational data source. If you do not use proactive caching, you need to process the SSAS objects explicitly to bring their data up to date. When an object is processed, the server sends a *SELECT* statement to the data source and uses the results to load the object.

Understanding SSAS Processing Options

The objects that you can process in SSAS are database, cube, measure group, partition, dimension, mining structure, and mining model. Among these objects, only dimensions, partitions, and mining structures store data.

When you process an object, the server creates a processing plan. For example, when processing the dimension attributes, the server analyzes the attribute relationships and first processes the attributes that do not depend on other attributes. The server then creates internal jobs that read, process, and write the data to the object physical stores.

A full discussion of SSAS processing internals is beyond the scope of this book. For details about the SSAS processing architecture and guidance about how and when to use the various processing options, read the white paper "Analysis Services 2005 Processing Architecture" by T. K. Anand (see References).

Processing Options

The SSAS server supports several processing options to address various processing requirements. Table 7-7 summarizes the processing options for OLAP objects only. Chapter 9, "Working with SSAS Data Mining," discusses processing for data mining objects.

TABLE 7-7 Processing Options for OLAP Objects

PROCESSING OPTION	DESCRIPTION	APPLIES TO
Process Default	Performs the minimum number of tasks required to fully initialize the object. The server converts this option to one of the other options based on the object state.	All objects
Process Full	Drops the object stores and rebuilds the object. Metadata changes, such as adding a new attribute to a dimension, require Process Full.	All objects

PROCESSING OPTION	DESCRIPTION	APPLIES TO
Process Update	Applies member inserts, deletes, and updates without invalidating the affected cubes.	Dimension
Process Add	Adds only new data.	Dimension, partition
Process Data	Loads the object with data without building indexes and aggregations.	Dimension, cube, measure group, partition
Process Index	Retains data and builds only indexes and aggregations.	Dimension, cube, measure group, partition
Unprocess	Deletes the object data or the data in the containing objects.	All objects
Process Structure	Deletes the partition data and applies Process Default to the cube dimensions.	Cube

As you have probably guessed, choosing the right processing option is a compromise between processing time and management complexity. Process Full—that is, processing the entire database fully—is the easiest and cleanest way to process all of its objects, but it might also be the most expensive. It might take a very long time to process a very large dimension. If only new members are added to the dimension, rather than fully processing the dimension and the related cubes, consider using the Process Add option. Note that the Process Add option is available only through an XMLA script.

Understanding Object Dependencies

SSAS objects share intradependencies and interdependencies. Intradependencies reflect the logical relationships among objects. As noted, only dimensions, partitions, and mining structures store data; the rest of the objects act as containers. So when you process the cube, you process all measure groups in the cube. Processing a measure group means processing its partitions.

For processing, you also need to account for the project interdependencies. In some cases, processing one object might affect other objects, even if the first object does not contain the second object. The most common example of interdependency is dimension processing. A dimension might be referenced by one or more cubes. The side effect of fully processing a dimension is invalidating the cubes that reference it. This means that you will also have to fully process the affected cubes. For a full list of dependencies, see the white paper "Analysis Services 2005 Processing Architecture" (see References).

You have several options for processing SSAS objects. The two most commonly used options are BIDS and SSMS. However, SSIS provides an Analysis Services Processing Task to process SSAS objects within an SSIS package.

Processing SSAS Objects in BIDS

During design, BIDS shields you from the processing technicalities. As you learned in Lesson 2, "Deploying SSAS Objects," by default, the project-level processing option is Process Default. Consequently, when the project is deployed, BIDS identifies the changes that you have made and applies the correct processing option for your situation.

However, BIDS can track only metadata changes. If you make a change in the data source, for example, BIDS is unaware of the change. So you also need to understand the way to process objects manually. Experimenting with different processing options will help you select the right option for the processing task at hand when you move the cube to production.

In BIDS, you can process objects in Solution Explorer by right-clicking the object and then clicking Process. Or you can process objects in the Cube Designer and the Dimension Designer by clicking the Process button on the toolbar. In both cases, BIDS will prompt you to deploy the metadata changes if the object definitions have changed. Next, BIDS displays the Process Object(s) dialog box.

Understanding the Process Object(s) Dialog Box

You can process multiple objects, such as several dimensions and a cube, in a batch. To do so, select the objects in Solution Explorer by holding down the Ctrl key, right-clicking, and then selecting Process. Figure 7-23 shows the Process Object(s) dialog box, which displays the objects you have selected for processing.

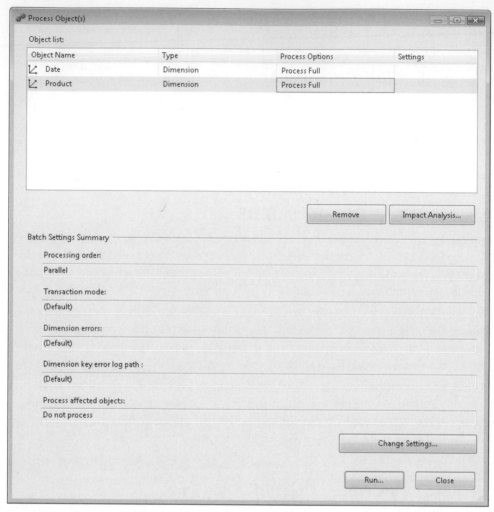

FIGURE 7-23 The Process dialog box supports batch processing of multiple objects with different processing options.

BIDS is intelligent enough to suggest a processing option for you. For example, if there are no structural changes to a dimension, BIDS will set the default processing option to Process Update because it assumes that you want to update the dimension data.

Analyzing the Processing Impact

As noted earlier, as a result of the object interdependencies, processing one object might mean that you have to process other objects. You can see the list of affected objects by clicking the Impact Analysis button in the Process dialog box. For example, if structural changes have been made so that you need to process a dimension fully, the Impact Analysis dialog box, shown in Figure 7-24, will list the cubes, measure groups, and partitions that reference this dimension.

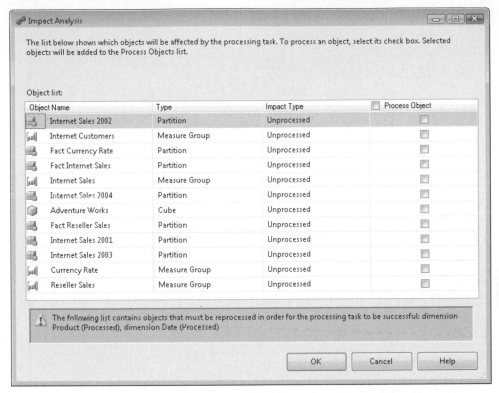

FIGURE 7-24 The Impact Analysis dialog box shows the objects that will be invalidated by a given processing task.

You can use the Process Object column to select the objects you want to process. Figure 7-24 shows the Adventure Works cube and all of its containing objects. Because, in this case, the cube contains the rest of the objects, you can select just the Adventure Works cube to process all objects, or you can select objects to be processed and leave the others in an unprocessed state.

Understanding Processing Settings

You can click the Change Settings button in the Process dialog box to change the default processing settings. Figure 7-25 shows the Change Settings dialog box.

By default, the server processes batch objects in parallel and chooses the number of concurrent jobs on its own. The Process Order setting lets you overwrite this behavior. You can limit the maximum number of processing tasks that run in parallel, or you can tell the server to process objects in a batch, sequentially.

The Writeback Table Option applies only to partitions that users can make data changes to. Writeback changes are written to a dedicated table in the data source. You can instruct the server to either create a new writeback table or use an existing one. Last, you can use the Dimension Key Errors tab if you need to overwrite the default error configuration—for example, you might want to abort processing if a duplicate dimension key is found.

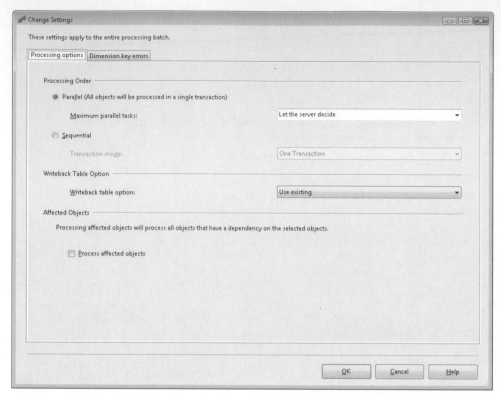

FIGURE 7-25 The Change Settings dialog box lets you overwrite the default server Processing Options and the Dimension Key Errors configuration.

EXAM TIP

If SSAS encounters a null value in a key column when processing dimension data, by default, it converts the value to zero for numeric columns or to an empty string for string columns. As you can see by inspecting the default ErrorConfiguration settings for the dimension and the Dimension Key Errors tab of the Change Settings dialog box, the server ignores the NullKeyConvertedtoUnknown error. However, if the dimension does not have an unknown member enabled, the processing task will fail. To enable the unknown dimension member, change its UnknownMember property from None to Visible or Hidden (if you do not want end users to see the unknown member). By default, the label of the unknown member is Unknown. However, you can specify a custom label by setting the dimension-level UnknownMemberName property. When the unknown member is enabled, end users will see all members with null keys grouped under the Unknown member. Although SSAS provides flexible processing options, as a best practice, you should resolve data inconsistencies during the ETL process.

Process errors usually result from data inconsistencies, such as referential integrity violations. Recall that you can specify custom error configurations at dimension, cube, measure group, and partition levels. The Change Settings dialog box's Dimension Key Errors tab lets you overwrite these settings for the duration of the processing operation.

Monitoring Processing Progress

When the server processes objects, it raises trace events to which client applications can subscribe to see progress reports. The Process Progress dialog box listens to these events and shows the progress of the processing operation. You can see which objects are being processed in parallel, the duration of the processing job, the SQL *SELECT* statement that the server sends to the data source to load data, and the number of rows retrieved, as Figure 7-26 shows. In the case of an error, the Process Progress dialog box shows the error message.

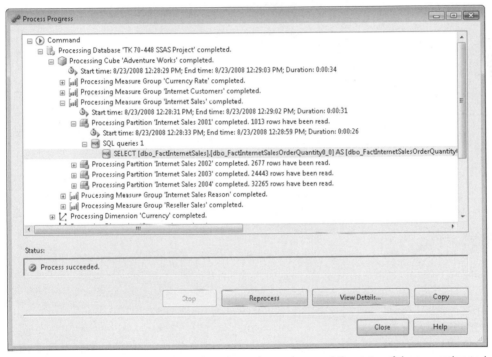

FIGURE 7-26 The Process Progress dialog box shows the progress and the status of the processing task.

Depending on the error configuration settings, errors might abort the processing operation. If this happens, you need to look at the error message or the error log file to find the problem, resolve the error, and restart the processing operation.

Processing SSAS Objects in SSMS

Administrators can use SSMS to process SSAS objects. Follow these steps to process an object in SSMS:

1. Connect to the SSAS server.

2. In Object Explorer, expand the tree to the object you need to process.

3. Right-click the object, and then select Process.

4. SSMS displays the Process Object(s) dialog box, as Figure 7-27 shows, which is similar to the BIDS Process Object(s) dialog box.

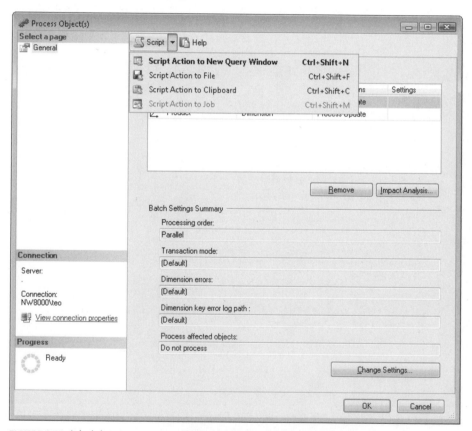

FIGURE 7-27 Administrators can use SSMS to script the processing operation.

To process multiple objects in a batch:

1. Select the containing folder (for example, Dimensions).

2. Hold down the Ctrl key and select each object in the Object Explorer Details window. If the Object Explorer Details window is not visible, select Object Explorer Details from the View menu or press F7.

3. Right-click the selection, and then click Process.

Generating the Processing Script

Unlike BIDS, SSMS lets you script management tasks, including processing. Almost every dialog box in SSMS has a Script drop-down list (as you can see in Figure 7-27), which lets you save the script in a new query window, in a file, or on the Windows Clipboard. Here is what the XMLA script might look like if you chose to process the Date and Product dimensions in a batch:

```
<Batch>
  <Parallel>
    <Process>
      <Object>
        <DatabaseID>TK 70-448 SSAS Project</DatabaseID>
        <DimensionID>Date</DimensionID>
      </Object>
      <Type>ProcessUpdate</Type>
      <WriteBackTableCreation>UseExisting
      </WriteBackTableCreation>
    </Process>
    <Process>
      <Object>
        <DatabaseID>TK 70-448 SSAS Project</DatabaseID>
        <DimensionID>Product</DimensionID>
      </Object>
      <Type>ProcessUpdate</Type>
      <WriteBackTableCreation>UseExisting
      </WriteBackTableCreation>
    </Process>
  </Parallel>
</Batch>
```

The *Batch* element encloses the objects to be processed. The *Parallel* element instructs the server to process the objects in parallel. And the *Type* element indicates the processing option. After you generate the script, you can execute it immediately, or you can use SQL Server Agent to schedule it to run at a later time.

Setting Advanced Processing Options with Proactive Caching

As Lesson 1 described, proactive caching lets you put the cube processing in an autopilot mode. When you enable proactive caching on a partition, you do not have to process the cube explicitly. Instead, the server automatically processes the MOLAP cache when changes are made to the data source.

The proactive caching discussion in Lesson 1 covered only standard proactive caching modes, such as Automatic MOLAP. However, as an administrator, you can fine-tune proactive caching by setting advanced options.

Understanding Advanced Processing Options for Proactive Caching

You can access the advanced proactive caching settings by clicking the Options button in the Partition Storage Settings dialog box. This displays the Storage Options dialog box, shown in Figure 7-28.

In general, the purpose of the advanced settings listed in Table 7-8 is to help you achieve a reasonable compromise between latency and performance. The key questions that you have to ask are: "How important is it to provide uniform response query times?" and "How much cache latency is acceptable?"

Table 7-8 summarizes the proactive caching settings and their purposes.

Depending on the database size, the ROLAP query performance might be much worse than its MOLAP equivalent. For example, suppose that you have a large relational database, and so reverting to ROLAP might slow query performance. Imagine that the user is browsing the cube while queries are answered in MOLAP mode, and the query performance is very fast, but suddenly, because a data change happens and proactive caching reverts to ROLAP, the system slows down so much that the user believes that the system has stopped responding. If query performance is your highest priority, you should not allow proactive caching to revert to ROLAP at all. In the Storage Options dialog box, disable the Latency setting (the Not Enabled item in the drop-down list) and clear the Bring Online Immediately check box. The net result of this combination is that the server will satisfy the queries from the old MOLAP cache until the new cache is ready.

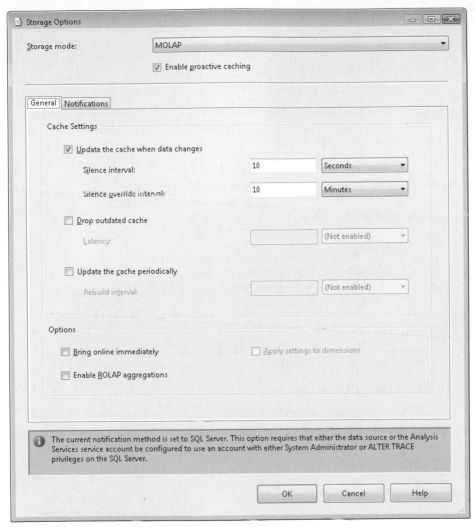

FIGURE 7-28 Use the Storage Options dialog box to fine-tune the proactive caching settings.

TABLE 7-8 Proactive Caching Advanced Processing Options

SETTING	DESCRIPTION	PREDEFINED SETTING
Silence Interval	Defines the minimum period to wait for a quiet time in the relational database.	–1 (Infinite) Ignore Database Notifications
Silence Override Interval	Defines the threshold period after which the server will start rebuilding the cache if no quiet period occurs—that is, if there are perpetual data changes.	–1 (Infinite) No Override Period

SETTING	DESCRIPTION	PREDEFINED SETTING
Latency	Defines the lifetime of the old MOLAP cache during which it is still used to respond to queries; data retrieved by those queries is out of date.	–1 (Infinite) Never Revert To ROLAP
Rebuild Interval	Schedules the new cache to be built automatically, whether or not there is data activity.	–1 (Infinite) No Periodic Update
Bring Online Immediately	When set to Immediate (On), the server satisfies queries from ROLAP while the cache is being rebuilt; when set to On-CacheComplete (Off), the server will never revert to ROLAP but will be in infinite latency.	
Enable ROLAP Aggregations	Attempts to create materialized SQL views for aggregations while queries are answered in ROLAP mode.	
Apply Settings To Dimensions	Applies storage mode and proactive caching settings to associated dimensions.	

Understanding Notification Options

Proactive caching supports three notification options to meet different deployment and security needs. You can set these options on the Notifications tab of the Storage Options dialog box (shown earlier in Figure 7-12).

SQL SERVER NOTIFICATIONS

This option is available only with SQL Server 2000 and later. It uses the SQL Server trace events, which are raised when data is changed. This option is the easiest to set up, but there are a few things to keep in mind. To begin, it requires SSAS to connect to the data source with administrator rights. When setting up the data source connection, you have to specify credentials of an account that has administrator rights to the data source.

SQL Server notifications also do not guarantee event delivery because no event queuing is supported. This can lead to data changes being lost in the proactive cache. For example, if SSAS is restarted while the data is being changed in the relational database, proactive caching will not pick up the data change events.

Last, SQL Server notifications always result in Full Process for partitions and Process Update for dimensions. One scenario in which this might be a problem is when only new data will be added to a partition or dimension. In this case, Process Add would be a more efficient option, but because the SQL Server notification option does not support Process Add, consider scheduled polling notifications.

CLIENT-INITIATED NOTIFICATIONS

Client-initiated notifications can be useful when you want an external application to notify the server when data is changed. For example, suppose that only the Adventure Works online sales application makes data changes to the FactInternetSales table. In this case, the application can notify SSAS that a data change took place. To do so, the application sends a *Notify-TableChange* XMLA command, as follows:

```
<NotifyTableChange>
  <Provider>SQLOLEDB</Provider>
  <DataSource>localhost</DataSource>
  <InitialCatalog>TK 70-448 SSAS Project</InitialCatalog>
  <TableNotifications>
    <TableNotification>
      <DBTableName>FactInternetSales</DBTableName>
      <DBSchemaName>dbo</DBSchemaName>
    <TableNotification>
  </TableNotifications>
</NotifyTableChange>
```

In this case, the *NotifyTableChange* command notifies the server that the data in the FactInternetSales table has changed. This client-initiated option is the most involved to set up, but it is also the most flexible. For example, if guaranteed event delivery is a must, the application can queue the events in case the SSAS server is offline.

SCHEDULED POLLING NOTIFICATIONS

The third and perhaps most commonly used notification option is to periodically poll the database for changes. The Scheduled Polling option assumes that the relational table has a column that indicates an update event. For example, if the FactInternetSales table in the AdventureWorksDW2008 database had a ModifiedDate column, you could use the following statement to detect a change:

```
SELECT MAX(ModifiedDate) AS ModifiedDate
FROM   FactInternetSales
```

The polling query must be a *singleton query*, meaning that it returns one row and one column. Each polling query tracks data changes from a single table. If you have a measure group that spans multiple tables based on a named query or SQL view, you need to add as many polling queries to the grid as there are tracked tables. Assuming that you have accepted the default polling interval of 10 seconds, the server will submit all polling queries to the database every 10 seconds. Internally, the server will keep track of the returned value from each query. For instance, the preceding example uses only one polling query. When data is changed, the query will return a new value for the ModifiedDate column, and the server will know that it is time to update the cache.

Often, data is only added to a table; it is never changed or deleted. In this case, you can improve the proactive caching performance by incrementally updating the cache. To do so, you must specify an additional processing query next to the polling query, as Figure 7-29 shows.

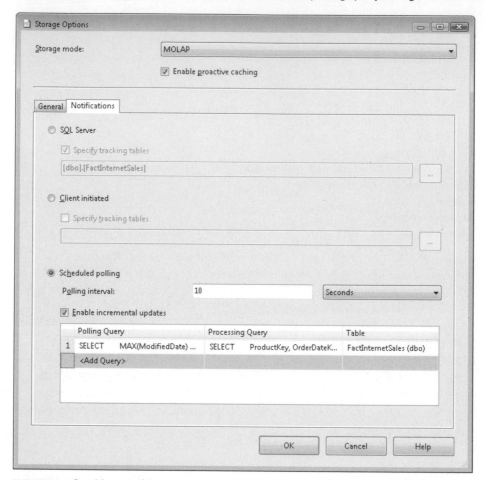

FIGURE 7-29 Consider specifying a processing query to incrementally update the MOLAP cache when data is only added to a partition or dimension.

For example, using the earlier polling query, you can define the following parameterized query to pick up new data only:

```
SELECT  * FROM FactInternetSales
WHERE   (ModifiedDate > ?) AND (ModifiedDate <= ?)
```

Notice that the query syntax is database-specific. It is very important to get the query *WHERE* clause correct to avoid data duplication or loss.

Here is how the server performs incremental updates to the cache. First, the server executes the polling query to retrieve the latest modified date. The server next executes the processing query, passing the returned *ModifiedDate* value from the polling query as a second parameter to the processing query. When the query is executed for the first time, the actual processing query is translated as follows:

```
SELECT * FROM   dbo.FactInternetSales
WHERE  (ModifiedDate > #old modified date#)) AND
(ModifiedDate <= #last modified date#)
```

The net result is that all table rows are loaded in the cache. During the next polling interval, the server will run the polling query again. If new data has been added, the server will pick up the new *ModifiedDate* value. Now the server has two date values: the old modified date and the last modified date. Next, the server passes the two dates to the two parameter placeholders, as follows:

```
SELECT * FROM   dbo.FactInternetSales
WHERE  (ModifiedDate > #old modified date#) AND
(ModifiedDate <= #last modified date#)
```

As a result, only the new rows will be retrieved and added to the cache. As you can imagine, incrementally processing a cache can greatly improve the server scalability.

EXAM TIP

Although SSAS is typically used in data warehousing projects that use ETL processes to extract, transform, and load data, sometimes it might make sense to build the UDM on top of the operational data source. For example, the database schema might not be that complex, and you might be able to "dimensionalize" it by implementing a set of SQL views on top of the schema. If business requirements call for low data latency, consider enabling proactive caching that polls the database for changes and processes the affected multidimensional objects in real time.

Using the Analysis Services Tasks in SSIS

The UDM commonly serves as an OLAP layer on top of a data warehouse or a data mart. Typically, implementing a data warehouse requires ETL processes to extract data from one or more data sources, cleanse and transform that data, and load the data into the data warehouse. As a last step of the ETL process, you can automate UDM processing. SSIS includes an Analysis Services Processing Task that can process SSAS objects. Follow these steps to configure the Analysis Services Processing Task:

1. Drag the Analysis Services Processing Task from the BIDS toolbox (available when you access the Control Flow tab in the SSIS Designer) to the Control Flow tab in your SSIS package.

2. Double-click the Analysis Services Processing Task to open the Analysis Services Processing Task Editor, and then select the Processing Settings page. This page is similar to the BIDS Process Objects dialog box.

3. Expand the Analysis Services Connection Manager drop-down list, and then select an existing connection manager, or click the New button to create a new connection to an existing SSAS database.

4. Click Add. In the Add Analysis Services Object dialog box, select the SSAS object(s) you want to process. For example, to process the entire SSAS database, select the database, and then click OK.

> **BEST PRACTICES**   **CONSIDER FULLY PROCESSING THE ENTIRE DATABASE**
>
> Fully processing the entire SSAS database is the cleanest and easiest solution to process all objects in the database, but it is not necessarily the fastest. Because SSAS processes objects in parallel and has a very efficient processing architecture that can handle some 10,000 records per second, you might find that you can process even large cubes within a reasonable time frame. Consider more advanced processing options, such as incremental processing *(ProcessUpdate)*, only when fully processing the database is not an option.

SSIS adds the objects you selected to the Object List grid, as Figure 7-30 shows.

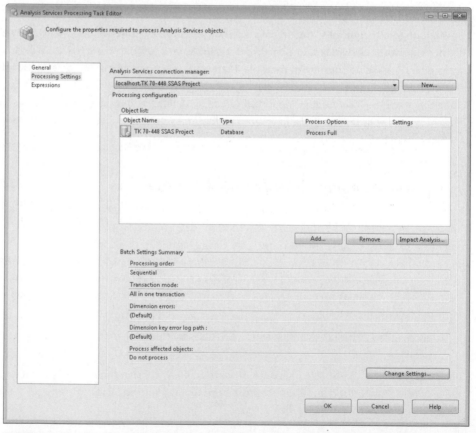

FIGURE 7-30 Use the SSIS Analysis Services Processing Task to automate UDM processing.

5. Optionally, click Impact Analysis to see how the processing task will impact the rest of the objects in the SSAS database. To change the default processing settings, click the Change Settings button. This displays the familiar Change Settings dialog box, which was discussed at the beginning of this lesson.

6. Connect the preceding ETL tasks to the Analysis Services Processing Task.

7. Run the SSIS package to execute the Analysis Services Processing Task and process the requested objects.

PRACTICE **Processing SSAS Objects**

In this practice, you will process SSAS objects in BIDS and SSMS and generate processing scripts. You will also work with the advanced proactive caching options.

EXERCISE 1 Process Dimensions Incrementally

Suppose that the cube is in production and that you know that no structural changes have been made to the Sales Territory dimension. Also assume that minimizing the cube's offline time is more important than minimizing the cube processing time. Rather than fully processing the Sales Territory dimension, you need to use a more lightweight dimension processing option. If only new members are added to the dimension, the best choice is Process Add because it detects new additions only. In this exercise, you will use the Process Update option to process the Sales Territory dimension incrementally. Process Update detects all member updates, inserts, and deletes.

1. In SSMS, connect to the SQL Server Database Engine, and then expand the Adventure-WorksDW2008 database.

2. Expand the Tables folder, right-click the DimSalesTerritory table, and then select Edit Top 200 Rows.

3. Change the SalesTerritoryGroup column of the France dimension member to **Pacific**. This step might not make much sense from a business standpoint, but it will help you understand how the Process Update processing option can be used to efficiently apply member changes.

4. In SSMS, right-click the Adventure Works cube, and then click Browse. Create a report with the Sales Territory multilevel hierarchy on rows and the Reseller Sales Amount measure on details, as Figure 7-31 shows. Notice that the France member is still a child of the Europe member.

Sales Territory Group ▼	Sales Territory Country ▼	Reseller Sales Amount
⊟ Europe	France	$4,607,537.93
	Germany	$1,983,988.04
	United Kingdom	$4,279,008.83
	Total	$10,870,534.80
⊞ North America		$67,985,726.81
⊞ Pacific		$1,594,335.38
Grand Total		$80,450,596.98

FIGURE 7-31 Create this report to see the effect of Process Update on the France dimension member.

5. In Object Explorer, right-click the Sales Territory dimension, and then click Process.

6. Process the Sales Territory dimension by using the Process Update option; this should already be set, by default, in the Process dialog box.

7. Go back to the report and reconnect. Notice that the France member is now found under the Pacific member. More important, the cube is not invalidated, and it does not have to be processed. In contrast, if you had fully processed the Sales Territory dimension, you would have had to process the entire Adventure Works cube because fully processing a dimension invalidates all cubes that reference the dimension.

> **BEST PRACTICES** **USE PROCESS UPDATE TO REMOVE AGGREGATIONS**
>
> If there is an aggregation on an attribute that is changed during a Process Update processing operation, the aggregation is temporarily removed from the cube, although it still exists in the aggregation design. At this point, queries give correct results, and aggregations that are not affected by the dimension processing are still in use. If you want to bring back the "lost" aggregations, you do not have to reprocess the whole cube, measure group, or partition; you need only to run a Process Index processing operation on it. When you use Process Index, the server rebuilds the missing indexes. If you are not sure which processing option you need, you can use Process Default. Process Default is the least expensive process type, so it gets the job done at minimum cost.

EXERCISE 2   Generate and Schedule Processing Scripts

Suppose that you need to create a SQL Server Agent job that fully processes an SSAS database. Follow these steps to automate processing with scripting:

1. In the SSMS Object Explorer, right-click the TK 70-448 SSAS Project database, and then click Process.

2. In the Process Database dialog box, expand the Script drop-down list, and then select Script Action To Clipboard.

3. In Object Explorer, connect to the SQL Server Database Engine.

4. In Object Explorer, right-click the SQL Server Agent folder, and then select Job.

5. In the New Job Step dialog box that appears, name the job **Process Database**.

6. Click the Steps page, and then click the New button to create a new step. Name the new step **Process database**.

7. Expand the Type drop-down list, and then select SQL Server Analysis Services Command.

8. Paste the script you created in step 2 into the Command box, as Figure 7-32 shows. Click OK to return to the New Job dialog box, and then click OK one more time to create the SQL Server Agent job.

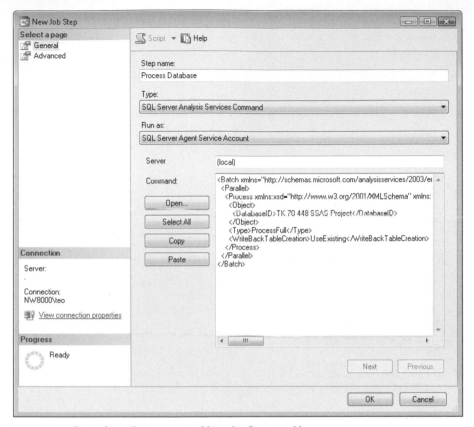

FIGURE 7-32 Paste the script you created into the Command box.

9. In Object Explorer, right-click the Process Database job you just created, and then click Start Job At Step to run the job.

10. Optionally, schedule the Process Database job to run on a schedule.

EXERCISE 3 Set Up Scheduled Polling Notifications for Proactive Caching

Suppose that you decide not to use SQL Server notifications with proactive caching because of their limitations. Instead, you want to set up scheduled polling notifications to let the server know when a change is made to the FactInternetSales table. In addition, assume that only new fact data is added to that table. As a prerequisite for setting scheduled polling, you need to decide how the polling query will detect data changes—typically, you would use a ModifedDate column.

1. Because FactInternetSales does not have such a date column, run the Scheduled-Polling.sql script (found in the ..\Source\Ch 07\TK448-ch07 Lesson 3\ folder) to add a ModifiedDate column to the FactInternetSales table and create an index on it. The script also prepopulates the ModifiedDate column with the order date.

2. Open the ..\Source\Ch 07\TK448-ch07 Lesson 2\TK 70-448 SSAS Project in BIDS.

3. Open the Adventure Works cube in the Cube Designer, and then navigate to the Partitions tab.

4. Expand the Internet Sales measure group, and then select the Internet Sales 2004 partition.

5. Click the Storage Settings link to open the Partition Storage Settings dialog box.

6. Select the Automatic MOLAP standard setting, and then click the Options button.

7. In the Storage Options dialog box, click the Notifications tab. Be sure that the Enable Proactive Caching check box is selected.

8. Select the Scheduled Polling notification option, and then select the Enable Incremental Updates check box.

9. Enter the following *SELECT* statement in the Polling Query column:

```
SELECT MAX(ModifiedDate) AS ModifiedDate FROM FactInternetSales
```

10. Enter the following *SELECT* statement in the Processing Query column:

```
SELECT * FROM FactInternetSales WHERE (ModifiedDate>?) AND (ModifiedDate<=?)
```

11. Click OK to return to the Partition Storage Settings dialog box, and then click OK again to return to the Partitions tab of the Cube Designer. Deploy the solution.

12. To test proactive caching, switch to the Cube Browser tab, and then create the report; it will look like the report shown in Figure 7-33.

Calendar Year ▼				
2001	2002	2003	2004	Grand Total
Internet Sales Amount	Internet Sales Amount	Internet Sales Amount	Internet Sales Amount	Internet Sales Amount
$3,266,373.66	$6,530,343.53	$9,791,060.30	$9,770,899.74	$29,358,677.22

FIGURE 7-33 This report demonstrates the effect of proactive caching with scheduled polling.

13. Open SQL Server Profiler, and then connect to SSAS.

14. In SSMS, open the FactInternetSales table. Copy the last record and paste it as a new record. Change the ModifiedDate column of the new record to **8/1/2004**.

15. Switch to SQL Server Profiler. You should see a trace notification event. In a few seconds, you should see a progress report event, which notifies you that the server has started processing the Internet Sales measure group.

16. In the Cube Browser, refresh the report, and notice that the total for year 2004 and the grand total values have changed. That is because the server received the scheduled polling notification and rebuilt the MOLAP cache automatically.

Case Scenario: Implementing Low-Latency OLAP and Deployment Strategies

1. You process the Adventure Works cube on a monthly basis as a last step of the ETL process that populates the AdventureWorksDW2008 database. However, some business users have reported that they would like to analyze sales data in real time. When a new Internet order is placed in the sales system, a lightweight ETL process enters the order data into the AdventureWorksDW2008 database. You need to enhance the Adventure Works cube to support low-latency reporting. In addition, based on some preliminary testing, the QA users have reported inadequate query response times when they browse the Adventure Works cube. You need improve the cube performance. How would you implement a low-latency partition to let business users browse the daily order data?

2. For the same scenario, what can you do to optimize the cube performance?

3. As an administrator, you follow an iterative design, test, and deploy cycle to implement a cube. You use BIDS to design the cube and test it locally. Periodically, you need to deploy your changes to a test server for user acceptance testing. To handle high reporting volumes, the production SSAS servers are load-balanced. Instead of processing all production cubes individually, you want to process the cube on a staging server and then deploy it to the production servers. Only new members are added to a large dimension, and you need to minimize the dimension processing time. What deployment options would you use to deploy the cube to testing and production environments?

4. For the scenario described in question 3, what processing option would you use to add only new members to a dimension?

Chapter Summary

- A measure group stores data physically in partitions. Partitions in a measure group can have different storage modes and aggregation designs.

- SSAS cubes perform best with MOLAP. Consider using HOLAP with very large and infrequently used partitions. Consider ROLAP to implement real-time partitions when you cannot use proactive caching.

- Aggregations are recalculated summaries of data. You might gain a remarkable performance increase by implementing useful aggregations. Useful aggregations are a byproduct of a good dimensional design.

- At design time, use the Aggregation Design Wizard to design aggregations using a cost/benefit algorithm.

- SSAS supports various deployment options to meet different management needs. During design time, use BIDS to deploy and process the changed object automatically.

- Deploying changes to a test or production environment typically requires more granular deployment. You can use the Deployment Wizard to preserve the existing management settings on the target server.

- Use the Synchronize Database Wizard to sync metadata and database changes between two SSAS databases.

- The SSAS processing architecture supports different processing options to minimize the database processing time. Processing a database fully is the easiest and cleanest way to process all objects contained in the database, but it might also take the longest.

- Proactive caching provides various advanced settings and notification options to meet different data latency needs.

CHAPTER 8

Securing and Administering SSAS

An enterprise-level platform, such as SQL Server Analysis Services (SSAS), must be trustworthy. A trustworthy system protects the data assets it captures by enforcing restricted access to sensitive data. A trustworthy system must also be easy to manage and monitor.

As an SSAS administrator, you will be performing various day-to-day tasks, such as managing the SSAS server instance(s); deploying, backing up, restoring, and synchronizing databases; automating repetitive tasks; managing storage; processing objects; securing the Unified Dimensional Model (UDM); and monitoring the server performance. SSAS provides a comprehensive management framework to help you perform all of these activities.

In this chapter, you will learn how to use SSAS security features to protect data in the cube. In addition, you will learn how to back up and restore databases and monitor the health and performance of your SSAS installations.

The source code for this chapter is available in the ..\Source\Ch 08\ folder within your Documents folder.

Exam objectives in this chapter:

- Configure permissions and roles in SSAS.
- Install and maintain an SSAS instance.
- Diagnose and resolve performance issues.

Before You Begin

To complete this chapter, you must have:

- Knowledge of Windows users and groups.
- Experience working with Windows services.
- Knowledge of dimensions and measure groups.

Lesson 1: Setting Up SSAS Server Security

Estimated lesson time: 30 minutes

As an administrator, you will not get very far with SSAS if you do not have a good grasp of how its security model works. You need to master this security model to meet real-life security requirements for protecting cube metadata and data. This lesson starts by discussing SSAS server roles and then teaches you how to implement restricted access to the cube data.

Understanding SSAS Security

The SSAS user security architecture is layered on top of Windows security. Users are authenticated based on their Windows accounts and authorized according to their role memberships.

Understanding Roles

To simplify security management, SSAS lets you group Windows users and groups into *roles*. The security policies you define in a role restrict the cube space that the user is authorized to access.

THE ADMINISTRATORS ROLE

When you install SSAS, the Setup program installs a predefined server-wide Administrators role. A user who is a member of this role has unrestricted access to the entire server. For example, members of the Administrators role can create SSAS databases and change server properties. You cannot delete the Administrators role.

Initially, the Administrators role is empty, but if you have local administrator rights on your machine, you can manage your local SSAS instance undeterred. Why? The reason is that the Setup program grants implicit SSAS administrative rights to the local members of the Windows LocalMachine\Administrators group.

> **IMPORTANT** **REVOKING LOCAL ADMINISTRATIVE RIGHTS TO SSAS**
>
> You can set the server *BuiltinAdminsAreServerAdmins* property to False if you want to revoke the predefined SSAS administrative rights to Windows local administrators. Before doing so, however, make sure that you assign some Windows users to the SSAS Administrators group to avoid a server lockdown.

To assign Windows users to the Administrators role, follow these steps:

1. In SQL Server Management Studio (SSMS), connect to the SSAS instance you want to manage.

2. Open the SSAS server properties by right-clicking the server node and then selecting Properties.

3. In the Analysis Services Properties dialog box, click the Security page.

4. Click the Add button to add Windows users or groups.

DATABASE ROLES

By default, users who are not members of the Administrators role are denied access to SSAS. To grant users access to SSAS objects, you must create one or more database roles and assign the users to a role that gives them the required permissions.

Database roles are additive—that is, if the user is a member of multiple roles, the effective permission set is the union of the allowed role permissions. Users who belong to multiple roles can choose the specific role they want to use to connect to the server.

EXAM TIP

The SSAS connection string property supports a Roles setting, which an end user or a client application can use to specify a comma-delimited list of database roles to be evaluated by the server. The following shows an example of a list of roles:

```
Data Source=(local);Initial Catalog="Adventure Works DW 2008";Roles=Adventure
Works,Sales Managers;
```

The server will evaluate and apply only the roles that the user is a member of.

Understanding Permissions

When you configure a role, you specify a set of security policies and attach these policies to an SSAS object, such as a cube or dimension. These security policies are saved as a collection of permissions inside the object metadata.

A *permission* defines a security policy for a given object. It references the role that uses the permission and has a common set of properties, described in Table 8-1.

TABLE 8-1 Permission Properties

PROPERTY	DESCRIPTION	SETTINGS
ID	Specifies the permission identifier.	
Role ID	References the role to which the permission applies.	
Read	The user can browse the object—that is, the user can view the cube object.	None, Allowed
Process	The user can process the object and its child objects.	
ReadDefinition	The user can view the definition of the object—that is, the user can script the object.	None, Basic, Allowed
Write	The user can modify the object data. The Write permission applies to dimension, cube, and mining models objects only.	None, Allowed

Suppose that you grant members of the Adventure Works database role rights to process the Adventure Works cube. In addition, you grant the members of the Sales Managers role rights to read the cube data. The resulting role definition contains a collection of two *Cube-Permission* objects, which are saved in the cube definition. The abbreviated definition of the *CubePermissions* collection might look like the following:

```
 <CubePermissions>
  <CubePermission>
    <ID>CubePermission</ID>
    <Name>CubePermission</Name>
    <RoleID>Adventure Works</RoleID>
    <Process>true</Process>
  </CubePermission>
  <CubePermission>
    <ID>CubePermission 2</ID>
    <Name>CubePermission 2</Name>
    <RoleID>Sales Managers</RoleID>
    <Read>Allowed</Read>
  </CubePermission>
</CubePermissions>
```

Each permission inside the permissions collection references the role to which the permission applies. The preceding example has two roles that define security policies for the Adventure Works cube: Adventure Works and Sales Managers. In addition to permissions for cubes, SSAS has corresponding permissions for the following SSAS objects: database, data source, dimension, attribute, cell, mining structure, and mining model. For example, if you define a dimension security policy, a *DimensionPermissions* collection will be created in the definition file of the affected dimension.

Permissions can be inherited. For example, if you let a role process a database, the role will be able to process all cubes in the database.

Creating Roles and Applying User Security to Cubes

You can create database roles in either SSMS or Business Intelligence Development Studio (BIDS). Database roles that you define in BIDS are included in the SSAS project, which lets you test them during development. Roles defined in SSMS are not included in the SSAS project, so working in BIDS is the recommended method. After the cube is deployed to production, the administrator finalizes the security setup by adding the required Windows users and groups as members of the database roles.

Creating a Database Role

To create a new database role in the BIDS Solution Explorer, right-click the Roles folder, and then select New Role. BIDS opens the Role Designer, shown in Figure 8-1, and adds a new role named Role under the Roles folder in Solution Explorer.

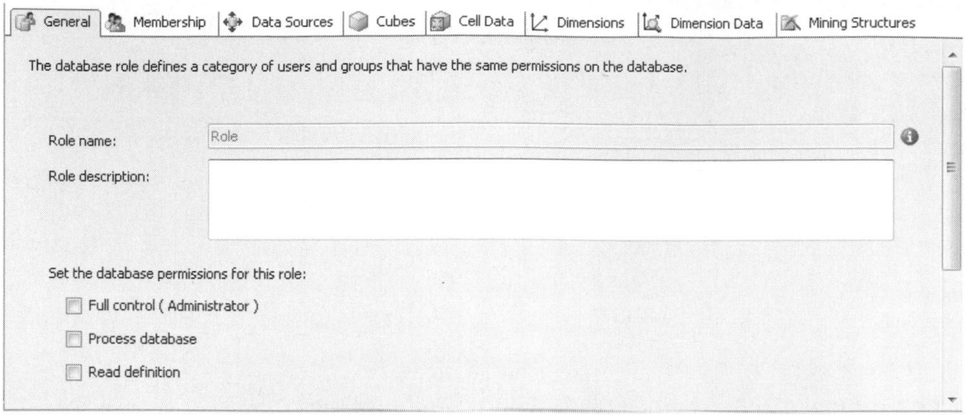

FIGURE 8-1 Use the Role Designer to create and maintain database roles.

To change the role name, right-click the role in Solution Explorer and select Rename, or rename the role in place by clicking the role twice. Be sure to use meaningful role names.

Click Yes in the message box that appears, to confirm that you want to change the role object identifier as well. The Role Designer tab interface lets you set up security permissions at different granularity. Use the General tab to control access to the entire database. If you select the Full Control (Administrator) check box, members of this role will become database administrators and will have unrestricted access to the database on which the role is defined.

Use the Membership tab to assign Windows users and/or groups to the role. Typically, users do not need access to data sources. However, one scenario in which users might need to access the data source is when they need to compare data in the data source with data in the mining model. To grant users access to the data source, switch to the Data Sources tab, and then change the Access column from None to Read.

By default, the members of a role do not have access to the cubes in the database. To let users browse the cube metadata and data, switch to the Cubes tab, and change the Access column from None to Read. If the cube has write-enabled partitions, giving the users Read/Write permission will let them change the partition data.

Recall that a dimension can be shared among cubes. The Dimensions tab lets you control access to cube dimensions (if the role has access to the cube) or database dimensions by using the Select Dimension Set drop-down list. You can grant a Read role, which is the default, and Read/Write permission to a dimension. The latter option lets users update the dimension members if the dimension has the Enable Dimension Writeback option enabled.

The Cell Data and Dimension Data tabs are discussed in the following sections, "Working with Dimension Data Security" and "Defining Advanced SSAS Cell Security." The last tab, Mining Structure, lets you restrict user access to mining structures and models. By default, members of a role have access to all dimensions in the database. Verify this by navigating to the Dimensions tab, shown in Figure 8-2.

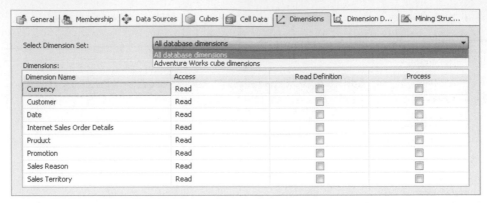

FIGURE 8-2 Use the Dimensions tab to grant the Read or Read/Write permissions to dimensions at a database or cube level.

Working with Dimension Data Security

Although SSAS lets you control security all the way down to the cube cells, most real-life security requirements are less granular. Usually, you will need to secure access to dimension members and data associated with these members. Dimension data security, defined on the Dimension Data security tab, is designed to do just that.

Use the Dimension drop-down list to set dimension data security at a database or cube level. If you select a database dimension, the security policies are inherited by cubes that reference that dimension and are stored in the database metadata. This might reduce the maintenance effort when an SSAS database contains more than one cube. In the case of a cube dimension, the security policies are scoped at that cube only and are stored in the cube metadata. This approach could be useful if the dimension is referenced by multiple cubes, but the dimension data security policies vary from one cube to another.

Real-life cubes might contain many attributes, and you might need to set up dimension security policies on several dimensions and/or attributes. You can easily tell which dimensions and attributes are secured by expanding the Dimension and Attribute Hierarchy drop-down lists. Secured dimensions and attributes will have an (attribute security defined) suffix after their names.

CONFIGURING BASIC DIMENSION DATA SECURITY

Remember that a dimension is simply a container of attributes. For example, the Sales Territory dimension contains Sales Territory Group, Sales Territory Country, and Sales Territory Region attributes. Figure 8-3 shows the Basic tab of the Role Designer's Dimension Data security tab.

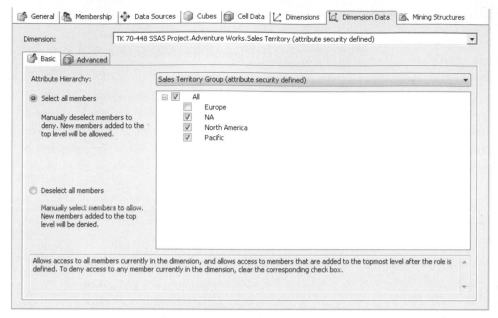

FIGURE 8-3 Use the Basic tab to configure basic dimension data security.

The Basic tab lets you secure dimension members explicitly by using one of two approaches: *pessimistic* or *optimistic*. With the pessimistic approach, you deny everything except a set of allowed members called an *allowed set*. The optimistic approach is the exact opposite: you allow all members except a set of denied members, called a *denied set*. For more information about allowed and denied sets, see Richard Tkachuk's blog entry "Dimension Security in Analysis Services 2005" (see References).

EXAM TIP

Suppose that you have an Employee dimension and you want to grant a role rights to view all employees except for a few. Should you define an allowed set or a denied set? Because the role would allow the viewing of most employees, consider implementing a denied set that contains the employees that the role is not authorized to view.

To create an allowed set of members, expand the Attribute drop-down list, and then select the attribute you want to secure. Select the Deselect All Members option, and then select the check boxes for only the attribute members that the role is allowed to view. To specify a denied set, choose the Select All Members option, and then select the check boxes for the attribute members that you do not want to let end users view.

Securing one attribute automatically secures the rest of the attributes in the same dimension. For example, given the security setup shown in Figure 8-3, if members of the role request a report that shows the Sales Territory Region attribute, they will not see the European regions. Behind the scenes, the server applies a special behavior called Autoexists to propagate the security filter to all other attributes within the same dimension.

CONFIGURING ADVANCED DIMENSION DATA SECURITY

Although explicitly selecting the allowed or denied attribute members might be sufficient to meet basic security needs, most real-life business requirements demand more flexibility. For example, you might need an MDX expression that returns a different allowed or denied set based on the identity of the interactive user. Figure 8-4 shows the Dimension Data tab's Advanced tab, which lets you use Multidimensional Expressions (MDX) language expressions to construct the allowed and denied sets.

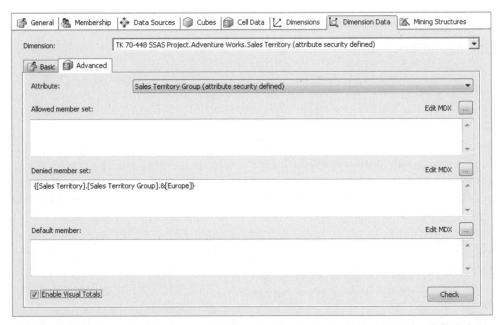

FIGURE 8-4 The Advanced tab lets you use MDX expressions to construct the allowed and denied sets.

When you select members on the Basic tab, the Advanced tab is automatically updated. You can use any set-producing MDX functions that return an MDX set containing the allowed or disallowed members. You can click the Edit MDX button, which lets you create the set by dragging metadata objects in the MDX Builder.

You can enter an MDX expression in the Default Member box when you need to customize the default member for different roles. A server property named Visual Total controls the totals a user should see when he or she browses the cube by another dimension. If the Enable Visual Totals check box is not selected (the default setting), the server aggregates data without regard to the denied attribute members. For example, even if the Europe member is denied, the Sales Territory Group totals will include its contribution. To exclude the denied members from contributing to the aggregated values, select the Enable Visual Totals check box.

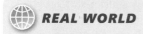 **REAL WORLD**

Teo Lachev

For one of our projects, we needed to implement rather complex application-based security policies in the cube. These policies would define the bank accounts that a given user would be allowed to see. Instead of replicating the entire security infrastructure to the cube and duplicating the management effort, we enhanced the Extract, Transform, and Load (ETL) process to import only the allowed set into a "factless" fact table. This fact table had only two columns: UserID, which stored the user domain identity, and AccountID. We then defined a Security Filter measure group that mapped to the fact table and referenced the Account and Employee dimensions. After this was in place, we used the following MDX expression for the allowed set of the Account dimension key:

```
Exists([Account].[Account].[Account].Members,
StrToMember("[Employee].[Login ID].&[" + Username + "]"),
"Security Filter")
```

The MDX *Username* function returns the Windows user account name for the user, in the format *domain\userid*. The *StrToMember* function resolves the text login to a member in the Employee dimension. Executed over the Security Filter measure group, the *Exists* MDX function returns a set of the accounts owned by the interactive user.

After evaluating different implementation approaches, we found that the factless measure group approach gave us the best performance. If importing the allowed set into the cube is not an option, consider dynamic dimension security by implementing an SSAS stored procedure that calls the security service to obtain the allowed dimension members and construct an allowed set. The *SQL Server Magazine* article "Protect UDM with Dimension Data Security," by Teo Lachev, describes this process in more detail (see References).

Defining Advanced SSAS Cell Security

By default, if a role is allowed to view an attribute member, the role can see all cells associated with that member. However, you can use cell security to hide cell values from the end user. For example, implement cell security when you need to prevent users from viewing sensitive measures, such as profit and account balances. Cell security is the most detailed level of SSAS security. You can define cell security policies on the Cell Data tab of the Role Designer, as Figure 8-5 shows.

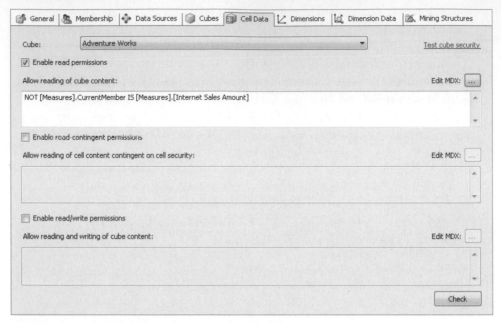

FIGURE 8-5 Use the Cell Data tab to define cell security policies.

There are three types of cell permissions that you can use to define cell security policies:

- **Read** This permission determines the cells that members of the role can view. If the MDX expression evaluates to True, access to the cells is granted. In Figure 8-5, the role is allowed access to all measures except Internet Sales Amount.

- **Read-Contingent** This permission determines whether cells derived from restricted cells are permitted. For example, in Chapter 6, "Extending SSAS Cubes," you defined the Sales Amount measure as a sum of the Internet Sales Amount and Reseller Sales Amount measures, as follows:

```
[Sales Amount]=[Internet Sales Amount]+[Reseller Sales Amount]
```

If you do not define an explicit read-contingent policy, the role will be able to read the Sales Amount–derived measure despite the fact that it does not have access to the Internet Sales Amount measure. You could add the Sales Amount measure to the list of read permissions, but this could become counterproductive if you have many calculated members using the Internet Sales Amount. Instead, you could broaden the security scope not only to disallow Internet Sales Amount but also to disallow all measures that derive from Internet Sales Amount. To do so, you need to clear the Enable Read Permissions check box and then select the Enable Read-Contingent Permissions check box. Then, to disallow access to the Internet Sales Amount measure and to the calculated members such as Sales Profit that derive from it, use the following expression:

```
NOT Measures.CurrentMember IS [Measures].[Internet Sales Amount]
```

- **Read/Write**   This permission identifies the cells that users can update when writing back to the cube, assuming that the partition is enabled for writeback. The measure group partition must be write-enabled for read/write permission to take effect. By default, if the cell is disallowed, it will show *#N/A*. Alternatively, the client application can use the Secured Cell Value connection string setting to specify a different text, such as *NULL*, for disallowed cells.

Setting Drillthrough Security

Recall from Chapter 6 that you can define a drillthrough action to let the user view the lowest level of detail behind a cell. For example, the Reseller Details drillthrough action that you defined in Chapter 6 lets the user see the source reseller data as it was loaded from the FactResellerSales fact table. By design, drillthrough actions ignore any calculations defined in the cube. Because this might present a security risk, a database role by default does not have drillthrough permissions.

The Cubes tab, shown in Figure 8-6, lets you enable cube drillthrough for a given database role.

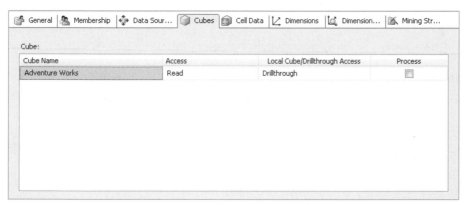

FIGURE 8-6 Set the Local Cube/Drillthrough Access drop-down list to Drillthrough to let the user view the lowest level of detail behind a cell.

To grant the role drillthrough rights, change the Local Cube/Drillthrough Access drop-down list value to Drillthrough, and then deploy the solution.

Testing Database Role Security

After you set up the database role, you need to make sure that it works as you intended. You can assign a Windows user account to a role and log in as that user, or you can use the Windows Run As feature. But BIDS supports a faster way to test the role security, as follows:

1. Open the cube in the Cube Designer, and then click the Browser tab.
2. Click the Change User button on the toolbar to open the Security Context dialog box, shown in Figure 8-7.

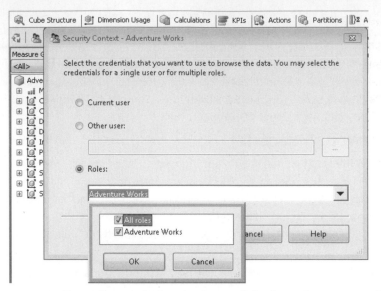

FIGURE 8-7 For testing, use the Security Context dialog box to impersonate a Windows user or a database role.

3. Select the Roles option, and then expand the drop-down list below it.

4. Select the role that you want to test, click OK to return to the Security Context dialog box, and then click OK again to return to the Browser tab.

After you have changed the security context, BIDS will use the selected role or roles when you browse the cube.

EXAM TIP

Real-life Windows security can be complicated. Suppose that you have a Web application deployed to a Web server that queries an SSAS cube on a different server. By default, the Web server will not delegate the end user identity to the SSAS server, and the connection will fail. To get around this limitation, you need to configure the Web server for Kerberos delegation. Read the Microsoft Knowledge Base article "How to Configure SQL Server 2005 Analysis Services to Use Kerberos Authentication" to learn how to implement Kerberos delegation (see References).

PRACTICE **Implementing User Security on SSAS Cubes**

In this practice, you create a database role and implement dimension and cell security. You also grant the role drillthrough access to the cube.

EXERCISE 1 Create Roles and Apply User Security to Cubes

You need to delegate the management of the Adventure Works cube to other users. Follow these steps to create a new database role that will grant its members rights to process the database but will prevent them from seeing sensitive information.

1. Open the TK 70-448 SSAS Project in BIDS (from the ..\Source\Ch 08\TK448-ch08 Start Here\ folder in your user account's Documents folder).

2. In Solution Explorer, right-click the Roles folder, and then select New Role.

3. BIDS creates a new role named Role and opens the Role Designer. In Solution Explorer, change the role name to **Adventure Works.role**.

4. On the General tab of the Role Designer, select the Process Database check box to let the role process the database and its objects.

5. By default, a new role cannot access any cubes in the database. Click the Cubes tab, expand the Access drop-down list, and then select Read to grant the role access to the Adventure Works cube.

6. Click the Dimension Data tab to configure basic dimension data security.

7. Now you want to prevent the members of the Adventure Works role from seeing sales for the Europe member of the Sales Territory dimension. Expand the Dimension drop-down list, and then select the Sales Territory cube dimension listed beneath the Adventure Works cube, as Figure 8-8 shows. Click OK.

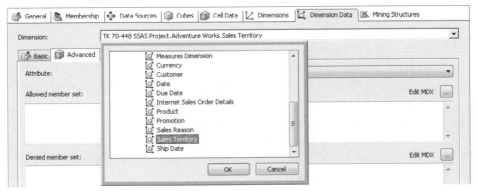

FIGURE 8-8 Select the Sales Territory cube dimension to limit the dimension data security to the Adventure Works cube.

8. Expand the Attribute Hierarchy drop-down list, and then select the Sales Territory Group attribute.

9. Clear the Europe check box.

10. Click the Advanced tab, and notice that the Role Designer has generated the following denied member set:

```
{[Sales Territory].[Sales Territory Group].&[Europe]}
```

11. Select the Enable Visual Totals check box to exclude the contributions of the Europe member from the aggregated totals.

12. Deploy the solution, and then navigate to the Browser tab in the Cube Designer.

13. To test the new role, click the Change User button on the toolbar. In the Security Context dialog box, select Roles and then from the Roles drop-down list, select the Adventure Works role check box and click OK. Click OK again to close the Security Context dialog box.

14. Create the report shown in Figure 8-9 by dragging the Sales Territory Group attribute of the Sales Territory dimension onto rows and the Internet Sales Amount measure onto data.

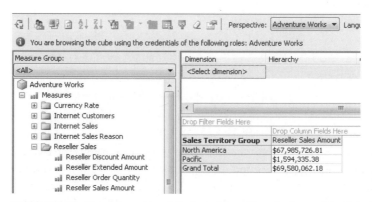

FIGURE 8-9 The Europe member is excluded from the members of the Sales Territory group.

Notice that the Adventure Works role does not have access to the Europe member. In addition, as a result of enabling Visual Totals, the report totals exclude the Europe data. If Visual Totals was off, the report totals would have included the Europe contribution as though Europe appeared on the report.

15. To test Autoexists, replace the Sales Territory Group attribute with the Sales Territory Region attribute. Notice that the European regions are now excluded even though you have not defined explicit dimension data security on the Sales Territory Region attribute. That is because the server returns only the members of the attribute hierarchies that relate to one another in the same dimension.

16. Optionally, use SSMS to add Windows users and/or groups as members of the Adventure Works role. Log on as one of the role members, and then test the role rights.

EXERCISE 2   Define Advanced SSAS Cell Security

Next you deny the Adventure Works role access to the Internet Sales Amount measure by setting up cell security policies.

1. Open the Adventure Works role in the Role Designer by double-clicking it in Solution Explorer, and then clicking the Cell Data tab.

2. Select the Enable Read Permissions check box.

3. To let the Adventure Works role read all cells except Internet Sales Amount, enter the following MDX expression in the Allow Reading Of Cube Content box:

```
NOT Measures.CurrentMember IS [Measures].[Internet Sales Amount]
```

4. Click the Check button to verify the expression syntax. Save the role definition, and then deploy the solution.

5. In the Browser tab of the Cube Designer, click the Change User button on the toolbar, and then select the Adventure Works role in the Security Context dialog box.

6. Create the report shown in Figure 8-10 by dragging the Sales Territory Group attribute of the Sales Territory dimension onto rows and the measures Reseller Sales Amount and Internet Sales Amount onto data.

Sales Territory Group ▼	Reseller Sales Amount	Internet Sales Amount
NA		#N/A
North America	$67,985,726.81	#N/A
Pacific	$1,594,335.38	#N/A
Grand Total	$69,580,062.18	#N/A

FIGURE 8-10 When cell security protects cells, the cell values show #N/A.

Notice that the Adventure Works role does not have access to the Internet Sales Amount, so all Internet Sales Amount cells show *#N/A*.

7. Optionally, drag the Sales Amount measure onto the report data. Notice that although you denied the role access to the Internet Sales Amount measure, the Adventure Works role can view the Sales Amount measure. That is because Sales Amount is a calculated member that uses Internet Sales Amount. If you want to deny access to both Internet Sales Amount and Sales Amount, you need to set up read-contingent permissions.

EXERCISE 3 Set Drillthrough Security

Now you want to let the members of the Adventure Works role execute the Reseller Sales drillthrough action that you implemented in Chapter 6.

1. In the Browser tab of the Cube Designer, click the Change User button on the toolbar, and then select the Adventure Works role.

2. Create the report shown in Figure 8-11 by dragging the Product Categories attribute of the Product dimension onto rows, the Calendar hierarchy of the Date dimension onto columns, and the Reseller Sales Amount measure onto data. Expand the Calendar hierarchy all the way down to the Date level.

3. Right-click a Reseller Sales Amount cell, and then select Reseller Details to execute the Reseller Details drillthrough action. Notice that the server shows an error message: *The permission required for this operation has not been granted*. That is because, by default, a role is denied drillthrough rights.

4. Open the Adventure Works role in the Role Designer, and then click the Cubes tab.

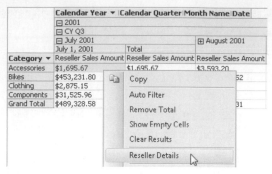

FIGURE 8-11 Initiate the Reseller Details drillthrough action and notice that, by default, a role is denied cube drillthrough access.

5. Expand the Local Cube/Drillthrough Access drop-down list, and then select Drillthrough.

6. When you have cell security permissions defined, even if you grant drillthrough permissions to a role, the server will deny the drillthrough actions. Click the Cell Data tab, and then clear the Enable Read Permissions check box.

7. Deploy the solution, and again initiate the Reseller Details action on the report shown in Figure 8-11. Notice that this time the Adventure Works role can drill through the cube to see the source data.

✔ Quick Check

1. Which server property do you need to change to disallow local Windows administrators administrative access to the SSAS server?

2. Is a new role allowed cube access by default?

3. What do you need to do to prevent a role from viewing calculated members that use a given measure?

Quick Check Answers

1. To disallow local administrators the rights to become SSAS administrators, change the Security\BuiltinAdminsAreServerAdmins property for the Analysis Services instance to False.

2. By default, a new role is not allowed cube access. You need to grant the role at least read permission to the cube so that its members can browse the cube.

3. To prevent a role from seeing calculated members that derive from a measure, you need to set a read-contingent permission that revokes that measure.

Lesson 2: Managing SSAS High Availability, Backups, and Object Scripting

Estimated lesson time: 20 minutes

An important management task that every administrator needs to master is preparing for disaster recovery. A well-designed and tested backup and restore plan is necessary for recovering your SSAS databases after a disaster. This includes backing up SSAS databases on a regular basis and knowing how to restore them when needed. Scaling out UDM lets you support increased query loads. In addition, operational requirements might call for high availability. By using the Microsoft clustering technologies provided in the Windows Server operating system, you can implement scalable and highly available SSAS solutions by configuring two or more SSAS servers in a cluster.

Backing Up an SSAS Database in SSMS

Backing up an SSAS database on a regular basis is a routine maintenance task. A common reason for backing up a database is so that you can revert to the latest saved copy as part of your disaster recovery plan. Another scenario in which backing up a database can be useful is when you are working on a prototype database and you want to send the database metadata and data to someone else as a single file.

A database backup copies the entire database: metadata, data, and aggregations. The backup operation is not intrusive, meaning that users can continue querying the cubes in the database while the backup operation is running. In Analysis Services 2008, Microsoft has redesigned the backup storage to enhance performance in all backup and restore scenarios.

You can use SSMS to back up a database by following these steps:

1. In SSMS, connect to the SSAS instance.

2. Expand the Databases folder. Right-click the database you need to back up, and then select Back Up.

3. SSMS displays the Backup Database dialog box, shown in Figure 8-12, to let you specify details about the backup operation.

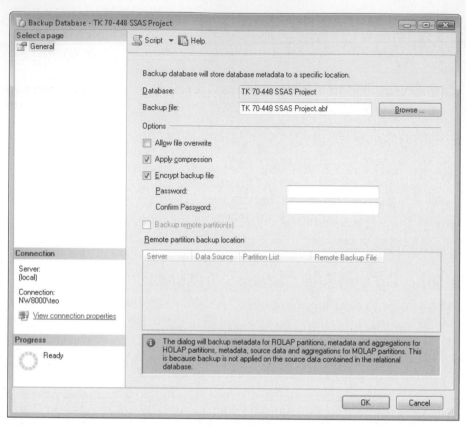

FIGURE 8-12 Use the Backup Database dialog box to specify the details for the backup operation.

Understanding the Backup Database Dialog Box

The Backup File box and the Browse button let you specify the file path and the name of the backup file. The Allow File Overwrite option lets you overwrite a backup file with the same name.

EXAM TIP

Allowed backup folders are listed in the *AllowedBrowsingFolders* advanced server property. The default backup folder is \Program Files\Microsoft SQL Server\MSAS10.MSSQLSERVER\ OLAP\Backup, as specified by the BackupDir server property. If you want to save the backup file to a different folder, add that folder to the *AllowedBrowsingFolders* server property. Use a semicolon as a delimiter. You can specify local folders only.

If you select the Apply Compression check box, the server will compress the data in the backup file, but be aware that this will increase backup time. Multidimensional OLAP (MOLAP) data is already stored in compressed format, so you will not gain much storage space if you select this option.

Consider encrypting the backup file if the SSAS database contains sensitive information. To do so, leave the default Encrypt Backup File check box selected, and then specify a password. Although the server does not enforce any password policies, you should still follow security best practices and use passwords that are difficult to guess. Save the password in a safe place—you will need it to restore the database.

Last, if your cube has remote partitions—that is, if some partitions are managed by another server—and you want to back them up, select the Backup Remote Partitions check box. SSMS will list the remote partitions in the Remote Partition Backup Locations grid.

Restoring Databases

Although we all hope we never have to, a common scenario in which you must restore a database is when you need to revert to the latest backup as part of a disaster recovery effort. To restore a database, follow these steps:

1. In SSMS, right-click the Databases folder, and then select Restore to open the Restore Database dialog box, shown in Figure 8-13.

2. Click the Browse button to locate the backup file, or type the full path in the Backup File box.

3. Expand the Restore Database drop-down list and select the database that you want to restore, or type the database name in the Restore Database box.

4. By default, the server will restore the database in the folder specified by the DataDir server property. If this is not what you want, you can click the Browse button to specify a different location.

5. Select the Allow Database Overwrite check box to restore the backup over an existing database. If you do not want to overwrite the database, you can enter a different database name in the Restore Database box instead of selecting an existing database from the drop-down list.

6. By default, the Include Security Information drop-down list is set to Copy All, and the server will copy the role membership information from the backup file. If you do not want to restore the role membership, select the Skip Membership drop-down list item.

7. If you have encrypted the backup file, which best practice suggests that you should, enter the password in the Password box.

8. Click OK to restore the database.

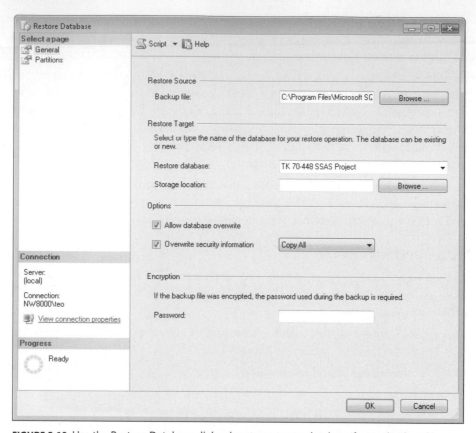

FIGURE 8-13 Use the Restore Database dialog box to restore a database from a backup file.

Attaching and Detaching Databases

In addition to backing up and restoring databases, SSAS lets you move an SSAS database to a new location by detaching and attaching the database, as follows:

1. In SSMS, right-click the SSAS database, and then select Detach.

2. In the Detach Database dialog box that appears, you can optionally specify a password to encrypt certain files that might contain confidential information. Click OK to detach the database.

3. Use any operating system mechanism or your standard method for moving files to move the database folder to the new location. For example, you can use file copy to move the TK 70-448 SSAS Project database from \Program Files\Microsoft SQL Server\ MSAS10.MSSQLSERVER\OLAP\Data\ to another folder.

4. In SSMS, right-click the Databases folder, and then select Attach.

5. In the Attach Database dialog box, click the ellipsis (...) button, and then navigate to the new folder. The *AllowedBrowsingFolders* server property controls which folders you can browse.

6. If you specified a password when detaching the database, enter the same password in the Password box.

7. Last, SSAS lets you attach a database in read-only mode by selecting the Read-Only check box. When the database is in read-only mode, the server disallows certain management operations, such as processing and synchronizing the database. For a full list of the restrictions with read-only databases, see the SQL Server 2008 Books Online topic "Database ReadWriteModes" (see References).

Scheduling SSAS Backups in SQL Server Agent

As a savvy SSAS administrator, you might want to automate the backup operations. The SQL Server Agent service, a component of Microsoft SQL Server, can execute backup scripts to help you do that. To schedule an SSAS backup, follow these steps:

1. In the Backup Database dialog box, expand the Script drop-down list, and then select Script Action To Clipboard (or press Ctrl+Shift+C). .

2. Connect to the SQL Server Database Engine instance where the job will run. Make sure that the SQL Server Agent service is running. In Object Explorer, right-click the SQL Server Agent node (it should be the last node in Object Explorer), select New, and then select Job.

3. In the New Job dialog box that appears, give the new job a name.

4. A job can contain one or more steps. In the Select A Page pane, click the Steps page, and then click New to create a new step.

5. Expand the Type drop-down list, and then select SQL Server Analysis Services Command as a step type.

6. Enter the name of the server that will execute the script—**(local)**, for example.

7. Paste the backup script that you copied to the Clipboard into the Command box, as Figure 8-14 shows. Click OK to close the New Job Step dialog box.

8. In the New Job dialog box, click the Schedules page to schedule the job execution when you want it to run. If you want to run the job immediately, click OK to create the job. Expand the Jobs folder under SQL Server Agent, right-click the job you just created, and then click Start Job. SQL Server Agent will start the job and display its progress in the Start Jobs dialog box.

9. To view the job history log, right-click the job, and then click View History.

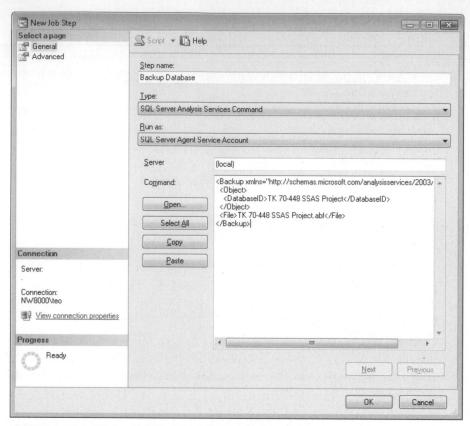

FIGURE 8-14 Use SQL Server Agent to automate database backups.

Scripting SSAS Objects in SSMS

Although backing up and restoring databases would probably meet most of your disaster recovery requirements, sometimes you might need to back up the object definition only. For example, before making extensive changes to a cube, you might want to back up the cube definition so that you can undo your changes later if needed. One way to meet this requirement is to implement source control in BIDS. However, you will undoubtedly perform some management changes, such as partition and role management, outside of BIDS. In this case, you can script the object in SSMS by generating an XML for Analysis (XMLA) script.

SSMS can script the definitions of all major objects, including databases, dimensions, cubes, measure groups, and partitions. You can generate scripts for creating, altering, and deleting objects. For example, to script the cube definition for creating the cube, you would follow these steps:

1. In SSMS Object Explorer, right-click the cube you want to script.

2. Select Script Cube As, Create To, and then New Query Editor Window, as Figure 8-15 shows.

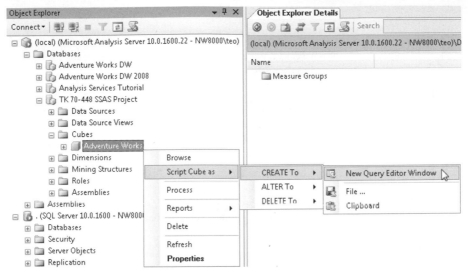

FIGURE 8-15 Use SSMS script support to back up and restore object definitions.

Alternatively, you can generate the script in a new query window or copy it to the Windows Clipboard.

3. SSMS generates a Create XMLA script in a new query window, as Figure 8-16 shows.

FIGURE 8-16 SSMS generates a Create XMLA script to back up and restore object definitions.

As with any XMLA command script, you can execute the object script manually at a later time. To do so, click the Execute button on the toolbar. Alternatively, you can schedule the script by using SQL Server Agent.

Clustering SSAS

More demanding operational requirements might call for fault tolerance and scalability. Windows Clustering in Windows Server provides two different but complementary technologies to provide scalable and highly available SSAS solutions. Table 8-2 provides a high-level comparison of the Network Load Balancing (NLB) and Microsoft Cluster Service (MSCS) technologies.

TABLE 8-2 Windows Clustering Technologies

CRITERIA	NLB	MSCS
Usage	Load balancing TCP and user-defined functions (UDF) traffic	Failover support
Windows Server editions	Web Edition, Standard Edition, Enterprise Edition, Datacenter Edition	Enterprise Edition, Datacenter Edition
Maximum number of nodes	32	8

NLB is primarily used to distribute the user load across several servers. In contrast, the main goal of MSCS is to provide high availability. MSCS is supported in Windows Server Enterprise and Datacenter editions.

Clustering for Scalability

You can use NLB to scale out SSAS to two or more servers. Scaling out should be your last resort to increase the performance of your SSAS solution. Before deciding to scale out, focus first on good design practices, such as partitioning your cubes, implementing useful aggregations, and tuning MDX calculations and queries. Figure 8-17 illustrates how you can use NLB to scale out SSAS.

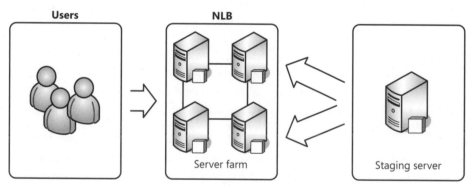

FIGURE 8-17 Use NLB to build highly scalable SSAS solutions.

User load is balanced across several SSAS servers (called *nodes*) configured in a cluster, also called a *server farm*. The SSAS servers participate in a Web farm by using NLB. To implement this scenario, configure NLB in multiple-host configuration mode so that all nodes can handle incoming requests. A client (user or application) sends query requests to the virtual IP address of the server farm. NLB maintains utilization statistics of all clustered servers and sends the request to the least utilized server. In this way, the SSAS site can scale out almost linearly by adding new servers to the NLB cluster.

Instead of processing the UDM on each server, consider building and validating the cubes on a designated staging server. Then, during off-peak hours, deploy the staging UDM to the nodes by using SSAS database synchronization.

You can also use a load-balancing cluster to ensure availability in the event that a node fails. However, NLB is not designed to check availability of services—for example, to ensure that the SSAS service on a particular node is functional—and so NLB might redirect the user to a nonfunctional SSAS server. If failover is the primary design goal, consider clustering SSAS servers in an MSCS failover cluster.

Clustering for Availability

SQL Server 2008 supports MSCS. Within the SQL Server 2008 business intelligence (BI) components, SSAS is cluster-aware and can be installed in an MSCS installation. For SQL Server clustering, MSCS uses a *shared-nothing model*, which means that the drive volumes (which hold the database and cube data) can be controlled by only one machine at a time in the cluster. This provides automatic failover of the drives if a server has a hardware or software problem that causes the SQL Server 2008 service to stop. Figure 8-18 illustrates an SSAS failover cluster.

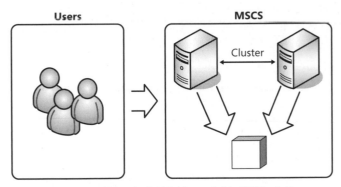

FIGURE 8-18 Use MSCS to build highly available SSAS solutions.

In this case, the failover cluster consists of two nodes, each of which is an independent server. Together, these independent servers create a server cluster that appears to users as a single server. Unlike NLB, cluster resources, such as a disk, are hosted on only one node at any time. The servers are in constant communication with each other by exchanging packets (called a heartbeat) to ensure that a node's network interface is still active. If the primary server crashes, the backup server is activated and takes over the cluster.

You cannot configure the same server to use both NLB and MSCS. Implementing a failover cluster solution requires additional steps to configure MSCS before you install SQL Server 2008. To learn how to configure a server cluster, see the Windows Server documentation topic "Server Clusters" (see References). The steps to install an SSAS cluster are identical to the steps to set up a SQL Server Database Engine cluster. For step-by-step installation instructions, see the SQL Server 2008 Books Online topic "Installing a SQL Server 2008 Failover Cluster" (see References).

In this practice, you use SSMS to back up the TK 70-448 SSAS Project database. You also use SQL Server Agent to schedule the backup script to run on a schedule.

EXERCISE 1   Create a Database Backup

In this exercise, you will back up the TK 70-448 SSAS Project database.

1. Open SSMS, and then connect to SSAS.

2. In Object Explorer, expand the Databases folder. Right-click the TK 70-448 SSAS Project database, and then select Back Up.

3. In the Backup Database dialog box that appears, click the Browse button, and notice that, by default, the backup file will be saved to the C:\Program Files\Microsoft SQL Server\MSAS10.MSSQLSERVER\OLAP\Backup\ folder.

4. Type **TK448** in the Password and Confirm Password boxes.

5. Click OK to create the database backup.

6. Optionally, restore the database from the backup file you have just created by right-clicking the TK 70-448 SSAS Project database and then selecting Restore. In the Restore Database dialog box, click the Browse button, and then select the backup file in the Locate Database Files dialog box.

7. Type **TK448** in the Password box.

8. Select the Allow Database Overwrite option, and then click OK. SSMS restores the database from the backup file.

EXERCISE 2   Schedule a Database Backup

Your second task is to schedule a backup script by using SQL Server Agent.

1. In the SSMS Object Explorer, right-click the TK 70-448 SSAS Project database, and then click Back Up.

2. Fill in the fields in the Backup Database dialog box as necessary.

3. In the Backup Database dialog box, in the Script drop-down list, select Script Action To Clipboard (or press Ctrl+Shift+C). If you assigned a password to encrypt the database, SSMS will prompt you as to whether you want to include the password in the script. Click Yes. SSMS generates the backup script. Close the Backup Database dialog box.

4. In SSMS Object Explorer, click the Connect button, and then select Database Engine. Connect to SQL Server when the script is scheduled to run. Ensure that the SQL Server Agent service is running.

5. Expand the SQL Server Agent folder. Right-click the Jobs node, and then select New Job.

6. In the New Job dialog box that appears, type **Back Up TK 70-448 SSAS Project** as the name of the job.

7. Select the Steps page, and then click New to create a new step.

8. In the New Step dialog box, type **Database Backup** as the name of the step.

9. Expand the Type drop-down list, and then select SQL Server Analysis Services Command.

10. Type the server name in the Server box. For example, type **(local)** if the SSAS server is installed on your local machine.

11. Paste the backup script in the Command field. Click OK to return to the New Job dialog box.

12. Click the Schedules page, and then create a new job schedule. Click OK to close the New Job dialog box.

13. When the schedule interval has passed, right-click the Jobs folder, and then select View History to see the status of the job.

✔ **Quick Check**

1. What should you do to protect a backup file from being accessed by unauthorized users?

2. What SQL Server Agent step type do you need to run a backup script?

3. How can you script the CREATE definition of a cube in SSMS?

Quick Check Answers

1. To protect a backup file, select the Encrypt Backup File check box in the Backup Database dialog box, and then enter a password.

2. To run a backup script in a SQL Server Agent job, you need to select SQL Server Analysis Services Command as a step type.

3. To script the CREATE cube definition in SSMS, right-click the cube, and then click the Script Cube As, Create To option.

Lesson 3: Managing SSAS Tuning and Logging

Estimated lesson time: 20 minutes

SSAS supports several server-level properties that control the behavior of the SSAS installation; such properties enable you to change the location of the data files or to optimize server memory. The default settings of these properties will satisfy most deployment scenarios. You can use SSMS to change the server properties when the default settings are inappropriate or when you want to optimize the server. After the UDM is in production, you might need to enable the query log so that you can fine-tune the cube aggregation design. You also need to know how to log and troubleshoot errors. SSAS supports various options for troubleshooting error conditions that range from comprehensive error logging to preparing and sending crash dumps of the server state.

Editing SSAS Server Properties

SSAS includes server-level properties that apply to the entire instance. The settings include system properties to manage and fine-tune how some functionality is applied as well as properties that allow various levels of logging.

To access the server properties, follow these steps:

1. In SSMS, connect to the SSAS instance you want to manage.

2. In Object Explorer, right-click the server node, and then select Properties.

Figure 8-19 shows the General page of the Analysis Server Properties window, which includes a list of server properties that you can manage.

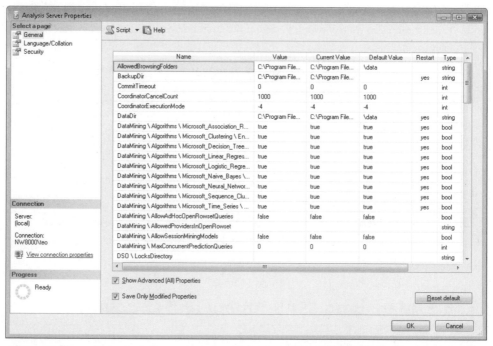

FIGURE 8-19 To manage SSAS server properties, connect to SSAS through SSMS, right-click the server, and then select Properties; you manage properties on the General page.

SSMS reads the property values from the msmdsrv.ini file, whose default location is \Program Files\Microsoft SQL Server\MSAS10.MSSQLSERVER\OLAP\Config\. The properties are assigned a category, either Basic or Advanced, and by default, only the Basic properties are displayed. To display the Advanced properties, select the Show Advanced (All) Properties check box.

A general best practice is to keep the property defaults unless a specific requirement dictates a change. These changes might be recommended through white papers or other SSAS resources. For the purposes of this Training Kit, you should note two general property categories:

- **Folder locations**   Define default locations for data, backups, and logs.
- **Logging**   Defines settings for the server query log, which is used for usage-based optimization aggregation design.

Setting Folder Locations

Table 8-3 lists some common folder location properties.

TABLE 8-3 SSAS Server Folder Location Properties

PROPERTY NAME	DESCRIPTION
AllowedBrowsingFolders (Advanced)	Use this property to define a pipe-separated list of the names of the folders where logs, backups, and other objects are allowed to be created on the server.
BackupDir	Set this to the name of the folder in which SSAS backups should be stored by default. The backup location can be overridden, but this assigns the default backup folder.
DataDir	Set this to the name of the folder in which SSAS data should be stored by default. Note that all dimension data will be stored in this location, but partitions and aggregates can be customized within the cube and partition properties.
LogDir	Set this to the name of the folder in which logs should be written by default.

Suppose that you added a new, fast hard drive to your server and you want to move the SSAS data directory to the new drive. You can do so by following these steps:

1. Detach all SSAS databases, as Lesson 2 explains.
2. Copy the SSAS databases to the new data folder.
3. Change the DataDir server property to the new data folder.
4. Attach the SSAS databases.

Alternatively, instead of detaching the databases, you can back up and restore them.

Configuring Error Logging and Reporting

As a first stop in troubleshooting SSAS server error conditions, you should inspect the Windows Event log by using the Event Viewer console (found under the Administrative Tools program group). The SSAS server outputs various informational and error messages to the application log.

You can help the Microsoft Product Support team investigate server issues by using Dr. Watson minidumps. A *minidump* captures stack traces of the server process (msmdsrv.exe) and could help the Microsoft Product Support staff explore the internal state of the server. One example of when you might want to perform a minidump is when you submit a support case when the server is not responding.

The Dr. Watson minidump feature is turned on by default. You can control it through the *CreateAndSendCrashReports* setting in the msmdsrv.ini configuration file, which has three possible values: 0 (minidump is not generated), 1 (create a minidump), and 2 (create and automatically send the minidump file to Microsoft Product Support). When this property is enabled, the server automatically generates minidumps when it encounters a critical (STOP) server error. The minidump files (*mdmp) are sequentially numbered and are generated in the log folder, whose default location is \Program Files\Microsoft SQL Server\MSAS10.MSSQLSERVER\OLAP\Log\ folder. You can configure this location by changing the *CrashReportsFolder* server property in the msmdsrv.ini configuration file.

Defining Aggregations with the Usage-Based Optimization Wizard

Recall from Chapter 7, "Managing SSAS Storage, Processing, and Deployment," that you can speed up query response times tremendously by designing useful aggregations. An *aggregation* contains the summarized values of all measures in a measure group by a combination of different attributes. At design time, you can use the Aggregation Design Wizard to define aggregations based on your dimensional design and data statistics. After the cube is in production and representative query statistics are available, you should consider running the Usage-Based Optimization Wizard to fine-tune the aggregation design based on the actual queries submitted to the server.

The Usage-Based Optimization Wizard uses the same cost/benefit algorithm as the Aggregation Design Wizard, but it also performs an additional ranking of the aggregation candidates in the query log. Before running the Usage-Based Optimization Wizard, you need to enable and populate the query log.

Enabling the Query Log

The query log captures the query activity as users and applications interact with the server. To enable the query log in SSMS, right-click the Analysis Services server node, and then select Properties. Next, in the Analysis Server Properties dialog box, shown in Figure 8-20, set the QueryLog properties.

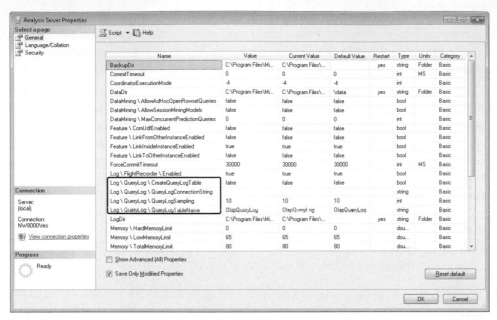

FIGURE 8-20 As a prerequisite for using the Usage-Based Optimization Wizard, you need to enable the query log by setting the QueryLog properties.

Table 8-4 describes the QueryLog server properties.

TABLE 8-4 QueryLog Properties

PROPERTY	DESCRIPTION
CreateQueryLogTable	When set to True and if the server account has sufficient privileges, the server will create the log table if it does not already exist.
QueryLogConnectionString	A valid connection string to a SQL Server database; the query log is disabled if this property is empty.
QueryLogSampling	The frequency for query sampling. By default, every tenth query is logged.
QueryLogTableName	The name of the table in a SQL Server database that will capture the query statistics. The default table name is OlapQueryLog.

After you set the QueryLogConnectionString property, the server will attempt to establish a connection by using the connection string you specified in the QueryLogConnectionString property. If the connection fails, the SSAS service ignores the error. Monitor the Windows event log for error messages if no queries are logged in the query log.

EXAM TIP

You want to run the Usage-Based Optimization Wizard to produce an aggregation design based on the actual server usage. You have a SQL Server database named SSAS_Logging. You want to configure the server properties to save every fifth query to a table named QueryLog inside the SSAS_Logging database. Which server properties do you need to change? You need to change all of the four Log\QueryLog properties. Set the Log\Query-Log\CreateLogTable property to True so that the server can create the table. Set Log\QueryLog\QueryLogConnectionString property to specify a valid connection string to the SSAS_Logging database. Change the Log\QueryLog\QueryLogSampling property to 5 to sample every fifth query. Last, change the Log\QueryLog\QueryLogTableName property to QueryLog.

Populating the Query Log

After the query log is enabled, let the server gather query statistics for a given period of time, such as a week. The server does not log the actual MDX queries. Instead, it logs certain query information, which includes the dimensions requested by the query and the attributes that the server used to satisfy the query. The server logs these statistics in the query log table, whose schema is shown in Figure 8-21.

	MSOLAP_Database	MSOLAP_ObjectPath	MSOLAP_User	Dataset	StartTime	Duration
1	TK 70-448 SSAS Project	NW8000.TK 70-448 SSAS Project.Adven...	NW8000\teo	00000000,000,00000000000000000,000000,000000,0,0...	2008-08-27 12:54:54.000	173
2	TK 70-448 SSAS Project	NW8000.TK 70-448 SSAS Project.Adven...	NW8000\teo	0,0	2008-08-27 12:54:54.000	19
3	TK 70-448 SSAS Project	NW8000.TK 70-448 SSAS Project.Adven...	NW8000\teo	00000000,000000,00000000,000,000000,0,000000	2008-08-27 12:54:54.000	67
4	TK 70-448 SSAS Project	NW8000.TK 70-448 SSAS Project.Adven...	NW8000\teo	0,000000	2008-08-27 12:54:54.000	62
5	TK 70-448 SSAS Project	NW8000.TK 70-448 SSAS Project.Adven...	NW8000\teo	00000000,000,00000000000000000,000000,000000,0,0...	2008-08-27 12:54:54.000	286
6	TK 70-448 SSAS Project	NW8000.TK 70-448 SSAS Project.Adven...	NW8000\teo	00000000,001,00000000000000000,000000,000000,0,0...	2008-08-27 12:55:46.000	0
7	TK 70-448 SSAS Project	NW8000.TK 70-448 SSAS Project.Adven...	NW8000\teo	00000000,000,00000000000000000,000000,000000,0,0...	2008-08-27 12:55:46.000	0
8	TK 70-448 SSAS Project	NW8000.TK 70-448 SSAS Project.Adven...	NW8000\teo	00000000,000000,00000000,001,000000,0,000000	2008-08-27 12:55:46.000	0
9	TK 70-448 SSAS Project	NW8000.TK 70-448 SSAS Project.Adven...	NW8000\teo	00000000,000000,00000000,000,000000,0,000000	2008-08-27 12:55:46.000	0
10	TK 70-448 SSAS Project	NW8000.TK 70-448 SSAS Project.Adven...	NW8000\teo	00000000,001,00000000000000000,000000,000000,0,0...	2008-08-27 12:55:46.000	119
11	TK 70-448 SSAS Project	NW8000.TK 70-448 SSAS Project.Adven...	NW8000\teo	10000000,000000,00000000,001,000000,0,000000	2008-08-27 12:55:46.000	56
12	TK 70-448 SSAS Project	NW8000.TK 70-448 SSAS Project.Adven...	NW8000\teo	00000000,000,00000000000000000,000000,000000,0,0...	2008-08-27 12:55:46.000	1

FIGURE 8-21 The queries are logged in the query log table.

Table 8-5 describes the columns in the query log table.

TABLE 8-5 Columns in the Query Log Table

PROPERTY	DESCRIPTION
MSOLAP_Database	The name of the SSAS database
MSOLAP_ObjectPath	A period-separated list of database, cube, and measure group names
MSOLAP_User	The Windows logon of the interactive user submitting the query
Dataset	A comma-separated attribute list
StartTime	The time the query request began
Duration	The length of the query, in milliseconds

The most important column for the Usage-Based Optimization Wizard is the Dataset column, which captures the attributes used to resolve the query. Each comma-separated section represents a dimension. The dimensions are in the order in which they appear in the Dimensions pane of the Cube Structure tab. Each bit in a section represents an attribute. If the bit is 1, the attribute is used in the query. For example, looking at the sixth row in Figure 8-21, you can see that the third bit in the second section is set to 1. Looking at the Dimensions pane in the Cube Structure tab of the Cube Designer, notice that the second dimension is Sales Territory, and its third attribute is Sales Territory Region. This means that the server used the Sales Territory Region attribute to satisfy the query.

Running the Usage-Based Optimization Wizard

When you have the query log populated, you are ready to create usage-based aggregations. You can do this by using BIDS or SSMS. Use BIDS if you want the aggregation design to become a part of the project, which means that it is saved in the cube definition. Follow these steps to run the Usage-Based Optimization Wizard in BIDS:

1. Open the cube in the Cube Designer, and then click the Aggregations tab.

2. On the Aggregations tab, select the measure group for which you want to change the aggregation design.

3. Click the Usage-Based Optimization button on the toolbar to start the Usage-Based Optimization Wizard.

4. The Specify Query Criteria page, shown in Figure 8-22, displays a summary of the query statistics and lets you specify a query filter if you want to include a subset of the logged queries. For example, if you want to filter the queries by date, you can specify a beginning date and an ending date. Or if you want to include queries based on their frequency, use the Most Frequent Queries filter option.

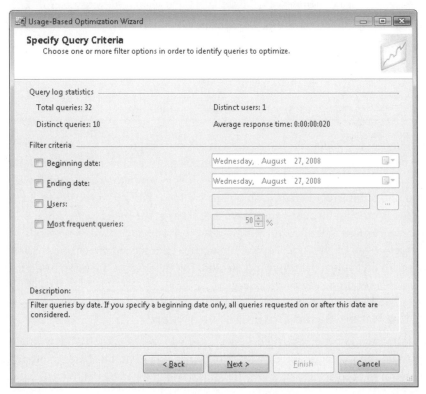

FIGURE 8-22 You can use the Specify Query Criteria page to filter the queries that the Usage-Based Optimization Wizard will examine.

5. On the Review The Queries That Will Be Optimized page, shown in Figure 8-23, you can select the attributes that will be considered for the aggregation design. The Occurrences column shows how often a given attribute has been used in the queries. Clear an attribute check box to exclude that attribute from the aggregation design.

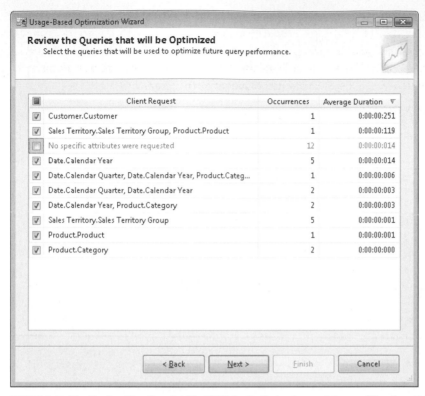

Client Request	Occurrences	Average Duration ▽
☑ Customer.Customer	1	0:00:00:251
☑ Sales Territory.Sales Territory Group, Product.Product	1	0:00:00:119
☐ No specific attributes were requested	12	0:00:00:014
☑ Date.Calendar Year	5	0:00:00:014
☑ Date.Calendar Quarter, Date.Calendar Year, Product.Categ...	1	0:00:00:006
☑ Date.Calendar Quarter, Date.Calendar Year	2	0:00:00:003
☑ Date.Calendar Year, Product.Category	2	0:00:00:003
☑ Sales Territory.Sales Territory Group	5	0:00:00:001
☑ Product.Product	1	0:00:00:001
☑ Product.Category	2	0:00:00:000

FIGURE 8-23 The Review The Queries That Will Be Optimized page lets you filter the attribute hierarchies that will be examined.

6. The Usage-Based Optimization Wizard next displays the familiar Specify Object Counts page, which you encountered when working with the Aggregation Design Wizard in Chapter 7. Use this page to specify the counts for dimension members and measure groups.

7. The Set Aggregation Option page should look familiar to you as well. As a best practice, use the Performance Gain Reaches 100 design aggregation option when running the Usage-Based Optimization Wizard.

8. The Completing The Wizard page lets you create a new aggregation design, as Figure 8-24 shows, or merge the Usage-Based Optimization design with an existing aggregation design. You also have the option to process the affected partitions immediately by selecting the Process Partitions Immediately check box.

FIGURE 8-24 You can create a new aggregation design or merge it with an existing aggregation design.

PRACTICE Setting Up SSAS Query Logging

Suppose that the Adventure Works cube has been deployed. As a best practice, you should use the Usage-Based Optimization Wizard to fine-tune the aggregation design using real-life query statistics. Here is how to do that.

EXERCISE 1 Enable and Populate the Query Log

In this exercise, you set up SSAS query logging to capture user queries against the databases on the SSAS instance.

1. Open SSMS, and then connect to the Database Engine in the Server Type drop-down list. Enter **(local)** in the Server Name box, and then click Connect.

2. In Object Explorer, open the (local) Database Engine instance, right-click the Databases folder, and then select New Database.

3. In the Database Name box, type **SSAS_Logging**, and then click OK to create the database.

4. In Object Explorer, click Connect, and then select Analysis Services from the list.

5. Type **(local)** or **localhost** in the Server Name box, and then click OK to connect.

6. In Object Explorer, right-click the SSAS server, represented by the yellow cube icon, and then select Properties.

7. In the Log\QueryLog\QueryLogConnectionString property, click in the value field, and then click the ellipsis button to open the Connection Manager dialog box.

8. In the Connection Manager dialog box, enter **(local)** in the Server Name box, and then in the Select Or Enter A Database Name drop-down list, select the SSAS_Logging database that you created in step 3. Click OK to save the connection string.

9. Locate the Log\QueryLog\CreateQueryLogTable property, and then change it to True.

10. Change the Log\QueryLog\LogSampling property to 1.

11. Click OK in the Analysis Services Properties dialog box to save the changes. Note that none of these changes requires a service restart because they take effect immediately.

12. In the Object Explorer window, browse to the SSAS_Logging database in the Databases folder of the (local) Database Engine connection.

13. Right-click the Tables folder, and then click Refresh.

14. Open the Tables folder, and notice that there is an OlapQueryLog table, which SSAS created for query logging. This table will initially be empty, but if you return to it after running a query, it will contain logging information.

15. Use the Browser in the Cube Designer or your favorite reporting tool to create a few reports from the Adventure Works cube. Browse the OlapQueryLog table to ensure that the server has captured query statistics.

EXERCISE 2 Run the Usage-Based Optimization Wizard

After you have gathered enough query statistics, you can run the Usage-Based Optimization Wizard to produce an aggregation design based on the actual queries sent to the server.

1. Open the Adventure Works cube in the Cube Designer, and then click the Aggregations tab.

2. Select the Internet Sales measure group.

3. Click the Usage-Based Optimization button on the toolbar to start the Usage-Based Optimization Wizard.

4. On the Specify Query Criteria page, accept the defaults to use all statistics captured in the query log table, and then click Next.

5. On the Review The Queries That Will Be Optimized page, clear the No Specific Attributes Were Requested row, if present. Leave the rest of the attributes selected, and then click Next.

6. On the Specify Object Counts page, click the Count button to count the objects. Click Next.

7. On the Set Aggregation Options page, accept the defaults, and then click Start. When the wizard has finished, click Next.

8. On the Completing The Wizard page, name your design **UOBAggregationDesign**. Leave the Create A New Aggregation Design option selected, and then click Finish.

9. Deploy the solution to process the cube and build the aggregations.

✔ **Quick Check**

1. Which server property do you need to set to change the location of where SSAS saves data files?

2. Can you enhance an existing aggregation design (custom or produced with the Aggregation Design Wizard) with an aggregation design from the Usage-Based Optimization Wizard?

3. Does the query logging feature in the SSAS server properties let you capture the MDX statements to a file for later review?

Quick Check Answers

1. You need to change the DataDir property to change where SSAS saves data files.

2. Yes, on the last page of the Usage-Based Optimization Wizard, select the Merge With An Existing Aggregation Design option.

3. No, the QueryLog table does not store the actual MDX statements. It stores the levels for each of the attributes and hierarchies that are used by the query. You can use SQL Server Profiler to capture SSAS activity by tracing MDX.

Lesson 4: Tracing and Monitoring SSAS Instances

Estimated lesson time: 25 minutes

It is unrealistic to expect that your SSAS management duties will end after the database is deployed to the production server. In real life, end users might occasionally report errors or degradation of server performance. By monitoring the server, you can ensure that it functions correctly and is performing optimally. You can use SQL Server Profiler and the Windows Performance console to track the health and performance of your server.

Working with SQL Server Profiler for SSAS Tracing

You can use SQL Server Profiler to trace SSAS events and monitor the server activity and performance of MDX queries. SQL Server Profiler supports filtering trace events and saving the trace events to a file to replay them later.

To start SQL Server Profiler in SSAS mode, do the following:

1. From the Start menu, select All Programs, Microsoft SQL Server 2008, Performance Tools, and then select SQL Server Profiler.

2. On the File menu, select New Trace, and then connect to the SSAS server that you want to monitor. SQL Server Profiler opens the Trace Properties dialog box.

Configuring Trace Properties

After you are connected to the SSAS server, you are ready to configure an SSAS trace by using the Trace Properties dialog box, shown in Figure 8-25.

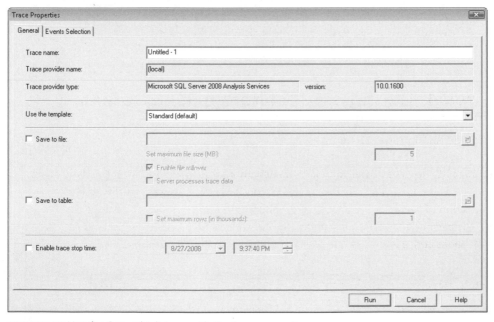

FIGURE 8-25 Use the General tab to specify the trace properties.

Use the General tab of the Trace Properties dialog box to configure the trace properties. Expand the Use The Template drop-down list to select a trace template. A trace template contains a subset of events that you want to monitor. Out of the box, SQL Server Profiler supports Standard, Replay, and Blank templates. The Standard template contains several useful predefined events. The Replay template selects only events that can be replayed, such as security-related and query processing events. And the Blank template does not contain any events.

> **BEST PRACTICES   CREATE CUSTOM TRACE TEMPLATES**
>
> After you configure a trace, you can save the configuration as a custom template by selecting Save As on the File menu and then selecting Trace Template. You can reuse the trace configuration later, saving the time and effort of selecting the same events each time you run SQL Server Profiler.

In addition to watching the events in real time, you can save the output to a file or a database table. Capturing the events is useful if you want to run the trace in an unattended mode and analyze the output later. Last, you can configure the trace to be deactivated at a given time by setting the Enable Trace Stop Time property.

Selecting Events

When you have finished making changes to the trace properties, click the Events Selection tab to select the trace events you want to monitor. Figure 8-26 shows a subset of the default events included in the Standard trace template.

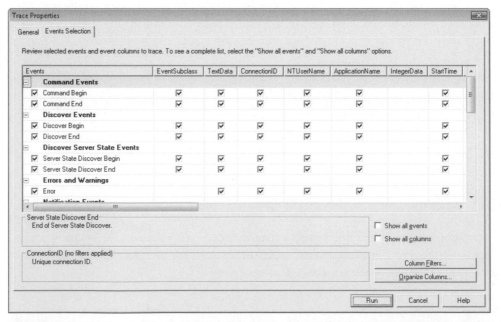

FIGURE 8-26 Use the Events Selection tab to select the check boxes for the events you want to monitor.

TYPES OF EVENTS

The Events column lists the events, grouped in collections. Command events are raised when action-oriented statements are sent to the server. Examples of action-oriented statements are management tasks, including deploying, synchronizing, backing up, and restoring databases. Discover events are generated when you query the SSAS metadata, such as when you retrieve the key performance indicator (KPI) schema to identify the KPIs implemented in a given cube. Discover Server State events are subsets of the Discover events raised as a result of querying the server state—you can use them, for example, to find the number of currently open connections, sessions, transactions, and locks.

As the name suggests, the Errors And Warnings collection contains events that the server raises when it encounters an error condition. For example, if you send a syntactically incorrect MDX query to the server, an error event will be generated. These events are helpful when you want to troubleshoot failed queries. Every now and then, the server raises Notification events when it performs tasks triggered by internal events that are not explicitly initiated. For example, if proactive caching is enabled, the server will raise this event when it detects that the underlying data has changed. You are already familiar with the Progress events, which the server raises to inform the client about the progress of a given task, such as backing up or processing a database.

The Query events output the MDX statements sent to the server. As a first stop for troubleshooting query-performance issues, you should track the query sent to the server and find how long it takes to execute; this information is displayed in the Duration column. You can monitor Security Audit events to find out who has logged in to or out of the server. Last, the Session Events collection lets you know when a session starts or ends. Undoubtedly, you have already experienced session time-out events when the MDX Query Designer was inactive for a long time in SSMS.

> **IMPORTANT** **USER SESSIONS**
>
> Most requests to the server work in the context of sessions. A *session* encapsulates the server state, just as an ASP.NET session can be used to hold user state. An SSAS session stores such things as the current catalog, the state of calculations in each cube that the session has accessed, and so on. Because sessions can be expensive, the server has a mechanism for ending old sessions. The default time-out is one hour with no activity. The administrator can change this time-out interval by setting the *MaxIdleSessionTimeout* server property.

To avoid having too many events in the trace output, you should select only the events that you want to monitor. To remove an event, simply clear its check box. To view all SSAS events, select the Show All Events check box.

EVENT COLUMNS

Each SQL Server Profiler event has additional information associated with it, organized in a set of columns. Point to the column header to see a brief description of its purpose. Table 8-6 lists the most important event columns.

TABLE 8-6 Important SQL Server Profiler Event Columns

PROPERTY	DESCRIPTION
Duration	The event duration in milliseconds. For example, the Duration column of the Query End event shows the duration of the query.
EventSubclass	Events can be further organized into subclasses. For example, the Progress Report events include the subclasses ExecuteSQL, Write-Data, BuildIndex, and so on.
IntegerData	Numerical information associated with some events. For example, the ReadData subclass of the Progress Report Current event shows the number of records read from the data source.
NTUserName	The Windows identity of the user or process that initiated the action.
TextData	A text description of the event. For example, the TextData column of Query events shows the MDX statement.

The sheer number of events and columns in the trace output could be overwhelming. To limit the number of events shown in the trace output, click the Column Filter button to display the Edit Filter dialog box, shown in Figure 8-27.

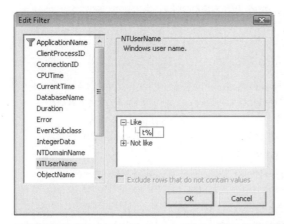

FIGURE 8-27 Consider setting up a column filter to limit the number of events in the trace output.

For example, to view only events raised by a given user, follow these steps:

1. In the Trace Properties dialog box, click Column Filters.
2. In the Edit Filter dialog box, select the NTUserName item.

3. In the right pane, expand the Like node, and then enter the user logon name. You can use the % wildcard for partial matching. So, for example, *t%* will match Windows logons *tlachev* and *teo*.

4. Click OK to save the filter.

Running a Trace

After you configure the trace, you can run it by clicking the Run button in the Trace Properties dialog box. SQL Server Profiler will start outputting the event information as the trace captures events.

The trace that Figure 8-28 shows was produced by browsing the Adventure Works cube in SSMS.

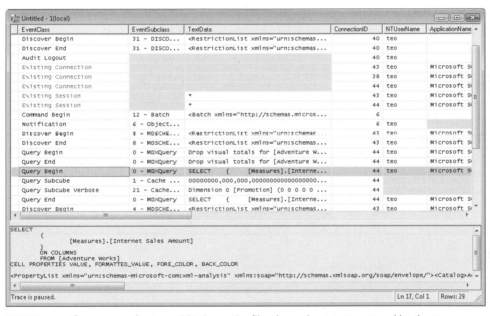

FIGURE 8-28 After you run the trace, SQL Server Profiler shows the events captured by the trace.

The Command Begin TextData column (not shown in Figure 8-26) contains the text of the *CREATE* command that the server used to create the trace. The server generated a *Notification* event when the trace was created. The *Discover* events were triggered as a result of browsing the database metadata in SSMS, such as expanding the database folder to see the cubes in the database. The *Audit Login/Logout* events indicate that the server has successfully authenticated the user.

The server raises the *Query Begin* event when it receives an MDX query and the Query End event when it has finished executing the query. The *Query Subcube* event shows which attributes the server used to satisfy the query. When configuring the trace, you can check the *Query Subcube Verbose* event to see these attributes in a human-readable format.

To stop a trace temporarily, click the Pause Selected Trace button on the toolbar. To resume the trace, click the Start Selected Trace toolbar button. Click the Clear Trace Window toolbar button to delete the trace output. To go back to the Trace Properties window, click the Properties toolbar button.

> **BEST PRACTICES**   **CHANGE THE TRACE PROPERTIES**
>
> If you need to change the trace properties after the trace is run, you first need to pause the trace and then click the Properties button on the toolbar. If you do not pause the trace, the Properties window will be read-only.

Working with the Flight Recorder Trace

Sometimes, you might need to investigate the server state after a problem has occurred. For example, an MDX query might have caused the server to stop responding, or a customer might have reported performance degradation. Every administrator knows that one of the most frustrating aspects of troubleshooting problems is not being able to reproduce them. To help you diagnose server issues, SSAS has a special trace object called the *flight recorder*. Working similarly to an airplane's "black box," the flight recorder trace automatically captures the server state and activity.

By default, the server runs the flight recorder trace every two minutes to take snapshots of the server activity. The current flight recorder trace file is named FlightRecorder-Current.trc, and it is located in the default log folder (\Program Files\Microsoft SQL Server\ MSAS10.MSSQLSERVER\OLAP\Log\). By default, the flight recorder captures the server state for the past hour only. After the flag duration period is exceeded, the server archives the current file to a FlightRecorderBack.trc file and starts a new trace file.

To configure the flight recorder, in SSMS, right-click the SSAS server and choose Properties to open the Analysis Server Properties dialog box. Select the Show Advanced (All) Properties check box. The flight recorder properties are found in the Log\Flight Recorder section, as Figure 8-29 shows.

To open and replay a flight recorder trace, follow these steps:

1. In SQL Server Profiler, select Open on the File menu, and then select Trace File.

2. Click the Start Replay button on the toolbar, or press F5.

3. You will be asked to connect to the target server. Enter the server name and login credentials in the Connect To Server dialog box.

4. In the Replay Configuration dialog box that appears, configure the server replay. For example, you can configure SQL Server Profiler to replay only those statements that were recorded within a given time frame.

When you click OK in the Replay Configuration dialog box, SQL Server Profiler will start executing the recorded statements against the server, simulating the server state and load as closely as possible. For example, the server will create the same number of open connections and sessions as existed during the capture.

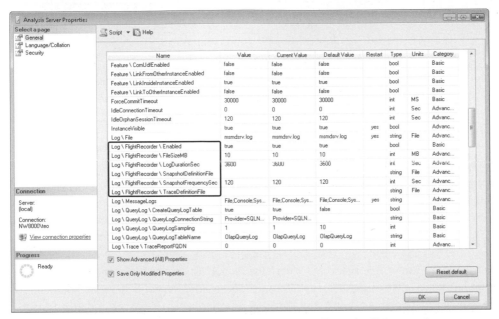

FIGURE 8-29 Use the Log\Flight Recorder server properties to configure the flight recorder trace.

Using Performance Monitor to Analyze SSAS Performance

Another way to track server utilization is to use Windows Performance Monitor (PerfMon), which you can find in the Reliability And Performance Monitor console in Windows Vista. As with SQL Server Profiler, PerfMon lets you monitor the server utilization of local or remote servers in real time or record the information to a file for later analysis.

Unlike using SQL Server Profiler, however, you cannot use PerfMon to identify the cause of a performance issue. For example, PerfMon might show high CPU utilization, but it cannot show the MDX queries that are being sent to the server. A common scenario for using Perf-Mon is when you need to conduct high-level performance or load testing. You might need to do additional work to find the cause of the performance bottleneck.

Understanding SSAS Performance Counters

As a part of the setup process, SSAS installs various performance counters that cover essential server statistics, including caching, connection management, memory utilization, MDX query coverage, processing, and more. Table 8-7 lists some important counters that are commonly used for performance testing.

TABLE 8-7 Important Performance Counters

OBJECT\COUNTER	DESCRIPTION
MSAS 2008:Connection\Current Connections	Displays the number of the connections to the server.
MSAS 2008:Memory\Memory Limit High KB	Represents the upper limit of memory that the server uses to manage all SSAS operations.
MSAS 2008:Memory\Memory Usage KB	Displays the memory usage of the server process.
MSAS 2008:Processing\Rows read/sec	Displays the number of rows read from the data sources per second. Ideally, this should be between 40,000 and 60,000.
MSAS 2008: Threads\Query pool job queue length	A nonzero value means that the number of query jobs has exceeded the number of available query threads. In this scenario, you might consider increasing the number of query threads.

Many more counters are available for PerfMon, including counters for system resources, such as hardware and the operating system, and specific counters for SQL Server and SSAS. For more information about how to use the SSAS counters for performance and load testing, read the white papers "Microsoft SQL Server 2008 Analysis Services Performance Guide," by Microsoft, and "SSAS Load Testing Best Practices," by Jaime Basilico and Dmitri Tchikatilov (see References).

Configuring Performance Monitor

Follow these steps to configure PerfMon to display SSAS performance counters:

1. Click Start, Run, and then type **perfmon**. Click OK to start PerfMon.

2. Click the plus sign (+) button on the toolbar to add a performance counter. In Windows Vista, you need to select the Performance Monitor tool under the Monitoring Tools folder and then click the + toolbar button.

3. Select the server name in the Select Counters From Computer drop-down list, or leave it set to <Local Computer> if you want to monitor a local SSAS instance, as Figure 8-30 shows.

4. Scroll down through the performance objects until you see the MSAS 2008 category, as shown in Figure 8-30.

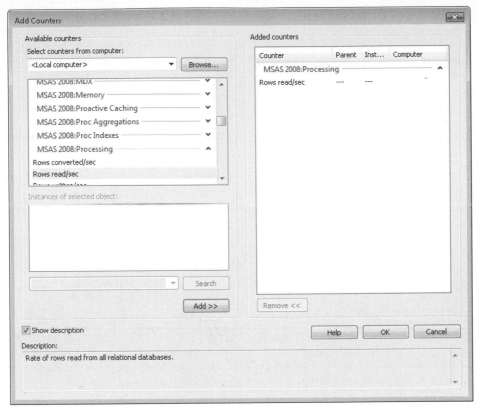

FIGURE 8-30 The SSAS performance counters are found under the MSAS 2008 performance object.

5. Select an SSAS performance object, such as MSAS 2008:Processing.

6. In the Select Counters From Computer list, select the performance counter you want to monitor. In Windows Vista, expand the performance object to see the counters below it.

7. Click Add to add the performance counter to the chart and display it in the chart legend, and then click OK.

In the PerfMon graph, shown in Figure 8-31, you can watch how the performance counter changes over time.

Select a performance counter in the legend to observe the last, average, minimum, and maximum values of the performance counter over time, as well as how long the counter has been monitored.

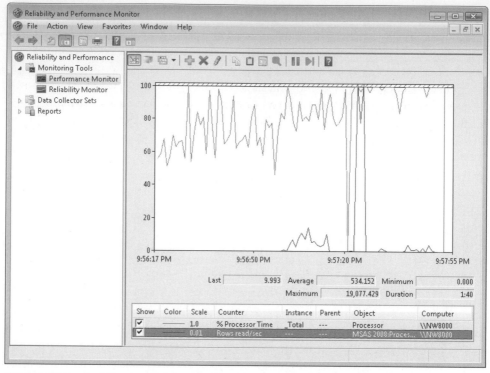

FIGURE 8-31 Use PerfMon to watch how performance counters change over time.

Using Dynamic Management Views

Microsoft introduced dynamic management views (DMVs) in SQL Server 2005 to help database administrators monitor the health of a server instance, diagnose problems, and tune performance. SSAS 2008 provides schema rowsets that you can use to examine the UDM and retrieve support and monitoring information from an SSAS instance. What is new in SSAS 2008 is that these schema rowsets plug into the SQL Server DMV framework and can be queried using SQL-like *SELECT* statements, just as you can query a SQL view. SSAS 2008 has also added new schema rowsets for discovering the run-time state of the server.

Table 8-8 lists some of the schema rowsets you might find particularly interesting. For a full list of the schema rowsets, see the SQL Server 2008 Books Online topic "XML for Analysis Schema Rowsets" (see References).

TABLE 8-8 Analysis Services Schema Rowsets

SCHEMA ROWSET	DESCRIPTION
DISCOVER_COMMANDS	Provides resource usage and activity information about the currently executing or last executed commands in the opened connections on the server.
DISCOVER_COMMAND_OBJECTS	Provides resource usage and activity information about the objects in use by the referenced command.
DISCOVER_CONNECTIONS	Provides resource usage and activity information about the currently opened connections on the server.
DISCOVER_OBJECT_ACTIVITY	Provides resource usage per object since the start of the service.
DISCOVER_OBJECT_MEMORY_USAGE	Provides information about memory resources used by objects.
DISCOVER_SESSIONS	Provides resource usage and activity information about the currently opened sessions on the server.

What is interesting about DMVs is that they contain in-memory the configuration since the start of the service. For example, the DISCOVER_CONNECTIONS rowset can tell you how long a given connection has been idle, how many bytes were received or sent through this connection, and when the last statement was sent.

Follow these steps to query the SSAS schema rowsets:

1. In SSMS, connect to your SSAS instance.
2. Right-click the server node, and then select New Query, MDX.

3. Enter a *SELECT* statement that queries the rowset by prefixing it with **$SYSTEM**. For example, to discover information about the connections made from the Windows logon 'nw8000\teo', type the following *SELECT* statement:

```
SELECT * FROM $SYSTEM.DISCOVER_CONNECTIONS
WHERE CONNECTION_USER_NAME = 'nw8000\teo'
```

4. Click the Execute button on the toolbar, or press Ctrl+E. The server returns the requested dataset, as Figure 8-32 shows.

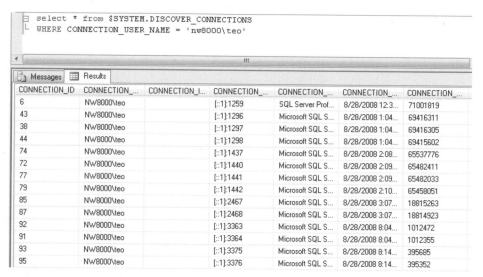

FIGURE 8-32 Query the DISCOVER_CONNECTIONS schema rowset to obtain information about the connections made to the server.

PRACTICE   Tracing and Monitoring SSAS Instances

In this practice, you use SQL Server Profiler's trace capabilities to watch server activity. You then use the Windows Performance Monitor to determine how many rows per second the server loads when a cube is processed.

EXERCISE 1   Use SQL Server Profiler to Trace SSAS Activity

A common use of SQL Server Profiler with SSAS is to determine how long a given MDX query takes to execute. Tracing MDX queries helps you isolate and troubleshoot query performance issues.

1. On the Start menu, select All Programs, Microsoft SQL Server 2008, Performance Tools, and then SQL Server Profiler.

2. Connect to your SSAS server.

3. Accept the default settings in the Trace Properties dialog box, and then click Run to start the trace.

4. Use SSMS to create and send the following MDX statement to the Adventure Works cube in the TK 70-448 SSAS Project database:

```
SELECT {[Measures].[Internet Sales Amount],
        [Measures].[Reseller Sales Amount]} ON COLUMNS,
[Product].[Product].[Product].Members ON ROWS
FROM [Adventure Works]
```

5. In SQL Server Profiler, you should now see a *Query Begin* event followed by a *Query End* event. The TextData column for both events should contain the text of the MDX statement. Scroll to the right, and notice the value in the Duration column of the *Query End* event. In this case, the query took 344 milliseconds to execute.

6. In SSMS, enter the *ClearCache* command after the query. Select the command, and then execute it to clear the query results cache, as Figure 8-33 shows.

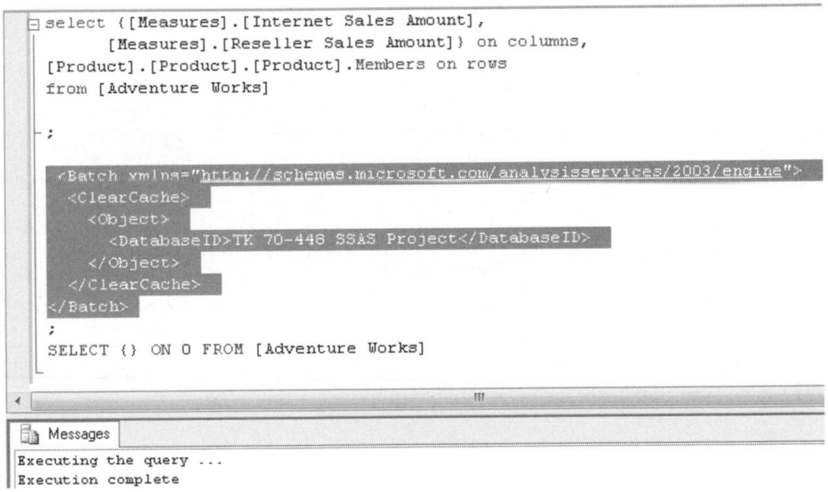

```
select {[Measures].[Internet Sales Amount],
        [Measures].[Reseller Sales Amount]} on columns,
[Product].[Product].[Product].Members on rows
from [Adventure Works]

;

<Batch xmlns="http://schemas.microsoft.com/analysisservices/2003/engine">
  <ClearCache>
    <Object>
      <DatabaseID>TK 70-448 SSAS Project</DatabaseID>
    </Object>
  </ClearCache>
</Batch>
;
SELECT {} ON 0 FROM [Adventure Works]
```

Messages
Executing the query ...
Execution complete

FIGURE 8-33 Use the ClearCache command to clear the query results.

7. Enter the following MDX statement, and then execute it to initialize a session:

```
SELECT {} ON 0 FROM [Adventure Works]
```

8. You can use the *NON EMPTY* clause to instruct the server to exclude the empty tuples from the result set. Change the MDX query as follows, and then execute it again:

```
select NON EMPTY {[Measures].[Internet Sales Amount],
[Measures].[Reseller Sales Amount]} on columns,
NON EMPTY [Product].[Product].[Product].Members on rows
from [Adventure Works]
```

9. Switch to SQL Server Profiler. You should see new *Query Begin/Query End* events. Notice the value in the Duration column of the *Query End* event; it should be less than the duration of the first query.

EXERCISE 2   Use SQL Server Profiler to Monitor Aggregation Usage

When the server parses an MDX query, it determines whether it can use an aggregation to satisfy the query. If the query results in an aggregation hit, the server can answer the query using the aggregation instead of having to scan the fact data. In this exercise, you will use SQL Server Profiler to monitor whether a query results in an aggregation hit.

1.   Start SQL Server Profiler, and then create a new trace to SSAS.

2.   In the Trace Properties dialog box, click the Events Selection tab, and then select the Show All Events check box. Scroll down in the Events grid, and then below Query Processing in the Events list, select the Get Data From Aggregation event check box.

3.   In SSMS, create and execute an MDX query. For example, the Usage-Based Optimization Wizard aggregation design includes the [Sales Territory].[Sales Territory Region] attribute, so use a query that requests this attribute, such as the following:

```
select [Measures].[Internet Sales Amount] on 0,
[Sales Territory].[Sales Territory Region].Members on 1
from [Adventure Works]
```

4.   Switch to SQL Server Profiler, and then analyze the trace. If the server has decided to use an existing aggregation, you will see a Get Data From Aggregation event, as Figure 8-34 shows.

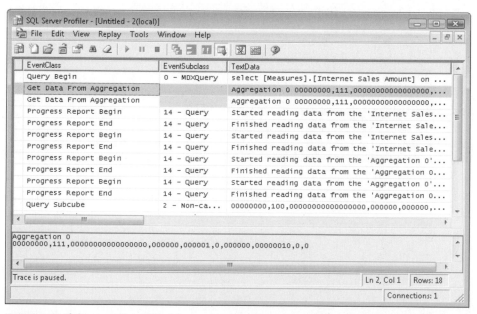

FIGURE 8-34 If the query is satisfied from an aggregation, you will see a Get Data From Aggregation event in SQL Server Profiler.

EXERCISE 3 Use Performance Monitor to Understand SSAS Performance

A cube is taking an unreasonably long time to process, so you decide to use PerfMon to determine how fast the server loads rows from the relational data source.

1. Start Windows Performance Monitor from the Windows Administrative Tools program group.

2. Click the plus sign (+) button on the toolbar to add a performance counter.

3. If necessary, enter the server name in the Select Counters From Computer box or select the server from the drop-down list.

4. Expand the Performance object drop-down list, and then scroll up until you see the MSAS 2008 performance objects.

5. Select the MSAS 2008:Processing performance object. This performance object exposes several processing-related metrics, which you can use to monitor the server processing activity.

6. In the Select Counters From drop-down list, select the Rows Read/Sec counter. This counter shows how fast the server processes rows from the relational database, expressed in rows per second.

7. Click Explain to view a brief description of the selected counter. Click Add to add the counter to the performance graph.

8. To monitor the Rows Read/Sec performance counter, go back to SSMS, and then fully process the Adventure Works cube.

9. While the server is processing the cube, navigate to the Performance console, and then watch the Rows Read/Sec counter. You should see a spike as the server starts extracting and processing rows from the AdventureWorksDW2008 data source.

10. Click the Rows Read/Sec counter to select it. Observe the Average field, which shows how many rows per second the server has read on average.

EXERCISE 4 Use Schema Rowsets to Discover Aggregation Misses

In this exercise, you will query the DISCOVER_OBJECT_ACTIVITY schema rowset to determine which partitions have the most aggregation misses and require more aggregations. To obtain more meaningful results, query a cube that has been in use for while, such as a production cube.

1. In SSMS, connect to the SSAS instance. Right-click the server node in the Object Explorer pane, and then select New Query, MDX.

2. Enter the following statement:

```
SELECT TOP 20 *
  FROM $SYSTEM.DISCOVER_OBJECT_ACTIVITY
  WHERE InStr(OBJECT_PARENT_PATH, '<SSAS Database Name>')>0
ORDER BY OBJECT_AGGREGATION_MISS DESC;
```

This statement requests the top 20 rows from the DISCOVER_OBJECT_ACTIVITY schema rowset, sorted by aggregation misses in descending order.

3. Replace <SSAS Database Name> with the name of the SSAS database you will use for the test.

4. Execute the query. The query should return a list of partitions. The ones that have resulted in the most misses should be at the top of the list. Consider enabling the query log and running the Usage-Based Optimization Wizard to add more aggregations to these measure groups or partitions.

✔ Quick Check

1. Which SSAS trace can you use to monitor the server activity for the past hour?

2. Which tool would you use to determine how long a given query takes to run?

3. Which schema rowset can you use to find the currently opened connections to the server?

Quick Check Answers

1. To monitor the server activity for the past hour, you can use the flight recorder trace.

2. You can use SQL Server Profiler to determine how a long a query takes to run. The Duration column will give you the execution time.

3. You can use the DISCOVER_CONNECTIONS schema rowset to discover information about current connections.

Case Scenario: Administering and Securing SSAS Cubes

You need to set up dimension data security on an SSAS database that contains several cubes. You want all cubes in the database to inherit the dimension data security allowed set for an attribute hierarchy. In addition, you want to know which users have been authenticated successfully by the server for a given time period.

1. How can you set up dimension data security so that all cubes share the allowed set?

2. How can you find out which users have been successfully authenticated by the server?

Chapter Summary

- SSAS supports a comprehensive role-based security model that is layered on top of Windows security.

- Members of the SSAS Administrators role have unrestricted access to SSAS. You can create database roles to protect the cube data and control security all the way down to the individual cube cells.

- Dimension data security protects dimension members and data associated with those members. To enforce dimension data security, you define allowed sets and denied sets.

- Cell security lets you define security policy at the most granular level—that is, at the cube cell level.

- Backing up and restoring SSAS databases are essential disaster-recovery tasks. You can automate them by using the SQL Server Agent service.

- With SQL Server Profiler, you can audit server activity and troubleshoot performance problems. Windows Performance Monitor (PerfMon) lets you identify high-level performance bottlenecks. Query the SSAS schema rowsets to retrieve support and monitoring information from an SSAS instance.

CHAPTER 9

Working with SSAS Data Mining

Probably the simplest business intelligence (BI) tools an organization can take advantage of are reports created with SQL Server Reporting Services (SSRS). However, end users have limited dynamic capabilities when they view a report. You can extend the capabilities of SSRS with the help of report models, which are covered briefly in Chapter 11, "Extending and Deploying SSRS Reports." But using report models to build reports is an advanced skill for end users, and the reports' performance is limited. In addition, classic reports do not show analysis over time.

You can eliminate both the need for SSRS advanced skills and problems with limited performance by using SQL Server Analysis Services (SSAS) to implement data warehouses and online analytical processing (OLAP) systems. End users can get information for analysis at lightning speed, and they can change the view of information in real time, drilling down to see more details or up to see summary information. However, end users are still limited in a few ways with these systems. Typically, users do not have time to examine all possible graphs and PivotTable dynamic views using all possible attributes and hierarchies. In addition, they can search only for patterns they anticipate, and OLAP analysis is typically limited to basic mathematical operations, such as comparing sums across different groups.

SSAS data mining addresses most of these limitations. Data mining is data-driven analysis. With data mining, you as the analyst do not anticipate patterns in advance. You examine data through advanced mathematical methods instead, and then you examine patterns and rules that your algorithm finds. Because the mining algorithms work automatically, they can check millions of different pivoting options in a very limited time.

In this chapter, you will learn how you can use SSAS data mining to give users the BI capabilities they need to make better, more informed decisions. First you will learn how to develop several SSAS data mining models and select from those the best models for deployment into production. You will learn how to assess the accuracy and reliability of the models and compare the performance of the models so that you can choose the best model for your business needs. Then you will see how to secure the models and how to create prediction queries. In addition, you will learn how to deploy a mining model by using it in an SSRS report.

Exam objectives in this chapter:

- Implement data mining.

Before You Begin

To complete this chapter, you must have:

- Knowledge of SSAS features and components.

- Experience working with Microsoft SQL Server 2008 Business Intelligence Development Studio (BIDS) projects and solutions.

- Experience working in SQL Server Management Studio (SSMS).

- The SQL Server 2008 AdventureWorksDW2008 database installed.

Lesson 1: Preparing and Creating Data Mining Structures

Estimated lesson time: 60 minutes

This lesson starts with some basic definitions. First, what does the term *data mining* mean? Data mining enables you to deduce some hidden knowledge by examining, or *training*, the data. The knowledge you find is expressed in patterns and rules. Your unit of examination is called a *case*, which can be interpreted as one appearance of an entity, or a row in a table. In the process, you are using attributes of a case, called *variables* in data mining terminology. An additional data mining goal is to perform predictions based on found patterns. A data mining *model* stores information about the variables you use, the algorithm you implement on the data, and the parameters of the selected algorithm. In addition, after training is complete, the model also holds the extracted knowledge. A data mining model does not store the data used for training, but you can use drillthrough queries to browse the training data.

Data mining techniques are divided into two main classes: the *directed approach* and the *undirected approach*. The directed approach uses known examples and then applies gleaned information to unknown examples to predict a selected target variable. In using the undirected approach, you are trying to discover new patterns inside the dataset as a whole. You use a directed approach to find reasons for purchases of an article, for example, and an undirected approach to find out which articles are commonly purchased together.

With data mining, you can project the answers to typical business questions such as:

- What is the credit risk of a customer?

- Are there any interesting groups of customers based on similarity of values of their attributes?

- What products do customers tend to buy together?
- How much of a specific product can your company sell in the next year?
- What is the potential number of customers shopping in this store?
- Are there any specific patterns in our Web site usage?
- Is a transaction fraudulent?
- Is this e-mail message spam?

Understanding the Data Mining Project Life Cycle

A data mining project has a well-defined life cycle. The life cycle consists of four main parts:

1. Identifying the business problem
2. Using data mining techniques to transform the data into actionable information
3. Acting on the information
4. Measuring the result

Figure 9-1 illustrates this life cycle.

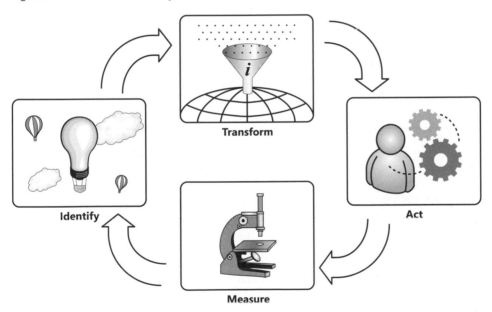

FIGURE 9-1 The four parts of a data mining project life cycle

In the Transform phase of the life cycle, you prepare the data, create the models, examine and evaluate the models, and then deploy selected models. This is the core phase of the data mining project. In this lesson, you will first learn about data and model preparation, and in later lessons, you will focus on model evaluation, deployment, querying, and security.

Preparing Data for Data Mining

After you understand your business problem and have defined a question for data mining, you need to prepare your data to be mined. Before you start creating data mining models, you must develop a basic understanding of your data. Begin with a data overview. To get a comprehensive view, you can use descriptive statistics, such as frequency distribution for discrete variables. For continuous variables, at a minimum you should check the mean value and the spread of the distribution. For example, you should check the average value and the standard deviation. OLAP cubes are handy for helping you understand your data. You can use a data source view (DSV) to get a quick overview of your variables in table, PivotTable, graph, or PivotGraph format. Microsoft Office Excel statistical functions and PivotTable and PivotGraph dynamic views also are useful tools for data overview.

> **IMPORTANT** **DATA PREPARATION IN A DATA MINING PROJECT**
>
> Data preparation and understanding are the most important factors in the success of a data mining project.

You should also check the ways your variables measure data values. Not all algorithms support all kinds of variables. You can measure values by using different kinds of variables, including the following:

- **Categorical or nominal attributes** These variables have discrete values but do not have any natural order. Examples are states, status codes, and colors.

- **Ranks** These are discrete variables with an order, but they do not allow arithmetic. Examples include opinion ranks and binned true numerics.

- **Intervals** These are continuous variables with an order that allows some arithmetic, such as subtraction, but they typically do not allow summations. Examples are dates, times, and temperatures.

- **True numeric variables** These variables support all arithmetic operations. Examples include amounts and quantities.

After you understand your data, you need to decide what your case is. Each case encapsulates all you know about the entity. Cases can be simple or complex, with nested tables in one or more columns. Traditionally, data mining techniques were used on a single table, but modern tools, such as SSAS 2008, support the use of nested tables. For example, with SSAS 2008, you can mine a customer list that is followed by a nested purchases table. If a nested table exists in the dataset, each nested key, such as a product in the purchases table, is considered an item. Nested tables are not relations; they are not in relational shape anymore, and thus, they are not allowed in the SQL Server relational Database Engine. When nested tables are queried from SQL Server, you have to flatten, or normalize, them into standard rowsets. With flattening, you are performing joins between parent and child tables.

In understanding your data, you next need to decide how to handle outliers and missing values. *Outliers* are rare and far-out-of-bounds values in a column. They can have a big influence on the model and its results. You have several approaches for dealing with outliers, including doing nothing, filtering the rows that contain outliers, ignoring the column that contains the outliers, or replacing outliers with common (mean) values or bin values of the variable.

EXAM TIP

SQL Server Integration Services (SSIS) can be very useful for preparing data for data mining. For example, you can use a different path in the SSIS data flow for regular missing data, and then later when the missing data is handled, you can merge both datasets.

Missing data—empty values, nonexistent values, and uncollected data—can also be a problem for effective mining. Methods for handling missing data are similar to those for handling outliers: do nothing, filter the rows containing missing data, ignore the column with missing data, and so on. You should also check to see whether there is any pattern in outliers and missing data such as specific groups of cases that typically contain them.

For predictive models, you need to see how well the models perform the predictions. To evaluate predictive models before you implement them, you need to split your data into a training set and a test set. The data mining algorithms learn the patterns on the training sets. You can then see how the models perform by letting them predict values of target variables on the test set. Because you already know the actual values of the target variables, you can measure the performance of the predictions.

The key to properly preparing the training set and the test set is to statistically split the data randomly. You should not create any pattern as you split the data. You can use the SSIS Row Sampling and Percentage Sampling Transformations to get a random split of the data. In addition, you can use the Transact-SQL (T-SQL) *SELECT TABLESAMPLE* clause to randomly select a specific percentage of the data. However, this clause works on pages, not on rows, so it is appropriate only for large tables. In SSAS 2008, this splitting task is easier than ever to perform. You do not have to create the training and the test set in advance. You can partition the data while you are creating the mining structure by using the Data Mining Wizard, you can use the Data Mining Designer to modify the structure to partition data, or you can partition data programmatically by using Analysis Management Objects (AMO) or XML data definition language (DDL).

After you perform the data split, you need to verify that it is random. To do this, you can check the first four moments (mean, standard deviation, skewness, and kurtosis) of continuous variables. The *mean value* identifies the center of the distribution of values; *standard deviation* measures the spread of the distribution. *Skewness* describes asymmetry in probability distribution; it shows if a distribution is skewed to one side—for example, if the distribution is concentrated on one side and has a long tail on the other side. *Kurtosis* measures peakedness of probability distribution; it shows whether the distribution is narrow and high around the center and has quite high tails or whether it is lower close to the center and has lower tails. You can also use a predictive data mining algorithm such as a Decision Trees algorithm to try to predict set membership with variables in your sets. If the split is random, no patterns will be created.

Creating Data Mining Models

After you have examined and prepared your data, you need to create your mining structure and models. You create your models by using the Analysis Services Project template in BIDS. For data mining models, you define the data source and DSV objects in the same way you create them for Unified Dimensional Model (UDM) dimensions and cubes. You then create a data mining structure.

The data mining structure is a data structure that defines the domain from which you build your mining models—it specifies the source data through a DSV, the columns, and training and test set partitioning. A single mining structure can contain multiple mining models.

> **BEST PRACTICES** **CREATE MULTIPLE MODELS**
>
> You should always create multiple models using different algorithms and different algorithm parameters for a task, evaluate all of them, and then deploy the one that works best. You should never rely on the results of a single model; if different models give you similar results, you can be more confident that the results are useful.

You can easily compare the performance of the models that share the same mining structure. The mining structure columns describe the data that the data source contains. They are bound to source data, which can be a relational database or an OLAP cube. These columns contain information such as data type, content type, and data distribution. In a mining structure, you can also have nested tables. A nested table is a table in a column of each row of your case table. You get a nested table from a one-to-many (1:M) relationship between the entity of a case and its related entities. For example, you can analyze orders, define the orders table as your case table, and add order details in a column of the case table as a nested table. With nested tables, you combine the information into a single case. The order identifier is the entity, and the order details are the related attributes. You will use a nested table in the next lesson.

With data mining models, you apply an algorithm to the data of your mining structure. As with the mining structure, the mining model contains columns. The model inherits all the values of the column properties that the mining structure defines. You can use all the columns from the structure in a model, or you can use a subset of columns.

In the mining model, you define the use of the column as input, predictable, or input and predictable. *Predictable columns* are the target variables in predictive models. For example, to predict reasons for purchases of an article, you would add a derived column showing that a customer has purchased the article you are interested in and declare it as predictable. You would use other columns as *input columns*—that is, as columns that explain the reason for purchases of those articles. Last, you can define the derived column that shows whether a customer purchased the article as input and predictable. In this way, you can try to explain purchases of an article by using previous purchases of the same article. In addition, you need key columns to uniquely identify each case. Later in this chapter, you will learn how to use BIDS to create a mining structure and mining models.

Selecting Data Mining Algorithms

A key to data mining success is selecting an algorithm that is appropriate for your task. SSAS 2008 provides nine algorithms. In addition, SSIS includes two text-mining transformations. Table 9-1 summarizes the SSAS algorithms and their usage.

To analyze texts, such as articles in magazines, you need to use text mining. Although text mining is part of modern data mining, it is not part of SSAS. Instead, you can use two SSIS transformations for text mining: Term Extraction and Term Lookup.

The Term Extraction Transformation extracts terms from Unicode text in a transformation input column and then writes the terms to a transformation output column. You can use this transformation on Unicode columns of your SQL Server tables and on XML data. Using Term Extraction, you can discover the content of a dataset by extracting important terms that can include nouns only, noun phrases, or nouns and noun phrases. You can store the results of the Term Extraction Transformation in a table, and you can also edit this table to add, delete, or change the terms extracted manually. The transformation works only with the English language; it uses its own English dictionary and linguistic information about English. For other languages, you can manually define terms in a SQL Server table.

The Term Lookup Transformation provides the opposite functionality. It applies a dictionary of terms stored in a table to a new dataset to find out which terms from the dictionary are in which documents. You can create the dictionary manually or by using the Term Extraction Transformation. The Term Lookup Transformation adds two columns to the output: term and frequency. In these two columns, you will find the terms that appear, the frequency with which they appear, and the documents in which they appear. You can use this information to classify your documents manually or with a data mining method, such as the Clustering or Association Rules algorithm.

As you can see, this extensive selection of algorithms and transformations lets you use data mining for many tasks. For example, you could use the Association Rules algorithm to make purchase recommendations on your company Web site. You could use any of the predictive algorithms to predict customer churn and then concentrate your actions on critical customers. Advanced e-mail SPAM filters already use the Naïve Bayes algorithm, which is easy and quick to implement. And you can use predictive models to better understand the mortality rate at a hospital, for example. With data mining, you are limited only by your imagination.

TABLE 9-1 Data Mining Algorithms and Usage

ALGORITHM	USAGE
Association Rules	The Association Rules algorithm is designed for market basket analysis. The algorithm defines an *itemset* as a combination of items in a single transaction. The algorithm scans the dataset and counts the number of times the itemsets appear in transactions. You should use this algorithm to find cross-selling opportunities.
Clustering	The Clustering algorithm groups cases from a dataset into clusters containing similar characteristics. Using these clusters, you can explore the data and learn about relationships among your cases. Additionally, you can create predictions from the clustering model that the algorithm creates. You can use the Clustering method to group your customers for your Customer Relationship Management (CRM) application, for example. In addition, you can use Clustering to search for anomalies in your data. A case that is not part of any cluster is a case worth further inspection. This is useful for fraud detection: a transaction that does not fit in any discovered cluster might be a fraudulent transaction.
Decision Trees	You can use Decision Trees, the most popular data mining algorithm, to predict discrete and continuous variables. The results are easy to understand, which is the main reason the algorithm is so popular. If you predict continuous variables, you get a piecewise multiple linear regression formula with a separate formula in each node of a tree. The algorithm uses the discrete input variables to split the tree into nodes. A tree that predicts continuous variables is a regression tree.
Linear Regression	The Linear Regression algorithm predicts continuous variables only, using a single multiple linear regression formula. The input variables must be continuous as well. Linear Regression is a simple case of a regression tree, but it is a tree with no splits.
Logistic Regression	As a Linear Regression algorithm is a simple regression tree, a Logistic Regression algorithm is a Neural Network without any hidden layers.
Naïve Bayes	Given each state of the predictable attribute, the Naïve Bayes algorithm calculates probabilities for each possible state of the input attribute. You can later use those probabilities to predict an outcome of the target attribute you are predicting based on the known input attributes. Because this algorithm is quite simple, it builds the models very quickly. Therefore, you can use this algorithm as a starting point in your prediction task. The Naïve Bayes algorithm does not support continuous attributes.

ALGORITHM	USAGE
Neural Network	The Neural Network algorithm comes from artificial intelligence research. You can use this algorithm for predictions as well. Neural Network algorithms search for nonlinear functional dependencies. They perform nonlinear transformations on the data in layers, from the input layer through hidden layers to the output layer. Because they are harder to interpret than linear algorithms such as Decision Trees, Neural Network algorithms are not used as commonly in business as are algorithms that search for linear dependencies, such as regression trees that express dependent variables as a linear function of independent ones.
Sequence Clustering	Sequence Clustering searches for clusters based on a model rather than on similarity of cases. It builds models from sequences of events by using Markov Chains. *Markov Chains* first define a matrix with combinations of all possible states, and then, in the cells of the matrix, probabilities for transition from one state to another. With these probabilities, you can calculate probabilities for sequences, or chains, of transitions by multiplying probabilities of state transitions in the sequence. The sequences with highest probabilities give you the models for the clusters. After the algorithm finds those models, it clusters cases around them based on similarity of the cases' transitions. You can use this algorithm on any sequential data. Typical usage would be an analysis of your company's Web site usage.
Time Series	The Time Series algorithm is created for forecasting continuous variables. Internally, the algorithm uses two different algorithms. For short-term forecasting, the algorithm uses regression trees on automatically transformed data, called Auto-Regression Trees (ART). For long-term prediction, Time Series uses the Auto-Regressive Integrated Moving Average (ARIMA) algorithm. By using mining model parameters, you can modify the blend of algorithms used. In the next lesson, you will learn how to set up model parameters.

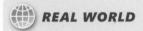
Understanding the Data Mining Tools

BIDS includes three main tools for creating mining models: the Data Mining Wizard, the Data Mining Designer, and Data Mining Viewers. This section briefly introduces them; you will use them in the practice for this lesson.

Data Mining Wizard

You start building a mining structure by using the Data Mining Wizard. With this wizard, you define the DSV and the tables and columns from the DSV that you want to use, add an initial model to the structure, and partition the data into training and test sets. You start the wizard in a BIDS Analysis Services project by right-clicking the Mining Structures folder in Solution Explorer and then selecting the New Mining Structure option. The wizard walks you through the following pages:

1. On the Welcome page, you learn what you can do with the wizard. Click Next.
2. On the Select The Definition Method page, shown in Figure 9-2, you define whether your source is a relational database or a UDM cube. Make the appropriate selection, and then click Next.

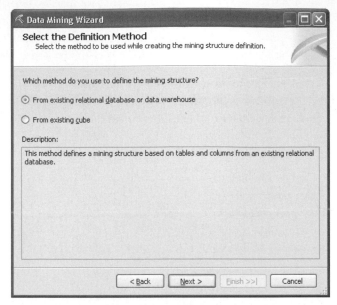

FIGURE 9-2 The Select The Definition Method page of the Data Mining Wizard

3. On the Create The Data Mining Structure page, you choose whether to add an initial model to the structure. If you decide to add an initial model, you also have to select the algorithm for this model. Click Next.

4. On the Select Data Source View page, select the DSV you want to use, and then click Next.

5. On the Specify Table Types page, you define which table is your case table and which tables you are going to use as nested tables, and then click Next.

6. On the Specify The Training Data page, you define column usage. You can define key, input, and predictable columns. Click Next.

7. On the Specify Columns' Content And Data Type page, you revise and correct column data types and content. For numeric columns, you can also automatically detect whether the content is discrete or continuous. Click Next.

8. On the Create Testing Set page, you specify the percentage of data or the maximum number of rows from the data to use for the test set. The rest of the data is used as the training set, for training the mining models in the structure. Specify a percentage, and then click Next.

9. On the Completing The Wizard page, you specify names for the mining structure and initial model. You can also enable drillthrough to the source data for the initial model by selecting the Allow Drill Through check box. Click Finish.

The Data Mining Designer

After you complete the wizard, the powerful Data Mining Designer opens automatically, as shown in Figure 9-3. You specify which actions you want to take by clicking the appropriate tab of the Data Mining Designer.

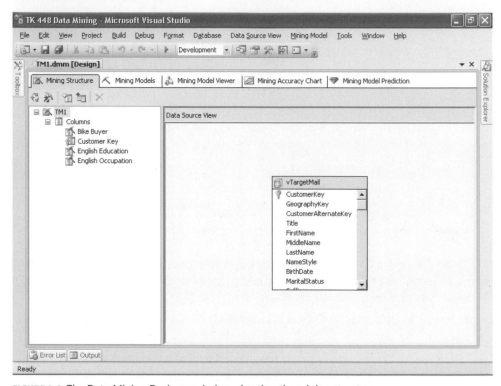

FIGURE 9-3 The Data Mining Designer window, showing the mining structure

In the Data Mining Designer, you can perform the following tasks:

- Modify the mining structure, including adding or deleting a column and changing the properties of a column or structure.

- Add additional mining models to the structure, and change the parameters of any model in the structure.

- Process the structure and browse the models by using Data Mining Viewers.

- Check the accuracy of the models by using a lift chart and other techniques. You will learn more about evaluating the models in Lesson 3 of this chapter.

- Create DMX prediction queries using your models. You will also learn more about the DMX language and prediction queries in Lesson 3 of this chapter.

Data Mining Viewers

Understanding the patterns and rules found by a mining model is not always an easy task. Therefore, it is important to be able to view the information from the models in an intuitive way. Data Mining Viewers, built into BIDS and SSMS, help you understand the models. In BIDS, you can access the viewers by clicking the Mining Model Viewer tab in the Data Mining Designer window. There are several viewers available—different ones for different algorithms. You will learn more about the viewers by using them in this chapter's practices. As an example of how intuitively these viewers display information from the models, Figure 9-4 shows the Microsoft Tree Viewer for the content of a Decision Tree model. The nodes of the tree show subgroups of the population. Decision Trees have split the population into nodes by using input variables in such a way as to maximize buyers in some nodes and non-buyers in other nodes. In the Background drop-down list, the value 1, meaning buyers, is selected. This means that nodes with a darker background include more buyers than nodes with a light background. This way you can easily spot interesting nodes.

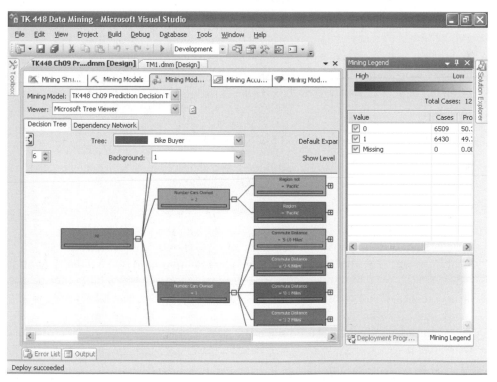

FIGURE 9-4 The Microsoft Tree Viewer, showing which nodes contain more bike buyers

Preparing Data for Data Mining and Creating Predictive Models

Adventure Works wants to boost bike sales by using a mail campaign. However, the company wants to target only those who are likely to buy bikes. The company wants to use existing data to find out which groups of customers tend to buy bikes. This data is already joined together in the vTargetMail view, from which you will create training and test set tables.

In this practice, you will get an overview of your data and prepare it for data mining by using the Data Mining Wizard and a DSV. You will modify a DSV to add the objects you need for data mining and explore the data. You will create a simple cube from a single view to examine your data further. Using the Data Mining Wizard, you will create a structure, map the structure columns to relational source columns, split the data into training and test sets, and create your first mining model. You will use the Data Mining Designer window to add additional models to the same structure. Last, you will use Data Mining Viewers to explore your models.

EXERCISE 1 Examine the Prepared Views

The AdventureWorksDW2008 sample database includes four views already prepared for data mining and a fifth view that you need only for the preparation of the four other views for data mining. First, you will examine their definitions.

1. In SSMS, connect to your SQL Server Database Engine, expand the Databases folder, expand the AdventureWorksDW2008 database folder, and then expand the Views subfolder.

2. You can script a view by right-clicking the name of the view, and then on the Script View As shortcut menu, selecting Create To and then New Query Editor Window, as Figure 9-5 shows. Script the following views: dbo.vTargetMail, dbo.vTimeSeries, dbo. vAssocSeqOrders, and dbo.vAssocSeqLineItems.

3. Examine the views' code. Notice that they all refer to an additional view, dbo.vDMPrep. Script that view as well.

4. Select the data from each of the views you scripted, and look at the data. Notice that the vTargetMail view joins the customer demographic data with a single column named BikeBuyer, which shows whether a customer has purchased a bike in the past. The vTimeSeries view gives you information about sales of different bike models in regions over time. The dbo.vAssocSeqOrders and dbo.vAssocSeqLineItems views provide information about individual orders and line items on those orders.

5. Close all the windows that contain scripts for creating the views.

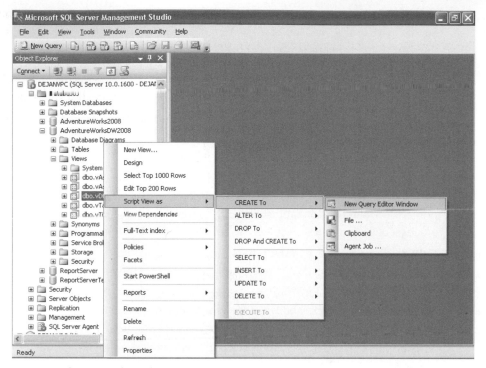

FIGURE 9-5 Steps to script a view

EXERCISE 2 Create a DSV and Examine Data

Now that you understand the DSV definitions, your task is to create a new project, add a data source and DSV to it, add the views you explored in the previous exercise to the DSV, and examine the data.

You will find complete solutions for this chapter's practices exercises in the installed practice files. The installed practice files are located in the C:\Users*username*\Documents\Microsoft Press\MCTS Training Kit 70-448\Source\Ch 09\ folder.

1. Open BIDS, and then create a new Analysis Services project and solution. Name the solution **TK 448 Data Mining** and the project **TK 448 Mining Models Project**.

2. In Solution Explorer, right-click the Data Sources folder, and then create a new data source. Use the Native OLE DB\SQL Server Native Client 10.0 provider. Connect to your SQL Server using Windows Authentication, and then select the AdventureWorks-DW2008 database. For the impersonation information, select the Inherit option. Use the default name (Adventure Works DW2008) for the data source.

3. In Solution Explorer, right-click the Data Source Views folder, and then select New Data Source View. In the Data Source View Wizard, on the Select A Data Source page, select the data source you just created. On the Select Tables And View page, select only the vTargetMail view. Use the default name (Adventure Works DW2008) for the DSV.

4. Now you need to add to the DSV other views that you will need for creating mining models. The DSV Designer should be open at this stage; if it is not, in Solution Explorer, double-click the Adventure Works DW2008 DSV to open it in the DSV Designer. Right-click in the pane containing the graphical representation of the DSV, and then select Add/Remove Tables.

5. Add the vTimeSeries, vAssocSeqOrders, and vAssocSeqLineItems views. Notice that the vTimeSeries view does not have a primary key defined yet. You have to set up a logical primary key. Notice also that there is no relationship between vAssocSeqOrders and vAssocSeqLineItems views. You have to set up a logical Foreign Key to associate them.

6. Hold down the Ctrl key and select the ModelRegion and TimeIndex columns of the vTimeSeries view in the DSV to select both columns, and then right-click the columns and select Set Logical Primary Key.

7. Set the logical foreign key between the vAssocSeqOrders and vAssocSeqLineItems views. Drag the OrderNumber column from the vAssocSeqLineItems to the vAssocSeq-Orders view. When you have finished, your Data Mining diagram should look like the one shown in Figure 9-6.

8. Explore the data of the vTargetMail view. Right-click the view in the DSV, and then select Explore Data. Initially, you get the first 5,000 rows of the view, shown in table format. But you can also examine the data by using a PivotTable, a chart, or a Pivot-Chart view.

9. Click the Chart tab. In the drop-down list above the distribution graphs, select the following columns: BikeBuyer, CommuteDistance, EnglishEducation, MaritalStatus, and NumberCarsOwned.

10. After you check the distribution of the attributes, close the Explore vTargetMail Table window in BIDS, and then save the project. Do not close BIDS.

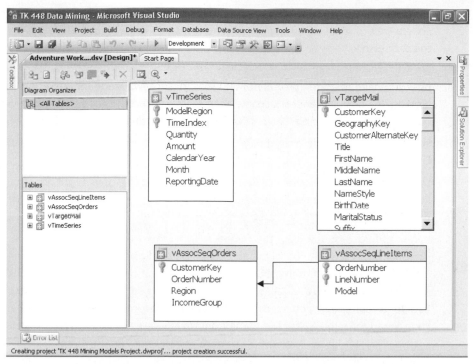

FIGURE 9-6 Data mining DSV, with database views used for analyses

EXERCISE 3   Create a UDM Cube to Examine Data

You have not finished your data overview yet. Now you need to create a UDM cube to examine the data more thoroughly. You will use this cube as a source for data mining in another practice later in this chapter.

1. In BIDS, use the TK 448 Data Mining project you created in the previous exercise. If you closed it, reopen it.

2. In Solution Explorer, for the TK 448 Mining Models project, right-click the Cubes folder, and then select New Cube. On the Welcome page of the Cube Wizard, click Next. On the Select Creation Method page, use the default option (Use Existing Tables) and then click Next.

3. On the Select Measure Group Tables page, select the vTargetMail check box from the Adventure Works DW2008 DSV, and then click Next. On the Select Measures page, select only the check box for the Bike Buyer attribute as a measure. Click Next.

4. On the Select New Dimensions page, use the default (the vTargetMail view) as the only dimension. Notice that you are using the same view for the measures and for the dimension. Click the dimension name to select it, and then right-click it so that you can rename it. Rename the dimension **TargetMailDim**. Click Next.

5. On the Completing The Wizard page, name the cube **TargetMailCube**, and then click Finish.

   Do not worry about the blue squiggly lines in the Cube Designer. Right now, you are not concerned about best practices warnings.

6. Next, add interesting attributes to your dimension. In Solution Explorer, in the Dimensions folder, double-click the TargetMailDim dimension to open the Dimension Designer window. From the Data Source View pane, drag the following columns to the Attributes pane: Age, CommuteDistance, EnglishEducation, EnglishOccupation, Gender, HouseOwnerFlag, MaritalStatus, NumberCarsOwned, NumberChildrenAtHome, Region, TotalChildren, and YearlyIncome. Again, disregard the best practices warning. Your dimension should look like the one shown in Figure 9-7.

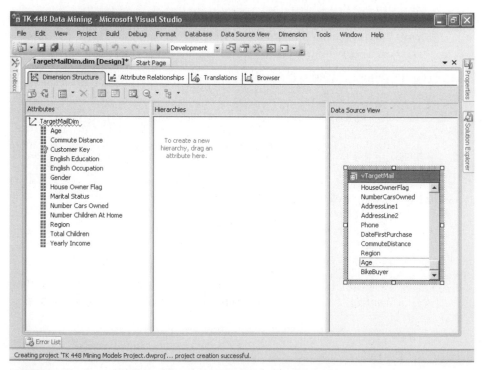

FIGURE 9-7 The TargetMailDim dimension in the Dimension Designer

7. The Age and Yearly Income attributes in your dimension have continuous values. Continuous attributes are not very useful for PivotTable and PivotGraph overviews. You need to discretize them—that is, group them into a discrete number of bins.

8. Select the Age attribute, and then use the Properties window to set the Discretization-BucketCount property to 5 and the DiscretizationMethod property to Automatic. You can find these two properties in the Advanced Properties group. Repeat this step for the Yearly Income attribute.

> **BEST PRACTICES** **USE DISCRETIZATION METHODS**
>
> In SSAS 2008, you can use two built-in automatic discretization methods: EqualAreas and Clusters. EqualAreas divides the population into groups with an equal number of cases in each group. Clusters tries to find the best discretization by using the Clustering data mining algorithm. With the Automatic option, you let SSAS determine which of the two methods to use automatically. However, in a real-life application, you should do the discretization manually, in the data preparation phase, and make your discretization decision from a business perspective.

9. Save the project, and then deploy and process it.

10. Use the Browser tab in the Cube Designer to examine the data. For example, create a PivotTable with the number of bike buyers broken down by number of cars owned across rows and marital status over columns.

11. Save the project. Do not close BIDS.

EXERCISE 4   Use the Data Mining Wizard

Now you can start mining your data. In this exercise, you will first create a mining structure, then split the data into training and test sets, and last create a mining model by using the Data Mining Wizard.

1. In the Solution Explorer window, right-click the Mining Structures folder, and then select New Mining Structure to start the Data Mining Wizard.

2. On the Welcome page of the Data Mining Wizard, click Next.

3. On the Select The Definition Method page, leave the first option selected to use the existing relational database or data warehouse. Click Next.

4. On the Create The Data Mining Structure page, in the What Data Mining Technique Do You Want To Use drop-down list, select Microsoft Decision Trees (the default). Click Next.

5. On the Select Data Source View page, select the Adventure Works DW2008 DSV and then click Next.

6. On the Specify Table Types page, select vTargetMail as a case table by selecting the Case check box for this table. Click Next.

7. On the Specify The Training Data page, select the appropriate check boxes to define CustomerKey as a key column (selected by default); BikeBuyer as an input and predictable column; and Age, CommuteDistance, EnglishEducation, EnglishOccupation, Gender, HouseOwnerFlag, MaritalStatus, NumberCarsOwned, NumberChildrenAtHome, Region, TotalChildren, and YearlyIncome as input columns. Click Next.

8. On the Specify Columns' Content And Data Type page, click Detect. Notice that the wizard detected that the Age and Yearly Income attributes are of the continuous content type. Click Next.

9. On the Create Testing Set page, you can specify the percentage of the data or number of cases for the test set (that is, the *holdout data*, data that is not used for training). Use the default splitting, using 30 percent of the data as a test set. Click Next.

10. Type **TK448 Ch09** Prediction as the name of the mining structure and **TK448 Ch09 Prediction Decision Trees** as the name of the model.

11. Click Finish to close the wizard and open the Data Mining Designer.

12. Save the project. Do not close BIDS.

EXERCISE 5 Use the Data Mining Designer

Your next task is to refine the structure and the model you created. You can then add more predictive models based on the same structure. You can also filter a specific model to use only a subset of data for training.

1. The Age and Yearly Income attributes are continuous attributes; you discretized them in the dimension of the cube you created in Exercise 3 of this practice, not in the relational data warehouse. You need to discretize them into five classes by using the Automatic discretization method.

2. Select the Age column in the Mining Structure pane. Open the Properties window if it is closed. Change the Content property to Discretized, the DiscretizationBucketCount property to 5, and the DiscretizationMethod property to Automatic.

3. Repeat the discretize process for the Yearly Income attribute.

4. To add a Naïve Bayes model, in the Mining Structure pane, right-click the TK448 Ch09 Prediction Decision Trees model, and then click New Mining Model. Type **TK448 Ch09 Prediction Naïve Bayes** as the name of the model. In the Algorithm Name drop-down list, select the Microsoft Naïve Bayes algorithm, and then click OK.

5. To add a Neural Network model, right-click the TK448 Ch09 Prediction Decision Trees model, and then click New Mining Model. Type **TK448 Ch09 Prediction Neural Network** as the name of the model, select the Microsoft Neural Network algorithm, and then click OK.

6. To add a Clustering model, right-click the TK448 Ch09 Prediction Decision Trees model, and then click New Mining Model. Type **TK448 Ch09 Prediction Clustering** as the name of the model, select the Microsoft Clustering algorithm, and then click OK.

7. To add a filtered Decision Trees model, right-click the TK448 Ch09 Prediction Decision Trees model, and then click New Mining Model. Type **TK448 Ch09 Prediction Decision Trees Filtered** as the name of the model, select the Microsoft Decision Trees algorithm, and then click OK.

8. Right-click the last model, the TK448 Ch09 Prediction Decision Trees Filtered model, and then select Set Model Filter. In the Model Filter dialog box, in the Mining Structure column, select the House Owner Flag attribute from the drop-down list. Use the default (equality) operator, and type **1** in the Value column. You are creating a separate mining model for house owners only. If you apply a filter to the model, you control the subset of the data that is used to train the model. In this way, you can assess the performance of the model on a subset of the data. Click OK.

9. Save, deploy, and process the complete project. Do not exit BIDS.

EXERCISE 6 Use the Data Mining Viewers

After you successfully create and deploy the models, you can analyze them by using the Data Mining Viewers.

1. View the Decision Trees model. In BIDS, in the Data Mining Designer window, click the Mining Model Viewer tab, and then select the TK448 Ch09 Prediction Decision Trees model from the Mining Model drop-down list.

2. Verify that you have the Decision Tree tab open. In the Background drop-down list, select value 1 of the Bike Buyer attribute. Check the potential buyers only. Notice the color of the nodes: the darker the color, the more bike buyers appear in the node. For example, you can see that the color of the node that groups people for whom the Number Cars Owned attribute is equal to 0 and the Age attribute is less than 40 is dark blue, which means that there are a lot of potential buyers in this node.

3. To identify the two variables that most influence the Bike Buyer attribute, click the Dependency Network tab, use the slider on the left side of the screen to show the strongest links only. Figure 9-8 shows the Dependency Network viewer with the three strongest links highlighted. The strongest links show input variables with the highest influence on the target variable.

4. View the Naïve Bayes model. Navigate to the Mining Model Viewer tab, and then select the TK448 Ch09 Prediction Naïve Bayes model.

5. The first viewer listed should be the Dependency Network viewer. Check whether the Naïve Bayes algorithm identifies the same two variables that the Decision Trees algorithm identified as having the most influence on the Bike Buyer attribute.

6. In the Attribute Profiles viewer, you can check the distribution of the values of input attributes in classes of the predictive attribute.

7. In the Attribute Characteristics viewer, you can identify the values of input attributes that are characteristic for particular values of the Bike Buyer attribute.

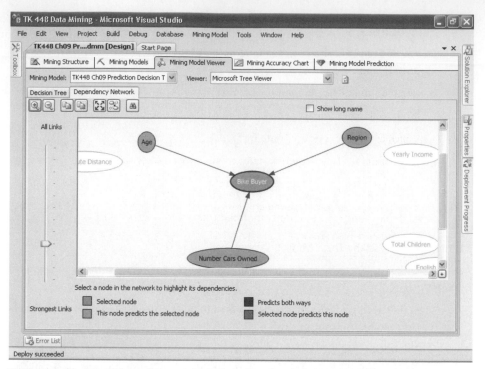

FIGURE 9-8 The Dependency Network viewer, showing the three variables with the most influence on the Bike Buyer variable

8. In the Attribute Discrimination viewer, you can see the values of input attributes that favor value 1 of the Bike Buyer attribute and the values that favor value 0.

9. Check the Clustering model as well. The viewers for the Clustering algorithm are similar to those for Naïve Bayes, although the Cluster Diagram view, which shows the number of clusters and how close these clusters are to one another, is different. You should see 10 clusters. You can shade the clusters based on a value of any variable. For example, you can use the Bike Buyer as the shading variable and select state 1 of the Bike Buyer variable to quickly see the clusters that have more bike buyers. In the Cluster Profiles viewer, you can see the distribution of values of variables in each cluster. In the Cluster Characteristics viewer, you can see the values that are characteristic of a specific cluster. Using the Cluster Discrimination tab, you can compare pairs of clusters to identify the values of input variables that favor particular clusters of the pair.

10. Check the Neural Network model. The only viewer you will see is the Attribute Discrimination viewer, in which you can identify the values of input attributes that favor value 1 of the Bike Buyer attribute and values that favor value 0. In addition, you can filter the viewer to show the discrimination for specific states of input attributes only.

11. Last, also check whether you got a different tree for the filtered Decision Trees model compared to the unfiltered one.

12. Save the solution, and then close BIDS.

✔ Quick Check

1. You need to predict which customers are about to leave your company. How can you accomplish this task?

2. What are the different components that make up the SQL Server BI suite?

3. Why would you prepare separate training and test sets?

4. Which algorithm is appropriate for fraud detection?

5. In the practice, why do you think you had to discretize the continuous attributes?

6. Do you get the same results when you use different algorithms for predictions?

7. How can you prepare training and test sets?

Quick Check Answers

1. Predicting which customers might leave your company is a typical task for data mining. You should use a predictive algorithm such as Decision Trees to discover patterns in the data that you have about customers who have already left your company. You should then use the same algorithm to predict the churn based on data from existing customers.

2. The SQL Server BI suite includes SSAS cubes, SSAS data mining, SSRS, and SSIS.

3. Whenever you use predictive models, you have to test the predictions. You train the models by using the training sets and then test the models by making predictions with the trained models on the test set.

4. For fraud detection, you can use the Clustering algorithm. You can cluster the transactions and then find the transactions that do not fit well in any of the clusters.

5. You had to discretize the continuous attributes because of the Naïve Bayes algorithm, which accepts discrete attributes only. If you did not discretize them, you would have to ignore them in the Naïve Bayes model.

6. No, different algorithms and even different parameters of a single algorithm give you different results—for example, slightly different predictions. That is why you have to evaluate the models by using them to make predictions on the test set.

7. To prepare training and test sets, you can use the Data Mining Wizard and Data Mining Designer in BIDS to specify the percentage of the holdout data for the test set. You can also use the *TABLESAMPLE* option of the T-SQL SELECT statement or the SSIS Row Sampling Transformation and Percentage Sampling Transformation.

Lesson 2: Creating Models and Applying Algorithms

Estimated lesson time: 70 minutes

In Lesson 1, you used a relational source to create quite a few predictable models, and you used columns from a relational source for different purposes in your mining structure and models. In this lesson, you will learn more about column usage and about an advanced column type called a *nested table*. You will then use this knowledge in a practice to create association, sequence, and forecasting models. You will also use a cube as the source for a data mining model and learn how to set up the most important parameters for different data mining algorithms.

Mapping Mining Structure Attributes to Source Columns

When you define how you are going to use source columns in your mining structure and models, you are actually defining the content type of a column and a prediction clause. A prediction clause is quite simple; you just have to define which columns you are going to predict. You can use a column in a mining model in the following ways:

- **Input column**   The input of a model.
- **Predictable column**   The target variable of directed models.
- **Input and predictable column**   The target variable also serves as input.
- **Ignored column**   The column is treated as if it does not exist in the mining structure; it is ignored in a specific model.

Column content types define how the column measures data values and whether the column is used as a key. You have already learned about different ways you can measure values. The supported content types are listed here:

- **Discrete**   The column has discrete values.
- **Continuous**   The column has continuous values.
- **Discretized**   You used this option to discretize continuous columns in your mining structure.
- **Ordered**   This is a discrete column that has ordered ranks.
- **Cyclical**   This special kind of column contains values in a cyclical ordered set, such as numbers of days in a week.

Key columns correspond to and are mapped to a single column that represents a Primary Key in the source. However, you can have two additional key column types:

- **Key Sequence column**   A specific type of key having ordered values that represent a sequence of events
- **Key Time column**   A specific Key Sequence type in which values are ordered based on a time scale and are an equal distance apart

Using Case Table Definitions and Nested Tables

If a column is a nested table, you have multiple options for how to use columns from the case table and columns from the nested table. In this section, you will look at several examples of how to use these columns. In the AdventureWorksDW2008 database, you have the dbo.vAssocSeqOrders and dbo.vAssocSeqLineItems views; you will use the first view as a case table and the second view as a nested table. Nested tables provide a lot of flexibility for modeling business problems. The following examples show you how to use the columns from the case table and the nested table from the views in different ways to answer different business questions.

Example 1: Association Rules

Table 9-2 shows the column usage for predicting associations. Note that the dbo.vAssocSeqLineItems view is used as a column of the case table—that is, as a column of the dbo.vAssocSeqOrders view.

TABLE 9-2 Example 1: Case and Nested Table for Association Rules

CASE TABLE COLUMN	NESTED TABLE COLUMN	USAGE
Order Number		Key
Customer Key		
Region		
Income Group		
vAssocSeqLineItems		
	Order Number	
	Line Number	
	Model	Key, input, predictable

In this example, you use the Model column of the nested table as a key, input, and predictable column. You are looking for the values of the Model column that predict other values of this column. This means you are searching for models that appear together on the same customer order; if they appear together many times, the appearance of one model predicts the appearance of another model. You are searching for the existence of rows of the nested table for each customer order; you do that through a row's key. Because a model is unique in an order, you can use it as a key. Because you want to predict the models, you use the Model column as both input and predictable.

Example 2: Sequences

You can use the Line Number attribute of the dbo.vAssocSeqLineItems view to define the sequence of purchases of models inside a single customer order. With multiple orders, you can try to find rules in sequences. Table 9-3 shows the usage of columns for predicting sequences.

TABLE 9-3 Example 2: Case and Nested Table for Sequence Clustering

CASE TABLE COLUMN	NESTED TABLE COLUMN	USAGE
Order Number		Key
Customer Key		
Region		
Income Group		
vAssocSeqLineItems		
	Order Number	
	Line Number	Key Sequence, input
	Model	Input, predictable

This example uses Line Number as the Key Sequence column, indicating that it has a sequence in it. Because the sequence predicts a model, you use this column as input. The Model column is predictable, but because you want to find not just sequences, but *sequences of models*, you have to use it as input as well.

EXAM TIP

Although Microsoft developed Sequence Clustering for clickstream analysis (that is, analysis of sequences of clicks on a Web site's pages), you can use the algorithm on any sequences.

Example 3: Predicting a Case Table Column

The third example shows how you can predict a column of the case table by using the values in the nested table. Table 9-4 shows the column usage you specify to perform this task.

TABLE 9-4 Example 3: Case and Nested Table for Predicting a Case Table Column

CASE TABLE COLUMN	NESTED TABLE COLUMN	USAGE
Order Number		Key
Customer Key		
Region		Input
Income Group		Predictable
vAssocSeqLineItems		
	Order Number	
	Line Number	
	Model	Key, input

In this example, you are predicting Income Group, using the Region column from the case table as input. You are using the Model column of the nested table as input as well. You are searching for the income of your customers based on the region they come from and the models they purchase. You can use your own creativity to find other business questions that you can model by using nested tables.

Using Cube Sources

Up to now in this chapter, you have used only relational sources for data mining. But you can also use a UDM cube as a data mining source. Using UDM cubes as sources for data mining is quite simple. When you mine OLAP cubes, your case table is a dimension. Any measure from any measure group—that is, any fact table—connected with the selected dimension can be used as a case-level column. Additionally, you can add other dimensions connected to the same measure group as nested tables.

OLAP cubes are often appropriate sources for data mining. In an OLAP cube, you already have data that has been collected over time, merged, and cleansed. However, adding derived variables and additionally modifying the data is much easier in a relational source.

> **BEST PRACTICES** **LIMIT HISTORICAL DATA IN OLAP CUBES**
>
> OLAP cubes might actually contain too much data, especially too much historical data, for effective mining. Your results could be accurate predictions for past behavior but not for the future. For example, mobile phone models change several times a year, so if you used 10-year-old data, your predictions would reflect what happened in the past. You can bypass this problem by filtering, or *slicing*, the OLAP data you want to use in your mining models. In addition, you could use data from higher levels of natural hierarchies—for example, you could use product categories rather than product models. Categories do not become obsolete as quickly as models do. Generally, you should not use too much history for data that changes frequently.

The opposite process, using cubes as destinations for a data mining process, is even more interesting. You can deploy a mining model as a new dimension in a UDM database and use it in cubes. This is probably the easiest way to deploy a mining model in production. However, you cannot use a mining model as a dimension in the same cube in which you used it as the source for the model. You would get a cyclical reference for processing, and therefore, processing would never stop. However, you can create a new linked cube, linked to or based on the source cube, with the mining model as a dimension. You can do this with just a few clicks in the Data Mining Designer, as you will also see in the practice for this lesson:

1. Right-click the mining model, and then click Create A Data Mining Dimension.

2. In the Create Data Mining Dimension dialog box, name the dimension, and then select the Create Cube check box.

3. Name the cube, and then click OK.

Configuring Algorithm Parameters

You have not yet changed any of the default parameters for any of the algorithms you have used in this chapter. Did you ask yourself, for example, whether you have any influence on the number of clusters in Clustering and Sequence Clustering techniques? The answer is yes, and in this section, you will learn how you can configure data mining algorithms.

Every mining algorithm has its own set of parameters. You can use these parameters to modify the behavior of the algorithm and thus influence the patterns and rules that the algorithm finds. Table 9-5 summarizes the most important parameters for each algorithm and defines their usage. For a detailed list of all parameters for each algorithm, see the SQL Server 2008 Books Online topic "Customizing a Data Mining Model (Analysis Services—Data Mining)" (see References).

TABLE 9-5 Most Important Algorithm Parameters

ALGORITHM	PARAMETER	USAGE
Decision Trees	MINIMUM_SUPPORT	Higher support for a node means fewer splits and thus a shallower tree.
	COMPLEXITY_PENALTY	A higher complexity penalty means fewer splits and thus a shallower tree.
	SPLIT_METHOD	With the split method, you can force binary splits only or complete splits on all values of an attribute.
Naïve Bayes	MAXIMUM_STATES	This parameter specifies the maximum number of states allowed for an attribute. If you have more states, you have to discretize the values.
Neural Network	HIDDEN_NODE_RATIO	This parameter influences the number of nodes in the hidden layer. If you set this parameter to zero, you have no hidden layer, so you create a Logistic Regression model.
Clustering	CLUSTER_COUNT	As the name of this parameter implies, you use it to control the number of clusters.
Association Rules	MINIMUM_PROBABILITY	This parameter specifies the minimum probability for a rule. You can have greater confidence in rules with higher probability.

ALGORITHM	PARAMETER	USAGE
	MINIMUM_SUPPORT	This parameter specifies the minimum number of cases that must contain the itemset before a rule is generated. With lower minimum support and minimum probability, you get more rules.
Sequence Clustering	CLUSTER_COUNT	In this algorithm, the CLUSTER_COUNT parameter gives only an approximate number of clusters found. The algorithm adds additional clusters to this number if it finds distinguishable models.
Time Series	PERIODICITY_HINT	With this parameter, you inform the algorithm that you have periodical data. Periods are very typical for a time series. For example, if your time points are based on months, the same month repeats every twelfth time.
	FORECAST_METHOD	With this parameter, you control the method used for training. Possible values are Auto-Regression Trees with Cross-Predict (ARTXP), ARIMA, or MIXED. The default is MIXED.
	PREDICTION_SMOOTHING	This parameter specifies how the model should be mixed between ART and ARIMA algorithms to optimize forecasting. You can enter any value between 0 and 1—lower values favor ART and forecasting is optimized for fewer predictions, while higher values favor ARIMA and forecasting is optimized for more predictions.

You can set the algorithm parameters by right-clicking the mining model in the Data Mining Designer and then clicking the Set Algorithm Parameters option.

PRACTICE Creating Mining Models and Setting Algorithm Parameters

In this practice, you will use advanced types of keys, including Key Sequence and Key Time columns, and nested tables to build association, sequence, and forecasting models. You will then create a clustering model, using a UDM cube as the source. You will also deploy the models as a dimension of a cube. Last, you will modify the algorithms' behavior by setting parameters and, in a clustering model, rename the clusters to meaningful names.

EXERCISE 1 Configure Association Rules, Sequence Clustering, and Time Series

First, you need to build a model to explore association rules for model purchases. You will search for any sequences that exist in model purchases and then forecast quantities and amounts of sales of bike models in different regions.

1. Open the TK 448 Mining Models Project you created in the previous lesson in BIDS.

2. In the Solution Explorer window, right-click the Mining Structures folder, and then select New Mining Structure to start the Data Mining Wizard.

3. On the Welcome page of the Data Mining Wizard, click Next.

4. On the Select The Definition Method page, select From Existing Relational Database Or Data Warehouse. Click Next.

5. On the Create The Data Mining Structure page, from the Which Data Mining Technique Do You Want To Use drop-down list, select the Microsoft Association Rules technique. Click Next.

6. On the Select Data Source View page, verify that the Adventure Works DW2008 DSV is selected, and then click Next.

7. On the Specify Table Types page, specify vAssocSeqOrders as the case and vAssocSeqLineItems as the nested table. Click Next.

8. On the Specify The Training Data page, clear the check box showing that the CustomerKey column is the key column (it is selected by default), and specify OrderNumber as a key column and Model as a key, input, and predictable column, as Figure 9-9 shows. Click Next.

9. On the Specify Columns' Content And Data Type page, click Detect. Click Next.

10. On the Create Testing Set page, set the percentage of data for testing to 0. Because this is not a predictive model, you do not need the testing set. Click Next.

11. Type **TK448 Ch09 Association** as the mining structure name and **TK448 Ch09 Association Rules** as the model name, and then click Finish

12. In the Solution Explorer window, right-click the Mining Structures folder, and then select New Mining Structure to start the Data Mining Wizard.

13. On the Welcome page of the Data Mining Wizard, click Next.

14. On the Select The Definition Method page, select From Existing Relational Database Or Data Warehouse. Click Next.

15. On the Create The Data Mining Structure page, from the Which Data Mining Technique Do You Want To Use drop-down list, select the Microsoft Sequence Clustering technique. Click Next.

16. On the Select Data Source View page, verify that the Adventure Works DW2008 DSV is selected, and then click Next.

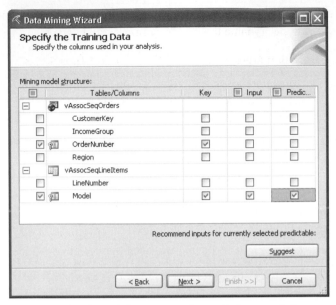

FIGURE 9-9 The data mining structure for analyzing associations among models

17. On the Specify Table Types page, specify vAssocSeqOrders as the case and vAssoc-SeqLineItems as the nested table. Click Next.

18. On the Specify The Training Data page, clear the check box showing that the Customer-Key column is the key column (it is selected by default), and specify OrderNumber as a key column, LineNumber as a key and input column, and Model as an input and predict-able column, as Figure 9-10 shows. Click Next.

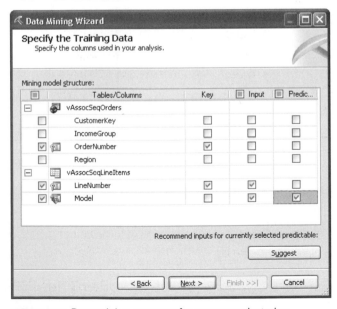

FIGURE 9-10 Data mining structure for sequence clustering

19. On the Specify Columns' Content And Data Type page, click Detect. Click Next.

20. On the Create Testing Set page, set the percentage of data for testing to 0. Because this is not a predictive model, you do not need the testing set.

21. Type **TK448 Ch09 Sequence** as the name of the mining structure and **TK448 Ch09 Sequence Clustering** as the name of the model, and then click Finish.

22. In the Solution Explorer window, right-click the Mining Structures folder, and then select New Mining Structure to start the Data Mining Wizard.

23. On the Welcome page of the Data Mining Wizard, click Next.

24. On the Select The Definition Method page, verify that From Existing Relational Database Or Data Warehouse is selected, and then click Next.

25. On the Create The Data Mining Structure page, select the Microsoft Time Series technique, and then click Next.

26. On the Select Data Source View page, verify that the Adventure Works DW2008 DSV is selected, and then click Next.

27. On the Specify Table Types page, select the Case check box for the vTimeSeries table. Click Next.

28. On the Specify The Training Data page, select the Key check box for the ModelRegion and TimeIndex columns and the Input and Predictable check boxes for the Amount and Quantity columns, as Figure 9-11 shows. Click Next.

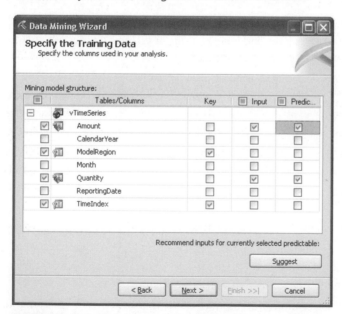

FIGURE 9-11 Data mining structure for forecasting

29. On the Specify Columns' Content And Data Type page, click Detect. When detection completes, click Next.

30. On the Create Testing Set page, set the percentage of data for testing to 0. Because this is not a predictive model, you do not need the testing set. Click Next.

31. On the Completing The Wizard page, type **TK448 Ch09 Forecasting** as the name of the mining structure and **TK448 Ch09 Forecasting Time Series** as the name of the model, and then click Finish.

32. Save, deploy, and process the project. Do not exit BIDS.

EXERCISE 2 Use the Data Mining Viewers

After you successfully create and deploy the models, you can analyze them by using the Data Mining Viewers.

1. In Solution Explorer, below the Mining Structures folder, double-click TK448 Ch09 Association to display the TK448 Ch09 Association Rules model in the Data Mining Designer.

2. Click the Mining Model Viewer tab. Within the Mining Model Viewer, click the Item-sets tab to view the itemsets that were found. In the Show drop-down list, select Show Attribute Name Only. In the Minimum Itemset Size box, type **2** to display only those itemsets with two or more items in the set.

3. On the Rules tab, check the first 10 rules that were returned.

4. Click the Dependency Network tab. Identify the models that predict other models in the same market basket. For example, if you lower the bar on the left to show strong links only, and click Touring Tire, you will find that Touring Tire Tube is often in the same market basket.

5. In Solution Explorer, below the Mining Structures folder, double-click the TK448 Ch09 Sequence structure.

6. In the Data Mining Designer, click the Mining Model Viewer tab and then click the Cluster Diagram viewer tab. In the Shading Variable drop-down list, select Model. In the State drop-down list, select Cycling Cap to identify the clusters that include Cycling Cap.

7. In the Data Mining Designer, click the Mining Model Viewer tab, and then click the Cluster Profiles tab. Check the distribution of models in different clusters. In addition, check the Model.Samples area of this viewer for typical combinations of models in clusters.

8. Click the Cluster Characteristics tab to use the Cluster Characteristics viewer to see typical models and transitions in a cluster.

9. Click the Cluster Discrimination tab. Use the Cluster Discrimination viewer to compare two clusters to identify the models and transitions that favor specific clusters.

10. Last, click the State Transitions tab to use this viewer to show transitions from a state to a state—that is, from a model to another model—in population or in a specific cluster and to predict the probability for transitions.

11. In Solution Explorer, double-click the TK448 Ch09 Forecasting mining structure to display it in the Data Mining Designer.

12. Click the Mining Model Viewer tab. In the Decision Tree viewer (the Model tab of the viewer), in the Tree drop-down list, select the tree for R250 Europe: Amount, if it is not selected by default. Select any node, and in the Mining Legend window, check the multiple linear regression formulas in the selected node.

13. Use the Charts view to show the forecasted values for the next five time points for R250 Europe: Amount, R250 North America: Amount, and R250 Pacific: Amount. You can find six models/regions selected by default on the chart legend at the right side of the chart. Use the drop-down list at the top of the chart legend to change the selection of models/regions that chart shows.

14. Close all Data Mining Designer views. Save the project. Do not exit BIDS.

EXERCISE 3 Create a Model from a Cube

Your next task is to create a Clustering model from an existing cube.

1. In the Solution Explorer window, right-click the Mining Structures folder, and then select New Mining Structure to start the Data Mining Wizard.

2. On the Welcome page of the Data Mining Wizard, click Next.

3. On the Select The Definition Method page, select From Existing Cube. Click Next.

4. On the Create The Data Mining Structure page, from the Which Data Mining Technique Do You Want To Use drop-down list, select the Microsoft Sequence Clustering technique. Click Next.

5. On the Select The Source Cube Dimension page, verify that TargetMailDim as the source cube dimension and the TargetMailCube cube are selected, and then click Next.

6. On the Select The Case Key page, click Next to accept the Customer Key attribute as the key column.

7. On the Select Case Level Columns page, below Attributes, select the Age, Commute Distance, English Education, English Occupation, Gender, House Owner Flag, Marital Status, Number Cars Owned, Number Children At Home, Region, Total Children, and Yearly Income check boxes. Below v Target Mail, select the Bike Buyer measure check box, and then click Next.

8. On the Specify Mining Model Column Usage page, if necessary, select the Input check box in the column heading to use all the selected columns as input attributes.

9. Do not add nested tables. Click Next.

10. On the Specify Columns' Content And Data Type page, click Next to accept the default settings.

11. On the Slice Source Cube page, click Next to continue without slicing the cube.

12. On the Create Testing Set page, set the percentage of data for testing to **0**. Because this is not a predictive model, you do not need the testing set. Click Next.

13. Type **TK448 Ch09 Cube Clustering** as the name of the mining structure and **TK448 Ch09 Cube Clustering** as the name of the model, and then click Finish.

EXERCISE 4   Change Algorithm Parameters

Now you need to refine two models by changing the parameters of an algorithm. You will change the number of clusters for the Clustering algorithm, and lower the threshold conditions for the Association Rules algorithm to get more associations. You will also inform the Time Series algorithm about periodicity in your data.

1. To change the TK448 Ch09 Cube Clustering model, in Solution Explorer, double-click the structure to open it in the Data Mining Designer. In the TK448 Ch09 Cube Clustering structure, click the Mining Models tab.

2. Right-click the TK448 Ch09 Cube Clustering model (displayed as a column heading), and then select Set Algorithm Parameters.

3. For the CLUSTER_COUNT parameter, double-click in the Value cell, enter 4,, and then click OK. Save and then close the TK448 Ch09 Cube Clustering model.

4. Open the TK448 Ch09 Association structure in the Data Mining Designer by double-clicking this model in Solution Explorer. To change the TK448 Ch09 Association model, click the Mining Models tab.

5. Right-click the TK448 Ch09 Association Rules model, and then select Set Algorithm Parameters.

6. Change the value of the MINIMUM_PROBABILITY parameter to 0.1 and the MINIMUM _SUPPORT parameter to 0.01, and then click OK. Save and close the TK448 Ch09 Association model.

7. To change the TK448 Ch09 Forecasting Time Series model, open the TK448 Ch09 Forecasting structure, and then click the Mining Models tab.

8. Right-click the TK448 Ch09 Forecasting Time Series model, and then select Set Algorithm Parameters.

9. Change the PERIODICITY_HINT parameter to **string literal {12}**, and then click OK. Do not forget to include the curly brackets. You can actually define more than one periodical cycle in your data; therefore, you are creating a set of periodicity hints.

10. Save, deploy, and process the project.

EXERCISE 5   Review Changes and Rename Clusters

Now you need to review the changes you made and then rename the clusters to meaningful names.

1. Check and change the TK448 Ch09 Cube Clustering model by going to the Microsoft Cluster Viewer—you should see only four clusters. (From Solution Explorer, open the TK448 Ch09 Cube Clustering model and then click the Mining Model Viewer tab. The Microsoft Cluster Viewer is displayed by default.)

2. Click the Cluster Discrimination tab to display this view. Use the Cluster Discrimination view to find the values of attributes that characterize each cluster. Compare each cluster to its own complement. This way, you can easily notice characteristics of each cluster. For example, compare Cluster 1 (selected by default in the left drop-down list on the top of the cluster discrimination graph) and Cluster 2 (you select this manually from the right drop-down list). You should see that if the number of children at home is zero, this favors Cluster 1, and if the number of children at home is between 1 and 5, this favors Cluster 2.

3. After you see what characterizes each cluster, click the Cluster Diagram tab and rename each cluster by right-clicking it and then selecting Rename Cluster. Enter a name for the cluster, and then click OK. For example, you could type **No Children At Home** as the business name for Cluster 1, **Many Children** as the business name for Cluster 2, **No Children** as the business name for Cluster 3, and **Europeans** as the business name for Cluster 4.

4. Open the TK448 Ch09 Association structure. Click the Mining Model Viewer tab, and then click the Dependency Network tab. You should immediately see many more associations than you saw before you refined the parameters.

5. Open the TK448 Ch09 Forecasting structure. In this model, you should not see significant differences from what you saw before you refined the PERIODICITY_HINT parameter. That is because you do not have enough time points in the past for the algorithm to detect periodicity. As its names suggests, this parameter really is just a hint.

EXERCISE 6   Deploy a Model as a Cube Dimension

Last, you are ready to deploy a model as a new dimension.

1. Open the TK448 Ch09 Cube Clustering structure, and then click the Mining Models tab. Right-click the TK448 Ch09 Cube Clustering model, and then select Create A Data Mining Dimension.

2. Select the Create Cube check box.

3. Rename the dimension to **CustomerClusteringDim** and the cube to **CustomerClusteringCube**, and then click OK.

4. Save, deploy, and process the project.

5. After the deployment and processing are complete, use the Browser tab in the Cube Designer to browse the new cube. In Solution Explorer, double-click the CustomerClusteringCube cube. Click the Browser tab.

6. Drag the Bike Buyer measure to the browser, and then drag the CustomerClusteringDim dimension to the rows area of the browser.

You should see the sum of bike buyers over the four clusters you created in this practice. If you renamed the clusters, you should see the business names of the clusters.

7. Save the project, and then close BIDS.

✔ **Quick Check**

1. When you created a new cube and a dimension from the mining model, did you notice any objects other than the database and a cube dimension that were created in the Analysis Services project?

2. How can you limit the depth of a Decision Tree?

3. Can you precisely control the number of clusters in the Sequence Clustering algorithm?

4. Can you always use order line items for sequences?

5. For how many time points in the future should you do forecasting?

6. Which algorithm would you use to find the best way to arrange products on shelves in a retail store?

Quick Check Answers

1. BIDS also created an additional DSV for this dimension.

2. You can use the MINIMUM_SUPPORT and COMPLEXITY_PENALTY parameters to control the growth of the tree.

3. No, the Sequence Clustering algorithm can add additional clusters if it finds distinctive and important sequences.

4. It depends on the way you do sales. With Internet sales, you typically can collect data that shows the sequence of items a customer placed into a market basket. However, in retail stores, you cannot rely on sequences because the sequence of purchasing gets completely remixed at the cashier.

5. The further you go into the future, the less you can rely on the forecasts. However, this also depends on the algorithm you use for forecasting. The ARIMA algorithm is much better than ART for long-term forecasting.

6. You should use the Association Rules algorithm for this task. For example, you can order the products that are commonly in a basket close together to help your customers remember to buy all, rather than just one, of them in a single purchase.

Lesson 3: Validating Models, Using DMX Queries, and Using Prediction Queries in Reports

Estimated lesson time: 60 minutes

As you have learned up to now in this chapter, to find the best solution for your company, you need to try to resolve a business problem by using a number of data mining models, using different algorithms and different algorithm parameters. You should deploy into production the model that performs best. In this lesson, you will learn how to evaluate the performance of the different models. Generally, you can measure a model's accuracy, reliability, and usefulness.

Accuracy is probably the most used measure, determining how well an outcome from a model correlates with real data. *Reliability* assesses how well a data mining model performs on different datasets—in other words, how robust a model is. You can trust a model if it generates similar predictions or finds similar patterns regardless of the test data that is supplied. If a model creates good predictions for one subset of data but worse ones for other subsets, you cannot trust the model for general predictions. *Usefulness* measures how helpful the information gathered with data mining is. Usefulness is typically measured through the perception of business users, using questionnaires and similar means.

Validating Predictive Models

Testing the accuracy of predictive models is simple. The model that predicts most accurately has performed the best. So how can you check the quality of the predictions? Remember that when you prepare the data, you split it into training sets and test sets. You train the model using the training set, and then you use the model to make predictions on the test set. Because you already know the value of the target variable in the test set, you can measure how accurate the predictions are. Because this measurement of predictive models is a recurring task, standard methods of showing the quality of predictions have evolved. These standard methods include lift charts, profit charts, and classification matrices.

In SSAS 2008, you can test the reliability of predictive models using *cross validation*. With cross validation, you partition your training dataset into many smaller sections. SSAS then creates multiple models on the cross sections using one section at a time as test data and other sections as training data, trains the models, and creates many different accuracy measures across partitions. If the measures across different partitions differ widely, the model is not robust on different training and test set combinations.

Using Lift Charts and Profit Charts

A *lift chart* is the most popular way to show the performance of predictive models. It is very intuitive and easy to understand. Figure 9-12 shows a lift chart for the predictive models you created in Lesson 1 for the value 1 (buyers) of the predicted variable (Bike Buyer), without the filtered Decision Trees model, which was removed to get a less cluttered picture.

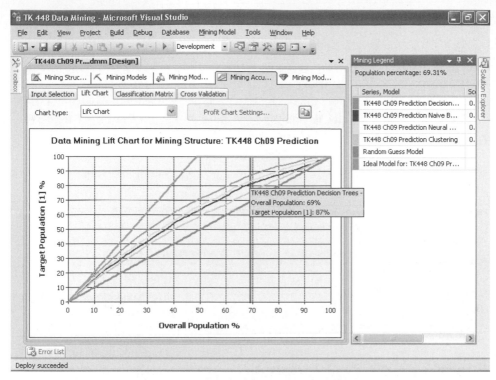

FIGURE 9-12 Lift chart comparing performance of four models when predicting a single value

From this chart, you can easily identify the performance of different models. As you can see in Figure 9-12, the chart shows four curved lines and two straight lines. The four curves show the predictive models (Decision Trees, Naïve Bayes, Neural Network, and Clustering), and the two straight lines represent the Ideal Model (top) and the Random Guess (bottom). The x-axis represents the percentage of population (all cases), and the y-axis represents the percentage of the target population (bike buyers). From the Ideal Model line, you can see that approximately 50 percent of Adventure Works customers buy bikes. If you could predict with 100 percent probability which customers will buy a bike and which will not, you would need to target only 50 percent of the population. The Random Guess line indicates that if you were to pick cases out of the population randomly, you would need 100 percent of the cases for 100 percent of bike buyers. Likewise, with 80 percent of the population, you would get 80 percent of all bike buyers, with 60 percent of the population 60 percent of bike buyers, and so on.

Data mining models give better results in terms of percentage of bike buyers than the Random Guess line but worse results than the Ideal Model line. From the lift chart, you can measure the *lift* of the data mining models from the Random Guess line, which explains where the name *lift chart* comes from.

Of course, a model predicts the outcome with less than 100 percent of probability in all ranges of the population—therefore, to get 100 percent of bike buyers, you still need

100 percent of the population. Data mining models give you interesting results somewhere between zero and 100 percent of the population. For example, if you take the highest curve, directly below the Ideal Model line, you can see that if you select 70 percent of the population based on this model, you would get nearly 90 percent of bike buyers. From the Mining Legend window, you can see that this is the Decision Trees curve. In terms of accuracy of predictions from the sample data used for analysis, the Decision Trees algorithm generates the best predictions, the Neural Network algorithm generates the second best, the Naïve Bayes algorithm generates the third best, and the Clustering algorithm generates the fourth best. In this case, you should deploy the Decision Trees model into production.

The question is what is the correct percent of the population to target in order to maximize profit. This question is answered by another graph called a *profit chart*. A profit chart displays the estimated profit increase that is associated with using a mining model. Figure 9-13 shows a profit chart, which is based on the lift chart.

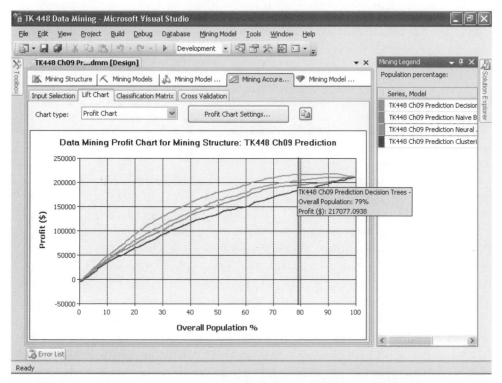

FIGURE 9-13 Profit chart for comparing potential profit if using different mining models

From this profit chart, you can see that with predefined settings, you can expect profits to increase with the percentage of the target population, up to nearly 80 percent of the overall population. This result would use Decision Trees to select the 79 percent target population; if you target more prospective customers, profit would start to fall because of the expenses required to reach each additional customer. For example, we used the default settings for the profit chart: the overall population is 50,000 cases, the fixed cost of the campaign is 5,000 units, the individual cost per targeted customer is 3 units, and you expect 15 units of revenue per individual. You can change these settings by clicking the Profit Chart Setting button above the chart. If you change these settings, you will generate a different profit chart and would need to select a different cutting point—that is, you would select different a percentage of target population.

Figure 9-14 shows the second form of lift chart, which measures the quality of global predictions. This means that you are measuring predictions of all states of the target variable. In this example, the chart measures the quality of predictions for both states of the Bike Buyer attribute—that is, for buyers and for no buyers. You can see that the Decision Trees algorithm predicts correctly in approximately 70 percent of cases.

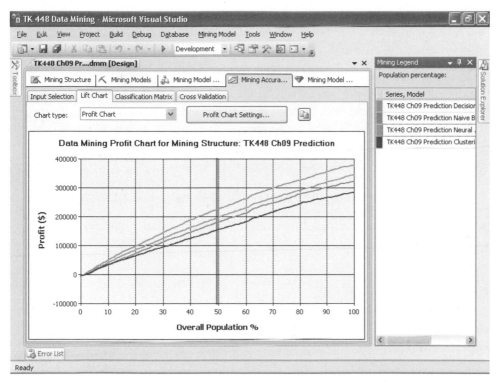

FIGURE 9-14 Lift chart for global statistics

Using a Classification Matrix

Another way of representing the quality of predictions is through a classification matrix. A *classification matrix* shows actual values compared to predicted values. Figure 9-15 shows the classification matrix for the predictive models from Lesson 1.

There are four matrices, one for each model. The rows show the predicted values, and the columns show the actual values. For the Decision Trees algorithm, for example, you can calculate from the first row that the algorithm predicted 2,510 buyers (744 + 1,766). Of these predictions, 1,766 were correct, while 744 predictions were false, meaning that customers from the test set did not actually purchase a bike.

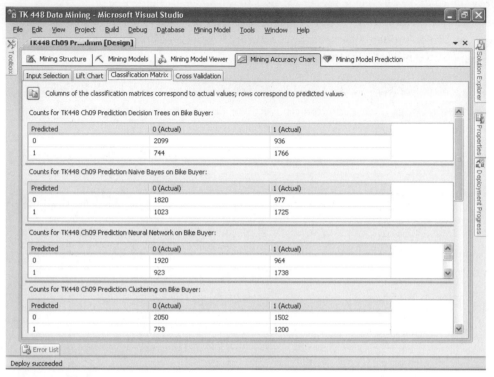

FIGURE 9-15 Classification matrix

Configuring Cross Validation

Figure 9-16 shows the settings for cross validation and the results of cross validation of the predictive models.

The cross-validation settings you can define are as follows:

- **Fold Count** With this setting, you define how many partitions you want to create in your training data. In Figure 9-16, three partitions are created: when partition 1 is used as the test data, the model is trained on partitions 2 and 3; when partition 2 is used as the test data, the model is trained on partitions 1 and 3; and when partition 3 is used as the test data, the model is trained on partitions 1 and 2.

- **Max Cases** You can define the maximum number of cases to use for cross validation. Cases are taken randomly from each partition. This example uses 9,000 cases, which means that each partition will hold 3,000 cases.

- **Target Attribute** This is the variable that you are predicting.

- **Target State**   You can check overall predictions if you leave this field empty or check predictions for a single state that you are specifically interested in. In this example, you are interested in bike buyers (state 1).

- **Target Threshold**   With this parameter, you set the accuracy bar for the predictions. If prediction probability exceeds your accuracy bar, the prediction is counted as correct; if not, the prediction is counted as incorrect.

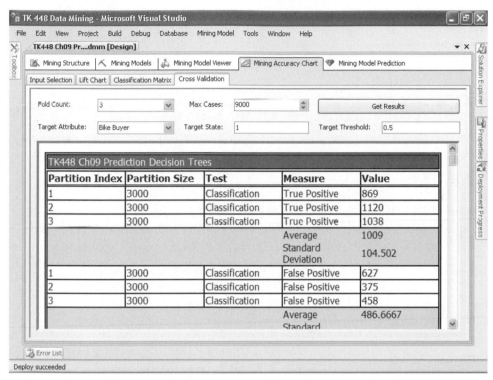

FIGURE 9-16 Cross validation of predictive models

In the cross-validation report below the settings, you can see many different measures that help you check the reliability of your models. For example, classifications True Positive, False Positive, True Negative, and False Negative count cases in the partition where prediction probability is greater than your accuracy threshold and predicted state matches target state.

You can see from Figure 9-16 that the True Positive classification of Decision Trees does not give you constant results across partitions. The True Positive classification counts cases predicted as positive (bike buyers, in this example) that are actually positive. Also, the standard deviation of this measure is quite high. You will cross-validate your models in the practice for this lesson—when checking the Neural Network model, you will see that it is much more constant for the True Positive classification, which means that this model is more robust on different datasets than the Decision Trees model. From the cross-validation results, it seems that you should deploy the Neural Network model in production—although the accuracy is slightly worse than the accuracy of Decision Trees, the reliability is much higher. Of course, in production, you should perform many additional accuracy and reliability tests before you decide which model to deploy.

> **BEST PRACTICES** **BUDGET THE TIME SPENT ON DIFFERENT PHASES OF A DATA MINING PROJECT**
>
> When working on a real data mining project, you should spend most of the time in data preparation. After that, the second most time-consuming task is the validation of predictive models. If you have tens of different models and you cross-validate them using different settings, this task could take even longer than the data preparation phase.

Measuring the Accuracy of Other Models

Measuring the accuracy of nonpredictive models can be trickier than measuring the accuracy of predictive models. Evaluating the performance of the model depends on the algorithm you are looking at.

Measuring the Accuracy of Association Rules

You can measure the quality of an Association Rule prediction directly from the viewers for this algorithm. In the Itemsets tab of the Mining Model Viewer, you can see the Support measurement for the itemsets. Support measures the number of cases in which the itemset is included. Figure 9-17 shows itemsets sorted in descending order by Support.

Support is an undirected measure that simply tells you how many times items were found together in the basket. However, there is typically a direction in purchasing habits. For example, in the United States, customers who buy a frozen pizza typically buy a soda as well. (In Europe, the typical combination is pizza and beer.) However, customers who buy a soda do not always buy a frozen pizza; they might buy only a soda or a soda with another product. You have to measure the probability of the rule, not the probability of the itemset, to get the direction. You express a rule by using a conditional sentence such as, "If a customer purchases a frozen pizza, the customer purchases a soda as well." You can see the probabilities of the rules by using the Rules tab in the Mining Model Viewer, as Figure 9-18 shows.

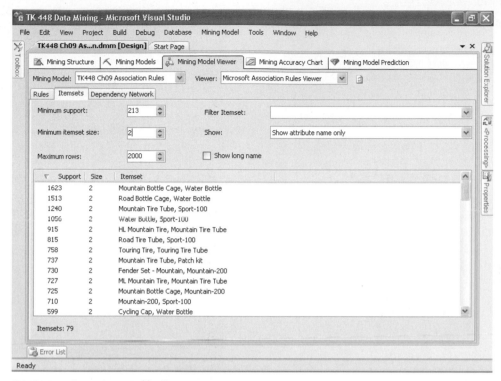

FIGURE 9-17 Itemsets sorted by Support

Figure 9-18 also shows the Importance measurement for each of the rules. Importance is the score of a rule. Positive Importance tells you that the probability that product B will be in the basket increases when product A is in the basket. Negative Importance means that the probability for product B goes down if product A is in the basket. Zero Importance means that there is no association between products A and B. All three measures—Support, Probability, and Importance—give you information about the quality of the rules that the Association Rules algorithm found.

EXAM TIP

Three measures—Support, Probability, and Importance—give you information about the quality of the rules that the Association Rules algorithm finds.

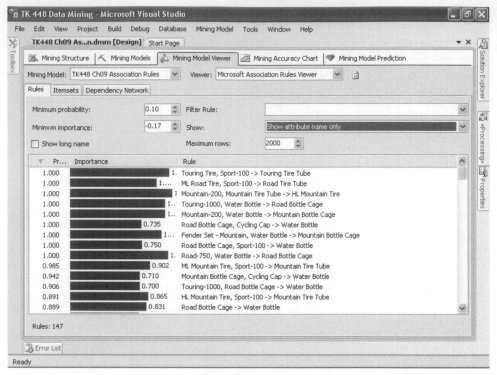

FIGURE 9-18 Rules showing Probability and Importance measures

Measuring the Accuracy of Clustering and Sequence Clustering

When you use the Clustering algorithm only to find groups of cases and not to make predictions, or when you use Sequence Clustering, measuring the quality of the models mathematically is typically not as important as it is when you are using predictive models. Of course, you still must measure the quality of the outcome of the algorithm somehow—you should base your decision about which model to deploy in production on the business needs. Even if a model gives you a good mathematical score for quality, that does not mean that it will be useful in production. The model could have clusters that contain input variable values that are hard to use. For example, depending on your business, it might not be easy to prepare a special offer that will appeal to everyone in a group of customers that includes wealthy customers older than 50 and all customers of any age with three children. Therefore, you need to analyze the clusters generated by different models by using the Clustering viewers and then decide which model to implement from a business perspective.

If you really need to evaluate your clusters mathematically, you can use the MSOLAP_NODE_SCORE attribute from the model content. A data mining model stores the knowledge extracted from the data in a table. (This is not a relational table, because it contains nested tables.) Mining Model Viewer shows the content of these tables graphically. For any algorithm, you can select the Generic Content Tree Viewer from the Viewer drop-down list to see the content in tree and tabular form. Figure 9-19 displays the content of the Clustering model of a cube you created earlier in this chapter, with the MSOALP_NODE_SCORE attribute shown.

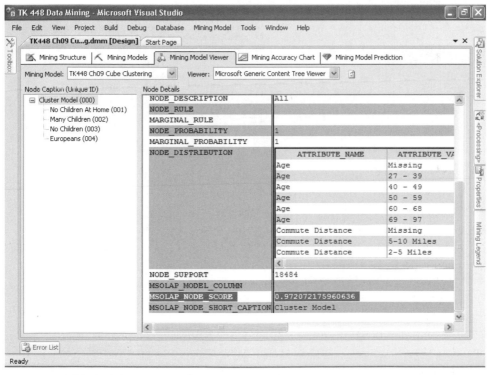

FIGURE 9-19 MSOLAP_NODE_SCORE of a clustering model

Measuring the Accuracy of Time Series

How can you measure the quality of forecasted values with the Time Series algorithm when you do not yet have the actual data? It probably is not very practical to wait until the data is available because by that time, you might already have made incorrect decisions based on your forecasting model. There is a better way to measure the performance of the Time Series algorithm.

Using a specific number of periods from the past, you can try to forecast present values. If the model performs well for forecasting present values, there is a better probability that it will perform well for forecasting future values. You control the creation of historical models by using two algorithm parameters: HISTORICAL_MODEL_COUNT and HISTORICAL_MODEL_GAP. The first parameter controls the number of historical models built, and the second parameter controls the number of time slices between historical models.

Figure 9-20 shows the historical predictions on the Charts view, with the dotted line representing sales quantity of the M-200 model in the Pacific region.

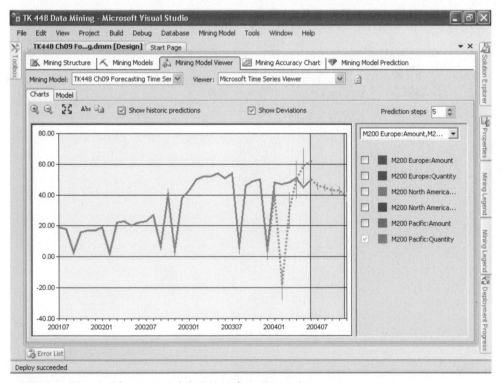

FIGURE 9-20 Historical forecasts and deviations for a time series

In addition, you can see the deviations (the thin vertical lines) from the forecasted values. Higher deviations represent a more unstable model and thus indicate that the forecasts are less reliable.

Creating Data Mining Queries and Reports

When you evaluated predictive models in Lesson 2, you actually created a *prediction query*. You used the DMX language by using the prediction *SELECT* statement to join the model that was trained on the training set with new data from the test set. In this section, you will learn how to create a prediction query by using the Prediction Query Builder. You will also review DMX language basics and see how to use the DMX language for SSRS reports.

Creating Prediction Queries in BIDS and SSMS

The easiest way to start learning DMX is with the help of the Prediction Query Builder, which is included in BIDS and SSMS. In BIDS, you can find the Prediction Query Builder on the Mining Model Prediction tab in the Data Mining Designer. In SSMS, you can right-click a model and then click Build Prediction Query. Figure 9-21 shows the Prediction Query Builder.

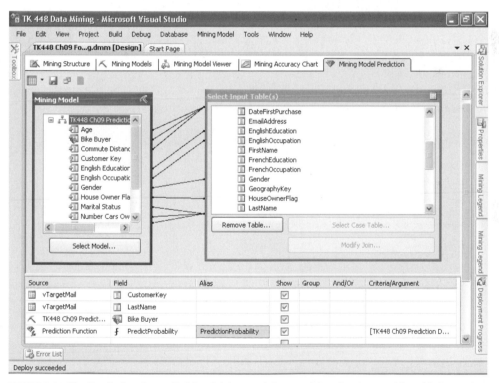

FIGURE 9-21 The Prediction Query Builder, joining a mining model and an input table, with four columns defined

In the Prediction Query Builder, you start by selecting a mining model. You then select the input table, which is the table with new data that you want to use for predictions. The Prediction Query Builder links as many columns as possible, based on the same column name. You can delete any link that the Prediction Query Builder creates. You can also create a new link by dragging a column from the mining model onto a column from the input table or by dragging a column from the input table onto a column from the mining model.

In the grid at the bottom of the window, you select the columns for your prediction *SELECT* statement. You can select a predicted column from the mining model, any column from the input table, or a DMX prediction function. You can also create a computed column by using a custom expression. You can define an alias name for any column, and prediction functions accept input parameters.

Using the drop-down list in the top-left corner of the Prediction Query Builder, you can switch between Design, Query, and Result views. In Figure 9-21, the Decision Trees model is selected, the source view (vTargetMail) is used as the input table, and the prediction query includes three columns. The first and second columns are the CustomerKey and LastName attributes from the input table. The third column is the predicted Bike Buyer attribute from the mining model, which shows the predicted value (0 or 1) for cases from the input table. The third column uses the PredictProbability DMX function. The PredictProbability function shows how good a prediction is—meaning that it shows the probability that the predicted value is correct. Of course, in a real-life scenario, you would not predict outcome on the input data, where the outcome is known. You would perform predictions on new data—for example, on potential customers, to see how likely they are to buy your product. You will create a prediction report on new data in the practice for this lesson.

Figure 9-22 shows the results of the example prediction query from Figure 9-21.

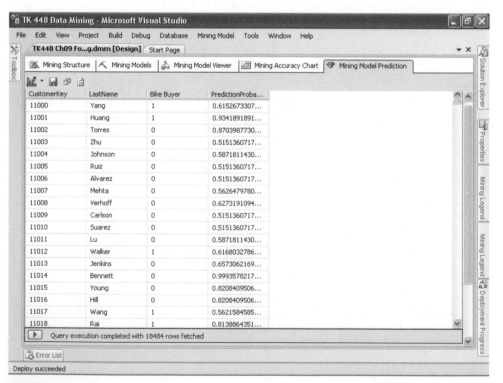

FIGURE 9-22 Prediction query results

You can see, for example, that for the customer with CustomerKey equal to 11001 and last name Huang, the model predicted buying a bike (value 1 in the Bike Buyer column) with more than 93 percent probability.

Understanding the DMX Language

The prediction *SELECT* statement is just one of several valuable DMX statements that you should master for data mining. DMX is a simple and limited language that resembles SQL. If you know T-SQL, you can probably learn DMX in two or three hours. For details, refer to "Data Mining Extensions (DMX) Reference" in SQL Server 2008 Books Online (see References). There are two kinds of DMX statements: data definition language (DDL) statements and data manipulation language (DML) statements.

The DMX DDL statements include the following:

- **CREATE MINING STRUCTURE** Creates the structure
- **ALTER MINING STRUCTURE** Adds a mining model to an existing structure
- **CREATE MINING MODEL** Creates a mining model and an associated mining structure simultaneously
- **EXPORT** Exports a mining model from an SSAS database
- **IMPORT** Imports a mining structure to an existing SSAS database
- **SELECT INTO** Copies the structure of an existing mining model into a new model and trains it with the same data
- **DROP MINING MODEL** Removes a model
- **DROP MINING STRUCTURE** Removes a complete structure

The DMX DML statements include the following:

- **INSERT INTO** Trains a mining model. This statement does not insert the source data into a data mining model; instead, you use it to train the model, to extract knowledge from the source data, and to store data in the model object in tabular format.
- **SELECT** Creates predictions, browses the content of the model, browses the source cases, and creates a copy of a model by using the *INTO* keyword. The different types of *SELECT* queries are listed here:
  - **SELECT DISTINCT FROM <model >** Returns all possible states of a column.
  - **SELECT FROM <model>.CONTENT** Shows the contents of a model; used by the Mining Content Viewer.
  - **SELECT FROM <model>.CASES** Browses the source cases; requires that drillthrough is enabled on the model. In SSAS 2008, you can also return mining structure columns not included in the model; however, drillthrough must be enabled on the mining structure and on the mining model.

- **SELECT FROM *<model>.SAMPLE_CASES*** Returns sample cases that are representative of the cases used to train the model; also requires that drillthrough is enabled. This statement works on Sequence Clustering models only.

- **SELECT FROM *<model>.DIMENSION_CONTENT*** Shows the content of the dimension that comes from a mining model.

- **SELECT FROM *<model> PREDICTION JOIN*** Performs predictions on new data; probably the most useful DMX statement.

- **SELECT FROM *<model>*** The simplest prediction query; also called an empty prediction join. Returns the most probable value for the columns specified in the query.

- **SELECT FROM *<structure>.CASES*** Returns the cases used to create the mining structure; drillthrough must be enabled. In SSAS 2008, drillthrough on structures is enabled by default. You can control drillthrough on a structure through the *CacheMode* property of the structure and on a model through the *AllowDrillThrough* property of the model.

■ **UPDATE** Updates a name of a node in the Clustering and Sequence Clustering models.

■ **DELETE** Cleans up the contents of a model or a complete structure. If you want to use the model after you have run the DELETE statement, you must retrain it.

As you can see, the DMX language uses only a subset of SQL statements. And as you saw earlier, you can use the Prediction Query Builder to write prediction queries. In addition to prediction queries, you can write any DMX query in SSMS. You have many templates you can use as a starting point for building a query, or you can write a DMX query directly in the DMX Query window in SSMS. Just be sure to open a new Analysis Services DMX Query window by choosing File, New, and then Analysis Services DMX Query. You should also be sure to select the correct database in the Databases drop-down list in SSMS. Following are a few examples of DMX queries.

This first example shows how you can browse the content of the Clustering model you created in the practices earlier in this chapter:

```
SELECT *
 FROM [TK448 Ch09 Prediction Clustering].CONTENT;
```

The next query shows you the 1,000 most likely bike buyers from the dbo.Prospective-Buyer table, provided in the AdventureWorksDW2008 database, with new customers and prospective buyers of bikes. The query bases the predictions on the Decision Trees model. The probability of the predictions is not very high because the query uses only *Gender* and *NumberCarsOwned* attributes in the prediction join. The more attributes you have in the new dataset to join with the model input columns, the better the predictions will be.

```
SELECT TOP 1000
        t.[LastName],
        t.[FirstName],
        [Bike Buyer],
        PredictProbability([Bike Buyer],1) AS DTPredictProbability,
        t.[Gender],
        t.[NumberCarsOwned]
   FROM [TK448 Ch09 Prediction Decision Trees]
    PREDICTION JOIN
        OPENQUERY([Adventure Works DW2008],
         'SELECT [LastName],
                 [FirstName],
                 [Gender],
                 [NumberCarsOwned]
            FROM [dbo].[ProspectiveBuyer]') AS t
         ON [Gender] = t.[Gender] AND
            [Number Cars Owned] = t.[NumberCarsOwned]
  WHERE [Bike Buyer] = 1
ORDER BY PredictProbability([Bike Buyer],1) DESC;
```

In the DMX language, you can also use Microsoft Visual Basic for Applications (VBA) functions, and you can extend the language with your own functions. The following example shows how to use VBA *Left* and *UCase* functions in a query from the Time Series model, showing the forecasted quantity and amount for the next three periods for the M200 model in Europe, North America, and Pacific regions. It uses the *PredictTimeSeries* DMX function for forecasting.

```
SELECT [Model Region],
       UCase(Left([Model Region],10)),
       PredictTimeSeries(Amount, 3),
       PredictTimeSeries(Quantity, 3)
  FROM [TK448 Ch09 Forecasting Time Series]
 WHERE [Model Region] >= 'M200' AND [Model Region] < 'M300';
```

Using Prediction Queries in Reports

You can also use DMX queries as the source for the report dataset in an SSRS report, but remember that dataset tables do not support nested tables. The Prediction Query Builder is included in SSRS, in the Report Designer and the Report Wizard. This builder already creates output without nested tables (that is, it creates flattened output). If you write a DMX query manually, you have to include the *FLATTENED* DMX keyword in the query, right after the *SELECT* keyword. In the practice for this lesson, you will create a report based on a DMX prediction query.

Testing Model Accuracy, Creating a DMX Report, and Using DMX Queries

In this practice, you will examine the quality of the predictive models by using a lift chart and a classification matrix and by performing cross validation of the models. You will also create an SSRS report based on a DMX prediction query. You will then create a simple mining structure with two predictive models. Last, you will train the structure and query the models by using DMX.

EXERCISE 1   Measure Model Performance

In this exercise, you are going to evaluate prediction models by using Lift Chart, Classification Matrix, and Cross Validation.

1. Open the TK 70-448 Mining Models Project you created in the previous practices.

2. Double-click the TK448 Ch09 Prediction mining structure to open the Data Mining Designer. On the Mining Models tab, right-click the filtered Decision Trees model (displayed in the last column on the right), and then select Delete. Click OK to confirm the deletion. You are deleting the model to get a less cluttered lift chart.

3. Deploy and process the solution.

4. Click the Mining Accuracy Chart tab.

5. In the top pane, make sure that the check boxes for all mining models are selected in the Select Predictable Mining Model Columns To Show In The Lift Chart and that the Synchronize Prediction Columns And Values check box is selected. Also verify that in the Select Data Set To Be Used For Accuracy Chart area, the Use Mining Model Test Cases option is selected. Leave the Filter Expression box empty.

6. In the Predict Value column of the Select Predictable Mining Model Columns To Show In The Lift Chart, select 1 in the drop-down list of any row. Because the Synchronize Prediction Columns And Values check box is selected, you should get the same value in all rows of the Predict Value column automatically. Your completed selection should be similar to the one shown in Figure 9-23.

7. Click the Lift Chart tab. Examine the lift chart.

8. Click the Classification Matrix tab. Examine the matrix.

9. Click the Cross Validation tab. Use the following parameters: Fold Count equal to 3, Max Cases equal to **3,000**, Target Attribute equal to **Bike Buyer**, Target State equal to **1**, and Target Threshold equal to **0.5**. Click Get Results, and then examine the results. For example, check the True Positive measure for each of the models (the first measure for each of the models). The True Positive measure shows how many times positive predictions (such as Bike Buyer = 1) were actually positive. You should see that the standard deviation of the number of the True Positive predictions for three different splits of the training data is higher for Decision Trees than for Neural Network, although the number of True Positive predictions is higher for Decision Trees; this means that although the Decision Trees

algorithm gives more accurate positive predictions, these predictions are not as stable as Neural Network predictions when using different data sets.

10. Save the project. Do not exit BIDS.

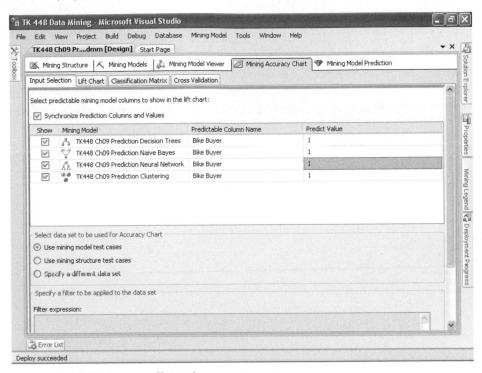

FIGURE 9-23 Mining Accuracy Chart tab

EXERCISE 2 Modify the DSV

In this exercise, you will use a new dataset of prospective customers and perform predictions on this dataset. This dataset is in the AdventureWorksDW2008 database in the dbo.Prospective-Buyer table.

1. If you closed the TK 70-448 Mining Models Project in BIDS, reopen it.

2. In Solution Explorer, double-click the Adventure Works DW2008 DSV to open it in the Data Source View Designer. Right-click in the blank space in the pane that contains the graphical presentation of your DSV, and then select Add/Remove Tables.

3. Add the dbo.ProspectiveBuyer table to the DSV.

4. Save, deploy, and process the project.

EXERCISE 3 Create the Report

Your next task is to create a report with predictions on the prospective customer dataset.

1. In BIDS, with the TK 70-448 Mining Models Project open, on the File menu, select Add, New Project. Select the Report Server Project Wizard template. Type **TK 70-448 SSRS DMX Project** for the project name, and then save the project in the folder for this lesson.

2. On the Welcome page of the Report Wizard, click Next.

3. On the Select The Data Source page, select New Data Source, and then type TK 70-448 Data Mining as its name. In the Type drop-down list, select Microsoft SQL Server Analysis Services. Click Edit, and then select the following options:

    a. Use **(local)** as the server name.

    b. Select the TK 70-448 Mining Models Project Analysis Services database. Test the connection, and then click OK.

    c. Click the Credentials button to verify that Windows Authentication (Integrated Security) is used, and then click OK.

4. Click Next.

5. On the Design The Query page, click Query Builder.

6. Change the command type to DMX by clicking the Command Type button (which resembles a pick tool) on the toolbar, and then click Yes.

7. In the Mining Model pane, click Select Model. In the Select Mining Model dialog box, expand TK448 Ch09 Prediction, and then select the TK448 Ch09 Prediction Decision Trees model. Click OK.

8. In the Select Input Table(s) pane, click Select Case Table, and then select the ProspectiveBuyer table. Click OK.

9. In the column list (that is, in the Source column of the table in the bottom of the Query Designer), select the following columns:

    a. Bike Buyer from the mining model. Click the Source column in the first row of the table in the lower part of the Query Designer window, and from the drop-down list, select the TK 448 Ch09 Prediction Decision Trees mining model. In the Field column, the Bike Buyer field should be selected by default. If it is not, select it from the drop-down list in this column.

    b. Use the Source and Field columns in the second and third rows to select Prospect-AlternateKey and LastName from the ProspectiveBuyer table.

    c. Use the Source column in the fourth row to select the Prediction Function option from the drop-down list. Select the PredictProbability prediction function in the Field column. Type **Prediction Probability** in the Alias column for this function. Drag the Bike Buyer column from the mining model onto the Criteria/Argument column of the function, and then click OK to close the Query Designer.

10. Review the query, and then click Next.

11. On the Select The Report Type page, select Tabular and then click Next.

12. On the Design The Table page, add Bike Buyer to the Group box and Prospect-AlternateKey, LastName, and Prediction Probability columns to the Details box, and then click Next.

13. On the Choose The Table Layout page, select Stepped. Enable drill-down by selecting the Enable Drilldown check box, and then click Next.

14. On the Choose The Table Style page, select the Slate table style, and then click Next.

15. On the Choose The Deployment Location page, check the deployment location. Note that in SSRS 2008, typically port 80 is used, unless SSRS is installed on a computer running the 32-bit Windows XP SP2 operating system and Internet Information Services. In this scenario, the default port is 8080. Therefore, you might have to change the Report Server Deployment option to, for example, **http://localhost:8080/ReportServer**. You can check the SSRS Web service URL in the Reporting Services Configuration Manager tool or in SSMS by right-clicking your Report Server in Object Explorer and then clicking Properties. Click Next.

16. On the Completing The Wizard page, type **Prospective Bike Buyers** as the report name, and then click Finish.

17. In the Report Designer, in the Design window, select the properties of the Prediction_Probability text box, and then change the format to N4. Click OK.

18. In the group row (which should be the second row, between the header row and the details row), in the Prospect Alternate Key column, add the expression **=Count(Fields!ProspectAlternateKey.Value)** to the cell. You will see the number of cases in this column for each group and the actual prospect alternate key in the details rows when you expand the group.

19. Preview the report. Check the number of cases in each group, and then expand each group. For example, if you expand the group where Bike Buyer equals 1, you get potential bike buyers with their alternate key, last name, and the probability that the prediction is correct.

20. Save all projects, and exit BIDS.

EXERCISE 4 Create and Train Models by Using DMX

Now you will use DMX to create a mining structure with two predictive models and then train the structure.

1. Open SSMS, and then connect to Analysis Services on your local SSAS server.

2. On the File menu, select New, and then select Analysis Services DMX Query. Connect to the local SSAS server again (for the query window).

3. Be sure to select the TK 70-448 Data Mining Project Analysis Services database from the Databases drop-down list in the upper-left corner of SSMS.

4. Create a mining structure named TK 448 Ch09 DMX Prediction with the following attributes:

- CustomerKey, data type LONG, content KEY
- Gender, data type TEXT, content DISCRETE
- [Number Cars Owned], data type LONG, content DISCRETE
- [Bike Buyer], data type LONG, content DISCRETE

You can examine the *CREATE MINING STRUCTURE (DMX)* command in SQL Server 2008 Books Online (see References) and use the code example here to view the command syntax. Your code should look like this:

```
CREATE MINING STRUCTURE [TK 448 Ch09 DMX Prediction]
(
    CustomerKey LONG KEY,
    Gender TEXT DISCRETE,
    [Number Cars Owned] LONG DISCRETE,
    [Bike Buyer] LONG DISCRETE
);
```

In the installed practice files, you can use the file named ..\Source\Ch 09\TK 448 Ch09 DMX Queries.dmx to copy and paste the queries used in this exercise.

5. Add Naïve Bayes and Decision Trees models to the structure you just created; you can read about the *ALTER MINING STRUCTURE (DMX)* command in SQL Server 2008 Books Online (see References). Use Bike Buyer as the predictable attribute. Enable drillthrough for the Decision Trees model. Your code should look like the following. (Note that in SSMS, you can execute only a single statement at a time.)

```
ALTER MINING STRUCTURE [TK 448 Ch09 DMX Prediction]
ADD MINING MODEL [TK 448 Ch09 DMX Prediction Naïve Bayes]
(
    CustomerKey,
    Gender,
    [Number Cars Owned],
    [Bike Buyer] PREDICT
)
USING Microsoft_Naïve_Bayes;

ALTER MINING STRUCTURE [TK 448 Ch09 DMX Prediction]
ADD MINING MODEL [TK 448 Ch09 DMX Prediction Decision Trees]
(
    CustomerKey,
    Gender,
    [Number Cars Owned],
    [Bike Buyer] PREDICT
)
USING Microsoft_Decision_Trees
WITH DRILLTHROUGH;
```

6. Process the structure by using the *INSERT INTO DMX* statement. Your code should look like this:

```
INSERT INTO [TK 448 Ch09 DMX Prediction]
(
    CustomerKey,
    Gender,
    [Number Cars Owned],
    [Bike Buyer]
)
OPENQUERY([Adventure Works DW2008],
  'SELECT CustomerKey,
          Gender,
          [NumberCarsOwned],
          [BikeBuyer]
     FROM [dbo].[vTargetMail]');
```

7. In SSMS, in the Object Explorer window, expand the TK 70-448 Data Mining Project database folder. Expand Mining Structures, select the mining structure you just created, and then select the Mining Models subfolder. Right-click either of the two models you created, and then select Browse. You should see the Data Mining viewers you are already familiar with from BIDS. Of course, the decision tree does not have as many levels as the one you created with BIDS in the practice in Lesson 1 because, for code brevity, you used only two input variables. Close the browser.

EXERCISE 5   Browse Models by Using DMX

Last, you are going to browse the models you created by using the DMX *SELECT* statement.

1. List all distinct values from the Gender attribute of the Naïve Bayes model.

2. List the contents of the Decision Trees model.

3. List the source cases of the Decision Trees model. (Note that if you try to do this for the Naïve Bayes model, you will get an error because the Naïve Bayes model does not support drillthrough.)

4. Make a prediction on the data for a new, unmarried, male customer with zero cars owned. Use the *PredictHistogram* DMX function to get the complete statistics for the prediction as a nested table. To see how to make predictions on a singleton query, review the syntax for prediction *SELECT* statements in the SQL Server 2008 Books Online topic "SELECT FROM <model> PREDICTION JOIN (DMX)" (see References).

5. Make a prediction on the data of the dbo.ProspectiveBuyer table. Use the *Predict-Probability* DMX function to see in the output only the probability of the prediction, not the complete set of statistics. This way, the output should already be flattened (without a nested table). For information about how to make predictions on the table returned by the DMX *OpenQuery* function, see the prediction *SELECT* syntax in SQL Server 2008

Books Online, as referenced in step 4, and for the *OpenQuery* function syntax, see the SQL Server 2008 Books Online topic "OPENQUERY (DMX)" (see References).

Your code for these tasks should look like this:

```
-- Select Distinct from Naïve Bayes
SELECT DISTINCT [Gender]
  FROM [TK 448 Ch09 DMX Prediction Naïve Bayes];


-- Decision Trees model content
SELECT *
  FROM [TK 448 Ch09 DMX Prediction Decision Trees].CONTENT;


-- Decision Trees model cases
SELECT *
  FROM [TK 448 Ch09 DMX Prediction Decision Trees].CASES;


-- Prediction join - singleton query
SELECT [Bike Buyer],
       PredictHistogram([Bike Buyer])
  FROM [TK 448 Ch09 DMX Prediction Decision Trees]
       NATURAL PREDICTION JOIN
       (SELECT 'M' AS [Gender],
               0 AS [Number Cars Owned]) AS t;


-- Prediction join - Openquery
SELECT t.[LastName],
       t.[FirstName],
       [Bike Buyer],
       PredictProbability([Bike Buyer]),
       t.[Gender],
       t.[NumberCarsOwned]
  FROM [TK 448 Ch09 DMX Prediction Decision Trees]
       PREDICTION JOIN
       OPENQUERY([Adventure Works DW2008],
        'SELECT [LastName],
                [FirstName],
                [Gender],
                [NumberCarsOwned]
           FROM [dbo].[ProspectiveBuyer]') AS t
        ON [Gender] = t.[Gender] AND
           [Number Cars Owned] = t.[NumberCarsOwned];
```

6. Drop the mining structure. Your code should look like this:

```
DROP MINING STRUCTURE
[TK 448 Ch09 DMX Prediction];
```

Lesson 4: Securing and Processing Data Mining Models

Estimated lesson time: 40 minutes

As with any object in any database, you need to be careful about the security for your data mining models. In previous chapters, you learned about SSAS security in general and cube security in particular. In this lesson, you will learn about SSAS properties that pertain to mining models and about SSAS roles and their permissions for data sources, mining structures, and mining models.

Remember that SSAS uses only the Windows Authentication model. Therefore, unless you explicitly permit anonymous authentication, any user who wants to use SSAS first needs a valid Windows user name and password. You can then create SSAS roles and add the user or an entire Windows group to a role. SSAS has a single fixed server role and multiple database roles. In this lesson, you will also examine database roles and the permissions that relate to mining objects.

Configuring SSAS Properties

There are a few SSAS server properties that let you control mining models and algorithms. You can modify server properties by right-clicking an SSAS instance in SSMS and then selecting Properties. All names of properties that deal with data mining objects start with the string *DataMining *, so they are easy to locate. Some of the properties are basic, and you can see them immediately when you open the Properties window. Others are advanced, and to see them, you need to select the Show Advanced (All) Properties check box, as shown in Figure 9-24.

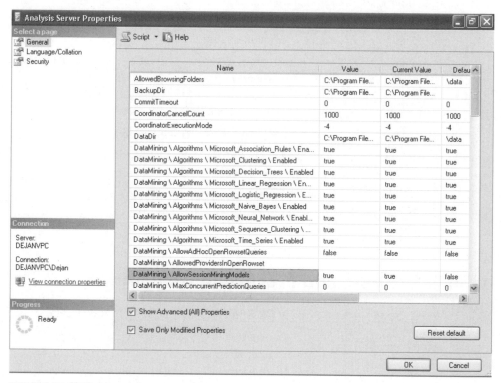

FIGURE 9-24 SSAS data mining properties

Here are the SSAS general data mining properties and what they control:

- **AllowSessionMiningModels** This Boolean property controls whether you can create session mining models. Session mining models are models that are automatically removed from the server when the connection closes or the session times out; they do not persist in an SSAS database after the session ends. Session models let applications use the SSAS data mining features. You can create an ad hoc model in your application to make a quick prediction, for example. Some 2007 Microsoft Office system applications can use session models. You can download Microsoft Office Data Mining Add-Ins for Excel 2007 and Visio 2007. Then, for example, you can use SSAS data mining features to find outliers in an Excel worksheet.

- **AllowAdHocOpenRowsetQueries**   Ad hoc distributed queries that use the Open-Rowset function are not allowed by default. You will need to use a data source and the OpenQuery function instead. This is similar to default security in SQL Server. In the T-SQL language, you can use the OpenQuery function, which uses linked servers by default, but you cannot use ad hoc OpenRowset queries. Because this is an important property, it is also included in the properties that you can control with the Surface Area Configuration tool.

- **AllowedProvidersInOpenRowset**   This string property identifies the providers you can use in your ad hoc OpenRowset queries.

- **MaxConcurrentPredictionQueries**   As its name suggests, this property controls the maximum number of concurrent prediction queries.

SSAS properties include nine Boolean properties that control whether a specific data mining algorithm is enabled or disabled. These properties are listed here:

- Microsoft_Association_Rules\ Enabled
- Microsoft_Clustering\ Enabled
- Microsoft_Decision_Trees\ Enabled
- Microsoft_Naïve_Bayes\ Enabled
- Microsoft_Neural_Network\ Enabled
- Microsoft_Sequence_Clustering\ Enabled
- Microsoft_Time_Series\ Enabled
- Microsoft_Linear_Regression\ Enabled
- Microsoft_Logistic_Regression\ Enabled

Configuring SSAS Roles, Permissions, and Data Sources

SSAS retrieves data from data sources for two reasons: to process SSAS database objects and to perform prediction joins and drillthrough operations in the DMX *SELECT* statement. For SSAS to securely introduce itself to a source for each task, you must configure the impersonation information of a data source. You have the following options:

- **Use A Specific Username And Password**   With this option, you create a specific Windows user for a data source and then give permissions on source data to this user. You can control SSAS permissions on sources through permissions of the Windows user you created.

- **Use The Service Account**   With this option, SSAS always connects to a source by using its own Windows account. However, this might be a security threat if the privileges on the sources for the SSAS service account are too high. In addition, you should use a domain account for the SSAS service to access remote sources.

- **Use The Credentials Of The Current User**   With this option, SSAS impersonates the current user for any activity on a data source. Typically, a current user is an end user for prediction queries and a SQL Server Agent service account user for scheduled processing (if you use SQL Server Agent scheduled jobs for processing). Note that the user you use for processing must have sufficient privileges on the source.

- **Inherit** This option means that SSAS uses the default settings. By default, with this option selected, SSAS 2008 impersonates current users for DMX queries that use the DMX OpenQuery function in the prediction join.

For data mining, you grant just a few permissions to an SSAS role, as follows:

- Data Sources permissions

  - **Access—Read or Access—None** Note that the end user needs read permission on a data source to execute prediction join queries.

  - **Read Definition** This permission controls access to metadata. With this permission, end users can view the connection string to the data source, which includes the server name and might include the login name. Granting this permission to an end user does not allow the end user to modify the connection string.

- Mining Structures permissions

  - **Access—Read or Access—None** Of course, if an end user needs to use a mining model in a structure, the user must have read permission on the structure.

  - **Drill Through** End users need this permission to drill through from a mining structure to source cases. Note that for queries that drill through to data sources, an end user needs appropriate permissions on the data source as well as on the source database system.

  - **Read Definition** As with data source permissions, this permission controls access to the metadata of the structure. End users typically do not need this permission.

  - **Process** With this permission, a user can process the structure. End users typically do not need this permission.

- Mining Models permissions

  - **Access—Read, Access—Read/Write, or Access—None** End users need read permission to read the model. They need read/write permission to update a model. However, in SSAS 2008, updating is limited to updating Clustering and Sequence Clustering cluster node names.

  - **Drill Through** End users need this permission to drill through from a mining model to source cases (or sample cases). Note that an end user needs appropriate permissions on the data source as well.

  - **Read Definition** This permission controls access to the metadata of a mining model.

  - **Browse** End users need this permission to browse the contents of a model.

You can grant a user the Read Definition permission for a complete SSAS database. This permission is then inherited on all database objects. Granting this permission to end users might not seem to be a good practice in production, but a user must have this permission to connect to an SSAS database through SSMS or BIDS.

Processing Data Mining Objects

Data mining shares many components with the OLAP layer of SSAS, including its processing architecture. In fact, the server creates an internal specialized cube for each mining structure. When the mining structure is processed, the server loads this cube and its dimensions with the case data.

As described earlier in this chapter, SQL Server Analysis Services data mining defines two main objects: a mining structure and a mining model.

Using Mining Structures and Mining Models

As you saw in Lesson 1, a data mining structure is a blueprint of the database schema that is shared by all mining models inside the structure. A structure encapsulates the logical mining domain at hand. From an implementation standpoint, the mining structure defines the data type and contains content definitions of the columns in the case table.

A structure can contain one or more mining models that use all or some of the columns defined in the structure. The practical rationale for having multiple models inside a structure is to compare several models to find the model that gives you the most accurate predictions. When you process a structure, the server loads the structure with the model training data.

> **IMPORTANT CACHING TRAINING DATA**
>
> By default, the data mining structure caches the data mining model training data (the structure *CacheMode* is set to *KeepTrainingCases*). This option lets the user issue drill-through queries to see the source data. If you do not want to keep the training data with large data volumes, set the *CacheMode* property to *ClearAfterProcessing*.

Remember that before you can use a mining model for predictions, you need to train the model by loading it with training data. Training the model is also called *model processing*. When you train the model, the server analyzes the data correlations and derives patterns.

Understanding Data Mining Processing Options

Data mining supports a subset of the OLAP processing options. Table 9-6 describes these processing options for the data mining structure.

TABLE 9-6 Data Mining Structure Processing Options

PROCESSING OPTION	DESCRIPTION
Process Default	Performs the minimum number of tasks required to fully initialize a mining object. For example, if you change a model and send Process Default to the structure, the server will process that model only.
Process Full	Drops the object stores and rebuilds the model. Metadata changes, such as adding a new column to a mining structure, require Process Full.
Process Structure	Reads and caches the training data in the structure. Does not affect the mining models inside the structure.
Process Clear Structure	Drops the cached data without affecting the mining models inside the structure. Disables drillthrough features. Consider Process Clear Structure if you need to dispose of the source data used to train the models to reduce the disk footprint.
Unprocess	Deletes data from the mining object. When this command is sent to a structure, it deletes the cached training data in the structure and the model patterns.

Because mining models and structures are contained in an SSAS database, fully processing the SSAS database fully processes not only the OLAP objects but also all data mining objects in the database.

Processing Mining Structures and Models

Processing a mining structure requires the following steps:

1. In BIDS, if you have finished the development of a project, save the changes by clicking the Save button on the Designer toolbar.

2. On the Mining Structure tab, click the Process The Mining Structure And All Its Related Models button on the toolbar, or in the BIDS Solution Explorer or SSMS Object Explorer, right-click the structure and then click Process.

3. In the Process dialog box, select the desired processing option, and then click Run.

4. In the Process Progress dialog box, watch the progress as the server executes the processing operation.

Securing and Processing Data Mining Models

In this practice, you will disable an algorithm and then test the data mining permissions for a test user. After you test the security, you will process data mining structures and models in SSMS.

EXERCISE 1   Disable an Algorithm

Your first task is to disable an algorithm. You should use an account with high privileges for this exercise; you need administrative permissions on SSAS and read permissions on the SQL Server AdventureWorksDW database to manage SSAS and perform drillthrough actions.

1. In SSMS, connect to Analysis Services on your server. Right-click your local SSAS instance, and then select Properties.

2. Select the Show Advanced (All) Properties check box to show the advanced properties. Click in the Value column of the DataMining \ Algorithms \ Microsoft_Decision_Trees \ Enabled row. Select the False option from the drop-down list to disable the Decision Trees algorithm. Click OK to close the Analysis Server Properties dialog box.

3. Restart SSAS. (Right-click the local SSAS instance in SSMS and choose Restart.)

4. In BIDS, create a new Analysis Services project named **TK 448 Algorithm Disabled**. Next, attempt to create a data mining model that uses the Decision Trees algorithm, as follows:

   a. Create a data source for the AdventureWorksDW2008 SQL Server database.

   b. Create a DSV with only the vTargetMail view.

   c. Try to create a new Decision Trees model. If you started BIDS after you restarted SSAS with the Decision Trees algorithm disabled, you should not be able to select the Decision Trees algorithm in the Data Mining Wizard or in the Data Mining Designer. If you opened BIDS before you restarted SSAS, you should still be able to select the Decision Trees algorithm; however, you should get an error when processing the model. If you can create the Decision Trees model, use Bike Buyer as an input and predictable attribute and use several other attributes as input only. Make sure that the Bike Buyer attribute content is discrete. Allow drillthrough. Name the structure **TK 448 Algorithm Disabled** and the model **TK 448 Algorithm Disabled Decision Trees**.

5. Reenable the Decision Trees algorithm, and then restart SSAS.

6. If you could not create the Decision Trees model, close and reopen BIDS. Open the project, and then create the model as described earlier: Use Bike Buyer as an input and predictable attribute, and use several other attributes as input only. Make sure that the Bike Buyer attribute content is discrete. Allow drillthrough. Name the structure **TK 448 Algorithm Disabled** and the model **TK 448 Algorithm Disabled Decision Trees**. If you created the model successfully, skip this step.

7. Try to deploy the project again. This time, deployment and processing should work.

8. Browse the model. Check drillthrough as well. (It should be working because you should be logged in as a user with high—probably administrative—privileges.) Right-click a node in the Decision Tree viewer, and then click Drill Through. Use either of the two options on the Drill Through submenu.

9. Save the project. Do not close BIDS.

EXERCISE 2 Manage Permissions

In this exercise, you will control permissions for a test user.

1. If you closed BIDS, restart it, and then open the TK 448 Algorithm Disabled project.

2. In Solution Explorer, double-click the Adventure Works DW data source to open it in the Data Source Designer dialog box. Click the Impersonation Information tab, and then make sure that the Inherit option is selected. Click OK.

3. Double-click the TK 448 Algorithm Disabled structure to open the Data Mining Designer. Click the Mining Models tab. Open the Properties window for the TK 448 Algorithm Disabled Decision Trees model. Make sure that the AllowDrillThrough property is set to True to enable drillthrough for this model.

4. Save, deploy, and process the project.

5. Create a local Windows user named **TestUser** with a password of **Pa$$w0rd**. Make sure that the User Must Change Password At Next Logon option is not selected. Do not add this user to any specific Windows group. (See the operating system documentation for ways to create a local user; one way is to use the Net User command.)

6. In SQL Server, create a login for this user, and then grant the user access to the AdventureWorksDW2008 database as follows:

    a. In SSMS, expand the Security folder, and then select the Logins subfolder of your SQL Server. Right-click the Logins folder, and then select New Login.

    b. On the General page, select the local TestUser you just created. Use Windows Authentication.

c. In the Select A Page area, click the User Mapping page. Give the user login access to the AdventureWorksDW2008 database, and then add the user to the db_datareader role, as Figure 9-25 shows.

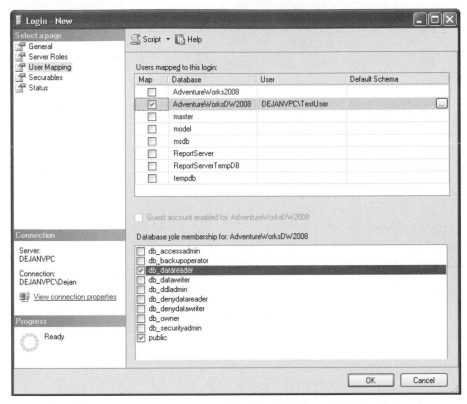

FIGURE 9-25 Give the TestUser login access to the AdventureWorksDW2008 database.

d. On the General page, change the default database for this login to Adventure-WorksDW2008, and then click OK.

7. Create a new SSAS role in the TK 448 Algorithm Disabled database.

8. In SSMS, expand the Analysis Services Databases folder, expand the TK 448 Algorithm Disabled database, right-click the Roles subfolder, and then select New Role.

9. Type **TestRole** as the name of the role, and then select the Read Definition check box, as Figure 9-26 shows.

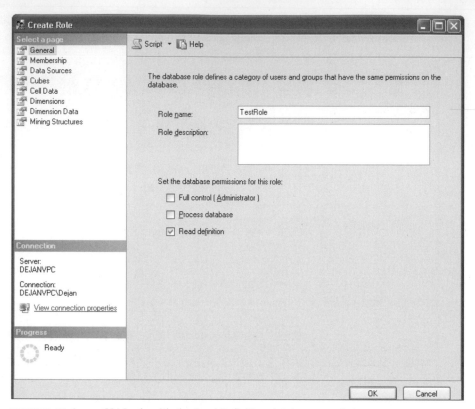

FIGURE 9-26 A new SSAS role with the Read Definition database permission

10. Use the Membership page to add the Windows local TestUser user to the role.

11. Give the role Read permission on the Adventure Works DW2008 data source, Read permission on the TK 448 Algorithm Disabled structure (this will also give the user Read permission on the models), and Browse permission on the TK 448 Algorithm Disabled Decision Trees model. Do not give Drill Through permission on the model to the TestRole role. The permissions settings should look like those shown in Figure 9-27. Click OK.

12. Use the Run As Windows functionality to run SSMS in the context of the TestUser Windows user.

13. Connect to your SSAS instance, expand the Databases folder, and then expand the TK 448 Algorithm Disabled database. Expand the Mining Structures, TK 448 Algorithm Disabled structure, and then expand the Mining Models subfolder.

14. Right-click the TK 448 Algorithm Disabled Decision Trees model, and then click Browse. You should be able to browse the model to see the Decision Tree viewer.

15. Right-click any node, click Drill Through, and then select either of the two options on the submenu. This time, you should see an error message, as Figure 9-28 shows. Click OK.

16. Close the SSMS window you opened with the TestUser credentials.

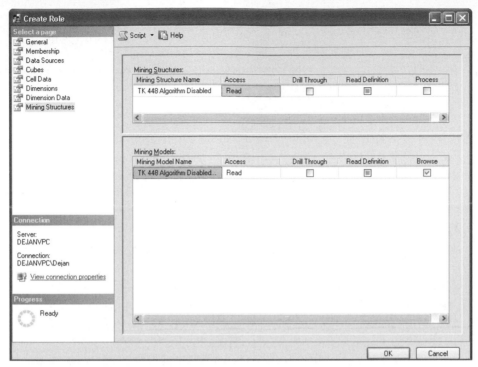

FIGURE 9-27 Data Mining Structures permissions and Mining Models permissions for the TestRole

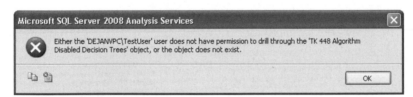

FIGURE 9-28 Drill Through permissions error

EXERCISE 3   Process a Mining Structure

You have built several mining structures so far, including the TK448 Ch09 Prediction structure used to predict the probability that a given customer will purchase a bike. This mining
structure contains four mining models. To fully process the TK448 Ch09 Prediction mining
structure and its mining models, follow these steps:

1.   Open SSMS, and then connect to your SSAS instance.

2.   In Object Explorer, expand the TK 70-448 Mining Models Project database folder, and
     then select the Mining Structures folder.

3.   Right-click the TK448 Ch09 Prediction mining structure, and then click Process.

4. Accept the defaults in the Process Mining Structure dialog box, and then click OK. The Process Progress dialog box displays the progress of the processing operation, such as the number of cases read.

5. Fully processing a structure trains the mining models in the structure. After the structure is processed, right-click the structure, and then click Browse to see the mining models in the structure.

EXERCISE 4   Dispose of the Structure Data

Suppose that you used a large input dataset to train the mining models in the TK448 Ch09 Prediction mining structure. By default, the structure caches the dataset to make drillthrough possible. To minimize the structure storage space, you need to dispose of the structure data without affecting the mining models.

1. In SSMS, right-click the TK448 Ch09 Prediction mining structure, and then click Process.

2. In the Process Mining Structure dialog box, expand the Process Options drop-down list, and then select Process Clear Structure. Click OK to start the process operation.

3. When processing is complete, right-click the TK448 Ch09 Prediction mining structure in Object Explorer, and then click Browse. Notice that you can browse the mining models successfully even though you purged the input dataset. That is because Process Clear Structure deletes the structure data without affecting the mining models in the structure.

✔ Quick Check

1. Can you use SQL Server logins for SSAS authentication?

2. Do end users need the Process permission on a mining structure?

3. As an administrator, how would you prevent usage of the Clustering data mining algorithm?

4. What processing option deletes the training data in a mining structure without affecting its mining models?

Quick Check Answers

1. No, you cannot use SQL Server logins for SSAS authentication. SSAS supports Windows Authentication only.

2. No, end users typically do not need any Process permission.

3. You can disable the Clustering algorithm by using the Analysis Services Properties dialog box in SSMS.

4. Use the Process Clear Structure option to purge the structure data without affecting the models inside the structure.

Case Scenario: Working with SSAS Data Mining

The Adventure Works Sales Department wants to know the reasons for its customer churn. The department has requested that you implement one or more mining models to uncover these reasons. You have to prepare the data as well. The Adventure Works Finance Department is satisfied with the Decision Trees model it uses to predict the payment discipline of new customers. However, to better understand the reasons behind the predictions, staff members would like to see the source cases that the model used for training. The Finance Department also gets information about potential customers in the form of Excel 2007 worksheets. They would like to perform advanced checks on this data. For example, they would like to test the data for suspicious rows.

1. How would you prepare the data for finding the churn information?

2. Which algorithms would you use?

3. How many models would you create?

4. How can you allow the Finance Department to see the source cases that the data mining model used for training?

5. How can you use SSAS data mining in Excel 2007 to find the suspicious rows?

Chapter Summary

- Creating a data mining model is easy with the Data Mining Wizard and Data Mining Designer tools in BIDS. And Data Mining Viewers display a model's findings in intuitive ways.

- Preparing data for mining can be a complex and time-consuming task.

- You can mine relational data or cube data.

- You can create models that use simple cases based on a single table or complex cases with nested tables.

- Nested tables provide a lot of flexibility for modeling business questions.

- You can influence algorithms by setting their parameters.

- After creating the mining models, it is important to evaluate their accuracy.

- For evaluating predictive models, you make predictions on the test dataset. You can show the quality of predictions with lift chart, profit chart, or classification matrix tools.

- You browse the mining models by using the DMX language. You can write DMX queries in SSMS. You can also use the Prediction Query Builder in SSMS and BIDS to create prediction DMX queries.

- An SSRS report can use a mining model as its source.

- You control access to data sources, mining structures, and mining models through SSAS roles.

- SSAS supports Windows Authentication only.

CHAPTER 10

Developing SSRS Reports

S QL Server Reporting Services (SSRS) plays an important role in the Microsoft SQL Server 2008 business intelligence (BI) platform. Reports built in SSRS query relational and multidimensional databases and other data sources and distribute information throughout the organization. In SQL Server 2008, SSRS features significant enhancements. You can create interactive reports that contain rich data regions, including the new Tablix report item, charts, and gauges. In this chapter, you will first learn how to create SSRS projects and reports in Business Intelligence Development Studio (BIDS). You will also see how to develop report objects by using the Report Designer and how to work with advanced report object properties. You will then see how to use a SQL Server Analysis Services (SSAS) database as the source for your report. And last, after looking at how to create a dataset from a data source, you will learn how to apply dataset filters and groups.

Exam objectives in this chapter:

- Implement report data sources and datasets.
- Implement a report layout.
- Create an SSRS report by using an SSAS data source.
- Implement interactivity in a report.
- Implement report items.

Before You Begin

To complete this chapter, you must have:

- Administrative access to an SSRS server.
- General understanding of the SQL Server BI platform.
- Familiarity with the SQL Server Database Engine.
- Experience working with SQL Server 2008 BIDS projects and solutions.
- Experience working in SQL Server Management Studio (SSMS).
- The SQL Server 2008 AdventureWorks2008 and AdventureWorksDW2008 databases installed.
- The Lesson 1, Exercise 3, "Create a UDM Cube to Examine Data," practice in Chapter 9, "Working with SSAS Data Mining," completed and deployed.

Lesson 1: Creating SSRS Projects and Reports in BIDS

Estimated lesson time: 40 minutes

SSRS supports several ways of creating reports. You can design reports by using the Report Designer, Report Builder, or third-party tools. You can also import reports from Microsoft Office Access 2002 or later. BIDS includes the Report Wizard as well as the Report Designer, which is the primary developer tool for creating reports.

Report Builder in SSRS 2008 is a completely new tool compared to Report Builder in SSRS 2005. Report Builder 1.0 in SSRS 2005 is a limited tool, available from Report Manager, which is used mainly by business users to create reports based on previously created report models. Report Builder 2.0 in SSRS 2008 is an entirely new, stand-alone authoring tool similar to Microsoft Office–applications that can take advantage of all of the SSRS features. Report Builder 2.0 is not included with SQL Server 2008 release-to-manufacturing (RTM), but you can download it from the Microsoft Download Center (see References). Note, however, that Report Builder 1.0 is still part of the product. In this lesson, you will learn how to use the Report Wizard and the Report Designer in BIDS to create reports.

Understanding the SSRS Report Templates

BIDS is the preferred tool for developers to create SSRS reports. BIDS extends Microsoft Visual Studio 2008 with project types that include three specific templates for SSRS.

- **Report Server Project**   The first SSRS template is the Report Server Project, a Visual Studio template that contains SSRS items, including data sources and reports. The Report Server Project template also contains deployment information. Creating a Report Server project produces a blank project with two folders in the BIDS Solution Explorer window: Shared Data Sources and Reports.

    You can add a new report by right-clicking the Reports folder and then selecting Add New Report to start the Report Wizard. You can also add a report by right-clicking the Reports folder, selecting Add, selecting New Item, and then selecting either the Report Wizard template or the Report template. The Report Wizard template, of course, starts the Report Wizard. And the Report template opens the Report Designer, a collection of BIDS design surfaces and graphical tools that let you develop reports that use the full capabilities of SSRS.

    Each report has a data source, a database that the data for the report comes from. You can create a report-specific data source or a shared data source. A shared data source can be shared among all reports in a project. You can add a new shared data source by right-clicking Shared Data Source and selecting Add New Data Source.

- **Report Server Project Wizard**   The second SSRS template is the Report Server Project Wizard, which is very similar to the Report Server Project template except that it automatically starts the Report Wizard when you create a project based on this template.

This is actually the same wizard mentioned in the previous bullet. The Report Wizard is an automated tool that facilitates the creation of tabular and matrix reports. *Tabular reports* are reports that have a predefined number of columns. *Matrix reports* use data as the source to define the columns that the report will contain. SSRS 2008 provides both Table and Matrix data regions as well as a List data region, but all three regions are just templates for the powerful new Tablix data region. You will learn more about different data regions later in this chapter. You can also manually launch the Report Wizard by adding a report to the project. After you complete the creation of a report with the Report Wizard, you can enhance your report in the Report Designer.

- **Report Model Project** The third SSRS template in BIDS is the Report Model Project template. A *report model* is a metadata description, from a business point of view, of a data source and its relationships. Chapter 11, "Extending and Deploying SSRS Reports," gives you an overview of the Report Model Project template and report creation.

Using the Report Wizard

In this section, you learn how to use the Report Wizard to create a report. Remember, you can use this wizard by creating a new project using either the Report Server Project template or the Report Server Project Wizard. The Report Wizard walks you through the following steps, which are illustrated in Figure 10-1.

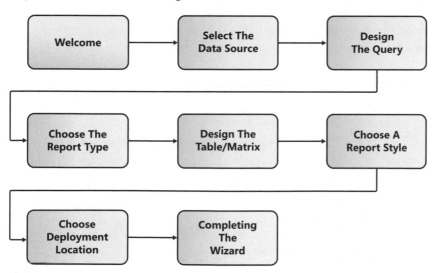

FIGURE 10-1 Report Wizard steps

1. On the Welcome page, you can review the basics of the Report Wizard and the steps it will follow.

2. On the Select The Data Source page, you select a previously defined data source or create a new data source. The data source defines the connection type, connection

string, and security configuration that SSRS will use to pull data from the database or data provider.

3. On the Design The Query page, you enter a SQL statement to query the database, or you can click Query Builder to design the query that will generate the data for your report.

> **BEST PRACTICES** **OPTIMIZE YOUR QUERY**
>
> To avoid any unnecessary burden on the database, make sure that you query only the data your report needs. Avoid the use of the *SELECT* * statement, and specify only the columns you require.

4. On the Choose The Report Type page, you select the report type that you want the wizard to generate. The Report Wizard supports tabular or matrix reports; however, both table and matrix regions are just templates for the new Tablix data region. You can enhance your Tablix later in the Report Designer. The wizard does not support chart or free-form reports, so if you want a chart or a free-form report, you must use the Report Designer to create the report interface.

5. On the Design The Table/Matrix page, based on the report type you select, the wizard lets you configure the table or matrix component of the report. In either scenario, you configure the general layout of the report. If you are configuring a table report, the wizard lets you configure Page, Group, and Details elements. If you are designing a matrix, the Report Wizard lets you configure Page, Columns, Rows, and Details elements.

6. Report styles define general formatting configurations such as fonts, colors, and borders. On the Choose A Report Style page, you can use one of the predefined templates. Note that you can extend BIDS with your customized templates.

7. If you launch the Report Wizard by creating a project with the Report Server Project Wizard template, on the Choose Deployment Location page, you have the opportunity to configure the SSRS deployment server and deployment folder. This configuration is stored at the project level rather than in the report. If you add a report to an existing project, this step is skipped.

8. On the Completing The Wizard page, the final step of the configuration is to review the defined report configuration and name the report.

Modifying Project Properties

After the report project is created, you might want to change some of the project properties, such as saving the deployment configuration to another folder. To change the properties of the project, right-click the project in Solution Explorer, and then select Properties. Table 10-1 lists the properties shown in the *ProjectName* Property Pages dialog box.

TABLE 10-1 Properties in the *ProjectName* Property Pages Dialog Box

CATEGORY	PROPERTY	DESCRIPTION
Debug	StartItem	Lets you configure the report that will be automatically displayed when running the project for debugging purposes.
Deployment	OverwriteDataSources	When set to Yes, this property will replace the shared data sources in the deployment server.
Deployment	TargetDataSourceFolder	Folder in which shared data source will be deployed.
Deployment	TargetReportFolder	Folder in which reports will be deployed.
Deployment	TargetServerURL	URL of the deployment server.

Note that by default in BIDS, the TargetServerURL points to http://localhost/ReportServer; however, you should also note that SSRS 2008 in native mode uses port 80 by default except when installed on a computer running the 32-bit Windows XP SP2 operating system, where the default port is 8080. This means that you should take special care to modify this property accordingly. You can find the correct link on the Report Services Configuration Manager Web Service URL page or by right-clicking your target SSRS instance in SSMS Object Explorer, selecting Properties, going to the General page, and looking at the URL box.

Modifying Report-Level Properties

You might also want to change some report properties after the report is created. Often you will want to change the report layout and set width and height properties that are different from the default report margins. Before changing the report, it is important to understand two fundamental concepts of report layout:

- Page layout is configured at the report level.
- Different rendering extensions are paginated differently. *Rendering* is the SSRS process of generating an image or document from data. You can select rendering in many ways: in Report Manager; in an ASP.NET application for a default report site in native mode, when viewing the report in default HTML format; in an application that uses the *MicrosoftReportViewer* control; and when you define a subscription to the report. Each document type has a rendering extension.

Table 10-2 summarizes the ways that different extensions are paginated.

TABLE 10-2 Rendering Extension Pagination

RENDERING EXTENSION	PAGE TYPE
CSV	None
Excel	Logical page
HTML	Logical page
Image	Physical page
PDF	Physical page
Word	Physical page
XML	None

Physical pages let you precisely control the way the pages will break in the report. *Logical pages* are calculated at run time based on the number of columns and rows, and you do not have precise control over how the pages break.

The physical page size is the paper size. The paper size that you specify for the report controls how the report is rendered. By default, the page size is 8.5 by 11 inches. Two properties, PageHeight and PageWidth, let you configure the physical page size. Other reports are not affected by these settings. There are several ways to configure these properties. You can select Report in the Properties window, you can select Report Properties from the Report menu, or you can right-click in a blank area of the report in the Report Designer, select Report Properties, and then set the values accordingly.

You can also specify report page size by setting up margins with the TopMargin, Bottom-Margin, LeftMargin, and RightMargin properties. But if a report item extends into the margin area, it is clipped so that the overlapping area is not displayed. If this happens, you can change the width of the report body, which contains data regions and other report items, by selecting Body in the Properties window. The size of headers and footers also affects pagination.

Just remember that you could create a report to be one page wide, for example, but when you use different rendering formats, it is displayed across multiple pages. To troubleshoot, check that the width of the report body, including margins, is not larger than the physical page size width. You can also enlarge or reduce the container size to prevent empty pages from being added to your report.

EXAM TIP

Be sure you understand how to control pagination and how pagination is implemented in different rendering formats.

Developing Report Objects with the Report Designer

After you have created a report through the Report Wizard, you will often need to add elements or change elements generated by the wizard. You use the Report Designer to modify report item properties and enhance the user report navigation experience.

The most common items that you need to change after the Report Wizard generates a report are fonts, colors, and date and number formatting.

Modifying Fonts

Changing the font of a report item is as simple as selecting the report item and using the Properties window to change the font. Table 10-3 lists the font properties.

TABLE 10-3 Font Properties

PROPERTY	DESCRIPTION
FontFamily	The fonts installed on your computer. If the font you need does not appear in the Properties window, type in the name of the font. If the font does not exist on the machine that is rendering the report, the font automatically defaults to Arial.
FontSize	The size of the font.
FontStyle	Either Normal or Italic.
FontWeight	Configures the boldness of the font, including Normal, Thin, Extra-Light, Light, Medium, Semi-Bold, Bold, Extra Bold, and Heavy.
TextDecoration	Specifies special text formatting, including Underline, Overline, and LineThrough.

Changing Colors

SSRS uses three color properties to format reports: Background Color, Border Color, and Color. These colors use either HTML names or a hexadecimal HTML color string. The standard format for HTML color strings is *#RRGGBB*—which represents color by the combination of Red, Green, and Blue—with hexadecimal numbers. For example, the color white is #ffffff and black is #000000.

The color properties that you can configure in SSRS are Background Color, Border Color, and Color (which refers to Foreground Color). Fortunately, you do not have to write hexadecimal strings. When you select any of the color properties, you can choose from the Standard Colors Palette, which shows at the bottom the most recently used colors.

If you need special colors, you can write expressions directly by clicking the Expression link in the drop-down list for a color property, or you can click the More Colors link to access the Select Color dialog box. There are three advanced color options: Palette—Standard Colors, which lets you select a color by its name, and Palette—Color Circle and Palette—Color Square, which let you choose a custom color by pointing to and clicking a color in the circle or the square, respectively. You can also adjust brightness. After you select a color, you can check the expression generated to make sure it is the correct color. Not all color options are available for all report items. Table 10-4 summarizes SSRS's color support for different report items.

TABLE 10-4 Color Support for Different Report Items

REPORT ITEM	BACKGROUND COLOR	BORDER COLOR	COLOR
Body	Yes	Yes	No
Chart	Yes	Yes	No
Chart area	Yes	Yes	No
Chart legend	Yes	Yes	Yes
Image	No	Yes	No
Line	No	Yes	No
List (that is, Tablix)	Yes	Yes	Yes
Matrix (that is, Tablix)	Yes	Yes	Yes
Rectangle	Yes	Yes	No
Subreport	No	Yes	No
Subtotal	Yes	Yes	Yes
Table (that is, Tablix)	Yes	Yes	Yes
Text box	Yes	Yes	Yes
Title	Yes	Yes	Yes

To change the color of any report item, select the item in the Report Designer, and then use the Properties window to change the color.

Changing Date and Number Formatting

You will also often need to modify a report's date and number formatting. SSRS uses either the Microsoft .NET Framework formatting strings or customized formatting strings. Table 10-5 shows the .NET Framework standard formatting strings.

TABLE 10-5 .NET Framework Formatting Strings

NUMBERS		DATES	
FORMAT STRING	**NAME**	**FORMAT STRING**	**NAME**
C or c	Currency	d	Short date
D or d	Decimal	D	Long date
E or e	Scientific	t	Short time
F or f	Fixed-point	T	Long time
G or g	General	f	Full date/time (short time)
N or n	Number	F	Full date/time (long time)
P or p	Percentage	g	General date/time (short time)
R or r	Round-trip	G	General date/time (long time)
X or x	Hexadecimal	M or m	Month day
		O or o	Round-trip
		R or r	RFC1123 pattern
		S	Sortable date/time
		U	Universal sortable date/time
		U	Universal full date/time
		Y or y	Year month

You can also extend the standard .NET format strings to use your own customized versions of the strings. For example, you can use the string #,###.0 to specify a number or *yyyymmdd* to configure a date format.

Adding Report Objects to a Report

In addition to changing the properties of objects, sometimes you will want to add other objects to the report, such as the following:

- A header or footer
- A text box

- An image
- A chart
- A gauge
- A Tablix
- Other graphical items

All of these report items except headers and footers are included in the Toolbox window. The Tablix report item, for example, is available through Table, Matrix, or List elements, which you can configure by displaying the Toolbox window and dragging the component onto the design surface. Because headers and footers are not in the Toolbox window, you must configure them at the report level.

Adding a Page Header or Footer

Reports can contain *page headers*, which are information included at the top of each page, as well as *page footers*, which are information included at the bottom of each page. Headers and footers are frequently used to display general report identification information such as title, page numbers, date and time of the report execution, a company logo, and user name. You cannot add data-bound fields or images directly to the page header or footer, but you can write expressions that reference data-bound fields or images.

To add a page header or footer, follow these steps:

1. In the Report Designer, click on the design surface away from the report body.

2. From the main menu, select Report, Add Page Header (or Add Page Footer).

After you add the page header or footer, drag the report items you want to use onto the header or footer area.

A header or footer for a complete report is not the same as a page header or footer. Report headers and footers appear only once, as the first and last content in the report, and there is no special area for report headers and footers. You can create a report header by placing report items at the top of the report body, and you can build a report footer by placing items at the bottom of the report body.

Adding a Text Box

A *text box* is a report item that displays a text string. The string displayed by a text box can be static text, an expression, or a field from a dataset. You use the Value property to configure the displayed string. Table 10-6 shows some examples of string values you might use in a text box.

TABLE 10-6 Text Box String Value Examples

DESCRIPTION	VALUE
Expression	="Page:" & Globals!PageNumber & " of " & Globals!TotalPages
Field	=First(Fields!Name.Value)
Static text (such as a column heading)	Sales Amounts in US$

Other properties let you change the layout of the text box. The CanGrow and CanShrink properties let SSRS expand or contract the height of a text box based on its contents.

You can also use the Action property to configure the equivalent of a hyperlink that will let a user jump to another part of the report, browse a different report, or navigate to a standard URL. You will learn more about the Action property in the section "Defining Report Actions" in Lesson 3, "Working with Advanced Report Object Properties," later in this chapter.

Adding an Image

SSRS supports four image formats: JPEG, GIF, PNG, and BMP. Images can be embedded in the report, stored in the report server, stored in the database, or stored on the Web and referenced in the report. You can set up image properties when you drag an image report item from the Toolbox window to the Report Designer.

The Image Properties window includes the following groups of properties:

- **General**   In this group, you define the name, tooltip, source (embedded, external, or database), and path for the image. If the source is embedded, you have to import the image from a file. If the source is a database, you can select any of the fields in your report datasets. If the source is external, you can use a URL to access the image, and the URL can also point to your report server.

- **Size**   In this group, you define how to display the image and padding options. You can specify whether to retain the image size and resize the container for the image, to resize the image to fit inside its container, to fit the image proportionally by resizing it while maintaining the aspect ratio, or to clip the image to fit inside its container.

- **Visibility**   In this group, you define whether the image is visible initially and the expression to toggle visibility.

- **Action**   In this group, you define an action on the image. You will learn about actions later in this chapter.

- **Border**   In this group, you define borders for the image.

Adding a Chart

Another type of report item that you can add to a report is a Chart report item. Charts belong to a type of report item called *data regions*. Table, Matrix, and List report items are also data regions (and as was noted earlier, all three are simply templates for the Tablix report item). Data regions take rows from datasets and display the information to the user. Table, Matrix, and List report items display the information in a repeated rows format, and the Chart report item summarizes the information in a graphical interface.

To add a chart to a report, follow these steps:

1. In the Report Designer, click the Design tab.

2. In the Toolbox window, double-click the chart item or drag a chart item onto the report area.

3. Select the chart type. (You can change the chart type later by right-clicking the Chart report item and then selecting the chart type you want the report to display.)

4. From the Report Data window, drag the column you want to use as the category onto the Drop Category Fields Here section of the chart. *Categories* are groups of data that will be displayed together. By default, categories are displayed on the x-axis of a line or column chart.

5. From the Report Data window, drag the column you want to use as the series onto the Drop Series Fields Here section of the chart. *Series* are optional groups of data that will be displayed together. By default, series are displayed with different colors in line or column charts.

6. From the Report Data window, drag the column you want to use as the values onto the Drop Data Fields Here section of the chart. *Values* define the size of chart elements (lines, columns, and areas).

To understand the relationship between chart axes and data to a matrix, consider a chart as a matrix, in which you can treat chart categories as matrix columns, a chart series as matrix rows, and chart data as matrix data.

Adding a Gauge

In the Gauge data region, you can display a single value in your dataset. Gauges are useful for displaying key performance indicators (KPIs). You can also use a gauge inside a table or matrix to illustrate values inside each cell. A gauge is always positioned inside a *gauge panel*. You can add child or adjacent gauges in the *gauge panel*. You might want to use multiple gauges in a single gauge panel to compare data between fields.

You can use two types of gauges: *radial* and *linear*. Both types have pointers. A radial gauge has a pivot point around which one or more pointers rotate. A linear gauge displays the values as a portion of the scale of the gauge in a horizontal or vertical orientation. You select the gauge type when you add a gauge to your report by dragging the Gauge report item from the Toolbox window. However, you cannot change the gauge type in the same way you change a chart type—to change the gauge type, you must remove the gauge and then add a new gauge.

You can change the other gauge properties by right-clicking the gauge and then clicking Gauge or Gauge Properties. From the Gauge option, which is actually a submenu, you can define scale, range, pointer, and gauge panel properties. From the Gauge Properties option, you can change general properties, such as name and size, frame and fill options, and actions. When you right-click a gauge, you can also add a scale, a pointer, a range, a gauge label, and an adjacent gauge.

Adding a Tablix

The Tablix data region is probably the mostly used data region. You can use a Tablix to display fields from a dataset, grouped or detailed, and in a grid or free-form layout. You can add a Tablix to your report by dragging a Table, Matrix, or List template from the Toolbox window. The template choice gives you the initial shape of the Tablix; however, you are not limited to this initial choice. You can modify the Tablix design later by adding groups, totals, labels, nested groups, independent adjacent groups, or even recursive groups.

Use the Table template as your starting point when your goal is to display detail data and row groups. Use the Matrix report item as your starting point when you need to present aggregated data summaries, grouped in rows and columns similar to Microsoft Office Excel PivotTables. And use the List template as your starting point to create a free-form layout.

A single Tablix, as is the case with a single chart, is bound to a single dataset. You will learn more about designing a Tablix in the practices for this chapter and in Chapter 11.

EXAM TIP

If your report requires data from multiple datasets, add multiple data regions.

Adding Other Report Items

SSRS also lets you configure other graphical elements, such as lines and rectangles, to add visual effects to your report. To add a graphical item, drag the item from the Toolbox window onto the design surface in the Report Designer.

In addition, you can display another report—a *subreport*—inside the body of a main report. A subreport is similar to a frame in a Web page. Typically, you would use parameters to filter datasets in the subreport and then pass parameters from the main report to the subreport. For example, you could have a main report showing sum of sales per product and a subreport showing product details for a specific product, using ProductId as a parameter to filter the subreport's dataset. You would open the subreport through an action defined on the product name field in the parent report. You will learn about dataset filters in Chapter 11, and you will see how actions work later in this chapter.

In this practice, you will use the Report Wizard in BIDS to create a report. You will then change the report properties so that the report fits into a landscape layout and modify the report to make it easier for users to understand. You will also change some item properties and then add a footer and a chart to the report.

EXERCISE 1   Use the Report Wizard to Create a Report

In this exercise, you create a report project and then use the Report Wizard to create a report.

1. Open BIDS.

2. From the main menu, select File, New, and then Project to create a new project in which you can develop the report.

3. In the New Project dialog box, select Business Intelligence Projects, and then select the Report Server Project Wizard template.

4. Type **TK 448 Ch10 SSRS Purchasing** as the name of the project. Name the solution **TK 448 Ch10 SSRS**. You will use this project to create Adventure Works purchasing reports. Click OK to create the project and start the Report Wizard.

5. On the Welcome To The Report Wizard page, click Next to begin the report configuration.

6. On the Select The Data Source page, type **AdventureWorks2008** as the data source, and then click Edit to configure the connection string.

7. Leave the default data source type as Microsoft SQL Server. Click Edit to configure the connection string.

8. In the Connection Properties dialog box, type **(local)** as the server name. For the database name, type or select **AdventureWorks2008**. Leave the default security as Use Windows Authentication. Click Test Connection to validate the connection information, and then click OK to close the Connection Properties dialog box and continue the connection string configuration in the Report Wizard.

9. On the Select The Data Source page, select the Make This A Shared Data Source check box, and then click Next.

10. On the Design The Query page, click Query Builder to open the Query Designer dialog box. You use the Query Designer to enter the SQL command that will retrieve data for the report.

11. In the SQL pane, enter the following query to select monthly purchasing information by product category and subcategory:

```
SELECT
    YEAR(poh.OrderDate) * 100 + MONTH(poh.OrderDate) AS OrderMonth
   ,pc.Name AS ProductCategory
   ,psc.Name AS ProductSubCategory
   ,p.Name
   ,SUM(pod.OrderQty) AS OrderQty
   ,SUM(pod.LineTotal) AS Amount
```

```
FROM Production.ProductCategory AS pc
    INNER JOIN Production.ProductSubcategory AS psc
     ON pc.ProductCategoryID = psc.ProductCategoryID
    INNER JOIN Production.Product AS p
     ON psc.ProductSubcategoryID = p.ProductSubcategoryID
    INNER JOIN Purchasing.PurchaseOrderDetail AS pod
     ON p.ProductID = pod.ProductID
        AND p.ProductID = pod.ProductID
    INNER JOIN Purchasing.PurchaseOrderHeader AS poh
     ON pod.PurchaseOrderID = poh.PurchaseOrderID
        AND  pod.PurchaseOrderID = poh.PurchaseOrderID
GROUP BY pc.Name
        ,psc.Name
        ,p.Name
        ,YEAR(poh.OrderDate) * 100 + MONTH(poh.OrderDate)
ORDER BY ProductCategory, ProductSubCategory, p.Name, OrderMonth;
```

In the installed practice files, you will find completed solutions for this chapter's prac-tices. The installed practice files are located in the C:\Users*username*\Documents\ Microsoft Press\MCTS Training Kit 70-448\Source\Ch 10\ folder. You might want to copy queries—especially lengthy ones—from the folder to avoid a lot of typing.

12. Click OK to return to the wizard.

13. Click Next to accept the query and continue.

14. On the Select The Report Type page, select Matrix, and then click Next.

15. On the Design The Matrix page, configure the fields as shown in the following table.

FIELD	DISPLAYED FIELDS SECTION
ProductCategory	Page
OrderMonth	Column
ProductSubCategory	Row
OrderQty	Details
Amount	Details

16. Click Next to continue.

17. On the Choose The Matrix Style page, select Ocean, and then click Next.

18. On the Choose The Deployment Location page, verify the deployment location. Note that SSRS 2008 uses port 8080 on the 32-bit Windows XP operating system, so you might have to change the Report Server Deployment option to **http://localhost:8080/ ReportServer**, for example. You can verify the SSRS Web service URL in the Reporting Services Configuration Manager tool or in SSMS by right-clicking your report server in Object Explorer and then clicking Properties. For this step, leave the deployment folder as is, and then click Next.

19. On the last page of the Report Wizard, type **PurchasingSummary** as the name of the report, and then click Finish to generate the report.

20. To preview the report, in the Report Designer, click the Preview tab.

EXERCISE 2 Use the Report Designer to Modify Report Properties

In this exercise, you change the layout of the report and edit its general properties to configure the way the PDF version of the report will look.

1. Click the Preview tab in the Report Designer. Notice that the HTML version of the report is only three pages long. The HTML rendering format uses logical pages and not physical pages, and you get one page per product category.

2. Click the Export button on the Preview tab toolbar, and then select Acrobat (PDF) File. To review the file formatting, export the file to your desktop, accepting the default file name.

3. Open the exported file, and then browse the content. Notice that this version is 28 pages long, and it displays very few columns. Close the file, and then return to BIDS.

4. Select the Design pane in the Report Designer.

5. If the Properties window is not displayed, from the main menu, select View, Properties Window or press F4.

6. In the Object box in the Properties window, select Report.

7. Configure the properties as shown in the following table.

PROPERTY	VALUE
PageSize\Width	11 in
PageSize\Height	8.5 in
Margins\Left	.5 in
Margins\Right	.5 in
Margins\Top	.5 in
Margins\Bottom	.5 in

8. Click the Preview tab. Notice that the HTML version of the report has not been affected by the change.

9. Click Export on the Preview tab toolbar again, and then select Acrobat (PDF) File. Replace the previous exported file on your desktop.

10. Open the exported file, and then browse the content. Notice that the report is now only 14 pages long and displays more columns than the previous version. Close the file, and then return to BIDS.

EXERCISE 3 Edit Report Item Properties

In this exercise, you change some properties generated by the Report Wizard, widening the Name column and using a customized format to display the sales amount.

1. In the Report Designer, click the Design tab.
2. Select the TextBox3 element, which is the last row and last column of the matrix element.
3. In the Properties window, select the Number, Format property, and then type the value **$#,#.##**.
4. Select the ProductSubCategory box, which is the last row and first column of the matrix element.
5. In the Properties window, expand the Size property, and then change Width to **2in**.
6. Preview the report, noting the changes.

EXERCISE 4 Add a Page Footer

In this exercise, you continue your modifications by adding a page footer that displays the user name for the report and page numbers.

1. In the Report Designer, click the Design tab.
2. On the Report menu, select Add Page Footer. A new design area is added to the Report Designer.
3. Drag a Textbox report item from the Toolbox window to the page footer area. Position the text box in the top-left corner of the footer. Configure the properties of the text box, as shown in the following table.

PROPERTY	VALUE
Name	txtUser
Width	3 in

4. In the Report Data window, expand Built-in Fields. (If the window is not visible, open it from the View menu by choosing Report Data.) Drag the User ID field to the txtUser box. BIDS creates the full expression for you. You can verify the full expression by right-clicking the text box and then clicking Expression.
5. Drag another Textbox report item from the Toolbox window to the page footer area. Position the text box in the bottom-left corner of the footer, under the UserId box, as Figure 10-2 shows.

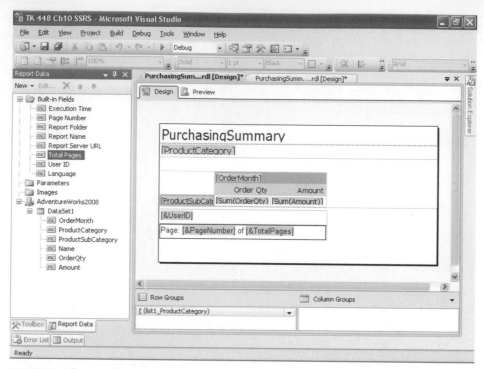

FIGURE 10-2 Report with page footer

6. Configure the properties of the text box, as shown in the following table.

PROPERTY	VALUE
Name	txtPage
Width	3 in

7. Type **Page:** in the txtPage box. (Important: Be sure to type a colon and a space following the label text.)

8. Drag the Page Number field after the space following the colon. Type **of** (with a space before and after the text) after the Page Number field, and then drag the Total Pages field to the end of the expression.

EXERCISE 5   Add a Chart

Now you are ready to add a chart to the report.

1. In the Report Designer, click the Design tab.

2. Select the Body element. Body is a transparent element in the body of the report, behind the matrix and before the page footer. You can select Body by clicking an empty area in the body of the report or by selecting Body from the Object drop-down

list in the Properties window. Because the wizard did not leave much empty space in the body of the report, it is probably easier to use the second method to select Body properties in this example.

3. In the Properties window, set the height of the Body element to **6 in**. Also change the width to **6 in**. You are making the Body element larger to make room for the Chart element.

4. Drag a Chart element from the Toolbox window to below the Matrix element. Select the Stacked Column chart type, and then click OK. Position the chart below the matrix, with left borders aligned. Leave some space for two matrix rows between the bottom of the matrix and the top of the chart. You will expand the matrix in the practice for Lesson 3 later in this chapter.

5. Right-click the chart, select Chart Properties, and then change the Name property to **chtAmount**.

6. In the Properties window, make sure that the chtAmount chart is selected and configure the properties as shown in the following table.

PROPERTY	VALUE
Height	4 in
Width	6 in

7. From the Toolbox window, select the Dataset pane. If the Dataset pane is not visible in the Toolbox window, from the main menu, select View, Datasets.

8. In the Design tab, select the chart. Drag the ProductCategory field from the Toolbox window onto the Drop Series Fields Here area of the chart. Drag the OrderMonth field onto the Drop Category Fields Here area. Last, drag the Amount field from the Toolbox window onto the Drop Data Fields Here area.

9. Right-click the ProductCategory field in the series area, and then select Series Group Properties. In the Series Group Properties window, select the Sorting pane. Click Add, and in the Column drop-down list, select the ProductCategory field.

10. Right-click the OrderMonth field in the Series area, and then select Category Group Properties. In the Category Group Properties window, select the Sorting pane. Click Add, and in the Column drop-down list, select the Order Month field.

11. Double-click the vertical axis title, and then rename it **Sales Amount**.

12. Double-click the horizontal axis title, and then rename it **Product Categories**.

13. Double-click the chart title, and then rename it **Sales Amount for Product Categories over Months**.

14. Save the report, and then select the Preview pane to review it.

Lesson 2: Creating a Dataset from a Data Source

Estimated lesson time: 20 minutes

Up to now in this chapter, you have worked with reports that contain single sets of data and that were defined by the Report Wizard. In this lesson, you will learn how to create datasets without the wizard and how to add additional datasets. You can use these datasets to enhance your reports and create composite reports.

Creating a New Report Dataset

A *dataset* is a collection of data. A dataset, like a table, consists of rows and columns. SSRS uses one or more datasets as the source of the report items. Note that this is a two-dimensional table, without nested tables, such as a SQL Server table. This distinction is important because when accessing multidimensional sources such as online analytical processing (OLAP) cubes, sources with nested tables such as data mining models, or sources with hierarchical data such as XML, you have to write the source query so that the result is flattened to a two-dimensional table.

A dataset has three main elements:

- **Data source** A data source configures the driver and connection properties to connect to the data.

- **Command type** The command type can be text, a table direct (which is equivalent to a *SELECT * FROM table* query), or a stored procedure. For many data sources—including a SQL Server relational database, SSAS cubes and mining models, and SSRS models—you can use graphical query designers.

- **Query string** Text commands use the query language of the data provider. For example, you use Transact-SQL (T-SQL) for the relational engine and Multidimensional Expressions (MDX) or Data Mining Extensions (DMX) for SSAS. You can call stored procedures by name.

A data source defines how SSRS connects to an underlying data source. SSRS supports nearly any source you might need, including SQL Server, SSAS, XML, report server model, SQL Server Integration Services (SSIS) package, Microsoft .NET Framework data providers, any OLE DB provider, and any Open Database Connectivity (ODBC) driver. In addition, you can create and install custom data processing extensions.

Datasets have other properties that are either optional or automatically generated when you configure the core properties. These properties are Timeout, Fields, Options, Parameters, and Filters.

Choosing a Shared or Private Data Source

You configure datasets in the Report Designer Design tab. But before you configure a dataset, you need to decide whether you want to use a shared data source or a private data source to connect to SQL Server or another data provider.

A *shared data source* is a report server item that has the following configuration information: the type of data provider, the connection string, and the security configuration to connect to the database or data provider. A shared data source is stored independently from the report and can be used to configure datasets in multiple reports.

You can also use private data sources. A *private data source* has the same provider type, connection string, and security configuration that a shared data source has. However, a private data source is not stored independently from the report but instead is embedded in the report. A private data source can be used only within the report for a single dataset.

Creating a Dataset

You create a new dataset by following these steps:

1. In the Report Designer, click the Design tab.

2. In the Report Data window, click New, and then select Dataset. You can create a data source while creating the dataset, or you can create a new data source from the New menu. Alternatively, if you already have a dataset created from a specific data source, you can add a new dataset from the same data source by right-clicking the data source and then clicking the Add Dataset option in the tree view of the data elements in the Report Data window.

3. In the resulting Dataset Properties dialog box, configure the name of the dataset and the data source.

4. To be able to use the graphical designer, leave the default query type as Text or use the Stored Procedure type and leave the query string empty. Click the Query Designer button.

You are probably already familiar with the Transact-SQL Query Designer. In the next section, you learn about the SSAS MDX Query Designer.

Working with an SSAS-Based Dataset

There are two query designers that work with SSAS data sources. The first is the Multidimensional Expressions (MDX) Query Designer, which lets you query OLAP cubes by using the MDX language. The second is the Data Mining Extensions (DMX) Query Designer. DMX is the language that lets you query and work with data mining models. In Chapter 9, you created a report that used a dataset based on a DMX query.

The Query Designer lets you switch between MDX and DMX by using the Command Type button on the Data pane toolbar. The Command Type button acts as a toggle between MDX and DMX. The Command Type MDX button deletes the previous DMX query and sets the designer to help you create a multidimensional query. And the Command Type DMX button deletes the MDX query and helps you create data mining queries.

Both designers have two modes: Design mode and Query mode. Design mode lets you create the query graphically, dragging different multidimensional structures or data mining elements. In Query mode, you can manually enter your MDX or DMX queries. When you work in Design mode to build an MDX query, the Query Designer automatically flattens the results of the query into two dimensions, using only the first two axes, which in MDX are named *COLUMNS* and *ROWS*. For a DMX query, the Query Designer does not flatten nested tables. After you create the DMX query graphically, do not forget to add the DMX keyword *FLAT-TENED* right after the *SELECT* and before the first column reference in the select list. Otherwise, you will get an error when trying to use a column that is actually a nested table. If you write an MDX or a DMX query manually, be sure to create a two-dimensional result.

Creating a Multidimensional Query

To create multidimensional queries, you need to be familiar with the MDX Query Designer. Figure 10-3 shows the different areas of the MDX Query Designer.

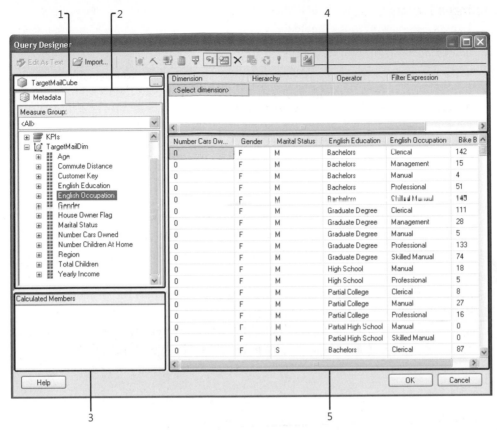

FIGURE 10-3 The MDX Query Designer window

In Figure 10-3, the main areas of the MDX Query Designer are marked with the numbers 1 through 5, which are used in the following list to describe the features of the designer window in greater detail:

- To change the cube or perspective, use the Cube Selection button (1).
- To add a hierarchy to the query, expand the dimension in the Metadata pane (2), and then drag the hierarchy to the Data pane (5).
- To add a level to the query, expand the dimension in the Metadata pane (2), and then drag the level or levels to the Data pane (5).
- To delete a level from the query, drag the column header from the Data pane (5) to any spot on the screen that is outside the Data pane.
- To delete a hierarchy from the query, drag each of the elements of the hierarchy from the column header in the Data pane (5) to any spot on the screen that is outside the Data pane.
- To add a measure to the query, expand the dimension in the Metadata pane (2), and then drag the hierarchy to the Data pane (5).

- To filter the query, expand the dimension in the Metadata pane (2), and then drag the level or hierarchy from the Metadata pane to the Filter area (4). In the Filter area, select the operator and filter expression to filter the dataset.

- To create a calculated member, right-click in the Calculated Members area (3), and then click New Calculated Member. Name the calculated member, and then write the MDX expression to calculate the cell. Drag the calculated member to the Data pane (5).

 REAL WORLD

Dejan Sarka

One of my customers recently had a problem delivering on the company's plan to share financial reports with partners on an extranet. The problem was that the reports from the relational data sources were simply too slow. The query to summarize accounting information for a partner for multiple years was taking about a minute.

As a solution, we introduced a Finance Unified Dimensional Model (UDM) cube. With proper aggregations and data, SSAS was able to return the results hundreds of times faster than SQL Server. The MDX query we created took only fractions of a second. And the partners were very pleased to be able to receive the reports on the extranet.

PRACTICE Creating Report Datasets

In this practice, you will use BIDS to create two reports without using the Report Wizard. One of the reports will have a relational data source, and the other will have an SSAS OLAP cube data source. You will use these datasets in the next lesson as well. This practice requires the completed and deployed solution named TK 448 Data Mining from Exercise 3 in the Lesson 1 practice for Chapter 9.

If you did not complete the practices from the previous chapter, you can find the solution in the ..\Source\Ch 09\ folder. Simply open and deploy the solution.

EXERCISE 1 Create the Relational Dataset and Add a Report

In this exercise, you create two shared data sources, a relational one and multidimensional one, as well as a relational dataset. This exercise will help you create the report interface in the next practice.

1. In BIDS, open the TK 448 Ch10 SSRS Purchasing project you created in the practice for Lesson 1 of this chapter.

2. In Solution Explorer, right-click the Shared Data Sources folder, and then select Add New Data Source. Name the data source **TMRelational**, click Edit, and then configure

the following options: Set the connection type to Microsoft SQL Server, the server name to (local), the database to AdventureWorksDW2008, and authentication to Windows Authentication. Click OK twice to save the new shared data source.

3. In Solution Explorer, right-click the Shared Data Sources folder, and then click Add New Data Source. Name this data source **TMOLAP**, and use the following options for the connection: set the type to Microsoft SQL Server Analysis Services, the server name to (local), the database to TK 448 Mining Models Project, and authentication to Windows Authentication. Click OK twice to save your changes.

4. In Solution Explorer, right-click the Reports folder, select Add, and then select New Item. Do not select the Add New Report option—that option starts the Report Wizard. In the Add New Item dialog box, select the Report template from Report Project Categories list. Type **TargetMail.rdl** for the report name, and then click Add.

5. In the Design tab, in the Report Data window, select New Dataset from the New menu. This will let you create a new dataset.

6. In the Dataset Properties dialog box, in the Query pane, type **TMRelational** as the dataset name. Click New next to the Data Source box to create a new data source for this dataset. Instead of creating a new data source, you will add a reference to a shared data source.

7. In the Data Source Properties dialog box, in the General pane, type the name **TMRelationalDataSource** as the data source name. Select the Use Shared Data Source Reference option, and then select the TMRelational data source from the drop-down list. Click OK.

8. In the Dataset Properties dialog box, in the Query pane, click Query Designer to display the Query Designer dialog box. Start by clicking the Add Table button (the rightmost button on the toolbar) to select the vTargetMail view with the following columns: CustomerKey, FirstName, LastName, MaritalStatus, Gender, EnglishEducation, EnglishOccupation, NumberCarsOwned, and BikeBuyer. Your query should look like this:

```
SELECT
    CustomerKey
    ,FirstName
    ,LastName
    ,MaritalStatus
    ,Gender
    ,EnglishEducation
    ,EnglishOccupation
    ,NumberCarsOwned
    ,BikeBuyer
FROM dbo.vTargetMail;
```

9. Still in the Query Designer, click the Run button (displayed as an exclamation mark [!]) to execute the query, and then verify the results.

10. Click OK to exit the Query Designer, and then click OK again to exit the Dataset Properties dialog box.

EXERCISE 2   Create the Multidimensional Dataset

In this exercise, you create a multidimensional data set.

1. In the Design tab, in the Report Data window, select New Dataset from the New menu to create a new dataset.

2. In the Dataset Properties dialog box, in the Query pane, type **TMDimensional** as the dataset name. Click the New button next to the Data Source box to create a new data source for this dataset. Instead of creating a new data source, you will add a reference to a shared data source.

3. In the Data Source Properties dialog box, in the General pane, type the name **TMDimensionalDataSource** as the data source name. Select the Use Shared Data Source Reference option, and then select the TMOLAP data source from the drop-down list. Click OK.

4. In the Dataset Properties dialog box, in the Query pane, click the Query Designer button to display the Query Designer dialog box.

5. Click the Cube Selection button to select the TargetMailCube, and then click OK.

6. From the Metadata tree, drag the following attributes from the TargetMailDim dimension and from Measures into the query area: Bike Buyer, Number Cars Owned, Gender, Marital Status, English Education, and English Occupation. Click the Design Mode button to show the query designed graphically. Your query should look like this:

```
SELECT
    NON EMPTY { [Measures].[Bike Buyer] } ON COLUMNS
    ,NON EMPTY {(
    [TargetMailDim].[Number Cars Owned].[Number Cars Owned].ALLMEMBERS *
    [TargetMailDim].[Gender].[Gender].ALLMEMBERS *
    [TargetMailDim].[Marital Status].[Marital Status].ALLMEMBERS *
    [TargetMailDim].[English Education].[English Education].ALLMEMBERS *
    [TargetMailDim].[English Occupation].[English Occupation].ALLMEMBERS
    )}
    DIMENSION PROPERTIES
      MEMBER_CAPTION
     ,MEMBER_UNIQUE_NAME ON ROWS
  FROM [TargetMailCube]
  CELL PROPERTIES
    VALUE
    ,BACK_COLOR
    ,FORE_COLOR
    ,FORMATTED_VALUE
```

```
,FORMAT_STRING
,FONT_NAME
,FONT_SIZE
,FONT_FLAGS;
```

7. Click the Click To Execute The Query link in the Data pane of the Query Designer to execute the query, and then verify the results.

8. Click OK to exit the Query Designer, and OK again to exit the Dataset Properties dialog box. Save the solution and close BIDS.

✔ **Quick Check**

1. Can you use a stored procedure to provide data to an SSRS report?

2. You want to use a perspective in an MDX query. How do you select the perspective?

3. Can you use data mining models in SSRS?

Quick Check Answers

1. Yes, you can use a stored procedure to provide data to an SSRS report by configuring the dataset to use a stored procedure command type. However, your stored procedure should return only a single result set. If it returns multiple result sets, only the first one is used for the report dataset.

2. Use the Cube Selector in the MDX Query Designer to select a perspective.

3. Yes, you can use the DMX Designer to create data mining queries for SSRS reports. However, do not forget to flatten the result set returned by the DMX query.

Lesson 3: Working with Advanced Report Object Properties

Estimated lesson time: 25 minutes

Designing effective reports involves much more than adding new elements or enhancing the look and feel of the existing ones. A critical part of report development is creating an interactive user experience in which users can see the general summarized picture of the data and drill through the data to discover details. This lesson covers how to configure advanced object properties to build interactive reports.

Toggling Object Visibility

A primary concept in interactive reports is that they include groups, columns, rows, tables, or matrix elements that are hidden when the user first sees the report. The user can then click an element of the report to display hidden items only as they are needed. Interactive reports help users stay focused on the global perspective of the report and still have the ability to look into the details.

EXAM TIP

The design of interactive reports is closely related to the HTML rendering format. Microsoft Office Excel, Microsoft Office Word, Image, Acrobat (PDF) File, and Web Archive reports do not support the same type of interaction; details are hidden by default. XML and CSV reports display all information by default.

Some common reasons you might want to use the toggle visibility feature are as follows:

- To hide columns or rows with details in table and matrix report items
- To completely hide a table or matrix item
- To hide other report items

Hiding Groups

To hide groups in table and matrix items, follow these steps:

1. In the Report Designer, on the Design tab, select the table or matrix report item (that is, row or column group) from the Row Groups or Column Groups pane.
2. Right-click the table or matrix item, and then select Group Properties.
3. In the Group Properties dialog box, click the Visibility pane.
4. Change the display options by first changing the When The Report Is Initially Run option to Show Or Hide Based On An Expression.
5. Select the Display Can Be Toggled By This Report Item check box.
6. Select the report item that will toggle the visibility. Typically, this is a text box that shows the label of the parent group.
7. Click OK to accept the configuration.

Hiding a Whole Tablix

Sometimes you will want to hide not columns and rows but the whole table or matrix. The following steps will hide a table or matrix:

1. Select the table or matrix report item, right-click, and then select Tablix Properties.
2. In the Tablix Properties dialog box, click the Visibility pane.
3. Change the display options by first changing the When The Report Is Initially Run option to Show Or Hide Based On An Expression.
4. Select the Display Can Be Toggled By This Report Item check box.
5. Select the report item that will toggle the visibility.
6. Click OK to accept the configuration.

Hiding a Static Row, Column, or Text Box of a Tablix

If you need to hide items such as a specific row, column, or even text box, you need to select the item and change its Visibility property. For a row or column of a Tablix, click the Tablix to select it and display handles on the left and top borders. Right-click the row or column handle you want to hide, and then select either Row Visibility or Column Visibility. To hide an individual text box (or cell of a Tablix), right-click it and then select Text Box Properties. Then use the Visibility pane to change the Visibility property.

Hiding Other Report Items

Other report items can also be hidden initially and toggled automatically when users select another item. To hide other report items such as images, charts, and so on, follow these steps:

1. Select the report item you want to hide.
2. In the Item Properties window, use the Visibility pane to change the settings.

Defining Report Actions

Actions are another common feature of interactive reports. *Actions* are responses to user clicks on a report item. Actions let users navigate reports in the same way they navigate the Internet. SSRS supports three types of actions:

- **Go To Report** This action lets you configure a set of interlaced reports. Reports can use parameters to indicate what users want to navigate to. Go To Report is frequently used to drill through to details of summary information.

> ***NOTE* REPORT PARAMETERS**
>
> In Chapter 11, you will learn more about parameters and how reports use them to filter displayed information.

- **Go To Bookmark** This action lets users navigate quickly within complex reports. Users can click one item to rapidly move to another section of the same report.
- **Go To URL** This action lets developers integrate the report infrastructure with the Internet, an intranet, or an extranet. Reports can use hyperlinks to integrate with the rest of the Web infrastructure.

To implement one of these actions, take the following steps:

1. Select the item in which you want to configure the action.
2. In the Properties window, select the Action property.
3. Click the ellipsis button and then select the type of action you want to configure.
4. Add the expression required to set the URL.

Adding Bookmarks

Bookmarks provide a customized table of contents or customized internal navigation links in the report. Add bookmarks for locations you want to direct users to—for example, to a chart that graphically explains values in a Tablix.

To add a bookmark, follow these steps:

1. Select the text box, image, chart, or other report item on the Design tab.

2. The properties for the selected item will appear in the Properties window. If this window is closed, open it by pressing F4 or by selecting the Properties Window option on the View menu.

3. In the Bookmark box, type a string that is the label for this bookmark. Alternatively, use the drop-down list to select a value of a field of the bound dataset or to select and edit a custom expression used as the bookmark value.

PRACTICE **Modifying Advanced Report Object Properties**

In this practice, you will modify the report you created in this chapter's previous practices to initially hide some of the detailed information from users. Users can then interact with the report and expand only those areas they want to focus on. You will then configure a hyperlink action in the report.

EXERCISE 1 Hide Columns

In this exercise, you hide columns so that the user will first browse only summarized yearly information.

1. Open BIDS.

2. Open the TK 448 Ch10 SSRS Purchasing project you created in the previous practices for this chapter. You can open the project from the main menu by selecting File, Recent Projects or File, Open Project/Solution.

3. In Solution Explorer, double-click the PurchasingSummary report. The report will open in the Report Designer Design tab.

4. Add a calculated field to your dataset, as follows. You will calculate order year from the OrderMonth field.

   a. In the Report Data window, right-click DataSet1, and then click Add Calculated Field.

   b. In the Dataset Properties dialog box, the Fields pane should be selected, with all the existing fields and boxes for creating a new field showing.

   c. Type **OrderYear** as the name of the calculated field, and then click the Expression button and add the following expression for this field:

   ```
   =Fields!OrderMonth.Value\100
   ```

IMPORTANT USE THE INTEGER DIVISION SYMBOL

The preceding expression uses the \ symbol and not the regular division symbol /. The \ symbol is for integer division. Order month comes from a query as an integer with six numbers, in YYYYMM format, such as 200407 for July 2004. Performing an integer division by 100 on this number gives 2004 as the result.

Figure 10-4 shows the Expression dialog box, with the expression added.

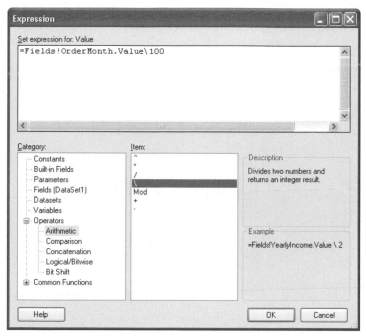

FIGURE 10-4 The Expression dialog box, showing how to build the OrderYear expression by using integer division

5. Click OK to close the Expression dialog box, and then click OK again to close the Dataset Properties dialog box.

6. In the matrix, click the OrderMonth column to select it. Make sure that only this column is selected, not the complete matrix. Right-click the OrderMonth column, select Add Group, and then select Parent Group. Figure 10-5 shows the correct selections.

7. In the Tablix Group dialog box, select the OrderYear field in the Group By drop-down list, and then click OK.

8. Click the new text box that has the OrderYear field in it to select it. In the Properties window, change the TextAlign property to Center.

9. Click the OrderMonth column header to see the column groups in the Column Groups pane at the bottom right of the Design window. In the Column Groups pane, right-click

Matrix1_OrderMonth, click Add Total in the Textbox pop-up menu, and then click After on the submenu.

10. In the Column Groups pane at the bottom right of the Design window, right-click Matrix1_OrderMonth, and then select Group Properties.

11. In the Group Properties dialog box, select the Visibility pane, and then change the When The Report Is Initially Run option to Hide. Now the monthly columns will not be displayed when the user sees the report.

12. Click OK to accept the new visibility settings.

13. Click the Preview tab to review the report. Notice that the user will be able to see only yearly sales and will not see the monthly details.

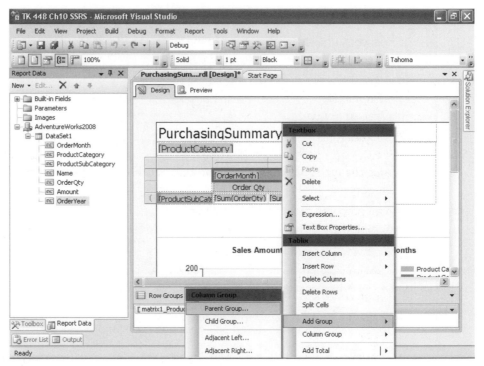

FIGURE 10-5 Adding a parent group to OrderMonth

EXERCISE 2   Unhide Columns

In this exercise, you change the report item properties so that the user can display month columns for a particular year. The idea is that the user will first browse yearly summarized information and, if more detailed information is needed, the user can expand any year to display the monthly details.

1. Switch to the Design tab.

2. In the Column Groups pane at the bottom right of the Design tab, right-click Matrix1_OrderMonth, and then select Group Properties.

3. In the Group Properties dialog box, click the Visibility pane. Select the Display Can Be Toggled By This Report Item check box. From the drop-down list under the check box, select Group1.

4. Click OK to accept the new visibility.

5. Click the Preview tab to review the report. Notice that the user will now be able to expand the yearly sales into monthly details.

6. Save the solution.

EXERCISE 3   Create a Hyperlink Action

In this last exercise, you enhance the usefulness of the report by adding a hyperlink action to the product name column so that users can browse the product home page in the Adventure Works portal.

1. Select the ProductSubcategory text box, which is the leftmost cell that is the last row in the matrix report item.

2. In the Properties window, make sure that the ProductSubCategory text box is selected. Change the Color property to DarkBlue (the sixth color in the first row of the color palette). Also change TextDecoration property to Underline so that users can see that the subcategory name value is a hyperlink.

3. In the Action property, click the ellipsis (...) button to open the Text Box Properties dialog box. Below Change Hyperlink Options, select the Go To URL option. Use the following expression to configure the URL:

    ```
    ="http://AdventureWorksIntranet/Products/"+Fields!Name.Value+".aspx"
    ```

4. The expression configures the hyperlink action to navigate to an imaginary Web site.

5. Click OK to configure the action, and then click OK again to close the Text Box Properties dialog box.

6. Click the Preview tab to preview the report. Try to click a product subcategory link. Internet Explorer should open, but because the URL points to an imaginary Web site, it should not open the URL.

7. Save the solution and close BIDS.

Lesson 4: Applying Dataset Filters and Groups

Estimated lesson time: 25 minutes

After you have created the dataset that will provide data to the report, you need to create the report items that will display the data to the user. These items are structured as data regions.

Assigning Datasets to Data Regions

As you saw earlier in this chapter, a *data region* is a report item that displays rows of data from the source datasets. SSRS has three data regions: Tablix, chart, and gauge. There is no Tablix report item in the Toolbox window; you start working with Tablix by using a List, Table, or Matrix report item. Up to now, you have used the Report Wizard to create data regions and assign datasets automatically, but you can also create data regions and assign the datasets manually. To create a data region, you need to navigate to the Report Designer's Design tab, and then drag one of the five report items described in the following sections to the report layout region.

The List Report Item

The List report item is a data region that lets you present information without any predefined structure. To use the List report item, drag the report item onto the Layout pane, and then drag a field from the Dataset pane and onto the List report item. The Report Designer will automatically create a new text box report item with the value of the dropped field and will automatically map the List report item to the dataset you dragged the field from. You can verify the bound dataset in the Properties window DataSetName property. You can use other report items inside the List report item to create the user interface for the report. You start with a single column and row; however, you can enhance your list design by adding additional detail rows and nested or adjacent row groups or column groups.

A list is actually a container—you can use it to display grouped data if you edit the Details group. You just have to specify a name and group expression. You can also have other data regions, such as Table or Chart data regions, embedded inside the list, bound to the same dataset as the list. Nested report items with grouped data repeat once for every group value.

The Table Report Item

The Table data region presents information in a tabular format. Table data regions have a predefined number of columns and present one row for each row in the dataset. The Table data region also allows multiple levels of data grouping over rows and the inclusion of graphical elements within the table. Of course, because the Table report item is just another template for the Tablix data region, you can enhance the table to use column groups, thus changing the table to a matrix.

The Table report item lets you sort, group, and filter information based on dataset fields and expressions, as Figure 10-6 shows. You will learn how to use these features in the section "Applying Filters, Groups, and Sorts to Data Regions" later in this lesson.

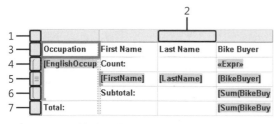

FIGURE 10-6 Table handles and headers

You can add totals for detail data. You can also change or add groups by using the Row Groups and Column Groups panes. In addition, when you select a table report item, the Report Designer displays handles, which you can use to configure different table options.

The table report item has the following handles. (The numbers correspond to the numbers in Figure 10-6.)

- **Table handle (1)** Lets you select the table. When you have the table selected, you can right-click the table item and then click Properties to display the Tablix Properties window, where you configure table properties such as sort order, visibility, and filters.

- **Column Header handle (2)** Lets you select a column. With a column selected, you can change the properties of all column cells simultaneously, change the visibility of a column, and add or delete columns.

- **Table Header handle (3)** Displays column titles for the table. With a table header selected, you can change the row visibility, add or delete rows, and change properties such as the font for all row cells simultaneously.

- **Group Header handle (4)** Can be displayed or hidden. With the Group Header handle, you can also edit row group properties and add additional row groups—either parent, child, adjacent above, or adjacent below.

- **Detail handle (5)** Lets you configure the final level of grouping of the table, including the row visibility. You can also add rows to the details section or delete them from the section.

- **Group Footer handle (6)** Displayed. You can change the row visibility, add or delete rows, change group properties, and add or delete row groups.

- **Table Footer handle (7)** Frequently used to present table totals. You can add or delete rows in this area and change visibility.

The Matrix Report Item

A Matrix data region is similar to a Table data region except that a Table data region has a predefined set of columns and the Matrix data region can dynamically expand the number of columns it contains in order to pivot information. Matrix data regions can have dynamic or static rows or columns, and you can use matrices to create crosstabs and PivotTable reports.

Working with a Matrix data region is similar to working with a Table data region, but it has two dimensions for working with data: columns and rows. You start with a single row and a single column group; you can add additional row and column groups, either parent, child, adjacent before, or adjacent after. Because the Matrix report item is again just another template for the Tablix data region, you can change a matrix to a table by adding detail rows.

The Chart Report Item

The Chart report item is different from other data regions in that it summarizes information from the dataset; other data regions render one row for each row in the dataset. You use charts to summarize data in a visual format.

The Gauge Report Item

The Gauge report item, new in SSRS 2008, is a one-dimensional data region. You can display a single value in it. However, a gauge is positioned in a gauge panel, where you can add additional gauges.

Applying Filters, Groups, and Sorts to Data Regions

After data has been assigned to a data region, you can filter, group, or sort the information that is presented to the user.

Grouping Data by Using Data Regions

A central feature of the Tablix data region is that it lets you configure multiple groups of data. The Table report item can use row groups, and the Matrix report item can use row and column groups. The List data region has only one grouping level: the detail group. And the Chart data region always groups all data in the set.

To add a group in a Tablix data region, follow these steps:

1. Select the Design pane, which lets you add groups in multiple ways.

2. If you have a table with detail data only, without any groups, you can right-click a column in the table header, and then on the Textbox shortcut menu, click Add Group. Then select either Column Group or Row Group. You can also add a group by simply dragging a grouping column to the Row Groups or Column Groups area in the Design window.

3. If you already have some row or column groups in the Row Groups or Column Groups area, you can right-click a group and then click Add Group.

4. In the Tablix Group window, you can define the grouping expression and add a group header and group footer.

5. When your group is created, you can change its properties by right-clicking the group and then clicking Group Properties. In the Group Properties window, you can change general properties (including Group Name and Expression), page break options, sorting, visibility, filters, group variables, and advanced properties (including Recursive Parent and Document Map).

Nesting Data Regions

In addition to using a data region with multiple grouping levels, you can also use nested data regions within other data regions. For example, you can use a List report item to group information by year and then drag another List report item onto the first List report item to group information within the Year List report item by quarter. Last, you can also drag a table element onto the Quarter List report item and configure the table with two groupings: Month and Week.

The List report item is not the only data region that can be nested. You can drag report items onto table and matrix report items and create a nested data region. For example, you can add a gauge inside a matrix to display summary data graphically.

Filtering Data

After data has been retrieved from the database, you can apply filters to the information that will be presented to the user. Filtering data is not the same as using parameters in the dataset; you will learn more about query parameters in Chapter 11. Filtering occurs after data has been retrieved from the source, and it lets you set two or more regions to use the same dataset but show different information to the user. For example, you could have a table show 6 months of data and a graph show 12 months of data—both from the same dataset.

SSRS lets you use filters in many different places:

- At the dataset
- At the data region
- At the row or column groups in a Tablix
- At the details group in a Tablix
- At the series or category groups in a chart

Filters at the dataset can be configured as follows:

1. Select the Report Data window.
2. In the Report Data window, right-click the dataset you want to filter, and then select Dataset Properties.
3. In the Dataset Properties dialog box, click the Filters tab.
4. In the Change Filters pane, click Add.
5. Configure the filter expression, data type, operator, and value. If your filter expression is simple, such as a single data field, the data type is assigned automatically from the field data type.

Filters at the dataset are very similar to parameters because they affect the data that is presented to all regions. However, filters always occur after data has been retrieved from the data source and might not perform as well as parameters because the query pulls all the data, not just the specific data that the user needs.

The main advantage of filters is that information can be shared between multiple users if you configure the report to use report execution snapshots. In *report execution snapshots*, the first execution of the report pulls the data from the server, and successive executions use the snapshot information stored in the report server.

> **BEST PRACTICES** **USE QUERY PARAMETERS INSTEAD OF FILTERS AT THE DATASET**
>
> Do not use filters at the dataset unless you plan to use report snapshots. Use query parameters instead to filter information before it gets to the report.

You can configure filters at the data region as follows:

1. In the Report Designer, click the Design tab.
2. In the design area, select the data region you want to configure.
3. Right-click the data region, and then select Data Region Properties.
4. In the data region Properties dialog box, click the Filters tab. (Note that there are different names for the data region properties dialog boxes for different data regions, such as the Tablix Properties dialog box for a Tablix data region.)

5. Configure the filter expression, data type, operator, and value.

Filters at data regions affect only the report item they are filtering, and different data regions can apply different filters to the same dataset.

Filters at the data grouping can be configured as follows:

1. In the Report Designer, click the Design tab.

2. In the Row Groups or Column Groups area, right-click the group you want to modify, and then click Group Properties.

3. In the Row Properties or Group Properties dialog box, click the Filters tab.

4. Configure the filter expression, data type, operator, and value.

Sorting Data in Data Regions

As with filters, sorting can be used in different places in your report. You can sort the data in your report in a dataset query, data region, or grouping. To sort data in the dataset query, use the appropriate syntax to sort the information. For example, in SQL, you use the *ORDER BY* clause to sort data in the dataset.

To configure the sort order in a data region, follow these steps:

1. In the Report Designer, click the Design tab.

2. Select the data region.

3. Right-click the data region, and then select Data Region Properties.

4. In the Data Region Properties dialog box, click the Sorting tab, and in the Change Sorting Option tab, click Add.

5. Configure the column to sort by and the order (that is, the direction of the sort).

6. Click OK.

To configure sorting at the grouping level, follow these steps:

1. In the Report Designer, click the Design tab.

2. In the Row Groups or Column Groups area, right-click the group you want to modify, and then click Group Properties.

3. In the Group Properties dialog box, click the Sorting tab, and in the Change Sorting Option dialog box, click Add.

4. Configure the column to sort by and the order.

5. Click OK.

EXAM TIP

Remember that you can sort data differently in different data regions.

Applying Aggregates to Data Regions

When adding groups to the data regions, you can also select to display header and footer rows for each group level. The headers and footers can be displayed or hidden by using table or matrix handles.

You can use the headers and footers to provide the user with data aggregates. The aggregates can include any of the aggregate functions such as *SUM*, *AVG*, *COUNT*, and many others.

To add an aggregate, click the icon displayed to the right within a text box from a header or footer and then select a dataset field, or drag a field from the Report Data window to the text box. If the field is numerical, the Report Designer will automatically use the *SUM* function to calculate the value. You can change the value with any other aggregate function. If the field is not numerical, the Report Designer does not use an aggregate function. In such a case, it is easier to right-click the text box where you want to have the aggregate, and then select Expression on the Textbox shortcut menu. You can then edit the expression manually in the Expression dialog box.

In your reports, you can also use a special type of aggregate—called a *running aggregate*—that adds one row at a time. A running aggregate is calculated in each of the rows, not only at group levels. Running aggregates are useful in studying the accumulated performance of a field.

SSRS supports two running aggregate functions: *RowNumber* and *RunningValue*. The *RowNumber* function returns a running count of rows in the dataset. The *RunningValue* function lets you specify the aggregate function that the report should use to calculate the value. For example, you can use the *SUM* function to have a running accumulated value, or you can use the *AVG* function to have a running average value.

PRACTICE   Creating Advanced Data Regions

In this practice, you will use BIDS to create a report based on two data sources. The report will have two sections. The first section will show summarized data in matrix format from an SSAS UDM cube, including a graphical presentation with a gauge. The second data region will show detail data with running totals from a SQL Server source. You will use the report with an empty layout and the two datasets you created in the Lesson 2 practice, "Creating Report Datasets."

EXERCISE 1   Create the Matrix Data Region

In this exercise, you create the first data section of the report and then configure a matrix that uses the TMDimensional data source.

1. In BIDS, open the TK 448 Ch10 SSRS Purchasing project.

2. In the Reports folder, double-click the TargetMail.rdl report to open the Design tab in the Report Designer for this report.

3. Select Body in the Properties window, and then change the size of the body by setting the Width property to **6.5in** and the Height property to **4in**.

4. In the Toolbox window, drag a Textbox report item to the top-left corner of the report.

5. In the Properties window, change the width of the text box to **2.5in**. Change the font to Arial, size 14pt, weight SemiBold. Type **Target Mail Overview** in the text box as the report header.

6. Drag the Matrix report item onto the report body, under the report header.

7. In the Report Data window, drag fields from the TMDimensional dataset, as shown in the following table.

FIELD	AREA
Bike_Buyer	Data
Number_Cars_Owned	Rows
Gender	Columns

8. Right-click the data text box containing the Sum(Bike_Buyer) expression. From the pop-up menu, in the Tablix section, select the Insert Column submenu. On the submenu, select the Inside Group —Right option. The new column should be inside the Gender column group.

9. Drag the Gauge report item to the new details cell, to the right of the Sum(Bike_Buyer) cell. Select the Bullet Graph gauge, the last one in the Linear group. Click OK.

10. Click the gauge inside the text box to select only the gauge. A new Drop Data Fields area should appear at the top of the gauge. Drag the Bike_Buyer column to the Linear-Pointer1 box inside the Drop Data Fields gauge area.

11. Right-click the gauge, and from the pop-up menu, select the Gauge submenu and then select Pointer (LinearPointer1) Properties.

12. In the Linear Pointer Properties dialog box, click the Pointer Fill tab. Change the secondary color to Red. In the left pane of the Linear Pointer Properties window, click the Pointer Border tab. Change the Line Style option to Solid, and then click OK.

13. Right-click the gauge again, and from the pop-up menu, select the Gauge submenu, and then select Linear Scale Properties.

14. In the Linear Scale Properties dialog box, click the General tab. In the Value And Interval Options group, change the Maximum value to 2,000, and then click OK.

15. Click the matrix to select it. Click the header (the first row) handle. Press Ctrl+B to make the text bold in the row. Enlarge the first column to be 1.8 inches wide (click the column header to select it, and then use the Properties window of this column to change the Width property).

16. Preview the report. You can see the total of bike buyers across gender and the number of cars owned in numbers and graphically.

EXERCISE 2   Add a Table Data Region

In this exercise, you add a table to show detailed data from the relational source.

1. In the Toolbox window, drag the Table report item to the Design window. Position the Table report item under the matrix.

2. In the Report Data window, from the TMRelational dataset, drag the following fields to the Data area: LastName in the first column, FirstName in the second, and BikeBuyer in the third.

3. In the Row Groups area, right-click the Details group, click Add Group, and then click Parent Group.

4. In the Tablix Group dialog box, use the Gender field as the Group By Expression. Select the Add Group Header check box, and then click OK.

5. In the Row Groups area, right-click the Group1 group, click Add Group, and then click Parent Group.

6. In the Tablix Group dialog box, use the NumberCarsOwned field as the Group By Expression. Select the Add Group Header check box, and then click OK.

7. In the Tablix header area (first row), change the value of the first text box to Number Of Cars Owned and of the second text box to Gender. Make the first column 1.8 inches wide.

8. In the NumberCarsOwned header area (second row), click in the Bike Buyer column (last column), and then click the displayed icon to view a list of the fields in the dataset. Select the BikeBuyer field. You should get the Sum(BikeBuyer) expression.

9. In the Gender header area (third row), click in the Bike Buyer column (last column) to get the quick field icon. Select the BikeBuyer field. You should get the Sum(BikeBuyer) expression.

10. In the Row Groups area, right-click Group1, and then click Group Properties. In the Group Properties window, click the Visibility tab. Change the initial visibility to Hide, and then select Group2 as the toggle item.

11. In the Row Groups area, right-click Details, and then click Group Properties. In the Group Properties window, click the Visibility tab. Change the initial visibility to Hide, and then select Group1 as the toggle item.

12. Preview the report.

EXERCISE 3   Create a Running Total

In the last exercise of this practice and this chapter, you add a running total to the table.

1. Right-click the BikeBuyer column in the detail area (last row, last column).

2. From the pop-up menu, from the Tablix section, select Insert Column, and then select Right.

3. Right-click the new detail column (last row, last column), and from the pop-up menu, from the Textbox section, select Expression. Enter the following expression to get the running sum of bike buyers in the scope of the Gender group:

    ```
    =RunningValue(Fields!BikeBuyer.Value, Sum, "Group1")
    ```

4. In the Tablix header area, in the running total column (first row, last column), type **Running Total** for the header.

    Your report design should look like the one shown in Figure 10-7.

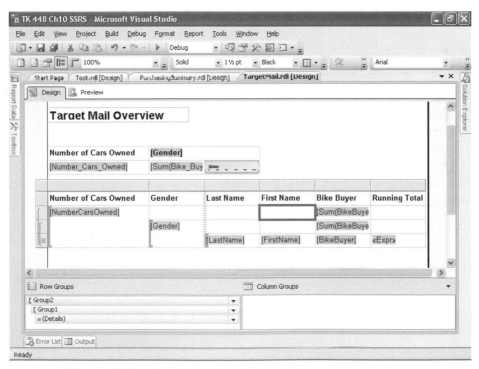

FIGURE 10-7 Target Mail Overview report

5. Preview the report.

6. Save the solution, and then close BIDS.

Case Scenario: Building Reports for the AdventureWorks Intranet

You have just successfully installed SSRS 2008. You have also created two shared data sources: one configured to retrieve data from the AdventureWorks relational database and the other to retrieve information from a sales and marketing data mart stored in an OLAP database. The data mart is populated once a week. The schemas of the relational and OLAP databases are the same as the sample databases provided by SQL Server 2008.

You are the main developer of a set of reports that will be used in the AdventureWorks portal, and you need to handle the following requirements:

1. Your end users want a report that gives them near real-time information about sales by Product Category, Product Subcategory, and Product model. The report should show only the past week's sales and should have only three columns: Name, Quantity, and Amount. Users also want the ability to drill through the report from summary information to greater detail. You do not want to use the Report Wizard. Given these requirements, what is the best way to create the report?

2. Your end users want a pivot table report that has Categories, Subcategories, and Models as columns and Year, Quarter, and Month as rows. The cell data should be filled with sales amount information. The information does not need to be real time. Given these requirements, what is the best way to create the report?

Chapter Summary

- Use the Report Server Project Wizard to create a new project and automatically start the Report Wizard to generate the first SSRS report. Then, use the Report Wizard to generate other reports. Use the Report Designer to enhance your reports and increase their functionality.

- Drag new items onto the Report Designer Design tab to add new report items, and use the Properties window to customize existing items.

- Use datasets to include more than one stream of data in your report.

- Hide columns and use the toggle properties to add interactivity to your report. Reduce the amount of information offered to the user at the beginning of the report, and let users expand and investigate areas they are interested in.

- Use groupings in Tablix data regions to summarize information by categories. You can also use multiple data regions.

CHAPTER 11

Extending and Deploying SSRS Reports

As you become more familiar with SQL Server Reporting Services (SSRS), you will probably find that you need to extend the functionality that is available in your reports. In this chapter, you will learn some techniques for using parameters to let users interact with reports and how to use these parameters to filter data. You will also learn how to enhance reports by using conditional formatting and how to extend SSRS features with custom code, either embedded in a report or made available to SSRS from a custom assembly. Last, you will see how to use SSRS reports in a client application.

Exam objectives in this chapter:

- Implement a report layout.
- Extend an SSRS solution by using code.
- Implement report parameters.
- Implement interactivity in a report.
- Implement report items.
- Embed SSRS reports in custom applications.
- Deploy an SSRS solution.

Before You Begin

To complete this chapter, you must have:

- Administrative access to an SSRS server.
- A general understanding of the Microsoft SQL Server business intelligence (BI) platform.
- A familiarity with SQL Server as a database engine.
- Experience working with SQL Server 2008 Business Intelligence Development Studio (BIDS) projects and solutions.
- Experience working in SQL Server Management Studio (SSMS).
- The SQL Server 2008 AdventureWorks2008 and AdventureWorksDW2008 databases installed.

- Microsoft Visual Studio 2008 Standard Edition or Visual Studio 2008 Professional Edition installed with the Microsoft Visual Basic .NET library. You must also have installed Visual Studio 2008 Service Pack 1 (or later) (see References).
- The practice from Lesson 1, Exercise 3, of Chapter 9, "Working with SSAS Data Mining," completed and deployed.
- The practices from Chapter 10, "Developing SSRS Reports," completed and deployed.

Lesson 1: Assigning Parameters Within Reports

Estimated lesson time: 20 minutes

SSRS uses two types of parameters: query parameters and report parameters. A *query parameter*, also called a *dataset parameter*, is a variable defined at the dataset level that affects the way SSRS queries the data source. For example, you might want to create a report that queries data only from a specific time range or that belongs to a specific user.

A *report parameter* is a variable defined at the report level that allows the personalization of a report at run time. Report parameters are often mapped to query parameters. For example, the user can select a department and use the report parameter to assign the query parameter value and filter expenses by departments. In addition, if a data source does not support query parameters, you can use report parameters to give users the ability to filter data after it has been retrieved for the report.

Filtering datasets after the data has been retrieved is also useful if you are using report snapshots. With report snapshots, SSRS caches the data and does not retrieve it from the source again to satisfy a user rendering request. If you want to present only a subset of data to the user, you need to use report parameters and filter the data in the report dataset or in any report data region.

Table 11-1 shows the differences between query and report parameters.

TABLE 11-1 Differences Between Query and Report Parameters

CONCEPT	QUERY PARAMETERS	REPORT PARAMETERS
Parameter runs on	Database server	Report server
Primary purpose of parameter	To filter data	To interact with user
Parameter properties	Name and value (can be an expression)	Name, type, value, prompt, available values, default values, and so on
Parameter is managed through	Dataset	Report Parameters dialog box

EXAM TIP

It is easy to misunderstand query and report parameters. To learn more about them, review the topic "Adding Parameters to Your Report" in SQL Server 2008 Books Online (see References).

In this lesson, you will learn how to create parameters in SSRS reports.

Creating Parameters in Report Datasets

The primary reason to create query parameters in SSRS is to filter the information that the report server queries from the data source. For example, you might want to create a report that selects information only from today or a report that uses the user ID to filter rows that the user can access.

However, query parameters are not limited to filtering information. You can use query parameters to change the way the server queries the data source. For example, you can create two queries and, based on the specific parameters in those queries, choose whether the report will show detailed information or summarized data.

Depending on the data provider, SSRS provides different ways of creating query parameters. Query parameters are frequently used to filter information through *WHERE* conditions in the *SELECT* statement. For example, if you want to filter information by day and you are using a SQL Server client, you could add the following condition to your query:

```
WHERE OrderDate=@Today
```

This condition causes the query to retrieve only rows that have a day equal to the *@Today* parameter. Other data providers might use different syntax to add variables and filter information. For example, in SQL Server Analysis Services (SSAS), the query might use a subcube clause or a *FILTER* clause to filter the information. The following code uses a subcube to filter a Multidimensional Expressions (MDX) query:

```
FROM (SELECT ( STRTOSET(@DateCalendar, CONSTRAINED) ) ON COLUMNS
FROM [Adventure Works 2008])
WHERE ( IIF(STRTOSET(@DateCalendar, CONSTRAINED).Count = 1
              , STRTOSET(@DateCalendar, CONSTRAINED)
, [Date].[Calendar].currentmember ))
```

How you add parameters depends on the query editor and mode you are using to edit the queries.

To add a parameter to a SQL Server client data provider by using the generic Query Designer, follow these steps:

1. In BIDS, open a project and then open a report.

2. In the Report Designer, open the Report Data window by using the tab displayed on the left side of BIDS (where you also access the Toolbox window). If the Report Data tab is not there, use the BIDS View menu and select Report Data to open this window.

3. Change the query syntax to add the parameters. Right-click a dataset to which you want to add parameters, and select Dataset Properties. On the Query tab in the Dataset Properties dialog box, edit the query to add the parameters. The SQL Server client uses the at symbol (@) as the first character of the name to define the parameters in the query. You can use parameters in the WHERE clause of the T-SQL query.

4. In the Dataset Properties dialog box, click the Parameters tab.

5. On the Parameters tab, assign a value to each query parameter. By default, a report parameter with an equivalent name is created for each query parameter, and query parameter values are assigned to corresponding report parameters. End users can change report parameters when they run the report, and SSRS replaces query parameters with report parameter values when executing the query. This is usually what you need; nevertheless, you could assign a constant or an expression to a value of a query parameter.

> **IMPORTANT ADDING REPORT PARAMETERS**
>
> Because query parameters are frequently mapped to report parameters, when BIDS creates the dataset parameter, it also creates a report parameter unless a report parameter with the same name exists. The simplest and recommended way to add parameters is to start with query parameters and let the Report Designer add report parameters automatically.

To add a parameter to a SQL Server client data provider by using the graphical Query Designer for T-SQL, follow these steps:

1. In the Report Designer, open the Report Data window.

2. Right-click the dataset, and then select Query.

3. If the Query Designer is not in the graphical mode (in which the Query Designer displays the tables used in the query in boxes in the top pane), click the Edit As Text button on the toolbar to enable the graphical mode. The Edit As Text button acts as a toggle and enables you to switch between the text mode and graphical mode of the Query Designer.

4. In the appropriate row, add the condition to the filter column. Use the @ symbol to define the parameter. Figure 11-1 shows an added parameter. You can also see the parameterized query in the query pane.

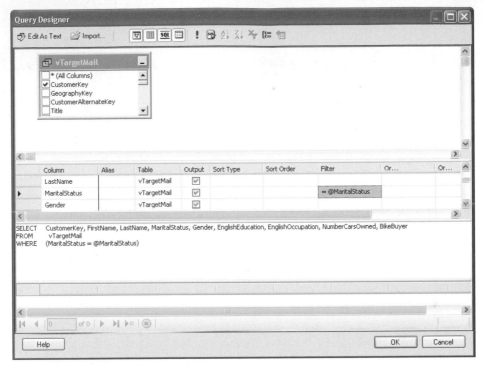

FIGURE 11-1 Adding a relational dataset parameter

To add a parameter to an SSAS client data provider by using the graphical Query Designer for MDX, follow these steps:

1. In the Report Designer, open the Report Data window.

2. Right-click the dataset, and then select Query.

3. From the Metadata pane, select the hierarchy, level, or attribute to filter and drag it onto the Filter Area pane.

4. Select the Parameter check box. Figure 11-2 shows the parameter added to a multidimensional query.

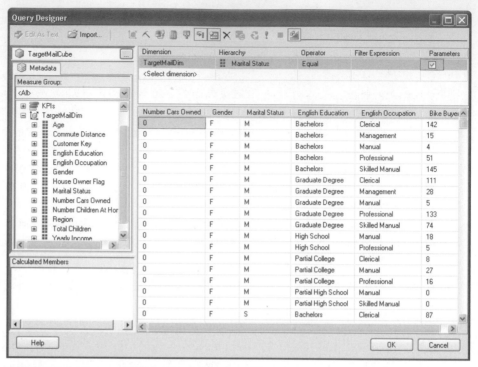

FIGURE 11-2 Adding a multidimensional dataset parameter

Exposing Parameters to Users

You usually use the second type of SSRS parameter, a report parameter, to give users ways to interact with reports. With report parameters, users can configure the values for the query parameters and change report formatting options.

To add or modify a report parameter, follow these steps:

1. In the Report Designer, click the Design tab, if necessary.

2. In the Report Data window, right-click the Parameters folder, and then select Add Parameter.

3. If you expand the Parameters folder, you can right-click an already defined report parameter and delete it or edit its properties.

Binding Datasets to Parameters

A common task in configuring parameters is assigning a list of values that users can select from. For example, if you want a report to display expense information for departments, you probably want users to select the department from a drop-down list rather than typing the department ID. To enable this functionality, you need to bind a dataset to a parameter.

To bind a dataset to the available values for a parameter, follow these steps:

1. In the Report Designer, open the Report Data window.

2. Right-click a data source, and then select Add Dataset.

3. In the Dataset Properties dialog box, on the Query tab, name the dataset, and then either enter your query manually or click Query Designer to define the query graphically.

    Be careful writing the query. These queries typically have two types of columns. The first type gathers primary key values, and the second type gathers descriptive information about the row. The first type of column is used for internal report filtering, and the second type is for user interaction. In addition, to populate the list of available values, this query can retrieve distinct values from only one column.

4. After the dataset is designed, in the Report Data window, right-click the report parameter you want to configure as a drop-down list, and then select Parameter Properties.

5. In the Report Parameter Properties dialog box, click the Available Values tab.

6. In the Choose The Available Values For This Parameter section, select Get Values From A Query.

7. Select the appropriate values for the Dataset and Value Field drop-down lists.

8. In the Label Field drop-down list, select the appropriate label, which is what users will see when they are prompted to provide values for a parameter.

9. Click OK to configure the parameter.

10. Click the Preview tab, and test that the parameter now works with a drop-down list.

Using Multivalued Parameters

You can also let a user select more than one value from a parameter's available values. Such parameters are called *multivalued parameters*. A query for a dataset must meet three specific conditions if you want to use multivalued parameters for the query:

- The data source must be SQL Server, Oracle, SSAS, SAP BI NetWeaver, or Hyperion Essbase.

- The source query cannot be a stored procedure—you cannot pass an array to a stored procedure in SSRS 2008.

- The query must use an *IN (@parameter)* clause to specify the parameter—for example:

```
SELECT * FROM dbo.vTargetMail WHERE EnglishOccupation IN (@Occupation)
```

If your parameter is used in the *IN* clause, on the General tab of the Report Parameter Properties dialog box, you can select the Allow Multiple Values check box. When a user views the report, the user can select all possible values, a single value, or two or more values of the parameter's available values.

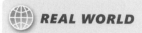
IMPORTANT CREATING AN EXPLICIT LIST OF VALUES FOR SECURITY

If your multivalued parameter is a string data type, make sure that you use an explicit list of available values, either created manually or from a dataset. If you let users enter the values manually in a text box, they could enter SQL code instead of the value and thus change the query to include malicious software—an attack appropriately known as *SQL injection*.

Working with Parameter Defaults

You can use the process described in the previous section to bind a default value to a pa-rameter, but the query that captures the default needs only the value column and not the description column. It should return only a single value.

To define a default value for a parameter, follow these steps:

1. In the Report Designer, open the Report Data window.

2. Right-click a data source, and then select Add Dataset to add the dataset you want to use for the default value.

3. In the Dataset Properties dialog box, on the General tab, name the dataset, and then either enter the query manually or click Query Designer to edit the query graphically.

   Be careful when you write the query. If the parameter you are creating the dataset for is not a multivalued parameter, this query should return only a single value.

4. After the dataset is designed, in the Report Data window, right-click the report parameter you want to configure as a drop-down list, and then select Parameter Properties.

5. In the Report Parameter Properties dialog box, click the Default Values tab.

6. In the Choose The Default Values For This Parameter section, select Get Values From A Query, or if you want to add a default value manually, select Specify Values.

7. If you selected Get Values From A Query, in the Dataset drop-down list, select the appropriate dataset. Then, in the Value Field drop-down list, select the field you want to use to provide a value for the parameter.

8. If you selected the Specify Values option, click Add to add a default value, and then type the value in the Value box. Figure 11-3 shows the default value for a parameter added manually.

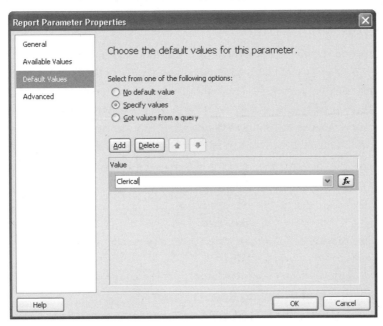

FIGURE 11-3 Defining a default value for a parameter

9. Click OK to configure the parameter.

10. Click the Preview tab, and verify that the parameter now works with a list box.

Working with Parameters in URLs

Although parameters are frequently used to provide users with interactive capabilities, you can also supply the parameter values through the URL used to run parameterized reports. This approach is useful when you need to embed reports in portal applications or line-of-business applications and you want to provide the values for users.

To assign values to the report, you use the standard Hypertext Transfer Protocol (HTTP) mechanism to provide parameters to a page. HTTP uses the equal sign (=) with the parameter name and the value pairs to map the values, and it uses the ampersand (&) for separation. For example, to set the department parameter in the URL, you would use the following query:

http://localhost/ReportServer?%2fExpense%2fExpensesForDepartment&rs:Command= Render&Department=12

The URL is broken down as follows:

- **Report server URL: *http://localhost/ReportServer?*** The report server name and protocol will reflect your specific installation. The question mark begins the parameter section.

- **Report path: *%2fLogistics%2fTracking+Numbers+by+Month&*** The path includes the folder and report name; for your reports, replace the names appropriately. Use *%2f* to replace the slash mark (/) and *%20* to replace spaces.

- **Command section: *&rs:Command=Render*** The command section configures the action of the report. The & symbol at the beginning separates the command section from the report path.

- **Parameters section: *&Department=1*** Use the & symbol to separate parameters, and use a name and value pair to configure the parameter. If you have multivalued parameters, you need to repeat the name and value pair once for each parameter.

If you want to hide parameters in the report, add **&rc:Parameters=false** to the URL. You can also hide the toolbar completely by adding **&rc:Toolbar=false**.

EXAM TIP

Remember that you can also use parameters in URLs to call a report.

<hr>

PRACTICE **Creating and Applying Report Parameters**

In this practice, you will use BIDS to create a report that uses parameters and then set the report parameters through the report URL.

EXERCISE 1 Create the Base Report

In this exercise, you create the report project and the basic interface.

1. From the BIDS main menu, select File, select New, and then select Project, which lets you create a new project in which to develop the report.

2. In the New Project window, below Project Types, select Business Intelligence Projects, and then select the Report Server Project template. You will create the report without using the wizard. Type **TK 448 Ch11 SSRS Logistics** as the name of the project and **TK 448 Ch11 SSRS** as the name of the solution, and then click OK.

3. In Solution Explorer, right-click the Shared Data Sources folder, and then choose Add New Data Source. Type **AdventureWorks2008** as the data source name.

4. Click Edit to configure the connection string.

5. In the Server Name box, type **(local)**. In the Database Name drop-down list, select AdventureWorks2008. Test the connection, and then click OK to configure the connection string.

6. Click OK to create the connection.

7. In Solution Explorer, right-click the Reports Folder, select Add, and then select New Item. In the Add New Item dialog box, select the Report template, and then type **Tracking Numbers by Month** as the report name. Click Add.

8. In the Report Data window, select the New option, and then select Dataset.

9. Type **TrackingNumbers** as the dataset name. Click New next to the Data Source box. In the Data Source Properties dialog box, name the data source **TrackingNumbers**, and then select Use Shared Data Source Reference. Select the AdventureWorks2008 shared data source, and then click OK.

10. In the Dataset Properties dialog box, on the Query tab, click Query Designer to display the Query Designer dialog box. The Query Designer lets you design the query graphically. Alternatively, you can create the query manually. Switch to the text-based design by clicking the Edit As Text button in the upper-left corner of the Query Designer. Write the following query. (You can find this and other T-SQL queries in the TK 448 Ch11 TSQL Queries.sql file in the installed practice files for this chapter. The installed practice files are located in the C:\Users*username*\Documents\Microsoft Press\MCTS Training Kit 70-448\Source\Ch 11\ folder.)

```
SELECT
     YEAR(sh.ShipDate) AS Year
    ,DATEPART(Month, sh.ShipDate) AS MonthNumber
    ,DATENAME(Month, sh.ShipDate) AS Month
    ,sm.Name
    ,sod.CarrierTrackingNumber
    ,SUM(sod.OrderQty) AS Quantity
    ,SUM(sod.LineTotal) AS Amount
FROM  Sales.SalesOrderDetail AS sod
      INNER JOIN Sales.SalesOrderHeader AS sh
       ON sod.SalesOrderID = sh.SalesOrderID
      INNER JOIN Purchasing.ShipMethod AS sm
       ON sh.ShipMethodID = sm.ShipMethodID
GROUP BY sm.Name
        ,YEAR(sh.ShipDate)
        ,DATEPART(Month, sh.ShipDate)
        ,DATENAME(Month, sh.ShipDate)
        ,sm.Name
        ,sod.CarrierTrackingNumber
ORDER BY Year, MonthNumber, sm.Name, sod.CarrierTrackingNumber;
```

This query lists all the carrier tracking numbers with the total sales quantities and sales amounts. Click OK to close the Query Designer dialog box, and then click OK again to close the Dataset Properties dialog box.

11. To design the report interface, click the Design tab.

12. From the Report Items window, drag a Table report item onto the report layout. In the Properties window, type **tblTrackingNumbers** as the table name. (You can configure the Properties window to sort all properties alphabetically by clicking Alphabetical on the Properties window toolbar.)

13. From the Report Data window, drag the CarrierTrackingNumber, Quantity, and Amount columns onto the detail row.

14. Select the tblTrackingNumbers table.

15. In the Row Groups section, right-click the Details group, select Add Group, and then select Parent Group. In the Group By drop-down list, select the Name column. Select the Add Group Header check box, and then click OK.

16. In the group header in the table, replace the default group header Group1 with **Carrier Name** and then click OK.

17. Click the Preview tab, and notice that the report has more than 80 pages. Note that the actual number of pages you get might differ, because you might have different defaults for page size and other settings.

EXERCISE 2   Create the Query Parameters

In this exercise, you create two query parameters and assign them fixed values. You are going to use parameters in the WHERE clause of the source query to limit the number of rows returned.

1. Click the Design tab. If necessary, open the Report Data window.

2. Add a WHERE condition to filter the information by year and month. (Right-click the dataset and choose Query.) After the query parameters are added, BIDS will automatically create report parameters for Years and Months. The statement after the change should look like this (note the query parameters in the WHERE clause):

```
SELECT
    YEAR(sh.ShipDate) AS Year
    ,DATEPART(Month, sh.ShipDate) AS MonthNumber
    ,DATENAME(Month, sh.ShipDate) AS Month
    ,sm.Name
    ,sod.CarrierTrackingNumber
    ,SUM(sod.OrderQty) AS Quantity
    ,SUM(sod.LineTotal) AS Amount
```

```
FROM   Sales.SalesOrderDetail AS sod
       INNER JOIN Sales.SalesOrderHeader AS sh
        ON sod.SalesOrderID = sh.SalesOrderID
       INNER JOIN Purchasing.ShipMethod AS sm
        ON sh.ShipMethodID = sm.ShipMethodID
WHERE YEAR(sh.ShipDate) = @Year
       AND MONTH(sh.ShipDate) = @Month
GROUP BY sm.Name
          ,YEAR(sh.ShipDate)
          ,DATEPART(Month, sh.ShipDate)
          ,DATENAME(Month, sh.ShipDate)
          ,sm.Name
          ,sod.CarrierTrackingNumber
ORDER BY Year, MonthNumber, sm.Name, sod.CarrierTrackingNumber;
```

3. Click OK to close the Query Designer.

4. Click the Preview tab. Type **2004** in the Year box and **1** in the Month box. Click View Report to preview the report. Notice that the report is now only three pages long. Again, note that the actual number of pages you get might differ, because you might have different defaults for page size and other settings.

EXERCISE 3   Add Datasets and Change the Parameters

In this exercise, you create two datasets to fill the report parameters and to let users select the year and month for their reports.

1. If necessary, open the Report Data window. Verify that you are working in the Design tab of the Report Designer.

2. Right-click the TrackingNumbers data source, and then select Add Dataset.

3. Type **Years** as the dataset name.

4. In the Query box, enter the following query, which selects the list of orders by year:

```
SELECT DISTINCT YEAR(sh.ShipDate) AS Year
FROM Sales.SalesOrderHeader AS sh
ORDER BY YEAR(sh.ShipDate);
```

5. Click OK to close the Dataset Properties dialog box.

6. In the Report Data window, expand the Parameters folder. You will use the Years dataset to populate the Year parameter.

7. Right-click the Year parameter, select Parameter Properties, and then click the Available Values tab. Select Get Values From A Query. In the Dataset drop-down list, select the Years dataset; in the Value Field drop-down list, select the Year field; and in the Label Field drop-down list, also select the Year field.

8. Click OK to configure the parameter.

9. You need another dataset that you will use to populate the available values for the Month parameter. In the Report Data window, right-click the TrackingNumbers data source, and then select Add Dataset.

10. Type **Months** as the dataset name.

11. In the Query box, enter the following query, which selects the list of months for the selected year:

```
SELECT DISTINCT MONTH(sh.ShipDate) AS MonthNumber
       ,DATENAME(Month, sh.ShipDate) AS MonthName
FROM Sales.SalesOrderHeader AS sh
WHERE YEAR(sh.ShipDate)=@Year
ORDER BY MONTH(sh.ShipDate);
```

Notice that the query refers to the *@Year* parameter. You are creating cascading parameters: the user will first have to select the year and then the month of that year to generate a report. Click OK.

12. In the Report Data window, expand the Parameters folder. You will use the preceding query to populate the available values for the Month parameter.

13. Right-click the Month parameter, select Parameter Properties, and then on the Available Values tab, select Get Values From A Query. In the Dataset drop-down list, select Months; in the Value drop-down list, select the MonthNumber field; and in the Label Field drop-down list, select the MonthName field.

14. Click OK to accept the parameter configuration.

15. Click the Preview tab, select different years and months as a test, and then click View Report to preview the resulting reports. Note that you must first select a year to be able to select a month.

✔ Quick Check

1. What is the main purpose of a report parameter?

2. What is the main purpose of a query parameter?

3. You want your users to select a parameter from a list of values in a list box. How should you configure the parameter?

Quick Check Answers

1. The main purpose of a report parameter is to add interactivity to your reports, letting users change the report behavior based on options they select.

2. The main purpose of a query parameter is to filter data in the data source.

3. You should create a data source that contains the possible values and then bind the data source to the parameter.

Lesson 2: Using Expressions to Perform Advanced Report Item Formatting

Estimated lesson time: 30 minutes

A critical part of any report implementation is the use of expressions to extend report functionality and to create reports that dynamically change object properties based on embedded functions or proprietary code. This lesson covers SSRS expressions, some of the functions they provide, and how to extend SSRS code with your proprietary code. You will also see how to use your code inside a report and how to create and deploy a custom assembly to extend SSRS functionality.

Extending Report Properties by Using Expressions

In Chapter 10, you learned how to personalize a report by using item properties to configure the report interface. Often, you know at design time the values you want to assign, so you can select the object you want to configure and then directly assign a value to the property. However, sometimes you want to set the value at run time rather than configuring it at design time. For example, when you use the table or matrix report items, dragging fields onto the items automatically creates a simple expression to reference the dataset field. But the value of that expression is not known at design time; it is resolved at run time. You can extend this same behavior to any report item property.

You can use expressions to calculate values for parameters, queries, filters, report item properties, group and sort definitions, text box properties, bookmarks, document maps, dynamic page header and footer content, images, and dynamic data source definitions. You can use this feature, for example, to dynamically change the color or format of text boxes based on the values you choose. Or you can use the functions included in SSRS to compute new values based on string, numeric, or data functions.

You write expressions in Visual Basic. You start an expression with an equal sign (=) and then use built-in collections, including dataset fields and parameters, constants, functions, and operators. Simple expressions that reference a single dataset field, parameter, or built-in field are created automatically by the Report Designer when you drag an item such as a dataset field to a text box. You can also enter expressions directly in a text box, including text boxes that are actually cells of a data region.

In a complex expression, you can reference multiple dataset fields, parameters, operators, constants, built-in report functions, Visual Basic runtime library functions, Microsoft .NET Framework common language runtime (CLR) classes, embedded custom code functions, and functions from a custom assembly. To create or change complex expressions, you use the Expression dialog box, which you can open from the Properties window of any report item that supports expressions.

To add an expression to a report item property, follow these steps:

1. Select the Report item.

2. In the Properties window, select the property that you want to configure.

3. Open the drop-down list for the property by clicking the drop-down arrow that is displayed to the right of the property value box and then select the Expression option. For many report items, such as text boxes, you can also right-click the item in the Report Designer and then select Expression.

4. Edit the expression in the Expression dialog box, as shown in Figure 11-4.

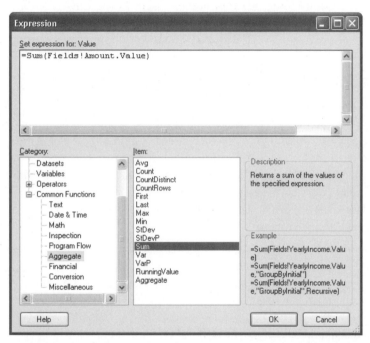

FIGURE 11-4 The Expression dialog box, showing the usage of the Sum aggregate function to summarize amount

SSRS provides a number of expression types that you can use to configure properties. The most common expressions include the following:

- **Field** A field expression can be a simple reference to a field in a dataset or a simple operation based on fields. Field expressions are not limited to the *Value* property. The following table lists some examples of field expressions.

PROPERTY	EXPRESSION
Value	*=Fields!LastName.Value*
Color	*=Fields!Color.Value*
Value	*= Fields!FirstName.Value+ " "+Fields!LastName.Value*

- **Control flow**   A control flow or a decision expression is one that, based on one or more conditions, returns a value to change the formatting or displayed value of the report. SSRS supports three control flow functions: *IIF*, *Switch*, and *Choose*. The following table lists some examples of conditional formatting.

PROPERTY	EXPRESSION
Value	*=Choose(Fields!NameStyle.Value, "Mr", "Mrs", "Miss")*
Color	*=IIF(Fields!Amount.Value < 0, "Red", "Black")*
BackColor	*=Switch(Fields!Amount.Value< 0.90*Fields!Goal.Value, "Red", Fields!Amount.Value<Fields!Goal.Value, "Yellow"* *, Fields!Amount.Value>=Fields!Goal.Value, "Green")*

- **Built-in function**   Built-in function expressions use built-in report functions to configure the property. In addition to the control flow functions, SSRS includes *Text*, *Date & Time*, *Math*, *Inspection*, *Program Flow*, *Aggregate*, *Financial*, *Conversion*, and *Miscellaneous* functions to help you create expressions. The following table lists some examples of built-in-functions.

PROPERTY	EXPRESSION
Value	*=Sum(Fields!Quantity.Value)*
Value	*=(Rate(Fields!TotPmts.Value, - Fields!Payment.Value, Fields!PVal.Value) * 12) * 100*

In addition to these expressions, you can use the .NET Framework and reference proprietary embedded functions to extend the functionality of your reports.

Using the *<Code>* Element in a Report

In addition to using the standard functions provided with SSRS, you might want to create your own embedded functions. The main advantages of using embedded code are extensibility and reusability, because the code embedded at the report level can extend SSRS functions and be reused in any expression of the report. You write embedded code in Visual Basic. In addition to custom functions, you can also add custom constants and variables to your report.

To add a *<code>* element at the report level, follow these steps:

1. In the Report Designer, click the Design tab.

2. From the Report menu, select Report Properties to open the Report Properties dialog box.

3. Click the Code tab.

4. Write the function by using Visual Basic code. For example, you can define a custom color version of your report by using the following code:

```
Function GetStockColor(ByVal Stock AS Short, ByVal Level AS Short) As String
        Dim returnValue As String
        returnValue = ""
        Select Case (100*Stock)/Level
            Case Is < 80
                returnValue = "Red"
            Case Is < 100
                returnValue = "Yellow"
            Case Is >= 100
                returnValue = "Green"
        End Select
        Return returnValue
End Function
```

This function generates a personalized color based on the stock and minimum stock level parameters.

After you create an embedded function, you can use the function in any expression. Use the *Code* prefix to reference the function. For example, you can use the following expression to assign the *BackgroundColor* property:

```
=Code.GetStockColor(Fields!Quantity.Value, Fields!ReorderPoint.Value)
```

Extending SSRS with Custom Assemblies

Instead of adding custom code to a report directly, you can create a custom assembly and reference it from multiple reports. Thus, custom assemblies provide even more reusability than embedded code. In addition, when you write custom assemblies, you are not limited to Visual Basic; you can use other .NET languages, such as Visual C#.

Before you can start using code from a custom assembly in your report, you have to deploy the assembly. To deploy a custom assembly, copy the assembly file to the application folders of your SSRS server and the Report Designer. You can also install your custom assembly in the global assembly cache (GAC).

Custom assemblies are granted Execution permission by default; this allows code execution in the scope of the report itself. If your code needs resources outside that scope—for example, if the code reads a file from the file system or a value from the registry—you must grant the assembly additional privileges. To grant these additional permissions, you need to edit the rssrvpolicy.config configuration file for the report server and the rspreviewpolicy.config configuration file for the Report Designer.

Here are the general steps for deploying a custom assembly in SSRS:

1. Copy your custom assembly to the report server bin folder and the Report Designer folder. The default location of the bin folder for the report server is C:\Program Files\ Microsoft SQL Server\MSRS10.MSSQLSERVER\Reporting Services\ReportServer\bin\. The default location of the Report Designer folder is C:\Program Files\Microsoft Visual Studio 9.0\Common7\IDE\PrivateAssemblies\.

2. If you need to add additional privileges beyond the default Execution permission, you need to change the two configuration files mentioned earlier. The default location of rssrvpolicy.config is C:\Program Files\Microsoft SQL Server\MSRS10.MSSQLSERVER\ Reporting Services\ReportServer\. The default location of rspreviewpolicy.config is C:\Program Files\Microsoft Visual Studio 9.0\Common7\IDE\PrivateAssemblies\.

3. Add a code group for your custom assembly. Custom assemblies are controlled through .NET code access security. For information about custom assemblies and code access security, see the topics "Using Custom Assemblies with Reports" and "Code Access Security in Reporting Services" in SQL Server 2008 Books Online (see References).

Sometimes you have to update an assembly that is already referenced by reports. If the assembly already exists in the deployment folders of the report server and the Report Designer and you increment the version number of the assembly, the reports that reference that assembly will no longer work properly. You need to update the version of the assembly referenced in the CodeModules element of the report definition and then republish the reports.

If you did not change any code elements already referenced in the published reports—say, you simply added a new function to your assembly and left the existing code unchanged— consider using the same version number for the updated assembly. If your published reports do not need to use the new functions from the updated assembly, consider deploying your custom assembly to the GAC. Because the GAC maintains multiple versions of an assembly, your currently published reports can reference the first version of your assembly, and your new reports can reference the updated version.

Before you start using code from your custom assembly, you must also add a reference to the assembly in your report. In addition, if you use the assembly in embedded custom code and this code references .NET Framework classes that are not in System.Math or System.Convert namespaces, you must also provide references to .NET Framework assemblies so that the Report Processor can resolve the names. To add a reference to an assembly in a report, follow these steps:

1. In the Report Designer, click the Design tab.

2. From the Report menu, select Report Properties.

3. Click the References tab.

4. In the Add Or Remove Assemblies section, click Add, and then click the ellipsis (...) button to browse to the assembly. Select the assembly, and then click OK.

5. In the Add Or Remove Classes section, click Add, type the name of the class, and then provide an instance name to use in the report. If you use static members only, use only the Add Or Remove Assemblies section.

After you have created a custom assembly, deployed it, added the appropriate security policy, and added a reference, you can access the members of the classes in your assembly by using report expressions. You can access static or instance-based members of your classes.

Static members belong to the class itself, and you do not need to instantiate objects to access them. Because you do not need to instantiate objects, static class members perform much better than object members. However, you should use only static methods in your class, not static fields or properties. Because all reports are executed in the same application domains, one user's static data is available to all users concurrently running the same report, and this can create a mess in your static fields and properties. You call a static method in your expression by using the format =*Namespace.Class.Method*, as this example shows:

```
=CustomColors.CustomColor.GetStockColorStatic(Fields!Quantity.Value,
Fields!ReorderPoint.Value)
```

For calling instance-based members, you must instantiate an object of your class type. You add an instance name for a class by using the Add Or Remove Classes section of the Code tab in the Report Properties window. Provide a class name and an instance name. You can then refer to your instance-based members by using the *Code* keyword followed by the instance and member name, as in the following example:

```
=Code.GetStockColorInstance(Fields!Quantity.Value, Fields!ReorderPoint.Value)
```

Creating a Custom Assembly

To create a custom assembly, you must have a full version of Microsoft Visual Studio 2008, with Visual Basic .NET, Visual C#, or other .NET language templates installed. You use the Class Library template. In the practice for this lesson, you can use the prepared dynamic-link library (DLL) available in the ..\Source\Ch 09\TK 448 Ch11 CustomAssembly\ folder within your Documents folder. However, if you have Visual Studio 2008 installed, you can use the following steps to manually create the custom assembly that you will use in the practice:

1. Start Visual Studio, and then create a new project. Navigate to Visual Basic, Windows, and then select the Class Library template. Give the new project the name **TK 448 Ch11 CustomAssembly**.

2. In Solution Explorer, right-click the Class1.vb module and rename it **CustomColor.vb**. In the message box that appears, click Yes to also rename all references to Class1 in the code generated by Visual Studio.

3. Add two public functions to the class: one shared (*Shared* is a Visual Basic keyword to create static members) and one instance-based. Your code should look like this:

```
Public Class CustomColor
    Public Shared Function GetStockColorStatic(ByVal Stock As Short, _
ByVal Level As Short) As String
        Dim returnValue As String
        returnValue = ""
        Select Case (100 * Stock) / Level
            Case Is < 80
                returnValue = "Maroon"
            Case Is < 100
                returnValue = "Turquoise"
            Case Is >= 100
                returnValue = "Gray"
        End Select
        Return returnValue
    End Function

    Public Function GetStockColorInstance(ByVal Stock As Short, _
ByVal Level As Short) As String
        Dim returnValue As String
        returnValue = ""
        Select Case (100 * Stock) / Level
            Case Is < 80
                returnValue = "HotPink"
            Case Is < 100
                returnValue = "Gold"
            Case Is >= 100
                returnValue = "Black"
        End Select
        Return returnValue
    End Function
End Class
```

4. In Solution Explorer, right-click the project name, and then select Properties. On the
    Application tab, which is selected by default when you open the Project Properties
    window, notice the root namespace TK_448_Ch11_CustomAssembly added automati-
    cally by Visual Studio. You need to know this namespace so that you can correctly refer
    to your functions in a report.

5. On the Build menu, select Build Solution. Save the project, and then exit Visual Studio.
    Your custom assembly is now prepared for deployment. In the practice for this lesson,
    you will deploy the custom assembly and use the functions you created.

EXAM TIP

Make sure that you understand the difference between embedded custom code and custom code in referenced assemblies.

Setting Properties and Making Them Dynamic

In this practice, you will create reports that use expressions and then use functions to dynamically change the properties of reports. You will also deploy a custom assembly and use embedded code as well as static and instance-based members of a custom assembly.

EXERCISE 1 Create the Base Report

In this exercise, you create the report project that contains the basic interface. You then use the report to personalize the interface.

1. In BIDS, open the TK 448 Ch11 SSRS Logistics project that you created in the practice in Lesson 1.

2. In Solution Explorer, right-click the Reports folder, and then select Add New Report to start the Report Wizard.

3. On the Welcome page, click Next.

4. On the Select The Data Source page, specify the AdventureWorks2008 shared data source. Click Next.

5. On the Design The Query page, in the Query String text box, enter the following query to select all the finished products and the properties required to create a Finished Products Stock Level report:

```
SELECT ProductNumber
      ,Name
      ,Color
      ,SafetyStockLevel
      ,ReorderPoint
      ,ListPrice
      ,CAST(SafetyStockLevel *
       (RAND(CHECKSUM(NEWID())%1000000000)+0.5)
       AS int) AS StockLevel
FROM Production.Product
WHERE FinishedGoodsFlag=1;
```

Notice that the query uses the SafetyStockLevel attribute and the StockLevel computed column. The StockLevel computed column calculates an imaginary stock level by using a random expression to make the stock level randomly higher or lower than the safety stock level. You will use the StockLevel and SafetyStockLevel fields as parameters to custom functions for defining colors. Click Next.

6. On the Select The Report Type page, select the Tabular report type, and then click Next.

7. On the Design The Table page, assign the ProductNumber, Name, SafetyStockLevel, and StockLevel fields to the Details box. (Below Available Fields, select a field and then click Details to add that field to the Details box.) Click Next to continue.

8. On the Choose The Table Style page, select the Slate table style, and then click Next.

9. On the Completing The Wizard page, type **Finished Products Stock Level** as the product name, and then click Finish.

10. Click the Preview tab to review the default report.

EXERCISE 2 Create a Dynamic Property in the Base Report

In this exercise, you set the background property and the color property of the text box to dynamically change colors based on an expression. You will use an *IIF* expression to change the color.

1. In the Report Designer, click the Design tab.

2. Select the Name box in the second column of the last row of the table report item.

3. In the Properties window, click the drop-down arrow to the right of the Background-Color property, and then select Expression.

4. In the Expression dialog box, in the Set Expression For Background Color box, delete the default expression (Transparent),and then enter the following expression:

```
=IIF(Fields!SafetyStockLevel.Value > Fields!StockLevel.Value, "Black", "White")
```

5. You can also use the Expression dialog box to create the expression by double-clicking the functions and fields you need in the expression and manually adding other parts of the expression. After the expression is created, click OK to close the Expression dialog box.

6. Click the Preview tab, and notice that the Name cell now changes the background color based on the expression.

   Notice also that the product names with a black background are unreadable because they use the same values for the color and background color (both are *Black*).

7. Click the Design tab, and then select the Name box, which is the second column in the last row of the table report item.

8. Select the Color Property list box, and then select Expression.

9. In the Expression dialog box, delete the *Black* expression, and then enter the following command:

```
==IIF(Fields!SafetyStockLevel.Value > Fields!StockLevel.Value, "White", "Black")
```

10. Click the Preview tab, and notice that the Products cell now changes the color to white if the background is black.

EXERCISE 3 Create a Dynamic Property with Embedded Code

In this exercise, you set the color property of the text box to dynamically change color based on a custom function in embedded code.

1. In the Report Designer, click the Design tab.

2. On the Report menu, select Report Properties, and then in the Report Properties dialog box, click the Code tab.

3. Enter the following code in the Custom Code box, and then click OK:

```
Function GetStockColor(ByVal Stock AS Short, ByVal Level AS Short) As String
        Dim returnValue As String
        returnValue = ""
        Select Case (100*Stock)/Level
            Case Is < 80
                returnValue = "Red"
            Case Is < 100
                returnValue = "Yellow"
            Case Is >= 100
                returnValue = "Green"
        End Select
        Return returnValue
End Function
```

4. Change the FontWeight property of the StockLevel box (the cell in the last row, last column of the table) to Bold. Change the Color property of the same field by using an expression. (Click the drop-down arrow to the right of the value for the Color property, and then choose Expression to open the Expression dialog box.)

5. In the Expression dialog box, delete the *Black* expression, and then enter the following expression:

```
=Code.GetStockColor(Fields!StockLevel.Value, Fields!SafetyStockLevel.Value)
```

6. After you have created the expression, click OK to close the Expression dialog box.

7. Click the Preview tab, and notice that the text in the Stock Level cell now changes color to red, yellow, or green based on the ratio between the stock level and the safety stock level.

EXERCISE 4   Use Methods from a Custom Assembly

In this exercise, you deploy a custom assembly and use a static and an instance-based method from the assembly to define the Color property for the Stock Level cell.

1. Use Windows Explorer to copy the TK 448 Ch11 CustomAssembly.dll file from the course data files located in the ..\Source\Ch 11\ folder to the C:\Program Files\Microsoft SQL Server\MSRS10.MSSQLSERVER\Reporting Services\ReportServer\bin\ folder and to the C:\Program Files\Microsoft Visual Studio 9.0\Common7\IDE\PrivateAssemblies\ folder (or change the folder appropriately if you did not install SSRS on the default drive and folders).

   You can find the DLL file in the ..\Source\Ch 11\TK 448 Ch11 CustomAssembly\TK 448 Ch11 CustomAssembly\bin\Debug\ folder within your Documents folder.

2. In the Report Designer, click the Design tab.

3. On the Report menu, select Report Properties, and then in the Report Properties dialog box, click the References tab.

4. In the Add Or Remove Assemblies section, click Add.

5. Click the ellipsis (…) button next to the Assembly box to display the Add Reference dialog box. Click the Browse tab, and then navigate to the C:\Program Files\Microsoft SQL Server\MSRS10.MSSQLSERVER\Reporting Services\ReportServer\bin\ folder (or to the folder where you copied the custom assembly) and select the TK 448 Ch11 Custom-Assembly.dll file. Click OK.

6. In the Add Or Remove Classes section of the References tab in the Report Properties dialog box, click Add. In the Class Name box, type **Ch11_CustomAssembly.CustomColor**. In the Instance Name box, type **MyCustomColor**. Click OK.

7. Change the FontWeight property of the ProductNumber and SafetyStockLevel boxes to Bold.

8. Use the static color function from the custom assembly by changing the Color property expression of the ProductNumber box to the following:

```
=TK_448_Ch11_CustomAssembly.CustomColor.GetStockColorStatic_
(Fields!StockLevel.Value, Fields!SafetyStockLevel.Value)
```

9. Use the instance-based color function from the custom assembly by changing the Color property expression of the SafetyStockLevel box to the following:

```
=Code.MyCustomColor.GetStockColorInstance(Fields!StockLevel.Value,
Fields!SafetyStockLevel.Value)
```

10. Click the Preview tab, and notice that the Product Name and Safety Stock Level columns now also change colors based on the ratio between stock level and safety stock level.

11. Save the project.

✔ Quick Check

1. What is the main benefit of using embedded code in a report?

2. What programming language would you use to create embedded functions in SSRS?

3. How do you reference an embedded function in a report expression?

Quick Check Answers

1. The main benefit of using embedded code in a report is that the code you write at the report level can be reused in any expression in the report.

2. An SSRS report supports only Visual Basic .NET embedded code.

3. Use the Code prefix and the name of the function to reference an embedded function in a report expression.

Lesson 3: Deploying New Reports and Changes

Estimated lesson time: 20 minutes

SSRS provides different options for deploying (also called *publishing*) and redeploying a report. In this lesson, you will learn how to deploy a report by using the Report Designer in BIDS and how to upload a file by using Report Manager. Before digging into the techniques for deploying reports, here is a short deployment checklist and deployment tasks you should consider:

- You have several choices for how to present reports to end users. You can deploy reports to the local report server so that users can use Report Manager to view the reports. If your company has an existing portal and you want to make the published reports available on the portal, you can embed URLs in reports so that they are published on the portal. If you use Windows SharePoint Services 3.0 or Microsoft Office SharePoint Server 2007, you and other SharePoint users can use SharePoint Web parts to explore the report server and view the reports. You can also use the .NET Framework report viewer controls to display the reports in a custom Windows or Web application. You will learn more about displaying reports in applications in Lesson 4 of this chapter.

- Before you allow end users access to the reports, you should first stage the reports— that is, temporarily deploy reports in separate locations—for testing. Create separate staging folders for the reports and have developers deploy the reports into the staging folders. You can even use a testing report server. After the reports are tested and, if necessary, corrected, an administrator can move them to the final production folders.

- After your reports are published, you should restrict access to the data sources. You should require user authentication for external sources and use the *principle of least privilege* for user accounts that access database servers. The principle of least privilege means that you give users the minimal possible permission set that still enables them to do what they need to do.

- Consider using query time-outs to prevent long-running queries on production servers. Although reports are usually short because they show only aggregated data, sometimes they can retrieve a huge amount of data to generate the summary information.

- Consider configuring the execution of long-running reports on a schedule rather than executing them on demand so that you can set them to run only in off-peak hours.

- Consider saving a snapshot of a report. End users can then render reports from the snapshot rather than rendering them from online data from a production server.

- Consider creating subscriptions. You can control report parameters, delivery channels, and rendering methods for each end user separately by using data-driven subscriptions.

Configuring Report Deployment Properties in BIDS

For the author of a report, the easiest way to deploy a report is through BIDS. However, note that before a report can be published, the author needs permission for publishing. Typically, a report server administrator grants permission for publishing by adding authors to the Publisher server role.

If a developer publishes a project, all reports in the project are published. You can use multiple deployment configurations. By default, the Report Designer in BIDS provides three configurations: DebugLocal, Debug, and Release. You should use the DebugLocal configuration to preview the reports in the Preview tab of the Report Designer, the Debug configuration for deployment to test or stage folders on a test server, and the Release configuration for publishing on the final production server or folder. You can also add your own configurations.

EXAM TIP

Be careful that you do not overwrite configuration properties when you deploy a project.

Through deployment configuration, you can control several properties, as described in Table 11-2.

TABLE 11-2 Deployment Configuration Properties

PROPERTY	DESCRIPTION
OverwriteData-Sources	This property indicates whether to overwrite data sources that are already deployed using the same name in the same folder. Typically, you will not want to overwrite a data source when you deploy a report in the production environment because an administrator might have changed the data source properties to connect to a production database server rather than the server the developer used when authoring and debugging the report.
StartItem	This is a debug property specifying the report to display in the Preview window or in the Browser window when you run the project. It is useful when the project has more than one report.
TargetData-SourceFolders	If your project includes shared data sources, this property holds the name of the folder on your target report server for the shared data sources deployment. If you deploy to a report server, you have to specify the full path of the folder hierarchy starting at the root—for example, you would specify root/folder1/folder2. If you deploy to a report server running in SharePoint integrated mode, you should specify the URL of the SharePoint library—for example, you might specify *http://<servername>/<site>/Documents/MyFolder*.

PROPERTY	DESCRIPTION
TargetReport-Folder	This is the name of the folder to which all reports in your project will be published. By default, this is the name of the project. If the folder does not exist on the target server, the Report Designer creates a new one. Again, when you deploy to a report server, you have to specify the full path of the folder hierarchy starting at the root. And if you deploy to a report server running in SharePoint integrated mode, you should embed a URL to the SharePoint library in the report.
TargetServerURL	Before you can publish a report, you must specify a valid report server URL for the *TargetServerURL* property. If you publish a report to a native report server, you should use the URL of the virtual directory of the report server—*http://servername/reportserver*, for example. If you are deploying a report to a report server running in SharePoint integrated mode, use the URL of a SharePoint top-level site or a subsite, such as *http://servername/site/subsite*.

You can modify configuration properties by right-clicking the project in the Solution Explorer window and then clicking Properties. The Property Pages dialog box for your current project opens, as Figure 11-5 shows.

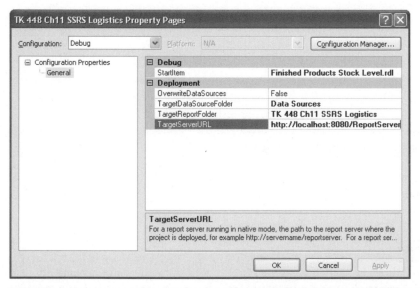

FIGURE 11-5 Project properties, showing *TargetServerURL* for the Windows XP SP2 operating system

You can select a configuration to modify from the Configuration drop-down list in the upper-left corner of the Property Pages dialog box. You can change the active configuration (in Figure 11-5, the active configuration is Debug), or you can add a new configuration by clicking the Configuration Manager button.

Deploying and Redeploying Reports in BIDS

You can deploy a project from BIDS in multiple ways. You can right-click the project name in Solution Explorer and then select Deploy. This forces the deployment immediately, but if you have errors in your reports, the deployment will not succeed. If you use other options, you can view errors, preview the report, or deploy the report.

You can access other options for running or deploying the report by clicking the Start button on the Standard toolbar. On the Debug menu, you can select Start Debugging, or you can press F5 to start the deployment. Two Configuration Manager properties—Build and Deploy—determine how BIDS deploys the project. You can configure these two properties by clicking the Configuration Manager button in the Project Properties dialog box. Figure 11-6 shows the Configuration Manager dialog box.

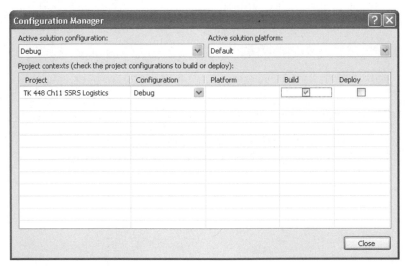

FIGURE 11-6 The Configuration Manager dialog box, showing that the project is going to be only built, and not deployed

Table 11-3 describes the Build and Deploy Configuration Manager property settings.

TABLE 11-3 Configuration Manager Build and Deploy Properties

PROPERTY SETTING	DESCRIPTION
Build—selected	BIDS builds the report project and reports errors in the Task List window.
Build—not selected	BIDS does not build the report. You can detect errors only when you preview the report or after deployment.
Deploy—selected	BIDS deploys the reports if there are no errors.
Deploy—not selected	BIDS shows the report in the local Preview window when you run the report.

Uploading a Report File in Report Manager

In production, an administrator often deploys the reports, but typically an administrator does not use BIDS for this task. Report Manager is the administrative tool you can use to deploy SSRS reports. You can also upload a shared data source and create and organize folders. You can create a new folder in Report Manager by clicking the New Folder button.

EXAM TIP

Note that in SSRS 2008, you can no longer deploy reports using SQL Server Management Studio (SSMS).

After you have the folders you need, you can upload files to the folders by clicking the Upload File button in Report Manager. Figure 11-7 shows the Upload File page in Report Manager.

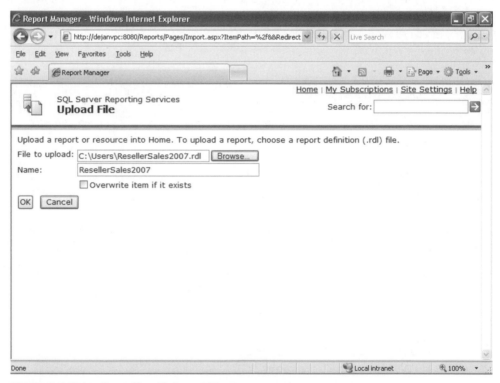

FIGURE 11-7 Uploading a file with Report Manager

Deploying Report Builder Models and Reports

With the Report Model Project template, you can create a semantic model, a description of your database. End users can then use the Report Builder 1.0 tool to create ad hoc reports based on your model. (Note that you can access Report Builder 1.0 through Report Manager;

see Chapter 10, Lesson 1, for an explanation of the different versions of Report Builder.) Deployment of a report model in BIDS is very similar to deployment of a report project. For example, you can right-click the project in a solution and then click Deploy. However, report models have only one configuration prepared by default, the Production configuration. Be sure to deploy the model in a test folder before putting it into the production folder.

> **BEST PRACTICES   STAGE REPORT MODELS**
>
> As you do with reports, you should stage report models for testing before you put them into the production folder.

It is extremely simple to deploy reports that end users create by using Report Builder 1.0. When you finish developing a report in Report Builder, on the File menu, select Save As. You can name the report in the Save As Report window and then select any folder that you have permissions to for deployment on your report server. When you save the report in Report Builder, you are publishing the report. If you want to save the report definition file in the file system so that you can edit it in BIDS or deploy it with Report Manager, you need to select the Save To File option on the Report Builder File menu.

PRACTICE   Deploying Reports

In this practice, you will deploy reports from BIDS, Report Manager, and Report Builder 1.0. You will also deploy a report model from BIDS.

EXERCISE 1   Create and Deploy a Report from BIDS

In this exercise, you create a simple report through the Report Wizard and deploy it by using BIDS.

1. In BIDS, add a new project to the TK 448 Ch11 SSRS solution by opening the solution, selecting Add on the File menu, and then selecting New Project.

2. Use the Report Server Project Wizard project template. Type **TK 448 Ch11 SSRS Deployment** as the project name, and then click OK.

3. In Solution Explorer, right-click Reports and choose Add New Report. On the Report Wizard Welcome page, click Next.

4. On the Select The Data Source page, create a new data source, and then type **AdventureWorksDW2008** as its name. Select the Make This A Shared Data Source check box, and then click Edit.

5. Specify the following options for the connection: in the Server Name list box, type **(local)**; select the Use Windows Integrated Authentication option; and then select the AdventureWorksDW2008 database, as Figure 11-8 shows. Click OK, and then click Next.

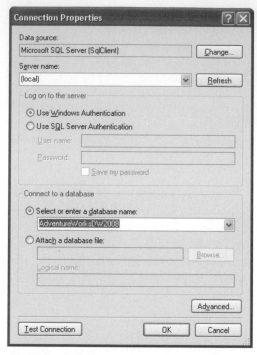

FIGURE 11-8 Configuring connection properties

6. On the Design The Query page, enter the following query, and then click Next:

```
SELECT FirstName + ' ' + LastName AS CustomerName
       ,NumberCarsOwned
       ,YearlyIncome
FROM dbo.DimCustomer;
```

7. On the Select The Report Type page, use the default type (Tabular), and click Next.

8. On the Design The Table page, select the following options for the report by selecting a column in the Available Fields pane and then clicking the appropriate button: Tabular report type, CustomerName and YearlyIncome columns in the table detail rows, and the NumberCarsOwned column in the group table rows.

9. On the Choose The Table Layout page, use Stepped table layout, and be sure to select the Include Subtotals and Enable Drilldown check boxes.

10. On the Choose The Table Style page, select the Slate table style.

11. On the Choose The Deployment Location page, correct the default report server URL to include the port your report server uses (for example, 8080), as Figure 11-9 shows.

12. On the Completing The Wizard page, type **Customer Income in Number of Cars Owned Groups** as the report name, and then click Finish.

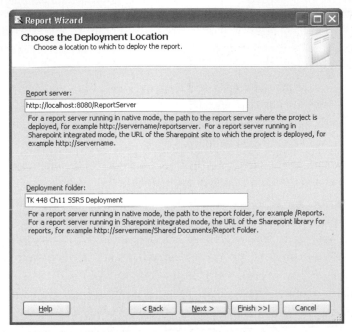

FIGURE 11-9 The Report Wizard Choose The Deployment Location page

13. Review the report layout in the Report Designer, and then preview it in the Preview tab.

14. Right-click the project, and then select Properties. Review the default configuration, including the properties of the configuration, and then close the *ProjectName* Property Pages dialog box.

15. Right-click the project, and then select Deploy. If there are any errors, correct them, and then repeat the process until the deployment is successful. Do not close BIDS.

16. Check the Deployment folder, and view the report in Report Manager. Check to see where the shared data source is deployed.

EXERCISE 2   Upload a Report with Report Manager

Now you can enhance the report you just created and redeploy it by using Report Manager.

1. In BIDS, in the Report Designer, click the Design tab.

2. Expand the third column (Yearly Income). The column must be wide enough to accept aggregated values in a single row.

3. Change the aggregate function in the grouping row of the Yearly Income column from the default Sum to Avg. To do this, click in the second row of the third column and simply overwrite the aggregate function, or select the cell, right-click it, and then click the Expression option in the Textbox group. You will test whether there is any dependency between customers' yearly incomes and the number of cars they own.

4. Change the Format property of the detail and group rows of the Yearly Income column to currency with two decimal places (C2). Simply click the appropriate cell (second-row and third-row cells of the third column), and in the Properties window, type **C2** for the Format property.

5. Preview the report by navigating to the Report Designer Preview tab, and refine the report if necessary. Save the report. Do not exit BIDS.

6. Open Internet Explorer, and then navigate to *http://localhost:8080/Reports*. Wait a couple of seconds while Report Manager loads.

7. On the home page, click the TK 448 Ch11 SSRS Deployment folder. (There should be an exclamation point and the word *New* in green beside the folder name.)

8. Click the Upload File button. In the Upload File dialog box, click the Browse button, and then navigate to your report folder. Select the Customer Income In Number Of Cars Owned Groups.rdl report. Be sure to select the Overwrite Item If Exists check box because you need to overwrite the report you deployed in the preceding exercise. Click OK.

9. In Report Manager, view the modified report. Review the enhancements you made. Check the dependency between number of cars owned and yearly income.

EXERCISE 3   Deploy a Report Model

In this exercise, you create a simple report model and deploy it.

1. In BIDS, on the File menu, select Add, select New Project, and then select the Report Model Project template. Type **TK 448 Ch11 SSRS Model** as the project name.

2. To add a data source, in the Solution Explorer window, right-click the Data Sources folder, and then click Add New Data Source. Create a connection to the (local) server and the AdventureWorksDW2008 database, using Windows Authentication. Change the name of the data source to **AdventureWorksDW2008**.

3. Right-click the Data Source Views folder, and then select Add New Data Source View. On the Select A Data Source page, select the AdventureWorksDW2008 data source you just created. On the Select Tables And Views page, select the DimProduct, DimProduct-Subcategory, and DimProductCategory tables. Type **AdventureWorksDW2008** as the name of the data source view (DSV), and then click Finish.

4. Right-click the Report Models folder, and then click Add New Report Model. On the Report Model Wizard Welcome page, click Next.

5. On the Select The Data Source View page, select the AdventureWorksDW2008 DSV you just created, and then click Next.

6. On the Select Report Model Generation Rules page, review the rules. Leave the default selection of the rules as is, and then click Next.

7. On the Collect Model Statistics page, click Next.

8. On the Completing The Wizard page, type **AdventureWorksDW2008** as the model name, and then click Run. When the wizard completes, click Finish, and then click OK. Click Yes in the message window that appears.

9. Right-click the TK 448 Ch11 SSRS Model project, and then click Properties to verify the deployment properties. Be sure to check the TargetServerURL property, and correct it if needed. Notice that the active (the only) configuration is the Production configuration.

10. Right-click the project name, and then click Deploy to deploy the report model. Verify in SSMS that the model appears in the Models folder.

EXERCISE 4 Deploy a Report Authored by Using Report Builder 1.0

For the final exercise in this practice, you create an ad hoc report by using Report Builder and then deploy the report.

1. In Report Manager, on the Home page, click the Report Builder button. When Report Builder opens, select the AdventureWorksDW2008 model on the right. Select Tabular format, and then click OK.

2. To create your report, in the Solution Explorer window, first select the Dim Product entity. Drag the English Product Name column onto the table on the design surface.

3. In the Entities pane, select the Product Subcategory entity. Drag the English Product Subcategory Name column onto the table to the right of the English Product Name column.

4. In the Entities pane, select the Product Category entity. Drag the English Product Category Name column onto the table to the right of the English Product Subcategory Name column. Your report is finished. In the Design Report window, it should look like the report shown in Figure 11-10. Click Run Report to preview it.

5. To deploy the report, on the File menu, select Save As to open the Save As Report window. In the Look In drop-down list, select the http://localhost:8080/Report Server/ TK 448 Ch11 SSRS Deployment folder. Type **Products Categories** as the report name, and then click Save.

6. On the File menu, select the Save To File option to save the report in an .rdl file that you can open later with the Report Designer. Select your working folder, and then name the file **Product Categories**.

7. Verify in Report Manager that the report was saved successfully, and then browse the report.

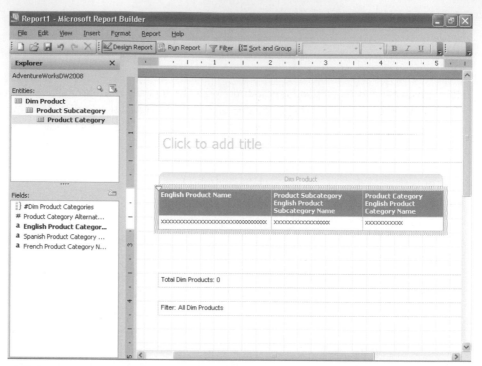

FIGURE 11-10 Designing a report in Report Builder

Quick Check

1. Which of the following are valid options for deploying a report? (Choose all that apply.)

   a. With BIDS

   b. With the Computer Management console

   c. With the .NET *START* command

   d. With SSMS

   e. With Report Manager

2. Why should you not overwrite a shared data source in production?

3. Can you edit a report that an end user created by using Report Builder in BIDS?

Quick Check Answers

1. The correct answers are a and e, BIDS and Report Manager.

2. You should not overwrite a production-shared data source because the administrator has probably already changed some connection string properties.

3. Yes, if an end user created a report by using Report Builder in BIDS and saved the report definition file, you can open the file in BIDS and edit it.

Lesson 4: Using Reports in Your Code

Estimated lesson time: 25 minutes

SSRS exposes all of its objects and methods through the Report Server Web service. You can use this service to work with SSRS programmatically. In addition, Visual Studio 2008 includes two report viewer controls: one for rich Windows applications and one for Web applications. You can use these controls to include server reports in your applications and to render reports locally on the client side.

Using the SSRS Web Service

You can access the full functionality of SSRS through the Report Server Web service. The SSRS Web service exposes dozens of collections, objects, and methods that you can use to manage folders, reports, and other resources in the report server database. You will learn about some of them through an example in this lesson. For more information about the SSRS Web service, see the "Report Server Web Service" topic in SQL Server 2008 Books Online (see References).

The SSRS Web service provides two kinds of endpoints—one for report execution and one for report management—with methods that expose the functionality of SSRS. So you can create your own tools and applications for any part of the report life cycle.

There are two different management endpoints: ReportService2005 and ReportService2006. You can use the ReportService2005 endpoint to manage objects if SSRS is configured in native mode. If your report server is configured in SharePoint integrated mode, use the ReportService2006 endpoint. In addition, for backward compatibility, SSRS 2008 also still includes the Web service that came with SSRS 2000, named ReportService.

To use the objects and methods exposed through a Web service, you need to add a service or a Web reference in your project. Using a Web Services Description Language (WSDL) file, the service must describe the members it is exposing. You can access the management endpoint WSDL of a report server configured for native mode by using the following URL:

```
http://<Server Name>:port/ReportServer/ReportService2005.asmx?wsdl
```

There is only one execution endpoint, ReportExecution2005. You can use it to customize report processing and rendering in both native and SharePoint integrated modes. You can access the WSDL file for the execution endpoint of a report server configured for native mode by using the following URL:

```
http://<Server Name>/ReportServer/ReportExecution2005.asmx?wsdl
```

Using the Windows Forms Report Viewer Control and the Web Forms Report Viewer Control

Visual Studio 2008 also provides two MicrosoftReportViewer controls that you can use to integrate report viewing into your applications. One version is for Windows Forms–based applications, and the other version is for Web Forms applications. Both controls provide similar functionality. In remote mode, you can use them to process reports on a report server, and in local mode, you can use them to process reports copied to a computer without a report server.

> **IMPORTANT** **RENDERING LIMITATIONS IN LOCAL MODE**
>
> The MicrosoftReportViewer controls that come with Visual Studio 2008 RTM and Service Pack 1 (SP1) cannot render SSRS 2008 reports in local mode. This means that Report Definition Language (RDL) reports created with the Visual Studio 2008 BI tools (that is, BIDS 2008) can be processed by SSRS 2008 servers but cannot be imported (and converted) for use in Visual Studio 2008 MicrosoftReportViewer projects (even after SP1). This limitation is expected to be corrected in a future release of Visual Studio.

If you use remote processing mode, you can use the full functionality of your report server, including all rendering and data extensions. You can use the full power of multiple report servers in a scale-out deployment or multiple processors of a report server in a scale-up deployment. In local processing mode, you get only a subset of the functionality. For example, the control does not process data; data processing is handled by the hosting application. And only PDF, Excel, and Image rendering extensions are available in local mode processing.

Using the SSRS Web Service and the Visual Studio 2008 Report Viewer in an Application

If you want to create an application that uses the SSRS Web service and the Visual Studio 2008 report viewer controls, you must have a full version of Visual Studio 2008, with Visual Basic, Visual C#, or other .NET language templates installed. For the short practice in this lesson, you will use a prepared application that you can find on the companion CD. However, if you have Visual Studio 2008 installed, you can use the following procedure to manually create the custom application that you will use in the practice:

1. Start Visual Studio, and then create a new project. Navigate to Visual Basic, Windows, and then select the Windows Forms Application template. Name the project **TK 448 Ch11 ReportViewer Win**.

2. In Solution Explorer, right-click the Form1.vb module, and rename it **Reports.vb**. In the message box that appears, click Yes to also rename all references to Form1 in the code generated by Visual Studio.

3. Modify the following properties of the Reports form, changing Text to Reports, Width to 800, and Height to 600.

4. In Solution Explorer, click the Show All Files button to show all the project's files.

5. Right-click the References folder, and then click Add Reference. In the Add Reference window, use the .NET tab to select the Microsoft.ReportViewer.WinForms library, and then click OK.

6. Right-click the References folder, and then click Add Service Reference. In the Add Service Reference window, click the Advanced button. In the Service Reference Settings

window, click the Add Web Reference button. In the Add Web Reference window, enter the following URL to the WSDL of the ReportService2005 endpoint:

```
http://localhost:8080/ReportServer/ReportService2005.asmx?wsdl
```

7. Click Go, and then wait until the Web service description is retrieved. In the Web Reference Name box, type **MyReportServer**, and then click the Add Reference button.

8. Double-click the Reports form to open the code window for this form so that you can create the load method for the form. Before the first row of code, add a row to import the MicrosoftReportViewer Windows control namespace, as follows:

```
Imports Microsoft.Reporting.WinForms
```

9. After the class definition but before the load method, add a constant that points to the SSRS report folder that contains the reports you created in this chapter, and then define a menu item. You will add menu items dynamically, one for each report in the folder. The code should look like this:

```
Const ReportFolder As String = "/TK 448 Ch11 SSRS Logistics"
Dim WithEvents mnuItem As ToolStripMenuItem
```

10. Switch to the Reports.vb [Design] window. From the toolbox, drag the MenuStrip control to the form. Type **Reports** in the Type Here box on the menu. Change the Name property of the menu to mnuReports.

11. From the toolbox, drag the MicrosoftReportViewer control to the form. In the Report-Viewer Tasks window that opens automatically (you can always open it later by clicking the small black arrow in the upper-right corner of the ReportViewer control), use the Choose Report drop-down list to select the <Server Report> option. Change the Report Server URL to point to your report server, as follows:

```
http://localhost:8080/reportserver
```

12. Select the Dock In Parent Container option.

13. Switch back to the code window. Clear any code that Visual Studio added to the form load method. You will manually add the code to the form load method. Create a Web service proxy and use default credentials, as follows:

```
Dim rs As New MyReportServer.ReportingService2005()
rs.Credentials = System.Net.CredentialCache.DefaultCredentials
```

14. To get a collection of all objects in the report folder, use the SSRS Web service CatalogItem type and the ListChildren method along with your constant that points to the SSRS report folder with reports from this chapter's practices, as follows:

```
Dim catalogItems As MyReportServer.CatalogItem()
catalogItems = rs.ListChildren(ReportFolder, False)
```

15. Create a For Each loop to loop through all items in the collection of SSRS Web service catalog items. If an item is a report, add a tool strip menu item to the mnuReports

menu, using the report name as the text of the menu item. Also add a handler method for the click event on each menu item by using the address of the mnuReportItem_ Click method. (Because this click event handling method does not yet exist, it should show a squiggly blue underline in Visual Studio; do not worry about this now.) The code should look like this:

```
For Each item As MyReportServer.CatalogItem In catalogItems
    If item.Type = MyReportServer.ItemTypeEnum.Report And Not item.Hidden Then
        mnuItem = New ToolStripMenuItem(item.Name)
        AddHandler mnuItem.Click, AddressOf mnuReportItem_Click
        mnuReports.DropDownItems.Add(mnuItem)
    End If

Next
```

16. Add the last menu item to the menu. This item is for exiting the application. Add a handler for the click event for this item. Use the address of the nuReportsClose_Click event handler (which also does not yet exist). The code should look like this:

```
mnuReports.DropDownItems.Add(New ToolStripSeparator())
mnuItem = New ToolStripMenuItem("&Close")
AddHandler mnuItem.Click, AddressOf mnuReportsClose_Click
mnuReports.DropDownItems.Add(mnuItem)
```

17. Last, clear the report viewer window. This should be the last line of the form load method:

```
Me.ReportViewer1.Clear()
```

18. In the Reports class, outside the form load method, create the menu item click event handler method. Assign the selected report to the ReportPath property of the Report- Viewer control. Set the processing mode to remote, and then use the RefreshReport method of the report viewer control to display the report. The code should look like this:

```
Private Sub mnuReportItem_Click(ByVal sender As System.Object, ByVal e As System.
EventArgs)
    'Assign the selected report to the ReportPath property
    Dim mnuItem As ToolStripMenuItem = CType(sender, ToolStripMenuItem)
    ReportViewer1.ProcessingMode = ProcessingMode.Remote
    ReportViewer1.ServerReport.ReportPath = ReportFolder & "/" & mnuItem.Text
    'Refresh the ReportViewer control
    ReportViewer1.RefreshReport()
End Sub
```

19. Create the close menu item click event handler, as follows:

```
Private Sub mnuReportsClose_Click(ByVal sender As System.Object, ByVal e As
System.EventArgs)
    Me.Close()
End Sub
```

20. Save the project, and then select the Start Debugging option on the Debug menu. Your Windows Form application should start. Correct any errors.

PRACTICE **Using the Windows Application**

In this short practice, you will use either the prepared Windows application from the ..\Source\ Ch 11\ folder or the application you just created manually by following the preceding instructions.

EXERCISE Run the TK 448 Ch11 ReportViewer Win Application

In this exercise, you use a small pre-prepared Windows application. The application dynamically builds menu of deployed reports; when you choose a report from the menu, the report is displayed in the MicrosoftReportViewer control.

1. In Windows Explorer, navigate to the bin\Debug\ folder of the TK 448 Ch11 Report-Viewer Win application, located in the ..\Source\Ch 11\TK 448 Ch11 ReportViewer Win\ TK 448 Ch11 ReportViewer Win folder.

2. Double-click the TK 448 Ch11 ReportViewer Win.exe file to start the application.

3. On the Reports menu, select the Finished Products Stock Level report. The report should be displayed in the report viewer control.

4. On the Reports menu, select the Tracking Numbers By Month report. This report is not rendered automatically because you have to provide values for the parameters.

5. Select the year 2002 and the month April, and then click the View Report button to display the report.

6. On the Reports menu, select Close Item to close the application. Also close BIDS and Visual Studio, if they are still open.

> ✔ **Quick Check**
>
> 1. How can you manage reports from your application if the report server is deployed in SharePoint integrated mode?
>
> 2. In which processing mode of a report viewer control can you use the full functionality of your report server?
>
> **Quick Check Answers**
>
> 1. Use the ReportService2006 endpoint of the SSRS Web service if your report server is deployed in SharePoint integrated mode.
>
> 2. You should use the remote processing mode to use the full functionality of your report server.

Case Scenario: Creating a Reporting Services Infrastructure

You just successfully installed SSRS 2008. You also created two shared data sources: one configured to retrieve data from the AdventureWorks relational database and the other configured to retrieve information from a marketing/sales data mart stored in an online analytical processing (OLAP) database. The data mart is populated once a week. The schemas of the relational and OLAP databases are the same as the sample databases provided by SQL Server 2008. You will be the main developer of a set of reports that will be used in the Adventure-Works portal, and you need to address the following requirements:

1. End users want the ability to create their own reports. The users are knowledge workers who have Excel expertise but no database experience. What is the best way to create the reports, without giving end users direct access to the database? How will you build the infrastructure?

2. In the previous version of the reports, users had a set of reports that were identical to each other except that each report grouped information at different levels of the organization. Users still want the flexibility to look at the information grouped in different ways, but you want to build a single report rather than multiple reports. Given these requirements, what is the best way to create the new report?

Chapter Summary

- Use report models to help users create their own reports without having to learn the complexity of the database schema or the SQL language.
- Use BIDS to create and personalize relational report models.
- Use query parameters to filter information retrieved from the database, and use report parameters to interact with end users. Create new datasets to provide a list of alternative values.
- Use expressions to dynamically change report formatting.
- Enhance expressions by using custom code, either embedded in the report or from a custom assembly.
- Manage the report server from your code by using the SSRS Web service.
- Include SSRS reports in your applications by using Visual Studio report viewer controls.

CHAPTER 12

Scheduling and Securing Deployed Reports and Data Sources

SQL Server Reporting Services (SSRS) is one of the tools with which users access information that is stored in different repositories, so the information must be secure in its original source and it must also be secure in any tool that displays it. With SSRS, you can use your existing knowledge of Windows technologies and infrastructure to secure your reports. From securing the server to securing individual objects, you can identify those who can access a given element inside the server and what kind of actions they can perform on it. You can also create *linked reports*, which let you use a report as a template to satisfy multiple users' needs. For the data sources that reports use and share, you also need to know how to manage, secure, and handle user credentials for various requirements.

After reports are deployed, users can view reports interactively by using a Web browser tool (such as Report Manager). In addition, they can subscribe to a report and receive it on a defined schedule through their chosen delivery channel and in their chosen rendering format. You can also create advanced subscriptions to reports by using a table to store data about each user and his or her preferred delivery method and rendering format. This approach is called a *data-driven subscription*.

After you learn how to secure and schedule your SSRS environment, you will see how to manage the execution environment for your report, how to decrease the workload pressure on the database servers, and how to keep a historical copy of the report so that you can always look back for a past report execution.

In this chapter, you will learn about Reporting Services site management and security, report and data source security, simple and advanced data-driven subscriptions, and report history and caching.

Exam objectives in this chapter:
- Implement report data sources and datasets.
- Configure report execution and delivery.
- Configure authentication and authorization for a reporting solution.

Before You Begin

To complete this chapter, you must have:

- Knowledge of SSRS features, components, and architecture.
- Experience working with Microsoft SQL Server 2008 Business Intelligence Development Studio (BIDS) projects and solutions.
- Experience working in SQL Server Management Studio (SSMS).
- The SQL Server AdventureWorks2008 and AdventureWorksDW2008 databases installed.
- Knowledge of Windows security concepts.
- The Report Server and Report Manager installed as follows:
  - Both are installed on the same computer.
  - The computer is the localhost.
  - SSRS 2008 is the default instance.
  - The Adventure Works 2008 reports samples are deployed to the report server.

Lesson 1: Administering SSRS Item-Level Permissions and Site Security Roles

Estimated lesson time: 60 minutes

The SSRS security model is based on objects, or *securables*, and roles. Objects can be secured through the assignment of permissions or functionality (called *tasks*) to a given role. Users or groups are then assigned to the roles.

There are two types of role definitions in SSRS: item-level roles and system-level roles. *Item-level roles* are used to assign permissions on report objects, and *system-level roles* are used to assign users to site-wide functionality. This lesson covers both the item-level role and the system-level role definitions. SSRS includes default roles, both item level and system level, to which users or groups can be assigned. You can also modify the default roles or create new roles to which users are assigned. In SSRS 2008, roles are modified, deleted, and created through SSMS. The assignment of roles to users or groups happens through the Report Manager Web interface.

Understanding SSRS Item-Level Roles

In SSRS, item-level role definitions reference the set of permissions, also called tasks, related to the server's content. This content includes reports created either with Report Builder or with BIDS, subscriptions, data sources, folders, report snapshots, and so on. (Creating report subscriptions is covered in Lesson 2, "Creating Report Subscriptions and Schedules.") These roles can be customized and modified to add or remove tasks.

By default, there are five item-level roles in SSRS, as follows:

- Browser
- Content Manager
- My Reports
- Publisher
- Report Builder

These default roles are given a set of task assignments that allow or prevent users from accomplishing certain activities based on whether they are assigned to a role and whether that role is given permission on a report object. The default task list assignments can be modified, and new roles can be given a custom set of tasks.

Table 12-1 lists the tasks available for item-level roles in SSRS 2008.

TABLE 12-1 Tasks for Item-Level Roles

TASK	DESCRIPTION
Consume Reports	Reads report definitions
Create Linked Reports	Creates linked reports and publishes them to a report server folder
Manage All Subscriptions	Views, modifies, and deletes any subscription, regardless of who owns the subscription
Manage Data Sources	Creates and deletes shared data source items and modifies data source properties
Manage Folders	Creates, views, and deletes folders and views and modifies folder properties
Manage Individual Subscriptions	Creates, views, modifies, and deletes subscriptions owned by the user
Manage Models	Creates, views, and deletes models and views and modifies model properties
Manage Report History	Creates, views, and deletes report history snapshots and modifies report history properties
Manage Reports	Creates, views, and deletes reports and modifies report properties
Manage Resources	Creates, modifies, and deletes resources and views, and modifies resource properties
Set Security For Individual Items	Views and modifies security settings for reports, folders, resources, and shared data sources

TASK	DESCRIPTION
View Data Sources	Views shared data source items in the folder hierarchy and views data source properties
View Folders	Views folder items in the folder hierarchy and views folder properties
View Models	Views models in the folder hierarchy, uses models as data sources for a report, and runs queries against the model to retrieve data
View Reports	Views reports and linked reports in the folder hierarchy and views report history snapshots and report properties
View Resources	Views resources in the folder hierarchy and views resource properties

Creating a New SSRS Item-Level Role in SSMS

To create a new item-level role in SSRS, you will need to use SQL Server Management Studio (SSMS). Perform the following steps:

1. Open SSMS, and then connect to Reporting Services. (Click the Connect button in Object Explorer, and then choose Reporting Services.) In the Connect To Server dialog box, type the name of the SSRS server you will be connecting to (or type **localhost** if the service is on your computer), and then click Connect.

2. In Object Explorer, expand the Security folder, and then right-click the Roles subfolder and select New Role, as Figure 12-1 shows.

FIGURE 12-1 The Object Explorer screen when connected to Reporting Services in SSMS

3. In the New User Role dialog box, type a name and a description for the new role.

4. Select the check boxes for several task items that the role should have access to perform.

5. Click OK.

Understanding Object Permissions and Assignment to Item-Level Roles

After you have created the new role, you can use that role to assign permissions to a given user or group to access an object.

SSRS 2008 security is based on the hierarchy of the report server's contents, where the root of the hierarchy is the Home folder. Every element inside that folder is considered to be a child in the hierarchy. For instance, consider a folder named Sales Report containing a report named Total Sales. The folder is considered to be a child of the root folder, and its parent is the root folder. The Sales Report folder is then the parent of the Total Sales report.

By default, the security configuration for a child is the same as that defined for the parent level. However, you can modify this configuration so that a given child has a completely different security configuration than that of the parent. Additionally, at any time, the security configuration can be changed back to the one defined by the parent. When this happens, the customized role assignments are deleted.

SSRS does not include its own catalog of users. It takes advantage of the Windows operating system users and groups. Windows users and groups are associated with roles, and that association is valid for a given element inside the report object hierarchy within SSRS.

Even though SSRS uses groups and users through Windows Authentication, in Internet deployment scenarios, this might not always be allowed. SSRS 2008 includes a complete framework for extensibility that allows you to have a custom security extension. For example, you could choose to have Forms Authentication with ASP.NET.

Note that a role, by default, has no association with any user. The role itself is the group of tasks. The only exception to this is the Content Manager role, which is assigned to the Home folder, with the BUILTIN\Administrators group in it. This role gives members of the Administrators group complete control over the server's content because the permission is defined at the root level.

Assigning Object Permissions to Roles

To assign permissions to a given Windows user or group, you use Report Manager. Follow these steps to assign a user to a role:

1. Open Report Manager (*http://*servername*/reports*), and then navigate to the item for which you want to define security (a folder or a report, for example).

2. Click the Properties tab to display the properties for the object, as shown in Figure 12-2.

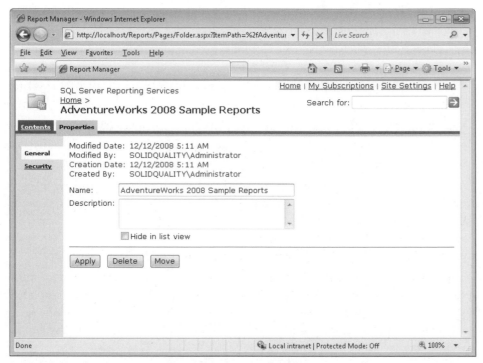

FIGURE 12-2 The Properties page for a folder in Report Manager

3. In the list of links on the left, click the Security link. Notice that, by default, there is one entry in the list of users/groups—in this case, the BUILTIN\Administrators Windows group with the Content Manager role. If you assigned more permissions to the root level, they should be visible as well.

4. Click Edit Item Security.

5. After you click Edit Item Security, a security message box appears. Click OK in the message box that appears. This message notifies you that the security for the current item is inherited from the parent folder. Clicking OK will define a different set of permissions from those that are defined for the parent folder.

6. Click New Role Assignment.

Roles can be assigned to report folders and other report objects directly without changing the security settings on other objects. This is handled in Report Manager by opening the object (such as a folder or a report) and then displaying the object's Properties tab. The Security property tab is available in the object properties if permission is granted to modify the object's security. Roles can be assigned, and either the security inheritance can be defined to inherit the properties of the parent object (such as a folder) or the security can be defined independent of other objects.

7. On the New Role Assignment page, as shown in Figure 12-3, in the Group Or User Name box, type the name of the Windows group or user to whom you want to grant permissions. Notice that in this text box, you can reference groups and users from the local computer or, if your server belongs to a domain, you can reference groups and users from Active Directory. In either case, you should qualify the group name by specifying the domain in the form *domain\group* or *domain\user*.

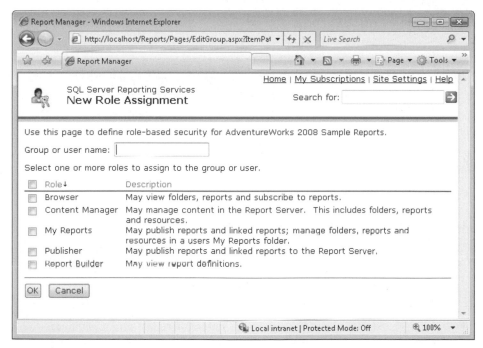

FIGURE 12-3 Windows users and groups may be assigned to SSRS roles for a report, folder, or data source.

8. Select the check boxes to the left of the roles you want to assign to the Windows entity. Remember that in SSRS, membership to roles is cumulative—if the Windows entity is assigned to multiple roles, that entity can perform all tasks associated with those roles.

9. Click OK.

Assigning Item Permissions and Site Security Access

Most of the objects in SSRS are embedded under the hierarchical namespace of the report object, which begins with the Home folder. However, some other components, even when they are securables, are scoped outside of this report object hierarchy. These types of permission sets are called system-level roles.

Understanding SSRS System-Level Roles

In SSRS, system-level role definitions reference the set of permissions, or tasks, related to the server's administrative objects and scoped outside the report object hierarchy. Because these roles are scoped outside the report object hierarchy, you manage system-level roles within SSMS, not Report Manager. The server's administrative objects include the report server itself, execution, events, jobs, shared schedules, and roles. System-level roles can be customized and modified to add or remove tasks.

By default, there are two system-level roles in SSRS, as follows:

- System Administrator
- System User

Assignment to the System Administrator role gives users the capability to manage roles and security, manage server properties, manage schedules and jobs, and execute reports. System Administrator users are allowed to view server properties and shared schedules and to execute reports. (Note that report execution task permission allows the role to generally execute reports but that the specific report objects still need item-level permissions assigned for the user or group.)

Just like the item-level roles, the creation and management of system-level roles is handled through SSMS.

Table 12-2 lists the tasks that are available for system-level roles in SSRS 2008.

TABLE 12-2 Tasks for System-Level Roles

TASK	DESCRIPTION
Execute Report Definitions	Starts execution from a report definition without publishing it to the report server
Generate Events	Provides an application with the ability to generate events within the report server namespace
Manage Jobs	Views and cancels jobs as they are running
Manage Report Server Properties	Views and modifies properties that apply to the report server and to items managed by the report server
Manage Report Server Security	Views and modifies system-wide role assignments

TASK	DESCRIPTION
Manage Roles	Creates, views, modifies, and deletes role definitions
Manage Shared Schedules	Creates, views, modifies, and deletes shared schedules used to run or refresh reports
View Report Server Properties	Views properties that apply to the report server
View Shared Schedules	Views a predefined schedule that has been made available for general use

Creating a New SSRS System-Level Role in SSMS

To create a new system-level role in Management Studio, follow these steps:

1. Open SSMS, and then connect to Reporting Services. (To do so, click the Connect button in Object Explorer, and then choose Reporting Services.) In the Connect To Server window, type the name of the SSRS server you will be connecting to (or type **localhost** if the service is on your computer), and then click Connect.

2. In Object Explorer, expand the Security folder, and then right-click the System Roles subfolder and select New System Role.

3. Type a name and a description for the new role.

4. Select the check boxes for the system task items that the role should have access to perform.

> **BEST PRACTICES** **ASSIGN MINIMUM TASK REQUIREMENTS FOR A NEW ROLE**
>
> A new system-level role requires that at least one task is assigned to the role definition.

5. Click OK.

Understanding Server Permissions and Assignment to System-Level Roles

After you create a new system-level role, you can use that role to assign permissions to a given user to access a server object. This assignment is handled through the Report Manager Web management site (*http://*servername*/reports*).

Because system-level roles are outside the report object hierarchy, they are defined once for each server. System-level roles are a complement to item-level roles. Like item-level roles, they are cumulative and are based on Windows users and groups.

Assigning Server Permissions to Roles

To assign permissions to a given Windows user or group, follow these steps:

1. In Windows Internet Explorer, open the Report Manager home page.

2. Click the Site Settings link in the upper-right corner of the window.

3. Click the Security link in the properties list on the left.

4. Click New Role Assignment.

5. On the New System Role Assignment page, in the Group Or User Name box, type the name of the Windows group or user to whom you want to grant permissions, as Figure 12-4 shows. Remember, you can reference groups and users from the local computer or a domain. Use the form *domain\group* or *domain\user* or *computer\group* or *computer\user*.

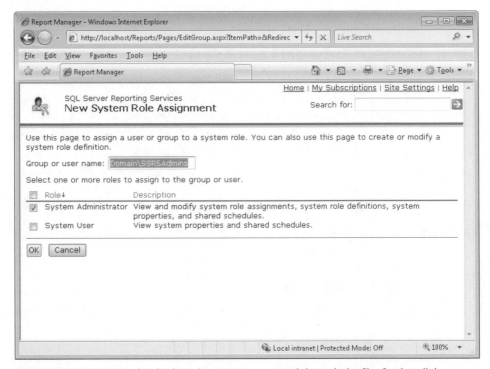

FIGURE 12-4 New system-level role assignments are created through the Site Settings link.

6. Select the check boxes to the left of the server-level roles you want to assign to the Windows entity. In SSRS, membership to roles is cumulative.

7. Click OK.

Understanding the Way My Reports Functions Within Reporting Services

In SSRS 2008, folders can be accessed by more than one user. However, because in real life there is often a need for a private space in which users can create their own reports, delete them, or modify them according to their particular needs, SSRS 2008 includes a space named My Reports. My Reports can be enabled or disabled at the server level. When My Reports is enabled, a user logging in to the SSRS Report Manager will see a My Reports folder under the Home folder.

Although each user sees a My Reports folder, that folder is not the same for every user. Internally, it is stored under the Users Folders*domain username*\ hierarchy. In this folder, the user inherits the permissions of the My Reports item-level role. This role allows the user to create and manage reports, data sources, and other resources inside this folder.

Understanding Linked Reports Within SSRS

Linked reports are entities that reference an existing report but with different configurations. For instance, suppose that in a report named Sales Representative Performance you want to see only the numbers that apply to you. You can create a linked report based on the existing Sales Representative Performance report in which you specify your name as a parameter. In this way, you have customized a report without needing to create a new report with the same structure.

Linked reports create a constant dependency on the base report. This means that the linked report has no internal .rdl file associated with it but instead takes all the report definitions from the base report. This dependency also implies that the linked report has no data source definitions of its own.

The base report can be updated, however, and the next execution of the linked report will use the new report definition. Keep in mind that some configurations, such as parameter information, must be consistent.

The linked report can also be redirected to a new report definition. This is useful for scenarios in which you want to redirect a report from a testing environment to the production environment. Additionally, a base report can be deleted without deleting the linked reports, and in that case, the linked report rendering process will fail.

Understanding the Correlation Between Linked Reports and My Reports Functionality

For users who do not have write access to public folders but who still want to have existing reports customized for their particular needs, the My Reports functionality is the solution. The My Reports item-level role includes the Create Linked Reports and Manage Reports tasks, which allow users to store linked servers inside their individual My Reports folders without having more permissions than are required in the public structures.

Managing Data Sources and Credentials

In Reporting Services, security is associated not only with the users who can access reports and data sources, but also with the credentials that are used to access the repositories the reports use to display data. In this lesson, you will learn about data source credentials and their impact on your Reporting Services management strategy.

Understanding Shared Data Sources

Shared data sources are the objects that represent the connection information to a data repository that a report will use. These data sources are stored in the Reporting Services ReportServer database.

When you are connecting to a data repository, you must define two main elements: the name of the service to which you can connect (often represented as the name of the server or the name of the database instance) and the credentials used to access that repository (in the form of a user name and password).

To modify the credentials of a shared data source, navigate to the shared data source in Report Manager, and then click the Data Sources link to display its properties. Figure 12-5 shows the Properties tab for the AdventureWorks2008 shared data source.

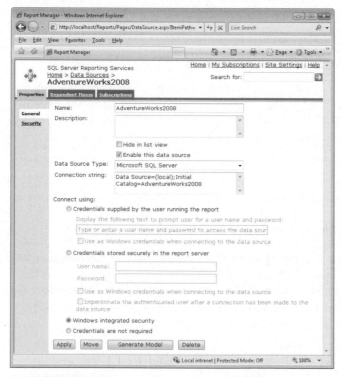

FIGURE 12-5 Shared data source connection properties

Reporting Services provides four mechanisms for specifying the credentials used to access the data repository, as follows:

- **Credentials Supplied By The User Running The Report**   Under this model, the user must manually enter a valid combination of user name and password to request the report. These credentials can belong to the internal directory of users for the database, or they can be Windows credentials. If this option is selected, each user must have a unique user name and password set to access the data repository. One of the advantages of this model is that database administrators can track the specific users who are accessing particular information.

- **Credentials Stored Securely In The Report Server**   Under this model, a single set of credentials is shared by all the users who are trying to connect to the data repository. Both the user name and the password are encrypted and stored in the Reporting Services catalog. The advantage of this model is that the end users do not have to specify any credentials to access the data repository. These credentials can belong to the internal directory of users of the database, or they can belong to Windows credentials.

- **Windows Integrated Security**   This option can be used when the credentials to access the data repository are the same as those that are used to log in to the local computer or to log in to the Active Directory domain. For instance, if you have a SQL Server Sales database running in a SQL Server instance on the same computer as the Report Server and you have the Windows users or groups mapped to SQL Server logins, you can use this option to allow Reporting Services to pass the token that the end user passed to Reporting Services to the SQL Server instance. However, if the data repository is on a different computer, you need to enable Kerberos to allow Reporting Services to pass the end user's token to a different computer. For more information about how to enable Kerberos, see the References section at the end of this book.

- **Credentials Are Not Required**   Under this model, the specified data source does not need any specific credentials.

Private report data sources have identical properties but are managed through the report properties in Report Manager.

PRACTICE   **Creating Roles in Report Manager and Managing Data Sources**

In these practice exercises, you will first create a new item-level role and will assign access to the root of the report object hierarchy. Next, you will apply system-level security to a role and then manage shared data sources deployed to a server.

EXERCISE 1   Create a New Role

In this exercise, you will create a new role for all users, and then you will assign Windows membership to the All Users item-level role in SSRS.

1. Open SSMS, and in the Connect To Server dialog box, select Reporting Services in the Server Type drop-down list.

2. In the Server Name box, type either **localhost** or the name of the server that you are administering, and then click Connect.

3. In the Object Explorer window, expand the Security folder.

4. Right-click the Roles subfolder, and then select New Role.

5. In the New User Role dialog box, type **All Users** as the name for the new role.

6. Type **Access to all the users of the development environment** as the description of the new role.

7. Select the View Reports check box, select the View Folders check box, and then click OK.

8. Open an Internet Explorer window, and then navigate to *http://localhost/reports* (or replace *localhost* with the name of the remote server that you administer). Click the Home link at the upper-right corner of the screen to verify that you are in the root Home folder.

9. Click the Properties tab. Notice that in the root folder, there is no Revert To Parent Security button. This is because the root has no parent folder.

10. Click New Role Assignment.

11. In the Group Or User Name box, type **Users** to assign this local Windows group to the role. There is no need to qualify the Users group of the local computer with the name of the local computer.

12. Select the All Users check box to assign the new role you just created to the local Users group, and then click OK.

EXERCISE 2 Create a New System-Level Role in Report Manager

In this exercise, you will create a system-level role. Then you will assign a Windows group to the role and define the Windows Users group as a member of the system-level role System All Users.

1. If necessary, open SSMS, and connect to Reporting Services.

2. In the Object Explorer window, expand the Security folder.

3. Right-click the System Roles subfolder, and then select New System Role.

4. Type **System All Users** as the name for the new role.

5. Type **Server access to all the users of the development environment** as the description of the new role.

6. Select the View Report Server Properties check box, select the View Shared Schedules check box, and then click OK.

7. If necessary, open an Internet Explorer window, and then navigate to *http://localhost/ reports* (or the remote server name that you administer).

8. In the current Internet Explorer window, click the Site Settings link at the upper-right corner of the screen.

9. Click the Security link in the list of site setting properties on the left.

10. Click the New Role Assignment button.

11. In the Group Or User Name box, type **Users**. There is no need to qualify the Users group of the local computer with the name of the local computer.

12. Select the System All Users check box, and then click OK.

EXERCISE 3   View the Properties for Data Sources

In this final exercise of this lesson, you will walk through the options and configurations available for reporting data sources.

1. If necessary, open Internet Explorer, and then navigate to *http://localhost/Reports*.

2. Click the AdventureWorks 2008 Sample Reports folder link. (This assumes that the AdventureWorks 2008 sample reports have been deployed as specified in this chapter's prerequisites.)

3. Click the Product Catalog 2008 report link, and then click the Properties tab.

4. In the list of links on the left, click the Data Sources link. Notice that a report can refer to either a shared data source or a custom data source. This report refers to the data source in the /Data Sources/AdventureWorks2008 element of the report object hierarchy. You can change the shared data source associated with a given report by clicking the Browse button and then selecting the new data source. This greatly increases your flexibility to make changes to reports even after they are deployed.

5. Click the Home link in the upper-left corner of the screen.

6. Click the Data Sources folder link.

7. Click the AdventureWorks2008 data source link. This data source uses the Windows Integrated Security option.

8. Select the Credentials Supplied By The User Running The Report option.

9. Select the Use As Windows Credentials When Connecting To The Data Source check box, and then click Apply.

10. Click the Dependent Items tab. On this tab, you can see the list of reports that depend on this shared data source.

11. Click the Product Catalog report link. Notice that the report is requesting credentials.

12. In the Log In Name box, type **Nancy**, and in the Password box, type **Pass@word1**.

13. Click View Report, and notice that Reporting Services notifies you that the logon operation failed.

14. Click the blue Change Credentials link. In the Log In Name box, type your Windows user account name, and then type your Windows password in the Password box. Click View Report. Notice that the report is generated this time.

15. Click the Home link in the upper-left corner of the screen.

16. Click the Data Sources folder link.

17. Click the AdventureWorks2008 data source link.

18. Select the Credentials Stored Securely In The Report Server option.

19. In the User Name box, type your Windows user name, and in the Password box, type your Windows password.

20. Select the Use As Windows Credentials When Connecting To The Data Source check box, and then click Apply.

21. Click the Dependent Items tab.

22. Click the Product Catalog 2008 report link. Notice that the report is no longer requesting credentials.

23. Click the Home link in the upper-left corner of the screen.

24. Click the Data Sources folder link.

25. Click the AdventureWorks2008 data source link.

26. In the list of links on the left, click the Security link. Notice that just as reports do, data sources have an Edit Item Security button. This confirms that they are securable objects as well.

✔ **Quick Check**

1. What types of roles are available in SSRS 2008, and what are their purposes?

2. Can a user or group belong to more than one item-level or system-level role?

3. When storing the credentials of a data source in the server, are those credentials safe?

Quick Check Answers

1. Item-level roles and system-level roles are the two types of roles available in SSRS 2008. An item-level role is a collection of tasks related to operations on an object of the report object hierarchy of SSRS 2008. A system-level role is a collection of tasks related to operations on server objects outside the report object hierarchy of SSRS 2008.

2. Yes, in SSRS 2008, a user or group can have more than one association to a system-level or an item-level role.

3. Yes, the data source credentials are safe because Reporting Services encrypts them and stores them in the ReportServer SQL Server database.

Lesson 2: Creating Report Schedules and Subscriptions

Estimated lesson time: 30 minutes

End users can always browse reports on demand. However, sometimes it is better to execute a report on a schedule. End users can also subscribe to regular deliveries of a report. You can create a shared schedule, which can be used by multiple reports and multiple subscriptions, or you can create report-specific schedules.

Before you can execute a report on a schedule, some prerequisites have to be met. SQL Server Agent must be running because it is the scheduling engine and SQL Server Agent jobs trigger the report execution. You also have to configure your report server to support scheduling and delivery operations. In addition, you must store new credentials to run a report on the report server because SSRS cannot rely on current user credentials to run scheduled reports. Typically, you would create a separate database login for running the reports and give this user only the following privileges:

- Read access to the ReportServer database
- Read access to the msdb database
- Read access to all objects from all databases included in a report

> **IMPORTANT CREATING SECURE REPORTS**
>
> Do not forget about security when you are executing and deploying reports. When you are executing reports on a schedule, for example, do not forget that you have to store the credentials in your report server database.

You should create a report-specific schedule only when either no shared schedule exists with the schedule you need or when that schedule is needed for a single report only. Shared schedules are typically more useful than report-specific schedules because you can use them in multiple reports and subscriptions. In addition, if a schedule changes, you will apply the change in only one place. However, to create a shared schedule, you need system-level permissions. The administrator is typically the person who creates shared schedules.

Creating Shared Schedules

You can create a shared schedule in Report Manager or in SSMS. In Report Manager, you click the Site Settings link in the upper-right corner, and then you click the Schedules link on the left. You can configure the same options that you can configure when you connect to Reporting Services in SSMS. If you want to create a shared schedule in SSMS, you right-click the Shared Schedules folder and then select New Schedule to display the New Shared Schedule dialog box, shown in Figure 12-6.

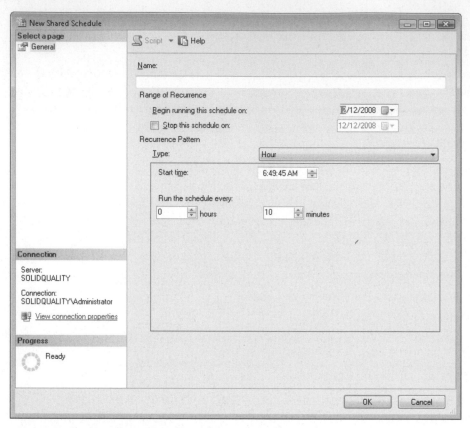

FIGURE 12-6 The New Shared Schedule dialog box in SSMS

In a shared schedule, you can define the following options:

- A descriptive name.

- A date to start the schedule; the default is the current day.

- A date to end the schedule; the default is no end date. After the end date, the schedule stops running, but the schedule is not deleted automatically.

- For a recurring schedule, you can select an Hour, Day, Week, or Month recurrence pattern. After you select the recurrence pattern, you can select additional options to fine-tune the schedule frequency, based on a particular hour, day, week, or month.

- You can also specify a schedule that is valid for a single run. Select the Once recurrence pattern, and then specify a Start Time.

Defining a Report-Specific Schedule

In addition to defining shared schedules, you can define a report-specific schedule for execution. You should create a report-specific schedule only if you do not have any appropriate shared schedule in place and you need to schedule only a single report. You can define a report-specific schedule when you define the execution properties of a report or when you subscribe to a report. You can manage execution properties and subscriptions in SSMS or in Report Manager.

To define a report-specific schedule, use the execution properties of a report, which are set in Report Manager. In Report Manager, open the report, click the Properties tab, and then on the Properties tab, click the Execution link, as shown in Figure 12-7. You will see options for using report-specific schedules or shared schedules for report caching and snaphot options (covered in the next lesson).

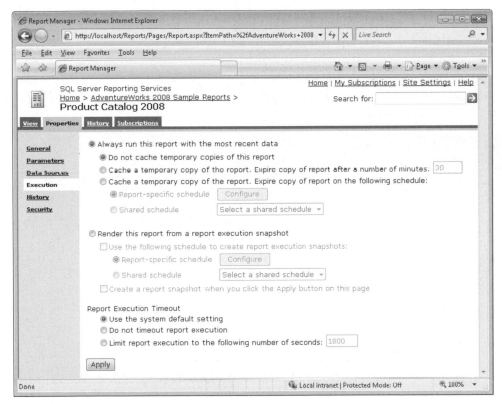

FIGURE 12-7 The Execution page of the Properties tab in Report Manager

Applying a Subscription to a Report

Running the reports on demand is considered to be a *pull delivery model*, where the user runs the report as needed. But you can also use a *push delivery model* for your reports—that is, the reports will be pushed out to fulfill a recurring demand. You can implement the push delivery model by using report subscriptions. A *subscription* is a standing request to have a report delivered at a specific time or in response to an event and in the format and delivery method that you have defined. You can use subscriptions to schedule and automate delivery of a report.

Subscriptions can use any of several delivery mechanisms. By default, SSRS includes file share and Simple Mail Transport Protocol (SMTP) e-mail delivery methods, and you can add custom delivery mechanisms. In addition, SSRS provides a Null delivery channel, which means that the report is not delivered anywhere but is loaded in the cache on a schedule. Creating the report only in the cache will improve the reporting performance for end users.

For a subscription, you must specify the following information:

- Delivery method
- Rendering type
- Conditions for processing the subscriptions, either on a schedule or when a snapshot of the report is updated on the report server
- Values for parameters if a report is parameterized

Report subscriptions are set for reports through Report Manager. To define a subscription for a report, in Report Manager, open a report, click the Properties tab, and then click the Subscriptions tab, as Figure 12-8 shows.

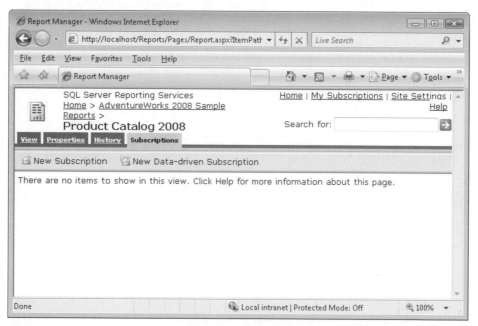

FIGURE 12-8 Report subscriptions are defined on the Subscriptions tab in Report Manager for each report.

To create a new subscription, click the New Subscription button. Each report delivery option contains a different set of properties to set. Figure 12-9 shows the properties of the Windows File Share delivery subscription.

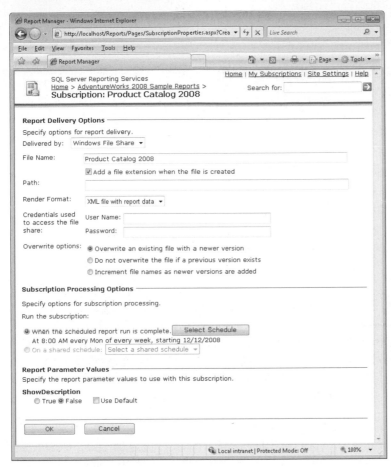

FIGURE 12-9 Subscription options for the Windows File Share option

If you use the file share delivery method, you must specify a Universal Naming Convention (UNC) name for the share as well as the Windows user credentials that SSRS will use to access the share. Of course, the user must have Write permission on the share and on the file system. If a file already exists in the share, you can specify that it should or should not be overwritten or that its file name should be incremented automatically when a new version of the file is added to the share. If you select the e-mail delivery method, you must specify a valid e-mail address.

Defining Data-Driven Subscriptions and Rendering Formats

Standard report subscriptions are quite useful. However, when you have multiple users who want to subscribe to the same report, you have to address diverse needs. Different users might want different rendering formats and different delivery mechanisms for the report. In addition, if a report is parameterized, different users might need to use different parameters. It would not be practical to create a new subscription for every single combination of delivery method and address, rendering format, and parameters. Instead, you can use data-driven subscriptions.

Creating Data-Driven Subscriptions

A data-driven subscription dynamically retrieves subscription data from an external data source at run time. You can also use some static values and default values that you can specify when you define the subscription. A data-driven subscription is especially useful in the following scenarios:

- Your list of subscribers is not fixed and changes often.

- You need to filter the report based on different parameters for each user, and you need to retrieve these parameters at run time.

- You need to use different rendering formats and delivery methods for different users, or you have to vary formats and methods for each execution.

 EXAM TIP

Report subscriptions are useful when a report needs to be sent by e-mail or saved to the file system on a recurring basis but the report needs to be run only one time for each time the schedule executes. A data-driven subscription is useful when you need to customize the report parameters and/or the type of subscription (for example, e-mail or file share). In addition, data-driven subscriptions can run the report several times for each scheduled execution occasion.

Data-driven subscriptions find data in tables in external data sources. The data source must provide the information in tabular format. Every row from a query that is used to retrieve the data for the subscription makes a new subscription, and columns returned by the query are used to dynamically specify subscription properties for each subscription. All the data that is needed for a data-driven subscription must be retrieved in a single query. If the query does not provide all the information you need, you must use static text and default values. You can use SQL Server relational data, SQL Server Analysis Services (SSAS) databases, SQL Server Integration Services (SSIS) package data, Oracle, Open Database Connectivity (ODBC) data sources, and OLE DB data sources for storing the data-driven subscription data. Data-driven subscriptions are available only in Evaluation, Developer, and Enterprise editions of SQL Server 2008.

The following steps demonstrate how to set up a data-driven subscription that uses the file share delivery option and runs the Employee Sales Summary 2008 report for a combination of parameters.

1. Because data-driven subscriptions use a query to populate the report parameters and subscription properties, the first task is to test the query. For this example, in SSMS, connect to the Database Engine and then open a new query window. In the AdventureWorks2008 database, run the following query. Confirm that the query

returns 97 rows of parameter combinations. This query will be the basis for the report parameters and output file name that the data-driven subscription will use. This query is also available in the Lesson 2 Data Driven Subscription Query.sql file available in the ..\Source\Ch 12\ practice files folder.

```
-- Preparing data for data-driven subscription
select distinct
    SalesPersonID, OrderYear = year(OrderDate), OrderMonthNum = month(OrderDate),
    replace(Employee.LoginID,'adventure-works\','') +
    convert(varchar(6),year(OrderDate)*100 + month(OrderDate)) as PDFFile
from Sales.SalesOrderHeader
    inner join Sales.SalesPerson
        on SalesOrderHeader.SalesPersonID =
            SalesPerson.BusinessEntityID
    inner join HumanResources.Employee
        on SalesPerson.BusinessEntityID =
            Employee.BusinessEntityID
where datepart(year, SalesOrderHeader.OrderDate) > 2003
```

2. In Report Manager, execute the Employee Sales Summary 2008 report found in the AdventureWorks 2008 Sample Reports folder. Notice that the report parameters match the columns in the query. To create a new data-driven subscription, go to the Subscriptions tab, and then click New Data-Driven Subscription. This step assumes that the credentials of the data source are stored on the server (a requirement for subscriptions).

3. On the Step 1 page, you would enter a Description for the data-driven subscription, and then select Windows File Share as the delivery method. Also on this page, you can use a shared data source for the query. To do this, you would choose the Specify A Shared Data Source option.

4. On the Step 2 page, to specify the data source for the recipients and properties query, expand the Data Sources folder and choose AdventureWorks2008.

5. On the Step 3 page, copy and paste the query tested earlier into the Delivery Query box. The Validate button will confirm that this query will run against the underlying database.

6. The Step 4 page allows you to define the subscription details, which can either be hard-coded in the properties, or defined by a column from the query. Figure 12-10 shows an example of the subscription properties and how they have been filled out for this example.

7. On the Step 5 page, you specify the parameter values for the specific report. This example report contains Report Month, Report Year, and Employee parameter options. For each parameter, select Get The Value From The Database and then select the appropriate database fields OrderMonthNum, OrderYear, and SalesPersonID for each parameter. For the ShowDescription parameter, leave False selected.

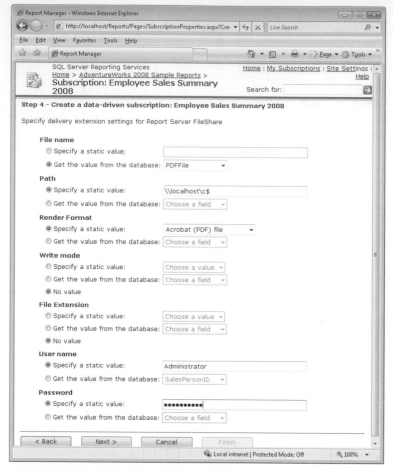

FIGURE 12-10 Data-driven subscription extension settings

8. On the Step 6 page, you specify the subscription schedule, which could either be a custom schedule or a shared schedule. For this example, select the On A Custom Schedule option, click Set Schedule, and then select Once as the recurrence pattern. Set the start time to a time about two minutes from the current time, so that you can observe the results. After clicking Finish, wait for the start time to pass, then check whether the share contains several PDF files for the sales reports.

Specifying the Subscription Delivery Format and Location

When you create the data source for your data-driven subscription, you must manually prepare the type of delivery method, rendering format, and other options you select for standard subscriptions through Report Manager.

You can easily find the values for the report parameters you need if you run the report manually in Report Manager. If a parameter gets the value from a static drop-down list, you have the list of all possible parameters. If the parameter list comes from a query, you can export the report in the Report Definition Language (RDL) file, open the file with BIDS, and check the query. You can use the same query to prepare the data for the data-driven subscription. For any report parameter, you can find the usage and the possible values if you use the report definition file and edit the report in BIDS.

PRACTICE **Creating Report Schedules and Subscriptions**

In this practice, you will prepare the infrastructure and then create a shared schedule and a subscription on a file share.

EXERCISE 1 Set Up the Infrastructure

In this exercise, you will verify that you have everything in place to create subscriptions, including SQL Server Agent and appropriate login credentials and permissions.

1. Verify that the SQL Server Agent service is running. If it is stopped, start the service.

2. Create a SQL Server login named ReportExecution for executing the reports. Create a database user for this login in the AdventureWorksDW2008, msdb, and ReportServer databases. Add the database user to the db_datareader role in all three databases. You can achieve this by using the following script in SSMS while connected to the Database Engine (the code below is available in the file named Lesson 2 ReportExecution Login Creation.sql, available in the ..\Source\Ch 12\ folder of the practice files):

```
USE master;
GO
CREATE LOGIN ReportExecution
WITH PASSWORD=N'Pa$$w0rd';
GO
USE AdventureWorks2008;
GO
CREATE USER ReportExecution FOR LOGIN ReportExecution;
GO
EXEC sp_addrolemember N'db_datareader', N'ReportExecution';
GO
USE msdb;
GO
CREATE USER ReportExecution FOR LOGIN ReportExecution;
GO
EXEC sp_addrolemember N'db_datawriter', N'ReportExecution';
GO
USE ReportServer;
GO
CREATE USER ReportExecution FOR LOGIN ReportExecution;
GO
EXEC sp_addrolemember N'db_datareader', N'ReportExecution';
GO
```

3. Create a Windows user to use for accessing the file share.

4. Create a new folder, or use an existing folder and share it. Make sure that the Windows user you just created has Write NTFS and Share permissions on the folder. See Windows Help for the details on sharing a file system folder.

5. Modify the AdventureWorks2008 shared data source. In Report Manager, click the Data Sources folder link, click the AdventureWorks2008 report link, and then click the Properties tab. For this connection, choose the Credentials Stored Securely In The Report Server option. Use the ReportExecution login name and Pa$$w0rd as the password, as shown in Figure 12-11.

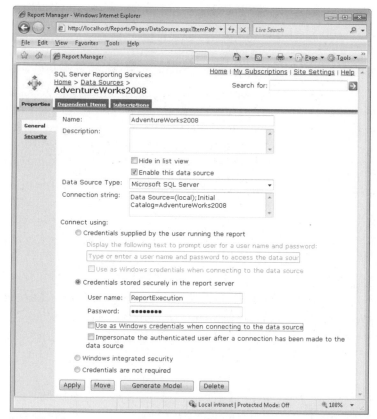

FIGURE 12-11 AdventureWorksDW2008 data source connection properties

6. Click Apply.

EXERCISE 2 Create a Shared Schedule

Now you are ready to create a shared schedule.

1. In SSMS, connect to Reporting Services, and then right-click the Shared Schedules folder of your report server and select New Schedule.

2. Type **AdventureWorks2008 Schedule** as the name of the schedule.

3. Select Once as the recurrence pattern type.

4. Set the start time to about 10 minutes from the current time.

5. Click OK to save the schedule.

6. In Report Manager, click the Site Settings link, and then click the Schedules link.

7. Check to see whether the shared schedule you created in SSMS appears in Report Manager.

EXERCISE 3 Create a Subscription

In this exercise, you will create a file share subscription for the Product Catalog 2008 report in the Adventure Works 2008 Sample Reports.

1. Open Report Manager by entering **http://localhost/reports** (or the server name) in Internet Explorer. Browse to the AdventureWorks 2008 Sample Reports folder and then click the Product Catalog 2008 report link.

2. In the Report Manager window, click the Subscriptions tab, and then click New Subscription.

3. In the Delivered By drop-down list, select Windows File Share.

4. In the File Name box, leave the default value of Product Catalog 2008.

5. Select the Add A File Extension When The File Is Created check box.

6. Change the Path to a valid Windows file share UNC path (such as *ServerName**Share*).

7. Change the Render Format property to Excel.

8. Type your Windows user name and password in the credentials text boxes.

9. Leave the Overwrite An Existing File With A Newer Version option selected.

10. In the Subscription Processing Options section, select the On A Shared Schedule option.

11. Confirm that the AdventureWorks2008 Schedule option is selected in the On A Shared Schedule drop-down list.

12. Leave the ShowDescription parameter set to False. Your settings should look similar to those shown in Figure 12-12.

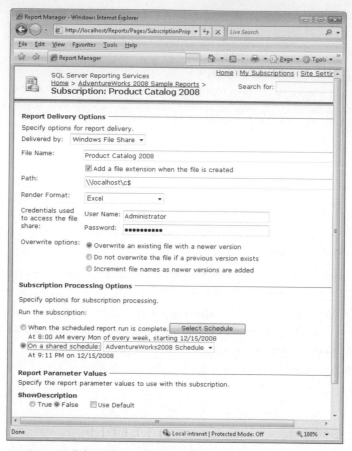

FIGURE 12-12 Subscription general properties

13. Click OK to save your subscription.

14. When the time comes for your shared schedule execution, check to see whether Product Catalog 2008.xls has been created.

15. After you deliver a file, do not stop sharing the folder and do not delete the shared schedule—you will need them in the practice at the end of the next lesson. You can delete the subscription.

Lesson 3: Managing Report Caching and Execution Properties in Report Manager

Estimated lesson time: 45 minutes

Security and subscriptions are just two of the components that you need to consider when defining management properties for SSRS. Another important component is report execution, which includes caching and snapshots. Understanding the way a report is executed inside SSRS will help you make decisions about the specific method you will use and will help you be aware of the impact that decision will have on your system performance.

Report execution includes defining how the report source data is handled and what Reporting Services should do with the data after the report is rendered.

Understanding Report Execution Behavior

To best understand the report execution process, examine the following process steps that a report with the default execution settings goes through when a report request is received:

1. Report Server receives a request, generally in Hypertext Transport Protocol (HTTP) format, for a given report.

2. Report Server validates the properties associated with the object requested.

3. Report Server accesses the SQL Server catalog database (ReportServer) and extracts the RDL definition of the report.

4. From the definition, Report Server extracts the information related to data sources.

5. Reporting Services connects to the data sources and executes the commands that retrieve data.

6. After the data has been retrieved, the data is mixed with the RDL definition and generates an intermediate format report.

7. The intermediate format report is rendered in the format that was requested by the client; this could be HTML, Excel, PDF, and so on.

This process implies the following:

- Every time a report is requested, the underlying queries defined for each of the different datasets within the report must be executed.

- For every single request, the intermediate format is generated.

- Query parameters are enabled in the report, dictating the number of rows returned by the data provider and rendered in the report.

For scenarios in which the data sources have high concurrency and large datasets, these actions could generate the following issues:

- The report or query runs slowly because the dataset is large.

- The performance of the underlying systems that are used to create the report might be compromised. If the query is scanning a large number of records, locking can occur.

Using Report Caching

Reporting Services has two mechanisms to reduce the overhead associated with a large number of concurrent users, large datasets, and long-running queries: report caching and report snapshots. Report snapshots are reviewed in the next section.

By default, a report is rendered using the most recent data. This means that every execution starts by reading the database data. This could be a large processing burden on a production server. To reduce the load on your server, you can cache a temporary copy of a report. SSRS caches the report in the ReportServer database with all the data but without any of the rendering information. If a report exists in the cache, when the next user runs the report, the user gets the data from the cache, and there is no need to reread data from the database. Because the rendering information is not stored in the cache, a user can use any rendering format on the data. The data in the cache might become outdated after time, so you can define an expiration period for the cached report. You can define an expiration time in minutes, or you can force expiration on a shared or report-specific schedule. Caching is enabled through the execution properties of a report, as Figure 12-13 shows.

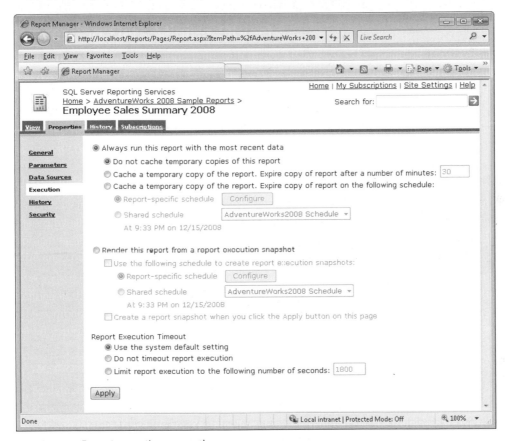

FIGURE 12-13 Report execution properties

The Execution properties are grouped by caching options, report execution snapshot, and report execution time-out.

After caching is enabled and the report is run for the first time after you enabled caching, the server stores the report data, and you can specify when the cache expires in one of two ways. First, the cache can be invalidated by specifying a number of minutes for which the cache is valid or by defining a report-specific schedule, or second, the cache can be invalidated through a shared schedule. The cache of a report will also be invalid if the data source credentials are changed or no longer stored on the report server.

To enable caching for a report, you can choose the Expire Copy Of Report After A Number Of Minutes option and set the expiration minutes. Alternatively, you can choose the Expire Copy Of Report On The Following Schedule option and then select the Report-Specific

Schedule option. Then you can configure a report-specific schedule with the same recurrence types and detail patterns that you set in shared schedules.

With report caching, Reporting Services can create and store a copy of the intermediate format report in a temporary SQL Server database named ReportServerTempDB in the Execution-Cache table. Even when the first request from a user follows the schema presented earlier, the processing of subsequent requests is altered as follows:

1. A request is sent to Report Server.

2. Report Server validates the properties associated with the object requested. If report execution is set to use the cache, and an item already exists in the ExecutionCache table of the ReportServerTempDB database for the ReportID of the requested report and the parameters passed are the same, Report Server renders the report from the stored intermediate format.

> **IMPORTANT MODIFYING REPORTING SERVICES CATALOG DATABASES**
>
> Do *not* modify the Reporting Services catalog databases. Doing so could jeopardize your environment by making your Reporting Services installation invalid.

When a report cache is available, the dataset queries do not execute, and the intermediate format is not created. This greatly increases the response time. However, for every combination of parameters, the report will create a new cache. In other words, if the parameters passed in the second request do not match those of the first request, the process is considered a brand-new request.

Using Report Snapshots for Report Execution

If you cache a report, the first user who runs the report after the cache has expired will have to wait longer to view the report than the users who follow, because the first user triggers the data being read from the database. You can prevent this problem by creating a snapshot of the data in advance of the first report being run. To do this, select the Render This Report From An Execution Snapshot option in the execution properties of a report. You can create a snapshot based on a shared or a report-specific schedule. In addition, you can create the first snapshot immediately after you save the execution settings.

Another caching consideration is determining whether previous versions of the cache should be persisted. Persistence of previous values in reports might be required by business users for comparison purposes or to be able to refer to those numbers later. Using snapshots, you can create persistent copies of a report and store those copies in the report history.

You can also store multiple snapshots in the report history. You can use the History page of the report properties to define a schedule to add snapshots to the report history. Additional history snapshots are stored in the ReportServerTempDB database. As you can see in Figure 12-14, on the History page, you can also limit the number of snapshots that are kept in the report history. This option can help you prevent the ReportServerTempDB database from becoming too large and from storing data that is too outdated to be useful to end users. After a report has snapshots available, you will see the snapshots on the History tab of the report viewer (instead of on the History page that is shown in Figure 12-14).

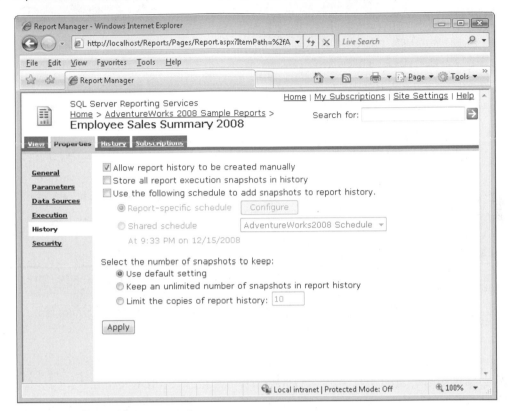

FIGURE 12-14 Report history properties

The number of report snapshots stored can be controlled. The Select The Number Of Snapshots To Keep option in Figure 12-14 shows that you can either keep an unlimited number of snapshots or define a limited number. The default can be set in the SSRS server properties.

When you run a report, you have to select which snapshot to use, and data from different snapshots cannot be compared. So if you anticipate that your end users might need five years of historical data, or they might want to compare older snapshots with newer ones, for example, you should create a data warehouse and an online analytical processing (OLAP) solution that will allow users to look at archived data.

One difference between the cache and snapshots is that the intermediate format of a report snapshot is stored in the ReportServer database rather than in the temporary database. Also, in contrast to cached copies, snapshots do not allow any change in the query parameters used to render the report.

> **NOTE** **CONFIGURING THE REPORT HISTORY PROPERTIES**
>
> The report history options are available in the Properties area of a deployed report. You will see a History link in the left pane of the report window. Three behaviors can be associated with report history, depending on which mechanisms you want to use to add elements to the history, as follows:
>
> - You can select the Allow Report History To Be Created Manually check box. This option enables the New Snapshot button on the History page of the report.
>
> - You can select the Store All Report Snapshot In History check box. This option is limited by the number of snapshots to keep in memory defined either at the History–Report level or at the server level—you find this server-wide setting in the Site Settings area.
>
> - You can select the Use The Following Schedule To Add Snapshots To Report History check box. This option is useful for keeping track of certain forms of data at certain times, independent of decisions made by users to create new snapshots.

Setting a Time-Out and Restricting Linked Reports

A couple of important advanced settings for reports and users include setting a query time-out and defining whether linked reports are allowed. Often you will need to limit the maximum execution time for a report. This will limit the impact of a runaway query. In addition, you might want to restrict the ability to create linked reports for a user.

Defining a Report Time-Out

Although there are techniques (such as caching and snapshots) that help control the performance of a report, performance at the server level can be affected by one poorly performing report. To avoid this scenario, you can define the maximum time spent rendering a report. You can configure this option either at the report level—found on the Execution page on the Properties tab for the report—or at the server level, on the Site Settings page.

Controlling Linked Report Use

Content Manager is one of the item-level roles available in Reporting Services 2008. This role has the capability to remove the item-level task Create Linked Reports from a given role in order to define the groups that can or cannot create linked reports. Also, in order for a user to define the location in which the linked report is going to be stored, the destination folder requires that the user has the Content Manager or the Publisher role.

Linked reports abide by the same rules for execution that regular reports follow. For linked reports, you can create cache versions and snapshots, and the execution snapshots can be stored in the History section of the linked report.

PRACTICE Using Report Manager to Modify Report Properties

In this practice, you will create a linked report and modify its properties.

EXERCISE   Create and Manage a Linked Report with Report Caching

Suppose that you want to create a personalized copy of the Product Line Sales 2008 report. You want to be able to see specific information in this report, and you want to validate the fact that there is a dependency between the base report and the linked report.

1. Open Internet Explorer, and then navigate to *http://localhost/Reports*.

2. Click the AdventureWorks2008 Sample Reports folder link.

3. Click the Product Line Sales 2008 report link. Notice that, by default, the value for the Category query parameter is Bikes, and the value for the Subcategory parameter is Road Bikes.

4. Click the Properties tab. Notice that there is an area named Report Definition, which includes two links: Edit and Update. Clicking the Edit link will allow you to get the RDL file. This is possible because this is a base report.

5. Click the Create Linked Report button.

6. Type **My Sales Report** as the report name, and then type the following description: **A linked report that I can use to view my sales**. Notice that the label contains the location information.

7. Click OK, and notice that the header for the report now reads *My Sales Report 2008*, so you know that you are looking at the linked report rather than the base report.

8. Click the Properties tab. Notice that in the Report Definition area, there are no links for editing or updating the RDL; instead, there is now a button that will allow you to change the link to the base report.

9. In the list of links on the left, click Parameters.

10. Change the default value of the ProductCategory parameter to 4, and then clear the Prompt User check box.

11. Change the default value of the ProductSubCategory parameter to 31, and then clear the Prompt User check box.

12. Click Apply.

13. Click the View tab. Notice that the parameters ProductCategory and ProductSub-Category are not visible. Also notice that immediately below the Adventure Works Cycles logo in the report, the sales for Accessories (Helmets) are displayed.

EXAM TIP

Report parameters can be set to default values either through the report designers or through the report properties in Report Manager. When report parameters are set to default values, the report can execute without requiring immediate user input.

14. Click the AdventureWorks2008 Sample Reports link in the upper-left corner.

15. Point to the report icon on the left side of the My Sales Report 2008 report. Notice that the tooltip states that this is a linked report. Also notice that the icon itself is different from the icon for the other reports in the same folder.

16. Click the Product Line Sales 2008 report link. Notice that the Category and Sub-Category parameters are still visible and that the parameters have retained their default values.

17. Click the AdventureWorks2008 Sample Reports link at the upper left.

18. Click the My Sales Report link.

19. Click the Properties tab.

20. In the list of links on the left, click Execution. Notice that this is the page in which you can define the execution options. Pay special attention to the Report Execution Time-out area. This value defines the maximum period of time that a given report request can take. By default, every report refers to the defined server value. You can set the time-out for a single report by using the properties you see on the Execution page. If you want to modify this parameter at the server level, you will find it by clicking the Site Settings link in the upper-right corner.

21. On the Execution page of the Properties tab for the report, select the Cache A Temporary Copy Of The Report. Expire Copy Of Report After A Number Of Minutes option. By default, Reporting Services sets this value to 30 minutes.

22. Click Apply. If the underlying data source does not have credentials stored (credentials were stored in the Lesson 2 practice exercises earlier in this chapter), you will receive an error stating *Credentials used to run this report are not stored*. This reflects the fact that there is a dependency with the underlying data source of the base report. The section "Managing Data Sources and Credentials" in Lesson 1 of this chapter provides more information about managing data sources.

23. Click the AdventureWorks2008 Sample Reports link in the upper-left corner.

24. Click the Product Line Sales 2008 report link.

25. Click the Properties tab.

26. On the General page, click Delete to delete this report.

27. In the message box that asks *Are You Sure You Want To Delete Product Line Sales 2008?*, click OK.

28. You will be redirected to the AdventureWorks2008 Sample Reports folder. Notice that the linked report My Sales Report that you created earlier is still listed.

29. Click the My Sales Report report link. You will see the error message *The report server cannot perform the operation on the report. The report link is no longer valid (rsInvalid-ReportLink)*.

30. Click the Properties tab. Notice that the report definition area contains a message stating that the report definition is no longer valid. Also notice that in the list of links on the left, there is no Parameters link. This does not mean that the information from the parameters configuration is lost. As soon as you change the link to a valid report, the link will appear again, with the previously defined values intact.

31. Click the Home link in the upper-left corner.

> ✔ **Quick Check**
>
> 1. What mechanisms do you identify to reduce the overhead of Reporting Services data sources?
> 2. Can you always create a cache of a report?
> 3. Can you edit the .rdl code associated with a linked report?
>
> **Quick Check Answers**
>
> 1. Snapshots and cached reports can help reduce the processing pressure on data sources and improve report response time.
> 2. No, you can create a cache of a report only when certain requirements, such as having credentials stored in the Report Server, are met.
> 3. No, because a linked report has no .rdl code of its own. It refers to the .rdl code of the base report.

Case Scenario: Managing the Report Environment for Adventure Works

Reporting Services has been deployed in Adventure Works, and multiple departments are requesting access to the new server. However, some employees need to access reports from departments other than their own. At the same time, some users from the call center require the flexibility to create reports based on their customers.

Adventure Works uses a mixed database environment, with most applications running on SQL Server 2008 but some running on Oracle.

1. What is the general security infrastructure required to support the reporting needs of the Adventure Works departments and employees?

2. From a data source security standpoint, how can you satisfy the requirements to access both Oracle and SQL Server from Reporting Services?

Chapter Summary

- Reporting Services has two main role types: item-level roles and system-level roles. These roles can be customized to meet your particular security requirements.

- Item-level roles handle the security of the object contained within the hierarchical namespace of report objects in Reporting Services, whereas system-level roles handle the objects and operations outside the hierarchy.

- My Reports functionality allows users to have private space to work with their own reports, without the need for high privileges in public folders. My Reports is disabled by default.

- Shared schedules are easier to maintain than report-specific schedules. Shared schedules give more control to an administrator.

- End users can subscribe to reports.

- To execute reports automatically on a schedule, you must store credentials for connecting to data sources in your report server database.

- You can quickly create multiple subscriptions with different properties by using a data-driven subscription.

- Reporting Services lets you improve report performance by using cached reports and report snapshots.

- Data sources represent access to data repositories. Credentials can be predefined and set to apply to everyone who accesses a report, or they can be defined at run time.

CHAPTER 13

Configuring and Administering the SSRS Server

This chapter examines the configuration and administration of SQL Server Reporting Services (SSRS) instances, including configuring advanced settings and developing a scale-out architecture for SSRS. Configuring SSRS includes working with the Reporting Services Configuration Manager tool, the command-line utility named RSConfig.exe, and the command-line utility named RSKeyMgmt.exe to set up the SSRS database repository, configure the Web management and report virtual Web directories, and manage the encryption keys. In addition, to work with SSRS, you might need to change the rendering output settings or to control Secure Sockets Layer (SSL) connections.

The standard installation of SSRS is reviewed in this book's Introduction and prerequisites.

Exam objectives in this chapter:

- Install and configure SSRS instances.
- Configure SSRS availability.

Before You Begin

To complete this chapter, you must have:

- Experience installing Microsoft SQL Server 2008 business intelligence (BI) components.
- Understanding of Windows security groups.
- Experience working in SQL Server Management Studio (SSMS).
- Administrative access to a full installation of SQL Server 2008 with Reporting Services configured for installing and configuring SSRS instances.

Lesson 1: Installing and Configuring Initial Instances of SSRS

Estimated lesson time: 45 minutes

When SSRS is installed with the default configuration, it is immediately ready to use for report deployment and report access by users. However, if you install a second instance of SSRS that needs to be configured separately, or if you need to set up an SSRS server farm, or if you need to configure SSRS for Internet deployment, your SSRS environment will require special configuration. This lesson focuses on these SSRS configuration scenarios.

Reviewing the Reporting Services Components

The Reporting Services 2008 architecture includes several components that work together to provide the full reporting experience, including report design, report management and security, report rendering, data caching, and Microsoft Office SharePoint application integration. Figure 13-1 shows an overview of the SSRS components.

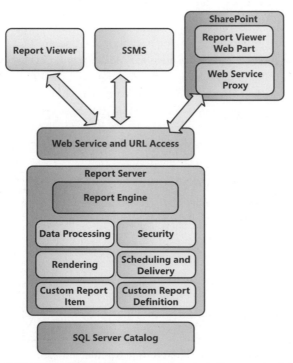

FIGURE 13-1 SSRS 2008 components include the report catalog, the Report Server service, the Web service, SSMS, and the Report Viewers.

A complete SSRS installation includes the following components:

- **SQL Server catalog** Two databases in SQL Server, ReportServer and ReportServer-TempDB, that are used for storing and caching data.

- **Report Server service** The report engine that handles report rendering, data processing, security access, scheduling, and delivery.

- **Web Service and URL Access** The two report server virtual directories named Reports and ReportServer allow URL access to the Reporting Services Web service. The Reports virtual directory is used by the Report Manager Web interface, and the ReportServer virtual directory provides direct access to the SSRS Web service.

Installing Reporting Services

As noted earlier, Reporting Services is configured during setup and is ready to use at the completion of installation when you allow the SQL Server installation process to configure it with the default settings on the default instance.

During installation, the Reporting Services Configuration page of the SQL Server 2008 Setup Wizard provides three configuration options, as shown in Figure 13-2.

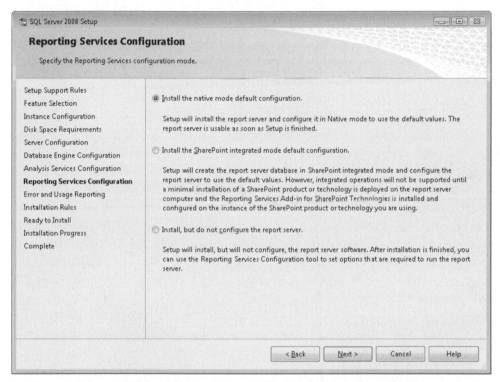

FIGURE 13-2 During installation, you can specify whether to use the default configuration or to use SharePoint as the report management tool, or you can install SSRS without configuring it.

The default option, Install The Native Mode Default Configuration, performs a full installation and configuration with all the default options. In *native mode*, you use the Report Manager Web management interface to manage, process, view, and deliver reports on the installation computer. Unlike in previous versions of Reporting Services, IIS is not required. Reporting Services uses HTTP.sys, included with Windows Server 2003 and Windows Server 2008.

Alternatively, you can allow SSRS to use Microsoft Office SharePoint Server 2007 or Windows SharePoint Services 3.0 as the report management interface. When you choose the Install The SharePoint Integrated Mode Default Configuration option, SharePoint Services needs to be available, and SSRS will be installed with the default options. Report Manager cannot be installed with this option because SharePoint is the exclusive report management tool.

Be aware that this is different from simply using the SSRS Web Parts in SharePoint, which can be used with any installation choice.

Last, the SSRS installation can also allow installation of the report server and catalogs without any configuration. The Install, But Do Not Configure The Report Server option will require a manual configuration of the service and allows for custom installations and multiple instances of SSRS installed on the same server.

Naming SSRS Instances

Reporting Services allows multiple instances to be installed on the same computer that use different report catalogs. The default instance does not have a name, and when the default settings are used, Report Manager is accessed through the URL *http://<ComputerName>/Reports*.

If you need to install a second instance of Reporting Services, you can name the instance (or use the default instance if you used a named instance for the first installation). During the Reporting Services installation, you can specify a different named instance. When you name an instance, you will not be able to use the default configuration, and you will have to manually configure the instance, as described in this lesson. The default Report Manager URL for a named instance is *http://<ComputerName>/Reports_<InstanceName>*.

A second instance of SSRS is useful in two common scenarios. First, if you have strict security requirements, a second instance of SSRS will allow you to divide site-level security among multiple groups of administrators. Second, if you have limited hardware for development, test, and production servers, you can use multiple instances on a single server to simulate multiple environments.

In Lesson 2 of this chapter, you will see how to configure SSRS for a scale-out solution when multiple instances of SSRS are installed on one or more servers and they share the same report catalog.

When the installation of Reporting Services is complete, you might need to configure Reporting Services with the Reporting Services Configuration Manager tool.

Using the Reporting Services Configuration Manager Tool for Server Setup and Management

The installation of the SSRS server component includes the Reporting Services Configuration Manager tool, a user interface (UI) administration tool for configuring SSRS server settings. To access the tool, on the Start menu, select All Programs, then select Microsoft SQL Server 2008, select Configuration Tools, and select Reporting Services Configuration Manager.

The Reporting Services Configuration Manager tool performs common setup and configuration tasks required to implement an SSRS instance, including the following:

- Creating the virtual directories
- Configuring the Service Startup account

- Defining the ASP.NET account
- Setting up the database connection to the SSRS repository
- Managing the symmetric encryption keys
- Performing initialization steps to enable new instances for a scale-out deployment
- Defining operational accounts for e-mail and other administration tasks

When you install SSRS and you choose not to apply the default configuration to SSRS during the installation, you will need to use the Reporting Services Configuration Manager tool to configure the components and settings that are required for the SSRS instance to be enabled. Figure 13-3 shows the Reporting Services Configuration Manager tool as it will appear for an instance that was installed without the default configuration options.

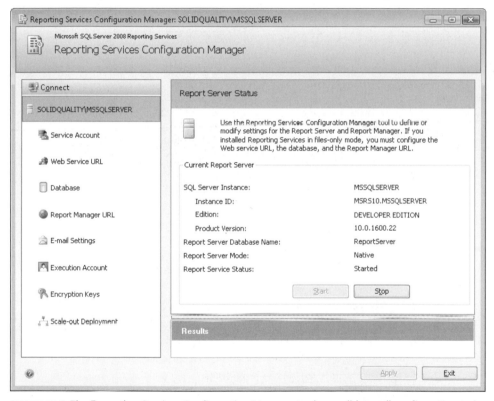

FIGURE 13-3 The Reporting Services Configuration Manager tool consolidates all configuration tasks needed to set up SSRS after installation.

If you are configuring a new instance of SSRS, you can follow these steps to enable an instance for development and reporting:

1. On the Service Account property page, you can select a local or domain user account to enable the Reporting Services service to log on to Windows.

2. On the Web Service URL property page, you set the Web service URL and security properties. On this page, you have the option to set the Virtual Directory for the Report Server Web service. Figure 13-4 shows the Web Service URL property page.

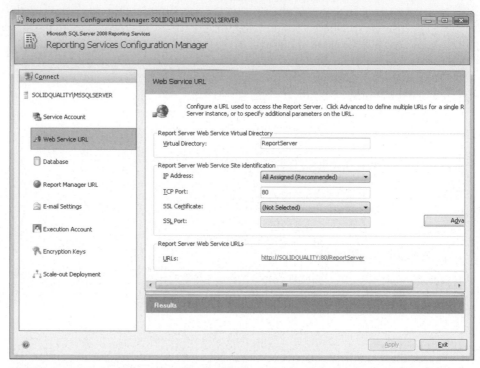

FIGURE 13-4 You can set the virtual directory, TCP port, and security properties for the Web service on the Web Service URL property page.

The Web service that SSRS uses to perform report management, publishing, and rendering operations is located in the Report Server Web service virtual directory. By default, the virtual directory is named ReportServer, but you can change this name if you have an instance that uses this virtual directory name already or if your application requires a name that is directly related to the application. In addition to the virtual directory, you can configure the IP address, port, and SSL certificate settings. Click Advanced to specify multiple certificates and ports.

3. On the Database property page, you configure the SSRS repository database, which is used by SSRS to store the report definitions, data sources, virtual folders for Report Manager, and security. In addition, Reporting Services Configuration Manager creates a second database for storing temporary data and temporary operations such as report caching. Reporting Services Configuration Manager automatically generates a name for this temporary database by combining the name of the repository database

with the name *TempDB*. By default, the repository database is named ReportServer, and the default temporary database name is ReportServerTempDB.

The databases can be created on the same local computer or on a remote computer. To create or change the databases, click Change Database. Figure 13-5 shows the Report Server Database Configuration Wizard, where you can configure the Reporting Services database name and the credentials needed for database creation rights.

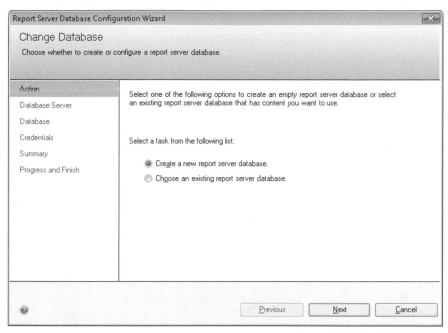

FIGURE 13-5 SSRS uses a SQL Server database to store report definitions, data sources, and security settings.

The Database property page also allows the configuration of the credentials that should be used to connect to the report catalog databases. To change the credentials, click Change Credentials. The credentials can use the current user or a specific SQL Server login account.

4. On the Report Manager URL property page, you can set or create the virtual directory for Report Manager, which is the Web-based management tool for Reporting Services. Configure this in the same way you configured the ReportServer virtual directory in step 2. After you set or change the virtual directory, click Apply, and the new virtual directory will be created if necessary. The default name for the virtual directory for Report Manager is Reports. Using Report Manager is reviewed in Chapter 12, "Scheduling and Securing Deployed Reports and Data Sources."

5. On the E-Mail Settings and Execution Account property pages, you can configure e-mail subscriptions and data sources that do not require credentials, respectively. The e-mail settings require you to specify the name of a Simple Mail Transfer Protocol (SMTP) server and a sender e-mail address. The Execution Account property page requires a Windows account that has appropriate access to remote servers or resources.

6. On the Encryption Keys and Scale-Out Deployment property pages, you can manage encryption keys and define a scale-out deployment. Encryption key management is described in the next section of this lesson as well as in the "Using the Reporting Services Command-Line Utilities to Manage SSRS" section in Lesson 2. Lesson 2 also examines building a scale-out deployment with multiple SSRS instances.

If you have just configured SSRS for the first time or have made changes to service account or database settings, you will need to start or restart the service. To do this, select the server icon in the upper-left corner of the Reporting Services Configuration Manager window. Click Start, or if you need to restart the service, click Stop, and then click Start.

Managing Report Server Encryption Keys

All sensitive information is encrypted between the Reporting Services database catalogs and the Report Server Web service and the Report Manager application (or SharePoint in Share-Point integrated mode). This includes data source connection strings, user names and passwords, reports with embedded data sources, the connection strings for the catalog database, and the service account information. Furthermore, access to the report server databases or a backup copy of them will not allow unwanted access to the data source connection information.

It is a good idea to back up your report server's encryption key in case you need to reinstall the report server on the same computer or a different computer and need access to the same report catalog database. If you do not have the encryption key file, you will not be able to connect the report server instance to an existing report server catalog.

To back up the encryption key, navigate to the Encryption Keys property page in Reporting Services Configuration Manager. Figure 13-6 shows the available options.

Your options are to

- Back up the key to store it in a password-protected file.
- Restore a key in the case of rebuilding a stand-alone instance.
- Change the key, which will reencrypt the content with a newly generated encryption key.
- Delete the encrypted content, which will remove the deployed content items from the Report Server database.

When you back up your report server's encryption key, you will need to specify a file name with an .snk extension and a password for the file. Be sure to keep the file and know the password if you ever need to restore the encryption key to recover an installation or to reinstall.

Managing the keys is also a function of the RSKeyMgmt.exe command-line utility. See the section "Using RSKeyMgmt.exe to Manage Encryption Keys" in Lesson 2 to learn about encryption key management.

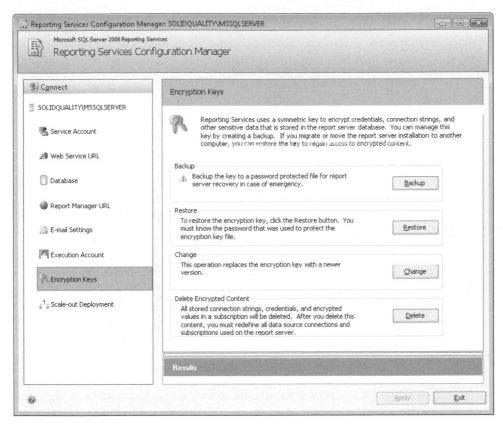

FIGURE 13-6 Reporting Services Configuration Manager lets you back up and restore your encryption keys.

EXAM TIP

When faced with a system failure where you lose your SSRS instance and/or database, you will first need to reinstall SSRS. After the installation is complete, you can optionally restore the latest backup of your report server catalog database (if it was also lost). After the service and catalog databases are in place, your final step is to restore the encryption key onto the newly installed instance of SSRS. This will enable the report server to be able to decrypt the catalog security, reports, and data sources.

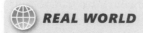

REAL WORLD

Erik Veerman

As you know, nothing works flawlessly in the real world—there are always hardware and software environment problems such as compatibility issues, hardware failures, and software bugs. Therefore, it is always best to plan for a failure so that you are ready to respond at a moment's notice!

Sometimes planning for failures takes a back seat to design and development, and at one client, unfortunately, the worse came about. I was working on architecting the extraction, transformation, and loading (ETL) and cube design for an analytic solution and was approached by one of the client's database administrators (DBAs) to assist in restoring the client's Reporting Services solution. The problem was that the production report server had an internal hardware failure and the server had to be rebuilt. Reporting Services was reinstalled, and the DBA pointed the report server to the report catalog located on another server. The problem? Well, the report server was giving an encryption key error.

I told the DBA that this was no problem. He simply had to restore the backup encryption key from the first installation and the server would then be able to decrypt the report structures, definitions, and data sources. The response? "We don't have a backup of our encryption key."

The truth is that this is not the end of the world. But the DBA did have to find all the report projects that had been deployed before and redeploy them to the new server. It took a couple of days to get things completely back in order. Luckily, the client was not keeping report history snapshots, so they did not lose any historical data, but it did cost them in down-time and administrative time to recover.

PRACTICE **Using Reporting Services Configuration Manager**

In this practice, you will use Reporting Services Configuration Manager to change the report server catalog and change the Report Manager virtual Web directory to get comfortable with the configuration of Reporting Services.

EXERCISE 1 Create a New Report Catalog Database

In this first exercise, you will generate a new report server catalog database and create some folders and data sources and then change back to the original report server catalog database.

These practice exercises assume that you have administrative rights to a local installation of SQL Server 2008.

1. Open the Reporting Services Configuration Manager tool from the Start menu by selecting All Programs, Microsoft SQL Server 2008, Configuration Tools, and then Reporting Services Configuration Manager.

2. In the Reporting Services Configuration Manager Connection window, connect to your local instance of Reporting Services, MSSQLSERVER, on your local computer.

3. In the property page list on the left, select the Database property page.

4. Click Change Database to start the Report Server Database Configuration Wizard.

   a. On the Action page, confirm that the Create A New Report Server Database option is selected, and then click Next.

   b. On the Connect To The Database Server page, confirm that your local computer name is entered where the Database Engine has been installed, and then click Next.

   c. On the Select A Report Server Database page, change the name of the Database Name property to **ReportServerNew**. Leave the Report Server Mode set to Native Mode, and then click Next.

   d. On the Credentials page, leave the authentication set to Service Credentials, and then click Next.

   e. On the Summary page, click Next. Wait for the database scripts to be generated and executed as indicated by the status bar, and then click Finish.

5. Start Internet Explorer, and then open Report Manager by entering **http://localhost/reports** in the Address box.

   Notice that the Home folder is empty because the report server is now using a newly created version of the report server database that has no reports, folders, data sources, or site settings created.

6. To reset the report server to the previous environment, go back to Reporting Services Configuration Manager, and on the Database property page, again click Change Database.

   a. On the Action page, select the Choose An Existing Report Server Database option, and then click Next.

   b. On the Connect To The Database Server page, leave the current settings, and then click Next.

   c. On the Select A Report Server page, choose the ReportServer database from the Report Server Database drop-down list, and then click Next.

   d. On the Credentials page, click Next to accept the default security credentials.

   e. On the Summary page, click Next. Allow the scripts to run to reconfigure Reporting Services to use its original database, and then click Finish.

7. Return to Report Manager in Internet Explorer, and then refresh the page.

Notice that all the folders, reports, and data sources have been restored to their previous state because the original version of the report server catalog database has been reconnected.

8. (Optional) Start SSMS, and then connect to the local Database Engine and delete the ReportServerNew and ReportServerNewTempDB databases.

EXERCISE 2 Modify the Report Manager Virtual Directory

In this exercise, you will change the Report Manager virtual directory, observe the results, and then change the directory back.

1. Open the Reporting Services Configuration Manager tool from the Start menu by selecting All Programs, Microsoft SQL Server 2008, Configuration Tools, and then Reporting Services Configuration Manager. When prompted, click Connect to connect to your report server instance.

2. Select the Report Manager URL property page, change the virtual directory name to **MyApp**, and then click Apply.

3. When the scripts have finished executing in the Results window, open Internet Explorer and attempt to start the local Report Manager application with the URL ***http://localhost/Reports***. Observe that the Web page cannot be displayed because the virtual directory name has changed.

4. Next, change the URL to **http://localhost/MyApp**, and then refresh the browser. Notice that Report Manager is now accessible under this new HTTP path because the virtual directory was changed.

5. Return to Reporting Services Configuration Manager, and then select the Report Manager URL property page.

6. Change the virtual directory name back to **Reports**, and then click Apply.

7. Return to Internet Explorer, and then navigate to *http://localhost/Reports* to confirm that Report Manager now runs under this default virtual directory name and URL.

✔ Quick Check

1. Which of the tools and utilities described in this lesson can change or create the virtual directories for the report server and Report Manager after installation?

2. What is the file name extension for an encryption key backup?

Quick Check Answers

1. Only Reporting Services Configuration Manager can enable and name the virtual directories for the report server and Report Manager.

2. Encryption key backups have an .snk file name extension.

Lesson 2: Configuring Advanced SSRS Settings and Scale-Out Deployment

Estimated lesson time: 35 minutes

Report Server Configuration Manager allows configuration for most of the SSRS settings. Many of these settings, such as setting the connection to the report server catalog and the encryption keys, can also be controlled through a set of command-line utilities. In fact, setting up a scale-out deployment model for SSRS involves sharing encryption keys between instances pointed to the same report server database and can be done either through Reporting Services Configuration Manager or through the command line.

In addition to configuring the report server catalog connection and managing the encryption keys, the report server also contains several server-level properties that are set through SSMS and through the RSReportServer.config XML file, such as device-specific rendering settings and Internet deployment.

This lesson covers these advanced configuration methods and settings.

Using the Reporting Services Command-Line Utilities to Manage SSRS

The installation of the SSRS server component includes three administration command-line utilities to assist in configuring SSRS server settings. The RSConfig.exe utility assists in managing the SSRS instance connection to the repository database. The RSKeyMgmt.exe utility assists in the management of the encryption keys for operations such as backup, restore, and create. Last, the RS.exe command-line utility assists in the Microsoft .NET scripting of report management operations.

EXAM TIP

SSRS includes three command-line utilities: RSConfig.exe, which handles configuring the connection properties from the Report Server to the catalog database; RSKeyMgmt.exe, which provides command-line support for managing encryption keys; and RS.exe, which allows scripting of report deployment.

Using RSConfig.exe to Manage Report Server Database Connections

The RSConfig.exe command-line utility manages the connection and settings for the SSRS instance, mainly to manage the repository database connection, but also to set up the default credentials for report execution against databases. The RSConfig.exe command parameters define the connection to the SSRS instance and then define the database connection to the Report Server database.

Use the parameters in Table 13-1 for the connection to the SSRS server and instance.

TABLE 13-1 RSConfig.exe SSRS Connection Parameters

COMMAND PARAMETER	DESCRIPTION
/m remote server name	The name of the server installed with SSRS. This is an optional parameter, with localhost used when it is not explicitly defined.
/i instance name	If a named instance has been installed, you use this to define the instance.

If you are configuring the Report Server database connection, you will need to specify the connection details. Use the command-line parameters in Table 13-2 to set these.

TABLE 13-2 RSConfig.exe Database Connection Parameters

COMMAND PARAMETER	DESCRIPTION
/c	Indicates that you are defining the connection information with other parameters. This parameter does not use a value and is required if you are defining the connection.
/s database server name	Used to identify the SQL Server name and instance of the host Report Server database.
/d database name	Defines the database name of the Report Server database on the specified SQL Server instance.
/a Authentication Method	Indicates whether the database connection will use Windows or SQL authentication to connect to the Report Server database.
/u username	Defines the user name that will be used if SQL Server authentication is specified; if a Windows domain account other than the SSRS service account is used, this represents the *domain/account*. This parameter is also used for the default source database connection, mentioned in Table 13-3.
/p password	Defines the password for the account specified in the /u parameter. This parameter is also used for the default source database connection, mentioned in Table 13-3.
/t	Optionally writes out error messages to the SSRS trace log.

Note that quotation marks are necessary if the values for any of the parameters in Tables 13-1 through 13-5 contain a space. Also note that you can precede the parameters with either the forward slash character (/) or the hyphen character (-).

Last, the RSConfig.exe command-line utility can be used to define the credentials that are used for unattended report execution. An unattended report might be triggered by a Reporting Services event, such as a scheduled report. Use the parameter described in Table 13-3 with RSConfig.exe to define the account to be used.

TABLE 13-3 RSConfig.exe Unattended Account Parameter

COMMAND PARAMETER	DESCRIPTION
/e	Indicates that you are setting the data source account to be used for an unattended report execution. This parameter requires that you also use the /u and /p user name and password parameters. Although it is not required, the /t parameter can also be used.

Examples: Using RSConfig.exe for Database Connection Management

The first example shown here uses the RSConfig.exe command-line utility to connect a locally installed SSRS instance to a local database named ReportServer using Windows Authentication:

```
rsconfig.exe /c /s (local) /d ReportServer /a Windows
```

In the next example, a locally installed SSRS instance is connected to a remote database server named ProdSQLSvr using the specified domain account Corporate\SSRSSvc:

```
rsconfig.exe /c /s ProdSQLSvr /d ReportServer /a Windows /u Corporate\SSRSSvc
/p pass@word1
```

Notice the difference between the preceding command-line example and the one that follows. In the next example, the /m switch is added, which specifies a remote SSRS instance. Also, the /a SQL parameter is added to specify that SQL authentication is used for the connection to the ReportServer database on ProdSQLServer:

```
rsconfig.exe /c /m ProdSSRSSvr /s ProdSQLSvr /d ReportServer /a SQL
/u SSRS_Login /p pass@word1
```

This last example sets the account to be used for unattended report execution to a domain account named Guest and logs any errors to the SSRS trace:

```
rsconfig.exe /e /u Corporate/Guest /p pass@word1 /t
```

Using RSKeyMgmt.exe to Manage Encryption Keys

SSRS includes a second command-line utility to assist in the management of the symmetric encryption keys that SSRS uses to secure and encrypt content in the Report Server database. This utility can perform common operations such as backup and restore, but it is also used to help in the management of SSRS instances that are part of scale-out deployments. This first set of properties is used for encryption key management tasks. In the next section, which discusses scale-out deployment, the RSKeyMgmt.exe switches are defined to join or revoke a report server in an existing scale-out deployment.

The parameters in Table 13-4 are used for general management of encryption keys such as backup, restore, and delete.

TABLE 13-4 RSKeyMgmt.exe Key Management Tasks

COMMAND PARAMETER	DESCRIPTION
/e	Specifies that the SSRS encryption key should be extracted to a file for backup.
/a	Specifies that the SSRS encryption key should be restored from a file and overwritten.
/d	Deletes the encryption key on the SSRS instance or instances and deletes all the encrypted data.
/s	Replaces the existing encryption key with a newly generated one and reencrypts all the existing content with the new key.
/f file path	Specifies the location of the file for the encryption key if the /e or /a parameter is used.
/p file password	Specifies the password used to secure the encryption key file so that if the file is found, the encryption key is still secure.
/i local SSRS instance name	Optional argument used to specify a named instance of SSRS if the SSRS instance is local to the command-line execution. This is not required if SSRS has been installed with the default (no name) configuration.
/t	Captures errors to the SSRS trace log.

Examples: Using RSKeyMgmt.exe for Encryption Key Management

The following statement backs up the encryption key to a file named SSRS_Keys (no extension) with a password set:

```
rskeymgmt.exe /e /f c:\SSRS_Keys -p pass@word1
```

In the next example, the backed-up keys are restored to the local server with the named instance SSRSAdmin:

```
rskeymgmt.exe /a /f c:\SSRS_Keys /p pass@word1 /i SSRSAdmin
```

The final example deletes all the keys and encrypted content on the Report Server database that the local instance is connected to:

```
rskeymgmt.exe /d
```

It is important to note that when you are performing any of the operations described earlier, you cannot run them against a remote server. They must be executed locally on the server. If, rather than the default, a named instance of SSRS exists, use the /i command-line parameter to specify the instance name.

Using RS.exe for Report Deployment

The final command-line utility, RS.exe, lets you script SSRS report operations such as deployment and management and run scripts through the command line. The RS.exe tool references a Report Server Script (.rss) file, which contains Microsoft Visual Basic .NET code based on the Web Services Description Language (WSDL) application programming interface (API). To learn how to build an .rss file, read the SQL Server 2008 Books Online topic "Scripting with the rs Utility and the Web Service" (see References). The RS.exe tool works similarly to other SSRS command-line utilities, using the command-line parameters listed in Table 13-5.

TABLE 13-5 RS.exe Report Deployment and Management

COMMAND PARAMETER	DESCRIPTION
/i input .rss file	Specifies the .rss file to execute.
/s SSRS Server URL	Defines the URL path to the SSRS Report Server virtual directory.
/u username	To override the user running the command, this parameter can define a different domain\user account to be used to connect to the Report Server instance.
/p password	Used to specify the password for the associated user name of the account defined with the /u parameter.
/l timeout seconds	Used to override the default time-out of 60 seconds; the /l (lowercase L) parameter is measured in seconds, with 0 representing an unlimited execution time.
/b	Runs the commands in a batch so that if a failure occurs anywhere in the script, the entire operation will be rolled back.
/e SOAP endpoint	Defines the Simple Object Access Protocol (SOAP) SSRS Web service endpoint to use for SSRS 2005 installations. By default, the SSRS 2005 management endpoint mgmt2005 is used.
/v Global Variable mapping	If the script contains embedded variables, the /v parameter can pass values into the variables.
/t	Captures errors to the SSRS trace log.

In the following example, an RSscript.rss script is executed against a local instance of SSRS that was installed with the default ReportServer virtual directory for Report Server:

```
rs.exe /i RSscript.rss /s http://localhost/ReportServer
```

In the more complicated example here, a script is executed under the corporate\SSRSSvc account while passing the value *ProdSQLSvr* into the script for the variable named *vDataSource*:

```
rs.exe /i RSscript.rss /s http://localhost/ReportServer /v
vDataSource=ProdSQLSvr /u Corporate\SSRSSvc /p pass@word1
```

Configuring SSRS for Scale-Out Deployments and High Availability

Scale-out SSRS deployments involve connecting more than one report server instance to a shared report server catalog. This allows report execution load to be shared across multiple servers. In addition to achieving a higher level of scalability, scale-out deployments also provide a higher level of availability in the case when a report server instance goes offline for whatever reason.

Figure 13-7 shows a typical architecture of a scale-out deployment of SSRS.

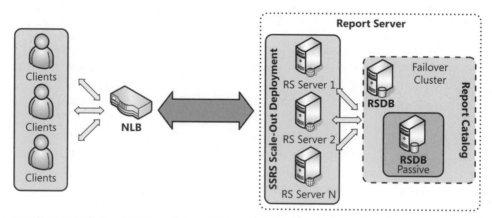

FIGURE 13-7 Scaling out SSRS involves multiple report server instances, a shared report server catalog, and Network Load Balancing (NLB) to distribute the requests.

The following elements are involved in a scale-out deployment:

- Network Load Balancing (NLB) provides the ability for the clients to distribute the requests to multiple report server instances.

- Multiple report server instances installed on multiple servers allow the report execution workload to be shared where report requests can be directed through NLB to different report server instances.

- A shared report server catalog provides the connection between the multiple report server instances. The report server catalog databases contain sensitive information such as report data sources and data caching that each of the report servers can access by sharing the encryption key.

- (Optional) A Microsoft Cluster Service (MSCS) installation with the shared report server catalog can be added to the cluster. This optional element in a scale-out solution provides higher availability because it provides high availability for the shared catalog databases.

Configuring the Report Server Catalog in a Failover Cluster

The report server catalog databases, ReportServer and ReportServerTempDB (by default), use the SQL Server relational Database Engine. Therefore, if the server or database engine fails, the SSRS instance will also fail. When you are configuring a scale-out deployment, it is important to also consider that the report server catalog is a single point of failure unless it is added to a clustered instance of the Database Engine.

The report server instances themselves, independent of the shared catalog databases, are not cluster aware. In other words, they should be installed on stand-alone servers, and their high-availability path has multiple instances on multiple servers in a scale-out federated environment, sometimes called a *Web farm*.

EXAM TIP

The report server is not installed in a cluster, and therefore cluster resource groups do not apply to the Report Server service. Only the report catalog databases can be created on an existing clustered SQL Server Database Engine instance. For the Report Server service, high availability and scale come through creating an SSRS scale-out deployment environment.

Enabling the catalog is simply a matter of creating the catalog databases (or restoring them) on a cluster with a SQL Server database instance installed. Clustering the SQL Server relational engine is handled through SQL Server setup and is documented in the SQL Server 2008 Books Online topic "Installing a SQL Server 2008 Failover Cluster" (see References).

Using Reporting Services Configuration Manager to Manage Scale-Out Deployments

There are two ways to configure SSRS for a scale-out deployment. The first method is to use Reporting Services Configuration Manager, and the second method is to use the RSKey-Mgmt.exe command-line utility, which is addressed in the next section.

The main steps involved in connecting a new report server instance to an existing report server installation using Reporting Services Configuration Manager are to point the database connection to the shared repository and then synchronize the encryption keys, as follows.

1. Open Reporting Services Configuration Manager, connect to the new instance, and then select the Database property page and click Change Databases to display the Report

Server Database Configuration Wizard (as shown earlier in Figure 13-5). Select the Choose An Existing Report Server Database option, and then run through the property pages, connecting to the shared ReportServer database on the remote server. Figure 13-8 shows the Database page where the ReportServer database is connected to the new report server instance.

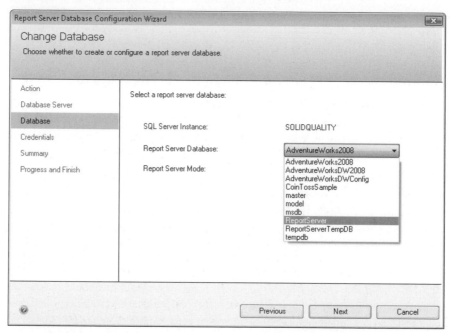

FIGURE 13-8 When creating a scale-out deployment of SSRS, connect the report server instances to a shared ReportServer catalog.

2. After the new instance has been pointed to the shared repository, the next step is to validate the addition by synchronizing the encryption keys. In Reporting Services Configuration Manager, you will need to connect to the original or first instance and then select the Scale-Out Deployment property page, as Figure 13-9 shows.

3. In the Status column, the new server will have a status of Waiting To Join. Select the instance, and then click Add Server. The instance will now be added to the scale-out deployment.

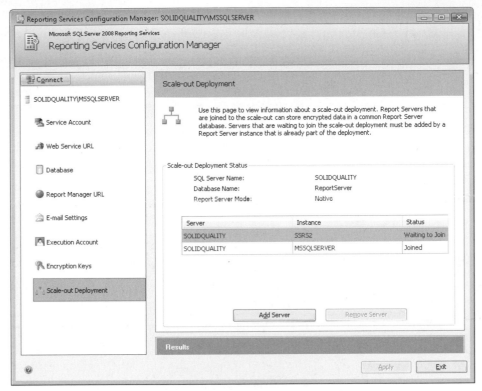

FIGURE 13-9 When you point a new instance of Reporting Services to a shared catalog, you need to add it to the scale-out deployment through the Scale-Out Deployment property page.

Using RSKeyMgmt.exe to Manage Scale-Out Deployment

Using the command-line utility RSKeyMgmt.exe, you can also add a report server instance to an existing report server scale-out environment. To do this, you would use the set of parameters in Table 13-6 to add and remove SSRS instances to help manage a scale-out SSRS deployment. These share the /i and /t parameters described earlier in Table 13-4. The difference here is that you can reference a remote SSRS instance that you want to add or remove from a scale-out deployment.

TABLE 13-6 RSKeyMgmt.exe Scale-Out Instance Management

COMMAND PARAMETER	DESCRIPTION
/j	Adds a remote instance of SSRS to the Report Server database of a local instance. The remote server and instance are specified with the /m and /n parameters, and if a named instance is used locally, it is specified using the /i parameter.
/r GUID Installation ID	Removes an instance of SSRS from a scale-out deployment implementation. The instance to be removed is identified by the *Installation ID*, a unique identifier mapped to the instance and specified in the RSReportServer.config file.
/u account name	Specifies the account of a local administrator on the server where the remote SSRS instance (the instance that will be joining a scale-out deployment) runs. This parameter is optional if the user who is executing RSKeyMgmt.exe has local administrator rights on the remote server.
/v password	This defines the password of the local administrator account specified by the /v parameter.
/m remote SSRS Server Name	In connecting to an SSRS instance on a remote computer, this parameter is used to specify the server.
/n remote SSRS instance name	This is used in conjunction with the /m parameter to specify the SSRS instance name on a remote computer. If the default instance is used, this is not required.

Examples: Using RSKeyMgmt.exe for Scale-Out SSRS Installation Management

In the following example, the remote SSRS instance ProdSSRSSvr1 is joined to the scale-out implementation of SSRS shared by the local SSRS instance. The remote local administrator account is *Corporate\SSRSSvc* with the associated password:

```
rskeymgmt.exe /j /m ProdSSRSSvr1 /u Corporate\SSRSSvc /v pass@word1
```

The next example removes an instance of SSRS that is part of a scale-out deployment. The report server globally unique identifier (GUID) installation ID was acquired from the RSReportServer.config file:

```
rskeymgmt.exe /r {632e859c-53513-47113-a9e5-f28a0206a68f}
```

Changing Report Server Properties in SSMS

At the report server level, SSRS contains properties that apply to the overall instance such as logging, enabling My Reports, and security. Some of these properties are found in the Site Settings link in Report Manager. However, other properties are accessible through SSMS when connected to an SSRS instance. After connecting to SSRS in SSMS, right-click the report server instance, and then select Properties. Figure 13-10 shows the Advanced property page of the Server Properties dialog box and some of the properties that you can configure.

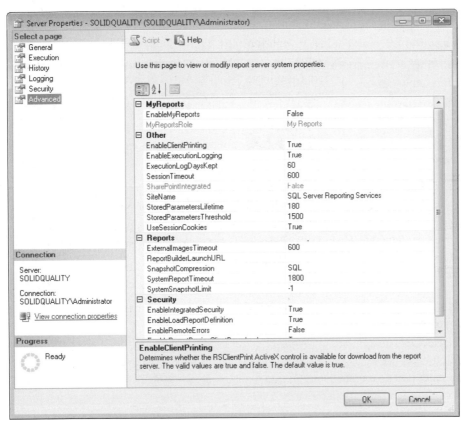

FIGURE 13-10 Some Report Server properties are found in the Server Properties dialog box for an instance in SSMS.

Understanding Configuration Files in Reporting Services 2008

SSRS uses several XML configuration files to handle advanced service settings, user defaults, and policy implementation, as follows:

- **RSReportServer.config** Primary configuration file that contains settings for the Report Server Web part and Report Manager.
- **RSSrvPolicy.config** Stores policy settings for the Report Server Web service.
- **RSMgrPolicy.config** Contains policy settings for the Report Manager application.
- **Web.config** Contains ASP.NET settings for the Report Server and Report Manager.
- **ReportingServicesServices.exe.config** Contains trace and logging settings for the Report Server service.
- **RSReportDesigner.config** Contains configuration settings such as rendering devices for the Report Designer application.
- **RSPreviewPolicy.config** Contains security policies for the server extensions.

Each file is stored in the Installation directory for SQL Server, relative to the component that the file primarily relates.

EXAM TIP

The primary configuration file in SSRS 2008 is RSReportServer.config. It contains rendering settings and HTTPS. SSRS 2008 does *not* use RSWebApplication.config. The SSRS policy settings are stored in the RSSrvPolicy.config and RSMgrPolicy.config files.

Modifying the RSReportServer.config File

The RSReportServer.config is one of several configuration files, but it is the main configuration file for both the Report Server Web service and Report Manager. In Reporting Services 2005, Report Manager had a separate configuration file named RSWebApplication.config, but this file is no longer used in Reporting Services 2008.

The RSReportServer.config file is found in the %Program Files%\Microsoft SQL Server\ MSRS10.<*InstanceName*>\Reporting Services\ReportServer\ folder.

The settings in Reporting Services Configuration Manager are saved as configuration entries in the RSReportServer.config file. However, the configuration manager also performs critical steps that are not handled by a configuration file, such as creating the virtual Web directories and generating the application as well as creating the structures and initial entries in the report catalog when a new database is specified.

Nonetheless, the RSReportServer.config file contains many more advanced settings and properties that are not available to set within Reporting Services Configuration Manager or through the report server properties in SSMS.

Example: Limiting the List of Report Rendering Options

A common configuration setting in RSReportServer.config is to limit the user choices for the report rendering.

For example, if you wanted to exclude Microsoft Office Excel as a choice for rendering reports, you would look for the entries under the *<Render>* tag in the XML .config file to find the following line:

```
<Extension Name="EXCEL" Type="Microsoft.ReportingServices.Rendering.ExcelRenderer.
    ExcelRenderer,Microsoft.ReportingServices.ExcelRendering"/>
```

To turn off Excel in the rendering options, you would add a *Visible="false"* entry to the line, like this:

```
<Extension Name="EXCEL" Type="Microsoft.ReportingServices.Rendering.ExcelRenderer.
    ExcelRenderer,Microsoft.ReportingServices.ExcelRendering" Visible="false"/>
```

PRACTICE **Managing SSRS Encryption Keys**

In this practice, you use RSKeyMgmt.exe to back up and restore an encryption key to experience the importance of having a backup copy of the symmetric encryption key. The practice exercise assumes that the default SSRS instance was installed on your local computer and was configured to use the default settings during installation. The command-line examples in this practice are in the Lesson 2 Practice Exercise Code.txt file in the ..\Source\Ch 13\ folder of the installed practice files.

EXERCISE Back Up and Restore an Encryption Key

In this exercise, you will back up and restore an encryption key.

1. Open Internet Explorer, and then navigate to the Report Manager Web interface by connecting to the Reports virtual directory of your SSRS instance (*http://localhost/ Reports*).

2. Click New Folder in the Reporting Services Home folder, and then create a folder named Test Encryption and click OK.

3. Open the new folder you created. Click New Data Source, and then name the new data source **Test Data Source**. In the Connection String box, enter the following code:

   ```
   Data Source=(local);Initial Catalog=AdventureWorks2008
   ```

4. Keep the connection defaults as they are, and then click Apply to save the changes.

5. Open a new Command Prompt window by clicking Start, selecting Run, and then typing **CMD** and clicking OK.

6. Back up the current SSRS encryption key by running the following command:

   ```
   rskeymgmt.exe /e /f c:\SSRS_Key_OLD.snk -p pass@word1
   ```

7. When prompted, confirm that you want to back up the encryption key by typing **y**.

8. Next, to generate a brand-new key and encrypt the existing SSRS content with the new key, run the following command-line statement:

```
rskeymgmt.exe /s
```

9. When prompted, confirm that you want to grant the report server access to the newly generated key by typing **y**. This will enable the content to use the newly generated key instead of the old key.

10. In the Report Manager browser, press F5 to refresh the window, and then confirm that you still have access to the content. Then click the Test Data Source link to open the Test Data Source Properties page.

11. Back in the Command Prompt window, run the following statement to back up the new key:

```
rskeymgmt.exe /e /f c:\SSRS_Key_NEW.snk -p pass@word1
```

12. When prompted, confirm that you want to back up the key.

13. Next, you will restore the original encryption key to your SSRS instance. Run the following command:

```
rskeymgmt.exe /a /f c:\SSRS_Key_OLD.snk -p pass@word1
```

14. The Report Manager browser should still have the Test Data Source Properties page open. If it is, press F5 to refresh the content; if it is not, browse to the Test Data Source that you created in step 3. At this point, you will receive the error *The report server is unable to access encrypted data. Apply a back-up key or delete all encrypted content.* This is because the existing content was encrypted with a new key, but the old key was restored. If you did not have the new encryption key, you would not be able to access the encrypted content, and it would have to be deleted.

15. Restore the new encryption key to enable the existing content to be unencrypted by the SSRS instance, and then run the following command:

```
rskeymgmt.exe /a /f c:\SSRS_Key_NEW.snk -p pass@word1
```

16. Navigate back to the Test Data Source Properties page in the Report Manager browser, or if you are already there, press F5 to refresh the content and confirm that the properties are viewable and modifiable.

Case Scenario: Scaling Out Your SSRS Servers

As you begin the process of setting up a SQL Server 2008 BI environment, you are planning out your hardware architecture. Your solution will consist of an SSRS installation that will access online analytical processing (OLAP) data in SSAS built from a SQL Server data mart. Your manager has approved two blade servers for SSRS so that the service can be configured for scale-out deployment—that will help to balance the workload and will provide some load balancing. Additionally, your system administrator has set up Network Load Balancing (NLB) to distribute the report requests. How will you handle the following two setup requirements?

1. Your SSRS implementation requires that you set up a scale-out deployment of SSRS on the two allocated servers. You have already installed the first SSRS instance on one of the servers that points to a Report Server database on your database server. You are now ready to install an instance of SSRS on the second computer. How do you use command-line utilities to install and configure this instance to be part of the SSRS scale-out deployment?

2. To prevent a single point of failure for SSRS, you also need to handle failures at the report server catalog database level. In the case of a server hardware failure, you do not want the SSRS implementation to also fail. Which is the best high-availability technology to use for this situation and why?

Chapter Summary

- A Reporting Services installation includes the report server catalog, which contains all the metadata necessary to run reporting services, including the encrypted report definitions, encrypted data sources, and site and report security settings.

- The Reporting Services Configuration Manager tool helps in the setup of an SSRS instance after installation, including setup of virtual directories, service accounts, Report Server database access, and encryption keys.

- The RSConfig.exe command-line utility provides SSRS connection administration to the Report Server databases, ReportServer and ReportServerTempDB.

- The RSKeyMgmt.exe command-line utility helps manage encryption keys for backup, restore, scale-out instance management, and deletion of encrypted content.

- The RS.exe command-line utility provides a way to run SSRS script files at a command line.

- The SSRS encryption keys need to be backed up to an .snk file and stored securely to allow for a restore at a later point in the case of a sever failure or a reconfiguration of hardware.

- SSRS can be implemented in a scale-out architecture by sharing the report server catalog between multiple instances of the report server. The Reporting Services Configuration Manager tool can synchronize the encryption keys between the servers in order to access the shared catalog, or you can use the RSKeyMgmt.exe and RSConfig.exe command-line utilities to set up the scale-out environment.

- Reporting Services uses several configuration files for advanced settings and management. The main file is the RSReportServer.config file, which contains service settings, Report Manager settings, rendering device properties, delivery method settings, and so on.

Answers

Chapter 1: Case Scenario Answers

Creating an ETL Solution

1. The best practice for creating a set of packages that all work together is to create a single SSIS project within BIDS. You would then create multiple packages within the project, one for each of the different dimensions and fact tables. Because all the packages would use the same source connection string to the ERP system and the same destination connection string to the data mart, you should create two data sources within the project: one for the source and one for the destination. Last, each package would need to reference the project data sources, so within each package, you would create package connections based on the project data sources.

2. The SSIS data flow contains a Slowly Changing Dimension Transformation that can handle changes and new records in the dimension tables. Before using the Slowly Changing Dimension Transformation, you need to create a source adapter to the ERP system that pulls the data to be compared with the dimension tables. You might need to use a transformation to clean and correct any data anomalies, and after those steps are complete, you can connect the data to the Slowly Changing Dimension Transformation. Ideally, you would create a separate SSIS package for each dimension package so that they could be reused for different groups of package executions.

3. Fact tables contain surrogate keys that reference the dimension tables but also contain the business keys from the source. So as you are pulling the reseller sales data and the sales quotas, you can use a Lookup Transformation to get the surrogate keys from dimension tables by joining across the business keys. You can then insert new rows into the fact tables by using the surrogate keys and measures. As you do when using dimensions, you will typically have a separate package for each fact table that needs processing.

Chapter 2: Case Scenario Answers

Troubleshooting and Handling Errors in SSIS Packages

1. When you are developing in the control flow, you can use breakpoints to pause packages during execution so that you can examine the intermediate state and the results of your tasks and constraints. When you are working in the data flow, you can use data viewers on your

data paths and error paths to catch errors, and you can watch the rows to isolate any errors and help determine the best way to fix them.

2. Because the commit level is configured on a table-by-table basis, all the data flow and control flow tasks that operate on a single task need to be grouped together in a container, and the *TransactionOption* property must be set to *Required* for each container. You should also implement checkpoints on the containers, which will let you restart the packages at the point of failure after you have resolved any problems. You can simplify this implementation by creating a master package that has checkpoints turned on and that uses the Execute Package Task to call child packages for each destination table that has transactions enabled.

3. To capture the destination row count, you add several Row Count Transformations to your package. Place a Row Count Transformation in the pipeline before each destination. The Row Count Transformation will store in a predefined variable the number of rows that flow through the component, so you can create a separate package variable for each destination. To capture the variable values, set the *RaiseChangeEvent* property to *True* for all new variables and add the *OnVariableValueChange* event handler. This event fires when each Row Count Transformation updates the identified variable, which subsequently calls a SQL statement that adds the *VariableName*, *count*, and *EventHandlerStartTime* to a tracking table.

4. Using the *OnError* event, you create a new event handler on the package executable file level. This event handler contains a single Send Mail Task that you configure to use the *SourceName* variable, which is the task or container name that experienced the error as the e-mail message subject and the *ErrorDescription* variable as the e-mail message body. You hard-code your e-mail Simple Mail Transport Protocol (SMTP) server and your support team's Distribution List (DL) address so that all parties will be e-mailed when a failure occurs.

Chapter 3: Case Scenario Answers

Deploying SSIS Packages

1. To make the connection strings configurable without manual package editing every time a server or user name and password changes, you should implement package configurations. Across the 25 packages, only two source systems contain user names and passwords (the files are on a network share), so you should create a single XML file that contains the connection strings. First you would create the configurations file in one package by using SSIS package configurations, and then you would have all the packages point to the same file. If your policies prevent storing user names and passwords in a flat file, you can choose to use a Microsoft SQL Server table to store these items. If you do use a SQL Server table, be aware that you will have a second configuration entry that will be applied first—it will point to the SQL Server database in which the connection strings are entered. You will need to replicate

the SSIS package configurations on the test and production computers, being sure to use the appropriate server, user name, and password entries where applicable. This way, as changes happen, you can modify the connections without opening the packages.

2. Because SQL Server is the package destination for both the test and production environments, an easy way to automate your deployment is to create a deployment installer set by using the Package Deployment Utility in BIDS. You can run the Package Installation Wizard on your test server and deploy all the packages to SQL Server in one step. When the tests are complete, the same installer set can be deployed on your production server through the Package Installation Wizard.

3. You can deploy single SSIS packages manually, but a better choice is to use the DTUtil command-line tool, which lets you write a command for the deployment and then automate the process. You could deploy the package to the local SQL Server using Windows Authentication by including a simple command, such as this:

    dtutil.exe / FILE c:\IntegrateCRM.dtsx / COPY SQL;IntegrateCRM

    Other command-line switches let you specify the destination SQL Server and SQL Server user name and password as needed.

Chapter 4: Case Scenario Answers

Securing and Scheduling SSIS Packages

1. To encrypt all the content of the packages, you need to use the DTUtil utility with the */ENCRYPT* command-line parameter, running the utility from the folder of the packages. Each DTUtil statement will look like the following:

    dtutil.exe /file MyPackage.dtsx /encrypt file;MyPackage.dtsx;3;EncPswd

    In addition, because all the packages contain a shared connection user name and password, you can use SSMS to deny access to the configuration table from all accounts except the SQL Server Agent service account or the SQL Server Agent Proxy account that will be executing the package.

2. To schedule the packages to be run, create a SQL Server Agent job and several job steps to execute the packages. When you identify the package, you need to enter the password that you specified in the DTUtil command-line statement in step 1 to encrypt the packages (EncPswd). The job could also be run by using a proxy account. That account would need to have the proper security credentials to access the SQL Server configuration table so that the connection user name and password are updated at execution time.

Chapter 5: Case Scenario Answers

Building an SSAS Solution as a Prototype

1. To build an initial prototype, you would create a new SSAS solution and add a data source and a data source view (DSV) on top of the database whose schema defines dimension and fact tables. You could then use the Cube Wizard to generate a cube with measure groups for Internet and reseller sales data, along with dimensions for business entities such as time, products, customers, geography, sales reasons, employees, and sales territories. After processing the new SSAS database, you could use the browsers within BIDS or Microsoft Office Excel to review the resulting design, possibly even sharing it with a few of your end users, to better understand the available data and the end users' analytical requirements.

2. To improve the usability of the cube, you would first want to ensure that all the measures, measure groups, dimensions, and attributes have business-friendly names. Next, you would likely need to define format strings for all the measures that show currencies and other numbers appropriately. Last, within each dimension, consider adding additional attributes that create useful attribute hierarchies.

Chapter 6: Case Scenario Answers

Extending SSAS Cubes

1. In general, you can accommodate reseller sales by creating a new Reseller cube or by adding a Reseller measure group to the existing cube. If you need to handle large data volumes, you might find that a new cube will give you better performance. On the downside, you will not be able to author consolidated reports that draw data from separate cubes. With smaller cubes, consider adding a new measure group to the existing cube. Incorporate a performance-testing plan early in the design cycle to gauge the performance of the single-cube approach.

2. As an OLAP server, SSAS is a natural choice for implementing calculated measures and KPIs. OLAP browsers and third-party applications can use the MDX KPI functions to query the cube and retrieve the KPI properties.

Chapter 7: Case Scenario Answers

Implementing Low-Latency OLAP and Deployment Strategies

1. You could partition the Internet Sales measure group and set up a low-latency partition. The definition slice of the low-latency partition could filter the sales data for the current month only. In addition, you could enable proactive caching on that partition so that you do not have to process it explicitly.

2. Start by optimizing the dimensional design of your cube. Make sure that you have set up correct attribute relationships and have defined useful user hierarchies. Set the Aggregation-Usage property of infrequently used attributes to None. Run the Aggregation Design Wizard to create the preliminary aggregation design. When the cube has been deployed, you can turn on query logging and then use the Usage-Based Optimization Wizard, which is discussed in Chapter 8, to tune the aggregations that are designed for the cube.

3. If you want to retain the partitions and security settings on the test server, your best deployment option is to use the Deployment Wizard. Rather than processing the production cubes individually, consider processing the cube on the staging server and then using the Synchronize Database Wizard to synchronize each of the production cubes with the staging cube.

4. If only new members are added to a dimension, you can process the dimension by using the Process Add option.

Chapter 8: Case Scenario Answers

Administering and Securing SSAS Cubes

1. To propagate the allowed set to all cubes in a database, you need to set up dimension data security on the database dimension rather than on the cube dimension. To do so, expand the Dimension drop-down list on the Dimension Data tab, and then select the dimension below the database name.

2. To find the users who have been successfully authenticated by the server, use SQL Server Profiler to configure a trace based on the Standard template. Inspect the Audit Login/Audit Logout events to find the authenticated users. You can also query the DISCOVER_CONNECTIONS schema rowset to see a list of the current connections.

Chapter 9: Case Scenario Answers

Working with SSAS Data Mining

1. Preparing the data for customer churn is not an easy task. The problem is that you typically do not have a simple Churn attribute in your source data. You should find out from the Sales Department how it wants to define churn. For example, you could create a new attribute that shows whether a customer has purchased anything from Adventure Works in the past six months and then use this as a predictable attribute. Do not forget to randomly split the existing data into training sets and test sets.

2. You can use Decision Trees, Naïve Bayes, Neural Network, Clustering, Logistic Regression, and Linear Regression algorithms for predictions.

3. In a real-life project, you should create multiple mining models by using different algorithms and different parameters of the algorithms. Alternatively, you could try to define the attribute that measures the churn differently and apply the models on the new predictable variable. Last, you could use different input attributes for different models. You could have a single mining structure and ignore some attributes in some models. You would then deploy the model with the best performance into the production environment.

4. To allow the Finance Department to see the source cases that the data mining model used for training, you have to enable drillthrough on your mining model. To do this, first give the Drill Through permission to the SSAS database role that includes the Finance Department users. In addition, you should give this role the Read Access permission and the Read Definition permission for the data source. Last, the Finance Department users must have permissions that allow access to the source data. For example, if the source is in a SQL Server table, the users need Select permission on that table.

5. You can download the Microsoft SQL Server 2008 *Data Mining Add-ins for Microsoft Office 2007* (see References) and install them on the computers in the Finance Department. Then, with the help of an ad hoc Clustering model, the Finance Department users will be able to use Excel 2007 Add-ins to analyze the worksheet data. With the Clustering model, you can easily find outliers, which are cases that do not fit well in any cluster. Outliers typically include suspicious data. Of course, you must allow session mining models on your SSAS.

Chapter 10: Case Scenario Answers

Building Reports for the AdventureWorks Intranet

1. You can add a new report to the SSRS solution to satisfy this user requirement. Create a dataset that uses the AdventureWorks relational database. In the dataset's query, filter the information to retrieve only the last week's sales by product category, subcategory, and model. Use a Table data region and create two additional groupings, one by category and

another by subcategory. Set the initial visibility status of the Subcategory and Detail rows to hidden, the toggle property of the Subcategory grouping to change based on Category, and the toggle property of the Detail grouping to change based on Subcategory.

2. For this requirement, you can use the Report Wizard to create the report. On the Data Source page, select the multidimensional database, and then use the MDX Query Builder to create the MDX query. In the Data pane, drag the Product Model Categories hierarchy, the Date.Calendar hierarchy, and the SalesAmount measure onto the Results pane. Remove the Calendar Semester and Calendar data levels. Select a matrix report, and then assign the date-related information to columns and the product category information to the rows. Last, assign the amount as detail information.

Chapter 11: Case Scenario Answers

Creating a Reporting Services Infrastructure

1. You can configure report models that will let users create their own reports. You need to create two separate models, one for the relational engine and another for the SSAS database. The relational database model should be created and configured in BIDS, and the OLAP data source should be created from SSMS or Report Manager.

2. You could create a parameterized report that prompts the user for the desired level of aggregation and then dynamically creates the *group by* statement. Alternatively, you could use the same query for all the aggregation levels, use a table or matrix report item, and hide the grouping level based on the user selection. The main advantage of the first approach is that it pulls only the required data when the report is executed. The main advantage of the second option is that it allows the reuse of the cache if the report uses report caching.

Chapter 12: Case Scenario Answers

Managing the Report Environment for Adventure Works

1. In general, because item-level roles are cumulative, for each department's folder, you can assign the Browser role to the Active Directory group that represents the employees of each division. Additionally, you can add the Browser role to each person who needs access to more than one department's folder.

2. To allow access to the Oracle databases, you will need to define a user with low-level privileges and store the credentials for that user in Report Server. For the SQL Server databases, given the fact that Adventure Works uses a Windows domain, you can enable Kerberos and use the Integrated Windows Authentication mechanism.

Chapter 13: Case Scenario Answers

Scaling Out Your SSRS Servers

1. Because the first SSRS server has been installed and configured, your next task is to install an unconfigured instance of SSRS, without having the installation use the default configuration, on the second server. You will then need to configure the virtual directories through Reporting Services Configuration Manager and set the service accounts. Before joining the new instance to the scale-out deployment, connect the SSRS instance to the same Report Server database by using RSConfig.exe with the /c parameter. At this point, you should run the RSKeyMgmt.exe tool with the /j command parameter to join an existing SSRS. (See Lesson 2 in this chapter for the other parameters needed to point to the servers.) You need to run this command statement on the server that is already configured and then reference the new instance that will join the existing scale-out deployment.

2. High availability at the database level can be handled by clustering, database mirroring, replication, or log shipping. However, the best choice is to use clustering. Clustering will prevent a server hardware failure from affecting the SSRS implementation, as the Database Engine will fail over to another available node in the cluster. In addition, this will be seamless to Reporting Services, as the database connection uses the virtual instance name of the database server, which also moves to the other server. With the other technologies, the SSRS implementation would need the catalog database connection to be repointed to the backup database from the mirroring, log shipping, or replication.

References

Implementing an SSIS Solution

Configuring, Deploying, and Maintaining SSIS

The following references offer more information on both of the SSIS objective domains for Exam 70-448.

- *Professional Microsoft SQL Server 2008 Integration Services*. Wrox, 2008. Brian Knight, Erik Veerman, et al.
  http://www.wrox.com/WileyCDA/WroxTitle/Professional-Microsoft-SQL-Server-2008-Integration-Services.productCd-0470247959.html

- SQL Server Integration Services, official Microsoft site
  http://www.microsoft.com/sqlserver/2008/en/us/integration.aspx

- "Project Real, Business Intelligence ETL Design Practices," best practices white paper for designing SSIS packages for data warehouse ETL
  http://www.microsoft.com/technet/prodtechnol/sql/2005/realetldp.mspx

- SSIS Data Sources references
  http://ssis.wik.is/Data_Sources

- TechNet Integration Services links
  http://technet.microsoft.com/en-us/sqlserver/cc510302.aspx

Implement Auditing, Logging, and Event Handling

- Troubleshooting Integration Services
  http://technet.microsoft.com/en-us/library/bb522581.aspx

Install and Maintain SSIS Components

- "Configuring Integration Services in a Cluster Environment," MSDN white paper
  http://msdn.microsoft.com/en-us/library/ms345193.aspx

- Building, Deploying, and Debugging Custom Objects
  http://msdn.microsoft.com/en-us/library/ms403356.aspx

Deploy an SSIS Solution

- **Deploying Integration Services packages**
  http://technet.microsoft.com/en-us/library/ms137592.aspx

Configure SSIS Security Settings

- **Integration Services Security Overview**
  http://technet.microsoft.com/en-us/library/ms137833.aspx

Implementing an SSAS Solution

Configuring, Deploying, and Maintaining SSAS

The following references offer more information on both of the SSAS objective domains for Exam 70-448.

- **The Adventure Works DW BI sample database, which includes the Adventure Works SSAS projects**
  http://www.codeplex.com/MSFTDBProdSamples/Release/ProjectReleases.aspx?ReleaseId=18407

- **"Microsoft SQL Server 2008 Analysis Services Performance Guide" white paper by Microsoft**
  http://www.microsoft.com/downloads/details.aspx?FamilyID=3be0488d-e7aa-4078-a050-ae39912d2e43&displaylang=en

- *The Data Warehouse Toolkit: The Complete Guide to Dimensional Modeling* (Second Edition). **Wiley, 2002. Ralph Kimball and Margy Ross.**
  http://www.wiley.com/WileyCDA/WileyTitle/productCd-0471200247.html

- **New Database Dialog Box (Analysis Services), SQL Server 2008 Books Online**
  http://msdn.microsoft.com/en-us/library/ms189710.aspx

- **XML for Analysis (XMLA)**
  http://www.xmla.org

Implement Measures in a Cube

- **Configuring Measure Group Properties, SQL Server 2008 Books Online**
  http://technet.microsoft.com/en-us/library/ms365411.aspx

- **Configuring Measure Properties, SQL Server 2008 Books Online**
  http://technet.microsoft.com/en-us/library/ms175623.aspx

Implement Custom Logic in a Cube by Using MDX

- **Multidimensional Expressions (MDX) Reference**
  http://msdn.microsoft.com/en-us/library/ms145506.aspx

- **Mosha Pasumansky, Microsoft OLAP blog entry "MDX in Katmai: Dynamic Named Sets"**
  http://sqlblog.com/blogs/mosha/archive/2007/08/25/mdx-in-katmai-dynamic-named-sets.aspx

Implement Data Mining

- **SQL Server Analysis Services—Data Mining, SQL Server 2008 Books Online. See the following topics:**
  Data Mining Concepts
  Designing and Implementing
  Querying Data Mining Models
  Operations
  Security and Protection

  http://msdn.microsoft.com/en-us/library/bb510517.aspx

- **The following topics in SQL Server 2008 Books Online:**
  - **Customizing a Data Mining Model (Analysis Services – Data Mining)**
    http://msdn.microsoft.com/en-us/library/cc280427.aspx

  - **Data Mining Extensions (DMX) Reference**
    http://msdn.microsoft.com/en-us/library/ms132058.aspx

  - **CREATE MINING STRUCTURE (DMX)**
    http://msdn.microsoft.com/en-us/library/ms131977.aspx

  - **ALTER MINING STRUCTURE (DMX)**
    http://msdn.microsoft.com/en-us/library/ms132066.aspx

  - **SELECT FROM <model> PREDICTION JOIN (DMX)**
    http://msdn.microsoft.com/en-us/library/ms132031.aspx

  - **OPENQUERY (DMX)**
    http://msdn.microsoft.com/en-us/library/ms132173.aspx

- **SQL Server 2008 Data Mining Add-ins for Microsoft Office 2007**
  http://www.microsoft.com/downloads/details.aspx?FamilyID=896a493a-2502-4795-94ae-e00632ba6de7&DisplayLang=en

- ***Data Mining with Microsoft SQL Server 2008**. Wiley, 2008. Jamie MacLennan, ZhaoHui Tang, and Bogdan Crivat.*
  http://www.amazon.com/Data-Mining-Microsoft-Server-2008/dp/0470277742/ref=sr_1_2?ie=UTF8&s=books&qid=1218702291&sr=8-2

- **SQL Server Data Mining community site**
  http://www.sqlserverdatamining.com/ssdm/default.aspx

Configure Permissions and Roles in SSAS

- "Introduction to Dimension Security in Analysis Services 2005," by Richard Tkachuk (Richard Tkachuk's Analysis Services Web site)
  *http://sqlserveranalysisservices.com/OLAPPapers/
  IntroductiontoDimensionSecurityinAnalysisServices2005.htm*

- "Protect UDM with Dimension Data Security," by Teo Lachev (SQL Server Magazine, July 2007)
  http://www.sqlmag.com/Articles/ArticleID/95998/95998.html

- Microsoft Knowledge Base article "How to Configure SQL Server 2005 Analysis Services to Use Kerberos Authentication"
  http://support.microsoft.com/kb/917409

Deploy SSAS Databases and Objects

- Analysis Services Product Samples
  http://www.codeplex.com/MSFTASProdSamples

- Analysis Management Objects (AMO), SQL Server 2008 Books Online
  http://msdn.microsoft.com/en-us/library/ms124924.aspx

Install and Maintain an SSAS Instance

- Database ReadWriteModes, SQL Server 2008 Books Online
  http://msdn.microsoft.com/en-us/library/cc280582.aspx

- Server Clusters, Windows Server 2003 Product Help
  http://technet.microsoft.com/en-us/library/cc783714.aspx

- Installing a SQL Server 2008 Failover Cluster, SQL Server 2008 Books Online
  http://msdn.microsoft.com/en-us/library/ms179410.aspx

Diagnose and Resolve Performance Issues

- "SSAS Load Testing Best Practices" white paper by Jaime Basilico and Dmitri Tchikatilov
  http://www.codeplex.com/SQLSrvAnalysisSrvcs/Release/ProjectReleases.aspx?ReleaseId=3505

- XML for Analysis Schema Rowsets, SQL Server 2008 Books Online topic
  http://msdn.microsoft.com/en-us/library/ms126221.aspx

Implement Processing Options

- "Analysis Services 2005 Processing Architecture" white paper by T. K. Anand
  http://msdn.microsoft.com/en-us/library/ms345142.aspx

Implementing an SSRS Solution

Configuring, Deploying, and Maintaining SSRS

The following references offer more information on both of the SSRS objective domains for Exam 70-448.

- SQL Server 2008 Books Online topics "Development (Reporting Services)" (*http://msdn.microsoft.com/en-us/library/bb522683.aspx*) and "Designing and Implementing Reports (Reporting Services)" (*http://msdn.microsoft.com/en-us/library/bb522712.aspx*), especially the subtopic "Adding Interactive Features" (*http://msdn.microsoft.com/en-us/library/ms159701.aspx*).

- *Applied Microsoft SQL Server 2008 Reporting Services*. Prologika Press, 2008. Teo Lachev. *http://www.amazon.com/Applied-Microsoft-Server-Reporting-Services/dp/0976635313/ref=pd_bbs_sr_2?ie=UTF8&s=books&qid=1219314632&sr=8-2*

- .NET Framework Developer's Guide: Formatting Strings on MSDN *http://msdn.microsoft.com/en-us/library/fbxft59x.aspx*

- To download a 90-day trial version of Microsoft Visual Studio 2008 Professional Edition: *http://www.microsoft.com/downloads/details.aspx?FamilyID=83c3a1ec-ed72-4a79-8961-25635db0192b&displaylang=en*

- To download Microsoft Visual Studio 2008 Service Pack 1: *http://www.microsoft.com/downloads/details.aspx?FamilyId=FBEE1648-7106-44A7-9649-6D9F6D58056E&displaylang=en*

- For more information about code access security for your custom assemblies in SSRS 2008, the following topics in SQL Server 2008 Books Online:
  - Understanding Security Policies *http://msdn.microsoft.com/en-us/library/ms154466.aspx*

  - Using Reporting Services Security Policy Files *http://msdn.microsoft.com/en-us/library/ms152828.aspx*

  - Code Access Security in Reporting Services *http://msdn.microsoft.com/en-us/library/ms154658.aspx*

- *Microsoft Visual Basic 2008 Step by Step*. Microsoft Press, 2008. Michael Halvorson. *http://www.amazon.com/Microsoft-Visual-Basic-2008-Step/dp/0735625379/ref=pd_bbs_sr_1?ie=UTF8&s=books&qid=1219651763&sr=8-1*

- Adventure Works 2008 Sample Reports *http://www.codeplex.com/MSFTRSProdSamples/Wiki/View.aspx?title=SS2008%21AdventureWorks%20Sample%20Reports&referringTitle=Home*

- Security and Protection (Reporting Services), SQL Server 2008 Books Online
  http://msdn.microsoft.com/en-us/library/bb522728.aspx

- Operations (Reporting Services), SQL Server 2008 Books Online
  http://msdn.microsoft.com/en-us/library/bb522794.aspx

- *Applied Microsoft SQL Server 2008 Reporting Services*. Prologika Press, 2008. Teo Lachev.
  http://www.amazon.com/Applied-Microsoft-Server-Reporting-Services/dp/0976635313/ref=pd_bbs_sr_2?ie=UTF8&s=books&qid=1219314632&sr=8-2

- "Reporting Services in SQL Server 2008," Microsoft SQL Server 2008 white paper
  http://www.microsoft.com/sqlserver/2008/en/us/wp-sql-2008-reporting-services.aspx

- "Reporting Services Scale-Out Deployment Best Practices," Technical Notes
  http://sqlcat.com/technicalnotes/archive/2008/10/21/reporting-services-scale-out-deployment-best-practices.aspx

- "Scaling Up Reporting Services 2008 vs. Reporting Services 2005: Lessons Learned," Technical Notes
  http://sqlcat.com/technicalnotes/archive/2008/07/09/scaling-up-reporting-services-2008-vs-reporting-services-2005-lessons-learned.aspx

- RSReportServer Configuration File, SQL Server 2008 Books Online
  http://msdn.microsoft.com/en-us/library/ms157273.aspx

- Customizing Rendering Extension Parameters in RSReportServer.Config, SQL Server 2008 Books Online
  http://msdn.microsoft.com/en-us/library/ms156281.aspx

- Microsoft SQL Server Reporting Services Report Builder 2.0
  http://www.microsoft.com/downloads/details.aspx?FamilyID=9f783224-9871-4eea-b1d5-f3140a253db6&displaylang=en

- For advanced information about designing reports, see SQL Server 2008 Books Online, especially the Working with Report Expressions topic
  http://msdn.microsoft.com/en-us/library/ms159238.aspx

Implement Report Data Sources and Datasets

- SQL Server 2008 Books Online topics "Development (Reporting Services)" (*http://msdn.microsoft.com/en-us/library/bb522683.aspx*) and "Designing and Implementing Reports (Reporting Services)" (*http://msdn.microsoft.com/en-us/library/bb522712.aspx*), especially the following subtopics:
  - Working with Data Regions subtopic
    http://msdn.microsoft.com/en-us/library/ms156394.aspx
  - Formatting Reports and Report Items
    http://msdn.microsoft.com/en-us/library/ms157448.aspx
  - Filtering Data in a Report
    http://msdn.microsoft.com/en-us/library/ms157307.aspx
  - Creating a Report Dataset
    http://msdn.microsoft.com/en-us/library/ms156288.aspx

Extend an SSRS Solution by Using Code

- For more information about the SSRS Web service and report viewer controls, see the following topics in SQL Server 2008 Books Online:
  - Report Server Web Service
    http://msdn.microsoft.com/en-us/library/ms152787.aspx
  - Integrating Reporting Services Using the ReportViewer Controls
    http://msdn.microsoft.com/en-us/library/aa337090.aspx
  - Using Custom Assemblies with Reports
    http://msdn.microsoft.com/en-us/library/ms153561.aspx

Implement Report Parameters

- For advanced information about designing reports, see SQL Server 2008 Books Online, especially the Adding Parameters to Your Report topic:
  http://msdn.microsoft.com/en-us/library/ms155917.aspx

Install and Configure SSRS Instances

- Scripting with the rs Utility and the Web Service, SQL Server 2008 Books Online
  http://msdn.microsoft.com/en-us/library/ms162839.aspx
- Installing a SQL Server 2008 Failover Cluster, SQL Server 2008 Books Online
  http://msdn.microsoft.com/en-us/library/ms179410.aspx

Configure Authentication and Authorization for a Reporting Solution

- How to: Configure Windows authentication in Reporting Services
  http://msdn.microsoft.com/en-us/library/cc281253.aspx
- Configuring Authentication in Reporting Services
  http://msdn.microsoft.com/en-us/library/bb283249.aspx

Index

A

D

N

About the Authors

 ERIK VEERMAN (SQL Server MVP) is a mentor for Solid Quality Mentors focusing on training, mentoring, and architecting solutions on the Microsoft SQL Server business intelligence (BI) platform. His industry recognition includes the Microsoft Worldwide BI Solution of the Year and *SQL Server Magazine* Innovator Cup. Erik has designed dozens of BI solutions across a broad business spectrum—telecommunications, marketing, retail, commercial real estate, finance, supply chain, and information technology. As an expert in OLAP design, ETL processing, and dimensional modeling, Erik is a presenter, an author, and an instructor. He led the ETL architecture and design for the first production implementation of SQL Server Integration Services (SSIS) and helped drive the ETL standards and best practices for SSIS on the Microsoft SQL Server 2005 reference initiative, Project REAL. Erik is coauthor of the four Wrox books that focus on SQL Server Integration Services and was also the lead author for *MCTS Self-Paced Training Kit (Exam 70-445): Microsoft SQL Server 2005 Business Intelligence—Implementation and Maintenance* (Microsoft Press, ISBN 978-0-7356-9156-8).

 TEO LACHEV (MCSD, MCT) works as a technical architect for a leading financial institution, where he designs and implements Microsoft-centric BI solutions. A Microsoft SQL Server MVP since 2004, Teo is also the author of *Applied Microsoft SQL Server 2008 Reporting Services* and *Applied Microsoft Analysis Services 2005*, and the coauthor of *MCTS Self-Paced Training Kit (Exam 70-445): Microsoft SQL Server 2005 Business Intelligence—Implementation and Maintenance* (Microsoft Press, ISBN 978-0-7356-9156-8). Based in Atlanta, Teo maintains a personal Web site, *www.prologika.com*, where he blogs about Microsoft business intelligence.

 DEJAN SARKA focuses on development of database and BI applications. In addition to projects, he spends about half of his time on training and mentoring. He is a frequent speaker at some of the most important international conferences, such as PASS, TechEd, and SqlDevCon. He is also indispensable at regional Microsoft events—for example, at the NT Conference, the biggest Microsoft conference in Central and Eastern Europe. He is the founder of the Slovenian SQL Server and .NET Users Group. Dejan Sarka is the main author or coauthor of seven books about databases and SQL Server. Dejan Sarka also developed two courses for Solid Quality Mentors—Data Modeling Essentials and Data Mining with SQL Server 2008.

ALEJANDRO LEGUIZAMO is a SQL Server MVP and mentor for Solid Quality Mentors. He has been working with SQL Server since version 6.5 and with Microsoft Office Access since Office 97. His core area is data warehousing and BI, including ETL. He has wide experience in deployment and training in Business Intelligence Strategies, with a degree in Business Management strongly focused on Executive Information Systems. Alejandro often speaks at Microsoft events in Spain, Peru, Ecuador, and Venezuela.

What do you think of this book?

We want to hear from you!

To participate in a brief online survey, please visit:

microsoft.com/learning/booksurvey

...and enter this book's ISBN number (appears above barcode on back cover).

Tell us how well this book meets your needs—what works effectively, and what we can do better. Your feedback will help us continually improve our books and learning resources for you.

Thank you in advance for your input!

Where to find the ISBN on back cover

ISBN: 000-0-0000-0000-0

9 0 0 0 0

0 000000 000000

Example only. Each book has unique ISBN.

Stay in touch!

To subscribe to the *Microsoft Press* Book Connection Newsletter—for news on upcoming books, events, and special offers—please visit:

microsoft.com/learning/books/newsletter